Transport Economics
3rd Edition

Kenneth Button

*University Professor, School of Public Policy, George Mason
University, USA*

Edward Elgar
Cheltenham, UK • Northampton, MA, USA

Published by
Edward Elgar Publishing Limited
The Lypiatts
15 Lansdown Road
Cheltenham
Glos GL50 2JA
UK

Edward Elgar Publishing, Inc.
William Pratt House
9 Dewey Court
Northampton
Massachusetts 01060
USA

Paperback edition reprinted 2014

A catalogue record for this book
is available from the British Library

Library of Congress Control Number: 2009937750

ISBN 978 1 84064 189 9 (cased)
ISBN 978 1 84064 191 2 (paperback)

Printed and bound in Great Britain by TJ International Ltd, Padstow

Contents

Preface

• •

Publishers are always pressing for new editions of books, and particularly text-books. This is logical, after all they are commercial enterprises, and new editions of a book make the old ones redundant and the used books, collectors' items. The more editions they publish, the larger the sales checks. Authors get paid royalties and are often enthusiastic collaborators. In practice, however, one should never rush into writing a new edition; there should be motivation besides money.

A new textbook becomes important when the old one becomes outdated. In subject areas such as economics, much of the basic theory is well established, although not always liked or accepted, by policy makers; perhaps this unpopularity is not surprising, after all Thomas Carlyle did call economics 'The dismal science' some two centuries ago. There are, however, movements forward in our basic understanding of the economics, including that which is particularly germane to transport matters. There are also developments in the techniques available for estimating the effects of transport on society, and conversely on the way social change impacts on transport. This, combined with a continual accumulation of data over time, and the ability to mine previous studies to look at time trend affects or, in exceptional cases, adds to our knowledge.

There are also continual shifts in the way that policy makers treat transport; the political economy of the subject. Just consulting daily newspapers clearly shows the importance of transport in public perception. Transport issues of all kinds fill the column inches of these publications, as does the time spent on transport and travel in television news programs and documentaries. This public interest inevitably draws the attention of policy makers sensitive to the perceptions of their constituents.

Since the last edition of the book, some 14 years ago, quite a lot has changed. Our understanding of the factors influencing demand for transport services has moved forward, and our approaches to modeling and estimating the ways in which a variety of factors influence the use of transport has evolved. Challenges that were pertinent in the early 1990s remain but many, such as global warming emissions and concerns over terrorism, have grown in importance. International transport is now more important, as globalization has grown, driven in part by institutional changes, but also facilitated by developments in such things as information technology. The role of logistics, which has a major economics component, has grown as trade has expanded.

Of course, not all things have changed. The basic economic principles of supply and demand remain as valid as ever; it is the context and focus that has changed. Nevertheless, more up-to-date examples make their understanding easier; context helps the assimilation of ideas. Equally the scale and details of the transport system have inevitably responded to internal and external factors over nearly a decade and a half, and it is time to update the factual background against which transport economics is set, even if it does not materially affect the underlying theories.

So this new edition takes on board these important changes. But it also has a different physical form. It is longer. This is because the original edition was aimed mainly, although far from completely, at the UK market where universities normally had a 10-week term. There was basically a chapter per class. Changes have taken place in the educational world, and the earlier edition seems to have found a wider market than expected. This edition is thus longer, some 14 chapters and more suited to a semester system. This is not just padding added to fill in students' time; there is serious restructuring, redrafting of material seen in editions one and two, and new material.

Additionally, the referencing is slightly different. The Harvard Manual, with its author–date format, which forms the basis of most economics journal and monograph referencing has been set aside for a simple Chicago approach. There are no extensive lists of references but rather a few important citations are offered together with a brief section of further reading at the conclusion of each chapter. This is in response to comments from users of the earlier editions who found the Harvard system distracting in what is essentially a textbook.

As before, the book is a mixture of prose, tables, figures and equations. The aim is to help understanding rather than to overpower, or impress, the reader with technique.

I hope that teachers, students and other readers find the new edition useful.

Kenneth Button

1 Transport and Economics

· ·

Economics is extremely useful as a form of employment for economists
— John Kenneth Galbraith

1.1 Transport* Economics

Over a quarter of a century ago I opened the first edition of *Transport Economics* with a quote from an address to the UK's Chartered Institute of Transport by K.J.W. Alexander[1] which made the rather sober point that despite the importance of transport in the economy, 'the number of academic economists who specialize exclusively in transport could probably be counted on two hands. If one adds to these economists the applied economists employed in the transport business and the specialist consultants working exclusively in that field I would be surprised if the total number exceeded sixty or seventy'. This is actually rather strange given the fascination that transport has held more generally for very eminent economists; indeed John Maynard Keynes once confessed when young, 'I find economics increasingly satisfactory, and I think I am rather good at it. I want to manage a railway, or organize a trust or at least swindle the investing public'.

Unfortunately, the situation as seen by a knowledgeable expert in the mid-1970s, continued to largely pertain in the 1990s when the second edition of *Transport Economics* was published. One may now have to bring one's feet and toes into Alexander's calculations, but even in 2009 there are still relatively few academics that specialize in the subject. There still remains, however, quite a lot of, often not very helpful, dabbling by those whose interest lay more in lobbying for a favorite mode of transport than social welfare, and who try to use economics to justify their own personal prejudices.

Alexander's statement also highlighted the fact that many transport economic issues have traditionally been under-researched and often poorly understood, particularly by non-economists. The situation has changed somewhat since that time, as witnessed by the introduction of a number of serious academic journals over the years that regularly publish papers on transport economics.

---

* The word 'transport' is used throughout this book rather than the US 'transportation' despite the use of American vocabulary elsewhere. This is to avoid confusion for British readers, and it avoids obvious problems for Australians for whom the term 'transportation' has peculiar connotations.

[1] K.J.W. Alexander, 'Some economic problems of the transport industry', *Chartered Institute of Transport Journal*, **36**, 306–8, 1975.

Most notable of these are the *Journal of Transport Economics and Policy*, which first appeared in 1967, and the *International Journal of Transport Economics*. Both of these date back to that general era, but so do journals such as the *Journal of Urban Economics* and *Regional Science and Urban Economics* which also often carry transport material. In addition, mode-specific journals have emerged, such as *Maritime Economics and Logistics*, which focus on particular transport industries. But, nevertheless, compared to many areas of economic study, transport still remains remarkably neglected.

This does not mean that there have not been periodic surges of interest in some particular aspects of transport economics. Indeed, in the mid-1980s Clifford Winston,[2] when examining developments in transport economics, was able to comment on 'a current intensity [of interest in the field] not witnessed for more than fifty years'. This surge was mainly related to the analysis of the impacts of more liberal, or to use the American term, 'deregulated', transport markets that were emerging. More recently, the role of transport as a facilitator of economic growth has attracted attention both at the micro and at the macroeconomic levels. Matters of transport security and the financing of transport networks have been themes attracting attention in the early part of the twenty-first century, as has the role of transport in international trade.

This relative lack of contemporary academic interest in transport economics is surprising because transport problems have in the more distant past stimulated major developments in economic theory (including the development of the notion of consumer surplus by French economists/engineers, such as Jules Dupuit, in the 1840s; the refinement of cost allocation models by such famed US economists such as John Bates Clark and Frank Taussig in the early part of the last century; and the examination of the marginal cost pricing principle to improve the charging of rail service and work on congestion and the environment by Arthur Pigou in the 1920s).

More recently, the advent of computers has encouraged work on applied econometrics (for example, the development of discrete choice models in consumer theory by Dan McFadden, and refinements to flexible form cost functions) and on mathematical programming (for example, the use of data envelopment analysis to assess the relative efficiency of different suppliers) using transport case studies as a basis for analysis. Nonetheless, transport economists in universities are thin on the ground, and their numbers in businesses and government are not much larger.

In part, the relatively small number of clearly identifiable specialist transport economists may be attributed to the diverse nature of the industries involved in their work which range from taxi-cabs to oil transportation, with their various institutional and technical peculiarities. Non-economists – lawyers and engineers – often have specialist knowledge of the industry and a limited background in economics. At the applied level, numerous, small firms do not have the resources

---

[2] C. Winston, 'Conceptual developments in the economics of transportation: an interpretive survey', *Journal of Economic Literature*, **23**, 57–94, 1985.

to employ full-time specialists that characterize a 'transport economist' although that does not mean they do not have individuals that fulfill some economics role in the organization.

It may also be explained by the tendency, which to some extent still remains, for physical planners and transport engineers to dominate substantive investment and policy decision making within the sector. The emphasis in this case is, on the personal transport side, more to do with the physical manifestation of travel, namely trips and journey numbers, rather than the demand for movement and the ability of the system to meet these aspirations. Where economics is used, it is often within the engineering framework and carried through by engineers – the so-called 'engineering economics'. This situation has only gradually been changing with innovations in management and planning, and in the way that political institutions have evolved. So what is 'modern transport economics', how did it evolve and what are the intellectual and practical driving forces behind it?

1.2   The Emergence of Modern Transport Economics

Economics is not easy to define.[3] Famously the Chicago economist Jacob Viner is meant to have said, 'economics is what economists do'; not exactly helpful to the outside. But it is generally agreed that it is about human behavior and resource allocation, and in particular about the allocation of scarce resources. It focuses a lot on the role of markets in doing this, but not exclusively so. Various aspects of it border on a variety of other disciplines such as law, sociology and engineering, often making boundaries vague. It also may be essentially descriptive in the sense of it approaching a value-neutral science – it tells us that in most conditions the quantity demanded of something will fall if its price rises – but it can also contain elements of prescription: it is a 'good' thing for social welfare for prices to be low. The latter is often called 'political economy'. All these elements, and some others, become important when studying the economics of transport.

What has been called 'Modern Transport Economics' by Michael Thomson[4] in his book of the same name, began slowly to take shape about 45 years ago. Up until that time, as Rakowski[5] points out, 'the field had essentially been in a state of semi-dormancy since the 1920s', and while considerable institutional studies had been conducted, very little analytical work as we would understand it today had been attempted. Indeed, the two standard American textbooks on transport economics into the late 1960s were D.F. Pregrum's *Transportation: Economics and Public Policy*, and Philip Locklin's *Economics of Transportation*, which had only five or so line drawings between them and no equations.

---

[3] R.E. Backhouse and S.G. Medema, 'On the definition of economics', *Journal of Economic Perspectives*, **23**, 221–33, 2009.

[4] J.M. Thomson, *Modern Transport Economics*, Harmondsworth: Penguin, 1975

[5] J.P. Rakowski, *Transport Economics: A Guide to Information Sources*, Detroit: Gale Research Co., 1976.

If one looks for a watershed in the history of modern transport economics it would probably be the publication of John Meyer, Meston Peck, Walter Stenason and Charles Zwick's *Economics of Competition in the Transportation Industries* in 1959, which provided a state-of-the-art review of resource allocation problems in the sector coupled with rigorous statistical analysis. There had been a number of seminal economic papers relating to transport that appeared prior to this, including James Buchanan's re-examination of congestion and Martin Beckmann and co-workers' set of studies, but Meyer et al.'s book really set the tone for the way in which transport issues are analyzed.

Interest in transport issues expanded throughout the 1960s with, for example, William Vickery's analysis of road charging and the role of public transit subsidies, Ian Little and James Mirrlees's development of work on investment appraisal, and in particular on cost–benefit analysis, Richard Quandt and William Baumol's improvements in methods of transport demand modeling based on Daniel McFadden's work and the ideas of Kelvin Lancaster, Leon Moses and Harold Williamson's development of innovative methods of travel time evaluation, and so on. All these are topics that we shall return to later, albeit in their more modern manifestations, and in many cases with some real-world examples of applications.

The changes were not all academic. This period also saw public policy makers become more interested in the role of economics in improving actual decision making. In many countries, specialist departments were established in national or municipal governments to examine the economic implications of various transport policy options.

The 1960s and early 1970s saw a slew of official reports appear, for example, in the United Kingdom, including studies on *Road Track Costs*, the Smeed Report on *The Economics of Road Pricing*, the Beeching Report on *The Reshaping of British Railways* and the report of the Commission on the Third London Airport, which set out the framework for ways in which economics helps in mega-project investment appraisal. The European Union, then just established as the European Economic Community, produced reports and plans in the early 1960s for integrating and coordinating economic approaches to transport provision across much of Europe. In the United States this was the period of the large land-use transport studies that included the Chicago Area Transportation Study from the late 1950s, the Puget Sound Regional Transportation Study, and the Detroit Regional Transportation and Land-use Study. These were essentially engineering studies seeking to deal with mounting congestion problems, but economic analysis was part of the assessment process.

While it is never easy to explain the timing of change, the renewed research interest in transport in the 1960s, especially in the United States, Rakowski attributes to 'the problems of physical distribution and the development of a new field which has come to be called business logistics', 'expanded interest in all phases of urban transportation' and 'a great deal of research in the areas of transportation in the developing countries'. Ken Gwilliam[6] echoes these themes

---

[6] K.M. Gwilliam, 'Review of "Transport Economics"', *Economic Journal*, **90**, 677–8, 1980.

but places particular emphasis on the growing problems of urban transport in the 1960s and the recognition that land use and transport needed to be considered together, and usually simultaneously, if the problems were to be tackled successfully. As a result of this, he argues, 'the boundaries between transport economics and urban and regional planning were obscured'.

While the broad underlying intellectual thrust of modern transport analysis has not changed significantly since the 1970s and early 1970s, namely the use of economic theory to enhance transport efficiency, in the broadest sense the topics of focus have shifted to some extent and the economic tools used have been improved and fine-tuned. The late 1970s saw particular concern in many parts of the world with the macroeconomic problems associated with 'Stagflation': the simultaneous occurrence of high levels of unemployment and poor economic growth with inflation. The failure of a large part of the US railroad industry may be seen as a catalyst for some of the particular changes in transport. The adoption of Reaganomics in the United States, and Thatcherism in the United Kingdom, involving similar approaches towards what became known as 'supply-side economics', led to a honing-in on reducing costs in heavily regulated industries such as transport.

The empirical analysis of those such as Bill Jordan and Michael Levine provided evidence of excess costs associated with regulation, the theories of Baumol and others on contestable market structures offered a new way of looking at competitive forces, and Harold Demsetz's work provided a basis for enhancing the efficiency with which transport infrastructure is provided and maintained. Work by a variety of Chicago economists, including George Stigler and Sam Peltzman, began to focus on the motivations of those responsible for framing and administrating economic regulatory regimes, arguing that they seldom served the public interest. The outcome was what some have called the 'Age of Regulatory Reform',[7] which focused on removing distorting regulations and allowing greater market flexibility.

More recently, public concern combined with academic curiosity has led to economists switching more of their attention to matters pertaining to the environmental implications of transport supply, the role that economics can play in enhancing the transport logistics supply chain, and the financing of infrastructure. Transport, as we shall see later in the book, can impose considerable strains on the environment and, although this has long been recognized, the scale and nature of transport has changed, as has scientific knowledge on the implications of these strains – and especially in the context of global impacts.

Equally, globalization, internationalization and domestic economic growth within many countries have been, in part, the result of improved logistics, including just-in-time supply chain management. Although often not appreciated, many of these improvements in logistics are the result of the application of basic economic principles. Finally, modern transport requires an extensive infrastructure

---

[7] K.J. Button and D. Swann (eds), *The Age of Regulatory Reform*, Oxford: Oxford University Press, 1989.

of roads, rail tracks, ports, air traffic control systems, bridges and so on. The construction and the maintenance of this infrastructure have to be paid for. While in the past transport economics has focused primarily on deciding which elements to build or repair, the taxpayer bearing much of the financial burden, there is now concern about the methods of finance to use and the overall amount of national resources that have to be devoted to this type of infrastructure. This issue is increasingly important in many developed economies as old infrastructure becomes obsolete or needs maintenance, but is perhaps more critical in lower-income nations that lack many key transport networks.

When considering this background, it is important to emphasize that transport economics is not distinct from all other branches of economics. Indeed, many of the seminal papers on the subject have appeared in the general economics literature and have often been produced by individuals with a broad interest in economics rather than transport specialists. Nevertheless, in most areas of study, as our knowledge has increased, it has become difficult, if not impossible, for economists to follow developments in all branches of their discipline; the Renaissance man or woman of economics is in the past. There has been an inevitable increase in specialization. Transport economics has, in general terms, a long history but, as Rakowski and others suggest, it was only in the 1970s or so that it become a major field of academic study within universities and only subsequently did a substantial body of specialists emerge. So the modern transport economist is a relatively new beast. But what is it that he/she studies?

1.3   The Scope of the Subject

The scope of each of the subdisciplines within economics (for example, agricultural economics, development economics and public sector economics) is determined not by particular schools or philosophies but rather by the type of subject matter examined and the problems tackled. Transport economists are interested in the economic problems of moving goods and people – they are not normally so concerned with either the industries producing the vehicles and infrastructure (aircraft manufacturing, road construction companies, ship building and so on) or with some of the very wide implications of transport policy (for example, on the balance of payments), although matters to do with the environment certainly attract increasing amounts of their attention. Of course, this does not mean that transport issues are viewed in complete isolation from their wider context, but it does mean that the main emphasis and thrust of analysis is directed towards the more immediate transport implications.

While much of the economic analysis of transport issues is at the micro level (for example, looking at the decisions of individuals or firms) or at the meso level (focusing on transport industries or the importance of transport or a specific region) there is also some interest in the macroeconomic impacts of transport, for example, on its effects on national productivity, globalization of trade, or labor force migration.

This book seeks to give adequate coverage to all levels of aggregation. Initially, however, we step back a little and spend time considering the economic institutions within which transport services are supplied and individuals and firms seek its services. Much of the theoretical economics that we encounter is rather abstract and largely assumes away the role of economic institutions, although this is now changing gradually. But institutional structures are important. Elementary economics, for example, talks about such things as perfect competition, but such markets could not exist without laws giving property rights to their suppliers and without contracts between sellers and buyers. As the Nobel Prize-winning economist Ronald Coase[8] said in the context of economic reforms in the former USSR countries, 'These ex-communist countries are advised to move to a market economy, and their leaders wish to do so, but without the appropriate institutions no market economy of any significance is possible'.

Traditionally, however, within economics, institutions have been treated as endogenous and man-made – sometimes deliberately, sometimes not – rather than something that is to be given. Few economists spent time studying them and those that did, such as Thorstein Veblen and John Kenneth Galbraith, were treated in their day as rather marginal to main-stream economics – some even considering them to be 'sociologists'! However, this view is changing, and as Oliver Williamson[9] observed: 'We are still very ignorant about institutions. . . . Chief among the causes of ignorance is that institutions are very complex. That neoclassical economics was dismissive of institutions and that much of organization theory lacked scientific ambitions have also been contributing factors'.

The so-called 'New Institutional Economics' has moved the economic study of institutions away from being a largely descriptive, legalistic and traditional historical way of viewing the world to one that offers microanalysis of such issues as to why economic institutions have emerged the way they have. It has also moved away from a largely negative way of looking at neoclassical economics, to one with its own theoretical constructs and tools of analysis. This approach importantly sets the neoclassical economics that underlies most of the work in transport economics up until the 1990s, into a larger context. Figure 1.1 is a simplified diagram that sets out four levels of social analysis. It is fairly self-explanatory except that the thick arrows show constraints that come down from higher levels of analysis, while the dotted arrows indicate the direction of feedbacks. The data offered in the figure are the rough frequency in years over which change takes place.

Long-term issues tend to receive less attention in transport economics the further one moves from narrow resource allocation matters. Their importance cannot be neglected, however. There have been, perhaps, two major societal changes that have impacted on culture in the broadest sense over the past century or so, and have had important ramifications for transport.

---

[8] R.H. Coase, 'The institutional structure of production', *American Economic Review*, **82**, 713–9, 1992.

[9] O.E. Williamson, 'The new institutional economics: taking stock, looking ahead', *Journal of Economics Literature*, **38**, 595–613, 2000.

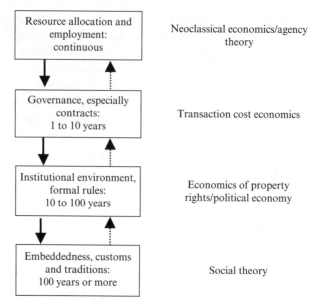

Figure 1.1   *Institutions and economics*

First, there was the demise of the Soviet Union and the move away from centralized planning, together with the gradual uptake of capitalism in China. These, and similar developments elsewhere, represent major shifts in the embedded attitude of these countries and with this have come new ways of thinking about the role of transport in society and the ways in which it should be provided. Second, there have been changing attitudes towards free trade, and with these have come 'globalization'. The resultant approach to tariffs and other barriers to international economic policies have had profound effects on shipping, air transport, and many forms of surface transport. Going back to the global conflict of 1914–18, the subsequent establishment of the League of Nations paved the way for this in modern times, and it has extended since the end of the Second World War. It is not just that such global institutions as the World Bank, the International Maritime Organization, and the International Civil Aviation Organization exist, but rather that there is now a belief that they have a durable role to play in society. This forms a basis for new economic systems and an embedded global view on how business can be conducted.

The institutional environment involves formal laws, regulations and rules, and at a higher level, 'constitutions'. It is also concerned with the instruments of law – legislatures and bureaucracies – and mechanisms of enforcement. For example, it relates to legal reforms such as the 1978 Airline Deregulation Act which liberalized domestic aviation in the United States, or the Single European Market Act in Europe in 1986 that led to a phased deregulation of transport and other markets within Europe. But it also importantly includes the issue of property rights and their enforcement. So-called 'Pigouvian externalities', such as pollution, and 'club good' problems of traffic congestion, are the most obvious areas of interest for transport economists in this regard. From an economics of transport perspective, the question becomes one of getting the rules right to meet societal demands.

Governance, basically the way business is done, is important, and here the economic emphasis is on notions of contracts. Strictly, it is about crafting order, and thereby mitigates conflict and realizes mutual gains. There are many factors – cultural, structural, cognitive and political – that influence the way in which these formal and informal institutions develop. If we take shipping as a case study, governance here may be seen as embodying such things as the evolving structure of coordination of shipping activities that began with 'conferences' – essentially cartels – in the 1970s and has developed through consortia into strategic alliances, whereby changes occur discretely rather than continuously. These, like their brethren in the airline industry, can involve agreements on such things as schedules and rates with flexibility about which vessels carry any particular assignments.

There are also contractual issues within the larger integrated supply chains that, for example, tie, to varying degrees, shipping with other elements in the logistics system, most immediately ports but extending beyond this. Governance is different from government in the sense that the former involves informal agreements within a legal structure. As an example, the United States deregulated its domestic airline industry by an Act of Congress, whereas the United Kingdom essentially got the same result because the Civil Aviation Authority reinterpreted the existing set of laws. Because of high transaction costs, the recent trend has been for a considerable amount of contract management and dispute settlement action to be dealt with directly by the parties involved – in other words, within market frameworks rather than by legal actions.

Finally, there are the ongoing processes involving the day-to-day activities that take place involving transport. This is essentially the traditional bread-and-butter of micro- and mesoeconomic analysis taking into account the specific nuances of transport. Resource allocation issues have since the days of Adam Smith, and more particularly Alfred Marshall in the late 1890s, centered on getting the marginal conditions right. To assess how this might be achieved in theory, and how it materializes in practice, requires some notion of the nature of the relevant cost and demand conditions – the guts of most introductory economics courses. The basic principles, although the nuances are still being refined, are well understood, and much of the recent attention in transport economics has therefore been on quantification and application in a network context.

Historically, however, this has not always been the case. Much of the analysis of market structures in transport, for example, paid scant heed to the network nature of the industry and *ipso facto* to network externalities. Much of the interest until 50 years or so ago, as we have hinted at previously, had been on traditional economic parameters such as market concentration ratios, the degree of product differentiation and the level of vertical integration. While all these can be important instruments in the economist's tool bag, the network nature of the transport, and the service nature of its outputs, received much less direct attention in the analysis. Much of the early work on transport demand modeling was also either devoid of any of these network features, or embraced them in a mechanical fashion. But network features are important, although they often add complexity to useful analysis.

All network service industries have essentially identical economic characteristics. Their output is non-durable, although they normally require significant amounts of infrastructure. There are also often very significant external benefits which, tied with various forms of scale effects, produce network economies. From the consumer's perspective, these external economies are related to the fact that the larger the number of links in a network the greater the degree of connectivity, and with this the larger the choice set available to him/her – often called 'economies of market presence'. On the cost savings side, the ability, where this is most efficient, to channel traffic through hubs, rather than carry traffic directly between origins and destinations, creates economies of scope (cost savings by combining traffic) and of density (the more intensive use of the mode). But complex networks can also create costs, and most especially congestion can develop on link roads or flight paths, or at hubs such as sea- and airports in the shipping and aviation context.

So what does all this mean regarding the day-to-day work of transport economists? In summary, an understanding of economic institutions is now generally seen as important for analyzing broad transport issues; nevertheless, the main 'tools' of the transport economist are still taken directly from the kit-bag of standard micro- and mesoeconomic theory, although one should add that the actual instruments used have changed significantly over the years. The pre-Second World War emphasis centered on the transport industries (that is, the railways, road haulage, shipping and so on.) and, in particular, on ways in which the transport supply could be improved within a largely regulated structure so that maximum benefit would be derived from public and private transport operations. The situation was summarized by one geographer who felt that transport economics at that time was concerned almost entirely with 'matters of organization, competition and charging, rather than with the effects of transport facilities on economic activities'.[10]

To some extent – particularly in relation to international transport and, to a lesser extent, inter-urban transport – this interest has remained. However, more recently it has been supplemented by concern with the wider welfare and spatial implications of transport. Greater emphasis is now placed on the environmental and distributional effects of the transport system and, in some cases, market efficiency is seen as an undesirably narrow criterion upon which to base major decisions. As Alexander argued, in the speech cited at the beginning of the chapter, one of the most important roles for economists is to make clear the overall resource costs of transport rather than just the accounting costs. It is no accident, perhaps, that much of the early work in cost–benefit analysis (CBA) was in the transport field.

[10] A.M. O'Connor, *Railways and Development in Uganda*, Oxford: Oxford University Press for the East African Institute of Social Research, 1965.

Transport economics has, like virtually all other branches of economics, become more quantitative in recent years. The dominant pre-war idea that economics is concerned mainly with establishing broad principles (for example, that the quantity demanded rises, *ceteris paribus*, as price falls) has given way, with the advent of econometric techniques and the computer age, together with improved data sources, to attempts at detailed measurement (that is, a rise of x tons in the quantity demanded will, *ceteris paribus*, follow from a $\$y$ fall in unit price). Transport economists are now heavily involved in trying to assess the precise quantitative effect of different policy options and with forecasting likely changes in transport demand.

At the public policy level, the increasing sophistication of transport operations, combined with both the long lead times that are required for full policy implementation and the financial costs involved, place mounting strains upon economists to produce useful, quantified predictions of future trends. The increased appreciation of the commercial benefits of better forecasting and costing as part of the supply-chain management process, has led to greater employment of numerate economists in the private sector.

From the relatively small base of the 1960s, transport economists have now become more established in most areas of transport policy making at all administrative levels. Their increased interest in the overall welfare consequences of different transport strategies, together with a willingness to attempt some form of quantitative assessment, has led to transport economists becoming more closely involved in major transport planning exercises. They have an established role in advising on appropriate actions at the national policy formulation level, but this has also spread down to a more specific function at the local planning level. At the strategic level, transport economists, for example, have made a significant contribution to the urban transport planning in industrial countries since the late 1960s, and have been involved in many detailed appraisals of traffic investment and management schemes in developed countries.

The particular advances made in transport investment appraisal – most notably the development of CBA techniques as practical tools of analysis – led to the adoption of economic criteria for the assessment of many large-scale investment projects in the 1960s and 1970s (for example, the Third London Airport scheme and Victoria Underground Line in the United Kingdom). Recent refinements have resulted in rather more standardization, and uniform CBA procedures are employed as a standard method of small-scale transport project appraisal (for example, the COBA package used in UK trunk road investment appraisal and the procedures favored by the World Bank for appraising transport schemes in low-income countries).

As argued earlier, the surge of regulatory reform and market liberalization from the late 1970s, which will be discussed later in the book stems, at least partly, from the empirical work of applied economists, and the regulatory regimes that subsequently emerged are largely economics based.

The dichotomy between the wealth of the industrial nations and the poverty of Third World countries has resulted in large-scale programs being initiated to stimulate the economic development of the Third World. Much of this aid has been in the form of monies and resources to improve transport provision. Over 20 percent of World Bank lending, for example, goes on transport projects, as does about 15 percent of total Bank assistance – grants, expertise and so on. Although it is not altogether agreed that aid actually stimulates growth[11] nor that, if it does, transport investments are the most suitable projects to finance, it is nevertheless important that within the narrow confines of transport efficiency these monies are spent wisely. Transport economists have become increasingly involved in the Third World in transport project appraisal work.

Large private transport businesses often employ economists but more often they, and smaller enterprises, make use of the many specialist consultancy companies that offer expert advice. The growth in interest in supply-chain logistics, which spans all movement and storage of raw materials, work-in-process inventory, and finished goods from point of origin to point of consumption, and within that just-in-time management, has led to a much more implicit incorporation of economics into transport activities.

One way of looking at this is through the notion of 'value chain' initiated by Michael Porter.[12] A value chain is a chain of activities. Products pass through all activities of the chain in order, and at each activity the product gains some value. The chain of activities gives the products more added value than the sum of added values of all activities. Capturing the value generated along the chain is the new approach taken by many management strategists. For example, a manufacturer might require its parts suppliers to be located near its assembly plant to minimize the cost of transport, or it may require regular delivery of components to keep production going, while holding minimum stocks of the component. By exploiting the upstream and downstream information flowing along the value chain, the firms seek to bypass intermediaries creating new business models, or in other ways create improvements in its value system.

Figure 1.2 provides a simplified generic value chain. The key point about it is the extensive number of linkages required through a production process from the initial extraction of raw materials to the final delivery of goods to a market and their subsequent servicing. Transport is, at various levels of aggregation and in different forms, important at all stages. Just-in-time management is, as we see in Chapter 10 when we look at the links between transport economics and transport logistics, important in ensuring that as few resources as possible are tied up in the process at any one time so that inventory holdings are optimized.

The remainder of this introduction is concerned with setting the scene for the body of the book. Initially, some of the main economic features of the transport sector are discussed. The intention is, however, not to point to the uniqueness of transport but rather to highlight the particular characteristics of the sector that pose special problems for economists. Recent trends in transport are then

---

[11] P. Baer, *Dissent on Development*, London: Weidenfeld & Nicholson, 1971.
[12] M.E. Porter, *Competitive Advantage: Creating and Sustaining Superior Performance*, New York: Free Press, 1985.

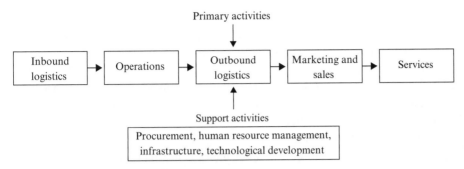

Figure 1.2 *The simple notion of the value chain*

reviewed and commented upon. To keep the subject matter manageable, much of the focus will be on the UK and US situations, although experiences elsewhere will not be neglected. This is followed by a brief review of what appear to be some of the longer-term factors that are going to attract the attention of transport economists. Finally, a detailed contextual section explains the format of the book and outlines briefly the rationale for the structure adopted.

1.4 The Economic Characteristics of Transport

Possibly the most important characteristic of transport is that it is not really demanded in its own right. As Munby[13] put it 40 years ago, 'Only the psychologically disturbed or inadequate want transport for its own sake'. In other words the demand for transport is a derived one, but its appropriate provision enables the benefits of a myriad of other, final benefits to be enjoyed. It is a major facilitator for enhancing personal welfare and for such things as economic development.

People wish, in general, to travel so that some benefit can be obtained at the final destination. The trip itself is to be as short as possible. Of course, there are 'joy riders' and 'tourists' but they tend to be in the minority. Similarly, users of freight transport perceive transport as a cost in their overall production function and seek to minimize it wherever possible. The derived nature of the demand for transport is often forgotten in everyday debate, but it underlies all economics of transport.

While the demand for transport has particular, if not unique, features, certain aspects of supply are entirely peculiar to transport. More specifically, part of the plant is 'mobile' – almost by definition – and is entirely different in its characteristics from the fixed plant (for example, rail track, airports and so on). The fixed component is usually extremely long-lived and expensive to replace. While most factories in the manufacturing sector may be thought to have a physical life expectancy of a hundred years at most, we still use ports and roads constructed in Roman times. Further, few pieces of transport infrastructure have alternative uses: some former waterways have been turned into leisure areas but these tend to be exceptions.

13 D. Munby, *Transport*, Harmondsworth: Penguin, 1968.

In contrast, most mobile plant is relatively short-lived and replacement usually occurs with physical rather than technical obsolescence as with the fixed components. It is also cheap, with the prospect of alternative employment if demand declines in one market; for example, a bus can be transferred to another route or another form of service – in technical terms, transport operators have few 'sunk costs'. Also, unlike fixed plant, the mobile components of transport are generally subject only to minimal scale economies. (Ships and aircraft may be seen as exceptions to this in some cases.)

The fixed component, on the other hand, is normally subject to quite substantial economies of scale. Once a rail track is laid, the marginal cost of using it falls until some maximum capacity is reached. This means that generally there is a minimum practical size below which the provision of transport infrastructure is uneconomical. There are minimum traffic flows, for example, below which it is not economically practical to build motorways.

As Michael Thomson[14] has pointed out, it is these features of the fixed and mobile components of transport that have influenced the present institutional arrangements in the sector. The high cost of provision, longevity and scale economies associated with the fixed components create tendencies towards monopoly control, while the ease of entry, flexibility and lack of scale effects tend to stimulate competition in the mobile sector. In common with many other countries, official reaction in Britain to this situation has, in the past, tended to be the nationalization and public ownership of transport infrastructure and the regulation of competition in the mobile sector. Nations differ in the degree to which fixed transport assets are publicly owned (there are entirely private railways in some countries such as the United States while several European states have privately operated motorways) and in the types of regulation imposed on mobile factors, but the overall impression is consistent.

While the rationale of directly controlling the provision and sale of the fixed components of transport can be linked to the containment of any monopoly exploitation which may accompany private ownership (although British experience in the nineteenth century suggests that control might equally well be enforced through price regulation), the need to regulate the mobile component stems from another aspect of transport operations. Transport generates considerable external effects (most obvious of which are congestion and pollution); as Thomson says, it is an engineering industry carried on outside the factory. It is, therefore, felt to be important at least to contain the harmful effects of transport and at best to ameliorate them. Coupled with this is the imperfect knowledge enjoyed by operators and, in particular, their inability to foresee relatively short-term change in demand.

Regulation is, therefore, often justified to ensure that excessive competition at times of depressed demand does not reduce the capacity of the transport system to an extent that it cannot meet higher demand during the upturn. Finally, there are political-economy arguments that transport is a social service that should

[14] J.M. Thomson, *Modern Transport Economics*, Harmondsworth: Penguin, 1974,

meet 'need' rather than demand and, hence, traditional market forces need to be supplemented to ensure that this wider, social criterion of transport operations is pursued rather than the simple profit motive.

1.5   The Framework of the Book

The remainder of the book is concerned with the application of economic theory to the transport sector. These are many books that concentrate on particular modes of transport, such as the railways or shipping, or specific sectors, such as the nationalized transport industries, or have a geographical bent such as, the transport policy of the European Union or urban transport problems. One of the main aims of this book, however, is to show that most challenges in transport are common to all modes (albeit with minor variations) and cover many different circumstances. Consequently, the approach is to show how economic theory may be applied to improve the overall efficiency of the transport sector; examples are, therefore, drawn from all forms of transport and many contexts.

Also while it is unavoidable, not to say desirable, that official transport policy must be implicitly incorporated in the analysis, this is not a book explicitly about transport policy. Economic forces do not operate in a vacuum but within the context of laws and governance structures. Indeed, economists of the public choice persuasion such as James Buchanan and Gordon Tullock put particular emphasis on this political economy dimension.[15]

It is felt useful, on occasions, to give brief details of institutional arrangements since they inevitably influence the type of economic analysis to apply (for example, a thumb-nail sketch of the historical and institutional framework of urban transport planning is included for this purpose), but, again, this is primarily for contextual reasons. The closing chapter is explicitly concerned with policy and institutions, and in particular with the matter of the economic regulation of transport markets.

At the theoretical level, the discussion is couched in terms of verbal and diagrammatic analysis. Mathematical expressions are not shunned, but equations are included rather as references, permitting readers to look up practical working models should they subsequently wish to undertake their own empirical investigations. There are virtually no mathematical derivations, but important equations are 'talked around' and the reader should find no difficulty in following the book even if his/her mathematical education has been neglected or forgotten.

Indeed the philosophy of the approach adopted here is very much akin to that espoused by the great economist, Alfred Marshall in a letter to a colleague, A.L. Bowley, in 1906,

> But I know I had a growing feeling in the later years of my work at the subject that a good mathematical theorem dealing with economic hypotheses was very unlikely to

[15] J.M. Buchanan and G. Tullock, *The Calculus of Consent: Logical Foundations of Constitutional Democracy*, Ann Arbor, MI: University of Michigan Press, 1962.

be good economics: and I went more and more on the rules – (1) Use mathematics as a shorthand language, rather than as an engine of inquiry. (2) Keep to them until you have done. (3) Translate into English. (4) Then illustrate by examples that are important in real life. (5) Burn the mathematics. (6) If you can't succeed in (4), burn (3). This last I did often.[16]

Although the Nobel Prize-winning economist, Paul Samuelson, and others have subsequently pointed to the fact that much of economics deals with quantitative concepts – prices, output, income and so on – and, therefore, inherently has a strong mathematic component, even they accept that there are limits to this.

Those interested in the mathematical extensions of the arguments on specific topics in the book are referred to the additional references set out at the end of each chapter, and to reading the material that is footnoted in more detail. The footnotes in particular are designed to direct readers to the more applied work in the field and the various challenges that economists encounter in trying to quantify various aspects of the transport system. An understanding of basic microeconomic theory is assumed and, while a knowledge of intermediate economic theory would be helpful, most of the theory does not go beyond that found in a standard introductory economics text.

Any divisions of material are partly arbitrary and really designed to make things digestible for readers; the chapters forming this book are no exception. Where to put material on the economics of transport security? Under logistics? – after all much of it is a business problem; under externalities? – part of it affects the public at large; under transport policy? – there is a large public policy element involved in delivering secure supply chains. Decisions have been made, but inevitably the material could have been arranged in a variety of alternative ways. The important point is simply to remember that economics is a way of helping to understand problems.

The book begins by looking at the nature and scale of transport at the beginning of the twenty-first century. It looks at it in global, national and local economies. It moves on in Chapter 3 to look at its broad interactions with other sectors of the economy, especially the land market. This interaction is often neglected in the explicit transport literature but is central to understanding the role of transport in society. This is followed by a related chapter concerned with the demand for transport services, the benefits derived from transport and methods of measuring these benefits, drawing particularly upon the tools of welfare economics.

While Chapters 3 and 4 are essentially demand oriented, the three following chapters are concerned with cost and supply aspects (costs here being seen both in terms of conventional financial cost problems and, also, in terms of wider external costs). The accountancy costs of running transport are now recognized as offering too narrow a picture of the overall social costs associated with the movement of goods and persons. The wider costs are those that are imposed by transport

---

[16] Letter form Marshall to Bowley, in A.C. Pigou (ed.), *Memorials of Alfred Marshall*, London: Macmillan, 1925.

users on one another, and that reduce the internal efficiency of the transport system, and the environmental costs that are inflicted on the larger society.

The remaining chapters concentrate on optimizing the size and use made of the transport sector both in the short and in the longer terms. Methods of pricing are reviewed in the context of the particular nature of transport activities and markets being served, with, once again, emphasis being directed to the wider social dimension as well as to narrow commercial criteria. Chapter 8, in particular, looks at methods of optimizing the environmental effects of transport on society in general, and Chapter 9 focuses on the challenges of dealing with the problems of traffic congestion, not only on our streets but also at air- and seaports. The importance of transport in the supply chain and modern logistics management is reviewed in Chapter 10.

Longer-term planning and investment decisions are considered in some detail. This is because of both the complexities of the issues involved and the size of the potential resource wastage if the wrong decision is taken. The sheer costs involved are also enormous, particularly where major pieces of new infrastructure are under consideration – for example, a Third London Airport for London or a 'Big Dig' for Boston. The problems of financing such undertakings are becoming more challenging and the respective roles and interactions of the government and private sectors are considered.

The long physical working life of projects, let alone the lead time often needed before they become operational, means that it is important to be able to forecast the future demands likely to be placed on transport infrastructure, and consequently, in Chapter 12, some space is devoted to economic demand forecasting techniques. The emphasis is, once again, on the economic assumptions involved rather than the econometric and estimation problems that may be encountered, although the latter are not entirely neglected.

The final chapters of the book take a much broader view of transport, considering both the role that transport policy may play in general economic development within the developed nations, and also in less developed countries. The question of appropriate regulations and the factors that have influenced official transport policy exercises over the years is explicitly examined in Chapter 14. The latter discussion is particularly concerned with the relative merits of central coordination and direction of transport *vis-à-vis* the use of the market mechanisms and competitive processes.

While each chapter is extensively referenced in footnotes throughout to permit readers to follow up specific points in more detail should they wish, it has also been thought useful to mention a few key references and some indication of further reading at the end of each chapter. These references are lightly annotated, and are really designed to help students and newcomers to the field. The intention is that they should be references to material that is relatively accessible to most readers rather than obscure reports, working papers and so on, which are often extremely difficult for those outside official circles or the academic sphere to obtain. Additionally, many of the references are to classic papers that can easily be found electronically.

Experience suggests that students often feel in the information age that any article or book written over five years or so ago is outdated. This is, of course, a folly of inexperience. Good studies that reveal universal principles are good studies whatever their vintage. Some cited here fall into the category of 'classics'. The lists of key references are also kept short so that the main items are immediately apparent to those interested. Many are to collections or surveys that go into greater depth on topics than we can in this short volume.

Further Reading

The book does assume some familiarity with basic microeconomic concepts, although in places, as an *aide-mémoire*, recaps of some important terms are offered. Those new to economics would find it useful to consult an introductory textbook such as: W.J. Baumol and A.S. Blinder, *Microeconomics: Principles and Policy* (10th edn), Cengage Learning, 2007; P.A. Samuelson and D. Nordhaus, *Microeconomics*, (19th edn), New York: McGraw-Hill, 2009; or N.G. Mankiw, *Principles of Microeconomics* (5th edn), Florence: Thomson, 2008.

There are a number of useful survey papers that provide broad overviews of the history of transport economics and more recent developments. In addition to those cited in the text, J.F. Due, 'Major recent contributions to the literature of transport economics: a review article', *Quarterly Review of Economics and Business*, **22**, 6–28, 1982 provides a look in the important literature of the 1970s and K.J. Button, 'Transportation economics: some developments over the past 30 years', *Journal of the Transportation Research Forum*, **45**, 7–30, 2006, brings this up to date. For a more technical approach to transport economics, and particularly to urban issues, the reader is referred to K.A. Small and E.T. Verhoef, *The Economics of Urban Transportation*, London: Routledge, 2007. Collected reprints of selected classic articles are to be found in H. Mohring (ed.), *The Economics of Transport* (2 vols), Aldershot, UK and Brookfield, VT, USA: Edward Elgar, 1994; and in K.J. Button (ed.), *Recent Developments in Transport Economics*, Cheltenham, UK and Northampton, MA, USA: Edward Elgar, 2003. For those seeking a detailed, but somewhat more policy-driven, and less technical approach, see the papers contained in J.A. Gómez-Ibáñez, W.B. Tye and C. Winston (eds), *Essays in Transportation Economics and Policy: A Handbook in Honor of John R. Meyer*, Washington, DC: Brookings Institute, 1999.

2 Transport, Transport Markets and Transport Industries

● ●

2.1 Introduction

Transport supply in the twenty-first century is, in both physical and financial terms, a major global industry, an employer of large numbers of people, the consumer of vast amount of raw materials, and it takes up a lot of personal time in its use. Whether it is, in some way, relatively more important than it was in the past is difficult to say. Certainly the major civilizations of yesteryear put considerable emphasis on their transport systems, and many, such as the Phoenicians, the Romans, the Chinese and the Dutch, centered their economies around their quite distinctly different transport systems. The Chinese have always been essentially a land power, whereas the Dutch and Phoenicians were maritime traders.

To understand just why there is such considerable interest in transport efficiency, and time and energy to improve it, it is helpful to offer a few facts and figures on transport's role globally, regionally and locally. The picture is far from complete because many of the implications and effects of transport lie outside the sector, including environmental effects, and we shall deal with these in separate chapters.

We should also perhaps hold in the back of our mind the words of the nineteenth-century UK Prime Minister and novelist, Benjamin Disraeli, who cautioned that, '[t]here are three kinds of lies: lies, damned lies, and statistics'. Basically he was referring to the persuasive power of numbers, and the use of statistics to support weak arguments, and the tendency of people to disparage statistics that do not support their position. We shall attempt to be as objective as possible in setting out the data.

It is impossible to paint anything like a complete quantitative picture of the nature and importance of modern transport. One could approach the challenge by focusing on a single country or sector – say shipping or roads – but this would inevitably be partial. Also looking at any single country's transport system can make it appear as if that country is special or unique. Certainly in some ways this will inevitably be so, but there are broader trends and features that transcend physical boundaries, and many of the economic challenges that confront policy makers are almost global in their incidence – traffic congestion being the most obvious example. Thus the examples and data provided are fairly wide ranging to offer illustrations of more general patterns and features.

We begin by looking at the very large pictures, international trade in transport services, and then gradually move down the level of aggregation with a diversion at the end to consider some emerging trends. Because local transport parameters can vary quite considerably, and because we deal with many specific local matters in subsequent chapters, this part of the description is less complete here. We also have a bias in that there is a disproportionate amount of American data and information provided, but this is supplemented in places with data from the United Kingdom and other countries.

In addition, it is important to remember that there can be quite large margins of error in the data that are presented here. Much of the data is based on surveys that have inevitable confidence intervals associated with them, many are not done often, and, like the US National Household Travel Survey, not at regular intervals. Questions differ over time and there are issues of definitions when making comparisons across countries, despite the efforts of the Organisation for Economic Co-operation and Development (OECD), EUROSTAT and other bodies, or at the more micro level across cities or regions.

Much of the transport that is provided is done so by the private sector, and the type of data collected can be significantly different from that gathered by public agencies. In particular, most of the private sector is commercially oriented and thus focuses on data that help in better business decision making, rather than those needed for good public policy analysis. This often means, for example, that the data are shorter term, because commercial activities are largely interested in timeframes involving cost recovery, and data are seldom gathered consistently, because private companies are generally only concerned with projects in which they have an immediate interest. Additionally, most private firms operate in markets, and commercial confidentiality engenders a reluctance to reveal data.

Even when census data are used, this type of information is normally collected only every decade with extrapolations to fill in the intervening years. Added to this most data that are collected on transport reflect physical characteristics of systems, and this is not always ideal for economic analysis.[1] This latter problem has become more acute in recent years as transport industries have become less regulated and there have been privatizations. With these institutional changes, commercial considerations have mitigated incentives to provide public data, and financial information in particular.

2.2 The Global Picture

International trade has existed ever since the formation of nation states, and indeed was the *raison d'être* for the establishment of many. Classical economists, when trying to explain the intensity and patterns of international trade, however, paid little attention to the role of transport; the focus was on the nation's comparative advantages in producing the commodities traded. Recently the emergence of

[1] K.J. Button, 'The usefulness of current international air transport statistics', *Journal of Transportation and Statistics*, **2**, 71–92, 1999.

the 'New Trade Theory' has changed this somewhat.[2] This approach recognizes that a large part of trade is intra-industrial, involving countries both importing and exporting very similar goods with each other (for example, Germany has both import and export trade in cars with Japan). Transport costs become one, but not the main, element in explaining these trade patterns.

In 2007, some $13,570 billion worth of recorded trade was conducted across international borders, and no doubt there was much more that fell out of the official statistics. While much of this involved the traditional industrial regions such as Europe ($5,769 billion, of which $1,327 billion involved Germany), the United States ($1,854 billion), and Japan ($710 billion), the new mega economy of China ($1,128 billion) is also now a major player.

Rising national incomes are one of the major factors influencing this growth as we see from Table 2.1. The table highlights the various geographical differences in trade and gross domestic product (GDP) in recent years. The more mature economies of North America and Europe have relatively stable growth rates of national income as one would expect, with a steady growth in trade. The asymmetrical pattern of trade with a considerably larger rise in imports and exports that characterizes the United States can be seen as not only posing potential balance of payments problems, but also impacts on the demands for transport services.

The rapid growth in the Chinese and Indian economies, and their importance in the globalization of economic activities, can be seen. The largely export-driven nature of their economic growth is reflected in the much faster growth in their trading activities than in their GDPs, and by the relative scale of imports and exports. The table also highlights the generally poor economic performance of Africa which in its entirety enjoyed only $422 billion of merchandise trade in 2007.

Figure 2.1 provides a longer-term picture that, from a time-series perspective, reinforces the link between economic performance and trade patterns. It also shows just how disruptive a shock to the world order can be for both economic growth and trade. The sudden decline in both global production and trade after the attacks on the United States in September 2001 are clear.

While these financial trends are insightful, and germane to many economic debates, they do not always provide insights into the physical nature of transport demands or the amount of resources that go into meeting it. For example, while international shipping carries some 90 percent of global trade measured by weight, air transport accounts for 40 percent by value despite carrying only 22.6 million tons[3] of freight in 2006. The value of what is moved is often unrelated to its economic importance, and air transport tends to move high-value, low-volume commodities where speed of delivery is at a premium. Table 2.2 offers some more general information concerning the growth of international air transport in the movement of people and freight.

[2] P. Krugman, 'Increasing returns, monopolistic competition, and international trade', *Journal of International Economics*, **9**, 469–79, 1979.
[3] All measures are expressed in their original units to allow readers to make subsequent comparisons with later data sets.

Table 2.1 *GDP and merchandise trade by region, 2005–07 (annual percent change at constant prices)*

	GDP			Exports			Imports		
	2005	2006	2007	2005	2006	2007	2005	2006	2007
World	3.3	3.7	3.4	6.5	8.5	5.5	6.5	8.0	5.5
North America	3.1	3.0	2.3	6.0	8.5	5.5	6.5	6.0	2.5
United States	3.1	2.9	2.2	7.0	10.5	7.0	5.5	5.5	1.0
South & Central America	5.6	6.0	6.3	8.0	4.0	5.0	14.0	15.0	20.0
Europe	1.9	2.9	2.8	4.0	7.5	3.5	4.5	7.5	3.5
European Union (27)	1.8	3.0	2.7	4.5	7.5	3.0	4.0	7.0	3.0
Commonwealth of Independent States	6.7	7.5	8.4	3.5	6.0	6.0	18.0	21.5	18.0
Africa and Middle East	5.6	5.5	5.5	4.5	1.5	0.5	14.5	6.5	12.5
Asia	4.2	4.7	4.7	11.0	13.0	11.5	8.0	8.5	8.5
China	10.4	11.1	11.4	25.0	22.0	19.5	11.5	16.5	13.5
Japan	1.9	2.4	2.1	5.0	10.0	9.0	2.5	2.5	1.0
India	9.0	9.7	9.1	21.5	11.0	10.5	28.5	9.5	13.0
Newly industrialized economies (4)	4.9	5.5	5.6	8.0	12.5	8.5	5.0	8.5	7.0

Note: Where applicable, number of countries in parentheses.

Source: World Trade Organization.

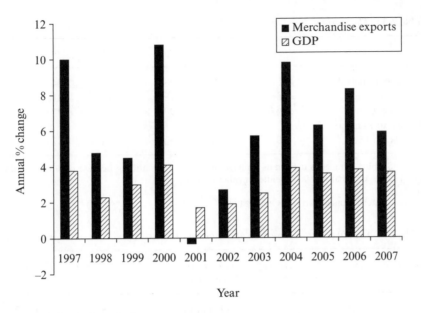

Source: World Trade Organization.

Figure 2.1   *Growth in the volume of world merchandise trade and GDP*

Table 2.2   *International air transport*

Year	Passengers	Freight (tonnes)	Passenger-kilometers	Freight (tonne-kilometers)
1996	412	13.6	1,380,680	75,510
1997	438	15.7	1,468,150	87,740
1998	458	15.8	1,512,040	87,050
1999	493	17.3	1,622,250	93,280
2000	542	18.8	1,790,370	101,560
2001	536	18.0	1,726,580	95,950
2002	547	18.8	1,736,070	101,590
2003	561	19.6	1,738,510	103,133
2004	647	21.8	2,015,070	115,120
2005	704	22.6	2,197,360	118,480

Source: International Civil Aviation Organization.

Transport supply has grown to cater for the demands of internationalization, and for globalization. The world's mercantile marine has increased considerably to handle the growth in international trade (Table 2.3 offers data on the global deadweight tonnage available) while the number of freighter aircraft doubled, from 1,789 to 3,563 airplanes, in the two decades to 2006. The world's fleets of trucks have expanded to meet demands for land transport.

Transport requires infrastructure as well as vessels, planes and vehicles, to move goods and people around the globe. This infrastructure is generally

Table 2.3   *The world's shipping fleet (million dwt)*

	1990	1999	2000	2001	2002	2003
World merchant fleet	658.4	799.0	808.4	825.6	844.2	857.0
Surplus tonnage	63.7	23.7	18.4	21.5	21.7	10.3
Active fleet	594.7	775.3	790.0	804.1	822.5	846.7
Surplus tonnage as % of world fleet	9.7	3.0	2.3	2.6	2.6	1.2

Note: Surplus tonnage is defined as tonnage that is not fully utilized because of slow steaming or lay-up status, or because it is lying idle for other reasons.

Source: International Maritime Organization.

Table 2.4   *Leading container service operators on the basis of number of ships and TEUs*

Operator		Country/ territory	Number of ships	TEU capacity
1	A.P. Moller Group	Denmark	328	844,626
2	MSC	Switzerland	217	516,876
3	Evergreen Group	Taiwan	152	442,310
4	P&O Nedlloyd	UK/Netherlands	157	419,527
5	CMA-CGM Group	France	150	299,174
6	Hanjin/DSR-Senator	Korea/Germany	76	290,677
7	COSCO	China	148	274,128
8	NOL/APL	Singapore	82	273,573
9	NYK	Japan	91	233,934
10	MOL	Japan	72	222,533
Top 10			1,473	3,817,358
Top 20			2,127	5,383,758
World fleet				8,354,000

Note: TEU is an inexact unit of cargo capacity used to describe the capacity of container ships and container terminals. It is based on the volume of a twenty-foot long shipping container, a standard-sized metal box that can be easily transferred between different modes of transport, such as ships, trains and trucks.

Source: United Nations Committee on Trade and Development, *Review of Maritime Transport*, Geneva: UNTAD, 2004.

physically large, and inevitably expensive and largely immobile that seldom have uses beyond those it was designed for – in economic terms infrastructure can be seen as a 'sunk cost'. As we shall see later, given technology improvements or new regulations, infrastructure can often become economically obsolete well before it is physically worn out.

To give some impression of the scale of some of the transport infrastructure in the world, Table 2.5 provides a list of the largest seaports in terms of what they handled, together with changes in their rankings since 2000. The increased importance of China is again seen in terms of the number of its ports that are listed and their movement up the table over time. Table 2.6 offers broadly comparable data

Table 2.5 *The world's largest seaports by TEU*

Rank in		Port	Country	TEUs
2000	2004			
1	1	Hong Kong	China	21.984
2	2	Singapore	Singapore	21.329
6	3	Shanghai	China	14.557
23	4	Shenzhen	China	13.615
3	5	Busan	South Korea	11.430
4	6	Kaohsiung	Taiwan	9.714
5	7	Rotterdam	Netherlands	8.281
7	8	Los Angeles	United States	7.321
9	9	Hamburg	Germany	7.003
13	10	Dubai	United Arab Emirates	6.429
10	11	Antwerp	Belgium	6.064
8	12	Long Beach	United States	5.780
12	13	Port Kalang	Malaysia	5.244
24	14	Quingdao	China	5.140
14	15	New York/New Jersey	United States	4.478
108	16	Tanjung Pelepas	Malaysia	4.020
not ranked	17	Ningbo	China	4.006
31	18	Tianjin	China	3.814
11	19	Tanjug Priok	Indonesia	3.597
25	20	Laem Chabang	Thailand	3.529

Table 2.6 *The largest international airports by passenger numbers (2007)*

Airport	International passengers
London Heathrow Airport	62,099,530
Charles de Gaulle International Airport	54,901,564
Amsterdam Airport Schiphol	47,677,570
Frankfurt Airport	47,087,699
Hong Kong International Airport	46,281,000
Singapore Changi Airport	35,221,203
Narita International Airport (Japan)	34,289,064
Dubai International Airport	33,481,257
Suvarnabhumi Airport (Thailand)	31,632,716
London Gatwick Airport	31,139,116
Incheon International Airport (Korea)	30,753,225
Madrid Barajas International Airport	29,339,784
Kuala Lumpur International Airport	26,938,970
Chatrapati Shivaji International Airport (India)	25,360,860
Munich Airport	23,988,612
Dublin Airport	22,339,673
John F. Kennedy International Airport	21,521,711
London Stansted Airport	21,201,543
Taiwan Taoyuan International Airport	20,855,186
Malpensa International Airport (Italy)	20,627,846

Note: There are a number of larger airports that handle primarily domestic traffic – e.g., Hartsfield-Jackson Atlanta International Airport handled 89,379,287 total passengers in 2007 and O'Hare International Airport some 76,177,855.

Source: Airports Council International.

Table 2.7   *Motorway networks of OECD states*

Country	Network of motorways (kms)	Motorways per capita (mm)	Motorway density (m per km²)
Austria	1,678	202.61	20.01
Belgium	1,763	167.73	54.17
Canada	16,900	534.59	1.69
Czech Republic	564	55.02	7.15
Denmark	1,340	236.04	31.09
Finland	693	131.85	2.05
France	10,843	176.20	19.67
Germany	12,363	149.97	34.63
Great Britain	3,555	60.41	15.46
Hungary	575	56.94	6.18
Iceland	0	0	0
Ireland	125	29.48	1.76
Italy	6,487	112.06	21.53
Japan	7,383	57.79	19.54
Korea	3,117	64.27	31.29
Luxembourg	147	319.57	56.84
Netherlands	2,274	139.01	54.76
New Zealand	171	41.30	0.64
Norway	194	41.81	0.60
Poland	662	17.36	2.05
Portugal	883	83.54	9.53
Slovenia	580	288.56	28.61
Sweden	1,740	192.31	3.87
Switzerland	1,361	182.46	32.97
United States	75,008	253.05	7.79

Source: Organisation of Economic Co-operation and Development.

on international passenger airports, in this case measured by the number of passengers that they handled.

It is more difficult to isolate international road and rail infrastructure. Although land modes play a significant role in international trade both as the main trunk-haul carrier and in providing feeder services to sea and air movements, they are used more extensively for domestic transport, and separating out the international component is less easy. An indication of the scale of road networks and how they vary between countries is seen in Table 2.7. A similar set of statistics, although listed in order of size, for railroads is seen in Table 2.8. It should be noted when comparing these tables, that while roads are used almost universally for the movement of both freight and people, this is less so for railways. For example, the Canadian and the US system, with the exception of Amtrak and some local services around larger cities, is primarily a freight system, whereas that of the United Kingdom, and many geographically smaller countries, is used mainly by passengers. The concept of infrastructure and the way in which it is measured can thus be contextual, whether one is looking at its importance to the freight or passenger sectors. As we shall see in Chapter 5, this can pose

Table 2.8 *Length of railway networks in the world's 36 largest systems (km)*

Country	Length of network
USA	210,437***
Russia	92,217
China	76,600
India	63,332
Canada	52,115***
Argentina	35,753 ***
Germany	34,192
Australia	33,819*
Japan	29,682
Brazil	29,487 ***
France	29,463
Mexico	26,662**
Ukraine	21,891
South Africa	20,247
UK	19,956
Poland	19,429
Italy	16,627
Spain	14,473
Kazakhstan	14,205
Romania	10,781***
Sweden	9,957
Czech Republic	9,496
Turkey	8,697***
Pakistan	7,791
Hungary	7,960
Iran	7,265
Indonesia	6,458
Finland	5,905
Chile	5,898***
Austria	5,827
Belarus	5,494
Sudan	5,478***
North Korea	5,214
Egypt	5,195***
Switzerland	5,063**
Cuba	4,226

Note: All 2006, except: *2002, **2004, ***2005.

problems when trying to allocate costs of infrastructure to various transport user groups.

Another, and linked, difficulty with all this type of data is the impossibility of devising a common unit of measurement – for example, freight moved from an airport is measured in tons, whereas passengers are seen as individuals and, while if looking at something like fuel use one may feel it reasonable to reduce everything to tons carried, this is hardly appropriate when looking at goods and people passing through an airport. The facilities needed for people and cargo movement

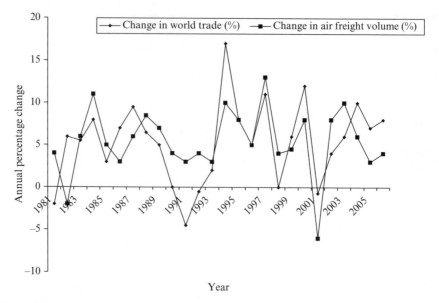

Figure 2.2 *Changes in international trade and freight airline volumes*

are entirely different. From another angle, it is possible to count physical units (for example, the number of cars or planes) but lack of homogeneity prevents meaningful comparisons over time for individual modes (for example, an average aircraft of 10 years ago is different from the average aircraft of today), let alone contrast of trends to be made between modes. Infrastructure data thus have to be treated with some care.

Output measures (for example, ton-miles or passenger-kilometers), although appearing to circumvent problems of comparability over broad categories of transport, in fact tend to be equally inadequate. Such measures, in particular, ignore the quality and costs of alternatives. Despite these comments it is still possible to look at official statistics and obtain a general feel for the way the transport "situation" is evolving in a very general sense.

What is important, and perhaps self-evident, although only implicitly so in the international data offered so far, is the strong correlation between international trade and trends in the use of transport services. A clearer illustration of this is to be found in Figure 2.2, which provides details of the long-term trends in air cargo volumes and changes in world trade. The figure also shows the short-term fluctuations that affect the demands for international transport services and, as we shall see later, pose particular challenges for capital-intensive industries such as shipping to adjust the levels of capacity that they offer.

While international trade, and transport with it, has grown globally, trade between and within certain blocs of countries has tended to expand more rapidly because of new institutional structures; most notably the creation of the North American Free Trade Agreement (NAFTA) and the continued widening and deepening of the European Union (which is discussed in more detail in Chapter 12). Table 2.9 shows just how important these trade blocs have become.

Table 2.9   *Value of merchandise trade by trade blocs as a percent of world trade (2006)*

	Exports	Imports
European Union	37.5	38.3
North American Free Trade Agreement	13.9	20.5
Association of Southeast Asian Nations	6.4	5.5
Gulf Cooperation Council	3.9	1.7
European Free Trade Association	2.3	1.7
Southern Common Market	1.8	1.1
South Asian Preferential Trade Agreement	1.3	1.9
South African Development Community	1.0	1.0
Common Market for Eastern & Southern Africa	1.0	1.0

Source: World Trade Organization, *International Trade Statistics*, WTO, 2007.

These new institutional arrangements have both fostered greater demand for transport services as barriers to trade in goods and services have come down, and also made it easier to provide transport as cross-border regulations have been relaxed.[4] In some cases, as with the EU, they also allow cabotage – the ability of a foreign transport operator to pick up and set down in another country – which increases transport flexibility and efficiency further. For example, the creation of the European Single Internal Market in 1992 alone has been estimated to have led to a 4.5 to 7 percent rise in the EU's GNP, with an increase of 30 to 50 percent in trans-frontier lorry traffic.

Reflecting on changes on the other side of the Atlantic, Table 2.10 provides some details of trade patterns, in monetary terms, across the US–Canada and US–Mexico borders as NAFTA has taken hold. NAFTA is a trilateral trade bloc in North America created by the governments of the United States, Canada and Mexico and, in terms of combined purchasing power parity GDP of its members, is the largest trade bloc in the world and the second-largest by nominal GDP comparison.

2.3   Transport at the National Level

Transport forms a major component of the national output and accounts for a large part of national expenditure in most developed countries; for example, it is over 14.5 percent of national expenditure in Great Britain. A substantial part of this is taken up for consumer expenditure, the remainder is undertaken by firms. While the UK's relative expenditure on transport is roughly in line with that found in the United States, it is slightly atypical within Europe where it is at the top end of the spectrum; for example, in Belgium 12.9 percent of income was spent on transport in 1989, in Italy it was 12.9 percent and in the Netherlands 11.3 percent. Table 2.11 gives a more detailed breakdown of the relative importance of

---

[4] K.J. Button, 'Transport policy', in A.M. El-Agraa (ed.), *The European Union: Economics and Politics* (8th edn), Cambridge: Cambridge University Press, 2007.

Table 2.10   *NAFTA trade by value (C$m)*

	1990	1995	1998	2000	2002	2004
Canadian imports from the US	87,865	150,683	203,578	229,644	218,329	208,553
Canadian exports to the US	108,586	207,752	269,908	359,289	345,366	347,933
US exports to Mexico	33,108	63,557	117,211	165,917	153,159	144,176
US imports from Mexico	35,205	84,684	140,501	201,842	211,578	202,833
Canadian exports to Mexico	656	1,161	1,467	2,035	2,420	2,975
Canadian imports from Mexico	1,749	5,352	7,682	12,066	12,732	13,398

Source: M.R. Brooks, *North American Freight Transportation: The Road to Security and Prosperity*, Cheltenham, UK and Northampton, MA, USA: Edward Elgar, 2008.

Table 2.11   *Weekly household expenditure in Great Britain (2001/2002)*

Average weekly expenditure all households (£)

Food & non-alcoholic drinks	41.80
Alcoholic drink, tobacco & narcotics	11.40
Clothing and footwear	22.90
Housing, fuel and power	35.90
Household goods & services	30.50
Health	4.50
Transport	57.80
Communication	10.40
Recreation and culture	54.10
Education	5.60
Restaurants and hotels	33.40
Miscellaneous goods and services	30.70
Other expenditure items	59.50
Total	398.30

Source: Family Expenditure Survey.

transport in overall expenditure in 2001–02 in Great Britain and Table 2.12 offers a time-series picture of national transport expenditure out of all expenditures. Table 2.13 provides similar data for the United States for comparative purposes.

Table 2.14, relating to the United States, reveals another important fact, namely the relative and absolute roles played by the different, individual modes of transport. It is quite clear from what we see in the table that expenditure on road transport dominates transport expenditures, and this is also reflected in the physical data; passenger-miles being the number of individual trips taken by each mode multiplied by the average length of those trips. Just to confirm that this is

Table 2.12   *Aggregate personal expenditure in Great Britain on transport (2003 prices)*

	2001	2002	2003	2004	2005	2006
Transport	35,100	36,057	38,016	39,107	39,571	40,365
Final consumption	309,917	323,931	340,339	357,152	363,896	379,431

Table 2.13   *Transport in US: final domestic demand*

	1990	1995	2000	2005	2006
Gross domestic demand	7,101.2	8,098.4	10,196.4	11,613.1	11,937.1
Domestic transportation-related final demand	n.a.	n.a.	1,198.5	1,287.2	1,295.2
Transport in GDD (%)	n.a.	n.a.	11.8	11.1	10.9
Personal consumption of transport	553.2	658.6	853.5	944.6	942.4
Motor vehicles and parts	226.6	272.3	386.5	451.3	437.3
Gasoline and oil	140.3	154.5	175.7	205.5	213.9
Transport services	186.3	231.8	291.3	287.8	291.2
Gross private domestic investment	n.a.	n.a.	167.4	151.1	161.7
Transport structures	n.a.	n.a.	6.6	6.0	6.5
Transport equipment	78.8	120.6	160.8	145.1	155.2
Government transport-related purchases	157.9	156.5	177.6	191.5	191.1
Federal purchases	18.4	18.0	19.2	25.4	25.6
State and local purchases	120.7	128.8	149.4	152.9	153.9
Defense-related purchases	18.8	9.7	9.0	13.2	11.6

Note: n.a. indicates not available.

Source: US Bureau of Transportation Statistics.

Table 2.14   *US passenger transport by mode (2007)*

Mode of passenger transport	Passenger-miles (millions)	Percent
Highway – total	4,884,557	88.79
Passenger vehicles, motorcycles	4,520,810	82.18
Trucks	222,836	4.05
Buses	162,908	2.96
Air carriers	583,689	10.61
Rail – total	30,972	0.56
Transit	16,118	0.29
Commuter	9,473	0.17
Intercity/Amtrak	5,381	0.10
All other modes (e.g., ferryboats)	2,091	0.04

Table 2.15   *Distance traveled per person per year by mode of transport, in Great Britain, 1999–2001*

		Walk	Pedal cycle	Cars and other private road vehicles	Bus	Rail	Taxi and other	All public transport	All modes of transport
Great Britain		189	39	5,713	245	425	205	874	6,815
	North East	177	–	4,651	448	–	211	858	5,737
	North West	173	36	5,407	265	249	204	717	6,333
	Yorkshire and Humber	190	42	5,490	279	282	199	761	6,483
	East Midlands	165	51	6,156	237	–	134	648	7,020
	West Midlands	175	31	5,694	269	–	222	613	6,513
	East	176	51	7,056	138	699	161	998	8,280
	London	237	32	3,647	333	996	206	1536	5,452
	South East	193	45	6,961	117	568	183	869	8,067
	South West	178	41	6,015	157	–	179	592	6,826
England		188	41	5,718	234	449	189	872	6,819
Wales		165	–	5,438	179	–	187	494	6,111
Scotland		220	30	5,835	393	366	369	1128	7,213

Source: UK Department for Transport.

not just a trend peculiar to the United States, Table 2.15 provides data for Great Britain. Although no time-series data are given, the trend has been for the car to continue to increase its modal share over time.

As we shall see later, the rise in private transport use is closely related to higher car ownership levels – although the question of cause and effect is a complex one (Chapter 4). What should also be remembered, however, is that while the relative use of private transport is rising, the role of public transport, especially for commuter trips into large cities, is still very important as we shall see later when discussing local transport, and often rises in absolute terms.

What the tables do not show is the share of household expenditure that goes on transport for different income groups. What is found looking at this data is that the proportion of expenditure that is devoted to transport tends to rise overall with household income, reflecting the 'superior good' nature of the activity. What official data also show is the use made by different income groups of the various modes. The railway mode is used primarily by those in the higher-income groups, as is the private car. In contrast, bus transport is used disproportionately more by the poorer sectors of the community. We shall return to this when looking at urban transport trends.

Within countries there are also distinctions in terms of how freight transport is moved, and the trends these movements have been taking over time. As we see in Table 2.16, inland freight transport in the United States is increasingly being dominated by trucking, although other modes, and particularly railroads, have a significant share. This is a pattern that is reflected in virtually all countries; Table 2.17 offers data on a number of higher-income nations.

Table 2.16 *US ton-miles of freight (millions)*

	1980	1990	2000	2006
Total ton-miles	3,404,015	2621,943	4,328,642	4,637,513
Air	4,840	10,420	15,810	15,357
Truck	629,675	848,779	1,192,825	1,294,492
Railroad	932,000	1,064,408	1,546,319	1,852,833
Domestic water transport	921,835	833,544	645,799	561,629
Coastwise	631,149	479,134	283,872	227,155
Lakewise	61,747	60,930	57,879	53,103
Internal	227,343	292,393	302,558	279,778
Intraport	1,596	1,087	1,490	1,591
Pipeline	915,66	864,792	927,889	913,202
Oil and oil products	588,00	584,100	577,000	584,700
Natural gas	327,666	280,692	350,889	328,502

Source: US Bureau of Transportation Statistics.

Table 2.17 *Freight moved by mode by country: 1995 and 2005 (billion tonne-kilometers)*

	Road		Rail		Inland waterways		Inland pipelines	
	1995	2005	1995	2005	1995	2005	1995	2005
UK	161.5	167.9	13.3	22.1	0.2	0.2	11.1	10.8
Austria	26.5	37.0	13.2	17.1	2.0	1.8	6.8	7.8
France	178.2	205.3	48.1	40.7	6.6	8.9	21.9	22.2
Germany	237.8	310.1	69.5	89.7	64.0	64.1	14.8	16.7
Italy	174.4	211.8	21.7	20.1	0.1	0.1	9.7	10.7
Spain	101.6	233.2	11.0	11.0	1.0	–	5.9	8.5
Sweden	31.6	38.6	19.4	21.7	–	–	–	–
Czech Republic	31.3	43.4	22.6	14.8	0.1	0.1	2.3	2.3
Poland	51.2	111.8	68.2	43.8	0.9	0.3	13.5	25.4
Switzerland	11.4	13.8	8.7	11.5	0.2	–	1.2	0.2
Japan	–	322.0	–	–	23.0	–	–	–
USA	1,521.0	1,845.0	1,923.0	341.0	534.0	476.0	878.0	861.0

We also notice in the table that pipelines are an important form of transport. Physical limits to the type of commodities which can be carried in this way, however, are likely to prevent pipelines from ever becoming more than a minority mode of transport. Rail transport tends to be declining irrespective of whether measured in absolute physical ton-kilometers or in the real monetary value of the revenues obtained.

While these aggregate data reveal interesting trends, they nevertheless hide quite important details. In particular, on the freight side the ton-kilometers statistics do not show that much of the increase in road haulage is attributable to longer hauls in larger vehicles. The average length of haul by road in the United Kingdom rose from 68 kilometers in 1980 to 86 kilometers in 2007, peaking at 95 kilometers in 1999, although 52 percent were lifted on trips of 50 kilometers or

Table 2.18   *Government expenditure on transport in Canada (C$m)*

	1971	1981	1991	1996
Transport equipment	174	734	1,571	1,222
Transport fuel	105	844	618	599
Highway and bridge maintenance	22	133	238	216
Transport industries				
Air	3	42	106	80
Water	10	23	37	24
Railway	2	3	1	2
Truck	52	191	286	254
Surface passenger	156	723	1,543	1,695
Other transport services	0	1	14	6
Pipeline	12	61	163	177
Transport margins	24	91	151	158
Rental of automobiles and trucks	40	169	300	349
Total, transport	600	3,015	5,028	4,782
Total, government input	23,694	89,697	195,471	213,48

less in 2007. Further, articulated vehicles over 33 tonnes gross weight continued to account for an increasing share of all goods moved: 73 percent of tonne-kilometers in 2007, compared with 65 percent in 1997. Similar trends are seen in the United States, where haul lengths rose from 272 miles in 1960, to 391 in 1990 and to 458 in 2001, and in most European countries.

The explanation for this probably is in part the greater geographical concentration of industry that has occurred, with a small number of production units now supplying the whole country and export demands, rather than numerous small factories meeting the needs of local markets. There have also been major changes in the way supply chains are managed, as we shall see later in the book.

The public sector plays an important role in the direct provision of transport services in most countries. It both provides and maintains a considerable amount of infrastructure, as well as being responsible for those modes operating within the nationalized transport sector, which can be significant in some countries.

Table 2.18 provides, by way of variety, some data breaking down overall government expenditure on transport in Canada. These figures are, however, likely to hide some transport expenditures and should, thus, be seen as lower limits. Transport, for instance, accounts, or is directly responsible, for additional expenditures under items such as law and order, environmental services and health. Another difficulty in looking at a snap-shot of expenditures, or even a series of snap-shots as here, is that public expenditure is subjected in aggregate to cycles that reflect such things as the state of a national economy and government policies, most notably Keynesian use it to counter act business cycles. The number of jobs created by injections of money into transport investments is not altogether clear, however, and varies between countries and the type of investment.[5]

[5] D. Tajgman and J. de Veen, *Employment – Intensive Infrastructure Programmes: Labour Policies and Practices – Guide*, Geneva: International Labour Organization, 1998.

Table 2.19 *Federal, state and local government transport-related revenues and expenditure ($m in current prices)*

	1980	1990	2000	2003
Total revenues	66,341	90,941	128,597	123,950
Federal	19,952	28,414	47,146	42,631
State and local	46,389	62,527	81,451	81,319
Total expenditures	95,431	131,270	195,398	227,529
State and local expenditures less federal grants	47,715	90,180	139,101	149,175
Federal grants	28,286	26,172	26,191	31,139
Federal expenditures less grants	19,429	14,919	30,106	47,214

Table 2.20 *Transport employment in the United States (thousands)*

	1960	1970	1980	1990	1995
Transport sector	2,471.3	2,694.3	3,175.0	3,731.8	4,098.0
Equipment manufacturing	1,772.9	1,949.0	1,995.3	2,073.3	1,864.8
Related industries	2,027.2	2,652.4	2,961.7	3,671.5	3,929.0
Government employment	532.0	711.0	670.8	673.3	101.0
Total transport employment	6,803.4	8,006.7	8,802.8	10,149.9	9,993.0
Transport in US employment (%)	10.4	10.2	8.8	8.5	8.0

A third problem in looking at this type of data in large, and especially federal countries is that they can miss outlays at the subnational level of government; for example, in the United States about a quarter of new road expenditure is by local government and over 55 percent of maintenance expenditure. At a more aggregate level, Table 2.19 provides a breakdown of US transport-related public expenditures (and also revenues) by level of government unit. It is clear that states act both independently in spending but also as agents of central government in terms of executing federal transport expenditures.

Transport is a major employer of labor in most countries. This extends through the infrastructure investment phase to operations. Some idea of the importance of transport employment in the US economy is seen in Table 2.20, which provides time series from 1960 to the mid-1990s. The table does not simply show those directly employed in transport but also embraces those engaged in related industries. The gradual decline in the relative national importance of transport employment is due to a number of factors, including the substitution of the car for public transport and for collection and delivery of goods at shops and the substitution of capital for labor (which ranges from the use of larger trucks to the smaller crews required in the cockpit of an aircraft).

In technical terms there is scope for factor substitutability in transport that allows for capital to replace labor; it can often be 'technologically progressive'.[6]

[6] W.J. Baumol, 'Macroeconomics of unbalanced growth: the anatomy of urban crisis', *American Economic Review*, **57**, 415–26, 1967.

This may come about through scale effects, the use of larger ships with the same size crew to carry more cargo, or the substitution of labor functions, like navigation on aircraft, by automated systems. Given the massive increase in freight and passenger traffic over time that we have seen in earlier tables, and the small overall rise in the number of transport and related workers, there has clearly been a very significant rise in labor productivity in the transport industries as a whole.

2.4 Local Transport

Local transport can conveniently be divided into urban and rural, although suburban transport can have its own particular features. Almost by definition there are only limited common features across cities; local transport conditions and use depend, among other things, on the geography of the area (for example, whether it is hilly, has waterways through it, or is close to another urban area), its history (for example, whether it has inherited a legacy of infrastructure more suited to a bygone era), its economic roles (for example, whether it is a political or commercial center, or has a large manufacturing base), and the political attitudes of local politicians (for example, whether they foster motor vehicle use or have a public transit bias). Similar factors influence transport in rural areas, including the nature of local agriculture or mineral extraction, the historical provision of infrastructure and the peculiarities of the area's geography.

Some very broad general patterns are identifiable in at least cities in the higher-income countries of the world, and to some extent in poorer nations. We have less data on rural areas in part because they tend to be less densely populated, especially in industrial nations, but also because traditional concerns of transport planners, most notably traffic congestion, tend to be much less pronounced.

Urban Transport

Increasing numbers of people are living in urban areas as agricultural efficiency improves and as industrialization spreads. Even in the long-industrialized countries there have been significant changes in land use, and in urban form more generally – as incomes have risen as the service sector has increased in importance, and there have been demographic changes. Interventions by urban planners have brought about their own impacts, a trend highlighted nearly half a century ago by Jane Jacobs.[7] There has been widespread urban sprawl from most cities as their populations have increased. This not only poses problems of a practical nature, such as the provision of public services and the delineation of appropriate areas for local government, but from a descriptive perspective, it means that data collected on old zoning systems can often obscure some of the newer trends in urban transport such as long-distance and reverse commuting. There have been some

---

[7] J. Jacobs, *The Death and Life of Great American Cities*, New York: Random House, 1961.

efforts to overcome this problem in recent years. The United States, for example, has sought to partially resolve it by providing data on 'metropolitan statistical areas' (MSAs) and 'combined statistical areas'; for example, the former combines data from administrative units within a contiguous area of relatively high population density.

Even in suburban areas, transport trends found in traditional city areas are not replicated because of lower densities of development than in central cities, dominated by single-family homes on small plots surrounded at close quarters by very similar dwellings. The planning authorities also tend to adopt zoning patterns that separate residential and commercial development, as well as different intensities and densities of development. At the simplest level this means that daily needs are not within walking distance of most homes and reliance on the car increases, and that over time the distance of the average commute has risen.[8]

To cope with some of these issues there are arguments that 'edge cities' have emerged – concentrations of business, shopping and entertainment outside a traditional urban area in what had recently been a residential suburb or semi-rural community.[9]

As a very broad generalization, most major cities in the world now suffer from serious traffic congestion problems, and this sometimes can extend well beyond traditional notions of the 'rush hour'. This is, however, a subject we shall deal with in some depth in Chapters 6 and 9. Here we focus more on the general characteristics of urban transport, and simply highlight some of the major differences that exist between cities.

Table 2.21 provides some basic details of the nature of eight major cities and the use that is made of passenger transport in each. Very significant differences can immediately be seen in the use of the various modes of transport, including walking and cycling. There is also a general correlation, as one may anticipate between the levels of car ownership in the cities and the use made of the motor car, although this may be deceptive if part of the mileage driven is outside of the city. What the data do not tell us, but which is a topic to which we shall devote considerable time to later in the book, are the policies that are being pursued in these cities to influence the amount of travel undertaken and the modes that are used.

The data in Table 2.21 offer a snap-shot across some cities in the world, and again it should be emphasized that this is just a small number of cities, but it offers no indication of trends. Table 2.22 partially fills this in by offering data on public transport use. The pattern that is clearly seen is, with one or two exceptions, a reduced relative importance for public transport in most cities. In part this is because of the difficulties of servicing physically spreading cities with public transport modes, but also links with the high levels of car ownership that can be found in most countries (Table 2.23), and this in turn, as we shall see later

---

8 A.M. Warnes, 'Estimates of journey-to-work distances from census statistics', *Regional Studies*, **6**, 315–26, 1972.

9 J. Garreau, *Edge City: Life on the New Frontier*, Garden City, NY: Doubleday, 1991.

Table 2.21 *Some basic features of a number of major cities (1995)*

Factor	Hong Kong	Singapore	Munich	Stockholm	New York	Phoenix	Perth
Population	6,311,000	2,986,500	1,324,204	1,725,756	19,227,361	2,526,113	1,244,320
Jobs	2,980,151	1,700,900	768,700	838,800	10,108,808	1,035,214	521,810
Metropolitan GDP per capita (in 1995 $s)	22,969	28,576	54,692	33,438	34,935	26,920	21,995
Urban population density (persons per km²)	46	116	469	386	444	531	658
Length of freeway per capita (meters per 1000 persons)	13.0	44.2	45.3	130.4	112.8	178.9	42.6
Passengers car (passenger-kilometers per passenger)	930	3,570	5,913	8,470	12,845	15,082	13,546
Public transport (passenger-kilometers per passenger)	3,675	3,143	2,622	2,317	1,266	100	642
Percentage of daily trips by walking and cycling	34.1	16.3	32.3	28.0	16.1	4.9	9.1

Source: T. Cameron, J. Lyons and J.R. Kenworthy, 'Trends in vehicle-kilometres of travel in world cities, 1960–1990: underlying drivers and policy responses', *Transport Policy*, **11**, 287–98, 2004.

Table 2.22   *Public transport use in urban areas (percentage of trips taken)*

Urban area	1980	Later year	
Adelaide	5.8	1990	4.9
Amsterdam	20.4	1995	16.9
Boston	4.0	2001	4.9
Brussels	19.9	1995	21.8
Calgary	8.8	1995	7.6
Chicago	8.0	2001	3.7
Denver	2.1	2001	1.5
Detroit	1.2	2001	0.5
Frankfurt	35.8	1995	14.2
Hong Kong	80.5	1995	73.0
Kuala Lumpur	30.2	1995	10.8
London (SE England)	19.8	1995	17.1
Los Angeles	2.7	2001	1.5
Manila	70.2	1995	34.0
Melbourne	7.1	1995	7.6
New York	14.1	2001	11.0
Paris	32.5	1995	24.1
Phoenix	0.5	2001	0.4
San Diego	1.2	2001	1.3
San Francisco	6.6	2001	4.5
Singapore	52.0	1995	40.1
Stockholm	25.6	1995	20.7
Sydney	13.7	1995	12.3
Tokyo	68.5	1995	56.6
Toronto	25.7	1990	15.2
Vienna	30.0	1995	24.8
Washington	5.0	2001	4.0
Zurich	23.2	1995	24.0

Source: Adapted from the *Millennium Cities Database* and P.G. Newman and J.R. Kenworthy, *Millennium Cities Database for Sustainable Transport, Cities and Automobile Dependence: A Sourcebook*, Aldershot: Ashgate, 1990.

when looking at transport demand, is influenced by income levels. There are also legacy effects to consider: many older cities have extensive rapid transit systems and metros that date back many years, and this acts to retain passengers on public transport modes.

Rural Transport

While there has been a global movement to urbanization there is still a significant amount of movement outside of cities which for convenience we call 'rural transport'. Much of this is transit traffic in the sense that it involves the movement of people and goods between urban areas and does not stop, except for breaks of various kinds, as part of this movement. Pure rural transport has its origins and destinations outside of urban areas, or involves movement between cities and non-city areas. Much of this transport involves the movement of agricultural

Table 2.23   *Car ownership per 1000 population in selected countries (2006)*

Country	Car ownership	Country	Car ownership	Country	Car ownership
USA	765	Greece	329	Cape Verde	30
Luxembourg	686	Bahrain	322	Colombia	29
Malaysia	641	South Korea	293	Senegal	18
Australia	619	Bahamas	289	India	12
Malta	607	Israel	263	China	10
Italy	566	Hungary	262	Pakistan	8
Canada	563	Poland	261	Burkina Faso	6
Japan	543	Bulgaria	239	Guinea	5
Norway	494	Slovakia	237	Niger	4
Belgium	484	Libya	234	Angola	4
Spain	471	Latvia	214	Somalia	3
UK	426	Uruguay	174	Rwanda	2
Netherlands	417	Argentina	170	Mozambique	2
Slovenia	413	South Africa	146	Bangladesh	2
Denmark	408	Mexico	138	Ethiopia	1

Source: United Nations.

products, and those involved in their production, although increasingly it can involve tourism. Further, although we focus here mainly on economically developed countries where urbanization is extensive, rural transport is a major subject of study in lower-income nations that still have a significant rural population.

Defining rural transport is not simple, and circumstances vary with country and regions within countries. For these reasons, only one small picture of a nation's rural transport situation is described. In the United States, the Office of Management and Budget definition of metropolitan areas (core counties with one or more central cities of at least 50,000 residents with a Census Bureau-defined urbanized area and a metro area population of over 100,000 or fringe counties that are economically associated with core counties) provides a residual of non-metropolitan counties located outside the areas that have no cities with 50,000 or more residents. This is defined as rural.

Overall, 92.7 percent of households in these rural areas had access to a car in 2000, compared with 88.9 percent of urban households. The highly carless rural communities were characterized by persistent poverty and had high concentrations of Black, Hispanic or Native American residents. Rural residents without access to cars are particularly dependent on public transport, especially in high poverty areas. During the 1990s public transport services grew, with non-metro providers offering 62 percent more passenger trips, 93 percent more miles traveled, and 60 percent more vehicles available. Public transport is available in 60 percent of rural counties, but with 28 percent of about 1,200 systems offering only limited service. About two-thirds of rural systems operate in single counties or are city/town in scope; only one out of four rural transit providers operates in a multi-county area. About 60 percent of rural providers are public agencies, and roughly a third are nonprofit groups; less than 5 percent are private companies or tribal entities.

The number of rural communities served by long-distance bus services declined sharply in the years following deregulation in 1982. The intercity bus industry serves about 4,300 locations, down from over 15,000 prior to 1982, with many of the service discontinuations concentrated in rural communities. Still, 89 percent of the rural population is served by long-distance bus services, the dominant mode of scheduled intercity passenger transport for most rural residents. One reason for this is that fewer than 200 non-metro places are served by passenger rail service, and, following the terrorist attacks of 2001, the airline passenger industry suffered a downturn, with smaller communities especially hard hit; the number of flights to small, non-hub airports dropped 19 percent between 2000 and 2003.

Overall, rural roads are in better condition than those in urban areas. While less than 14 percent of rural roads (as measured by miles) in the United States were in poor or mediocre condition in 2002, some 29 percent of urban roads were so classified. Less wear and tear because of lower traffic levels at least partly explains this.

2.5   Emerging Trends

The world is not static and there are a number of emerging, as well as ongoing, trends that are beginning to influence the issues that transport economists are addressing. One way of categorizing some of the more important trends is to isolate them according to the broad nature of the economic environment of the countries involved.

First, in the established industrial world the long-term trend, despite periodic downturns in the business cycle (including recessions in many countries which began in 2007) and periods of 'irrational exuberance', to quote Alan Greenspan, the then Chairman of the US Federal Reserve Board, would seem to be for continued economic expansion. The recent past has already witnessed significant increases in traffic and vehicle ownership in these countries (Table 2.23) and there are reasons to expect this trend to continue in broad terms over the years. Globalization does not seem to have been fully completed, although the economic success of the Single Internal Market within the European Community and NAFTA are providing demonstration effects of the benefits of removing trade restrictions. The natural growth in trade accompanying these developments will in itself create demands for more transport services, but this inevitably will take place in the context of limited infrastructure capacity. Even if there are major investment initiatives, it takes time to construct new ports, roads and so on.

Looking to Europe, a lot has been written on impacts for transport of the creation of the Single European Market in 1992, and certainly the new situation with an enlarged membership has implications for transport not only within the member states but also to countries of the European Free Trade Area involved in the larger European Economic Space (see Chapter 14). The problem is how to cater for such traffic growth in a fully economically efficient manner, a fact recognized by the European Union in its transport policy statements.[10]

Second, it is becoming clearer that the liberalization of Eastern Europe, coupled with the new political geography that is emerging, is posing problems as well as offering opportunities, for the countries in the region.[11] Liberalization has meant that the overall 'transport market' in Europe expanded considerably in line with major new urban and industrial centers being brought within the market system. It means, therefore, that many major transport links are now part of Europe's transport future. In many ways this may prove advantageous for the long-term development of European transport since it creates something more akin to a natural market for transport services than currently exists, but there are problems of defining priorities and financing investments in the system.

Short-term problems also remain because of the attitude regarding transport that has grown up in Eastern and Central Europe over the past 40 years and the impact this has had on the physical transport infrastructure now in place. In particular, the transport systems of Eastern Europe are dominated by rail (which itself suffered from low productivity and overmanning), tend to be of poorer quality than in Western Europe and were developed from the late 1940s to meet the trading patterns of the members of the Council for Mutual Economic Assistance.

North America has begun, albeit slowly, to integrate its economies through free trade arrangements that are shifting patterns of production and with this, the demands for transport services. Coupled with this, the general growth in importance of international trade for the US has put increasing strains on its international border crossing; a situation worsened by the costs of meeting enhanced security arrangements. As with Europe, there are pressures for seeking innovative ways to finance new infrastructure, maintain and upgrade what is already in place, and to make better use of existing capacity.[12]

It is not only in the industrialized nations, and in the post-communist states, that new conditions are emerging. If there is to be economic development in the low-income countries of Africa, Asia and South and Central America then transport will inevitably change. There is ample evidence from China, India and some other economies, that the economies of some of these states are beginning to expand, although not the lowest-income countries. Again returning to Table 2.23, we see low levels of car ownership in the poorest countries. Added to this

---

[10] European Commission, *European Transport Policy for 2010: Time to Decide*, European Commission, 2001.

[11] K.J. Button, 'Enlargement from the point of view of the economist', in German Ministry for Transport, Construction and Housing, *Transport Political and Economic Transport Strategies of EU Enlargement*, Berlin: Deutsche Verkehrswissenschaftliche Gesellscaft, 2003.

[12] Transportation Research Board, *Freight Capacity in the 21st Century*, Washington DC: TRB, Special Report 271, 2003.

they also tend to have some of the least safe transport systems: Botswana, for example has the highest road mortality rate on roads in the world at 30 deaths per 100,000 population.

Economic expansion, however, especially if it results in significant growth in some larger countries, could lead to substantial demands for car ownership, more mobility, and the need for major new infrastructure initiatives, as well impose serious environmental and safety challenges. As can be seen from earlier discussions, the link between per capita income and vehicle ownership is a positive one. It will also mean that there will be increasing strains put on the environment, both within these countries and in terms of global effects such as emission of greenhouse gases.

A significant feature of most low-income countries in recent years has been the secular drift of population into urban areas. Historically, the growth of car ownership in the largest cities in Third World countries was already of the order of 7 to 15 percent in the decade to 1970. Added to this, the cost of transport in these cities has risen significantly, with households spending over 5 percent of their income on transport, and in some cases 15 percent, and city governments spending 15 to 25 percent of their annual budgets on transport investments and operations.

Looking forward, the transport situation in the urban areas of the developing world is inevitably going to get worse in the short to medium term. The mid-1980s saw eight of the largest cities in the world with populations of over 10 million located in low-income countries. Predictions are that this number will have doubled by the end of the century while a further 18 agglomerations in the developing world will each have a population of between 5 and 10 million. A major difficulty is that the growth of urbanization and the level of motor car ownership and use are closely linked. While this is partly due to the concentration of wealth in the urban areas it is also entwined with the geographical spread which accompanies urbanization and the resultant increase in the average journey length.

Comparing Nairobi and Mexico City, for example, shows average trip lengths of between 1.5 to 2.8 miles for the former while those for Mexico City, which is much larger, are between 3.5 and 6.0 miles. Public transport is much less efficient at serving a spatially dispersed market and hence the automobile is used more often. How to plan and cater for the inevitable expansion in traffic as urbanization continues in these countries will be a mounting problem for transport economists, as will be finding resources. Some indication of the resources that are currently being spent in China, for example, is that $4.25 billion was invested in Beijing's infrastructure in 2004, and another $22 billion up to the 2008 Olympics to reduce the city's traffic congestion issues.

The emergence of the economies of China and India has seen further urbanization trends and with this has come new demands for consumer goods, including automobiles (see Table 2.24 for details of China). These countries combined account for about 37 percent of the world's population, and between 1980 and 2005 the real personal income of India more than doubled, and it more

Table 2.24 *Durable goods for 1,000 households (2006 or most recent prior year)*

	China		India		Total
	Urban	Rural	Urban	Rural	
Automobiles	4.3	–	4.0	0.7	1.7
Bicycles	117.6	98.4	51.9	57.2	55.7
Cameras	48.0	3.7	0.0	0.0	0.0
Computers	47.2	–	0.0	0.0	0.0
Microwave ovens	50.6	–	–	–	–
Motorcycles[a]	20.4	44.6	28.3	7.9	13.6
Refrigerators	91.8	22.5	30.8	4.8	12.1
Telephones	93.3	64.1	–	–	–
Mobile telephones	137.4	89.4	70.4	27.5	39.5
Televisions[b]	137.4	89.4	70.4	27.5	39.5
Video disc players[c]	70.2	–	8.2	1.7	3.6
Washing machines	96.8	43.0	12.5	0.9	4.1

Note: [a] Data for India include scooters; [b] Data for China include color TVs; data for India include all TVs; [c] Data for India include VCRs.

than quadrupled in China.[13] The outcome has been a tripling of motor vehicles in India and a tenfold increase in China. The transport situation has been exacerbated by the urbanization that has accompanied the macroeconomic trends in these countries; the development area of Chinese cities, for example, tripled between 1985 and 2005 while the population only doubled, producing significant urban sprawl. A similar pattern emerges for India. There are different patterns of travel in urban areas between the two countries, however, with over half the trips in Chinese mega-cities being non-motorized compared to only 25 per cent in India. In both cases, however, motorization is growing rapidly – especially in terms of motorized two-wheeled vehicles which, for instance, grew in number from 200,000 to over 50 million in China from 1981 to 2002.

But it is not only the local transport systems that are finding it difficult to cope with rising demands; as incomes rise in many developing countries, other elements of transport infrastructure networks are also coming under increasing pressure. The amount and quality of infrastructure varies widely between developing countries; Figure 2.3 offers some indication of the length of roads and paved roads, adjusted by populations, for global regions. In many cases, the issue is simply that there is insufficient infrastructure for the needs of a country, a particular problem that is compounded in Africa where many mineral countries have no access to the sea and not only have to move the output long distances over their own territory but also have to rely on the infrastructure of other nations. While this has been a long-standing problem for some countries, in other cases, there is simply a shortage of capacity to meet a sudden increase in demand for their products.

[13] J. Pucher, Z.-R. Peng, N. Mital, Y. Zhu and N. Korattyswaroopam, 'Urban transport trends and policies in China and India: impacts of rapid economic growth', *Transport Reviews*, **27**, 379–410, 2007.

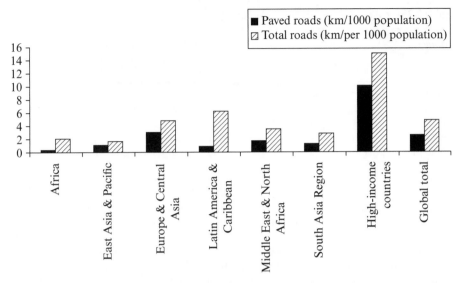

Figure 2.3   *Ratio of road networks to population by world region (2005)*

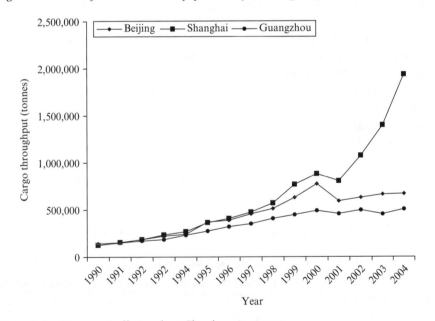

Figure 2.4   *Air cargo traffic trends at China's main airports*

In particular, countries like China and India that have seen large increases in their international trade from 1990, find themselves with pressure on their air- and seaports capacities to meet the globalized patterns of activities which they now engage. (Figure 2.4, for example, shows the growth in cargo traffic at China's main airports.) This pressure on capacity extends to national inter-urban transport systems as the domestic supply chain expands not just to feed the gateway ports but also as increased production itself puts pressure on the domestic freight networks.

Table 2.25   *Commitments by the World Bank for transport ($bn)*

Mode	Commitments			
	1996–2000	*Percent*	*2001–2006*	*Percent*
Roads	13.0	73	11.9	73
Railways	1.5	9	1.3	8
Ports	1.2	6	0.5	3
Aviation	0.1	0	0.5	3
General transport	2.2	12	2.2	13
Total	17.9	100	16.3	100

Source: World Bank, *A Decade of Action in Transport: An Evaluation of World Bank Assistance to the Transport Sector, 1995–2005*, Washington, DC: World Bank, 2007.

In terms of surface transport, in 2005 China had a road network of more than 3.3 million kilometers, although about 1.47 million kilometers were 'village roads'; paved roads comprised 770,265 kilometers of the total in 2004; the remainder were gravel, improved earth standard, or merely earth tracks. In 2003 they moved nearly 11.6 billion tons of freight and provided 769.6 trillion passenger-kilometers. Highways (some 130,000 kilometers) have been critical to China's economic growth, as they worked to mitigate a poor distribution network. Massive new investments mean that all major cities are expected to be linked by a 55,000-kilometer interprovincial expressway system by 2020. (By comparison, the US interstate freeway system is about 47,000 miles.) The highway and road systems carried nearly 11.6 billion tons of freight and 769.6 trillion passenger/kilometers in 2003.

Both bilateral and multilateral aid, most notably through the World Bank and the United Nations, but also from blocs such as the European Union, have been used in the past to help less economically advanced countries improve their transport systems. Table 2.25, for example, shows the recent expenditures of the World Bank, and future commitments are of the same order of magnitude, although with a somewhat broader focus in terms of how the monies will be spent.[14] Most of these funds are committed to enhancing the transport infrastructure of recipient countries, but there is increasing interest in ensuring that environmental and safety considerations are brought to bear at the project decision-making level.

It seems unlikely that the poorer nations of the world will require less assistance to maintain their transport systems in the future, although there are now more efforts by the aid-giving agencies to ensure that the monies provided are used effectively. Added to this, there is increased encouragement for these countries to do more by way of self-help in terms of imposing user charges on infrastructure to at least recover some of the costs and to limit its use to activities contributing most to economic development.

[14] World Bank, *Safe, Clean, and Affordable . . . Transport for Development, The World Bank Group's Transport Business Strategy for 2008–2012*, Washington, DC: World Bank, 2008.

Further Reading

Data on transport are widely available but differ in quality and the ways in which they are presented; for example, fuel use may be in kilometers per liter or in miles per gallon (and of course a US gallon is smaller that an imperial gallon to confuse things further). Governments at all level publish data, as do trade associations and transport undertakings. A few useful sites include the following. For the United States, national data are collected by the US Department of Transportation Bureau of Transportation Statistics (http://www.bts.gov/); for the United Kingdom, corresponding data is provided by the Department for Transport (http://www.dft.gov.uk/pgr/statistics/); EUROSTAT provides data for the European Union (http://epp.eurostat.ec.europa.eu); and for Canada a comparable site is http://www.tc.gc.ca/en/menu.htm. It is a simple matter to seek out national data for other countries. Internationally, the UN's International Civil Aviation Organization (http://www.icao.int/) and its International Maritime Organization (http://www.imo.org/) provide statistics on air transport and shipping, respectively, and its World Tourism Organization (http://www.unwto.org/) covers the important and growing tourism sector. The World Bank offers data and studies relating to the transport and related conditions in developing countries (http://www.worldbank.org/).

3 Movement, Transport and Location

3.1 The Desire for Movement

Robert Louis Stevenson once said, 'For my part, I travel not to anywhere, but to go. I travel for travel's sake. The great affair is to move' (from *Travels with a Donkey*). He is very much in the minority; few people travel for the sheer joy of it, although some modes of transport do arouse feelings of excitement, romance or sentiment. But even here there are fine lines to be drawn. Drifting down a Venetian canal in a gondola as the sun sets with the right person sitting beside you can clearly provide utility, but is this really from the transport? There are also, of course, people who take touring holidays each year where sight-seeing from a bus or car is an integral part of the enjoyment.

Most individuals, though, travel because they wish to benefit from the social, recreational, educational, employment and other opportunities that become accessible with movement. Similarly, freight transport opens up opportunities for greater efficiency in production, and it permits extensive geographical specialization with the accompanying benefits of increased division of labor. Larger markets can be served. More simply, transport permits the spatial disadvantages of separation to be reduced.

In more detail, over three decades ago the English economist Michael Thomson[1] provided a helpful classification of seven main reasons why people in the modern world desire to transport either themselves or their property:

- The heterogeneity of the earth's surface means that no one part of it is capable of providing all the products people wish for. An acceptable bundle of such goods can only be obtained by either moving around collecting them, or having them brought to you.
- The continuation of modern society and the high levels of material wellbeing rely upon a degree of productive specialization. Industry requires a multiplicity of diverse inputs which must be collected from wide-ranging sources and also, to permit the necessary level of specialization, extensive market areas must be tapped and served.
- In addition to specialization, high quality transport permits the exploitation of other major economies of scale. There are essentially technical economies associated with high levels of output and include automation, bulk handling, research and development activities, mass marketing, purpose-built equipment and so on.

[1] J.M. Thomson, *Modern Transport Economics*, Harmondsworth: Penguin, 1974.

- Transport has always served a political and military role. Internally, a country seeks good transport both to permit more effective defense of its borders, and to improve the political cohesion of the nation. The Romans were certainly well aware of this and most of their road building was to this end. Externally, good transport permits a country to dominate any colonial or subservient provinces, while more aggressive states require transport to pursue their expansionist policies. Politically, the ownership of expensive, modern transport infrastructure (especially aircraft or mercantile marine) is also treated as a symbol of power and status. In most developed countries the scale of transport required to meet strict needs normally exceeds that required to meet political or military criteria although individual components of a transport system (for example, specific roads or airports) may be provided explicitly for non-economic reasons.
- Without transport, social relationships and contacts are normally very restricted. Transport permits social intercourse, and with it may come a greater understanding of the problems and attitudes of various geographically distant groups. In the developed world the enhancement of social understanding brought about by increased international travel is well recognized, but in many less developed countries the introduction of much more basic transport technology can have profound effects upon the social relationships between inhabitants of formerly isolated towns and villages which are, by Western standards, very close together.
- Modern transport has widened cultural opportunities, permitting people to examine the artistic treasures of other countries and to explore their own national heritage. It also allows for the staging of international exhibitions, sports spectaculars, concerts, parades and fairs that stimulate new trends and innovations in the cultural and sporting spheres.
- Transport is desired to permit people to live and work apart; specifically it permits the geographical separation of employment from leisure. It increases the life-style options open to people, giving them a choice among residential locations away from cities but involving a heavy commitment to travel, or ones much closer to the main employment center but involving short commuting journeys. Transport, quite simply, widens the location choices open to households.

What becomes apparent from Thomson's listing is the close link between location decisions (of both individuals and firms) and the transport system. It is this link to which we now turn.

3.2 The 'Chicken or Egg' Problem

If one takes very broad statistics, then there is unquestionably a link between mobility and affluence. This is, for example, fairly clear from Table 3.1 which presents some of the findings contained in a classic study by Wilfred

Table 3.1 *Mobility across countries*

	GNP per capita	*Travel mobility*	*Freight mobility*
Switzerland	139	104	81
Sweden	119	96	151
USA	106	160	260
Netherlands	101	83	42
France	100	100	100
Canada	95	114	374
Australia	91	107	335
Japan	87	96	94
UK	63	78	47
Italy	53	86	49
Spain	43	54	44
Venezuela	24	32	55
Yugoslavia	24	32	55
Brazil	18	18	23
Mexico	15	14	42
Colombia	11	6	47
Nigeria	6	5	5
Egypt	5	5	13
Pakistan	2	3	10
China	2	3	16
India	2	5	26
Bangladesh	1	2	3

Owen[2] regarding levels of per capita GDP across a range of countries and the transport mobility (expressed as a combination of such things as passenger-miles per annum of automobile, rail and domestic air travel, miles of railway, number of lorries and so on) enjoyed by those living in these countries. While the correlation is apparent, what is less clear is the direction of causation involved. Does high income lead to or result from higher levels of mobility? Or to put it in more technical terms, is mobility a function of the supply of transport services, or does the supply of transport services result from an inherent demand for mobility? The answer is not immediately apparent.

At another level, in previous chapters it was suggested that one of the reasons for the increased interest in transport economics from the late 1960s was the recognition of the important link between transport and land-use patterns (especially those relating to urban form and intra-location). The effects of changes in the transport system on land use tend to be long term (hence they are often called 'activity shifts') but, given the longevity of much transport infrastructure, such interactions must to some extent concern transport policy makers. The changes that occur in land use will also, in turn, by altering the nature and size of the local residential population and industrial base, exert an enormous influence on future transport demand. A major new suburban underground

² W. Owen, *Transport and World Development*, London: Hutchinson, 1987.

railway system, for example, will immediately attract some travelers away from other modes of transport in addition to encouraging trips to be made by former non-travelers. In the longer term, sites near the underground termini will become desirable while those further away will appear relatively less attractive. There will, therefore, be important implications for residential and employment location patterns. Additionally, changing location and trip-making patterns will alter car ownership decisions.

While these interactions are now fully recognized, in practice it is difficult to construct a comprehensive theory that fully reflects all the linkages. The problem is further compounded by the fact that transport and land-use changes are ongoing modifications to the spatial economy. There are continual cycles of cause and effect, and it is impossible to decide upon a point where it is sensible to break into this continuum of change. Consequently, from a pragmatic standpoint one has to make a rather careful judgment whether to treat land use as influenced by transport or vice versa. To some extent the final decision must rest with the questions being considered.

Urban and regional scientists tend to treat transport as the influential variable because the focus of attention here is on the spatial dimension. Questions are posed, for example, in terms of why certain population densities occur or why specific urban economies interact. In contrast, transport economics usually accepts a given land-use pattern and looks at methods of providing efficient transport services within this constraint. Questions center, for instance, on problems of aligning routes or controlling traffic flows.

An example of this latter approach, which reveals both the methodology of conventional transport economics but also highlights some of the difficulties in the modeling of urban decision making, was developed by John Kain.[3] This econometric study, looking specifically at public transport subsidies and calibrated using information from a 1953 survey of 40,000 households in Detroit, adopts four steps in its argument:

1   Workers initially select a residential density in which to live depending upon their income, their preference for a specific plot size and the price of residential land.
2   Once a location has been selected the decision to purchase a car is treated as dependent upon the local residential density, family income, public transport availability and the composition of the worker's family.
3   The decision whether to use public transport for the journey to work, besides depending upon the previous decisions regarding location and car ownership, is thought to be influenced by the quality of local public transport, and the demands of non-working members of the household to make use of the car (if one is owned).

[3] J.F. Kain, 'A contribution to the urban transportation debate: an economic model of urban residential and travel behavior', *Review of Economics and Statistics*, **47**, 55–64, 1964.

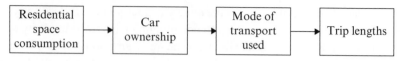

Figure 3.1   *The recursive view of location and travel*

4   Finally, the length of journeys is treated as dependent both on previous decisions of the worker and on the price of residential land adjacent to workplaces.

The implied chain of decision making is, therefore, unidirectional and of the form seen in Figure 3.1.

While Kain was clearly aware of the feedbacks from transport to land use, for a variety of statistical and theoretical reasons he could not adequately reflect them in his model. Besides not allowing for the longer-term feedbacks from travel behavior to land use, the sequence takes no account of the influence of public transport quality on the car ownership decision, or the length of journeys on the longer-term provision of public transport. What the sequence does do, however, is to permit Kain to examine the case for subsidizing public transport within the current urban land-use framework. The assumptions of the sequential type of framework used by Kain are analogous to the standard *ceteris paribus* assumptions of conventional partial equilibrium microeconomics; they suffer from the same limitations but do provide boundaries within which useful analysis can be conducted.

Another way of looking at this issue is suggested by Michael Wegener[4] who does focus on feedback cycles (Figure 3.2) and the recognition that trip and location decisions codetermine each other. It is also very much the approach used in many engineering-based and human geography-derived development theories. Essentially:

- The distribution of land uses, such as residential, industrial, or commercial, over the urban area determines the locations of human activities including living, working, shopping, education and leisure.
- The distribution of human activities in space requires spatial interactions or trips in the transport system to overcome distance between the locations of activities.
- The distribution of infrastructure in the transport system creates opportunities for spatial interactions, and can be measured by accessibility.
- The distribution of accessibility in space co-determines location decisions and so results in changes in the land-use system.

Most of this book is concerned exclusively with the transport sector and with short-run travel decisions. It assumes implicitly, therefore, that the causal

[4]   M. Wegener, 'Overview of land use transport models', in D.A. Hensher, K.J. Button, K.E. Haynes and P. Stopher (eds), *Handbook of Transport Geography and Spatial Systems*, London: Elsevier, 2004.

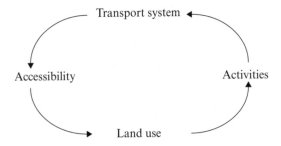

Figure 3.2   *The land-use transport feedback cycle*

link runs from land use to transport and, generally, that land use is predetermined. In a way this may be seen as a short-term view – land-use being less flexible than transport. It seems inappropriate, however, not to give some brief overview of the approach adopted by spatial scientists; not to do so would in effect ignore the part played by transport in both shaping land-use patterns and determining the size of the market areas served by various industries. In the remainder of this chapter, therefore, we shall present a brief introductory outline of modern location theory, concentrating primarily on that aspect of theory that gives a central role to transport. The theory is supplemented by some discussion of the applied work that offers quantification of the important role played by transport in this field. Later in the book (in Chapter 13) the subject of transport and location interaction will be touched upon again in the context of economic development.

3.3   Transport and Industrial Location

From the beginning, economic theories of industrial location argued that transport plays a key role in decisions concerning where industrial activities will be located. As we have seen, provision of good transport permits producers to be separated from both their sources of new materials and also their eventual customers. Alfred Weber[5] developed an early model for mobile plant with transport costs determining the location of manufacturing industry. In Figure 3.2 all potential customers are located at A_1 while the two raw materials required by manufacturing industry are located respectively at A_2 and A_3. The ds represent actual distances between the points of raw material supply and final demand. It is assumed that all other factors of production are freely available at all potential production sites and that, topographically, all activities are located on a uniform plane.

Transport costs are assumed proportional with respect to both distance covered and weight of goods carried. The location of a manufacturing plant will therefore depend on the relative pull of the various material locations and the

[5] A. Weber, *Theory of the Location of Industry*, Chicago, IL: University of Chicago Press, 1929.

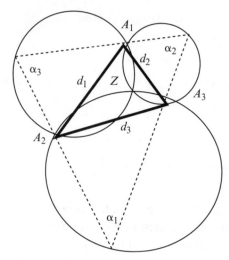

Figure 3.3   *Weber's model of industrial location*

market. The problem is then one of finding the site, Z, for manufacture which minimizes total costs, in other words the location which minimizes T where:

$$T = a_1 \mathbf{r}_{A_1} + a_2 \mathbf{r}_{A_2} + a_3 \mathbf{r}_{A_3} \tag{3.1}$$

where:

> a_1 is the physical amount of the final goods consumed at A_1;
> a_2 is the physical amount of the raw material available at A_2 required to produce a_1 of the final good;
> a_3 is the physical amount of the raw material available at A_3 required to produce a_1 of the final good; and
> $\mathbf{r}_{A_1}$, $\mathbf{r}_{A_2}$ and $\mathbf{r}_{A_3}$ are the distances from sites A_1, A_2 and A_3, respectively.

It is easily seen that if any two of a_1, a_2 and a_3 are exceeded by the third, then the location of production is determined at the site associated with this third variable (for example, if $a_2 > (a_1 + a_3)$, then production of the final commodity should be at site A_2). If no location is dominant, then graphical methods can be used to find the least-cost site. A second triangle is drawn with its sides (ds) proportional to a_1, a_2 and a_3 and the three angles measured. We denote the angle opposite the a_1 as α_1, that opposite a_2 as α_2 and finally that opposite a_2 as α_2. These angles then form the basis for erecting similar triangles around the original location triangle (see Figure 3.3). Circles are drawn which touch the points of each triangle and the optimal production site Z is then found at the location where all three circles intersect (if Z is found to be outside the original location triangle, then it is simple to prove that one of the corner solutions, A_1, A_2 and A_3 is preferable). This location minimizes transport costs as defined in equation (3.1).

This simple analysis implicitly assumes that transport costs are linearly

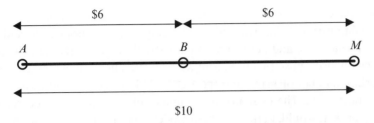

Figure 3.4   *The effects of tapered transport rates on industrial location*

related to distance, but there is ample evidence that there are often considerable diseconomies associated with short hauls and with partially full loads. While Weber originally suggested that one could adjust the sides of the location triangle to capture this, the situation requires rather more complicated modifications. The difficulty is that in these circumstances, location and transport costs are codetermined; without knowledge of the final location (that is, Z) it is impossible to assess the magnitude, if any, of economies of long-haul transport. There is a suggestion, however, that other things being equal, tapered transport rates (that is, when the rate per mile declines with distance) tend, in some circumstances, to draw industry to either the source of raw materials or the market for final products.

Suppose that only one raw material is needed to produce the final product (or that the range of raw materials required is located at a single point) and this is to be found at location A in Figure 3.4. Further, there is no loss of weight in the manufacturing process required to produce the final product that will eventually be sold at location M. Either the transport system offers a through service from A to M costing $10 per ton or alternatively there are services from A to the intermediate site B costing $6 per ton and one from B to M also costing $6 per ton, Since we assume no weight loss in production, the cost-conscious manufacturer is clearly indifferent between A and M but would not select site B because (AB + BA) > AM in cost terms.

To relax the assumption of no weight loss in manufacturing does not remove the disadvantage suffered by B relative to A which is now preferable to location M. (It is possible in this situation for B to be preferred to M if a location at A is impracticable for technical or planning reasons, but this would depend upon the relative importance of the taper *vis-à-vis* the weight loss in manufacture.) Weight loss will influence only the choice between A and M, and this may even be true if different rates are charged not simply by haul length but also by type of commodity.

Even if it is more expensive per ton to carry the final product it may still be preferable to locate production facilities at the material source rather than the final market. In the United States, for example, the meat-packing industry of the nineteenth century was gradually drawn westwards to the main source of beef (initially to Chicago and then to Omaha and Kansas City) even though rail rates per ton-mile favored transport of live animals rather than carcasses. The simple fact was that the dressed meat of a steer weighs only 54 percent of the live animal weight; hence locations near the raw material were favored.

Of course, firms do not in general locate in isolation from one another. Lösch[6] demonstrated that with all firms facing identical production and transport cost schedules, and confronted by a spatially uniform market, the market would be divided out so that each firm would serve a hexagonal market area. The equilibrium number of firms, and the area served by each, would be determined by transport costs. The existence of a number of different, but interdependent product markets would, in the Löschian model, tend to encourage concentrations of firms at particular locations.

Discussion of the details of these location and other models is beyond the scope of this volume (although some references are included in the further reading at the end of the chapter), but it should be becoming increasingly apparent that transport costs have increasingly been recognized to be only one of many factors which influence industrial location. The factors influencing location include (in addition to transport considerations) market structure, demand elasticities, external economies of geographical concentration, expectations of future market changes and processing costs. Melvin Greenhutt,[7] for example, suggests that in practice transport costs become of major importance only if freight costs form a large proportion of total costs or differ significantly among potential locations.

While theoretical models of industrial location offer useful insights into the role transport plays, its actual relevance in the real world requires detailed empirical study. If Greenhutt's argument is followed, in many cases transport costs are such a small component of overall production costs that it appears to be more costly to acquire the information necessary to find the least-cost location than to suffer the inefficiencies of a suboptimal situation. If, for example, we go back to Cook's[8] classic study of industrial location in the Black Country of the Midlands of the United Kingdom, we find that many firms were totally ignorant of their transport costs. One can attempt to isolate such transport cost-insensitive industries by looking at the relative importance of transport costs in their overall costs of production.

Table 3.2 offers some estimates of the percentage of the value of net output for a variety of US and Japanese industries attributable to transport costs in the mid-1980s. There are clear differences between the two countries, and between the various industries within them. It seems reasonable to conclude from this table that, *ceteris paribus*, industries producing primary products such as agriculture, petroleum and wood products are going to be more influenced in their location choices by transport considerations than others such as machinery, furniture and precision instruments. In particular, production of raw materials represent nodal solutions in the Weberian triangle, with production at the raw material source. (In

---

[6] A. Lösch, *The Economics of Location*, New Haven, CT: Yale University Press, 1954.

[7] M.L. Greenhutt, *Microecononiics and the Space Economy*, Glenview, IL: Scott-Foresman, 1963.

[8] W.R. Cook, 'Transport decisions of certain firms in the Black Country', *Journal of Transport Economics and Policy*, **1**, 344–56, 1967.

Table 3.2   *Transport costs as a percentage of final consumer costs*

Producer	Transport costs (%)	
	United States	*Japan*
Agricultural products	7.85	2.43
Food products	1.59	2.16
Textiles	0.58	6.33
Apparel and leather products	0.22	0.69
Paper and wood products	1.91	3.37
Furniture	0.53	2.03
Publishing	1.46	1.16
Chemical products	1.38	0.59
Petroleum products	2.60	1.56
Rubber and plastic products	1.79	0.99
Glass, clay and stone products	1.36	4.50
Primary metal products	2.54	1.34
Finished metal products	0.93	0.75
Machinery	0.47	0.64
Electrical equipment	1.08	0.71
Transport vehicles	2.56	0.88
Precision instruments	0.15	0.90
Other	0.69	1.13
Total	1.70	1.83

Source: Adapted from S.R. Pirog III and R. Lancioni, 'US–Japan distribution channel cost structures: is there a significant difference?', *International Journal of Physical Distribution and Logistics Management*, **27**, 53–66, 1997.

the United States it has often been suggested that Gary, Indiana, was originally chosen specifically by US Steel to minimize transport costs.)

Changes in industrial structure over the past 40 years, and especially the movement away from basic industries to manufactures and services, suggest that transport is experiencing a diminishing influence over location decisions, at least at the interregional level. Further, the existence of comprehensive transport and communications networks in virtually all industrialized countries suggests that proximity to good transport is much easier to achieve now than in the past.

These factors, however, may not be as new as sometimes supposed. In earlier work by Gudgin,[9] looking at the 1968 UK Census of Production, it was found 'that almost three-quarters of British industry incurs total transport costs at levels of less than 3 per cent of the value of gross output. In 95 per cent of industry, by value of production, the transport costs are less than 5 per cent of total costs'. This finding was reaffirmed by Diamond and Spence[10] in a study of 190 manu-facturing and service industries in the United Kingdom which found that most

[9] G. Gudgin, *Industrial Location Processes and Regional Employment Growth*, Westmead: Saxon House, 1978.

[10] D. Diamond and N. Spence, *Infrastructure and Industrial Costs in British Industry*, London: HMSO, 1989.

firms reported transport costs of between 3 and 6 percent of production costs. Interestingly, at 9.9 percent, transport costs represented a considerably higher proportion of costs in the service sector than for manufacturing firms (4.7 percent).

Cost statistics may, though, give a slightly distorted impression of the influence of transport factors. In particular, while transport costs may form only a relatively small portion of output costs in many sectors they may, nevertheless, have significant influence on levels of net profits – a fact long appreciated by economists. Again drawing on UK data, Michael Chisholm,[11] for instance, suggests that transport costs may have represented as much as 25 percent of profits in manufacturing industry during the 1960s. Additionally, while transport costs may, on average, be low for some industries they may vary considerably among areas. Edwards[12] suggested that there existed a range of about 20 percent in transport costs of manufacturing industry by region in 1963. It should also be remembered that simple cost estimates may disguise variations in other attributes of transport (speed, regularity and so on) which can influence decision makers. Reliable inter-urban transport, good international transport links and high-quality local transport (necessary to retain scarce skilled labor) are, for instance particularly important for modern high-technology industry. An analysis of the largest US commercial airports, for example has shown that they attract a considerable amount of high-technology employment: some 12,000 such jobs compared to cities without these facilities.[13]

Survey evidence, questioning industrialists about the motivations underlying their location or re-location decisions, also provides some guide to the importance of transport considerations. There are obvious difficulties in using such results – for example, the sample may be unrepresentative, respondents offer answers which they hope may further their individual interests, while others offer *ex post* rationalizations of their actions – but some information may be gleaned from them.

Some years ago now, for example, the UK Trade and Industry Sub-committee of the House of Commons Expenditure Committee,[14] when seeking information about the effectiveness of regional economic policies, was told by five of the 17 major industrial firms interviewed that transport costs were a specific disadvantage for locations in developed areas. While accepting this as an objective comment, it is important to note not simply the relatively small number of firms concerned but also their particular nature – for example, three were car

[11] M. Chisholm, 'Freight transport costs, industrial location and regional development', in M. Chisholm and G. Manners (eds), *Spatial Policy Problems of the British Economy*, Cambridge: Cambridge University Press, 1971.
[12] S.L. Edwards, 'Regional variations in freight costs', *Journal of Transport Economics and Policy*, **9**, 115–26, 1975.
[13] K.J. Button, S. Lall, R. Stough and M. Trice, 'High-technology employment and hub airports', *Journal of Air Transport Management*, **5**, 53–9, 1999.
[14] UK Trade and Industry Sub-committee of the House of the Commons Expenditure Committee, *Regional Development Incentives Report*, House of Commons Paper 85, London: HMSO, 1973.

manufacturers and one a large steel tube mill. These were large firms engaged in the production of bulky products whose per unit transport costs were likely to be high. The Armitage Committee[15] supported this line and concluded that:

> When industry and commerce make decisions about the location of factories or their systems of distribution, it is often less important to reduce transport costs than to reduce other costs such as those of stockholding or to take advantage of the grants for setting up factories in assisted areas.

Such a view is consistent with that of Cameron and Clark,[16] who in their study of 71 firms which located in UK assisted areas found that accessibility to main markets was ranked only third as a location factor (behind the availability of trained labor and local authority cooperation) while local goods transport facilities were listed fifth and accessibility to main suppliers ranked sixth.

One factor which emerges from these studies, and has limited support in econometric work, is that during the post-war phase of full employment and strengthened land-use controls, access to markets and raw material supplies was often overshadowed in location decisions by the availability of scarce skilled labor and factory space. International confirmation of this position is found in the West German context where in a survey of newly located plants conducted in 1971, Fischer[17] found that accessibility to motorways ranked only fourth in the list of location criteria.

More localized studies suggest that good passenger transport facilities may influence industrial location rather more than the quality of long-distance or freight transport. In retailing and some other activities this argument is further extended to embrace firms' desire to be accessible to customers. The importance of local transport is, for instance, seen in a study of factors affecting location choices of high-technology firms in Pennsylvania. Allen and Robertson[18] found that while proximity to market, proximity to family and commuting distance came first, second and fourth, respectively, in terms of factors influencing firms, regional surface transport and proximity to an airport came only thirteenth and sixteenth, respectively. This confirms the emphasis that has been placed upon the ready availability of trained workers.

It is certainly clear from a number of surveys (as shown, for instance, in Table 3.3 which reports the results of a study of 162 US branch plants) that the availability of suitable labor is a key factor in location choices of both high-technology and more traditional industries. There is also evidence that local

[15] UK Department of Transport, *Report of the Inquiry into Lorries, People and the Environment*, London: HMSO, 1980.

[16] G.C. Cameron and B.D. Clark, 'Industrial Movement and the Regional Problem', University of Glasgow Occasional Paper No.6, 1966.

[17] L. Fischer, *Die Berucksichtignung Raumordnungs Politiseler Zeilsetviengen in de Verkehrsplanung*, Berlin: Strassenbahn und Strassenverkesstectnick 1971.

[18] D.N. Allen and G.E. Robertson, *Silicon, Sensors and Software: Listening to Advanced Technology Enterprises in Pennsylvania*, Institute of Public Administration, Pennsylvania State University, 1983.

Table 3.3 *Factors influencing the location of branch plants in the United States*

Rank	High technology	Other plants
1	Labor	Labor
2	Transport availability	Market access
3	Quality of life	Transport availability
4	Market access	Materials access
5	Utilities	Utilities
6	Site characteristics	Regulatory practice
7	Communications characteristics	Quality of life
8	Business climate	Business climate
9	Taxes	Site characteristics
10	Development organizations	Taxes

Source: Adapted from H.A. Stafford, 'Environmental protection industrial location', *Annals of the Association of American Geographers*, **75**, 227–40, 1985.

transport can be influential in attracting or retaining such labor. Transport and transport-related considerations would seem, therefore, to still be very relevant in the location decisions of modern industries, although the specific transport attributes of importance may have changed somewhat over the years.

In addition to the appreciation that transport is often not the dominant factor in location choice, there is now the increasing view among economists that notions of cost minimization do not always motivate firms. Hence, even if one can isolate the factors of interest to firms it is not certain that they should be treated within a cost-minimizing framework. In many cases, provided that a site offers, *ceteris paribus*, a location where transport costs are below some threshold, it is considered acceptable. In other cases, the first acceptable location encountered is adopted rather than a protracted search pursued. The influence of social setting and amenities on those who make the decisions about location, and on the staff whose preferences they have to consider, were highlighted in this context many years ago by Eversley.[19] Firms often, therefore, adopt 'satisficing' policies in site selection rather than attempt to profit or revenue maximize, or to cost minimize. Under these conditions the exact role played by transport costs becomes almost impossible to define, but it seems likely that once a location has been chosen, a major rise in transport costs would be necessary to overcome the basic inertia which would seem to accompany such a managerial objective.

3.4 Gateways and Corridors

Economic activities clearly require the movement of resources: factors to points of production and goods and services to markets, and even in the information age, ideas and data from the generator to the user. The distances involved in this

[19] D.E.S. Eversley, 'Social and psychological factors in the determination of industrial location', in T. Wilson (ed.), *Papers on Regional Development*, Oxford: Blackwell, 1965.

have historically been increasing. The making of any final produce may now require many thousands of miles of transport input. Distance *per se*, however, is not always (and perhaps seldom) the crucial element that influences the relative success of competitive production sites; other things being constant, factors such as time, frequency, reliability and security are often more important. In this context, appropriate transport is relevant. Because of the attributes of transport and the costs of delivering them, this often leads to a channeling of movements through gateways and along corridors. This is not in itself the issue. The challenge concerns the nature and number of these gateways and corridors and their form.

As with any economic resource, transport services suffer from scarcity; they are not ubiquitous and, indeed, allocating resources to activity inevitably involves taking resources from elsewhere. In the past this scarcity, and with it an opportunity cost, was often neglected in trade theory and, by association, economic development theory. Classical Ricardian economics in the nineteenth century, for example, focused exclusively on the comparative advantages in production at different locations, while in classical spatial economics, albeit at a more local level, it was assumed that there existed infinite radial transport links within a concentric economic geographical space (a topic we look at implicitly in Section 3.6). But transport supply is constrained by its particular characteristics.

Transport is a network industry and it is, therefore, natural to think in terms of the role that transport may play both in stimulating economic development along links in transport networks and at various nodal points – normally towns and cities. Historians have long viewed the trade and migration passages that existed in prehistoric times as important for the spread of civilization as it emerged, and subsequent trade routes as facilitating economic progress and disseminating knowledge. Those living in early commercial cities, which Kenneth Hirth[20] called 'gateway communities', benefited from the flows passing through their area and they could exercise control over them and charge for their passage.

The much more recent opening-up of North America has attracted a lot of attention, in part one suspects because of the availability of written records. Whebell[21] explained the growth of Southern Ontario, Canada in terms of a five-stage corridor development process occurring over an extended period and embracing significant technical changes. In contrast, Andrew Burghardt[22] focuses on gateway cities, distinguishing between them and hubs and examining the ways in which they change over time. Gateways are explained in this case in economic terms by considering threshold values of distance and levels of productivity.

While discussions of gateways and corridors, together with their role in economic development, are not new, they aroused particular interest in the 1980s and

[20] K.G. Hirth, 'Interregional trade and the formation of prehistoric gateway communities', *American Antiquity*, **41**, 35–45, 1978.

[21] C.F.L Whebell, 'Corridors: a theory of urban systems', *Annals of the Association of American Geographers*, **59**, 1–26, 1969.

[22] A.F. Burghardt, 'A hypothesis about gateway cities', *Annals of the Association of American Geographers*, **61**, 269–85, 1971.

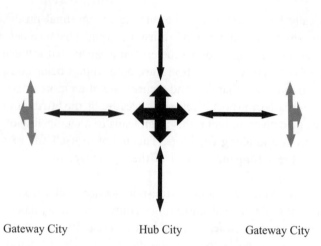

Gateway City   Hub City   Gateway City

Figure 3.5   *Notions of transport gateways, corridors and hubs*

1990s with the onset of the 'hi-tech boom'. Indeed, many concentrations were designated either explicitly or implicitly by their corridor geography – Silicon Valley, the M4 Corridor, Route 128 Corridor, the Dulles Corridor and so on – while others, such as a research triangle, were visualized in terms of having a gateway role. These concentrations highlight the synergies between transport and certain types of capital investment, but are more local in their orientation than the macro corridors and gateways that are seen as linking regions or countries to wider markets.

Gateways have tended gradually to move farther apart as it has become easier for traffic and individuals to both pass through them and, as transport systems have evolved, traverse the distance between them. Figure 3.5 represents the traditional view of gateways. At the national level in most countries there are one or more major hub cities that are linked to their borders by corridors that end at gateway cities offering links to the international market. Parallels can be drawn at the regional level. In spatial economic terms, the main distinction between the hub city is that, while it fulfills the classic role of serving a concentric hinterland, a gateway city services a cone-shaped market extending away from the border and along the corridor.

Corridors are essentially links between major nodes; in some ways they can be treated as 'super-links' and this is seen as distinguishing them from spokes in a hub-and-spoke network – a standard pattern of transport supply discussed in Chapter 5. A major difficulty, however, involves the level of aggregation that one is dealing with.

At the global–historic, macro–macro level, corridors are defined as routes that humankind used to populate the world – for example, the 'Bering land-bridge' allowing migration from Europe to the American continent. But in the modern, high-technology age a corridor may be an electronic channel over which a piece of information is sent. The term suffers from almost infinite vagueness. This is not very helpful when it comes to in-depth analysis or forecasting, but it does have its uses in general assessments of trends and can serve as a focal piece of terminology when policy makers want to coordinate actions – as, for example, in the creation of trade corridors.

It is also relatively easy to relate the picture seen in Figure 3.5 to specific contexts in more recent history. In the United States, for example, the two gateway cities may be seen as New York on one coast and San Francisco on the other in the mid-1800s. Once into the country, goods or migrants could move into the hinterland, often dispersing more broadly through a hub such as Chicago. Railroads largely facilitated this movement. The nature of international maritime and domestic railroad transport at the time, as well as institutional controls, led to this pattern of behavior. The gateways proved to be challenging barriers to cross over and, while trade and migration were extensive, it was not easy and it was costly, and reverse migration and visits to family left behind proved almost impossible for the vast majority of individuals, even if they did succeed in their new land.

The pattern of the Canadian railroad networks (Figure 3.6) provides a classic representation of the form that in theory a gateway/corridor structure looks like, and it is perhaps no accident that much of the early analytical writings on the subject came from Canada. The maritime gateways on the two coasts, and the inland crossing gateways to the United States, funnel goods and, more in the past, individuals to and from the major hub cities of the country – Toronto, Montreal and so on. Similar patterns emerge for the more recent road network.

The world is changing, and transport has been both a cause of this change and, mainly because of the derived nature of the demand for its services, has also had to react to it. These changes have implications for the demands that are placed on mobility of both people and goods. They have produced significant changes in the amount of geographical specialization and in both internal and external trade. The traditional barriers to trade, most obviously the physical geographical ones associated with oceans, mountains, rivers and distance, but also the institutional ones tied to tariff and non-tariff barriers and fragmented financial markets, and the social ones of cultural and linguistic diversity have had their potency reduced.

Transport costs for both passengers and freight have fallen considerably over the past three or four decades. This is, in part, a function of technology improvements, including those found in complementary sectors such as telecommunications and warehousing, but also stems from institutional developments and especially the liberalization of many transport markets, the economies of scale and scope that have come with the freeing of international trade more generally, and the adoption of innovative methods of supplying logistics services of all types by the private sector.

The increased volume of trade, both within and between countries, and changes in its nature, have led to the emergence of new gateways and corridors to handle it. The degree of competition between various gateway/corridor combinations, and their importance in economic development, even those involving existing combinations, have also changed for a variety of interacting

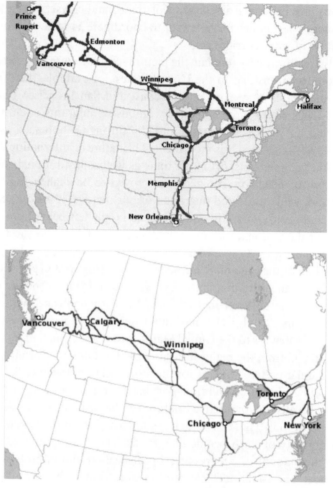

Figure 3.6   *Canadian National's (upper) and Canadian Pacific's (lower) railroad network*

reasons. The full picture of what has happened is complex and is still not fully documented or agreed upon. It is a topic that will be returned to in a slightly different way when the links between transport and development are discussed in Chapter 13.

3.5   Output, Market Area and Transport Costs

Transport costs are not only instrumental in influencing where firms locate, but they also play an important role in determining the market area served by each firm. Transport costs, given the place of industrial location, can determine the quantity of goods sold and their price and the spatial distribution of this output. Lösch conducted much of the early work looking at market areas, but here we focus on a specific transport-oriented model that was devised by van

Es and Ruijgrok.[23] The simple model treats transport demand as derived from the demand for the final product and assumes all supply and demand curves to be linear. For expositional ease the relevant functions are treated in a manner running counter to economic convention; specifically, price is treated as dependent upon demand rather than vice versa. Initially our firm, which produces a homogeneous product, supplies a single customer who is located some distance from its predetermined site. Hence we have,

$$P^s = a_0 + a_1 Q^s + P^t \qquad (3.2a)$$

$$P^d = b_0 - b_1 Q^d \qquad (3.2b)$$

$$Q^d = Q^s \qquad (3.2c)$$

$$P^s = P^d \qquad (3.2d)$$

where:

P^s is the supply price of the commodity;
P^d is the demand price of the commodity;
Q^s is the quantity of the commodity supplied;
Q^d is the quantity of the commodity demanded; and
P^t is a constant transport cost per unit carried to the customer and treated as a cost borne by the supplier.

Manipulation and combination of these equations yields the profit-maximizing supply, Q^e, that is,

$$Q^e = \left(\frac{b_0 - a_o}{a_1 + b_1}\right) - \left(\frac{P^t}{a_1 + b_1}\right) \qquad (3.3)$$

It is immediately clear that transport costs exert a negative influence on the quantity the profit-maximizing firm ought to supply, that is, if $P^t = 0$ then the equilibrium output would rise by $(P^t)/(b_1 + a_1)$. Further we can derive the equilibrium price (P^e) that should be charged to the customer:

$$P^e = \left(\frac{a_1 b_0 - a_0 b_1}{a_1 + b_1}\right) + \left(\frac{b_1 P^t}{a_1 + b_1}\right) \qquad (3.4)$$

Here we see that the transport cost component increases the equilibrium price by $(b_1 P^t)/(a_1 + b_1)$. The effects of this, together with the effects of transport costs on Q^e, are illustrated graphically in Figure 3.7. The vertical axis shows the final price per unit paid by the customer and the horizontal axis the quantity of goods sold. The introduction of the transport cost element to the diagram has the

[23] J. van Es and C.J. Ruijgrok, 'Modal choice in freight transport', in E.J. Visser (ed.), *Transport Decisions in an Age of Uncertainty*, The Hague: Martinus Nijhoff, 1974.

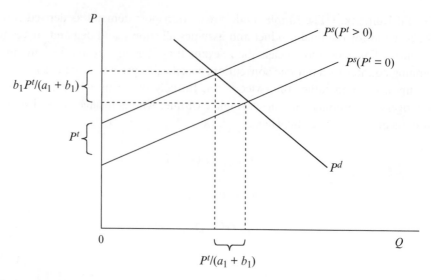

Figure 3.7 *The effect of transport costs on price and output*

effect of pushing the supply curve up from $P^s(P^t = 0)$ to $P^s(P^t > 0)$. It is evident that transport cost rises will push up final prices and reduce the quantity sold. The exact impact depends not only upon the magnitude of P^t but also the elasticities of supply and demand – greater inelasticity increases the influence on price exerted by transport cost considerations.

To estimate the market area served when potential customers are spread evenly around the production site, we shall initially assume that identical individuals are located at equal distances along a straight road from the site of the supplier. The customers will be confronted by prices that are composed of a fixed factory price reflecting production costs and a variable transport cost dependent upon the distance they live from the production site. Since each customer – by assumption – exhibits a similar demand response it is, therefore, the transport component that determines the amount each will buy. At the edge of the firm's market area, the amount supplied to the marginal customer vanishes to zero; this will be when $P^t = (b_0 - a_0)$. If j customers are served before this limit is reached, then from equation (3.3), we can see that the sales of the firm (Q^T) will amount to:

$$Q^T = \sum_j Q^e_j = j\left(\frac{b_0 - a_0}{a_1 + b_1}\right) - \left(\sum_j P^e_j\right)\left(\frac{1}{a_1 + b_1}\right) \qquad (3.5)$$

where Q^e represents sales to customer j.

This approach can be extended to show the entire geographical area served by the firm. In Figure 3.8, the vertical axis represents the quantity supplied to each customer, on the assumption that the customers are evenly spread over the plane. The amount sold to a customer falls from very high levels $Q^e = [(b_0 - a_0)/(b_1 + a_1)]$ immediately adjacent to the site of supply – where transport costs are zero – and falls to zero when transport costs become excessive.

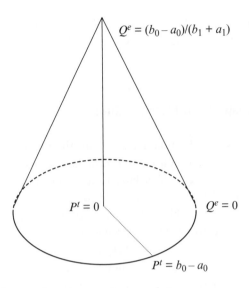

Figure 3.8 *The influence of transport costs on market area*

The amount sold can be measured by calculating the volume of the cone, that is:

$$D = b\pi \int_0^R (P + T) T dT \qquad (3.6)$$

where:

D is demand as a function of free-on-board (fob) price net of mill price P;

b is twice the population density of a square in which it costs 1 money unit to ship 1 unit of the commodity along one side;

$d = f (P + T)$ is an individual demand as a function of the price of the commodity at the place of consumption;

P is fob net mill price of the commodity;

T is freight cost per unit from the factory to the consumer; and

R is the maximum possible transport cost.

While this type of approach (relating the sales, prices and market area of production to transport costs) is obvious theoretical, interestingly it does rely upon many abstractions from reality for its internal consistency. As with many theories, some of the assumptions associated with the model may be relaxed: it is possible, for example, to allow for variations in population density, for heterogeneity in consumer tastes, and non-perfectly elastic supply conditions – but this does tend to add complexity to the analysis. The general impression conveyed, however, is always the same, namely that transport costs are key in determining the size of geographical market served by a firm and the total volume of its sales. Further, one situation where the effects of transport improvements may have a magnified effect on the market area is when the producing industry is capable of exploiting manufacturing scale economies. This is not a novel idea and, indeed, it was recognized over two centuries ago by the classical economist Adam Smith in his *Wealth of Nations*.

3.6   Urban Transport and Land Values

The previous sections have been concerned with the interaction between transport and the physical, spatial economy but little has been said regarding the way in which transport quality can affect land values. Location, to date, has tended to be viewed in terms of where a firm would locate and the area that would be served. Little has been said about the distribution of land among alternative uses either within one sector, such as manufacturing, or among sectors, notably between industrial and residential use. Very early work on this problem can be traced back to von Thünen's[24] land rent model which attempted to explain differences in agricultural land rent. He argued that concentric zones of crop specialization would develop around the central market, the key feature of the model being that land rent differentials over homogeneous space are determined entirely by transport cost savings. While the nineteenth-century agrarian economy provided the inspiration for 'bid–rent curve' (sometimes, 'rent–bid curve' is used) analysis, it is in the context of twentieth-century urban development that it has been most fully developed.

Haig[25] was the first to apply von Thünen's argument in the urban context arguing:

> Site rents and transportation costs are vitally connected through their relationship to the friction of space. Transportation is the means of reducing that friction, at the cost of time and money. Site rentals are charges which can be made for sites where accessibility may be had with comparatively low transportation costs.

People who are prepared to pay the highest price for improved transport provision (that is, outbid rivals) will enjoy the most accessible locations.

This approach is clearly dependent upon some very stringent assumptions that need to be spelt out before we proceed further. We focus initially upon the residential location of households. The city under review is seen as a featureless plain with all production, recreational and retailing activities concentrated at a single urban core (the central business district: CBD). The population is homogeneous with respect to family size, income, housing demands and so on, but while building costs do not vary with location, transport costs rise with distance from the CBD. With these assumptions, the sum of transport costs plus site rents is constant across the entire city (that is, if we take a ray out from the CBD to the

---

[24] J.H. von Thünen (1826), *Der Isolierte Staat in Beziehung auf Landwirtschaft und Nationalökonomie*, Stuttgart: Gustav Fischer (1966 reprint).

[25] R.M. Haig, 'Towards an understanding of the Metropolis', *Quarterly Journal of Economics*, **40**, 179–208, 1926.

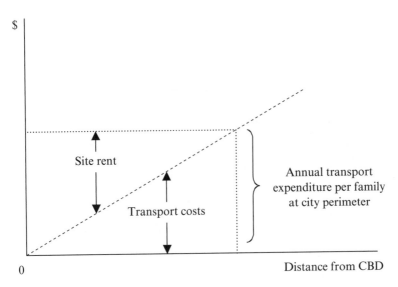

$

Site rent

Transport costs

Annual transport
expenditure per family
at city perimeter

0

Distance from CBD

Figure 3.9 *The site rent/transport cost trade-off*

perimeter of the city and concentrate exclusively on household decisions we have the situation depicted in Figure 3.9. Total site rent in the city may be estimated as the volume of the inverted cone centered on the CBD).

An improvement in the transport system will result in a fall in land values at each location and an outward expansion of the city – the extent of this outward expansion being dependent upon the elasticity of demand for transport services. If the demand for transport is perfectly inelastic then the boundary of the city remains unchanged. If *AB* in Figure 3.10 is the initial rent gradient then, with a perfectly inelastic demand for transport services, the result of, say, uniformly lower public transport fares is to shift the gradient to *A'B*. The city's perimeter remains at *B*.

With a degree of elasticity, however, the reduced transport cost will encourage longer-distance travel to work and recreational activities and the eventual rent gradient is likely to settle at a position such as *A"B"* and the city's boundary to extend out to *B"*. It should be remembered that this simple model assumes that transport costs vary linearly with distance from the CBD and that individuals are identical. If this is not the case then, as Herb Mohring[26] has pointed out, the precise relation between transport cost and location patterns would be obtained simultaneously rather than sequentially as above. Further, the change in relative site rentals may also result in households wishing to own different size plots of land; this complication is incorporated by allowing for some elasticity in the demand for quantities of land.

This model of urban location, which was subsequently greatly refined in a classic paper by William Alonso,[27] extends beyond the simple consideration

[26] H. Mohring, 'Land values and the measurement of highway benefits', *Journal of Political Economy*, **69**, 236–49, 1961.

[27] W. Alonso, *Location and Land Use*, Cambridge, MA: Harvard University Press, 1964.

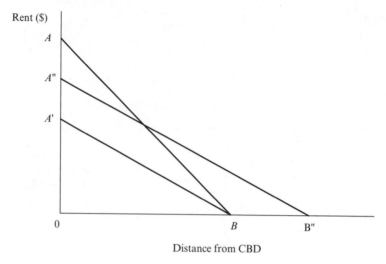

Figure 3.10   *The site rent/transport cost trade-off*

of residential land rent. The priorities of households differ and there is clearly competition in a free market land economy among the demands of industry, commerce and various classes of households for different sites. In general, there are so-called 'agglomeration economies' to be enjoyed by industry and commerce from locating both close to each other and at the city core – they present an identifiable geographical entity (for example, medicine in Harley Street and bespoke tailoring in Savile Row in London, and finance in Wall Street, New York), can be easily served by specialized suppliers, provide customers with a comprehensive range of services and so on. Consequently, given the potentially higher revenue associated with a core location, business tends to bid highly for central sites. Poorer people who cannot afford high transport fares and place a relatively low priority on large sites are willing to bid higher rents for small inner-area locations, while the wealthy will be more inclined to bid a higher rent for suburban locations.

Figure 3.11 shows in the bid–rent curves for three groups of urban land user: poor, middle income and wealthy households. We see, in this very simple example, that the poor will outbid both higher income classes of household for sites near the urban center, middle income households will locate adjacent to the CBD, while the wealthy will outbid the other groups for sites at the edge of the city. Clearly this is rather a stylized picture of urban land use and rents (Chapter 13 provides some further refinements), but it does offer some insight into the influence transport can have on intra-urban location patterns. Quite simply, high transport cost activities, *ceteris paribus*, will be located near to the CBD and low transport cost activities will take locations further away.

General support for this pattern of land use is seen in Table 3.4, which shows that the spatial concentration of poverty increased steadily in the three decades to 1998, with over 25 percent of core metropolitan area populations being made up of the country's poorest 20 percent by the end of the period. But there has also been a continual overlapping suburbanization process, with 61 percent of the

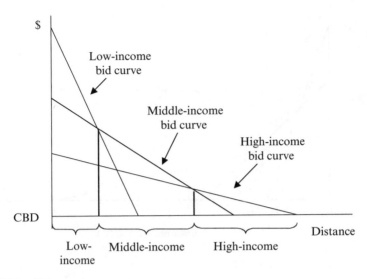

Figure 3.11   *Bid–rent curves*

Table 3.4   *Share of US central-city population by income class and year*

Year	All metropolitan statistical areas/ primary metropolitan statistical areas (%)	Central (%) cities	Suburbs (%)
Low income (national lowest 20%)			
1969	18.3	21.9	14.8
1979	18.5	23.7	14.5
1989	18.1	24.0	14.1
1998	19.0	25.5	14.9
Middle income (national middle 60%)			
1969	59.4	59.8	59.1
1979	59.4	59.0	59.8
1989	59.4	58.8	59.8
1998	58.8	57.9	59.3
High income (national top 20%)			
1969	22.3	18.3	26.2
1979	22.1	17.3	25.7
1989	22.5	7.2	26.1
1998	22.3	16.6	25.8

Source: US Department of Housing and Urban Development, *State of the Cities*, Washington, DC: HUD, 2000.

Americans living in suburbs by 1990 compared to 36 percent in 1948. The advent of cheap motoring was a major cause of this.

Changes in transport costs may affect the amount of land taken up by various activities, and some of the basic implications can be illustrated using the bid–rent curve.

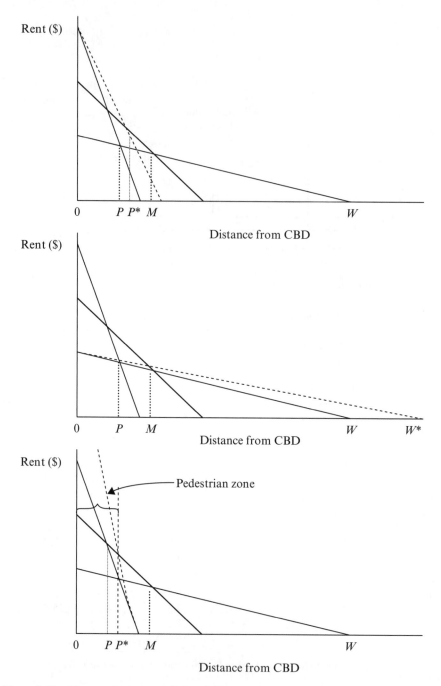

Figure 3.12   *The simple impacts of changing transport provision on urban land use*

Figure 3.12 replicates Figure 3.10 with $0 \Rightarrow P$ being the section around the CBD occupied by poorer people, $P \Rightarrow M$ that occupied by middle income people, and $M \Rightarrow W$ that occupied by the wealthy. The introduction of improved public transport with extremely low fares, for example, may well increase the willingness of poorer households to bid for locations further from the CBD and consequently the central ring of land use, as we see in the top section of Figure 3.12, may both widen and, more probably, move outwards to say *P**.

It was found, for example, that the construction of the Washington metro, with its cheap, good-quality service, increased the willingness of people to pay for land parcels near metro stations. Although not shown, the effect may well also produce a growth in economic activity at the CBD. In the urban center, retailers were even more willing to offer high rents for sites near metro services.

Alternatively, the construction of an extensive urban/suburban freeway network is likely to improve the access offered to car-owning, wealthy households, shifting their bid–rent curve upwards and to the right (the middle element of Figure 3.12). The ring of land occupied by this group will thus be extended out beyond the original city boundaries (that is, from $M \Rightarrow W$ to $M \Rightarrow W^*$). Work in the United Kingdom on its motorway building programs of the 1960s by Evans,[28] for instance, specifically attributes the 'flight to the suburbs' to 'the large-scale construction of urban motorways which increases commuting speeds and comfort for the commuter' and argues that the only way to get higher-income groups back into the central area is to 'Make the transport system slow, cheap and uncomfortable, and not fast, comfortable and expensive'.

Another possibility is that land-use planning may instigate a pedestrian-only zone around the CBD as seen in the lower part of Figure 3.12. This will make it cheaper for poorer households to move around and thus locations about the CBD more attractive places for them to live. Although the exact effect of such a policy depends upon its detailed design, in the bottom section of Figure 3.12 it is assumed that the final result is that the belt of lower-income households expands out to *P**.

Of course, the real world is a little more complicated than these examples suggest; for example, we have treated the city in isolation and as an abstraction, ignored variations in the geography of the area, assumed away any land-use planning agency, and treated location change as instantaneous. It also ignores important feedback effects including the ability to change times of travel and routes, and to use different modes of transport. The aim however, is to make it apparent that any attempt at formulating an urban transport policy, or any advance in transport engineering, will have important implications for urban form and for the people that live in the city even physically distant from the actual policy initiative.

3.7 Transport and Urban Wage Rates

Not only do transport costs influence urban land-use patterns, but they are also instrumental in determining spatial variations in urban wage rates. As Leon Moses[29] pointed out many years ago, 'the wage differential, positive or negative,

---

[28] A.W. Evans, *The Economics of Residential Location*, Basingstoke: Macmillan, 1973.
[29] L.N. Moses, 'Towards a theory of intra urban wage differentials and their influence on travel behavior', *Papers of the Regional Science Association*, **9**, 53–63, 1961.

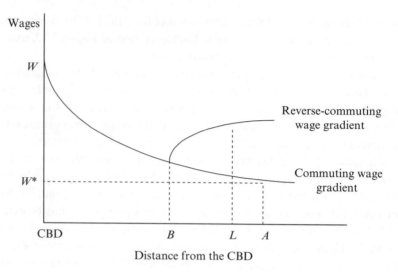

Figure 3.13   *Transport and wage costs*

a worker is willing to accept is completely determined by the structure of money transport costs'. We shall assume that all employment is either concentrated at the city center or else spread evenly over the surrounding, mainly residential, area. All households are assumed initially to be in equilibrium, all enjoying the same level of welfare. Moreover, all workers are paid identical wages, work the same hours and undertake the same number of commuting trips. Initially then, net monies after work-trip outlays will vary among workers according to the nature of their intra-urban transport costs and the distance of their homes from the CBD. Variations in land values with distance from the CBD, as we saw in the previous section, act as an adjustment mechanism to ensure uniformity of welfare. People living away from the urban core will pay more in transport costs, but their land rentals will be correspondingly lower.

In this simple world, however, workers could improve their well-being by giving up their job in the CBD (and thus saving commuting costs) and work at one of the jobs which are spread evenly over the urban area and which is near their home. They would be willing to accept a lower income in this situation; indeed, they would be willing to sacrifice their wage rate down to the point where it is cut by as much as the commuting costs that are saved. Thus there will be an equilibrium wage at locations nearer home than the CBD that will be lower than the core wage.

The result of this type of approach is the development of an urban wage gradient the shape of which is determined by commuting cost factors. In Figure 3.13, the downward-sloping curve then represents the fall-off in wages from W in the CBD needed at each location to be paid to a worker as the employment one moves from the urban center. This decline represents the decreasing amounts of compensation required to be paid by an employer to attract workers that have easier commutes because they do not have to go to the CBD. The cost of enticing a local worker to a job at, say, location A is only W^* and well below that at the

CBD. The worker living at A is indifferent between commuting to the CBD and earning $0W$ and working at home and earning $0W^*$. The commuter wage gradient curve traces out the wage rates at which a worker living at A would have to be paid to make him/her indifferent between working at home and at any intermediate site between A and the CBD. (It also shows the wage rates at which people living between A and the CBD will be indifferent between working at home and at the core.)

If we introduce the notion of some secondary employment concentration, say at L, then reverse commuting may develop. If employers at this subcenter require amounts of labor that they cannot attract from households to the right of L, they will need to compensate workers who travel out from areas between L and the CBD. Since the transport system tends to be less costly, in overall terms of money, time and comfort factors (see Chapter 4) for reverse commuting, the reverse commuting wage gradient is likely to be less steep than the commuting wage gradient. In this case, they can obtain the workers that they need by taking them from $B \Rightarrow L$ as well as to the right of L, with wages being determined by the reverse-commuting wage curve. The main influence on reverse-commuting costs *vis-à-vis* those for CBD commuters is the generally lower levels of traffic congestion away from the city center.

Just how does the wage gradient theory stand up to empirical investigation? There is remarkably little work on this question, but we can pull together some insights. Quite clearly the spread of national wage agreements, combined with imperfections in the land and transport markets (for example, public transport subsidies, the existence of company cars, and incomplete road networks), makes any exact testing of the theory difficult. American evidence from New York in the 1960s found wages to be higher in suburban counties than in the CBD and, even after allowing for variations in industrial structure, no wage gradient emerged.[30] However, a little later, Rees and Schultz[31] in their study of Chicago found a 'strong positive association of wages with distance traveled to work', but the wage gradient for blue-collar workers had its peak in the area of heavy industrial concentration (the south-west of the city) and sloped downwards towards the north-west. Similarly, analysis of the Panel Survey of Income Dynamics (basically looking at the activities of the same group of individuals over time) showed, 'Urban wage gradients exist in America'.[32]

More recently, Darren Timothy and William Wheaton[33] have provided further confirmation of the trade-off between commuting times and wages in the United States, taking account of the larger shifts that are taking place in urban form, notably suburbanization. They used a very simple model.

[30] M. Segal, *Wages in the Metropolis*, Cambridge, MA: Harvard University Press, 1960.
[31] A. Rees and G.P. Schultz, *Workers and Wages in an Urban Labour Market*, Chicago, IL: Chicago University Press, 1970.
[32] J.F. Madden, 'Urban wage gradients: empirical evidence', *Journal of Urban Economics*, **18**, 291–301, 1985.
[33] D. Timothy and W.C. Wheaton, 'Intra-urban wage variations, employment location, and commuting times', *Journal of Urban Economics*, **50**, 338–66, 2001.

$$W_i - W^0 = F_2(C_1) \qquad F'_2 > 0 \tag{3.7a}$$

$$C_i = F_1(E_i) \qquad F'_1 > 0 \tag{3.7b}$$

where:

C_i is the average commuting cost of workers in employment zone i;
E_i is the employment in zone i;
W_i is the wage rate in zone i;
W_i is the base metropolitan wage rate.

Using data for two large metropolitan areas they found, after adjusting for types of employment and such, that much of the 15 percent variation in urban wages could be related to commuting time differences between locations.

In Britain, Evans in his 1973 work suggested that while a wage gradient can be discerned for Greater London, there is little conclusive evidence of one else-where. Indeed, in provincial cities, clerical wages are often almost uniform across metropolitan areas. Clerical wages were, however, found to be higher in the City and the West End of London than in the suburbs.

Although these findings are not completely conclusive, it is clear that the evidence supporting the wage-gradient theory is at least balanced by that reject-ing it. The problems are that the studies to date fail to allow for the multiplicity of factors other than transport that affect wage levels. We have already mentioned some of the problems – notably, imperfections in certain markets – but to these we must add the tendency for employers to compensate workers for high trans-port costs by unrecorded payments (free meals, shorter working hours, more flexible timekeeping and so on). Additionally, in some cities there are unrecorded advantages of working in the city center (better out-of-work and shopping facili-ties, increased career potential and so on). The studies do not, therefore, refute the idea that transport costs influence urban wage patterns, but rather, the situation is more complex than the simple wage-gradient theory suggests.

Further Reading

Writings on the interactions between movement, transport and location are exten-sive. Although now over 30 years old, perhaps the best account of the various theories that manages to explain complex concepts in a very lucid way is H.W. Richardson, *The New Urban Economics and Alternatives*, London: Pion, 1977. A large number of reprinted classic papers are to be found in M.L. Greenhut and G. Norman (eds), *The Economics of Location* (3 vols), Aldershot, UK and Brookfield, VT, USA: Edward Elgar, 1995. For a collection of up-to-date survey papers of the various links between geography, spatial systems and transport, see D.A. Hensher, K.J. Button. K.E. Haynes and P.R. Stopher (eds), *Handbook of Transport Geography and Spatial Systems*, Oxford: Elsevier, 2004. K.J. Button,

S. Leitham, R.W. McQuaid and J.D. Nelson, 'Transport and industrial and commercial location', *Annals of Regional Science*, **29**, 189–206, 1995, offers a detailed analysis of the role of alternative modes of transport in the context of locations of different units of firms (for example, headquarters) and K.J. Button, 'High-technology companies: an examination of their transport needs', *Progress in Planning*, **29**, 79–146, 1987, looks specifically at more footloose companies.

Readers are also referred to journals such as the *Journal of Urban Economics, Regional Studies, Urban Studies* and the *Journal of Regional Science and Urban Economics*, which regularly publish material germane to the theme of this chapter.

4   The Demand for Transport

4.1   Introduction

Chapter 3 was concerned with the interrelationship between land-use patterns and transport; it thus offered some insights into a few of the factors influencing the demand for transport services. In this chapter the primary factors that influence demand for transport are considered in more detail. In particular, previous chapters laid stress on the derived nature of the demand for the vast majority of transport services, and it is this feature of demand that explains another characteristic of the transport market.

One of the most pronounced characteristics of the demand for transport, for instance, is its regular fluctuation over time. In urban areas, the demand for road space and public transport services is markedly higher in the early morning and late afternoon than during the rest of the day; in the inter-urban context the demand for passenger transport fluctuates regularly over a year with high seasonal peaks, while with international freight transport (especially shipping) there are long-term cycles in demand.

This tendency for peaks and troughs in the demand for transport is a reflection of fluctuations in the demand for the final products made accessible by transport services. In general, people wish to go on holiday in the summer; hence the seasonal peak in the demand for coach, rail and air services, while business finds it helpful to operate standard hours (that is, from 'nine-to-five') with the consequential concentration of commuter traffic. Longer-term fluctuations in the demand for shipping services reflect the state of business cycles in the trading nations – at the nadir of such cycles demand slumps, while at the zenith it is extremely buoyant.

There are also pronounced differences in the demands for different modes of transport according to the distance of a trip. This is largely a function of the technical features of the various modes that affect their overall attractiveness for shorter or longer trips. Figure 4.1 offers a very generalized picture of the way that different forms of transport dominate different lengths of personal trips, from walking and cycling being important to short journeys, to air transport dominating intercontinental travel. The extent of competition between modes, the issue of cross-elasticity of demand that we shall return to later, only really relates to cases where there is a genuine alternative.

Despite these regular fluctuations, it has been suggested that over time, and in another sense, there has been a remarkable stability in the demand for travel, with households, for example, on average making roughly the same number of trips during a day albeit for different purposes, over different routes, or by

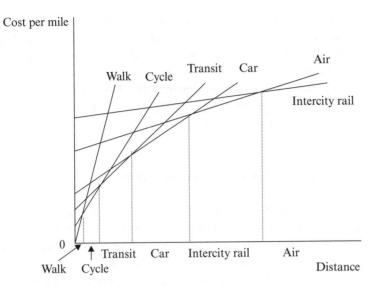

Figure 4.1   *Dominant modes of passenger transport*

different modes. There may be more leisure travel, but there are fewer work trips and greater use is now made of air transport and the automobile at the expense of walking and cycling. It is suggested that this situation reflects the obvious fact that there is a limit to the time people have available for travel, especially if they are to enjoy the fruits of the activities at the final destination. They therefore seek to use some notion of a 'travel time budget' more effectively as technology and choices change. Yacov Zahavi, for example found that people who made at least one motorized trip a day in an urban area, spent a constant 1.1 hours a day on travel.[1]

More recent work on travel time budgets indicates that the situation is more complicated than this and that the constancy suggested above should be sub-jected to a much closer inspection. In the United Kingdom, for example, there is evidence that average travel times have increased steadily throughout the twen-tieth century.[2] Explanations are difficult to find but one suggestion is that this is the result of rising incomes and that the constant time budget implied by Zahavi and others holds only for each income group. Thus peoples' travel changes as they move from low-income groups with low travel time budgets to higher-income groups with associated higher travel time budgets.

One example of a detailed analysis of this kind looking at the Netherlands, found that 'travel time budgets' increased over the last three decades of the twen-tieth century, but time expenditure on travel per head increased in relation to changes in travel costs and income levels. Such findings emphasize the importance

[1] Y. Zahavi, 'Equilibrium between travel, demand, system supply and urban structure', in E.J. Visser (ed.), *Transport Decisions in an Age of Uncertainty*, The Hague: Martinus Nijhoff, 1977.

[2] H.P. Gunn, 'Travel budgets – a review of evidence and modelling implications', *Transportation Research A*, **15**, 7–23, 1981.

of time as well as conventional monetary variables in travel demand analysis and, as we shall see in the following chapter, considerable emphasis is placed upon the role that time costs play in transport decision making.[3]

Given this rather general, aggregate background it is now relevant to look in much more detail at the actual influences and motivations that affect travel and transport-related demand. It seems appropriate to begin by considering the simple demand function as an *aide-mémoire*.

4.2   Factors that Influence Travel Demand

Initially we recap some basic demand theory. Demand is an abstract concept reflecting what individuals would like to consume under different scenarios. It is generally considered that the quantity demanded of a commodity, D_a, is influenced by its price, P_a, the price of other goods ($P_1, | P_2, \ldots, P_n$), tastes, T, and the level of income Y. The neoclassical demand curve entails focusing on the implications of price changes on demand, holding the other factors constant, that is,

$$D_a = f(P_a P_1, P_2, \ldots, P_n, T, Y) \tag{4.1}$$

A fall in price has two implications for demand – the price of the activity under consideration falls relative to other prices (substitution effect) and more can be bought for a given income (income effect) – both of which stimulate the quantity of the good or service demand. This means that normally there is a negative relationship between price and the quantity demanded, provided that other elements in equation (4.1) remain constant (Figure 4.2). It gives the 'downward-sloping demand curve'. The elasticity of demand reflects the relative sensitivity of a change in the quantity demanded to a change in price.

This curve shifts, however, if there are changes in other elements of equation (4.1). An increase in income by allowing more to be bought at any price level moves it out, whereas a fall in the price of a substitute, by making the good relatively more expensive, pulls the demand at any price down. In some cases, as with fashion goods or where public attitudes alter, the demand curve may shift because of changes in 'taste', essentially a catch-all concept used to mop up effects not captured in income or price effects.

For calculation purposes, as with many areas of demand analysis, a double logitharimic (or log-linear specification) of the form seen in equation (4.2) is often used to estimate the effects of the various factors on demand. This allows a simple interpretation of parameters as elasticities, but does assume that, for example, the price elasticity of demand is the same at all price levels:

---

[3] B. van Wee, P. Rietveld and H. Meurs, 'Is average daily travel time expenditure constant? In search of explanations for an increase in average travel time', *Journal of Transport Geography*, **14**, 109–22, 2006.

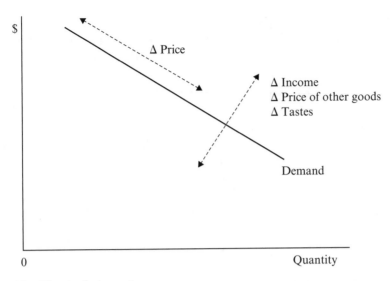

Figure 4.2 *The simple demand curve*

$$\ln Q_M = \alpha + \beta_1 \ln P_M + \beta_2 \ln Y + \beta_3 \ln P_N \qquad (4.2)$$

where: Q_M is the quantity of mode M demanded, P_M is the price of mode M, Y is income, and P_N is the price of an alternative, N. All variables are expressed as logs (ln) and the parameters would normally be estimated using multiple regression analysis. The price elasticity (defined as $\{\Delta Q/Q\}\{\Delta P/P\}$ is the parameter β_1 in a double logarithmic equation, the income elasticity of demand, reflecting the sensitivity of the quantity demanded to income changes, is β_2, and β_3 is the cross-elasticity of demand.

While this simple framework holds for transport, as for all other goods and services, there are refinements and detail that need to be highlighted if one is to gain an understanding of the way the transport markets operate. The individual terms in the equation are, in fact, often not simple variables but rather represent complex compounds of several interacting factors. Price, for instance, is not simply the fare paid but must embrace all the other costs involved in obtaining the transport service (of which 'time costs', as we noted above, are generally held to be the most important), while it may not be total income that influences travel demand by individuals but rather income in excess of some threshold subsistence level. Further, there is the need to be very clear on what exactly is being demanded: is it a trip *per se* or is it something more specific than this, for example, a bus trip or a journey over a particular route? Quandt and Baumol[4] have gone so far as to suggest that it is not transport at all which is being demanded but rather a bundle of transport services. (We shall look at this idea more fully in the context of forecasting in Chapter 12.)

These types of problems and issues are clearly difficulties that cannot be

[4] R.E. Quandt and W.J. Baumol, 'The demand for abstract transport modes, theory and measurement', *Journal of Regional Science*, **6**, 13–26, 1966.

entirely circumvented in a general discussion of the influences affecting transport demand, but they should be borne in mind as we move on to look in more detail at some of the items contained in the demand function set out as equation (4.1).

The Price of the Transport Service

As has been suggested, the price of transport embraces considerably more than the simple money costs paid out in fuel, fares or haulage fees. In transport modeling and quantitative work these other components of price (that is, time costs, waiting, insecurity and so on) may be combined to form a generalized cost index of the type we shall discuss later in Chapter 5 where we focus in more detail on cost, but here we concentrate on money prices and, in particular, on the sensitivity of transport users to the price of transport services.

Generalizations are obviously difficult, especially across all modes of transport, but in many cases it seems clear that price changes within certain limits have relatively little effect on the quantity of travel or transport services demanded. The demand for cargo shipping is, for example, very inelastic, in part because of the lack of close substitutes for shipping services, in part because of the short-term inelastic nature of the demand for the raw materials frequently carried, and in part because of the relatively small importance of freight rates in the final selling price of cargoes.

While in broad terms, demand elasticities exhibit a degree of stability, over time they do not remain constant in part because of shifts in the demand function due to such things as rising incomes and changes in consumer tastes. Studies of urban public transport in the 1970s, for example, covering a variety of countries, indicate relatively low price elasticities with a direct fare elasticity of around -0.3 being considered normal. Smith and MacIntosh[5] looking at British urban bus undertakings, for instance, produce figures ranging from -0.21 to -0.61, but the majority fall at the lower end of the spectrum. McGillivany's[6] suggestion of a figure of around -0.2 for bus trips in San Francisco and Charles Lave's[7] finding of a direct fare elasticity of -0.11 for transit trips in Chicago imply that the fare elasticity in the United States was slightly lower than in the United Kingdom at that time. In Canada an elasticity of -0.33 has for some time been used as a rule of thumb by operators.

Studies, in the 1980s surveyed by Goodwin[8] tend to produce similar figures

---

[5] M.G. Smith and P.T. McIntosh, 'Fares elasticity; interpretation and estimation', in *Symposium on Public Transport Fare Structure*, Crowthorne: Transport and Road Research Laboratory Report, SR37UC, 1974.

[6] R.G. McGillivany, 'Demand and choice models of modal split', *Journal of Transport Economics and Policy*, **4**, 192–207, 1970.

[7] C.A. Lave, 'The demand for urban mass transportation', *Review of Economics and Statistics*, **52**, 320–23, 1970.

[8] P.B. Goodwin, 'A review of new demand elasticities with special reference to short and long run effects of price changes', *Journal of Transport Economics and Policy*, **26**, 155–70, 1992.

to Smith and MacIntosh, although highlighting the fact that the short-term elasticities found in 'before and after' studies of fare change are in the order of a third of the size of longer-term elasticities covering a reaction time in excess of five years. Something of a rogue result, however, was obtained in the econometric study of bus and underground use in London during the late 1980s by Gilbert and Jalilian[9] which suggests long-run elasticities exceeding unity for buses and approaching unity for the underground; rail demand elasticity was at the more 'normal' low value.

The effect of price change on private car transport must be divided between the effect on vehicle ownership and that specifically on vehicle use. Most early UK studies of car ownership indicate an elasticity of about −0.3 with respect to vehicle price and −0.1 with respect to gasoline price.[10] American empirical work suggests a rather higher sensitivity (the Chase Econometrics Associates[11] model, for example, implies a −0.88 purchase price elasticity and a −0.82 fuel price elasticity), but responsiveness is still very low.

For car use, all the evidence suggests an extremely low fuel price elasticity in the short term which may be attributed to changing patterns of household expenditure between vehicle ownership and use and people's perception of motoring costs. Bendtsen brought early findings together[12] in an international comparison which shows that the petrol price elasticity of demand for car use was −0.08 in Australia for the period from 1955 to 1976; −0.07 in Britain for 1973/74; −0.08 in Denmark for 1973/4 and −0.12 for 1979/80; and −0.05 in the United States for 1968/75. Oum and co-workers[13] found a slightly greater degree of sensitivity when looking at seven studies covering the United Kingdom, the United States and Australia; they yielded car usage elasticities in the range from −0.09 to −0.52.

Table 4.1 provides a survey of more recent estimates of automobile and public transport elasticities. We immediately note the higher long-term elasticities in all cases, a topic we shall return to below, but also the relatively high-income elasticities reflecting the possibilities for modal switching or other changes in travel behavior as incomes change – an important consideration for policy makers in developing countries.

If we move to the other extreme of the transport market and look at airline operations, the evidence is that demand is slightly less elastic with long-term

---

[9] C.L. Gilbert and H. Jalilian, 'The demand for travel cards on London Regional Transport', *Journal of Transport Economics and Policy*, **25**, 3–30, 1991.

[10] M.J.H. Mogridge, 'The effect of the oil crisis on the growth in the ownership and use of cars', *Transportation*, **7**, 45–65, 1978.

[11] Chase Econometrics Associates, *The Effect of Tax and Regulatory Alternatives on Car Sales and Gasoline Consumption*, NTIS Report No. PB-234622, New York, 1974.

[12] P.R. Bendtsen, 'The influence of price of petrol and of cars on the amount of automobile traffic, *International Journal of Transport Economics*, **7**, 207–13, 1980.

[13] T.H. Oum, W.G. Waters and J.S. Young, 'Concepts of price elasticities of transport demand and recent empirical evidence', *Journal of Transport Economics and Policy*, **26**, 139–54, 1992.

Table 4.1 *Summary of demand elasticities provided by Graham and Glaister*

	Short/long run	Elasticity
Fuel demand with respect to fuel price	SR	−0.25
	LR	−0.77
Fuel demand with respect to income	SR	0.47
	LR	0.93
Traffic (car-km) with respect to fuel price	SR	−0.15
	LR	−0.31
Traffic (car-trips) with respect to fuel price	SR	−0.16
	LR	−0.19
Traffic (car-km) with respect to car time	SR	−0.20
	LR	−0.74
Traffic (car-trips) with respect to car time	SR	−0.60
	LR	−0.29
Traffic (car-km) with respect to income	SR	0.30
	LR	0.73
Freight traffic with respect to price	n.a.	−1.07
Car ownership with respect to cost	SR	−0.20
	LR	−0.90
Car ownership with respect to income	SR	0.28
	LR	0.74

Source: D.J. Graham and S. Glaister, 'Road traffic demand elasticity estimates: a review', *Transport Reviews*, **24**, 261–74, 2004.

demand (estimated from cross-sectional data) emerging as elastic. What these coefficients, and indeed, those cited above relating to other modes often disguise are quite significant differences in the elasticities for different groups of travelers and between individual services. Mutti and Mural[14] in an investigation of air travel across the North Atlantic air market generally found inelasticity, but with variability between routes. Examinations of internal air traffic within the United States, however, produce much more varied results. Brown and Watkins[15] and Gronau[16] show a remarkable degree of consistency by producing price elasticities of −0.85 and −0.75, respectively, but Jung and Fujii[17] came to a somewhat different conclusion, namely that demand for air travel for distances under 500 miles in the south-east and south-central areas of the United States is price elastic.

The relevance of this earlier work, other than in its technical innovations, is clouded by the considerable institutional changes that have taken place since the late 1970s when air transport, as we shall discuss in Chapter 14, began to be

[14] J. Mutti and Y. Mural, 'Airline travel on the North Atlantic', *Journal of Transport Economics and Policy*, **11**, 45–53, 1977.

[15] S. Brown and W. Watkins, 'The demand for air travel: a regression study of time-series and cross-sectional data in the US domestic market', *Highway Research Record*, **213**, 21–34, 1968.

[16] R. Gronau, *The Value of Time in Passenger Transportation: The Demand for Air Travel*, New York: Columbia University Press, 1970.

[17] J.M. Jung and E.T. Fujii, 'The price elasticity of demand for air travel – some new evidence', *Journal of Transport Economics and Policy*, **10**, 257–62, 1976.

deregulated. Table 4.2 provides a larger listing of some of the main studies that have examined air transport demand elasticities, including more recent ones. While no single figure emerges from these studies that can be isolated as the 'representative' fare elasticity, some general conclusions can be drawn.

There is a distinction between the fare elasticities for business and non-business air travel, with the latter being generally higher. This is a pattern also seen, as one might expect, in terms of the type of fare being paid. This conforms to the intuition that vacation travelers have more flexibility in their actions (destinations, times of flights) whereas business trips often have to be taken at short notice.

The lower sensitivity associated with first/business class fares also reflects the service requirements of users who often seek room to work on planes and in lounges. The estimates of the elasticities are also sensitive to the length of service with shorter routes generally exhibiting higher fare elasticities, in part because other modes of transport become viable options.

The difficulty with many statistics on demand sensitivity is, therefore, that they are elasticities averaged over several groups. In fact, the price elasticity of transport, as with the price elasticity of other goods, should ideally be set in a specific context. In the case of transport, four broad types of classification are important and we consider each in turn. Tables 4.1 to 4.3 provide a complement to the more specific discussions found in the body of the text.

Trip purpose

There is an abundance of evidence that the fare elasticity for certain types of trip is much higher than others. Business travel demand in particular seems to be relatively more insensitive to changes in transport price than other forms of trip. Kraft and Domenich[18] found that public transport work trips exhibited a fare elasticity of −0.17 in Boston compared with −0.32 for shopping trips. These figures conform closely to those found by London Transport in the UK. If we focus on the work that has looked at air traffic, Mutti and Mural attribute part of the variation they found in fare responsiveness on the North Atlantic to the fact that 'we expect personal travel to be more price elastic than business travel'. Straszheim[19] subsequently provides confirmation of this view and isolates elasticities for different types of service. In particular he concludes, 'First class fares can be raised and will increase revenue . . . The demand for standard economy service is about unity, and highest for peak period travel . . . The demand for discount and promotional fares is highly price elastic'. Oum et al.[20] came to identical conclusions when looking at North American data. Quite clearly, therefore, it is dangerous to attempt to analyze transport demand without considering the specific type of trip being undertaken.

[18] G. Kraft and T.A. Domenich, *Free Transit*, Lexington: Heath, 1970.
[19] M.R. Straszheim, 'Airline demand functions on the North Atlantic and their pricing implications', *Journal of Transport Economics and Policy*, **12**, 179–95, 1978.
[20] T.H. Oum, D.W. Gillen and S.E. Noble, 'Demand for fare class and pricing in airline markets', *Logistics and Transportation Review*, **22**, 195–222, 1986.

Table 4.2   *Air fare elasticity studies*

Study (publication year)	Focus of study	Values
Oum et al. (1993)*	United and American Airline hubs	−1.58 to −2.34
Oum et al. (1992)[†]	Trip purpose (business/non-business)	−1.15 to −1.52
	Mixed or unknown	−0.76 to −4.51
Oum et al. (1986)*	First class	−0.58 to −0.82
	Standard economy	−1.23 to −1.36
	Discount economy	−1.50 to −1.98
Royal Commission on National Passenger Transportation (1992)**	Business travel	−1.57 to −3.51
	Non-business travel	−4.38 to −4.50
	Short trip (under 500 miles)	−1.16 to −2.70
	Long trip (over 500 miles)	−1.34 to −2.56
Apogee Research Inc. (1994)*	Business travel	−0.59
	Non-business travel	−0.38
Morrison & Winston (1985)*	Non-business	−0.859
Abrahams (1983)*	Transcontinental	−1.81
	Florida vacation city pairs	−1.98
	Hawaiian-West Coast city pairs	−1.68
	Eastern medium-haul city pairs	−1.22
Ippolito (1981)*	440 mile trip (one way)	−0.53
	830 mile trip (one way)	−1.00
Straszheim (1978)[††]	First class	−0.65
	Economy, peak period	−1.92
	Economy, average	−1.48
	Economy, standard	−1.12
	Economy, promotional	−2.74
	Economy, high discount	−1.82
De Vany (1983)*	28 mile trip (one way)	−0.78
	400 mile trip (one way)	−1.02
	650 mile trip (one way)	−1.07
	1500 mile trip (one way)	−1.14
	2500 mile trip (one way)	−1.17
Gillen et al. (2002)[†¥]	Long-haul international business	−0.26
	Long-haul international leisure	−0.99
	Long-haul domestic business	−1.15
	Long-haul domestic leisure	−1.52
	Short/medium-haul business	−1.39
Brons et al. (2002)[†¥]	Meta analysis of 204 studies	−1.15
Pickrell (1984)*	Short routes	−2.0
	Business travel	−1.0 to −1.5
Bhadra (2003)*	Less than 250 miles	−0.67
	250–499 miles	−0.56
	500–749 miles	−0.74
	750–999 miles	−1.45
	1000–1249 miles	−1.82
	1250–1499 miles	−0.85
	1500–1749 miles	−1.08
	1750–1999 miles	−0.84
	2000–2249 miles	−1.06
	2250–2499 miles	−1.38
	2500–3000 miles	−0.86

Notes: * US data, ** Canadian data, [†] synthesis of previous studies, [††] North Atlantic data, [¥] from a range of international studies.

Table 4.3 *Elasticities of demand for passenger transport (expressed in absolute values)*

Mode	Range surveyed		Number of studies
	Market demand elasticities	*Mode choice elasticities*	
Air*			
Vacation	0.40–4.60	0.38	8
Non-vacation	0.08–4.18	0.18	6
Mixed+	0.44–4.51	0.26–5.26	14
Rail: Intercity			
Leisure	1.40	1.20	2
Business	0.70	0.57	2
Mixed+	0.11–1.54	0.86–1.14	8
Rail: Intracity			
Peak	0.15	0.22–0.25	2
Off-peak	1.00	n.a.	1
All day+	0.12–1.80	0.08–0.75	4
Automobile:			
Peak	0.12–0.49	0.02–2.69	9
Off-peak	0.06–0.88	0.16–0.96	6
All day+	0.00–0.52	0.01–1.26	7
Bus:			
Peak	0.05–0.40	0.04–0.58	7
Off-peak	1.08–1.54	0.01–0.69	3
All day+	0.10–1.62	0.03–0.70	11
Transit system:			
Peak	0.00–0.32	0.1	5
Off-peak	0.32–1.00	n.a.	3
All day+	0.01–0.96	n.a.	15

Notes: *The distinction between vacation and non-vacation routes is rather arbitrary in most studies and may partly account for the very wide range of elasticity estimates; +This includes studies which do not distinguish between categories (peak, off-peak or all day); n.a. = not available.

Source: T.H. Oum, W.G. Waters and X. Fu, 'Transport demand elasticities', in D.A. Hensher and K.J. Button (eds), *Handbook of Transport Modelling*, 2nd edn, Oxford: Elsevier, 2008.

The methods of charging

Users of different forms of transport (or, sometimes, different services of the same mode) are often confronted with entirely different methods of payment. Consequently, their perception of the price of a journey may differ from the actual monies expended. Sherman,[21] for example, has suggested that motorists perceive very little of the true overall price of these trips because they base decisions on a limited concept of short-run marginal cost. Forty years ago, in a pioneering study of UK traffic, Harrison and Quarmby[22] found that drivers perceived between

[21] R. Sherman, 'A private ownership bias in transmit choice', *American Economic Review*, 77, 1211–17, 1967.

[22] A.J. Harrison and D.A. Quarmby, 'The value of time in transport planning: a review', in *Report of the Sixth Round Table on Transport Economics*, Paris: European Conference of Ministers of Transport, 1969.

50 and 60 percent of their own costs (fuel, tire wear, vehicle maintenance and so on) and this did not included environmental effects and the costs of congestion imposed on others. Users of public transport, on the other hand, are usually made much more aware of the costs of their trip-making by the requirement to purchase a ticket, usually prior to beginning their journey. Nevertheless, given the range of season tickets (which permit bulk-buying of journeys over a specific route) and travel card facilities (which permit bulk-buying of journeys over a specified network), the distinction is not a firm one. The empirical findings are also not very helpful. Peter White's[23] review of the empirical information available on travel cards in the United Kingdom, for example, points to a much lower price elasticity for travel card systems than for conventional single ticket cash payment systems.

The time period under consideration

As with other purchasing decisions, people confronted with a change in transport price may act rather differently in the ultra-short run, the 'market period', the short run and the long run. Immediate reactions, in the ultra-short term, to a public transport fare rise may, for example, be dramatic, with people, almost on principle, making far less use of services, even boycotting them, but knee-jerk reaction is extremely short-lived and seldom considered by economists, although it is often of interest to politicians.

The ultra-short-term elasticity may, therefore, be extremely high but short-lived. This type of situation may be less common than is sometimes thought and, indeed, the reverse response may result in the slightly longer period. In the market period, for example, people may appear to be relatively unresponsive to a price change either because they do not consider it to be a permanent change or because technical constraints limit their immediate actions. The demand for gasoline, a major input into modern transport, offers a good example of how its demand varies with significant price rises – a situation found with the 'oil shocks', and more recently in 2007 to 2008.

In Figure 4.3 the price of oil rises from P_1 to P_2; ignoring any knee-jerk reactions in the ultra-short term the gasoline purchased will change little. The transport users are locked into a pattern of behavior that makes reducing their fuel consumption difficult; this is the 'market period'. In the short run, however, individuals can change their travel patterns by switching modes, combining trips, and cutting out some travel, and businesses can reschedule the use of their vehicle fleets and modify their collection and delivery patterns. The demand, therefore, becomes more elastic in relation to the new price and the amount bought falls to Q_2. In the long term, people can change the type of car they use, and their employment and residential locations, and industry can modify their entire supply chain. Hence, the quantity of gasoline demand will fall to Q_3 in the figure, and the demand curve will flatten out further.

[23] P.R. White, '"Travelcard" tickets in urban public transport', *Journal of Transport Economics and Policy*, **15**, 17–34, 1981.

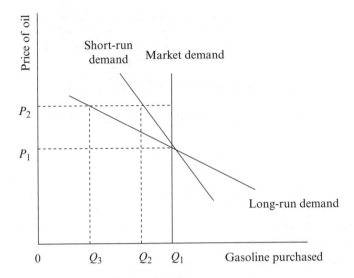

Figure 4.3   *Changes in demand elasticities over time*

Similarly, in a more direct transport context, when considering the effect of general rises on commuter travel costs, the necessity of having to make journeys to work is likely to result in minimal changes in travel patterns in the short term, but over a longer period relocations of either residence or employment may produce a more dramatic effect. This implies that one must take care when assessing elasticity coefficients, and it is useful to remember that cross-sectional studies tend to offer estimates of long-run elasticity while time-series studies reflect short-term responses.

Table 4.1 provided some general guidelines to variations in elasticities through time. Table 4.3 offers more explicit indications of how price and income elasticities can vary over time after a price shock in the gasoline market; a more detailed discussion of this appears in Chapter 7.

The absolute level of the price change
Elasticities are generally found to increase the longer the journey under consideration. This should not be seen simply as a function of distance but rather as a reflection of the absolute magnitude of, say, a 10 percent rise on a $5 fare compared with that on a $500 fare. It is also true that longer journeys are made less frequently, and thus people gather information about prices in a different way. Additionally, they often tend to involve leisure rather than business travel; this suggests that distance may be picking up variations in trip purpose. In the air transport market, for example, Arthur DeVany[24] found in a classic study that price elasticity rose from −0.97 for a 440-mile trip in the United States to −1.13 for an 830-mile trip. For similar journeys, Ippolito[25] found the respective elasticities to be −0.525 and −1.0.

[24] A.S. DeVany, 'The revealed value of time in air travel', *Review of Economics and Statistics*, **56**, 77–82, 1974.
[25] R.A. Ippolito, 'Estimating airline demand with quality of service variables', *Journal of Transport Economics and Policy*, **15**, 7–15, 1981.

Table 4.4 *Price and income elasticities of gasoline demand by automobiles users*

	Price elasticity	*Income elasticity*
Short run	−0.2 to −0.3	0.35 to 0.55
Long run	−0.6 to −0.8	1.1 to 1.3

Source: L.J. Basso and T.H. Oum, 'Automobile fuel demand: a critical assessment of empirical methodologies', *Transport Reviews*, **27**, 449–84, 2007.

While it is important to treat elasticities with care because of these type of aggregation issues, there is a further reason for counseling caution when considering such parameters. There are a number of statistical methods employed to calculate elasticities and these can influence the values obtained. In some instances these related to the time span of the elasticity being studied; some techniques are used mainly for short-term elasticity estimation while others are more relevant for cross-sections of data, and thus long-term elasticity calculations. The intention here is not to go into the technicalities of the various modeling frameworks, although some discussion of this is to be found in Chapter 12, which explicitly discusses demand modeling and forecasting, but rather to highlight what seem to be the two main trends:

- First, if aggregate data are used, for instance looking at demand for an entire railroad network, then, although it is far from universally true, elasticities tend to be higher than from 'discrete choice' type models that use data at the individual service or customer level.
- Second, even within a particular modeling framework (be it involving the use of aggregate data or disaggregate data) the exact mathematical form of the equation used influences the elasticity calculated. Equation (4.2) highlighted the log-linear, or 'Cobb–Douglas', specification, the generic features of which we shall return to in Chapter 5. Table 4.5 provides some general guidance to these specification issues with respect to estimated elasticities of demand for rail freight transport.

Income Levels

After housing and food, transport represents, at about 10 to 15 percent for a single-car-owning household, the largest element of expenditure out of income in industrialized countries. While there is ample evidence that transport is a normal good in the sense that more is demanded at higher levels of income, this generalization does not apply to all modes of transport or to all situations. As was seen in Chapter 2, at the national level, income exerts a positive influence over car-ownership decisions, and we shall consider this relationship at a more disaggregate level below. But the situation is not so clear-cut with public transport use, and in some cases this mode clearly becomes an 'inferior good' with its use falling after some level of income has been attained. As incomes have risen and car ownership has become more widespread, public transport has in many situations proved to

Table 4.5 *Demand elasticities for North American rail freight transport (expressed in absolute values)*

Commodities	Log-linear	Aggregate logit	Translog	Discrete choice
Aggregate commodities	1.52	0.25–0.35, 0.83	0.09–0.29, 0.60	n.a.
Chemicals	n.a.	0.66	0.69	2.25
Fabricated metal products	n.a.	1.27	2.16	n.a.
Food products	0.02, 1.18	1.36	2.58, 1.04	n.a.
Iron and steel products	n.a.	n.a.	2.54, 1.20	0.02
Machinery	n.a.	0.16–1.73	2.27–3.50	0.61
Paper, plastic & rubber products	0.67	0.87	1.85	0.17, 0.09
Petroleum products	n.a.	n.a.	0.99	0.53
Stone, clay & glass products	n.a.	2.03	n.a.	0.56
Transport equipment	n.a.	n.a.	0.92–1.08	2.68
Wood & wood products	0.05	0.76	1.97, 0.58	0.08

Source: T.H. Oum, W.G. Waters and J.S. Young, 'Concepts of price elasticities of transport demand and recent empirical evidence', *Journal of Transport Economics and Policy*, **26**, 139–54, 1992.

be an inferior good. Gwilliam and Mackie[26] suggest that the long-run elasticity of demand with respect to income was of the order −0.4 to −1.0 for urban public transport trip making in the United Kingdom during the 1970s. They argue that although car ownership rises with income, and hence some trips are diverted from public transport, there is still a limited offsetting effect inasmuch as wealthier households make more trips in total. This effect would seem to be less relevant today with much higher levels of automobile ownership in developed countries.

The income elasticity of demand for many other modes of transport is seen to be relatively high, and especially so for modes such as air transport. John Taplin,[27] for example, suggests a figure of the order of 2.1 for vacation air trips overseas from Australia. By its nature, air travel is a high-cost activity (the absolute costs involved are high even where mileage rates are low) so that high income elasticities of this level are to be expected. There is also some evidence that wealth influences the demand for air travel, and a study of the Israeli market found a wealth elasticity of 2.06.[28]

As with price, income changes exert somewhat different pressures on transport demand in the long run compared with the short. In general, it may be argued, a fall in income will produce a relatively dramatic fall in the level of demand, but as people readjust their expenditure patterns in the long term the elasticity is likely to be much lower. Looking at the responsiveness of car-ownership levels

[26] K.M. Gwilliam and P.J. Mackie, *Economics and Transport Policy*, London: Allen & Unwin, 1975.

[27] J.H.E. Taplin, 'A coherence approach to estimates of price elasticities in the vacation travel market', *Journal of Transport Economics and Policy*, **14**, 19–35, 1980.

[28] G. Alperovich and Y. Machnes, 'The role of wealth in demand for international air travel', *Journal of Transport Economics and Policy*, **28**, 163–73, 1994.

to income changes, British and US studies suggest a short-term income elasticity of between 2.0 and 4.5 while in the long run it appears to fall to around 1.5.[29] However, as with price elasticities, the relationships between long- and short-term effects are not completely clear-cut. Reza and Spiro,[30] for example, produce an estimate of 0.6 for the short-run income elasticity of demand for petrol, rising to 1.44 in the long run – findings that are generally in line with what we saw in Table 4.4. If one assumes that gasoline consumption is a proxy for trip making, then one could attempt to justify this in terms of a slow reaction to changing financial circumstances – a reluctance, for example, to accept immediately the consequences of a fall in income. In fact, the situation is likely to be more complex than this since the long run may embrace changes in technology, and possibly locations, which alter the fuel consumption–trip-making relationship. Thus these figures may still be consistent with the initial hypothesis regarding the relative size of short- and long-run income elasticities of demand for travel.

There is a literature on the possibility of a constant travel income budget akin to the travel time budget mentioned in Section 4.1 with households tending to spend a fixed proportion of their income on transport. Zahavi, for example, in his examination of data from a large sample of urban transport users, noticed that the proportion of disposable income spent on cars by car-owning households at any income level appears to be approximately constant at a given moment of time. (UK data suggest a proportion of around 15.5 percent – slightly larger for low incomes – for 1971 to 1975.) The evidence for bus transport is less clear, but Mogridge in his study suggests that while the proportion of disposable household income spent on bus travel seems to rise with income, a constant proportion still emerges if adjustments are made for the number of people in each household.

In the longer term there is evidence at the aggregate level that over the past 40 years or so there has been a steady increase in the overall proportion of income or disposable income allocated to travel in the United Kingdom. (This contrasts to a more or less constant proportion in Canada and the United States.) This may, though, be explained in terms of rising income levels but constant proportional travel budgets within each income group. The general conclusion about the idea that some overall budget mechanism governs individual travel decisions, however, must be that, to date, the evidence available still leaves many questions unanswered and the theory is still largely unproved. More recently, in an examination of 30 or so travel surveys from across the world, Andreas Schafer[31] finds some consistency in travel money budgets for countries with about 0.85 cars per household, but the link is weak and only applies at a very aggregate level.

[29] K.J. Button, A. Pearman and A. Fowkes, *Car Ownership Modelling and Forecasting*, Aldershot: Ashgate, 1982.

[30] A.M. Reza and H.M. Spiro, 'The demand for passenger car transport services and for gasoline', *Journal of Transport Economics and Policy*, **13**, 304–19, 1979.

[31] A. Schafer, 'Regularities in travel demand: an international perspective', *Journal of Transportation and Statistics*, **3**, 1–31, 2000

Table 4.6   *Greater London estimated Monday to Friday fare elasticities (1970–1975)*

Study	Elasticity of	With respect to	
		Bus	Local rail
Fairhurst and Morris (1975)	Bus	−0.60	0.25
	Rail	0.25	−0.40
Glaister (1976)	Bus	−0.56	0.30
	Rail	1.11	−1.00
Collings et al. (1977)	Bus	−0.41	n.a.
Lewis (1978)	Peak road traffic	0.03	0.06

Source: S. Glaister and D. Lewis, 'An integrated fares policy for transport in London', *Journal of Public Economics*, **9**, 341–55, 1978.

The price of other transport services

The demand for any particular transport service is likely to be influenced by the actions of competitive and complementary suppliers. (Strictly speaking, it is also influenced by prices in all other markets operating in the economy but, with the possible exceptions of the land market, which was discussed in Chapter 3, and electronic communications, which we shall look at in Chapter 8, the importance of these is less great.) We have only touched upon the importance of motoring costs *vis-à-vis* the demand for public transport services and more will be said on this topic later in the chapter. Moreover, there are the cross-price effects between modes of public transport. Table 4.6 presents the results from a number of different studies looking at elasticities of demand (both own fare and cross-fare) for transport in Greater London for 1970 to 1975.

The variation in results generally reflects the adoption of alternative estimation procedures and time-lag allowances. One of the more interesting points is the almost total insensitivity of the demand for urban car use to the fare levels of both bus and rail public transport modes. This fact, which has been observed in virtually all studies of urban public transport, is the main reason why attempts by city transport authorities to reduce or contain car travel by subsidizing public transport fares have, in the main, proved unsuccessful.

The table suggests that there is likely to be more switching of demand between public transport modes as a result of one changing its fare structure than between that mode and private transport. The more recent work by Gilbert and Jalilian cited earlier (see note 9), also provides London cross-elasticities between public transport modes but throws up somewhat different results with the indication, in particular, that bus travel in London is more sensitive to underground fares with a cross-fare elasticity of 0.90. Analysis of the cross-elasticity of demand between car and rail costs for intercity rail travel in the United Kingdom shows much less sensitivity: an average cross-elasticity of 0.09, falls to 0.027 to 0.028 on some freeways.[32]

[32] M.Z. Acutt and J.S. Dodgson, 'Cross-elasticities of demand for travel', *Transport Policy*, **2**, 271–7, 1995.

In other transport markets the cross-elasticity of demand may be higher, both between operators of the same mode of transport and between modes themselves. Recently, price reduction in non-conference shipping lines, for example, has attracted considerable traffic away from the cartel carriers. Similarly, scheduled airlines have experienced a contraction of demand as reduced-rate operators have entered the market.

Evidence on the cross-price elasticity of complementary transport services, such as feeder links to longer-distance trunk hauls, is scant. The expansion of the motorway network in the United Kingdom, the autobahns in Germany, and the freeways in the United States reducing motorway travel costs, certainly increased the demand for certain feeder roads while at the same time reducing it on competing routes. The exact implications of such network effects are much more difficult to trace out than changes in modal split but, in practical terms, are important features of the transport system.

The topic of cross-elasticities of demand between modes will be returned to in Chapters 8 and 9 when we discus their importance when trying to divert traffic to less environmentally damaging and congestive forms of transport

Tastes

One of the items which influences equation (4.1) and not mentioned to date, but which is often included in elementary discussion of demand, is the 'catch-all' variable, tastes. While there may be circumstances when such a term could and, indeed, should be included in the demand function, in general, tastes are more likely to influence the actual form of the demand equation: linear, log-linear, or whatever. Consequently, a change in tastes may be seen to affect the relationships between demand and the explanatory variables rather than result in some movement along a demand curve following the pattern of an established relationship.

The economic meaning of 'tastes' is seldom made clear, but in practice it seems to embrace all influences on demand not covered by the previous headings. Over time, tastes in transport certainly have changed. Some time ago, Burrell,[33] for instance, emphasized the increased car orientation of society towards private transport irrespective of cost or income considerations, while in freight transport the changing structure of the national economy (especially the switch from basic heavy industry to light industry producing high-value, low-weight products) has shifted the emphasis from price to other aspects of transport service. Both of these changes must to some extent be related to rising standards of living. With more wealth and greater free time there is likely to be an enhanced desire to benefit from the greater freedom and flexibility offered by private transport. A change in location patterns is also possible, with larger residential plots away from urban centers now becoming attractive for many people.

[33] J. Burrell, 'Recent developments in car ownership forecasting', in *Urban Traffic Model Research*, London: Planning and Transport Research and Computation, 1972.

Another aspect of 'taste' concerns inertia and asymmetry in decision making.[34] This has two implications:

- First, there may be discontinuities in the demand curve for transport, or at least parts of the demand curve, reflecting almost total insensitivity to price changes, as a result of habit and inertia on the part of individuals and firms.[35] It may be explained in some cases quite simply by the fact that there are costs involved in seeking out information about alternatives and continuing as before is thus the rational response until more major price changes occur.
- Second, there may be cases where responses are not symmetrical: a ratchet effect exists whereby the reaction to a price fall is not the same as the reaction to an identical price rise. Limited empirical work has been done on such 'path dependencies' although Blase[36] did find evidence of asymmetries in travel behavior in the context of fuel price variation, and Joyce Dargay[37] provided further support for this across a number of national studies.

Rather more effort has been put into the question of service quality. It is noticeable, for example, from empirical studies that public transport demand is sensitive to changes in service quality, especially to any reduction in the speed or frequency of services. Again this fact reflects the decreased importance attached to the purely monetary dimension. Market research in the West Midlands of the United Kingdom, for example, revealed that only 27.1 percent of people felt that keeping fares down would be the greatest improvement to local public transport; the remainder looked for service quality improvements – for example, 14.6 percent looked for greater reliability, 10.4 percent higher frequency, 10.4 percent more bus shelters, 10.0 percent cleaner vehicles and so on.[38]

An extensive survey by Lago et al.[39] examined a wide range of international studies concerned with urban public transport service elasticities. The general conclusion that services will generate less than proportional increases in passenger and revenue (that is, $\varepsilon_S < 1$) would seem to contradict the above findings, but this may be misleading. To begin with, the survey looks at a number of service quality attributes in isolation rather than at a package of service features. It also admits that many of the services sought by potential public transport users are qualitative rather than quantitative and, hence, are not amenable to the types of

[34] P.B. Goodwin, 'Habit and hysteresis in mode choice', *Urban Studies*, **14**, 95–8, 1977.
[35] D. Banister, 'The influence of habit formation on modal choice a heuristic model', *Transportation*, **7**, 19–33, 1978.
[36] J.R. Blase, 'Hysteresis in travel demand', *Transportation Planning and Technology*, **6**, 109–16, 1980.
[37] J.D. Dargay, 'Demand elasticities: a comment', *Journal of Transport Economics and Policy*, **27**, 87–90, 1993.
[38] J.K. Isaac, 'Price and quality in road passenger transport', *Journal of the Chartered Institute of Transport*, **38**, 359–61, 1979.
[39] A.M. Lago, P.D. Mayworm and J. McEnroe, 'Transit service elasticities – evidence from demonstration and demand models', *Journal of Transport Economics and Policy*, **15**, 99–119, 1981

analysis reviewed. The survey also highlights the fact that service quality is far more important when the initial level of service is poor: the general elasticities found for peak-period ridership, for instance, are much lower than those for the off-peak. The evidence presented suggests that service headway is one of the more important service variables; the studies examined indicate an elasticity of the order of −0.42 compared with, for example, −0.29 for in-vehicle bus travel time.

The available evidence suggests that today low price is also no longer the dominant determinant of freight modal choice. In a survey conducted in the United Kingdom by the Price Commission,[40] for instance, it was found that only in 52 percent of cases did consignors elect to use the cheapest road haulage operator available for local trips, 77 percent for intraregional trips and 64 percent for trunk-hauls. Many were so unconcerned about finding the lowest price that competitive quotations were not sought. An emphasis placed upon vehicle suitability is seen to reflect customer concern about such factors as weather protection, systems for securing loads and compatibility of vehicle with product. These are concerns unlikely to have been of paramount importance when heavy industry dominated the economy but are of much more concern for the more modern, high-technology firms.[41] These firms are increasingly turning to 'just-in-time' production methods whereby inventories are kept to a minimum. To optimize such processes reliability of supply is vital and companies are willing to pay the additional financial costs that this may entail.[42]

4.3 The Notion of a 'Need' for Transport

The demand function indicates what people would buy given a particular budget constraint, but it is often argued that allocation of resources on this basis results in inequalities and unfairness because of differences in household income or other circumstances. There are, thus, some advocates of the idea that transport services, or at least some of them, should be allocated according to 'need' rather than effective demand. The concept of need is seldom defined (or at best rather imprecisely so[43]), but seems to be closely concerned with the notion of merit goods – that is, needs 'considered so meritorious that their satisfaction is provided for through the public budget over and above what is provided for through the market and paid for by private buyers'.[44] The idea is that just as everyone in a civilized society is entitled to expect a certain standard of education, medical cover, security and

[40] Price Commission, *The Road Haulage Industry*, House of Commons Paper HC 698, London: HMSO, 1978.

[41] K.J. Button, 'High-technology companies: an examination of their transport needs', *Progress in Planning*, **29**, 81–146, 1988.

[42] L.M. Schneider, 'New era in transportation strategy', *Harvard Business Review*, **63** (March–April), 118–26, 1985.

[43] A. Williams, '"Need" as a demand concept (with special reference to health)', in A.J. Culyer (Ed), *Economic Policies and Social Goals*, London: Martin Robertson, 1974.

[44] R.A. Musgrave, *The Theory of Public Finance*, New York: McGraw-Hill, 1959.

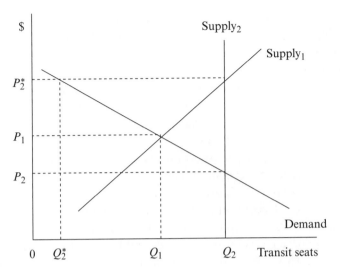

Figure 4.4   *Allocation by 'need'*

so on, so they are entitled to enjoy a certain minimum standard of transport provision. Looked at another way, the government or other donor provides such a good on the basis of 'merit', because it can better provide for individual welfare than allowing consumer sovereignty.

One can point to a number of transport policy initiatives over time which are based upon this idea. The 1930 Road Traffic Act in the United Kingdom, for example, introduced, besides other things, road service licenses into the bus industry which embraced the notion of public need. The traffic commissioners interpreted this to mean the provision of a comprehensive network of services for an area irrespective of the effective demand for specific routes. Licenses were granted on this basis and operators cross-subsidized the unremunerative services with revenue from the more profitable ones. More explicit were the social service grants given to the railways under the 1968 Transport Act whereby 222 services were subsidized for social reasons, once again despite deficit effective demand for their services. Additionally, the UK government has provided capital and operating cost subsidies to assist the shipping and air services to the remoter islands of Scotland.

In a different context, the 1978 Airline Deregulation Act in the United States has provided subsidies for services to small communities (the Essential Air Service Program) and the 1987 National Transportation Act in Canada provided explicitly for subsidies to 'essential' air services in the northern part of the country.

What allocation by some notion of need implies is that the market is not used to determine the output or price of a transport service. Figure 4.4 takes the simple case of a transit service that, under market conditions, would produce a fare of P_1 and offer Q_1 seats. If public policy requires that a higher level of services is warranted, say Q_2 seats, then this distorts the market. For a commercially driven market to offer Q_2 seats, a fare of P_2^* would be required, but only Q_2^* seats would be filled at this price. For the Q_2 transit seats to be efficiently used, a fare

P_2 is needed. The result is the necessity to subsidize the difference between this fare and the commercially necessary fare P_2^* for Q_2 seats. We shall deal with some of the issues involved in transport subsidies, and alternative methods of finance, later in the book.

This notion of need rather than effective demand raises two important issues. First, exactly what is the nature of 'need' in reality, and second, if one accepts that the concept has some operational meaning, how can it be incorporated into economic analysis? We look at these two questions in turn.

The need for adequate transport provision stems from the idea that people should have access to an acceptable range of facilities.[45] It is, therefore, essentially a 'normative' concept. Transport is seen as exerting a major influence on the quality of the lives of people and a certain minimum quality should be ensured. The United Kingdom has traditionally emphasized this view of mobility, for example: 'The social needs for transport also rank high – the needs of people to have access to their work, shops, recreation and the range of activities on which civilized society depends'.[46] Defining the exact level of mobility in this context is difficult, but it is helpful to look at the groups who, for one reason or another, seem in need of transport services in addition to those that would be forthcoming in the market.

The most obvious group is the poor, who cannot afford transport. Transport expenditure forms a substantial part of a household budget and, consequently, those on the lowest income must make fewer trips, shorter trips or trips on inferior modes of transport. A major problem is that, as we shall see later, as income levels rise, in general, there is a tendency towards higher car ownership, leaving only depleted and expensive public transport facilities for those at the lower end of the income distribution. A household with a car in the United Kingdom tends, for instance, to make on average about 300 fewer bus journeys a year than comparable households without a car. But there are also wider issues, in that this change in the transport sector has implications for population distribution. In particular, higher car ownership in rural areas, and the resultant reduction in the demand for local public transport, has put pressure on rural bus and rail services. Between 1970 and 1974, for example, in England the National Bus Company, which was responsible for most rural services in England and Wales, reduced its bus-kilometers by 7 percent. This, in turn, has been seen as one of the causes of rural depopulation. Similar trends were seen in Chapter 2 with respect to the United States. There is a long tradition of rural public and special transit services operating and capital assistance from federal and state government. The US Federal Transit Administration has over 5,300 rural and intercity transit programs, and there is special federal and state transport support for special mobility services. In addition, social services funding is available. The question then arises as to whether society, in general, needs a balance between urban and rural society.

[45] P.A. Stanley and J.R. Farrington, 'The need for rural public transport; a constraints-based case study', *Tijdschrift voor Economische en Societe Geografie*, **72**, 62–80, 1981.
[46] UK Department of Transport, *Transport Policy*, Cmnd 6836, London: HMSO, 1977.

While inadequate income poses one problem, there are other groups in society that are often felt to be in need of assistance. The old, infirmed and children are obvious examples where, irrespective of income, effective demand may be felt to be an inadequate basis upon which to allocate transport resources. The available evidence suggests that only about 10 percent of households in the aged or disabled category have private transport at hand in the UK. Even when a household does own a car (or has one made available through employment agreements) there are still members of it who may be deemed to be in need of additional transport.

Women enjoy less mobility than men, although the gap is closing, at least in wealthier countries. A study of mobility by Hillman et al.,[47] for instance, found that 70 percent of young married women in the outer metropolitan area of London had no car available for their everyday use – even 30 percent of those qualified to drive were in this position. Even in the mid-1990s, women in the United Kingdom aged between 26 and 59 years, the prime years of domestic caring responsibilities, only traveled about half the miles traveled by men, making fewer and shorter trips. While there are national differences, the British pattern is far from atypical.[48]

There are political-economy arguments, therefore, that these various groups are in need of adequate and inexpensive public transport services (or special transport provision in the case of the disabled) and that the normal market mechanism is inadequate in this respect.

If one accepts the notion that need is, in certain contexts, the relevant concept rather than effective demand, then, for practical purposes, this idea requires integration into more standard positive economic theory. (It should perhaps be noted that many people do not accept the idea of 'need' as an allocative device but advocate tackling problems of low income or disadvantage at their source through measures such as direct income transfers, but this is an issue outside our present discussion.) Perhaps the simplest method of reconciling the difficulties is to treat the monies paid out by government and other agencies in subsidies to social transport services, as the effective demand of society for the services. One can then perceive the situation as analogous to that of conventional consumer theory. Just as effective demand reflects the desire of an individual to purchase a particular service, so government's response to need reflects society's desire to purchase particular transport services for certain of its members.

4.4 The Valuation of Travel Time Savings

The importance of travel time in transport economics should by now be apparent. While the action of travel involves some time costs, it is perhaps more useful

---

[47] M. Hillman, I. Henderson and A. Whatley, *Personal Mobility and Transport Policy*, London: PEP Broadsheet 542, 1973.

[48] A. Root, L. Schintler and K.J. Button, 'Women, travel and the idea of "sustainable transport"', *Transport Reviews*, **20**, 369–83, 2000.

in this chapter to consider travel time that focuses on demand and benefits rather than costs. This is because travel or transport time savings are normally considered to be a major component of any scheme designed to improve transport efficiency. As we shall see in Chapter 11, travel time savings form the major component of inter-urban road investment benefits – a situation also found in most fields of transport. For reasons of comparability with other forms of benefit, a vast amount of intellectual energy has gone into devising methods of placing money values on such benefits.[49]

Two quite distinct methodologies have been developed for time evaluation, the distinction being made between time saved in the course of employment and time saved during non-work travel (including commuter trips when fixed working hours are involved). The distinction is drawn because work time involves lorry drivers, seamen, pilots and so on, not simply in giving up leisure but also in incurring some actual disutility from the work undertaken. Hence, if they could do the same amount of work in less time, these people would be able to enjoy more leisure and also suffer less disutility (or the employer must pay them more to encourage a continuation of the same work hours with a higher output). Savings in non-work time do not, by definition, reduce the disutility associated with work and, consequently, although more leisure may be enjoyed, they are likely to be valued below work travel time savings.

The valuation of work travel time (which embraces all journeys made when travelers are earning their living) is made simpler if we accept the traditional economic idea that workers are paid according to the value of their marginal revenue product. On this basis, the amount employers pay workers must be sufficient to compensate them for the marginal time and disutility associated with doing the job. Thus it becomes possible to equate the value of a marginal saving in work travel time with the marginal wage rate (plus related social payments and overheads). An alternative way of arriving at this cost savings approach is by reflecting upon the opportunity costs involved – as Benjamin Franklin, US statesman, once said, 'Remember that time is money'. Time savings at work permit a greater output to be produced within a given time period which, again drawing on the marginal productivity theory of wage determination, will be reflected in the marginal wages paid. Official policy in many countries is to value work travel time savings as the national average wage for the class of transport user concerned plus the associated costs of social insurance paid by the employer and a premium added to reflect overheads.

A major problem with the wage equivalence approach is that it assumes that employees consider the disutility of travel during work to be the same as the disutility of other aspects of their work that they may be required to undertake if travel time is reduced. In many instances, workers may consider the travel much less arduous than these alternative tasks. This implies that savings in

[49] H.F. Gunn, 'An introduction to the valuation of travel time-savings and losses', in D.A. Hensher and K.J. Button (eds.), *Handbook of Transport Modelling*, 2nd edn, Amsterdam: Elsevier, 2008.

work-time travel should, in such cases, be valued at less than the wage rate plus additions. Also some people may view travel time as highly productive – many rail and air travelers, for instance, certainly work on their journeys – suggesting that reduced travel time would not significantly alter output. Even time spent in car travel can be used to complete mental tasks – for example, Fowkes et al.[50] found that about 3 percent of business travel time by car was spent working. More recently, analysis of San Francisco Bay area travelers found that overall, commute time is not unequivocally a source of disutility to be minimized, but rather offers some benefits (such as a transition between home and work). Most people were found to have a non-zero optimum commute time, which can be violated in either direction – that is, it is possible (although comparatively rare, occurring for only 7 percent of the sample) to commute too little.[51] Examining the wage rate alone ceases to be a useful measure of work travel time savings in such cases.

While labor economics provides a useful foothold to obtain values of work travel time, rather more empiricism is required in the evaluation of non-work travel time. The behavioral approach involves using revealed preferences to consider trade-off situations that reflect the willingness of travelers to pay in order to save time. In other words, if a person chooses to pay X to save Y minutes then he/she is revealing an implicit value of time equal to at least (X/Y) per minute. More formally,

$$\Delta A = -\alpha \Delta T - \beta_1 \Delta C + \beta_2 \Delta E \qquad (4.3)$$

where the relative attractiveness of the alternatives, ΔA is the difference between the travel time cost, ΔC, and travel time, ΔT. ΔE is differences in everything else. The coefficients α and β_1 are both negative because a decrease in either the time or cost of a trip is seen to generate positive utility.

Empirical studies attempting to value non-work travel time in this way have looked at a number of different trade-off situations,[52] notably when travelers have a choice among:

- route;
- mode of travel;
- speed of travel (by a given mode over a given route);
- location of home and work; and
- destination of travel.

[50] A. Fowkes, P. Marks and C. Nash, 'The value of business travel time savings', Working Paper 214, Institute for Transport Studies, University of Leeds, 1986.

[51] L.S. Redmond and P.L. Mokhtarian, 'The positive utility of the commute: modeling ideal commute time and relative desired commute amount', *Transportation*, **28**, 179–205, 2001.

[52] For a survey see W.G. Waters, 'Value of travel time saving used in road project evaluation: a cross-country/jurisdiction comparison', Australian Transport Research Forum, 1992.

The standard approach in these trade-off studies is to employ a simple equation of the general form:

$$P_1 = \frac{e^y}{(1 + e^y)} \text{ where } y = \alpha_0 + \alpha_1(t_1 t_2) + \alpha_2(c_1 t_2) \tag{4.4}$$

Where:

P_1 is the probability of choosing mode (route and so on) 1;

y is choice of mode (route and so on); takes value of 1 for mode (route and so on) 1 and 0 for mode (route and so on) 2;

e is an exponential constant;

t_i is the door-to-door travel time by the j'' mode (route and so on); $i = 1,2$;

c_i is the door-to-door travel cost by the jth mode (route and so on); $i = 1, 2$; and

α_0, α_1 and α_2 are constants to be estimated.

A value of time is then inferred by looking at changes in the dependent variable that result from a unit change in either the time or the cost difference. Strictly it may be found as the ratio α_1/α_2 in equation (4.4).

Many of the early studies of non-work travel time concentrated on urban commuter trips because there was pressure at the time to provide information for cost–benefit analysis of urban transport investment plans. In consequence, mode and route choice evaluation techniques were developed to a high level of mathematical sophistication. Early work by Michael Beesley[53] specifically employed discriminant analysis to examine the journey to work mode choices of employees at the UK Ministry of Transport during 1965/66. This technique essentially finds the trade-off value of time that minimizes the number of misallocations of commuters to alternative modes with different time and cost characteristics.[54]

The upper part of Figure 4.5 considers the possible options available to a traveler when choosing between two modes. If the figure relates to mode A, and only time savings and costs are important, then Option 3 dominates. Conversely, mode B will dominate Option 2 where mode A is slower and more expensive. But in some cases travelers may not have such a clear-cut choice and will have to elect between Options 1 and 4 where there are trade-offs between time and money costs.

The lower portion of the figure gives some actual decisions by individuals regarding the choices that are made between the two modes (solid and empty circles). The line AB (where $\Delta C = \theta \Delta T$) provides the partitioning that leads to the minimum number of 'misclassifications' and reflects the trade-off between changes in travel time and travel costs being made. The slope of this line, θ, identifies the value of travel time savings.

[53] M.E. Beesley, 'The value of time spent in travelling: some new evidence', *Economica*, **32**, 174–85, 1965.

[54] D.A. Hensher, 'Measurement of the valuation of travel time savings', *Journal of Transport Economics and Policy*, **35**, 71–98, 2001.

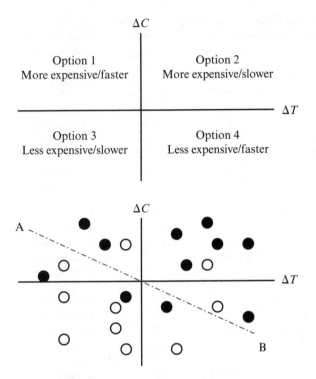

Figure 4.5   *The 'Beesley graph' travel time–cost trade-off*

The discriminate function used to determine the minimum number of mis-specifications takes the form:

$$Z_{ij} = \sum_{k=1}^{n} \alpha_k [f(X_{ki}, X_{kj})] + \sum_{1}^{m} \beta_1 U_1 \qquad (4.5)$$

where:

X_{ki}, X_{kj} are the values of the kth attributes of the ith and the jth trip packages;
U_1 are user attributes;
α_k are parameters associated with the alternative systems;
β_1 are parameters associated with user characteristics; and
$f(X_{ki}, X_{kj})$ is a function that may take either of the forms $(X_{ki} - X_{kj})$ or (X_{ki}/X_{kj}).

Beesley found that commuter trip time savings were valued at between 30 and 50 percent of the gross personal income of the commuters. One of the main problems with this pioneering study is that it failed to isolate on-vehicle travel time from the other components of journey time (for example, waiting and walking times). The defect was subsequently remedied in a larger study of mode choice in Leeds undertaken by David Quarmby[55] which embraced seven variables

[55] D.A. Quarmby, 'Choice of travel mode for the journey to work: some findings', *Journal of Transport Economics and Policy*, **1**, 273–314, 1967.

Table 4.7   *Computation of estimated values of travel time savings*

Study	Country	Value of time as % of wage rate	Trip purpose	Mode
Beesley (1965)	UK	33–50	Commuting	Auto
Quarmby (1967)	UK	20–25	Commuting	Auto, transit
Stopher (1968)	UK	21–32	Commuting	Auto, transit
Oort (1969)	USA	33	Commuting	Auto
Thomas & Thompson (1970)	USA	86	Interurban	Auto
Lee & Dalvi (1971)	UK	30	Commuting	Bus
		40	Commuting	Auto
Wabe (1971)	UK	43	Commuting	Auto, subway
Talvitte (1972)	USA	12–14	Commuting	Auto, transit
Hensher & Hotchkiss (1974)	Australia	2.70	Commuting	Hydrofoil, ferry
Kraft & Kraft (1974)	USA	38	Interurban	Bus
McDonald (1975)	USA	45–78	Commuting	Auto, transit
Ghosh et al. (1975)	UK	73	Interurban	Auto
Guttman (1975)	USA	63	Leisure	Auto
		145	Commuting	Auto
Hensher (1977)	Australia	39	Commuting	Auto
		35	Leisure	Auto
Nelson (1977)	USA	33	Commuting	Auto
Hauer & Greenough (1982)	Canada	67–101	Commuting	Subway
Edmonds (1983)	Japan	42–49	Commuting	Auto, bus, rail
Deacon & Sonstelie (1985)	USA	52–254	Leisure	Auto
Hensher & Truong (1985)	Australia	105	Commuting	Auto, transit
Guttman & Menashe (1986)	Israel	59	Commuting	Auto, bus
Fowkes (1986)	UK	27–59	Commuting	Rail, bus
Hau (1986)	USA	46	Commuting	Auto, bus
Chui & McFarland (1987)	USA	82	Interurban	Auto
Mohring et al. (1987)	Singapore	60–129	Commuting	Bus
Cole Sherman (1990)	Canada	93–170	Commuting	Auto
		116–165	Leisure	Auto

Source: W.G. Waters, 'Values of travel time savings used in road project evaluation: a cross-country/ jurisdiction comparison', Australian Transport Research Forum, 1992. This paper contains the full references to the studies cited.

including walking and waiting times as well as on-vehicle time. The findings indicate that savings in walking and waiting times are valued at between two and three times savings in on-vehicle time – parameters that have proved to be remarkably robust over the years.

Table 4.7 provides details of the non-work time values that have been revealed in these and subsequent studies. Many of these moved on from the discriminate approach to adopt logit and probit specification (which we discuss below in the context of car ownership modeling and, more generally, in Chapter 12) which offer more flexibility and more sophisticated models. Model specifications can influence the travel time values obtained and care is needed in their selection.[56] There is also a tendency to lump all non-work travel time together because it is not directly related to theories of labor productivity, but this may produce aggregation bias. Mark Wardman,[57] for example, in reviewing value of travel time savings in Britain found that the valuation of commuting time savings is about 35 percent higher than for leisure travel in London and South-East England, although only about 14 percent higher in studies pertaining to other parts of the country.

Stated preference, or experimental, techniques, whereby hypothetical questions are posed to travelers to gain information about trade-offs they would be willing to make have become more common in recent years. A pioneering example was that of Lee and Dalvi[58] who used questionnaires, rather than looking at actual choices, to discover the level of fare increase required before passengers switched from one mode of public transport to an alternative. Interestingly, in Manchester it was found that on-vehicle time, walking time and waiting time were not important separately, and travelers did not distinguish among them. Overall it was estimated that non-work travel time was being valued at 15 to 45 percent of hourly income. More recently David Hensher[59] has described additional analysis completed in New Zealand and Australia.

While most urban studies have tended to focus on mode choice decisions, the evaluation of non-work inter-urban travel time has tended to concentrate rather more on route and speed choice situations – although imperfections in travelers' knowledge of the latter make speed choice trade-offs suspect. Pioneering work on route choice by Claffey et al.[60] looked at choices made between tolled and free roads in the United States and attempted to allow for differing accident rates and levels of driver discomfort when assessing the time/money cost trade-offs. Mathematical weakness limits the value of this specific model but subsequent reworking suggests that time differences are unimportant in route choices of this type.

Thomas,[61] again using American data, conducted a study on a similar basis

[56] D.A. Hensher, 'The valuation of commuter travel time savings for car drivers in New Zealand: evaluating alternative model specifications', *Transportation*, **28**, 101–18, 2001.

[57] M. Wardman, 'A review of British evidence on time and service quality valuations', *Transportation Research A*, **34**, 171–205, 2001.

[58] N. Lee and M.Q. Dalvi, 'Variations in the value of travel time', *Manchester School*, **37**, 213–36, 1969.

[59] D.A. Hensher, 'Accounting for stated choice design dimensionality in willingness to pay for travel time savings', *Journal of Transport Economics and Policy*, **38**, 425–46, 2004.

[60] P.T. Claffey, C. St Clair and N. Weldes, 'Characteristics of passenger car travel on toll roads and comparable free roads, *Highway Research Bulletin*, no. 306, 1961.

[61] T.C. Thomas, *The Value of Time for Passenger Cars: An Experimental Study of Commuters' Values*, Washington, DC: US Bureau of Public Roads, 1967.

and here time differences did appear to be significant; he estimates that non-work travel time appeared to be valued at between 40 and 83 percent of average income. Dawson and Everall,[62] using a further modification and looking at route choices of motorists traveling between Rome and Caserta and between Milan and Modena, where autostrada offered alternatives to ordinary trunk roads, found that observed trade-offs indicate that commuting and other non-work travel time was valued at about 75 percent of the average wage rate.

It is clear from the selection of studies cited above that non-work time savings are, indeed, valued below the wage rate, but it is equally clear that the actual values obtained from the behavioral studies are extremely sensitive to the assumptions made and the estimation technique employed. Hensher[63] goes further and, in particular, points to the rather strong assumptions that are implicit in the not uncommon practice of taking time values obtained from, say, a mode choice study and employing them in route or speed choice situations. He also questions whether enough consideration is given to the composition of time savings beyond the in-vehicle/waiting time split and, in particular, to preferences between constant journey speed (with a lower average) and faster, variable speeds (with a higher average). There is also the common practical problem that it is difficult to separate the influence of comfort and convenience factors from travel time savings.

In Britain, the UK Department of Transport and its successors have since the 1960s recommended standard values of time for transport analysis purposes. The use of standard figures is to encourage uniformity in investment appraisal. While the work travel time figures are open to only minor criticisms (and even quite major errors here would seem unlikely to distort decisions), the use of standard non-work travel time values has met with more serious criticism.

Empirically, non-work travel time values have generally been shown correlated with income levels (Heggie's work being one of the few exceptions[64]), but on occasions an average value across all income levels has been used for policy formulation purposes. The argument supporting this 'equity' value is that if time values were directly varied with income, this would tend to bias project selection towards projects favoring the higher-income groups. In evaluation, the travel time savings of such groups would automatically be weighted more heavily than those of the less well-off. The Leitch Committee[65] in the UK, however, rejected this line of argument because it is not consistent with the way other aspects of transport investment are evaluated. Since the overall distributional effects of transport investment may be treated more directly in the appraisal process (see Chapter 11), the notion of 'equity' values was rejected in favor of income-based time evaluations.

[62] R.F.F. Dawson and P.P. Everall, *The Value of Motorists' Time: A Study in Italy*, Crowthorne: Transport and Road Research Laboratory Report, LR 426, 1972.

[63] D.A. Hensher, 'Formulating an urban passenger transport policy: a re-appraisal of some elements', *Australian Economic Papers*, **18**, 119–30, 1979.

[64] I. Heggie, 'A diagnostic survey of urban journey to work behaviour', in I. Heggie, (ed.), *Modal Choice and the Value of Travel Time*, Oxford: Clarendon Press, 1976.

[65] UK Department of Transport, *Report of the Advisory Committee on Trunk Road Assessment*, London: HMSO, 1978.

Even if generally acceptable values of travel time could be obtained, there are still difficulties associated with using them. One of the major problems is that some projects can result in a small number of large time savings while others produce a magnitude of extremely small savings. The problem becomes one of deciding if 60 one-minute savings are as valuable as (or more valuable than) one saving of an hour's duration. It could be argued that travelers, especially over longer routes, tend not to perceive small time savings or cannot utilize such times.[66] If this is so it would tend to make urban transport schemes appear less attractive *vis-à-vis* inter-urban ones because the main benefits of urban improvements have been small time savings spread over thousands of commuters.

One suggestion is that a zero value should be adopted in these contexts, small travel time savings with a positive value only being employed once a hold level of saving has been reached (say 10 minutes). This ignores the fact that small time savings may, in some circumstances, be combined with existing periods of free, or idle time to permit substantial increases in output or in leisure enjoyment. Further, if there are non-linearities in the value of travel time this would imply that widely used trade-off methods of time evaluation based upon average time savings must be giving biased estimates of the value of travel time. The debate over the handling of small travel time savings is unlikely to be resolved easily.

Finally there is the question of whether revealed or stated preference measures of the value of travel time savings are more 'accurate'. There is some indication from Table 4.8, which provides details of the travel time savings values used in the United Kingdom that, in fact, they are relatively consistent – a finding consistent with Wardman's review. The table relates to the values used in COBA, the program used to assess road investments. The method of determining the values changed between 1988 and 1994 from a revealed to a stated preference approach. While there are some clear differences, the broad pattern is very similar considering the very different methods of estimation used.

Transport studies in less developed countries tend to adopt the convention that while work travel time savings should be given a monetary value based upon the cost-savings approach (although the wage rate is generally modified to allow for imperfections in the local labor market), savings in non-work travel time – especially in rural areas – are given a zero value.[67] The justification for this is that the prime objective of improving transport infrastructure in the Third World is to assist in economic growth and thus the emphasis should be exclusively concentrated on economically productive schemes – leisure time is not seen as 'productive'. Thomas[68] has pointed to a serious anomaly, however, when this argument is carried into practice. While non-work travel time savings in rural areas are ignored, savings in vehicle operating costs for such travel is not. Not only is this

---

[66] D. Tipping, 'Time savings in transport studies', *Economic Journal*, **78**, 843–54, 1968.

[67] I.D.G.P Howe, 'Valuing time savings in developing countries', *Journal of Transport Economics and Policy*, **10**, 113–25, 1976.

[68] S. Thomas, 'Non-working time-savings in developing countries', *Journal of Transport Economics and Policy*, **13**, 335–7, 1979.

Table 4.8   *Overall values of time used in United Kingdom road investment analysis*

	1994 Study	COBA (1988)	COBA (1988) full income growth	COBA (1988) income elasticities	COBA (1988) income growth Adj.10
Driver Commuting	5.4				
Other	4.4				
Non-work total	4.9	5.6	6.2	5.9	
Employee (Business)	6.7				
Employer (Business)	14.7				
Working total	21.4	19.1	20.9	20.6	
Passenger					
Commuting	6.0				
Other	3.1				
Non-work total	4.03	5.6	6.2	5.9	
Employee (Business)	6.7				
Employer (Business)	14.7				
Working total	21.4	15.9	17.4	17.1	
Light goods vehicles					
Hire & reward	45.0				
Own account	35.0				
Total	40.06				
COBA 9		19.35			20.3
Heavy goods vehicles					
Hire & reward	45.0				
Own account	35.0				
Total	40.06				
COBA 9		14.05			14.7
Public service vehicles					
Scheduled coach	50.0–60.0				
Motorway charter	23.0–33.0				
Scheduled bus	17.0				
Trunk road charter	0.0–25.0				
Total Public good vehicles		84.17			88.4

Notes: All results are in 1994 £0.01/minute.

Source: H.J. Gunn, 'An introduction to the valuation of travel time-savings and losses', in D.A. Hensher and K.J. Button (eds), *Handbook of Transport Modelling*, 2nd edn, Amsterdam: Elsevier, 2008.

inconsistent but it also has important distributional implications because the main beneficiaries of low operating costs are almost invariably high-income car owners.

4.5   The Demand for Car Ownership

While the demand for cars is not strictly a direct transport matter, it is in some ways more to do with industrial economics and the demand for consumer durables, the importance of the automobile in affective travel behavior, land-use patterns and the environment makes it a matter of considerable interest to transport economists.[69]

Car ownership, as we saw in Chapter 2, has risen considerably since the First World War with only brief halts during periods of major military conflict and occasional decelerations in the trend during periods of macroeconomic depression. This upward trend is not unique to the United States or the United Kingdom but is also to be found in all other countries irrespective of their state of economic development, or the nature of their political institutions. The upward trend in car ownership is the result of both the considerable benefits that accompany car availability (notably improved access and greater flexibility of travel) and the long-term increases in income enjoyed by virtually all countries since the Second World War. The 'demonstration effect' has tended to accelerate the process in less developed countries as attempts are made to emulate the consumption patterns of more affluent nations.

Considerable effort has been focused on exploring both the rate of increase in vehicle ownership and reasons why this should differ between countries and between areas within a single country. Information on the underlying demand functions is sought for a variety of reasons. Car manufacturers need to know the nature of changing demands for new vehicles, both within the country and within their export markets, and to be able to forecast likely changes in the type of vehicles which are wanted. While work in this area often sheds some useful light on the workings of the car market, it is only of limited use to transport economists.[70] By contrast, central government is generally more interested in the aggregate number of vehicles in the country, mainly for road planning purposes, but also, to a lesser extent, to assist the finance authority in its fiscal duties. Regional variations, which can be quite pronounced within countries (Table 4.9), are also of interest for strategic planning purposes, particularly for developing national and international road networks.

The theory underlying much of the early forecasting work looking at car-ownership levels is closely akin to the management theory of a 'product life' cycle, where a product has a predetermined sales pattern almost independent of traditional economic forces, although taste and costs are not altogether absent from the model. The logistic curve-fitting model developed by the UK's Transport Research Laboratory (TRL; then the Road Research Laboratory and subsequently the Transport and Road Research Laboratory over the period), in its basic form, treats per capita vehicle ownership as a function of time (Figure 4.6) with the ownership level following a symmetric, sigmoid growth path through time until an eventual saturation level is approached.[71] Broadly, it is argued that

[69] J.D. Dargay and G. Giuliano, 'Car ownership, travel and land use: a comparison of the US and Great Britain', *Transportation Research A*, **40**, 106–24, 2006.

[70] K.J. Button, A.D. Pearman and A. Fowkes, *Car Ownership Modelling and Forecasting*, Aldershot: Gower, 1982.

[71] J.C. Tanner, 'Long-term forecasting of vehicle ownership and road traffic', *Journal of the Royal Statistical Society*, **141A**, 14–63, 1978.

Table 4.9   *Regional variations in Great Britain's car-ownership patterns*

Region	Automobiles per 1000 population	Average vehicle age
North East	403	6.0
North West	469	6.1
Yorkshire and the Humber	432	6.2
East Midlands	487	6.7
West Midlands	510	6.4
East of England	513	7.1
London	345	7.4
South East	542	6.9
South West	522	7.5
Total England	471	6.8
Wales	483	6.9
Scotland	433	5.8
Great Britain	480	6.7

Source: UK Department for Transport, *Transport Statistics Great Britain 2007*, London: DfT, 2007.

long-term growth in ownership follows a predictable diffusion process. Initially, high production costs and unfamiliarity will keep sales low, but after a period, if the product is successful, economies of scale on the supply side coupled with bandwagon effects on the demand side would result in the take-off of a comparatively rapid diffusion process. Finally, there is a tailing-off as the market becomes saturated and everyone wishing to own a car does so.

The initial form of model was a logistic curve that simply traced out per capita car ownership over time using national car-ownership data (Figure 4.6). The logistic equation took the form:

$$C = \frac{\alpha}{1 + \beta \exp(-\alpha c t)} \tag{4.6}$$

where C is per capita car ownership, t is a time trend and α, β, c are parameters to be estimated.

For calculation purposes it was necessary to feed an exogenous value of 'saturation level' (the parameter α) into the equation. This was done either by judgment based upon such things as the proportion of the population who would be able to drive if there were no constraints on car ownership (for example, taking out the young and the infirm from the population) or by calculation of 'mean reversion' parameters. The latter involved taking two periods of regional cross-sectional data on car ownership levels and regressing the levels of ownership in the base year against the changes in those levels. The constant term in the resultant equation (that is, when $\Delta C = 0$) is, *de facto*, the saturation level. Once the overall equation is fitted using up data to point t in Figure 4.7 then it is possible to extrapolate to produce forecasts.

The TRL extrapolative approach provided relatively good forecasts in the

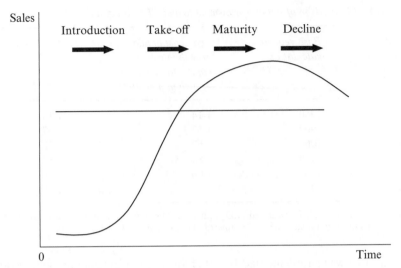

Figure 4.6   *The life cycle of a product*

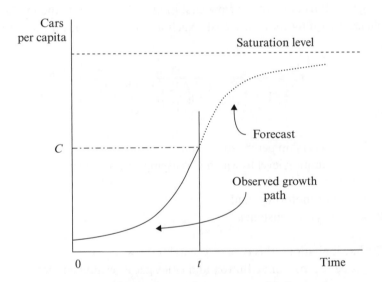

Figure 4.7   *The logistic growth curve approach to car-ownership forecasting*

United Kingdom in the 1960s (Table 4.10), but tended to be less reliable in later years and to suffer from a tendency towards overprediction.[72] Some of the difficulties were associated with problems of estimating key parameters such as the ultimate saturation level, or with the correct configuration of the growth curve – in later work a power function, which does not imply a symmetric sigmoid growth path, replaced the logistic (equation (4.7)).[73] In addition, the

[72] K.J. Button and A.S. Fowkes, 'An evaluation of car ownership forecasting techniques', *International Journal of Transport Economics*, **4**, 115–43, 1977.

[73] J.C. Tanner, *Car Ownership Trends and Forecasts*, Crowthorne: Transport and Road Research Laboratory Report, LR 799, 1977.

Table 4.10   *Comparison of actual car ownership and TRL forecasts*

Year of publication	Base year for calculation	(Forecast annual growth in cars per capita)/actual annual growth in pool 1975	Forecast car pool 1975
1962	1960	1.14	1.13
1965	1964	1.57	1.57
1967	1966	1.67	1.68
1969	1968	1.84	1.84
1970	1969	1.66	1.66
1972	1971	1.62	1.58

Source: K. Button, A.S. Fowkes and A.D. Pearman, 'Disaggregate and aggregate car ownership forecasting methods in Great Britain', *Transportation Research A*, **14**, 263–73, 1980.

time variable was supplemented by other variables to reflect changing costs of motoring and income. The resultant extrapolative model is still widely used to gain general insights into car ownership and also to gauge the implications of policies regarding motoring costs, such as fuel taxation, on the future car pool:

$$C_t = \frac{S}{1 + \left(\dfrac{S - C_0}{C_0}\right)\left(\dfrac{Y_t}{Y_0}\right)^{-k_1 S}\left(\dfrac{P_t}{P_0}\right)^{-k_2 S} e^{-k_0 S_t}} \tag{4.7}$$

where:

C_0 is car ownership per person at time $t = $ zero;
S is the saturation level to which C is asymptotic as t increases;
Y_t is income per head;
P_t is 'cost of motoring'; and
k_1, k_2 and k_3 are constants.

Despite limitations, this type of general framework can be useful when there are serious data constraints. Button and colleagues[74] examined factors affecting car-ownership levels across a range of very low-income countries where there is little information on many of the economic variables that one would like to consider – in this case just data on income and time were used in a quasi-logistic equation.

At least one school of thought rejects the underlying extrapolative philosophy as inadequate. In particular, it is argued, car-ownership forecasting should be based only upon explicit economic variables such as income and vehicle prices rather than 'proxy' variables such as time. (The counter argument being that 'time' somehow encapsulates changing tastes.) The final TRL forecasting framework attempted to meet this criticism by incorporating economic variables,

[74] K.J. Button, N. Ngoe and J. Hine, 'Modelling vehicle ownership and use in low income countries', *Journal of Transport Economics and Policy*, **27**, 51–67, 1993.

but a time trend is still retained and also the income and vehicle operating cost elasticities are not estimated internally within the model but derived from 'external' sources.[75] The demand model developed by Bates and others,[76] as part of a larger Regional Highway Traffic Model (RHTM) in the United Kingdom, in contrast is based entirely upon 'causal' variables and all the relevant elasticities are estimated directly within the forecasting model. This type of framework is now widely used in economic forecasting, especially at the local level, but also for national studies.

The basis for the underlying model is in economic utility theory.[77] It is assumed that the utility, U, a household, n, gets from owning something, j, is represented by:

$$U_{j.n} = V_{j.n} + \varepsilon_{j.n} \tag{4.8}$$

where $V_{j.n}$ is a deterministic component and $\varepsilon_{j.n}$ is a random factor.

For estimation purposes, a multinomial logit model is generally used in the car-ownership context, although in some cases alternatives are adopted, especially for local analysis where the interest may be in forecasting the number of cars per household rather than the national car pool. The logit model takes the general form:

$$V_n = \beta_n^1 + \sum_{k=1}^{p} \beta_{nk} X_{nk} \tag{4.9}$$

where:

p is the number explanatory variables;
β_n^1 is the 'alternative-specific' constant associated with having n vehicles;
β_{nk} is the 'weight' for variable k in the utility of having n vehicles; and
X_{nk} is the value of variable k for vehicle-ownership level n.

To show what this means in practical terms, a simple form of the actual type of equation calculated is provided by Fairhurst in the context of car ownership, not in the United Kingdom as a whole, but in London:[78]

$$\log \frac{P_0}{1 - P_0} = c + b\log Y + d\log H + f\log(B + 1) + g\log(R + 1) \tag{4.10}$$

[75] G. Whelan, 'Modeling car ownership in Great Britain', *Transportation Research A*, **41**, 205–19, 2007.

[76] J.J. Bates, H.F. Gunn, M. Roberts, *A Disaggregate Model of Household Car Ownership*, Department of the Environment and Transport Research Report 20, London: HMSO, 1978.

[77] K. Train, *Quantitative Choice Analysis: Theory, Econometrics, and an Application to Automobile Demand*, Cambridge, MA: MIT Press, 1986.

[78] H.M. Fairhurst, 'The influence of public transport on car ownership in London', *Journal of Transport Economics and Policy*, **9**, 193–208, 1975.

where:

P_0 is the proportion of households without a car;
H is persons per household;
B is a bus public transport index; and
R is a rail public transport index.

The data used in these types of model are not the time-series registration statistics employed by the TRL, but rather a series of cross-sectional sets of statistics generally obtained from household surveys. For forecasting purposes it is necessary to be able to predict reliably the level and distribution of future income and other variables. The approach also concentrates on the probability of households having a certain level of vehicle ownership rather than, as with the time-trend model, on forecasting the national average or regional ownership level; this conforms more closely to other recent trends in transport demand forecasting (see Chapter 12). In the case of the United Kingdom, for example, where the geographical size of the country makes national forecasting meaningful, this type of economic model makes use of data from the Family Expenditure Survey and the National Travel Survey. It relates household car ownership to household income, number of adults in a household, number of children in a household, number of employed household members, number of retired people, and the geographical nature of the location of the house.[79]

This type of economic framework is now regularly used in aggregate analysis. Dargay,[80] for example, examines trends in the growth of car stocks over past decades and make projections of its development over the next 25 years for 82 countries at different levels of economic development, from the lowest (China, India and Pakistan) to the highest (the United States, Japan and European nations). The countries account for 85 per cent of the world's population and 93 percent of the vehicle stock. The projections are based on estimates of a dynamic time-series model and an S-shaped function to relate the vehicle stock to GDP. The estimates are used, in conjunction with assumptions concerning income and population growth, to produce projections of the growth in the vehicle stock on a year-by-year basis.

Differences in the geographical demand for car ownership interest transport planners both because they need to be able to forecast future demand for links in the local road network and because, where ownership is low, social commitments may require that alternative public transport is provided. These models often need to be a little more detailed in terms of the variables included. For example, it seems likely that spatial variations at the local level may, once allowance has been made for differing income and demographic factors, be explained in terms of the quality of local transport services – as in the case of Fairhurst's work on London.

---

[79] G.A. Whelan, J. Fox and A.J. Daly, *Updating Car Ownership Forecasts*, London: Department of the Environment, Transport, and the Regions, 2001.

[80] J.D. Dargay, 'Road vehicles: future growth in developed and developing countries', *Proceedings of the Institution of Civil Engineers*, **151**, 3–11, 2002.

Good, uncongested roads combined with poor public transport increases the demand, *ceteris paribus*, for private car ownership. Regional econometric studies of car ownership have attempted to reflect this cost of transport effect by incorporating variables such as residential density in their models (it being argued that a densely populated area is normally well served by public transport while motoring is adversely affected by the higher levels of traffic congestion). More sophisticated local models have shown the frequency of public transport services to influence car-ownership rates; at least slowing the rise in automobile ownership but not reversing it.[81] If these studies are correct then there is some evidence that the long-term growth in car ownership may be contained by improving public transport services, although from a policy point of view the overall cost of such actions needs to be fully assessed.

Further Reading

Readers interested in the influence of different variables on transport demand, especially demand elasticities, should see T.H. Oum, W.G. Waters and X. Fu, 'Transport demand elasticities', in D.A. Hensher and K.J. Button (eds), *Handbook of Transport Modelling*, 2nd edn, Amsterdam: Elsevier, 2008, and T. Littman, 'Transit price elasticities and cross-elasticities', *Journal of Public Transportation*, **7**, 37–58, 2004. Discussion of 'need' is usually rather imprecise but D. Banister, M. Bould and G. Warren, 'Towards needs-based transport planning', *Traffic Engineering and Control*, **25**, 372–5, 1984, although a little old, offers a useful and more detailed assessment of many of the analytical problems. The literature and empirical work on valuing travel time savings is extensive; N. Bruzelius, *The Value of Travel Time*, London: Croom Helm, 1979 offers a good starting point. The problems of evaluating travel time savings in low-income countries is examined in K.J. Button and A.D. Pearman, 'The value of time in road investment appraisal in less developed countries', *International Journal of Transport Economics*, **11**, 135–48, 1984. Regarding car ownership modeling, a solid review is to be found in G. De Jong, J. Fox, M. Pieters, A. Daly and R. Smit, 'Comparison of car ownership models', *Transport Reviews*, **24**, 379–408, 2004.

---

[81] K.J. Button, A.S. Fowkes and A.D. Pearman, 'Car ownership in West Yorkshire: the influence of public transport accessibility', *Urban Studies*, **17**, 211–15, 1980.

5 The Direct Costs of Transport

5.1 The Supply of Transport

Elementary economic theory tells us that, in most circumstances, supply of any-thing is a positive function of its price. Suppliers are more willing to put the effort and resources of providing more output as prices rise. The detailed nature of the relationship is heavily influenced by the costs involved. This chapter and the one that follows look at the various costs associated with supplying transport services and, in particular, at the relationships between the resources required to provide these services and the types and amounts of output finally 'consumed' by travelers and freight consignors. This chapter is specifically concerned with the production functions perceived by the providers of transport, which relate the various factor inputs to the final services offered, and with the financial costs of these factor inputs.

The chapter differs from the following one in that it deals with only direct costs as borne by the supplying agency. These are normally, but not always, financial costs that are incurred as the result of purchasing factor services in the market (that is, the wages of labor, the interest on capital, the price of fuel, and so on). There is one very important exception, however, namely the actual cost of the travelers' or consignors' own inputs. Transport is special (but not unique) in that the actual person being transported has to contribute his/her own time inputs and, when private motor transport is involved, his/her personal energies, skills and expertise.

The opportunity costs of this time and the utilization of acquired skills will, therefore, directly enter the production function for trip making. The external costs, which we shall consider in the following chapter, although representing genuine resource costs, do not directly influence the decisions of transport suppli-ers in their provision of transport services. In brief, therefore, this chapter is exclu-sively concerned with the perceived or reaction costs that influence the supply of transport services. It should be pointed out, however, that the separation of direct and external costs is something of an expositional device and that in practice this distinction is becoming increasingly blurred as official policies attempt to make transport agencies fully cognizant of the full resource implications of their actions.

All these factors influence the shape of the transport supply function which, in its simplest form, is seen in Figure 5.1. There is nothing special in the general sense about the supply curve of transport services. It is normally positively sloped, reflecting the incentive that higher prices have on suppliers to put more of their services on the market. The importance of the need for consumers, at

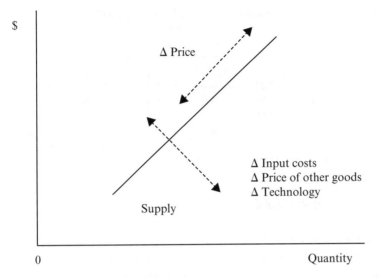

Figure 5.1 *The simple transport supply curve*

least in terms of passenger movements, to put their own time into the delivery of transport services, however, often means that one should treat price in a broader sense to embrace time costs. This gives us a notion of 'generalized costs', which we shall discuss in some detail later.

The supply curve is also responsive in terms of where it is actually positioned *vis-à-vis* factors such as levels of income, the price of alternatives to transport (which may be seen as teleworking or tele-shopping in the short term but can embrace relocating home or work in the longer run), and to the costs of the inputs required to provide the transport services (including the costs of the time of the travelers or of inventory holdings in the case of freight transport).

The financial costs of transport to immediate users have, as a broad generalization, been falling over the ages. The money cost of traveling from, say Washington to San Francisco, for example, has fallen considerably over the past century relative to incomes in the United States, and it is certainly a lot quicker. This has been due to technical progress, but also more recently to changes in the regulatory regimes that have controlled the supply of transport – a subject we shall return to in detail in Chapter 14. Not all transport users have enjoyed lower fares, and especially not so in the short run. As technology and demand patterns have changed so some modes or journeys have become more expensive, often because a superior service has replaced them. In other cases the subsidies given to the various modes have changed, again affecting the costs to the final user. Table 5.1 provides, in very broad terms, details of how passenger fares have changed in recent history in the United States. Of course, there are wide variations by route or region and in part this chapter offers some reasons for these micro and meso differences. Other modes exhibit different patterns.

Table 5.1 *Average passenger fares in the United States (2000 prices)*

	1960	1970	1980	1990	2000	2006
Domestic airlines	138.96	138.65	123.18	117.94	121.27	126.20
Intercity bus	17.71	20.46	22.63	23.31	29.46	–
All modes of transit	1.02	0.92	0.75	0.86	0.93	–
Commuter rail	4.60	5.04	3.97	3.81	3.32	–
Intercity rail	30.30	19.15	49.86	51.99	49.61	52.36

Source: US Bureau of Transportation Statistics.

5.2   Fixed and Variable Costs

Direct costs can be divided in a number of ways but two are particularly relevant to transport, namely distinctions according to variability over time and distinctions among the parties responsible for incurring the various elements of cost. The first of these distinctions is discussed in this section.

In the long run, or so the introductory texts tell us, all costs are variable, but the long run is itself an imprecise concept (even a tautology) and the ability to vary costs over time differs among modes of transport. The long run in the context of a seaport is, for instance, very different from that in road haulage or the bus industry. Port infrastructure is extremely long-lived, specific, indivisible and very expensive. It is, in reality, impossible to consider the standard question associated with long-run costs – namely, 'what is the cheapest way of providing a given capacity in the long run?' – when talking of time horizons 20, 30, or even 50 years hence. Trucking is different, capital costs are lower, physical durability less, and there is always the prospect of varying the use, within limits, of the vehicle fleet. Lorries are, unlike ports, mobile both among a range of potential employers and among a range of locations.

The nature of many costs, therefore, means that they may be considered fixed in the short term: there are temporal indivisibilities. The period under consideration will, as we have seen, differ among transport sectors, but it will also differ within a single transport undertaking. Railway operators owning track and rolling stock offer a useful illustration of this.

A railway service involves using a large number of factor services, many of these being highly specific and each with its own physical lifespan. When it comes to considering line closures, the essential questions revolve around deciding exactly which costs are fixed. Figure 5.2 offers a general illustration of the main cost items associated with a rail service together with an appropriate, although not exact, indication of the physical life of existing equipment. In the very short period, since all other items have already been purchased (that is, they are fixed), the only savings the railways can make are in very variable costs, notably those attributable to labor, fuel and maintenance. However, if the railways are earning sufficient income to cover these costs then there is no justification for closing the line. Wagons last 10 years, and applying the same logic, should be replaced if returns exceed the cost.

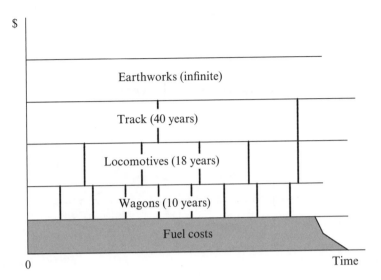

Figure 5.2   *Railway costs over time*

After a period of about 18 years, locomotives become due for replacement. Consequently locomotive costs become variable over a 18-year horizon and the managers must decide whether revenues justify replacement. Is 18 years, therefore, the long run? The answer is probably 'no' because other factors have still longer lives and track and signaling for 40 years. (Earthworks have an infinite life and once constructed do not enter into further decision-making processes.) Further decisions regarding closure must, therefore, be made after 40 years even if the line earns sufficient revenue to cover its locomotive replacement needs. Consequently, the long run for railways, in this text, is anything up to 40 years with, in the interim, a series of successive short-run cost calculations having to be made.

The reverse calculations are made regarding the expansion of services. If the wagons are covering their costs to an extent that they would also cover the costs of additional locomotives, then capacity expansion is commercially justified.

It should be quite apparent that the distinction between fixed and variable costs is a pragmatic device requiring a degree of judgment and common sense on the part of the decision maker. In the short term – whatever that may be – some costs are clearly fixed, resulting in a falling short-run average cost of use until capacity is reached. Just to show the generality of the principles we can switch to a different mode. Figure 5.3, for instance, may be seen to illustrate the average cost of increased use of a ship ($SRAC_1$) that falls steeply until capacity is fully utilized. A second ship may then, if demand is sufficient, be brought into operation exhibiting a short-run average cost curve of $SRAC_2$.

The fixed capacity constraint for each ship typifies that found in most modes of transport and tends to differ from the smooth, stereotypical, symmetrical 'U-shaped' $SRAC$ curves often assumed to be associated with manufacturing industry in economics texts. The long-run curve is, following elementary economics, formed from the envelope of the short-run average cost curves.

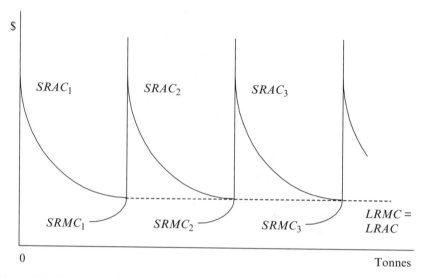

Figure 5.3   *The long- and short-run costs of shipping*

In many sectors of the economy the long-run average cost curve (*LRAC*) is not horizontal, as in our illustration, at least not to any high level of minimum cost, but is often found to be downward sloping as a result of economies of scale. These economies may potentially take a variety of forms in transport and may be thought to vary according to the type of transport involved and the mode of operation being undertaken.

The standard method of examining for scale effects is to look at the cost elasticity with regard to output. Evidence presented in a survey of studies of rail, road haulage and aviation sectors in the United States[1] suggests that scale effects exist in some modes with respect to output but not in others. All studies examined, irrespective of the modeling framework used, indicate scale effects in rail freight transport but the empirical evidence is contradictory for trucking although the more recent of the studies, employing state-of-the-art econometric techniques, suggest constant costs. Studies of US domestic aviation are almost unanimous that there are no scale effects, irrespective of how the cost function is specified. The more-specific studies tend to consider particular features of transport industries, fleet size, infrastructure and so on and these are looked at in turn.

Economies Associated with Larger Vehicle Size

One approach is to look at costs with respect to size of vehicle or vessel. The classic example of this is in shipping where capacity (in terms of volume) increases much faster than surface area but this is also a feature of most other modes of freight transport. Thermal processes (such as engine size) also generally

---

[1] C. Winston, 'Conceptual developments in the economics of transportation: an interpretive survey', *Journal of Economic Literature*, **23**, 57–94, 1985.

Table 5.2   *Economies of scale in bulk carriage by sea*

Ship size (thousand dwt)	15	25	41	61	120	200
Index of size	100	167	267	432	973	1318
Capital cost index	100	140	197	291	457	641
Operating cost index (excluding fuel)	100	121	134	155	201	275
Seagoing fuel consumption index	31	38	38	38	38	38

Source: R.O. Goss and C.D. Jones, *The Economics of Size in Dry Bulk Carriers*, Government Economic Services Occasional Paper 2, London, 1971.

Table 5.3   *Estimated savings by increasing the maximum weight of trucks in the United Kingdom from 32.5 tonnes*

Maximum weight	Savings (%)
35 tonnes, 4 axles	5–7
38 tonnes, 5 axles	5–9
40 tonnes, 5 axles	7–14
42 tonnes, 5 axles	9–13
44 tonnes, 6 axles	11–13

Source: UK Department of Transport, *Report of the Inquiry into Lorries, People and the Environment*, London: HMSO, 1980.

exhibit scale economies in all forms of transport and crew numbers do not increase proportionately with the size of mobile plant. Table 5.2 gives some indication of economies of scale in bulk carriers, but similar economies are also found in oil tankers. Such scale economies are not unique to shipping, but they are perhaps more pronounced in that mode. It should be said, however, that some econometric work indicates that there are limits to such economies and that they may become exhausted for larger-sized ships.[2]

Evidence produced in the early 1970s by Edwards and Bayliss[3] suggested that there may be limits to the cost advantages of using extremely large trucking vehicles. Diseconomies of scale appear to begin setting in after about 11 tonnes carrying capacity has been reached. Evidence from Britain's Armitage Inquiry into heavy trucks, however, indicated that there were economies of scale to be enjoyed by using commercial road vehicles in excess of the 32.5 tonnes gross maximum weight permitted in 1980 (see Table 5.3).

While for engineering reasons economies of scale clearly do exist in utilizing larger units of mobile plant at least up to some point, it should be noted that it is often impossible to take advantage of them even when demand for transport services is high. In many instances there may be physical limitations associated with

[2] W.K Talley, V.B. Agarwal and J.W. Breakfield, 'Economies of density of ocean tanker ships', *Journal of Transport Economics and Policy*, **20**, 91–9, 1986.

[3] S.L. Edwards and B.T. Bayliss, *Operating Costs in Road Freight Transport*, London: UK Department of the Environment, 1971.

Table 5.4   *Economies of large port operations*

	Vancouver	*Seattle*
Traffic	88,000	377,000
Number of berths	3	11
Wharfage ($)	23.63	33.75
Handling and through-port charge ($)	81.27	40.00
Vessel service and facility charge ($)	0	26.60
Tailgate loading ($)	22.28	0
Total of port charges per container ($)	127.18	95.35

Source: T.D. Heaver, *The Routing of Canadian Container Traffic Through Vancouver and Seattle*, Vancouver, WESTMAC, 1975.

complementary inputs and, in particular, the associated infrastructure cannot always handle the larger vehicles (sea and airports pose specific problems in this context) while in others the consignments of traffic are small and can be more efficiently handled in smaller vehicles.[4] Returning to our maritime example, large ships on liner routes often incur heavy costs as frequent landings and embarkation of individual consignments require rearrangements of the entire cargo. This is one reason why hub-and-spoke operations are gaining in importance – see Section 5.3.

Economies of Scale in Infrastructure Provision

Transport demand is not spread evenly over space but tends to be concentrated on links between particular trip-generating and trip-attracting points. For example, journey to work trips are concentrated along links between residential and industrial estates; summer holiday air transport demand in Europe is highest between the main cities in the 'cooler' countries such as the United Kingdom, Sweden and Germany and popular recreational resorts in the warmer areas of Spain, Greece, Italy and so on. Thus, there is a tendency in transport, as we saw in Chapter 4, for demand to be concentrated on certain portions of the network and, *ipso facto*, certain parts of the static infrastructure. Technically this concentration of traffic is possible because of substantial scale economies in infrastructure provision.

An examination of the costs associated with handling container traffic in an average port (Vancouver) and a large port (Seattle) in Table 5.4 (which assumes that the charges paid by container traffic reflect port costs) reveals the economies enjoyed from scale. It seems in port operations that a fourfold increase in size reduces costs by approximately one-quarter. Similarly, with internal transport, John Tanner[5] stated some years ago that the cost of four-lane UK motorways was on

---

[4] J.O. Jansson and D. Shneerson, 'Economics of scale of general cargo ships', *Review of Economics and Statistics*, **45**, 287–93, 1978.

[5] J.C. Tanner, *An Economic Comparison of Motorways with 2 or 3 Lanes in Each Direction*, Crowthorne: Road and Research Laboratory Report, LR. 203, 1968.

Table 5.5   *Average cost per mile of rail track in the United Kingdom, 1967 (current prices)*

	Number of tracks		
	1	*2*	*3*
Interest	£3,020	£4,260	£7,900
Revenue of track and structure	£1,400–2,840	£1,986–3,442	£3,422–4,474
Signaling	£2,600	£4,030	£8,070
Total	£7,020–8,460	£10,190–11,730	£19,380–20,430

Source: C.D. Foster and S, Joy, 'Railway track costs in Britain', in *Development of Railway Traffic Engineering*, Institution of Civil Engineers, 1967.

average 78 percent of those with six lanes. However, it should be said that evidence of scale economies in road provision is not altogether conclusive. The findings of Keeler and Small,[6] looking at 57 freeway segments in the San Francisco area, favor constant returns while Walters,[7] again employing American sources, finds evidence 'that there are increasing costs of (road) construction in urban areas'.

The difficulty here, as with other forms of infrastructure costing, is to isolate comparable construction costs from those costs associated with specific locations. In terms of railways, the move from a single- to a double-track system involves roughly a quadrupling of capacity by eliminating conflict between directions; that to quadruple track should more than double capacity by permitting segregation by speed. The estimated costs of these options in Britain (at 1967 prices) are seen in Table 5.5, and clearly they rise much less rapidly than the increase in potential capacities.

Economies from Large Fleet Size

Larger fleets of vehicles may offer economies in maintenance, standardization (or, in some cases, the availability of a mixed vehicle fleet to meet variable demand), crew scheduling and so on, although administrative problems and remoteness of decision maker from customer may temper these advantages. Evidence on the presence of fleet economies of scale, however, is far from conclusive for all modes of transport and indeed there seems to be a gradual emergence of constant returns for many modes with limited scale economies in specialized forms of transport.

The picture regarding bus operations, for example, provides a rather confusing picture. The oft-cited UK statistical analysis by Lee and Steedman,[8] looking at the accounts of 44 municipal bus undertakings for 1966/67, suggests the notion

[6] T.E. Keeler and K.A. Small, 'Optimal peak-load pricing investment and service levels on urban expressways', *Journal of Political Economy*, **85**, 1–25, 1977.

[7] A.A. Walters, *The Economics of Road User Charges*, Baltimore, MD: Johns Hopkins University Press, 1968.

[8] N. Lee and I.W. Steedman, 'Economies of scale in bus transport I: some British municipal results', *Journal of Transport Economics and Policy*, **4**, 15–28, 1970.

of constant returns to scale, a situation agreeing with Williams'[9] study of 11 American publicly owned operations. Wabe and Coles's[10] examination of 66 UK operators, however, 'provides evidence that diseconomies of scale exist in the provision of bus services'. Koshal's[11] work in India offers international support for the notion of constant returns in bus operations. The problem with most of these studies, however, is that they use econometric models which assume that scale effects do not extend over all levels of output.

The 1980s witnessed the development of more 'flexible' model forms in econometrics (a topic we shall address in more detail later) that allow for variation in scale effects as output changes – for example, they allow for testing for a U-shaped cost curve. Button and O'Donnell,[12] applying such techniques to UK urban bus data, found that economies of scale do seem to exist up to a point, although diseconomies set in for the larger undertakings. This broadly conformed to studies both of Israeli bus fleets[13] and for the US intercity bus industry.[14]

Alan Walters's work on the trucking sector produced evidence of constant returns in the United Kingdom, although the large number of owner drivers working in this sector makes exact costing difficult. Regarding British aviation, the Edwards Committee's[15] pioneering analysis found evidence of scale economies when there was fleet standardization but generally concluded that the optimal size of a fleet depends upon the task in hand. Looking at shipping, Tolifari et al. found evidence of scale effects in bulk fleets – see Figure 5.4. The difficulty with empirical work in this field, and in aviation, is the diversity of the market conditions that are encountered and the support that is often forthcoming from government to finance 'the nation's flag carrier'. As can be seen in the figure, the costs of a fleet with traditional registry (in one of the major industrial states) tend to be higher than when open registry (the adoption of a 'flag of convenience') is favored because of the standards demanded by the former. As we shall see below, these scale effects also become rather clouded with the introduction of economies of density.

One indication of constant returns to fleet size is sometimes thought to

[9] M. Williams, 'The economic justification for local bus transport subsidies', *International Journal of Transport Economics*, **8**, 79–88, 1981.

[10] J. S. Wabe and O.B. Coles, 'The peak and off-peak demand for bus transport: a cross-sectional analysis of British municipal operations', *Applied Economics*, **7**, 25–30, 1975.

[11] R.K. Koshal, 'Economies of scale in bus transport II: some Indian experience', *Journal of Transport Economics and Policy*, **4**, 29–36, 1970.

[12] K.J. Button and K. O'Donnell, 'An examination of the cost structures associated with providing urban bus services in Britain', *Scottish Journal of Political Economy*, **32**, 67–81, 1985.

[13] J. Berechman, 'Costs, economies of scale and factor demand in road transport', *Journal of Transport Economics and Policy*, **17**, 7–24, 1983.

[14] M. Williams and C. Hall, 'Returns to scale in the United States intercity bus industry', *Regional Science and Urban Economics*, **11**, 573–84, 1981.

[15] UK Board of Trade (1969), *British Air Transport in the Seventies*, Cmnd 4018, London: HMSO, 1969.

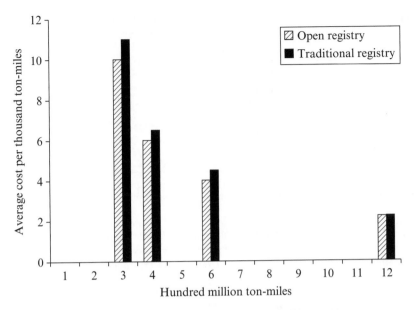

Source: S. Tolifari, K.J. Button and D. Pitfield, 'Shipping costs and the controversy over open registry', *Journal of Industrial Economics*, **34**, 409–27, 1986.

Figure 5.4   *Economies of scale in bulk shipping*

be diversity in the scale of operators in a sector of transport: large companies competing directly against one or two vehicle firms, suggesting that there is little advantage in large fleets. Road haulage is possibly the most extreme example of this phenomenon (Table 5.6 offers a British example) but throughout the whole of transport – except for areas directly regulated by government – one finds large and small firms competing with each other.

Differential managerial skills may permit some firms to grow larger than others but this does not imply that technical economies of scale exist. They may also be supplying slightly different services, perhaps in qualitative terms that are not easy to quantify, and thus strict cost comparisons become difficult to make. Evidence of this type, therefore, may be capturing differential demands rather than any strict scale effect.

The variable costs of transport – those related to the rate of output – are generally considered to be dominated by labor and fuel items because these are thought to be highly flexible in the short term. Their importance relative to each other can, however, vary considerably, even in the short term as seen by the increased importance of fuel costs for modes such as aviation in 2007 to early 2008 when oil prices rapidly rose to record levels. Since infrastructure costs are relatively fixed, it is the cost of the mobile plant that is normally treated as marginal. Table 5.7 gives some indication of the relative importance of these items in overall urban public transport operating costs in Australia, and Table 5.8 offers data on international airlines in a more stable period before the atypical fuel price rises.

Table 5.6   *United Kingdom's trucking fleet by size and number of operators (1977)*

Fleet size	No. of operators	No. of vehicles in fleet
1	25,100	25,100
2–5	14,300	44,400
6–20	5,500	53,700
21–100	1,400	49,500
Over 100	100	16,300
Total	46,400	189,000

Source: UK Department of Transport, *Road Haulage Operators' Licensing (Report of the Independent Committee of Enquiry into Road Haulage Operators Licensing)*, London: HMSO, 1979.

Table 5.7   *Cost components of urban public transport in Australia (%)*

Cost component	Train	Tram	Bus
Crewing	14	49	48
Station manning and signaling	7	–	–
Maintenance	32	23	22
Fuel	5	3	9
Administrative/other	9	9	9
Capital related expenses	23	16	12

Source: R. Kinnear, 'Financial realities: cost trends and productivity', *Transport Reviews*, **8**, 34–50, 1988.

Table 5.8   *Components of operating costs of scheduled international airlines (%)*

	1980	1990	1999
Direct operating costs			
Flight operations	44	32	35
Flight crew	8	7	8
Fuel and oil	28	15	8
Airport and en-route charges	5	4	7
Aircraft rental, insurance etc.	3	6	9
Maintenance	11	11	11
Depreciation: aircraft and ground facilities	6	7	7
Total direct costs	60	50	53
Indirect operating costs			
Station/ground services	11	12	11
Passenger services	9	10	11
Ticketing, sales, promotions	14	16	14
Administration and other costs	6	11	12
Total indirect operating costs	40	50	47

Source: International Civil Aviation Organization, *Digest of Statistics*, Montreal: ICAO, for years indicated.

It should perhaps be pointed out that even in the long term the costs of mobile plant are, in aggregate, likely to exceed those of infrastructure, but individual vehicle costs, in many cases, are relatively small. The costs of aircraft operations come within a sector with very high costs per unit of mobile plant, while road haulage is a sector where the operational costs per vehicle are low. The importance of both direct and indirect labor and fuel costs, however, is apparent at both ends of the spectrum.

The tables we have used for illustration represent broad averages across many different types of operation but variable costs differ not simply with level of vehicle usage but also with the type of transport operation undertaken. Vehicles, for example, have an optimal speed above or below which fuel costs tend to rise steeply; consequently operations involving continually stopping and starting will, *ceteris paribus*, increase variable costs.[16] Maintenance costs can also vary considerably with the type of terrain over which journeys are made. To some extent these variations may be offset by employing specialized vehicles whose variable cost profiles conform most closely to the type of operation undertaken. In the airline context there exists a whole range of different aircraft designed to meet the needs of different operational patterns – airbuses for short-haul, large-volume traffic, wide-bodied jumbos for long-range operations and so on. Equally, Table 5.9, from one of the most detailed studies on the subject, gives some indication of the running and standing costs of different forms of operation in the UK's trucking sector in the late 1970s. While these figures are not strictly variable and fixed costs, and they are very much case specific in that trucking hauls are relatively short in Britain compared, say, with the United States, but they do convey a general impression of how costs vary, even within sectors, with the type of transport operation performed.

The cost profiles also vary with the type of firm controlling the operations. Evidence from statistical studies of US urban public transit systems, for instance, suggests that public ownership can lead to higher costs of provision.[17] Wallis,[18] in his study of urban bus operations in major Australian cities, gave some reasons why private operators enjoy lower costs in certain areas than their publicly owned counterparts:

- greater flexibility and efficiency in use of labor;
- relatively small proportions of maintenance and administrative costs;
- lower basic rates of pay; and
- lower wage/salary add-on-costs (taxes, pensions and so on).

[16] I.D. Greenwood, R.C.M. Dunn and R.R. Raine, 'Estimating the effects of traffic congestion on fuel consumption and vehicle emissions based on acceleration noise', *Journal of Transportation Engineering*, **133**, 96–104, 2007.

[17] J. Pucher and A. Markstedt, 'Consequences of public ownership and subsidies for mass transit: evidence from case studies and regression analysis', *Transportation*, **11**, 323–45, 1983.

[18] I.P. Wallis, 'Private bus operations in urban areas – their economics and role', *Traffic Engineering and Control*, **22**, 605–10, 1980.

Table 5.9   *British trucking running and standing costs per mile in 1977 (current prices)*

	Fleet size	Bulk tankers	Tipping	Smalls & parcels	Long distance	Other general	Other sectors	All sectors
Running	100+	0.20	–	0.12	0.15	0.21	0.14	0.18
Standing	100+	0.27	–	0.30	0.18	0.31	0.42	0.28
Running	21–100	0.17	0.13	0.12	0.15	0.16	0.16	0.15
Standing	21–100	0.22	0.19	0.28	0.16	0.22	0.26	0.21
Running	1–20	0.19	0.15	0.12	0.13	0.12	0.16	0.14
Standing	1–20	0.31	0.12	0.19	0.19	0.14	0.25	0.18

Source: UK Price Commission, *The Road Haulage Industry*, House of Commons Paper HC 698, London: HMSO, 1978.

While in part cost variations may be explained in terms of either the size of the operator or the type of operation undertaken, cost differences may also reflect alternative operational objectives There is ample evidence that large national airlines often employ high-cost modern equipment to enhance their image. But even at the level of local public transport similar indications of X-inefficiency exists. Teal et al.,[19] for example, cite instances of local authorities preferring to operate their own para-transport system rather than make use of established private operators despite demonstrably higher costs.

Labor costs, although flexible, are usually much less variable than fuel costs. This is not simply because of imperfections in the labor market (for example, fixed working hours, union agreements on redundancies, training costs and so on) which often make it difficult to increase or reduce the size of the labor force – even in the sense of dividing up public transport crews to conform with daily peaks in travel demand – but also because of the nature of many types of transport operation. Once a particular form of transport operation has been decided upon, and capital invested, there are high labor costs associated with maintaining and servicing this equipment, irrespective of the traffic carried. Further, once an undertaking is committed to a scheduled service, labor becomes a fixed cost in providing this service.

One of the major problems in this latter context is the technologically unprogressive nature of many forms of transport operation that makes it difficult to substitute one factor input for another as their relative prices change. In the case of the mercantile marine it has proved possible to substitute fixed for variable factors (notably capital for labor) as labor costs have risen but this is much less easy in areas such as public transport provision. It is difficult to see how the basic operations of taxi-cabs, for example, could be retained with a substantial reduction in labor input. Attempts to reduce labor costs in the urban public transport sphere in the United Kingdom by introducing one-man operated vehicles, did seem to have some limited effect on costs (for example, Brown and Nash[20]

---

[19] R.F. Teal, J.V. Marks and R. Goodhue, 'Subsidized shared-ride taxi service', *Transportation Research Record*, **778**, 25–32, 1980.

[20] R.H. Brown and C.A. Nash, 'Cost savings from one-man operation of buses', *Journal of Transport Economics and Policy*, **6**, 281–4.

estimated a 13.7 percent cost saving), but this should be seen as a once-and-for-all step rather than the prospect of continual factor substitution.

5.3   Economies of Scale, Scope, Density and Experience

In recent years it has become increasingly appreciated that while economies of scale in its strictest form may be of considerable importance in many transport activities, there are instances where it is not simply the pure size of the undertaking or activity that is the prime determinant of cost variation. A number of other factors are of particular importance in the transport context.

Many transport undertakings provide a variety of outputs. Taking aviation as an example, at the most basic level these may be scheduled and charter services, but in more detail there is the matter of outward and return services and, at a more detailed level still, each particular flight may be viewed as a specific product. The economic question then becomes one of deciding whether there are cost savings in one supplier producing this range of services rather than there being a number of suppliers each specializing. Where there are cost economies from multi-product production, then economies of scope are said to exist. Just as with conventional scale effects, it is possible for economies of scope to exist at some levels of output but not at others. As a city expands, for example, there may exist economies of scope in bus service provision favoring a monopoly supplier but as it gets larger and demand rises so these economies may disappear and a number of much smaller operators prove more cost effective.

Technically, economies of scope are assessed when:

$$S = \{[C(Q^1) + C(Q^2)] - C(Q^1 + Q^2)\}/\{C(Q^1 + Q^2)\} \qquad (5.1)$$

where:

$C(Q^1)$ is the cost of producing Q^1 units of output one alone;
$C(Q^2)$ is the cost of producing Q^2 units of output two alone; and
$C(Q^1 + Q^2)$ is the cost of producing Q^1 plus Q^2 units of together.

Economies of scope exist if $S > 0$. There are economies scale if C/Q falls as Q expands.

There are also instances where there are cost economies from serving larger markets – it effectively allows the more intensive use of capital. Again, aviation provides an example of these so-called 'economies of density' where larger markets enable higher load factors to be enjoyed and hence lower unit cost per passenger.

The coming together of these economies of scope and of density has been characterized by the adoption of 'hub-and-spoke' operations. While US domestic aviation is the most-cited example of this phenomena, with all the main airlines basing their services on radial flights from a limited number of hubs it is also appearing in

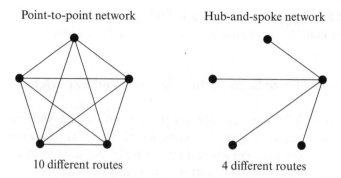

Figure 5.5   *Point-to-point versus hub-and-spoke networks*

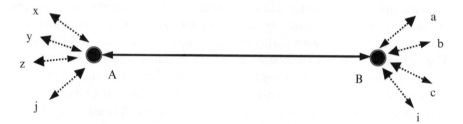

Figure 5.6   *The 'dog-bone' pattern of international hub-and-spoke operations*

shipping – with traffic into Europe coming by large ships to a small number of large ports to be distributed to other ports by smaller vessels – and in some spheres of bus operators, such as the importance of Victoria Coach Station in London as the hub for long distance intercity bus services in the United Kingdom. The Post Office has based its operations around hub-and-spoke networks since its inception.

Figure 5.5 offers an indication of the cost advantages of hub-and-spoke operations. With direct services between each city pair there would need to be 10 services provided, and many of these may be relatively thin with limited traffic. If, as in the right-hand side of the figure, traffic is hubbed through one of the cities with passengers being consolidated at this hub to go on to their final destinations, then only four services are required. This allows larger aircraft to be used, and potentially higher load factors enjoyed, thus reducing costs and fares. The penalty is that people traveling through, rather than stopping at the hub airport, will have longer flight times and spend some time waiting for their connecting flight.

For longer-distance travel, often international routes, there may be a number of changes. Figure 5.6 illustrates a typical 'dog-bone' or 'dumbell' route structure. Here a passenger wanting to travel from x to c would be routed as x $\Rightarrow$ A $\Rightarrow$ B $\Rightarrow$ c where A and B are major hub airports that consolidate traffic from cities x, y, z, . . .; j traveling to a, b, c, . . ., i. An example of these types of trip are found on North Atlantic air routes where, for example, an individual may fly with United Airlines from a small city in the United States to Washington, change plane and fly on to London, then change plane again and fly to a small European city.

Competition in this system is largely between interconnected airline networks,

Figure 5.7   *Network competition in the air cargo sector*

often involving alliances. Figure 5.7 again takes the long-distance movement x ⇒ c but now looks at the options that may be available when comparing different airline alliances rather than just the services of a single airline. The routing x ⇒ A ⇒ B ⇒ c is retained as the base case, but the airline offering this may also have alliance ties with other carriers and push traffic through one or more of their hubs; this may make x ⇒ C ⇒ A ⇒ B ⇒ c an option, or x ⇒ C ⇒ D ⇒ c. A competitive alliance may offer x ⇒ F ⇒ G ⇒ c. And so on.

Depending on schedules and routes served, there are thus numerous possibilities for moving from x to c. From a costing perspective, the costs of these various combinations will differ for the combinations supplying airlines involved. In the context of a discussion of fuel price rises, each overall routing would require a different surcharge that would need to reflect not only the weight of the consignment but also such things as the different distances involved and the forms of equipment used by the various members of an alliance.

A further recent development is the appreciation that there is a 'learning-by-doing' element in many activities that can reduce costs, and in some cases may also be a factor affecting demand. These 'economies of experience' tend to be under-researched in the transport sphere but technically exist when unit costs decline as more is produced or as a supplier stays in a market for an extended period. There may be a number of dimensions involved in this.

- *Goodwill.* When confronted with a number of carriers, potential users of aviation have varying levels of information, and especially about the quality of services. Risk aversion encourages a 'better the devil I know' mentality which favors incumbent suppliers. The need to combat this with advertising and promotions pushes up the costs of new entrants.
- *Knowledge.* Incumbent suppliers have more information about a market it serves and can tailor its services to specific customer groups. New entrants must sink resources into acquiring such information.
- *Organization.* New entrants must assimilate the requirements of new services within their networks and this entails learning costs throughout the remainder of their organization.

As for evidence, one early study of US domestic airline regulation found that after the opening-up of routes, incumbent carriers had a larger impact on markets than newly established carriers.[21] Similarly, analysis of Compass Airline's entry into the Australian domestic market highlights the problems of establishing goodwill and brand loyalty.[22] Switching mode, in the United Kingdom, it has been argued that these experience effects may have been advantageous to National Express in the period following the deregulation of the intercity bus network after 1980. It was the incumbent supplier and enjoyed, along with other things, considerable experience in the market that enabled it to dominate newcomers.[23]

The natural way for a transport undertaking to enjoy the various cost advantages of scale, scope and so on is for it to develop its own network and services on those networks efficiently. In many cases, however, suppliers try to accelerate this process by merging or taking over an existing network to add to their own. Mergers may take place for a number of specific reasons.[24] In some cases, and we shall return to this in Chapter 7, it may be to remove competition from a market so as to enjoy additional market power. Mergers involving overlapping transport networks are often seen as motivated in this way. In other cases, there may be synergies between non-overlapping (or at least involving limited overlap) that can add to economies of scope and density, and also bring in economies of experience because they do not involve developing routes from scratch. Added to this, the enlarged network may generate economies of greater market presence on the demand side by offering a wider range of services to transport users.

The decision to merge networks occurs, therefore, when the incentives exist for the businesses involved, be they driven by rent-seeking or cost-saving motivations. For simplicity we assume that the benefits of, say, a shipping network are proportional to the number of customers (n) that use it, and that the constant of proportionality is unity. Then following Metcalfe's Law the value of the network is n^2. A simple calculation shows that by combining two networks of size n_1 and n_2 yields:

$$\Delta v_1 = n_1(n_1 + n_2) - n_1^2 = n_1 n_2 \tag{5.2a}$$

$$\Delta v_2 = n_2(n_1 + n_2) - n_2^2 = n_1 n_2 \tag{5.2b}$$

Each network of sailings gets equal value (v_2) from the interconnection. Those on a smaller network (2) each get considerable value from linking with

[21] S.H. Baker and J.B. Pratt, 'Experience as a barrier to contestability in airline markets', *Review of Economics and Statistics*, **81**, 352–6, 1989.

[22] M. Nythi, P. Hooper and O. Heusher, 'Compass Airline; 1 December 1990 to 20 December 1991 – what went wrong?', *Transport Reviews*, **13**, 112–49, and **13**, 185–206, 1993.

[23] K.J. Button, 'Contestability in the UK bus industry, and experience goods and economies of experience', in J. Dodgson and N. Topham (eds), *Bus Deregulation and Privatisation: An International Perspective*, Aldershot: Gower, 1989,

[24] W.B. Tye and J. Horn, 'Transportation mergers: the case of the US railroads', in K.J. Button and D.A. Hensher (eds), *Handbook of Transport Strategy, Policy and Institutions*, Amsterdam: Elsevier, 2005.

the large number of nodes on the larger network (1), while a large number of consignors on the latter may each get a smaller additional utility, but there are a lot of them. This offers scope for reciprocation with the networks having free access to each other. The problem is that the large supplier may need to keep its market power to allow adequate price discrimination to recover costs and make an acceptable long-term return. In this case, the larger shipping company may merge with the smaller one and attain twice the value of offering interconnecting services:

$$\Delta v_1 = n_1(n_1 + n_2)^2 - n_1^2 - n_2^2 = 2n_1n_2 \qquad (5.3)$$

5.4 Specific, Joint and Common Costs

When dividing out costs, according to the groups of services produced, it is often useful to allocate responsibility to specific users or consignors. While the fixed/variable cost dichotomy poses problems about the relevant time period to consider, cost responsibility raises issues of the traceability of costs. Some costs are very specific and can, therefore, be allocated quite easily – the stevedore costs of loading and unloading a particular cargo onto and off a ship is a case in point. In other cases a degree of averaging may be necessary but, nevertheless, many costs can generally be traced to specific groups or classes of user.

But there is also a range of other costs which may be either 'joint' or 'common' to a number of users and are difficult to trace directly to any specific group. It is sometimes said that fixed costs may generally be treated as joint or common while variable costs may be treated as specific, but this is too simplistic. Many variable costs are, in practice, joint (for example, the fuel costs incurred in moving a train in one direction and bringing it back are joint to both movements) or common (for example, the basic maintenance costs of retaining a freight and passenger rail link) while certain fixed costs are clearly specific (for example, the capital costs of freight wagons have no connection with passenger demand).

In some cases the technology is such that two products can be delivered at the same time – the textbook wool and mutton case. An example of this in transport is the combination of passengers being carried on the upper deck of commercial aircraft and freight on the lower deck. Allocating the fixed costs of the aircraft between these two uses, other than for specific features such as seats, is challenging. Nevertheless, airlines do carry both on many aircraft as can be seen in the revenue composition in Figure 5.8.

Strictly, joint costs exist when the provision of a specific service necessarily entails the output of some other service. Jointness is a technical feature and exists at all points in time, that is, both before as well as after any investment decisions are made. Return trips (or 'back-hauls'), where the supply of transport services in one direction automatically implies the provision of a return service, are the classic examples in transport economics. The fact that true joint products are produced in fixed proportions means that there can be no variability in costs, making

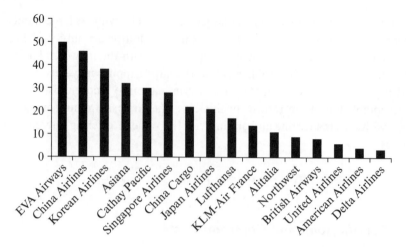

Figure 5.8   *Percentage of airlines' revenues from cargo*

it logically impossible to specify the cost of, say, an outward journey when only the overall cost of the round trip is known. Joint costs are, consequently, non-traceable. This further implies that joint costs can only be escaped jointly, with services in both directions being withdrawn together.

In a market situation, joint costs pose few problems in practice. If there is a competitive road haulage service offering a round trip between A and B and back again each week using *M* trucks, then equilibrium rates would soon emerge for each service (that is, from A to B and from B to A). Although there are specific delivery, terminal, pick-up costs and so on, little difference exists between the costs of running the lorries fully loaded or empty and hence prices would primarily be influenced by the differences in the demand in each direction. In the short term the combined revenues from the A to B and the B to A services may not be sufficient to cover joint costs but in such a situation the number of trucks offered would soon fall below *M*, increasing the price of trips in both directions until joint costs are recovered. Excess revenue above joint costs would have the opposite effect. The key point is that differences exist in the demands for the out and return services and that different prices should be charged for each in equilibrium. Consequently, knowledge of the relevant demand elasticities together with that of joint cost permits the problems of traceability to be avoided. We shall return to consider this problem in more detail in our discussion of pricing in Chapter 7.

Common costs are similar to joint costs, in that they are incurred as the result of providing services to a range of users, but differ in that the use of resources to provide one service does not *unavoidably* result in the production of a different one. The classic example of common costs in transport is the provision of track facilities. A road may be used in common by lorries and cars but the withdrawal of rights for hauliers still leaves costs to be borne by motorists. With several classes of user it is often possible to trace certain components of cost to those responsible, but there is still usually a large proportion that is untraceable.

We now turn to look at some attempts that have been made to allocate common track costs across different categories of traffic.

5.5   Problems of Common Cost Allocation – the Road and Rail Track Cases

The allocation of common track costs among users poses particular practical problems in transport and deserves specific attention. As Arthur Twining Hadley put it in 1885, before becoming President of Yale University, 'God Almighty did not know the cost of carrying a hundred pounds of freight from Boston to New York'.[25] The way costs are allocated differs between countries. The intercity road network in the United Kingdom, for example, is the responsibility of local and central government. Since the effective abolition of the Road Fund in 1937 and its legal death in 1955, users make no direct, hypothecated payments to use the network – save for a small number of toll bridges – but do pay considerable sums to government each year in the form of fuel tax, value added tax, car tax and vehicle excise duty. The United States has a national gasoline tax which since 1956 goes into a Highway Trust Fund that finances the nation's Interstate Highway system and some other roads. Individual states have a variety of mechanisms for financing their road networks.

When deciding upon the desirability of making a road journey, potential users are to some extent influenced by these taxes. Therefore, attempts have been made, on the grounds of economic efficiency, to allocate accurately the public costs of road provision (both the construction and maintenance of the track) to users. The European Union, for example, now wishes members to ensure that all road users pay at least their allocated short-run marginal costs of track provision and that the full long-term cost is recovered.[26]

There are problems of deciding exactly what constitutes the total cost of road track provision in any period – for example, should the maintenance costs be estimated in the same way as depreciation in nationalized industries or simply considered as they are incurred and what exactly constitutes the capital cost of any one year?

National comparisons of annual expenditures against tax revenue suggest that many governments of industrial countries recover from road users more than is spent on road track provision. There is also certainly no reason why, as some have advocated, the ratio of revenues to costs should approximate to unity. Part of the revenue raised from road users must be considered as a 'pure' tax in the same way that there are taxes on other expenditures. Also there are social costs associated with road transport (see Chapter 6) and motoring taxes may, in part,

---

[25] T. Hadley, *Railroad Transportation: Its History and Its Laws*, New York: G.P. Putnams, 1885.

[26] C. Creightney, 'Road user taxation in selected OECD countries', Washington, DC, SSATP Working Paper 3, World Bank, 1993.

be seen as a method, albeit a very imperfect one, of making road users aware of such costs. Additionally, if prices in other sectors of the economy deviate from costs, there are sound economic reasons for this to be also the policy on roads.

The UK's 'Road Track Costs' Allocation Method

While there is no sound reason why expenditure should match revenue in aggregate, it may still be desirable for each class of road vehicle to more or less cover its allocated track costs – this is the view, for example, of the European Union.[27] Allocation of track costs to vehicle categories is, therefore, still important. The difficulty is that roads provide a common service to a variety of modes of transport (cyclists, motor cars, light vans, heavy lorries, buses and so on) and the exact apportionment of marginal costs is, therefore, far from easy. The method of allocation favored by the UK Department of Transport is based upon a refined version of an approach pioneered in *Road Track Costs*, which crudely attempts to allocate long-run marginal costs to different classes of road users.[28] It is similar to the method that has been used in the United States from the 1980s.

The calculations in this study were done for the four standard categories of road: motorway, trunk, principal and other. Of total capital expenditure (made up of the average expenditure over the previous year, the current year and the forecast for the following year), 15 percent is allocated directly to heavy goods vehicles according to their maximum vehicle weight times the kilometers run, on the grounds that they necessitate higher engineering design standards. The remaining 85 percent is allocated out on passenger car unit (pcu) kilometers (pcu being an estimate of the amount of road required to accommodate a vehicle expressed in terms of car equivalents), on the argument that capital expenditure is determined by changes required in the physical capacity of the network.

Maintenance expenditures were allocated according to a series of *ad hoc* calculations that attempt to relate the various component items (such as resurfacing, grass cutting, lighting, road markings, traffic signs, drainage and so on) to different vehicle characteristics, namely their size, number of standard axles (high axle loadings doing considerable damage to road surfaces) and the use made of roads. The criteria used to decide how costs are affected by the vehicle characteristics are based upon 'expert advice from traffic engineers and research scientists'. Special items such as policing and car parks are treated separately.

The information contained in Table 5.10 provides a comparison of the cost allocations with revenues for different broad categories of road user in the United Kingdom for 1989/90. All classes cover their allocated cost, a situation that is also common in many other industrialized countries. A similar picture is seen within vehicle classes. For example, while all sizes of heavy goods vehicle pay tax in

---

[27] European Commission, *Fair Payment for Infrastructure Use: A Phased Approach to a Common Transport Infrastructure Charging Framework in the EU – White Paper*, Brussels, COM(98) 466, 1998.
[28] UK Ministry of Transport, *Road Track Costs*, London: HMSO, 1968.

Table 5.10   *Allocated taxation/revenue ratios by vehicle type in the United Kingdom (1989/90)*

Vehicle class	Tax to cost ratios
Cars/light vans/taxis	3.4:1
Motorcycles	2.3:1
Buses and coaches	1.1:1
Trucks over 1.525 tonnes gvw	
Not over 3.5 tonnes gvw	3.1:1
Over 3.5 tonnes gvw	1.3:1
Other vehicles	2.4:1
All vehicles	2.6:1

Source: UK Department of Transport, 'The Allocation of Road Track Costs 1989/90', DOT, London: 1989.

excess of the public road costs attributable to them, there is considerable variation in the revenue/cost ratio, and large vehicles with a small number of axles tend to have the lowest ratios. This may be particularly undesirable if these large vehicles are also responsible for generating a high level of external costs.

The UK Department of Transport's method of cost attribution has come under some criticism. At one level, Button[29] suggested that the detailed allocation within the Department's framework in the 1970s was biased against heavy goods vehicles because of:

- the excessive emphasis on vehicle weight in the allocation of capital costs when much of the network's design is determined by vehicle speed;
- the implied assumption in the calculation that the network is of optimal size;
- the rather dubious nature of passenger car units as a measure of road capacity; and
- the 'standard axle' (a computational device for comparing the damaging effects of different vehicles, taking account of the 'fourth power' rule of road damage') measure used in the calculations to reflect damage done per wheel.

In particular, there is evidence that there may be an element of double counting when calculating heavy goods vehicle costs. Cars are accredited with a small allocation and maintenance costs, but this is only possible because of the high engineering standards of roads required to carry heavy goods traffic. Hence, goods vehicles are allocated both the additional costs of high design standards and the bulk of maintenance costs whereas with lower design specifications, suitable for cars only, cars would be allocated much higher maintenance costs.

[29] K.J. Button, 'Heavy goods vehicle taxation in the United Kingdom', *Transportation*, **8**, 389–408, 1979.

Table 5.11   *Examples of actual and optimal road vehicle taxation in the United States (1988)*

Vehicle	Taxes (cents per mile)		
	Current	Marginal cost (existing roads)	Marginal costs (improved roads)
2-axle single unit			
26,000lbs	2.5	9.2	3.6
33,000lbs	3.0	23.8	9.3
5-axle tractor unit			
33,000lbs	4.0	1.2	0.5
80,000lbs	7.2	41.3	16.2

Source: K.A. Small, C. Winton and C.A. Evans, *Road Works: A New Highway Pricing and Investment Policy*, Washington, DC: Brookings Institution, 1989.

This last point has been examined in some detail by Ken Small and colleagues in a study of US road investment and pricing policy (see Table 5.11). The evidence strongly suggested that under the US regime, where certain federal road taxation revenue is partly hypothecated to road building and maintenance, the amount of investment has historically been suboptimal resulting in pavements that are, from an economic prospect, too thin. The result is the need for high maintenance and reconstruction outlays relatively soon after a road is opened.

The economic evidence from this study is that if higher taxes had been introduced initially and higher standard roads constructed then subsequent taxation to finance maintenance would, on average, have been much lower than it inevitably will have to be if the network is not to deteriorate. The actual structure of the taxation should also have been adjusted to correspond more closely to the damage associated with various class users. Table 5.11 provides data on actual taxation, the taxation needed in the near future to maintain the current road system and what it would have been if optimal taxation and investment policies had been adopted in the United States.

At a more fundamental level, Chris Nash[30] has suggested that the traditional road track cost approach is really asking the wrong question and that track cost allocation should be along altogether different lines. He suggests that the way ahead is to adopt a sequential approach where greater emphasis is placed upon differing demand elasticities among road users. Specifically he advises:

• Forecast traffic growth rates by vehicle type using alternative assumptions about future taxation levels and structures.
• Estimate the full costs of catering for different traffic growth rates.
• Identify the level and structure of taxes at which the revenue obtained from

[30] C.A. Nash, 'The track costs issue – a comment', *Journal of Transport Economics and Policy*, **14**, 113–6, 1979.

an incremental slice of traffic matches incremental costs both for traffic as a whole and for individual traffic types.

- To the extent that the resulting taxes fall short of government revenue requirements, raise taxes on vehicle classes along second-best lines (that is, according to demand elasticities).

Such calculations obviously place greater demands on informational sources but they do offer a rather more realistic basis for track cost allocation and pricing consistent with principles adopted elsewhere in the transport sector.

Allocating Costs in a State-owned Railroad

Railway track cost allocation is often done in a slightly different context because the railways, unlike the roads case, have traditionally been responsible in most countries for providing both track and rolling stock. In the United States, this has always involved private railroads, albeit until recently heavily regulated, but this has not, at least until recently, been the case in most other countries. The situation has changed somewhat is some European countries, not only because in countries like the United Kingdom rail operations have been separated from track provision,[31] but because EU regulations require open access to their networks and this necessitates track cost estimations for charging purposes. We focus on the situation where, as still is common, state ownership of track and operations remains and look at some of the challenges faced in the past by British Rail – a largely passenger system. The intensity with which this subject was studied provides insights of a more general nature.

In countries such as the United Kingdom, the necessity for devising a method of allocation pre-privatization, stemmed not simply from designs for internal efficiency but also to permit the allocation of common fixed costs between those services that are operated on commercial criteria (for example, intercity passenger services) and those that are operated on social criteria (for example, commuter services) and are given central government subsidies.

One of the difficulties with railway operations is that common costs (which must include signaling, termini and so on in addition to track) form a very substantial part of total cost. Normal commercial practice would be to use a 'cost-plus' method of pricing so that each customer would pay a rate covering his/her specific costs plus a contribution to overheads. Provided that this results in all costs being recovered in aggregate, the problem of common cost allocation is not a serious issue. Unfortunately, for the reasons mentioned above, plus the difficulty of devising a sufficiently sensitive price discrimination regime given the diversity of services offered (see Chapter 7 for a discussion of price discrimination), the railways have found it important to be able to allocate their track costs.

A major difficulty in this area is that the railway 'jargon' often does not

---

[31] R. Haywood, 'Britain's national railway network: fit for purpose in the 21st century?', *Journal of Transport Geography*, **15**, 198–216, 2007.

conform to conventional economic definitions. The railways talk of 'direct costs' and 'indirect costs' but the former (which embraces haulage costs, maintenance, marshaling, booking, insurance, collection and delivery by road) is clearly different from the economic notion of short-run escapable costs (and may or may not exceed them). As the UK's Select Committee on Nationalized Industries[32] said, 'The direct costs ascertained by traffic costing methods are not the same thing as short run marginal costs. Nor do they correspond with the savings that would flow immediately from the discontinuance of a small part of railway activities'. Equally, indirect costs, as defined by the railways (that is, track, signaling and general administration) are not sufficiently fixed costs that are common to all traffic. While certain costs (for example, earthworks) are invariant with traffic it is often possible to allocate track and signaling costs to particular services according to causation. The type and density of traffic determine whether a single-track route is operated with no signaling or a multi-track, multiple-aspect signaling system is provided.

Stewart Joy,[33] the chief economist at British Railways, first highlighted over 40 years ago how these costs can vary with the quality of service – an express Category A service on double track with 12 trains a day costs £8,250 per mile per annum in track costs (at 1961 prices); a less frequent, Category B service, £7,250; heavily used non-express Category C services, £6,250; and slow, Category D services, £3,500. It is possible with poorer-quality services to have more basic signaling and lower track maintenance standards. Furthermore, there are quite significant differences associated with the costs of track used exclusively for passenger services and that used only for freight. The Beeching Report,[34] which brought about major reforms in the British rail system 45 years ago, found that a single track maintained to passenger standards costs at least £3,500 per mile per annum but if it were only required to conform to freight standards it would cost £2,000 per mile per annum, and it has been argued that this could be reduced further.[35]

The improvement in costing in the United Kingdom came about in part because of the 1968 Transport Act and the introduction of social service subsidies for specific routes – the system required 'identification and costing of those services and facilities whose cost should properly be borne or aided by the community'. The common costs were allocated according to a formula developed by the consulting firm, 'Cooper Brothers' (which it should be noted was essentially an average, rather than marginal, cost type of framework), which endorsed the idea of allocating track costs on the basis of gross ton-miles and signaling costs on the basis of train-miles. With homogeneous traffic flows evenly spread this is reasonable, but with mixed traffic and peaks in use the allocation technique is unlikely to match causation with costs.

[32] UK House of Commons Select Committee on Nationalized Industries, *Report: British Railways*, London: HMSO, 1960.

[33] S. Joy, 'British Railways track costs', *Journal of Industrial Economics*, **13**, 74–89, 1964.

[34] British Railways Board, *The Reshaping of British Railways*, London: HMSO, 1963.

[35] S. Joy, *The Train that Ran Away*, London: Ian Allan, 1973

British Rail moved in the late 1970s to a system of 'contribution account-ing' which entailed breaking down revenue and costs into some 700 major sub-sectors (or 'profit centers'). These profit centers, which are composed of single traffic flows, groups of flows or specific passenger services, are defined so that resources allocated to them can be specifically identified with a minimum of con-troversy. Even so not all common costs could be so allocated and thus British Rail accounts revealed the surplus of revenue over directly attributed expenses that are a 'contribution' to the indirect costs. The sum of all avoidable costs recovered may not cover all business costs, however, and a 'basic facility cost' is likely to remain. British Rail argued though, that this approach, given the high proportion of indirect costs, 'ensures a high level of certainty in profit assessment'.[36]

The later privatization of railways in the UK and the deregulation of private networks as in countries such as the United States has meant that there has been more effort put into cost modeling of the type discussed in other sections of the chapter. The American railroads, an almost exclusively freight mover, have tradi-tionally varied in the way that they have allocated their costs and generalizations are not easy.[37] The removal of regulations under the 1980 Staggers Rail Act has provided the American railroads with more flexibility in their pricing and the ability to close or sell off unprofitable lines and with this has come the need for more specific costing. The growth of container traffic, with its own unique set of costing issues, has provided a further stimulus as has the common use of trade with Amtrack.

Prior to 1980 the US Interstate Commerce Commission regulated rates on a rate-of-return basis – essentially a cost-plus basis. For this it assigned each service those costs that could be directly and unambiguously attributed to it. In addi-tion to these directly attributable costs, each service was assigned a portion of common costs in such a way that all such costs were allocated somewhere. This was what is often called in the United States, a 'fully distributed cost approach'. In other words, the total allocated costs C of a service were defined by an affine function of the form $C = F + my$ where F represents fixed costs insensitive to traffic volume, m is a constant marginal cost and y is the level of output.

John Meyer[38] and others, criticized this approach over the years, pointing to the arbitrary allocation of common costs across services – a point initially made as early as 1891 by F.W Taussig, 'attempts have indeed been made at various times . . . to apportion the expenses, and assign to each item of traffic the sum which it costs . . . Yet surely the division is purely arbitrary'.[39] While any attempt to allo-cate all costs to a particular output is difficult, as we shall see later in this chapter,

[36] J.S. Dodgson, 'Railway costs and closures', *Journal of Transport Economics and Policy*, **18**, 219–236, 1984.

[37] E.C. Poole, *Costs – A Toll for Railroad Management*, New York: Simmons-Boardman, 1962.

[38] J.R. Meyer, 'Some methodological aspects of statistical costing as illustrated by the determination of rail passenger rates', *American Economic Review*, **48**, 209–22, 1958.

[39] F.W. Taussig, 'A contribution to the theory of railway rates', *Quarterly Journal of Economics*, **5**, 438–65, 1891.

the degree of arbitrariness has been reduced somewhat with the introduction of econometric costing analysis. They also pointed to the inappropriate assumption about output costs – for example, the Commission's methodology assumed that it cost as much to haul 100 tons one mile as to haul one ton a hundred miles.

From the two examples, the problems of allocating costs common to several services is, therefore, seen to be a difficult one. Economic principles advocate the notion of seeking avoidable costs associated with specific users and then allocating these accordingly. The problem is in defining the base from which to begin the series of allocations; in the case of roads, are they mainly designed for cars with lorries imposing additional costs or are they there to provide a quality of service with the faster car traffic necessitating higher engineering standards? We have seen that it is possible to allocate many items on an avoidable cost basis although practical application may necessitate a high degree of averaging.

5.6 Transport User Costs and the Notion of Generalized Costs

Simple observation shows us that different types of transport are associated, in a very broad way, with the distances of trips. Walking and cycling, together with the riding of mopeds, is largely reserved for local travel, whereas air transport dominates long-distance movements. Similar generalizations can be said about freight transport, although in this case it is shipping that dominates long-distance movements, at least in terms of physical movements. Of course there are cases where this very broad picture is not applicable. For example, where there are stretches of water to be covered, this is often by boat or aircraft if there is no road or rail infrastructure; and equally where these are mountains and it is costly to build surface infrastructure, air transport can play an important role. The boundaries also tend to vary slightly with culture – the United States is a car-oriented society and many even for the shortest of journeys do not consider walking or cycling.

In the previous chapter, Figure 4.1 provided a very stylized picture of the boundaries of the various transport modes. The crossover points represent 'distant boundaries' over which the modes compete. This competition takes a variety of forms. From the traveler's point of view, or that of a consignor of freight, a multiplicity of factors influences this type of decision.

In particular, travelers take notice of the time it takes to make a trip and the money costs involved and, frequently, also the quality of the service offered. Consignors are concerned not simply with the financial costs of carriage but also the speed, reliability and timetabling of the service. The demand for transport is not, therefore, simply dependent upon financial costs but rather on the overall opportunity costs involved. Transport is not unique in this, but it does differ from other services in that money costs may form only a relatively small part of overall costs. In terms of decision making, the money cost of a trip may have minimal influence over whether it is undertaken or the transport mode preferred – a fact that may explain the considerable use of private motorcars even when 'cheaper' alternative modes are available.[40]

User costs are also, according to Herb Mohring,[41] important in the urban public transport context for another reason. He argues that in the context of very frequent public transport in cities the main scale economy effects are associated with saving in passengers' time. These economies exist when the service is such that people do not arrive at a stop intending to catch a particular scheduled bus but rather know that headways are so close that at any time the wait will be short. If, say, the average headway is 10 minutes then the average wait, assuming random arrivals of passengers, will be five minutes. A reduction of headway to five minutes will reduce the average wait to two and a half minutes. Increased output of bus services, therefore, reduces average waiting time and thus the users' cost of traveling by bus.

In analyzing transport demand or when forecasting future consumer response it is often possible to assess responses to the individual components of overall cost, that is money costs, time costs, inconvenience costs and so on. In some situations, however, it has proved useful to have a composite measure. This may be true in situations where multidimensional cost functions are unwieldy or when a simple unidimensional measure, by focusing attention on general trends in cost, permits a clearer understanding of changes in the demand for transport services. A pragmatic device to reduce the wide range of costs involved in travel is to employ a single index expressing 'generalized cost'.

The generalized cost of a trip is expressed as a single, usually monetary, measure combining, generally in linear form, most of the important but disparate costs that form the overall opportunity costs of the trip. On occasions a generalized time cost measure may replace the financial index.[42] The characteristic of generalized cost is, therefore, that it reduces all cost items to a single index and this index may then be used in the same way as money costs are in standard economic analysis. Simply, generalized costs can be defined as:

$$G = g(C_1, C_2, C_3, \ldots, C_n) \tag{5.4}$$

where G is generalized cost and $C_1, C_2, C_3, \ldots, C_n$ are the various time, money and other costs of travel. This permits the demand for trips to be expressed as a function of a single variable – that is, $Q_D = f(G)$. While in simple indices, generalized cost is formed as a linear combination of time and money (or distance) costs, in most applied analysis the time and money components are divided into a number of elements (for example, walking time, waiting time, on-vehicle time and so on). This results in an expression of the general form:

[40] R. Sherman, 'A private ownership bias in transit choice', *American Economic Review*, **77**, 1211–17, 1967.
[41] H. Mohring, *Transportation Economics*, Cambridge, MA: Ballinger, 1976.
[42] P.B. Goodwin, 'Generalised time and the problem of equity in transport studies', *Transportation*, **3**, 1–24, 1974.

$$G = \sum_i M_i + \sum_j T_j, \tag{5.5}$$

where the M are the actual money costs of a journey, for example, fare or petrol costs, and T_j are the time costs, for instance, on-vehicle time and waiting time made up of the amount of time involved time the monetary value per unit of time (these were discussed in detail in Chapter 4).

For expositional ease, we take a fairly simple specific form of the generalized cost function that was used some time ago in the United Kingdom as part of the South-east Lancashire, North-east Cheshire (SELNEC) transport study conducted in the late 1960s,[43] which provides a useful illustration of actual application. It is dated, but it makes the key points rather neatly. The generalized cost index used in the combined trip distribution – modal split element of the analysis (see Chapter 12) was of the form:

$$G_{ij}^K = a_1 t_{ij}^K + a_2 e_{ij}^K + a_3 d_{ij}^K + p_j^K + \zeta^K \tag{5.6}$$

where:

G_{ij}^K is the generalized cost of travel by mode K between points i and j;
t_{ij}^K is the travel time from i to j by mode K (in minutes);
e_{ij}^K is the excess time (for example, waiting time for public transport) for the journey from i to j (in minutes);
d_{ij}^K is the distance from i to j that acts as a surrogate for the variable money costs of trips (that are assumed proportional to distance);
p_j^K is the terminal cost (for example, parking charges) at j (in pence);
ζ^K is a modal penalty reflecting the discomfort and lesser convenience associated with public transport journeys; and
a_1, a_2 and a_3 are parameters which, since p_j^K and ζ^K have unit coefficients, value other cost items in monetary terms.

An important issue is how these costs should be treated in analysis of transport decisions. Economics is concerned with costs that influence behavior in the short term and with those that affect long-term decisions. In the short term, people may well perceive only a limited range of costs or not fully appreciate the full magnitude of some cost items. Nevertheless, it is this set of costs that influences their immediate actions. The problem of perception is generally associated with the external costs that travelers generate by ignoring their actions (see Chapter 6) but here we are concerned with the misperception of the costs they bear themselves.

People misperceive the cost of their journeys (or of moving goods) for a number of reasons:

- The money or time cost may be so small that it is not worth taking into account.

[43] A.G. Wilson, H.F. Hawkins, G.J. Hills and D.J. Wagon, 'Calibration and testing of the SELNEC transport model', *Regional Studies*, **3**, 337–50, 1967.

- Certain variable costs may be regarded wrongly as fixed costs; included here would be the tendency for car users to take account only of petrol costs of journeys and ignore depreciation of the vehicle and its maintenance.
- Users may be unaware of the connection between a particular action and the costs to which it gives rise, for example, a fast driver may be unaware of the additional fuel costs he/she incurs.
- Habit can make regular trip makers unaware of changing cost conditions over time even if they were fully cognizant of the full resource costs of their actions at some earlier point in time. This is more likely to be a problem encountered by car users than public transport travelers who face regular ticket purchases.

While the final three reasons for misperception result from poor or inadequate information, the first represents a departure from the conventional economic idea of maximizing behavior. While this poses interesting theoretical questions, there are reasons for arguing that the last three are likely to be of greater quantitative importance for transport economists. Lack of good information is likely to result in different travel behavior from that anticipated in full information situations. Whereas perceived generalized costs offer a basis for travel behavior analysis, it is actual resource costs that are appropriate for investment decision taking. Where people accurately perceive the costs of their travel there is no difference between the perceived and resource generalized cost. Where there is misperception, however, resource costs, being the full opportunity cost of trip making, will exceed the perceived costs and this may result in overinvestment in transport facilities if adjustments are not made. (Of course, we are still ignoring external costs such as pollution but these complicate rather than change the argument.)

The social welfare gains associated with an investment are assessed by comparing the resource costs with the benefits generated. The difficulty is that the actual traffic levels using the facility depend upon perceived costs. In Figure 5.9 we have a linear demand curve for use of a road with an initial perceived generalized cost of usage equal to P^1. A widening of the road speeds traffic, causing the perceived generalized cost to fall to P^2.

If, however, the actual resource costs of trip making along the road are F^1 and P^2 for the respective pre- and post-investment situations, then there will be 'deadweight' welfare 'losses' generated at both the t^1 and t^2 traffic levels. (At the pre-investment traffic flow, t^1, this loss is equal to area c and at the post-investment flow, t^2, it is h.) If no account is taken of this, however, the apparent consumer surplus gain from the road widening is equal to (d + e + f + g). In fact, since the genuine resource costs are measured by F^1 and F^2, the investment will result in a net benefit of (b + c + d + e − h). The area (b + e + d) represents a straight resource cost saving under the demand curve by reducing the resource costs of travel, while (c − h) reflects the change in deadweight welfare loss between the two traffic flow situations. Henry Neuberger[44] generalized this calculation to

---

[44] H.L.I. Neuberger, 'Perceived costs', *Environment and Planning*, 3, 369–76, 1971.

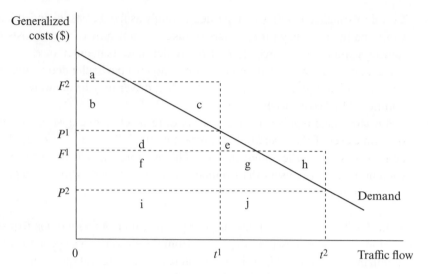

Figure 5.9 *Welfare gains from a cost reduction with misperceived transport costs*

take account of the effects of policies that alter costs and travel patterns over a network of roads.

The adoption of a single index idea of transport costs has permitted significant advances in transport forecasting and project appraisal to be made. This does not mean, however, that the concept is not without its critics, or that those choosing to ignore its existence have not made other advances. First, the inherent constraints implicit in aggregation of different elements of cost, in particular the aggregating of the various cost components into a unique index, restricts the separate elasticities of demand with respect to each individual cost component.[45] One ends up with an elasticity with respect to generalized costs but cannot, for example, assess the specific effect of a reduction in travel time costs.

Second, there is concern about the long-term stability of money as the numerator. Because income rises over time, it is argued, the utility of money will fall relative to other items, especially time, which is fixed in quantity. McIntosh and Quarmby,[46] therefore, argued that time should be used as the basis of measurement and the operational concept should be generalized time costs. Additionally, time is equally distributed (in the sense that everyone has 24 hours in a day) which circumvents some of the distributional difficulties of using money values of travel cost components. Third, even if the basic notion of generalized cost is accepted, there are critics who oppose the use of a 'universal' index for application throughout a country, for example of the form McIntosh and Quarmby put forward for the United Kingdom some years ago. A difficulty is that there is little evidence to support the universality of any weighting scheme employed. Although the use of official time valuations and formulae ensure consistency in approach, they may

[45] A. Grey, 'The generalised cost dilemma', *Transportation*, 7, 261–80, 1978.
[46] P.T. McIntosh and D.A. Quarmby, 'Generalized costs and the estimation of movement costs and benefits in transport planning', *Highway Research Record*, **383**, 11–23, 1972.

lead to inconsistencies in results if the overall index is accurate only in certain sets of circumstances.

Generalized cost is, despite these criticisms, a useful tool in helping us to understand, in broad terms, how variations in travel cost can influence travel behavior. Above all, it is an extremely useful pedagogical device that can help policy makers articulate their ideas and plans to a more general audience. It also serves as a pragmatic device for assisting in certain types of modeling and decision making where otherwise, as Searle[47] points out, no information would be forthcoming at all. In this context the index is likely to be an imperfect instrument but, when used with sufficient circumspection, it can yield useful insights into the possible effects of alternative transport policies.

5.7   The Bunching of Services

There often seems to be a bunching of buses on the roads, or a concentration of flights leaving at about the same time for a particular destination. In the bus case, this may simply be caused by traffic conditions that do not allow buses, with the frequency of their stops and their relative lack of dexterity, to keep up a schedule that on paper has more regular headways between them. But in many others cases bunching, and similar service features, result from deliberate actions on the part of suppliers of services. This may be because demand is peaked at certain times of the day and, therefore, that is the time that customers are willing to pay for having the 'bunch' of vehicles available. This logic extends to the large number of taxicabs at certain times waiting at airports, railway stations and other terminals. But the nature of supply and the product on offer can also lead to situations where the bunching is less desirable. This can also occur in terms of where transport infrastructure, such as gas stations, are located. Setting aside planning controls, even where there is a relatively free choice gas stations tend to be physically bunched.

The explanation for this phenomena, and the account of the costs that it creates, can be traced back to the work of Harold Hotelling over three-quarters of a century ago.[48] While his analysis was really designed to explain business location decisions and why manufacturers in markets with a limited number of large producers – known as 'oligopolies' these days – tend to produce very similar goods, it also has relevance to the issue of transport service bunching. The analysis can be explained by recourse to Figure 5.10.

The distances between points A ⇒ B ⇒ C in the figure represent 10-minute intervals. If there are potential users arriving continually and at an even rate then this flow can be taken as the lines between points A, B and C. We introduce two bus companies, X and Y, which offer identical fares and an infinite capacity to carry passengers. Thus passengers are indifferent as to which company's bus they

[47] G. Searle, 'Comment – generalized cost; fools gold or useful currency?', *Transportation*, **7**, 297–9, 1978.
[48] H. Hotelling, 'Stability in competition', *Economic Journal*, **39**, 41–57, 1929.

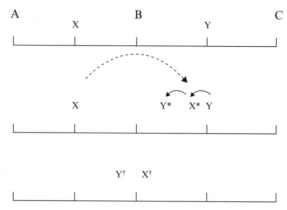

Figure 5.10   *The bunching of transport services*

make their trip in. Initially both companies operate their services at 20-minute headways, each offering seats midway along a time period. The average wait for a passenger is thus five minutes – if someone just misses the X's bus and has to wait for Y's then he/she has a 10-minute wait, but someone arriving coincidently with Y's bus has no wait. However, while this is an optimal situation, it is not an equilibrium because there is incentive for the bus companies to reschedule. X, for example, may reschedule its service to run just prior to Y's bus – say at X*. This will allow X to pick up virtually all the passengers that were waiting for Y's bus. Company Y, to remain in business, will then reschedule its service to, say, Y* and so take away most of the passengers that would be waiting for the X* service. This goes on until the companies time their 20-minute headways to coincide with each other – at X† and Y†.

This is an equilibrium because there is no incentive for either to change their services; alterations will mean smaller numbers of passengers. It is not, however, optimal from a passengers' perspective because now the average waiting time is 10 minutes – missing X's bus means a wait of 20 minutes for either X's or Y's next service with no wait for those that just turn up when a bus is due.

The nature of the competition and common costs for the two suppliers effectively cause an external cost for potential bus users, a topic we shall return to in Chapter 6. Of course the example is excessively simple, but there are records from the early part of the twentieth century of bus companies engaging in a whole series of practices akin to this – for example, missing out passengers at some stops to move ahead of another company's buses to collect a large line of customers later on in a route.[49] In reality, the degree of welfare loss due to a high level of waiting time is likely to be dissipated because consumers will not arrive at even intervals but will play their own 'games' with the bus companies to minimize their wait. Also the equilibrium conditions tend to break down with more than two bus operators and when complex networks of services come into play.

---

[49] C.D. Foster and J. Golay, 'Some curious old practices and their relevance to equilibrium in bus competition', *Journal of Transport Economics and Policy*, **20**, 191–216, 1986.

5.8 Elements of Economic Performance

It is generally assumed that firms seek to minimize their costs, and this is a common assumption when considering transport markets. In practice firms perform with varying degrees of efficiency. Further, performance can be measured in many dimensions; it may be in terms of whether costs of production are being minimized (X-inefficiency), whether output is at an optimal level (allocative efficiency), or whether resources are being wasted in protecting a particular, normally legal monopoly, market position (the so-called 'Tullock rent-seeking inefficiency').

We take the example of an airport and an airline and look at the potential implications for these various forms of efficiency when there are different market structures. The interest is in how actors seek to acquire rent (or profit) when there is no genuine capacity problem; in other words when they can exercise market power. Figure 5.11 represents, for simplicity, the short-run costs (MC) and demand (D) for take-off slots associated with a single runway airport. For ease of presentation the demand curve is drawn as linear, and the cost curve is horizontal. In most natural monopolies, because of various scale and scope economies, the cost curves would almost certainly be downward sloping. Introducing this, however, while more realistic, adds complexity but not substance to the argument.

There is assumed to be adequate capacity to meet all effective demand currently in the market. If there were a binding physical capacity constraint at a level before Q_C, as strict classic theory would require, then the MC curve would become vertical at the point where capacity is reached. This does not affect the fundamental tenure of the rent-seeking argument as presented here, and is thus ignored. But in these circumstances charges become a rationing device for the limited capacity as well as a reflection of the costs incurred in providing the existing capacity and as a means of extracting economic rent. The issue is the very simple one of the overall level and distribution of benefits from alternative allocating mechanism, assuming that only airlines and an airport are involved. It is assumed, unless stated otherwise, that both the airlines and the airport are seeking to be economic rent maximizers. This may be a strong assumption for those in public ownership where there may be valid arguments for considering other possibilities such as 'satisficing' with a series of lower objectives being sought, but it does provide the ability to keep the analysis manageable.

The ultimate outcome will depend on the nature of the market and the power of buyers and sellers,

- *Competitive airlines/competitive airport*   This yields the standard Pareto first best outcome of a price of P_C and an output of Q_C. The combined rent of buyers and sellers is maximized as the area ebP_C in Figure 5.11. The airlines enjoy the economic surplus from the use of the airport in this case because of the horizontal nature of the cost curve; with a positive slope the airport would also enjoy some rent but with a negative slope it would be losing

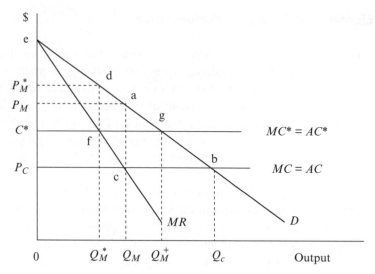

Figure 5.11   *Illustration of potential inefficiencies in a market for airport take-off/landing slots*

money. The same outcome in terms of overall slot use would emerge if the airport were a monopoly that is regulated requiring it to marginal cost price its slots or allocate them using a Vickrey[50] style of auction, whereby the highest bidder wins but pays an amount equal to the second-highest bidder, although here the airport would extract the rents from the airlines.

- *Monopoly airline (or strong strategic alliance)/competitive airport*   Since the airport has no market power, the airline, or cartel of airlines, will be able to force it to price its slots down to the airport's marginal cost of providing the slots, P_C. The airlines will again gain all of the economic rents, again ebP_C.
- *Competitive airlines/single pricing natural monopoly airport*   This is the neo-classic case of a monopoly with slot prices reaching P_M and the number of slots limited by the airport to Q_M. The gains from the airport's activities are shared between the airlines (eP_Ma) and the airport (P_MacP_C). But there is a welfare loss equal to the area abc – the Harberger[51] 'deadweight loss trian-gle'. This is the sort of institutional structure that one could imagine under a regime where the airport sets its slot prices at P_M and then allows any airline to take up slots at this rate with subsequent slot swapping allowed. If, once the slot fees have been paid, the airlines can buy and sell slots, then there would be transfers of benefits between them to the extent of aP_Me with no effect on either the airport's rent or aggregate welfare.
- *Competitive airlines/single pricing institutionalized monopoly airport*   Here the price and output combination is the same as the above but the airport will potentially enjoy a smaller rent and overall social welfare will be less.

[50] W. Vickrey, 'Counter-speculation, auctions, and competitive sealed tenders', *Journal of Finance*, **16**, 8–37, 1961.
[51] G. Harberger, 'Using the resources at hand more effectively', *American Economic Review Papers and Proceedings*, **59**, 134–47, 1959.

Gordon Tullock[52] argues that there is likely to be rent dissipation in this type of situation. The airport, to retain its institutional monopoly, will be willing to expend up to $P_M ac P_C$ in potential economic rent to defend this position – for example, through lobbying, political support, advertising or legal actions. Even a small amount of rent is preferred to none. Since such actions are essentially non-productive, at least in a non-Keynesian world, not only does it cost the airport money but it also represents a loss of social welfare.

- *Competitive airlines/perfect price discriminating natural monopoly airport*   In this case, through such actions as the auctioning of individual slots in a manner that allows first-degree price discrimination, the airport can extract slot prices down the demand curve. This action produces for the airport economic rent of $eb P_C$ with the airlines having none. The outcome is Pareto efficient and maximizes welfare. *De facto* this means that the demand curve represents the airport's marginal revenue curve with price differentiation. The outcome is Pareto optimal.

- *Competitive airlines/single natural monopoly airport with X-inefficiency* Harvey Leibenstein[53] argued that monopolies have limited incentive to minimize their costs but rather they often operate in an 'inert area' where there is little incentive to seek maximum efficiency. (Figure 5.12 illustrates the notion of an inert area. Managers can make trade-offs between the profits they may make by affecting costs and the efforts they put into the business. The additional profits tend to taper away with additional effort because more problems are encountered. At some point E^* the additional effort $(E_{Op} - E^*)$ is just not seen to justify the additional profit of $(\Pi_{max} - \Pi)$ required to maximize profits. Hence costs are not minimized.) This inertia may be brought on by a variety of factors such as the considerable managerial effort required to negotiate labor contracts when confronted by labor union demands. If this is the case then the cost curve will rise to MC^* in Figure 5.11 and the single profit-maximizing monopolist will limit the supply of slots to Q_M^* and extract rent amounting to $P_M^* df C^*$ The airlines will be left with $ed P_M^*$, but perhaps most important, the social welfare associated with slot use will be $P_M^* db P_C$ less than when there is competition in both the airline and airport markets.

- *Competitive airlines/perfect price discriminating natural monopoly airport with X-inefficiency*   The situation here is that the airport will provide Q_M^+ and enjoy economic rents of $eg C^*$, with the airlines taking none. Compared with the single pricing monopoly situation where there is no X-inefficiency, the aggregate social welfare is, though, reduced by $P_M ag C^*$

This categorization does not consider all possibilities – for example, there is no consideration of X-inefficiency among the airlines or of collusion between

52 G. Tullock, 'The welfare costs of tariffs, monopolies and theft', *Western Economic Journal*, 5, 224–32, 1967.
53 H. Leibenstein, 'Allocative efficiency vs "X-efficiency"', *American Economic Review*, **56**, 392–415, 1966.

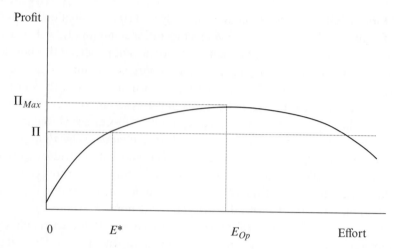

Figure 5.12 *The notion of an inert area*

the parties – but it does indicate the importance of the institutional, as well as technical, characteristics affecting efficiency in determining the levels of profits generated and the recipients of this rent.

5.9   Costs and the Measurement of Economic Efficiency

One can consider whether a transport undertaking is efficient, or whether its efficiency changes over time, by looking at either the costs of producing its outputs, which is the way we have discussed the subject so far, or the output that is generated from the inputs used: productivity. These measures are mirror images of each other. Cost functions relate costs to output quantities and input prices; production functions relate output quantities to input quantities.

Productivity improvement can come about in several ways. It could reflect reductions in inefficiency using existing technology, a shift in technological knowledge and capabilities, and/or differences in environmental or operating circumstances that affect input/output use. An example of the latter is a transport firm operating in adverse terrain. It will require more inputs per ton of cargo moved than firms operating in easy terrain; this is separate from questions of technological prowess. The concept of productivity of greatest importance is often that of technological change or 'shifts' in productive abilities. Improving efficiency using existing knowledge will encounter limits. Major long-term advances in industries' and society's wealth are causes by changes in productive abilities.

Returning to the strict cost side of the equation, the traditional method of assessing whether an undertaking is efficient was to rely on accountancy procedures that involved compiling data in relation to the various cost categories of interest and connecting these to the firm's outputs in largely an intuitive manner, generally assuming a linear relationship between the various costs and outputs. While useful for short-term decision making, the technique lacks any explicit causal link between inputs and outputs, which limits its usefulness for long-term decision making. Separating the impacts of fixed and variable costs is particularly problematic.

In the transport context, a somewhat more advanced accountancy framework is described by Ken Small,[54] and takes the form:

$$C = c_1 RM + c_1 PV + c_1 VH + c_1 VM \qquad (5.7)$$

where RM is route-miles, PV peak vehicles in service, VH vehicle-hours and VM vehicle-miles.

The accounts imply constant returns to scale, with total costs increasing by the same factor as any common increase across all the right-hand-side variables. If, however, RM is kept fixed and the other factors increase by a common factor, then the increase in total costs will be less than this, implying economies of density.

There are two broad approaches to quantitative performance ratings that are now more widely used than accountancy measures.[55] The first are statistical or econometric estimations of production or cost functions and the second, non-parametric or programming approaches. Before looking at these in detail, there is also a more basic, productivity indicator that entails 'benchmarking'. This is a generic concept referring to a process of identifying similar organizations or production activities, gathering quantitative and impressionistic data about the similarities and differences across the enterprises, and drawing conclusions about which are the most effective, and hence what other enterprises can learn from them. This may include quantitative performance comparisons but is not restricted to that. It often includes management organizational structures and practices. We do not discuss this in detail, but it is often used in practice (for example, by EUROCONTROL, the body overseeing European air traffic control, when comparing the efficiency of individual centers[56]) and focus on the more rigorous econometric and program approaches.

Statistical Cost and Production Functions

Statistical functions, with parameters normally estimated using regression analysis, are much more widely used in economic analysis. A statistical production function relates output to levels of inputs but because it is difficult to estimate a production function when firms produce more than one output, cost function approaches have been developed based on duality theory.[57] A cost function, is the dual to production technology in that it translates in a one-to-one fashion. The

54 K.A. Small, *Urban Transportation Economics*, New York: Harwood, 1992.
55 T.H. Oum, W.G. Waters and C. Yu, 'A survey of productivity and efficiency measurement in rail transport', *Journal of Transport Economics and Policy*, **33**, 9–42, 1999.
56 EUROCONTROL Performance Review Commission, Brussels, *6th ATM Effectiveness Benchmarking Report*, 2008.
57 D. McFadden, 'Cost, revenue, and profit functions', in M. Fuss and D. McFadden (eds), *Production Economics: A Dual Approach to Theory and Application*, Amsterdam: North-Holland, 1978.

cost function can be easily applied to multiple-output situations. Duality theory also recognizes that input prices replace the need for explicit measurement of input quantities. A cost function specifies the minimum cost of producing a given output obtainable from an input vector given the production technology, that is:

$$C = C(w, y, t) \tag{5.8}$$

where C is the cost, w is a vector of input prices, y is a vector of outputs, and t is the state of technology. (The production function approach relates outputs to inputs.)

Because the estimation involves the costing of producing y given the input vector, there is also the need to specify the motivations of the transport supplier and the technical relationship between the inputs and outputs involved.[58] Traditional econometric methods for estimating cost or production functions implicitly assume that all firms are successful in reaching the efficient frontier, and deviate only randomly. If, however, firms are not always on the frontier, then the conventional estimation method would not reflect efficient production or cost frontier against which to measure efficiency. For this reason, many studies now estimate frontier production or cost functions that recognize that some firms may not be on the efficient frontier, they are X-inefficient. We take this to be so here, although we shall return to the topic to in Chapter 6.

Logarithmically differentiating the cost function with respect to time decomposes the rate of growth of total cost into its sources: changes in input prices, growth of output, and rate of cost reduction due to technical progress:

$$\frac{\partial \ln C}{\partial t} = \left(\sum_{n=1}^{N} \frac{\partial \ln C}{\partial \ln w_n} \frac{\partial \ln w_n}{\partial t} \right) + \left(\frac{\partial \ln C}{\partial \ln y} \frac{\partial \ln y}{\partial t} \right) + \left(\frac{\partial \ln C}{\partial t} \right) \tag{5.9}$$

The rate of technical progress equals the negative of the rate of growth of total cost with respect to time, holding output and input prices constant. In a regression, this is the parameter measuring the shift in the cost function over time. When it comes to introducing technology into estimations, the accountancy approach, as seen in equation (5.7), assumes a linear relationship between inputs and outputs; often referred to as a Leontief technology. This means that there is no possibility of substituting one input for another in the production process. The Cobb–Douglas cost function, while being limited by having constant returns to scale, has been widely used in transport studies; for example, in the analysis of economies of scale in the British bus industry by Lee and Steedman cited earlier (see note 8), as well as American railroads.[59] It has the advantage that it does allow some factor substitution in production, and it is relatively easy to

[58] T.H. Oum and W.G. Waters, 'Recent developments in cost function research in transportation', *Logistics and Transportation Review*, **32**, 423–63, 1996.

[59] T.E. Keeler, 'Railroad costs, returns to scale, and excess capacity', *Review of Economics and Statistics*, **56**, 201–8, 1974.

estimate the coefficients in the model using regression techniques when expressed in natural logarithms. Its general form is:

$$\ln C = \beta_0 \sum_i \beta_i \ln y_i + \sum_j \gamma_j \ln w_j \qquad (5.10)$$

where i denote the inputs and j the outputs.

There may be systematic differences between firms otherwise employing the same technology, for example, differences in terrain or market location. Network variables could allow for differences in terrain, weather, or exogenous characteristics of the market area served such as more favorable directional flows of cargo and/or shorter average lengths of haul. Firm dummy variables (which by taking the value of unity or zero distinguish whether a firm is in a particular grouping or not) and firm-specific trend variables are sometimes incorporated to measure differences in productive efficiency across firms and over time. By controlling for these factors, the estimate with respect to time is a measure of the rate of technical change, that is, how the cost function is shifting over time. Bitzan and Keeler[60] have further separated out specific productivity changes (reduction in crew size and elimination of caboose) and show that there were sustained productivity gains in addition to the specific advances after railroad deregulation in the US.

A major constraint in using stochastic frontiers such as the Cobb–Douglas specification, and others such as the constant elasticity of substitution model, is the need to specify the detailed form of relationship between inputs and outputs. Additionally, none provide functions akin to the 'U-shaped' functions that are seen as the norm in economics as initially costs fall with production but ultimately rise as inputs become scarcer and thus more expensive. To circumvent this problem, variable 'flexible' forms of function have been developed. Perhaps the one most widely used in transport analysis is the translog model. This takes the general form in the case of total cost of:

$$\ln C = \beta_0 \sum_i \beta_i \ln y_i + \sum_j \gamma_j \ln w_j + \sum_i \sum_j \delta_{ij} \ln w_j \ln y_j$$
$$+ 0.5 \sum_i \sum_k e_{ik} \ln y_i \ln y_k + 0.5 \sum_j \sum_l \Phi_{jl} \ln w_j \ln w_l \qquad (5.11)$$

with the following cost share equations also being required:

$$S_j = \frac{\delta \ln C}{\delta \ln w_j} = \gamma_j + \sum_i \delta_{ij} \ln y_i + \sum_l \Phi_{il} \ln w_l$$

The flexible form approach does not need any prior specification of technology; it emerges from the estimation process. For example, Allen and Liu's[61] work on American trucking found constant to increasing returns to scale using

[60] J. Bitzan and T.E. Keeler, 'Productivity growth and some of its determinants in the deregulated US railroad industry', *Southern Economic Journal*, **70**, 232–53, 2003.

[61] W.B. Allen and D. Liu, 'Service quality and motor carrier costs: an empirical analysis', *Review of Economics and Statistics*, **77**, 499–510, 1995.

a translog model; Friedlander et al.,[62] by holding capital inputs constant, found increasing returns to density on the US railroads, as did Caves and associates[63] for airlines and Singh[64] for Indian urban buses.

The usual emphasis in cost function estimation is on the overall results, that is, the parameter values such as the degree of scale economies and measure of technological change. These are based on the common relationship revealed by statistical estimation across the set of firms and years. For performance comparisons, one also looks at individual firms relative to the estimated cost function. In estimating a cost function from combined cross-sections of firms and time-series data, it is common to include firm- and time-specific variables to remove the mean effect of systematic departures from the industry norm of particular firms or years. This is done to correct for possible omitted variables in the regression. For example, a particular trucking firm might enjoy unusually low costs because of some overlooked network advantage – perhaps the cities it serves are closer together than those for other firms. The cost and output data for this firm could distort the coefficients being estimated across the industry.

This practice, though, can sometimes prove to be counterproductive. Expressed as a 'fixed effects model', dummy variables are used to remove the mean deviation of the firm's observations from the common regression estimate. The firm in question may, however, be the largest in the industry. It might be scale economies explaining the firm's superior performance, and one would want to have left the firm's data unadjusted precisely to help measure scale economies. In terms of productivity comparisons, the firm dummies are capturing some of what is being sought: how does the firm compare to others? If it has systematically lower cost and this cannot be explained by known variables, the residual may be taken as an indicator of managerial performance. The value of a firm-specific dummy variable could be a performance indicator, but again, it could be that there are other factors explaining the firm's apparently superior performance. It is, therefore, important to examine the deviations of firms and years to see if there are possible explanations that need to be taken into account.

The total cost function formulation assumes that firms adjust all inputs instantaneously as outputs change. However, in reality they may not be able to adjust them all (especially capital stocks) as outputs change. To account for the short-run disequilibrium adjustment in capital stock, Gillen et al. in their work on airlines,[65] and others estimate variable cost functions, in which capital stock is treated as a

[62] A.F. Friedlander, E.R. Berndt, J.S. Chang, M. Showalter and C.A. Vellturo, 'Rail costs and capital adjustment in a quasi-regulated environment', *Journal of Transport Economics and Policy*, **24**, 9–34, 1993.

[63] D.W. Caves, R. Laurits and M.W. Tretheway, 'Economies of density versus economies of scale; why trunk and local airline costs differ', *Rand Journal of Economics*, **15**, 471–89, 1984.

[64] S.K. Singh, 'Costs, economies of scale, in urban bus transport: an analysis of municipal undertakings in India', *International Journal of Transport Economics*, **32**, 171–94, 2005.

[65] D.W. Gillen, T.H. Oum and M.W. Tretheway, 'Airline cost structure and policy implications', *Journal of Transport Economics and Policy*, **24**, 9–34, 1990.

fixed input, that is, the capital stock enters the cost function rather than the service price of capital. Separating out the influence of capital stocks and capital utilization is an important element in productivity studies, that is, distinguishing between productivity gains from capital investment or increased utilization of capital, as distinct from actual shifts in the function (technological change).

Productivity and cost measures irrespective of the way they are derived, assume that the quality of service provided is constant. This is a long-recognized shortcoming of most productivity measures, and the criticism remains. In the absence of acceptable quality measures, productivity measurement is biased because it measures quantity changes but not quality. Improving quality absorbs inputs, but the higher-quality output is not recognized except partially by a shift in weights if prices for higher-quality services rise relative to others. The inability to incorporate service quality is a major weakness of productivity measures.

An issue related to quality is that of capital utilization. If the flow of capital services is measured as strictly proportional to capital stocks (that is, the capital depreciates with the passage of time rather than actual use), then productivity gains can be obtained via higher utilization of the fixed or indivisible capital stocks. But high utilization of capital may be accompanied by deteriorating service such as congestion delays. Insofar as the deterioration of service is manifested by increases in the use of other inputs, this will offset the seeming productivity gain. But if congestion manifests itself in decreased service quality, standard productivity measures do not capture this. High utilization rates of capital may thus appear to imply high productivity but this might, in part, be misleading if there is deterioration in unmeasured service quality.

Programming Measures

Management programming methods directly compare quantities of outputs with quantities of inputs. The most widely used is data envelopment analysis (DEA), which is a mathematical programming technique that generates quantitative relative performance scores across 'decision-making units' such as bus companies or shipping lines, where multiple outputs and inputs are involved but there is no basis for assigning relative weights to the various inputs and outputs. Index numbers compare the growth in aggregate output to the corresponding changes in aggregate inputs. The aggregates are weighted sums of the growth rates of respective outputs and inputs, with economic weights (for example, revenues and costs) assigned to the outputs and inputs.

Programming measures of efficiency involve index number procedures that construct a ratio-type productivity/efficiency measure from measures of outputs and inputs. They are non-parametric; that is, a direct numerical calculation in contrast to the statistical estimation used in the production or cost function approach. They may take a number of forms, including partial productivity ratios, such as DEA, and total factor productivity (TFP). Once a measure of productivity is developed, it can be 'decomposed' into sources of productivity gains to isolate pure technological change in contrast to other influences on productivity, such as X-inefficiency.

Partial productivity measures relate a firm's output to a single input factor such as revenue tonne-kilometers divided by the number of employees to measure labor productivity. This is tracked over time or compared with other companies or operations. However, the productivity of any one input depends on the level of other inputs being used; high productivity performance in one input may come at the expense of low productivity of other inputs. Despite this limitation, partial productivity measures remain in wide use, and can provide useful insights into causes of differential performance across firms operating in similar operating environments or over time within a firm when the operating environment and input prices remain relatively stable.

DEA becomes useful when firms employ a number of inputs and generally produce a number of outputs. It can be used for ranking the relative efficiency of decision-making units, say different urban bus fleets or airports, in this context. With multiple outputs and inputs, weights are usually needed to aggregate the various output and input categories to construct an index to rate different units. DEA uses linear programming to solve for a set of weights that will maximize each unit's or firm's performance rating relative to others in the dataset.

In its most basic form, we can take a case where W and Z are the inputs in an airline-wide sample of n carriers and w and z are the corresponding observations of a typical airline. The airline's efficiency index, Θ, assuming free disposability and variable returns to scale is the solution to the linear program:

Choose $\{\Theta, \lambda\}$ to: min Θ such that: $\Theta w \geq \lambda' W$

$$z \leq \lambda' Z$$

$$\lambda_i \geq 0, \Sigma\lambda_i = 1, i=1, 2,\ldots, n \qquad (5.12)$$

An illustration is seen in Figure 5.13, which depicts production, rather than cost, frontiers. We consider the efficiency with which a number of bus companies with identical vehicle fleets use their labor input to provide peak (X) and off-peak (Y) services. The black dots represent the combinations of peak and off-peak passenger seat-miles each operator provides. Those enterprises on the 'old frontier' are deemed to be the most efficient users of their labor over the two periods, although no judgment can be made about whether company M, which offers a relatively large amount of peak services is preferable to N, which focuses on using its labor for off-peak services. To make that judgment one needs to know the demands for the different types of services. The filled stars indicate what may happen to the frontier over time as technology improves.

DEA can be a useful procedure for establishing relative performance scores where multiple outputs and inputs are present yet their relative importance (weights) are not evident. But it has its limitations. While other suppliers inside the frontier are relatively inefficient, being on the frontier does not imply maximum efficiency; indeed all the companies may be inefficient but differ in their degree of inefficiency. There are methods of measuring the extent to which suppliers fall behind those on the frontier, but these may be sensitive to the ways in which measurements are made; for example, is the measurement the vertical distance from

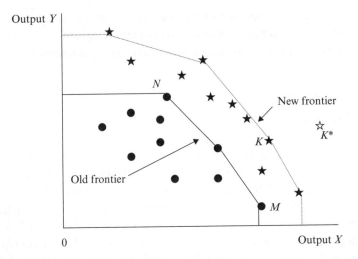

Note: ● denotes performance of firms in the first period; ★ denotes performance of firms in the second period.

Figure 5.13   *Production frontier for two outputs, observed at two different time periods*

the frontier, the horizontal distance, or some average of the two? The results are also sensitive to outliers. The shape of the frontier can differ considerably if there is, say, one supplier that is well away from the remainder. This can be seen in the figure if instead of producer K in the second period being located at the position denoted by the ★, it is located at the unfilled star ☆ (that is, $K*$). Finally, the technique does not in itself allow for any assessment of causality – it basically provides a ranking mechanism indicating levels of cost (or production efficiency), offering insights as to the underlying causes of the differences between suppliers.

Given the availability of easy-to-use software, there are numerous examples of applications of DEA in transport, for example, Bookbinder and Qu[66] who calculated DEA scores for seven large North American railroads, and explored the effects of different numbers of outputs and inputs as well as reducing the number of firms. Another case study is by Oum and Yu,[67] who analyzed OECD railways for the period from 1978 to 1989, employing two types of output measure, and evaluating and interpreting the relative efficiency scores. Button and Costa examined the efficiency of local transport in a number of European cities,[68] and Scheraga[69] and

[66] J.H. Bookbinder and W.W. Qu, 'Comparing the performance of major American railroads', *Transportation Research Form*, **33**, 70–85, 1993.
[67] T.H. Oum and C. Yu, 'Economic efficiency of railways and implications for public policy: a comparative study of the OECD countries' railways', *Journal of Transport Economics and Policy*, **28**, 121–38, 1994.
[68] K.J. Button and A. Costa, 'Economic efficiency gains from urban public transport regulatory reform: two case studies of changes in Europe', *Annals of Regional Science*, **33**, 425–38, 1999.
[69] C. Scheraga, 'Operational efficiency vs. financial mobility in the global airline industry: a data envelopment analysis and Tobit analysis', *Transportation Research A*, **38**, 383–404, 2004

Fare et al.[70] looked at airlines, just to provide a few examples. Some studies have used both parametric and non-parametric techniques to confirm their findings, as, for example, did Good and co-workers when comparing the efficiency of European and US airlines.[71]

Further Reading

A.A. Walters, 'The long and the short of transport', *Bulletin of the Oxford Institute of Economics and Statistics*, **27**, 97–101, 1965 is a classic paper offering a useful theoretical examination of the more technical issues involved in separating short- from long-run transport costs; it is also nonmathematical in its approach. R.R. Braeutigam, 'Learning about transport costs', in J.A. Gómez-Ibáñez, W.B. Tye and C. Winston (eds), *Essays in Transportation Economics and Policy: A Handbook in Honor of John R. Meyer*, Washington, DC: Brookings Institute, 1999, and E. Pels and P. Rietveld, 'Cost functions in transport', in D.A. Hensher and K.J. Button (eds), *Handbook of Transport Modelling*, 2nd edn, Amsterdam: Elsevier, 2008, provide up-to-date outlines of thinking about economic cost analyses of the transport industries.

Regarding particular issues, Bill Waters's study of railway costing (W.G. Waters, II, 'Rail cost analysis', in K.J. Button and D.E. Pitfield (eds), *International Railway Economics*, Aldershot: Gower, 1985) offers insights into the practical problems of applying these principles. J. Berechman and G. Giuliano, 'Economies of scale in bus transit: a review of concepts and evidence', *Transportation*, **12**, 13–32, 1985 provides a review of econometric work on scale effects in bus operations, and contains both a careful assessment of measuring problems and good coverage of recent findings. *The Road Track Cost Report* (London: UK Ministry of Transport, 1968) still provides interesting reading for those interested in the practical problems of finding a workable method of allocating track cost to users. Grey's paper on generalized costs (A. Grey, 'The generalized cost dilemma', *Transportation*, **7**, 261–80, 1978), although now somewhat dated, contains both a more detailed description of the theory behind the concept and an account of its uses besides being a carefully argued, stimulating and clearly presented criticism of generalized cost as a tool in transport economics. While almost an antique, R. Dorfman, P. Samuelson and R. Solow, *Linear Programming and Economic Analysis*, New York: McGraw-Hill, 1958, is still an excellent introduction to the subject, while C. Charnes, W. Cooper, A. Lewin and L. Seiford (eds), *Data Envelopment Analysis: Theory, Methodology and Applications*, Boston, MA: Kluwer, 1995 offers a good overview of DEA analysis.

[70] R. Fare, S. Grosskopf and R.C. Sickles, 'Productivity of US airlines after deregulation', *Journal of Transport Economics and Policy*, **41**, 93–112, 2007.

[71] D.H. Good, D.H. Röller and R.C. Sickles, 'Airline efficiency differences between Europe and the US: implications for the pace of EC integration and domestic regulation', *European Journal of Operations Research*, **80**, 508–18, 1995.

6   The External Costs of Transport

6.1   Introduction

Chapter 5 was concerned with showing the types of financial and other costs directly confronting transport users. It is quite clear from our everyday experience, however, that there are other costs associated with transport that are not directly borne by those generating them. Some of these affect those not traveling, such as when air travelers impose noise costs on those living below aircraft flight paths, and when road travelers inflict dirt and vibration on those living adjacent to major trunk routes while, at the same time, impeding the progress of pedestrians in towns. Maritime transports frequently pollute bathing beaches with their oil discharges, and the construction of ports disrupts local breeding grounds for birds and sea life.

These are external costs generated by transport users and inflicted on the non-traveling public. But they are not the only form of negative externality. A car driver entering a congested stream of traffic slows fellow drivers; an effect external to the driver but different from environmental effects in that the cost is contained within transport.

This chapter focuses initially on the former type of external effect – the imposition of uncompensated effects created by transport users on the general public or some part of it – and then moves on to look at the challenges imposed by various forms of traffic congestion, which is really about managing the internal workings of the transport system more effectively by optimizing the external costs that one set of users imposes on another. But we begin with some definitions and some clarifications.

6.2   What Are Externalities?

Formally, in economics externalities exist when the activities of one group (either consumers or producers) affect the welfare of another group (consumers or producers) without any payment or compensation being made. They may be thought of as relationships other than those between a buyer and a seller, and do not normally fall within the 'measuring rod of money' or within a complete market.

There are also external benefits as well as costs, although these are generally thought less important in the transport sector. The fact that wide streets, for example, act as fire-breaks, in addition to serving as transport arteries, may be thought of as an external benefit associated with urban motorways. One reason why external benefits are less common than their counterparts is that there is an incentive for those producing them to bring them into the market and charge for them. A simple example of this may be when railway enthusiasts (often called 'foamers' in the United States and 'gricers' in the United Kingdom) who formerly enjoyed standing on railway platforms watching trains – a benefit generated by the railway company and enjoyed free by the enthusiasts – are then charged for accessing platforms.

A vast theoretical literature has grown up over the last 70 years or more refining the rather complicated concept of external costs. There are, for example, often confusions between externalities and such things as public goods that we shall return to later. While much of the detail of this work has a greater or lesser importance in a transport context there are two major distinctions that need to be highlighted.

Pecuniary and Technological Externalities

The formal difference between these two categories of externality is that when the latter effects occur in production (or consumption) they must appear in the production (or utility) function, while this is not the case with pecuniary externalities. Pecuniary effects occur when, say, a firm's costs are affected by price changes induced by other firms' actions in buying and selling factors of production. An example can help to clarify this. A new motorway may block or destroy a pleasant view formerly enjoyed by the resident of an area. The fact that this directly enters the resident's utility function means that if no compensation is paid, this is a technological externality. If this new motorway also takes business away from a local garage and transfers it to a new motorway service station, then the reduced income suffered by the garage proprietor is a pecuniary externality since the effect is indirect, namely through changes in the prices charged by the two undertakings.

The distinction is a fine one, particularly since in practice both forms of externality usually occur simultaneously, but it is an important one. Technological externalities are real resource costs that strictly should be taken into account in decision making if optimal efficiency is to be ensured. Pecuniary externalities do not involve resource costs in an aggregate sense, but they do normally have important distributional implications (for example, in our motorway example the service station gains while the local garage loses).

The fact that there may be pecuniary externalities associated with a project does not reduce the aggregate net benefit, but rather reveals that there are adjustments in the economy which influence who is to enjoy the gains and who is to suffer the costs. The distinction between technological and pecuniary externalities is, therefore, important in the appraisal of public sector transport investments where one is concerned with the incidence of the costs and benefits in addition to their overall level (see Chapter 11). The pecuniary external effects can, for example, raises matters of environmental justice.[1]

---

[1] K.E. Haynes, 'Transportation location and environmental justice: a US perspective', in D.A. Hensher, K.J. Button. K.E. Haynes and P. Stopher (eds), *Handbook of Transport Geography and Spatial Systems*, Amsterdam: Elsevier, 2004.

The Distinction between Pollution and Congestion

Conventional welfare economics distinguishes between varieties of techno-logical externality categories according to the different types of agent involved. Rothenberg[2] offers a simple dichotomy that is possibly of more use in the transport context than some of the more complicated categorizations. He distinguishes between two forms of what he calls 'generic congestion'. The underlying idea is that externalities result from attempts by different agents to share a common service that is not provided in discrete units earmarked for each (in a technical sense, it has 'public good' characteristics). The presence of other users already affects the quality of service that is rendered to each. Generic congestion may, in technical terms, be divided into:

- *Pure pollution* 'The essence of pollution . . . is that there are some other users who do abuse the medium – the polluters – while others are relatively passive victims of such abuse – the public. Jet planes make the noise, house-wives are forced to submit to it.'
- *Pure congestion* 'If highway traffic is the classic example of congestion, then the central inter-personal distributive fact about it is that all users are using the medium (the public good) in much the same way, each is damaging service quality for both others and himself, and the ratio of self/other damage is approximately the same for all users . . . The whole user group loses homogeneously by their self-imposed interaction.'

Another way of looking at externalities, and one developed by Alain Bonnafus,[3] is according to the domain that they affect. The alternative typology is illustrated in Figure 6.1. Here we see a succession of overlapping spheres that address the question of 'external to what?'. The inner sphere is essentially the firm (which may be any producer of transport services, bus company or shipping line, but may also be treated as a driver of a car supplying transport services to him- or herself). The agent is the perpetrator of the externalities. The second ring reflects what are often called 'Marshallian externalities' and captures what we have termed 'pure congestion': a truck entering a congested road and slowing down others further. The third ring, reflects what Bonnafus sees as the external costs of a transport company paid for by the community; basically these are subsidies for operations and infrastructure maintenance not captured in user fees. The penultimate ring reflects interpersonal external effects, such as lack of safety or noise. Finally, the outer ring embraces the quality of the larger, potentially global, environment that is affected by the emissions of the truck.

The advantage of this type of approach from an economic perspective is that

---

2. J. Rothenberg, 'The economics of congestion and pollution: an integrated view', *American Economic Review, Papers and Proceedings*, **60**, 114–21, 1970.
3. A. Bonnafous, 'Summary and conclusions, in Organisation for Economic Co-operation and Development', *Internalizing the Social Costs of Transport*, Paris: OECD, 1994.

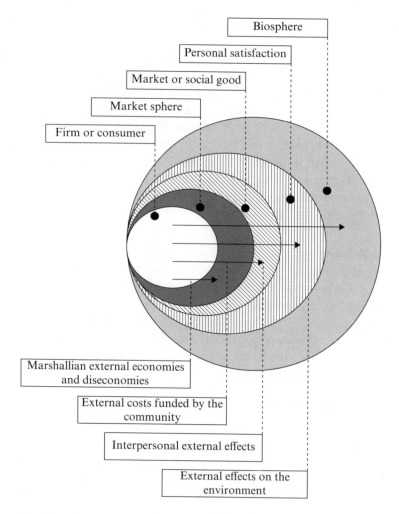

Figure 6.1   *The economic relationships between external effects*

it provides an indication of where the market failings are in the broader scheme of things, and also where the incidence of the external costs are being borne. The movement from conceptualization to practical valuation and analysis of alternative ways of dealing with the various forms of externality is, however, made no simpler. We do not, therefore, attempt to look at all the domains illustrated but focus on those particularly relevant for transport, namely those involving pure pollution and pure congestion.

6.3   Transport and the Environment

Transport pollutes the physical environment in a number of ways, which can also be seen in a stylized manner in relation to their broad geographical and temporal incidence in Figure 6.2:

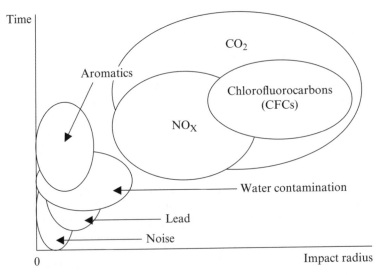

Figure 6.2   *The time and spatial coverage of exhaust gases and other environmental intrusions*

- Transport imposes many local environmental costs on those living, working or taking recreation near major pieces of transport infrastructure. These include such factors as noise, visual intrusion, local air pollution (for example, particulates, lead and carbon monoxide) and the disposal of obsolete vehicles. A major problem here is that, unlike many other forms of environmental intrusion, it is generally difficult to move transport facilities away from sensitive areas simply because users demand easy access and close proximity to roads and to public transport terminals.
- There are transboundary effects such as emissions that contribute to acid rain (such as NO_X) and maritime spillages that have impacts some distance from the transport activities themselves. This poses challenges of interjurisdictional authority at the national level, and often within federal systems at the state level.
- There is the contribution of transport to the global environmental problems of global warming (such as emissions of CO_2) and to upper-level ozone depletion (in particular CFCs). As we shall see in Chapter 8, these pose particular challenges because of their long-term effects and the need for coordinated, global approaches to handle them.

A very general indication of the contribution of transport to some of the atmospheric problems associated with light mechanized transport in the United States is set out in Table 6.1. Table 6.2 offers a similar breakdown for the United Kingdom, although here covering all transport modes. It is noticeable that many of the pollutants are becoming less of a problem per mile traveled, but of course, transport use is growing and partly offsets this.

Many environmentalist groups argue for substantial reductions or total elimination of these adverse environmental effects, but this ignores the cost

Table 6.1   *Average US light gasoline and diesel vehicle emission rates (grams per mile)*

	1990	1995	2000	2005	2007
Light-duty gasoline vehicles					
Exhaust HC	2.79	1.57	0.97	0.52	0.42
Nonexhaust HC	1.21	1.05	0.91	0.72	0.62
Total HC	4.00	2.62	1.88	1.25	1.04
Exhaust CO	42.89	26.60	18.53	0.58	10.28
Exhaust NO_X	2.70	1.78	1.29	0.92	0.73
Light-duty diesel vehicles					
Exhaust HC	0.68	0.77	0.80	0.60	0.36
Exhaust CO	1.49	1.69	1.78	1.57	1.21
Exhaust NO_X	1.83	1.89	1.81	1.32	0.85

Source: US Bureau of Transportation Statistics.

Table 6.2   *Pollutant emissions from transport in the United Kingdom (thousand tons)*

	1995	2000	2005	Percent of National Income in 2005
CO	4,180	2,500	1,124	46.5
NO_X	1,098	818	549	33.8
PM_{10}	53.6	38.6	33.7	22.5
Benzene	28.4	5.6	3.4	20.8
1,3 butadiene	7.4	3.8	1.6	60.8
P_b	1.049	2.2	2.1	1.7
SO_2	51.8	6.7	3.0	0.4

Source: UK Department for Transport.

associated with removing such nuisances. While some people suffer from the environmental intrusion associated with transport, others clearly benefit from being able to travel more freely or move goods more cheaply. In almost all cases, environmental improvements would reduce the net benefits enjoyed by transport users. Economists tend, therefore, to think in terms of optimizing the level of pollution rather than 'purifying' the environment entirely.

If we look at Figure 6.3, we see plotted on the vertical axis the money value of the costs and benefits of reducing the noxious fumes emitted by motorcars and, on the horizontal, the environmental improvements that accompany a reduction in such fumes. The marginal costs (*MC*) of reducing the emissions are likely to rise quite steeply. While more sophisticated filters may be fitted and fuel subjected to more extensive refining, both become increasingly costly to apply as the toxicity of the exhaust is reduced. Additionally, they reduce the efficiency of vehicles and may, in the case of improved refining, impose higher levels of pollution on those living around refineries.

The marginal benefits (*MB*) of 'cleaner' road vehicles, in contrast, are likely to fall with successive improvements. The public is likely to be relatively less conscious of lower levels of emission and be aware that many of the seriously toxic

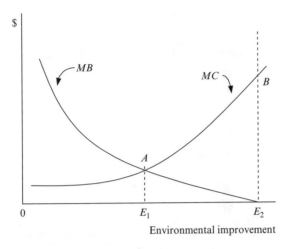

Figure 6.3   *The optimal environmental improvement*

materials (for example, lead) are likely to be among the first to be removed in the clean-up program. Consequently, the marginal cost and revenue curves associated with improved emission quality are likely to be of the form seen in Figure 6.3.

There is quite clearly an optimal level of improvement (that is, $0E_1$) beyond which the marginal costs of further emission reductions exceed the marginal benefits. If the clean-up program reduced emissions to the point where further reductions would yield no additional benefit (that is, exhaust fumes would be considered 'pure' although this may not mean zero toxicity if individuals' perceptions are faulty), then the situation is not optimal. Improvements beyond $0E_1$ to $0E_2$, in fact, result in a net welfare loss equal to the area ABE_2 in the diagram.

Consequently, when talking about the excessive environmental harm caused by various forms of transport it is important to remember that this is an excess above the optimal level of pollution, not above zero pollution or some perceived 'pure' environment. We shall return to this topic and methods of attaining the optimum in Chapter 8.

6.4   The Valuation of Externalities

Physical measures of environmental damage are helpful, and a necessary input into analyzing their economic implications, but the diversity of measurements used and impacts generated limit their usefulness. To compare the external costs and benefits of transport with other features of transport it is often found useful to convert such costs and benefits into monetary terms. This is no easy task but economists have developed a number of procedures that, at least in the case of some externalities, do provide reasonable guidance to the value of these external effects. In recent years the level of sophistication used in this process has risen considerably and only a very brief outline of some of the more common techniques is set out below.

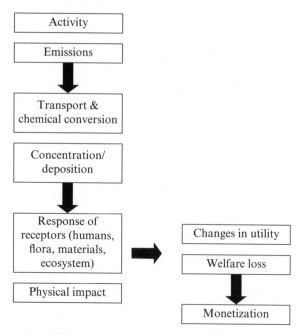

Figure 6.4   *The stages of putting a money value on an externality*

The various stages in valuation are shown in Figure 6.4. As can be seen, it is a sequential process embracing many disciplines beside economics: indeed, without good physical measurement and scientific understanding of the consequences of environmental intrusion the economic analysis would not be possible. The immediate focus will be on the various techniques that go into 'monetization' of the various externalities, and in the following section we shall consider some of the empirical work that has been conducted.

Precedents

Consistency over time is the prime reason for suggesting that historical precedents could be used as a means of valuing certain aspects of the environment. Precedents in this context largely comprise legal, judicial rulings on compensation for inflicting environmental damage. While having some superficial attractions, the procedure, however, has severe limitations.

The main applications of this approach in transport have been in terms of valuing injury and death in transport accidents although there are numerous instances of transport suppliers, and especially shipping companies, having to compensate for spillage of toxic pollutants, and there are often rulings on compensation on such things as the additional noise nuisance associated with an airport expansion.

Precedents exist only where there are established rights, and these extend to very few environmental attributes. Even without this practical limitation, the usefulness of the techniques is restricted by the nature of most legal systems. They normally apply to the need for victims (including relatives of people killed) of the incident to be cared for during the remainder of their life. Consequently, where the environmental damage causes death, the 'cost' to the deceased is not considered. Equally, damage to flora and fauna is generally outside of the scope of legal rulings on compensation. Finally, where evidence has been produced looking at legal precedence it tends to show little by way of a consistent pattern.

Averting Behavior

Many adverse environmental consequences of transport can be ameliorated by insulation. Noise nuisance can be reduced by double-glazing windows, the adverse effects of air pollution by installing air conditioning, and accident risk by the adoption of safer engineering design standards for transport infrastructure (for example, relating to road surfaces and air traffic control radar), the ways in which it may be used (for example, speed limits), and the design of vehicles that use it (for example, air bags and seat belts in cars). A widely deployed technique for assessing the costs of environmental damage is to equate them with the cost of avoidance, often called the 'prevention expenditure' method.

The main problem is the difficulty of isolating specific expenditures made for environmental reasons from the implicit joint expenditure on other benefits accompanying, for example, double-glazing (such as, reduced heating bills and so on) or air conditioning (for example, a cooler room temperature). Noise insulation is also only partial in that it does not offer protection when one is in the garden or when windows are open. More fundamentally, there are questions about the optimality of the level of avoidance adopted. In terms of safety, for example, the aviation industry provides an extremely safe product but only at a tremendous cost. In terms of potential lives saved, each is implicitly valued more highly than, say, a life saved on the roads where the per capita safety expenditure is much lower.

Assessing damage is the mirror image of this averting behavior, looking at the environmental costs of lost production or the damage done in repairing the problems caused by environmental damage – for example, adding lime to water polluted by traffic-related NO_X emissions. The cost of pollution on health can be related to the days of work lost by, for example, more frequent asthma attacks due to fuel additives or from lack of sleep due to aircraft noise. Isolating these costs can be difficult; there is a need to make a full life assessment of their impacts on individual or production.

Revealed Preference: Hedonic Prices

There are circumstances where consumers of environmental resources, through their actions, implicitly reveal the values that they place on them. They make trade-offs involving sacrificing some monetary benefits to limit the use of environmental resources, or to gain some environmental benefit. The classic case is the willingness of people to pay to live away from noisy airports or roads or to pay a

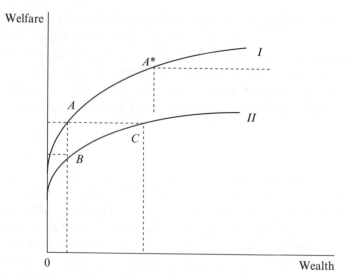

Figure 6.5   *The basic trade-off model*

premium for a hotel room away from a busy street. But these choices, as we saw earlier with the discussion of generalized costs, also extend to travel time values that involve trade-offs between such things as external and internal attributes of modes and travel speeds.

The underlying theory can be discussed in terms of Figure 6.5, which plots the welfare enjoyed by an individual at various levels of wealth. The diminishing marginal utility of money gives, for example, the trade-off curve *I* for an individual living in a quiet, rural setting. The construction of an airport adjacent to the house imposes measurable noise costs on this person and, for every level of wealth, this pulls the trade-off curve down, that is, it becomes *II*. If the person was initially at a point *A* on *I* then the imposition of the noise will reduce welfare to level *B*. To get that person back to his/her original welfare level, wealth compensation of *BC* would be needed, this being sufficient to move him/her around *II* until the original level of welfare is restored.

This approach assumes, however, that there is a finite level of compensation that satisfies the individual. If, however, one starts at an initial position *A** then it is not altogether clear that this is so. (This type of problem essentially arose as early as the late 1960s when researchers were trying to value the noise costs of aviation at alternative sites for a third London airport – eventually an arbitrary value was adopted for some individuals.[4]) Second, the onus of the technique as described is on compensation. One would normally get a different value by taking the amount adversely affected individuals would be required to pay to bribe the authorities not to construct the airport (that is, the amount necessary to get back to the higher trade-off curve at the new level of welfare *B*).

In practical terms, revealed preference techniques normally require sophisticated econometric analysis. This is because most goods involve a variety of

---

[4] Commission on the Third London Airport, *Report*, London: HMSO, 1971.

attributes of which environmental elements represent only a subset. In consequence, the normal approach is to use a hedonic price index that puts values on the diverse attributes of the good being examined (for example, the various features of houses in the noise case mentioned above). In general terms this means estimating:

$$C_h = F(c_1, c_2, c_3, \ldots, c_n) \tag{6.1}$$

where C_h is the consumption of housing services $c_1, c_2, c_3, \ldots, c_n$.

The specifications of individual models differ, indeed one of the problems with hedonic indices is that of model specification, but whatever form they take they seek to isolate the 'price' of each characteristic in the equation.

This leads on to a further problem. It is necessary to have a substantial amount of information on the determinants of, in our example, housing selection processes just to gain an insight into the value of one environmental influence. Many hedonic studies employ a wide variety of variables. It is also important that the characteristics used are the ones perceived to be important to house occupiers and buyers – the perceived housing market attributes. It is not the actual set of characteristics that determine hedonic prices, but rather the characteristics as seen by those active in the housing market. This often leads to the implicit, but seldom accurate assumption, that all those in the market have complete information of all housing attributes. The assumption is also that all such attributes are tangible and measurable so as to be incorporated in the econometric estimation.

Travel Cost Method

The travel cost method is a particular form of revealed preference analysis. New transport infrastructure can open up recreation sites such as parks and fishing facilities that have been provided at a zero price. People, however, travel to such locations to make use of the natural amenities and thus incur a measurable travel cost in terms of both time and money. Use can be made of this information to gain some idea of the value of such facilities.[5] This is a special case of the more general revealed preference approach.

Figure 6.6 offers guidance to the simplest travel cost approach. Surveys find that the number of visits to, say, a park from an origin A amounts to X_a and from B to X_b. Further, the actual average generalized travel costs (that is, including travel time costs) for these trips amount to Pa and Pb respectively, from the two origins. A succession of further surveys looking at other origins enables the distance decay function to be derived. From this the consumer surplus derived from visiting the park and enjoyed by an individual living in A is seen to be area

[5] V.K. Smith, 'Selection and recreation demand', *American Journal of Agricultural Economics*, **70**, 29–36, 1988.

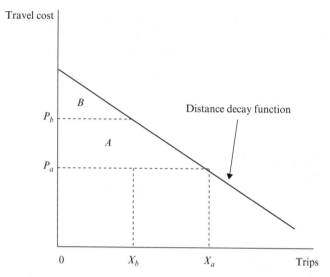

Figure 6.6   *The basic travel cost method*

$(A + B)$. The surplus for those making trips from B is equal to area B. Similar calculations can be carried out for each origin to get the aggregate surplus.

The main application of the technique is in evaluating specific types of environmental impact, but is of less use where there are a number of environmental factors involved and one wishes to evaluate them individually. Perhaps a bigger problem, however, is the need to specify the generalized cost function which itself should include a monetary value of travel time. While, as we have seen, the work on the value of travel time is extensive, the subject is itself at least as controversial as that in the field of environmental evaluation.

Stated Preference

Stated preference techniques (often called 'contingency valuations' in the environmental literature), which have their basis in experimental economics,[6] do not involve attempting to place values on environmental costs by observing actual trade-offs but rather seek to elicit information on the trade-offs individuals would make when confronted with particular situations. It provides individuals with a mental experiment, a pseudo-market that involves decision making within a controlled environment as far as the information they have and the options open to them.

The most widespread approach is that of asking, through questionnaires and surveys, or interactive computer games, a relevant group of individuals either what compensation they would need to keep them at their current level of welfare if some predefined transport-induced environmental degradation took place or, alternatively, what amount would they be willing-to-pay to prevent

---

[6] L.V. Smith, 'Microeconomic systems as an experimental science', *American Economic Review*, **72**, 923–55, 1982.

this occurrence.[7] The questions are set in an institutional context (for example, to make it clear what methods of finance are involved) and, so as to provide a market framework, the questioner initiates the process by suggesting an opening 'bid' to which the respondent reacts. The questions need to be couched carefully to ensure that the hypothetical trade-offs are clear and that the potential problems with the techniques are minimized.

Inevitably questions arise as to the extent the information gained through a stated preference approach is that which would emerge if an actual market existed. Strict comparisons are not possible, since, by definition, no actual market exists in the stated preference context, but comparisons with other techniques can, at least, give some indication of consistency. In their analysis of a number of case studies (which were not transport specific) where stated preference techniques were deployed alongside other methods of evaluation, Pearce and Turner[8] found that there was a 'reassuring' degree of overlap in the findings reported. Differences do, however, still exist and it is difficult to decide whether this reflects variations in the quality of individual studies or is a reflection of the usefulness of differing techniques.

One of the main problems in using the above set of procedures is that they do not all have the same theoretical underpinnings and this makes comparisons of results difficult. Is it valid, for example, to compare a value for noise pollution derived from an averting study with a value of air pollution derived from a stated preference study? It may also be argued that stated preference is more likely to yield meaningful results for local environmental effects such as traffic noise and road accidents because these are effects that people are more generally familiar with, and thus they are capable of making trade-offs in experimental situations.[9]

6.5   The Magnitude of the Environmental Externality Problem

The discussion so far has provided some general account about the nature of the external environmental costs of transport and explanations of some ways these may be expressed in a way useful for economic analysis. For example, Figure 6.3 presented hypothetical marginal cost and benefit curves associated with reducing motor vehicle exhaust emissions, but to make good practical use of these concepts, as we have emphasized, it is first necessary to measure physically the levels of pollution and then to put a monetary value on the units of pollution generated.

Here we look at the measurement problem and consider some of the ways in which pollution has been evaluated in practice and the results obtained. There

[7] R.T. Carson, 'Contingent valuations: a user's guide', *Environmental Science and Technology*, **34**, 1413–18, 2000.

[8] D.W. Pearce and R.K. Turner, *Economics of Natural Resources and the Environment*, Hemel Hampstead: Harvester Wheatsheaf, 1990.

[9] C.A. Nash, 'Transport externalities: does monetary valuation make sense?', in G. de Rus and C.A. Nash (eds), *Recent Developments in Transport Economics*, Aldershot: Ashgate, 1997.

is also an assessment of the economic importance of various forms of transport-associated environmental effects. These topics embrace many complex issues and have been subjected to major research efforts.[10]

Noise

The noise caused by traffic is associated with many things and is almost always increased by heavier traffic volumes, higher speeds, and a greater number of trucks. Vehicle noise is a combination of the noises produced by the engine, exhaust and tires. Defective mufflers or other faulty equipment on vehicles can also increase the loudness of traffic noise. From an economic perspective, it is often important to have engineering data on the causes of noise to assess optimal policies for remediation.

Noise associated with transport is seen as a major problem. A survey conducted by Market and Opinion Research in 1972 found that 12 percent of respondents thought that excessive noise was one of the three or four most serious problems in Britain. In pre-unified Germany, Frenking[11] found that 65 percent of the population were adversely affected by road traffic noise, with 25 percent seriously affected – by way of comparison this represented twice the problem of noise from neighbors and three times that from industrial noise. It is an especial nuisance in urban areas, in towns that suffer from a lot of through-traffic (for example, located astride major trunk arteries, such as railway lines, motorways, and so on) and at locations around transport terminals, such as airports, bus stations and car parks. It should also be remembered that noise is not only generated by traffic but extremely high levels of noise are also often associated with the construction of transport infrastructure – up to levels of 110 dB when piles are being driven.

It has been estimated that over 110 million people in the industrial world are exposed to road traffic noise levels of more than 65 dB(A) – a level considered unacceptable in OECD countries. While consistent data are somewhat sparse, there is also ample evidence that there are, in large part because of the nature of national land-use patterns, but also because of differing national legal structures, quite considerable differences between countries in terms of the populations affected by transport-related noise. Equally it is difficult, because of data limitations, to discern exact trends in population exposure to high noise levels. International comparisons provide tentative evidence of a decline in numbers suffering from serious noise problems – that is, over 65 dB(A) – in some countries but a rise in others, but there does seem to be a pattern of significantly increasing numbers of people falling into the grey area of intermediate noise nuisance of between 55 and 65 dB(A).[12]

[10] Organisation for Economic Co-operation and Development, *Effects of Traffic and Roads on the Environment in Urban Areas*, Paris: OECD, 1983.

[11] H. Frenking, *Exchange of Information on Noise Abatement Policies. Case Study on Germany*, Paris: OECD, 1988.

[12] Organisation for Economic Co-operation and Development, *Fighting Noise*, Paris: OECD, 1991.

Table 6.3   *Relative noise of different activities*

Perception example	Sound level dB(A)
Extreme jet take-off at 100 meters	120
Pop group	110
Loud car horn	100
Very loud heavy traffic	90
Noisy office	80
Loud busy street	70
Average office	60
Noisy normal conversation	50
Moderate quiet office	40
Quiet conversation	30
Quiet room	20
Very faint normal breathing	10
Threshold of hearing	0

Noise has several different effects on health and well-being. It affects activities such as communication (speaking, listening to radio and television) and sleep. These effects further induce psychological and physiological disorders such as stress, tiredness and sleep disturbance. Noise can also contribute to cardiovascular disease and, at high and prolonged exposure, hearing loss.

In practical terms there are, however, problems in measuring noise nuisance. First, noise nuisance depends upon both the intensity and the frequency of the noise. The 'A' weighted decibel scale (dB(A)) attempts to allow for this by offering a measure based on a weighted average of decibel readings where the weights reflect the level of unpleasantness caused by different frequencies and the decibels reflect the actual intensity of the noise. (While this measure is used in most transport-related work, a slightly different set of weights is employed in the perceived noise scale (PNdB) used in the measurement of aircraft noise.) The dB(A) scale is logarithmic and Table 6.3 gives some examples of dB(A) measured peak noise of different forms of transport relative to other sources of noise.

The dB(A) scale is sometimes prefixed by a term such as L_{10}, which means that it relates to a specific proportion of time (that is, L_{10} refers to the 10 percent peak noise level). On some occasions decibel measures have been combined with other indicators of noise annoyance in a composite index. The Noise and Numbers Index (NNI) developed for the economic appraisal of the Third London Airport, for example, combined the average peak level of noise at an airport (measured in PNdBs) with an indicator of the daily number of aircraft heard. The logarithmic nature of the NNI means that a one unit increase in the index represents a greater increase in noise nuisance, the higher the existing level of the index.

A scale against which noise nuisances may be measured does not, in itself, offer an economist trying to optimize noise emitted by transport much assistance in being able to place a monetary value on the noise so that the opportunity costs of different policies may be assessed. There are several ways in which noise has been evaluated, although revealed preference studies dominate in number.

In the 1960s, the Commission on the Third London Airport, in its pioneering study cited earlier, considered changes in property values with higher noise levels and in so doing established the adoption of hedonic indices as an evaluation method. Surveys were conducted at the existing Heathrow and Gatwick airports, seeking the actual and predicted sale prices of properties at different distances from them. While the Third London Airport method is useful it does present some difficulties. In particular, house prices vary for many different reasons and not simply because of the noise levels inflicted upon the area. House prices around Gatwick, for example, tended for a variety of reasons to be higher than those around Heathrow, which explains the greater fall in house values with respect to noise levels in the former. This does not invalidate the house valuation technique but it does suggest that values obtained by employing it should be used with circumspection. More specifically, that a value for noise nuisance derived using it in one area may be inappropriate for transport studies elsewhere without adjustments; in other words value transfer may be difficult.

A fairly typical hedonic index of the type now used, albeit probably with fewer variables, is provided by Nelson:[13]

$$\ln PV = 1.54 + 0.03(\ln X_1) + 0.20(\ln X_2) + 1.35(\ln X_3) + 0.02(\ln X_4)$$
$$+ 0.07(\ln X_5) - 000.33(\ln X_6) - 0.01(\ln X_7) \tag{6.2}$$

where: PV is a measure of property value differences, X_1 is a measure of the age of the house, X_2 reflects whether there is air conditioning, X_3 is the number of rooms, X_4 is the plot size, X_5 reflects whether the house has a riverside location, X_6 is time to reach employment and X_7 is the 'noise exposure forecast' (NEF). Examination of the NEF coefficient, the models calculated on data from around six major US airports thus suggests that a one unit increase in NEF results in a 1 percent depreciation in the value of a house. Table 6.4 provides some examples of the findings of such studies regarding airport noise.

More recently, meta-analysis was applied by John Nelson[14] to the negative relationship between airport noise exposure and residential property values. The analysis focuses on 20 hedonic studies covering 33 estimates of 23 airports in Canada and the United States that have looked at the percentage depreciation in property values per decibel increase in airport noise, or the noise discount. The weighted-mean noise discount across the studies is 0.58 percent per decibel with country and model specifications having some effect on the measured noise discount; the cumulative noise discount in the United States is about 0.5 to 0.6 percent per decibel at noise exposure levels of 75 dB or less, while in Canada it is 0.8 to 0.9 percent per decibel. These are findings in line with the literature review conducted by David Gillen, who found that aviation

[13] J.P. Nelson, 'Airport noise, location rent, and the market for residential amenities', *Journal of Environmental Economics and Management*, **6**, 320–31, 1979.

[14] J.P. Nelson, 'Meta-analysis of airport noise and hedonic property values: problems and prospects', *Journal of Transport Economics and Policy*, **38**, 1–28, 2004.

Table 6.4   *Estimates of noise nuisance on property values (percentage change per decibel increase)*

Study	% in house price	Country
Abelson (1979)	0.45	Australia
Collins and Evans (1994)	0.45	UK
De Vany (1976)	0.80	US
Dygert (1973)	0.60	US
Emerson (1969)	0.57	US
Gautin (1975)	0.35	UK
Levesqus (1994)	1.30	Canada
Maser (1977)	0.62	US
McMillan (1978)	0.50	Canada
McMillan (1980)	0.87	Canada
Mieszkowski (1978)	0.40	Canada
Nelson (1979)	1.10	US
O'Byrne et al. (1985)	0.52	US
O'Byrne et al. (1985)	0.57	US
Paik (1972)	0.65	US
Pennington et al. (1990)	0.60	UK
Price (1974)	0.83	US
Uyeno et al. (1993)	1.13	Canada

Source: K. Johnson and K.J. Button, 'Benefit transfers: are they a satisfactory input to benefit cost analysis?', *Transportation Research D*, **2**, 223–31, 1997. This paper contains the full references to the studies cited.

noise seems to reduce the price of similar houses by about 0.45 to 0.9 percent for each decibel.[15]

Atmospheric Pollution

Transport is a source of many harmful gases, and is one of the major contributors of several atmospheric pollutants. It is worth emphasizing, however, that while in some respects the environmental damage done by transport is increasing, in others, and in particular with regard to local pollution, there are reductions in many countries. Visual manifestations of this can be seen in the removal of the smog that used to hang over cities such as Los Angeles.

It is also worth remembering that exhaust fumes have a time and a spatial coverage. There is a time gap as the impacts move from one level to another. Figure 6.2 offered a broad picture of what happens. At the higher levels, the original impacts are connected to many other effects and systems, which are not exclusively related to transport. A potent cocktail of transport- and non-transport-related emissions, therefore, often exists. For ease of exposition, however, we deal with each of the main pollutants separately. The discussion below provides some indication of both these long- and short-term implications, as well as the nature of the spatial coverage, when this is particularly relevant.

[15] D. Gillen, 'The economics of noise', in K.J. Button and D. Hensher (eds), *Handbook of Transport and the Environment*, Oxford: Pergamon, 2003.

Fuel additive emissions

To enhance engine performance, additives are added to fuels. While some are relatively benign in their environmental effects, others have caused increasing concern over time. The organic lead compounds added to gasoline as an anti-knock agent, especially when used by automobiles in confined urban spaces, have been singled out for particular attention. Lead is a metallic element that can be retained in the body in the forms of its compounds and can have an adverse effect on the mental development of children and affect the kidney, liver and reproductive system.

In industrialized nations, transport is the single largest source of lead emissions with some 50 percent of lead associated with transport, but the figure can approach 100 percent in confined urban spaces. However, the tightening of maximum lead content in gasoline laws (for example, in the UK's case from 0.84 grams per liter to 0.40 grams per liter in 1981 and a further reduction to 0.15 grams per liter in 1985) and the fostering of increasing use of lead-free gasoline through fiscal and other measures which we shall discuss further in Chapter 8, has caused major changes in most major industrialized countries.

Particulate matters

These embrace fine solids or liquid particles found in the air or in emissions such as dust, smoke or smog. They are normally neither smelled nor tasted, or seen by the naked eye, but can penetrate the body through the lungs and cause major health problems. Sources include the fine asbestos and other particles stemming from wear and tear of tires and brakes as well as matter resulting from engine, and especially diesel engine, combustion.

Transport is the major source of particulate emissions in many industrialized countries including the United Kingdom and the United States. Particulate matter may be toxic in itself, or carry toxic (including carcinogenic) trace substances absorbed into its surfaces. It also imposes costs on physical structures, for example, in terms of the need to clean and repaint buildings. There is, however, no scientific consensus on the size of particles that may most harmful – for example, matter of less than 10 microns (PM-10) or 2.5 microns (PM-2.5) – making economic valuations difficult, and what estimates have been made generally relate to health aspects, and especially mortalities. In this context, however, McCubbin and Dellucci[16] found that particulate matter, because of the severity of its health implications, was the most serious road transport-generated pollutant in the United States. In terms of physical quantity, emitted by transport in the US, PM-2.5 matter has fallen from 7.3 million short-tons (2,000 lbs) in 1991 to 2.61 in 2006, but PM-10 has risen to 18.42 million short-tons to 18.4 over the same period.

Carbon dioxide emissions

The environmental concern here relates to CO_2 being generally seen by scientists as a major contributor to the greenhouse effect and consequential global

---

[16] D.R. McCubbin and M.A. Dellucci, 'The health costs of motor-related air pollution', *Journal of Air Transport and Policy*, **33**, 253–87, 1999.

Table 6.5   *Share of transport CO_2 emissions*

	1971	1990	1998
OECD			
North America	25	29	30
Europe	14	20	23
Pacific	16	20	22
Non-OECD			
Africa	20	18	17
Middle East	14	20	18
Europe	10	9	13
Former USSR	9	9	8
Latin America	31	33	34
Asia (exc. China)	14	16	18
China	4	6	8
World	19	22	24

Source: International Energy Agency, *CO_2 Emissions from Fuel Combustion 1971–1998*, Paris: IEA, 2000.

warming: 'the balance of evidence suggests a discernable human influence on the global climate'.[17] CO_2 emissions result from the combustion of fossil fuels. The contribution of CO_2 to the atmosphere varies considerably between countries but the industrialized countries as a whole are responsible for about 80 percent. Table 6.5 provides more details.

Since CO_2 is a natural constituent of air (although only about 0.03 percent) it is not strictly a pollutant. Additionally, excess amounts of the gas have no detrimental effect on personal health. The problem is that there is mounting, although some would argue not yet conclusive, evidence that high levels of CO_2 in the atmosphere, by preventing heat from escaping from the planet, will lead to global climate changes.

The issue is not really one about the merits of the greenhouse effect *per se* (without it, estimates suggest that the global average temperature would fall to about 19°C), but rather about the desirability of the effects that changes in its intensity will have. The exact geographical impacts of global warming, and its timing, are difficult to predict, and the long-term economic consequences are even harder to foretell. The types of problems which are feared, however, include: a rise in the sea level as a result of thermal expansion of the sea and the melting of land ice; changes of climatic zones, for example, of desert regions and regions affected by tropical storms; detrimental effects on water resources in many areas; and problems of adapting agricultural production. The wide-ranging potential impacts of global warning make it particularly problematic to place money values on them.

[17] Intergovernmental Panel on Climate Change, *IPCC Second Assessment Synthesis of Scientific–technical Information Relevant to Interpreting Article 2 of the UN Framework Convention on Climate Change*, Geneva: IPCC, 1995.

The Stern Report[18] concluded that 1 percent of global GDP per annum needs to be invested to avoid the worst effects of climate change, and that failure to do so could risk global GDP being up to 20 percent lower than it otherwise might be.

Nitrogen oxide emissions

These pose particular difficulties when combined with other air pollutants or in areas where residents already suffer ill-health. In the latter case they can lead to respiratory difficulties and extended exposure can result in oedema or emphysema. At the trans-boundary or regional level, NO_X emissions converted to nitric acid and combined with SO_2, form a significant component of 'acid rain' (or 'acid deposition') which has serious detrimental effects on ecosystems, for example, damage to fresh-water fish stocks and deforestation. About 50 percent of NO_X emissions stem from the transport sector, and the rest from the energy and industrial sectors, although in many countries their output is falling. The amount of million NO_X emitted in many countries by transport sources has also tended to fall in recent years. In the United States it fell from 26.9 million short-tons in 1970, to 22.6 by 2000, and to 18.2 million tons in 2006. The decline in transport associated with NO_X is largely due to the widespread adoption of autocatalysts: from 1990 all new cars in Norway, Sweden, Austria and Switzerland had these fitted, and most industrialized countries quickly followed.

Carbon monoxide emissions

Carbon monoxide (CO) can have detrimental effects on health by interfering with the absorption of oxygen by red blood cells. This may lead to increased morbidity, and adversely affects fertility. There is also evidence that it affects worker productivity. CO is an especial problem in urban areas where synergistic effects with other pollutants means that it contributes to photochemical smog and surface ozone (O_3). Concentrations of O_3 at lower levels have implications for the respiratory system. CO emissions result from incomplete combustion, which is most likely to occur at low air-to-fuel ratios in the engine. These conditions are common during vehicle starting when the air supply is restricted.

In the 1980s, some 90 percent of all CO emissions originated from the transport sector in most industrial countries, and about 80 percent were associated with automobile use. The figure reached 100 percent in the center of many built-up areas. CO emissions from transport more than halved in the United States in just over 35 years from 1970 to 100.6 million short-tons in 2006. As with the United Kingdom (see again Table 6.2), transport accounts for about half of all CO emissions in the United States.

Sulfur dioxide emissions

Emissions of this colorless but strong-smelling gas can result in bronchitis and other diseases of the respiratory system and they are, in conjunction with NO_X

---

[18] N. Stern, *Stern Review: The Economics of Climate Change*, Cabinet Office, London: HM Treasury, 2007.

emissions, the major contributor to acid rain. Transport is directly responsible for about 5 percent of SO_2 emissions, with diesel fuel containing more SO_2 per liter than gasoline. What is more important, coal-fired electricity generation is a major source of this gas and thus there are further transport implications for both electric rail transport and the manufacture of transport vehicles. Modern diesel engines are being adopted in wealthier countries, and reducing the sulfur problem and enhanced technology is combating the levels of SO_2 associated with coal-fired electricity generation.

There have been a number of studies at a local or regional level to try to place an economic value on the costs of acid rain on forestry. In an econometric study, Adams and co-workers, for example, by evaluating the lost production of soft and hardwood timber, estimated that it was costing the economy of the eastern United States some $1.5 to $7.2 billion a year in the mid-1990s.[19]

Volatile organic compounds

These comprise a wide variety of hydrocarbons and other substances (for example, methane, ethylene oxide, formaldehyde, phenol, phosgene, benzene, carbon tetrachloride, CFCs and polychlorinated biphenyls). They generally result from incomplete combustion of fossil fuels, although evaporated gasoline from fuel tanks and the carburetors is increasingly contributing to releases of aromatic hydrocarbons (HCs) such as benzene.

When combined with NO in sunlight, HCs and some volatile organic compounds (VOCs) can generate low-level ozone, the main component of photochemical smog. Besides producing respiratory problems and causing eye irritations, some of the compounds are suspected of being carcinogenic and possibly mutagens or teratogens (which can result in congenital malformations). Excluding methane, emissions of which largely stem from agricultural sources, about half of VOC emissions in industrialized countries are generally associated with road traffic, and the proportion in developing countries tends to be rising. About 30 percent of all VOC emissions are directly related to transport.

Accidents

Transport is a dangerous activity. Every year more than 1.17 million people die in road crashes around the world, and over 10 million are crippled or injured. These accidents generally concern not just those involved in transport itself but also third parties. The dangers inherent in the transport of dangerous and toxic substances are, in fact, increasing this latter problem. From a purely statistical perspective this is mainly seen in relation to road transport where there are, on

---

[19] R.M. Adams, C. Anderson, J.H.B. Garner, B.H. Hale, W.E. Hogsett, D.F. Kanesky, J. Lawrence, E.H. Lee, A.S. Lefohn, P. Miller, V. Rucecles, J.A. Weber and R.D. Yanai, 'Environmental effects of ozone and related photochemical oxidants', in *Air Quality Criteria for Ozone and Related Photochemical Oxidants*, Washington, DC: US Office of Research and Development, Environmental Protection Agency, 1996.

a day-to-day basis, many fatal and serious accidents. Less frequent, but from a public perception perspective, more alarming because of the degree of potential severity and geographical concentration associated with the impacts of each incident, are rail, maritime, and aviation disasters.

Some indication of the order of magnitude of the risks involved in transport is the fact that transport accidents cost over 44,900 lives in the United States in 2006, and only slightly less in the European Union. There are quite wide variations at a lower level of aggregation in the chances of being killed in a transport accident. For example, within the European Union in 2004 the number of road fatalities per million inhabitants ranged from 33 in Malta, 49 in the Netherlands and 53 in Sweden, to 218 in Lithuania and 150 in Poland. As a point of comparison, 146 deaths per million inhabitants were recorded for the United States in 2004.

It should be also be pointed out that in many high-income, developed countries the number of fatal road accidents is decreasing – for example, road fatalities for the United Kingdom reveal 4,753 deaths in 1991, falling to 3,743 in 1997 and to 3,368 in 2004, with the general pattern repeated for injuries. For Germany the decline has been even more pronounced, from 11,300 fatalities in 1991 to 5,842 in 2004, while for Italy the comparable figures are 8,109 and 5,625. This is not, however, the situation in many low-income countries: as private transport is expanding, the number of fatalities continues to rise, with about 70 percent of deaths now occurring in developing countries. Increased amounts of hazardous waste transported in recent years, and the related problem of spillage, is also adding to the risks borne by third parties throughout the world, but particularly so in lower-income countries..

If one considers the accident rates by mode then road transport incidents dominate statistics although, because of variations in modal split between countries, there are national variations in their relative importance. Some indication of different accident rates by mode and over time for the United States is, for example, seen in Table 6.6.

Interpretation of such data does, however, pose some particular problems; for example, there is the point of comparison against which numbers of accidents should be set. Commercial aviation is, from a statistical perspective, generally cited as the safest mode of transport but this may not be the case viewed in terms of time exposure.

Valuing the external accident costs of transport also poses a particular problem.[20] Accident risks are partly internalized within transport in the sense that individuals insure themselves against being harmed by them. However, many travelers have no insurance or, where it as been taken up, it is on the basis of a misperception of the risks involved. There are also third-party risks involved in the possibility of accidents during the transporting of dangerous goods or toxic waste. Attempts to devise methods for valuing accident risk have a long history, especially with regard to fatal accidents.

---

[20] M.W. Jones-Lee and G. Loomes, 'Valuation of safety', in K.J. Button and D.A. Hensher (eds), *Handbook of Transport and the Environment*, Oxford: Pergamon, 2003.

Table 6.6   *Transport accidents in the United States by mode*

	Air	Highway (thousand)	Railroad	Waterborne
Fatalities				
1992	989	39.2	170	1,032
1995	964	41.8	1,146	1,016
2000	764	41.9	937	888
2001	1,166	42.2	971	828
2002	616	43.0	951	857
2003	698	42.9	868	807
2004	636	42.8	895	759
2005	603	43.5	887	777
2006	766	42.6	911	797
Injuries				
1992	456	3,148	21,383	5,356
1995	452	3,593	14,440	6,165
2000	357	3,260	11,643	5,112
2001	368	3,100	10,985	5,008
2002	335	2,959	11,103	4,846
2003	375	2,919	9,245	4,666
2004	304	2,818	9,157	4,066
2005	302	2,728	9,402	4,095
2006	287	2,604	8,189	5,245

Source: US Bureau of Transportation Statistics.

The methods of valuation currently in use, however, still differ between countries, and agencies within countries. Some adopt cost avoidance calculations, others use lost production/consumption-type techniques, but the use of revealed and stated preference methods is becoming more widespread. The lost production (or *ex post*) method essentially asks what output the economy forgoes if, for example, someone is killed in a road accident – essentially a discounted calculation of the difference between what that person could have been expected to produce over the rest of his/her life and what he/she could have been expected to consume. The obvious problem is that a pensioner's death would be accorded a positive value using such a procedure. The lost consumption (or *ex ante*) method avoids this problem by assuming that the individual would gain utility by not dying and thus does not net out lost consumption, the ability to enjoy this consumption acting as proxy for the welfare of remaining alive.

Analysis based on microeconomic principles looks at choices that people make when trading off safer travel against riskier options and estimates the willingness to pay for the reduced risk. The revealed preference work focuses on actual choices, such as driving faster, which saves time but is more dangerous, or driving more slowly, which is more costly in time.

There is still no universally accepted value for accident prevention, and countries adopt a variety of valuations. The United Kingdom for example, uses a figure of £1.14 million (2000 prices) for a statistical life saved in road project appraisal based on stated preference analysis, and £128,650 and £9,922 for serious and slight non-fatal accidents, respectively. The United States uses a value of over $3 million for a fatality, and Canada, US$1.5 million (in 1991 prices). Academic studies also show some variability in their results. A review of such studies in the United States, the United Kingdom and Sweden using mainly stated preference methods concludes that the most reliable estimates from such studies give a distribution of values of life in 1989 with a median of $1.1 million and a mean of $3.4 million.[21]

While reservations must be expressed over the method of valuing lost life (in terms of lost production), and some of the other forms of accident damage, these types of figures can also be aggregated to give very broad national overall costs of accidents – for example, the American Automobile Association estimated that the costs of property damage, lost earnings, medical costs, emergency services, legal costs and travel delays due to road accidents amounted to $164.2 billion in 2007. It must be remembered, however, that such figures are gross of the internalization that takes place through insurance markets, and do not include the costs of lost lives and injuries.

Visual Intrusion

Transport infrastructure and mobile plant is frequently visually intrusive and often far from aesthetically pleasing. In addition, particulates and gases emitted by transport scatter and absorb light, adversely affecting visibility. The problem is measuring these effects. Some attempts have been made in the past to assess the intrusion of motorways on the landscape by looking at the percentage of the skyline obscured,[22] but this approach considers only one dimension of a multifaceted problem. In particular, transport infrastructure must be viewed in the context of its surroundings – a new freeway located in formerly unspoiled countryside is likely to be viewed differently from one that blots out an unsightly waste tip. Design is also important. Furthermore, it should be remembered that vehicles are as intrusive as infrastructure and large trucks or buses are, for example, often totally out of place in unspoiled areas or 'historic towns'. Whether it is the actual size of vehicles that is alarming or simply the level of traffic flow is difficult to disentangle.

A newer problem is that caused by the eyesores created by the difficulties of disposing of the old hardware of transport. The problem embraces not only disused infrastructure of road, rail and maritime transport but also increasingly the vehicles themselves: cars, ships and railway wagons. Variations in the number of scrapped vehicles over time are due to a variety of factors,[23] but as the overall vehicle population grows, disposal problems increase. Even a small country like

---

[21] M.W. Jones-Lee, 'The value of traffic safety', *Oxford Review of Economic Policy*, **60**, 39–60, 1990.

[22] P.E. Clamp, *Evaluation of the Impact of Roads on the Visual Amenity of Rural Areas*, London: UK Department of the Environment Research Report 7, 1976.

[23] A. Greenspan and D. Cohen, 'Motor vehicle stocks, scrappage, and sales', *Review of Economics and Statistics*, **81**, 369–83, 1999.

the Netherlands, for instance, scraps about 450,000 cars each year but of the 750,000 tons of waste generated only 450,000 tons are recycled leaving metals, oily products, paint, plastics and other materials to be dumped.

Pollution of Water Systems

Water systems, both fresh and saline, suffer considerable pollution and other environmental damage from transport. Maritime transport itself results in both accidental and intentional releases of waste and oil into the seas, lakes and rivers and ports, especially those requiring significant amounts of dredging, and are disruptive to wildlife. Other modes, however, can also cause damage, including the run-off from roads and airports of liquids such as de-icing fluids, and the diversion of natural water courses to allow for the construction of infrastructure.

Although most oil spillage (53 percent of incidents) is the result of transfers, major oil spillages due to maritime accidents attract considerable attention: for example the *Atlantic Express* spilled 287,000 tons of oil in 1979; the *ABT Summer*, 260,000 tons in 1991; the *Castillo de Bellver*, 252,000 tons in 1983; and the *Amoco Cadiz*, 233,000 tons in 1978. The quantity of oil spilt is not, however, a good indicator of the environmental damage done. The *Exxon Valdez* incidence in 1989, for example, because it occurred in a scenic area, Prince William Sound, is considered the most expensive in history despite the spillage being 37,000 tons. The costs of this in terms of clean-up ($2.2 billion), lost production in fishing and other industries ($300 million), and lost fishing output in south-central Alaska ($108 million), besides damages paid by the ship's owner are large, although strictly difficult to calculate exactly because of problems of double counting.[24] For example, while south-central Alaska may have lost business, other areas may have gained and some of the costs that have been included in calculations for damages paid by the ship's owners are already reflected in the direct damage and clean-up cost estimates. Ships are also generally insured and this means that at least part of the cost of spillage is internalized, as with many forms of accident risk.

There are also technical issues in physically assessing damage from spillage prior to any efforts at placing monetary values on them. A spill on marshland in winter does minimal damage to plant life, for example, because the plants have died back naturally, and weather conditions can affect the rate of evaporation and toxicity of oil.[25]

Vibrations

Low flying commercial aircraft, heavy goods vehicles and railway wagons create vibrations that can affect buildings. Vibration within vehicles also adversely

---

[24] M.J. Cohen, 'Technological disasters and natural resource damage assessment: an evaluation of the *Exxon Valdez* oil spill', *Land Economics*, **71**, 65–82, 1995.

[25] W.K. Talley, 'Oil spillage and damage costs: US inland water tank barge accidents', *International Journal of Maritime Economics*, **2**, 217–34, 2001.

affects drivers and passengers. Vibration within a 'cabin' starts from the engine and the response of the vehicle to the road surface. Vibration varies in response to the load of the vehicle: there is more vibration as the load becomes lighter. The most widely reported injury for whole of body vibration is back injury.

Again, useful measures are elusive. While it is known, for example, that ground-borne vibration is related to axle loads, it has proved impossible to relate this effectively to any measure of structural damage to buildings. The evidence suggests, however, that the physical damage caused may be less than is sometimes claimed. Improved engineering techniques have reduced the damage caused by road transport and much of the damage formerly thought 'caused' by heavy lorries is more likely to have simply been 'triggered' by them. As Whiffen and Leonard[26] point out, 'Attention can be drawn to vibration by the rattling of doors, windows, lids of ornaments, mirrors, etc. The association of these audible and visible signs with the possibility of damage to the building results in exaggerated complaints about vibration, even though, in fact, there may be no risk of damage'. Vibrations may still be a cost in an economic sense, however, even if there is no structural damage to buildings. Some years ago, for example, Martin[27] found that 8 percent of the UK population were considerably bothered by vibrations from road traffic, but his suggestion that this could be measured cardinally by looking at the spectra of emitted low-frequency noise has yet to be attempted.

Community Severance

Roads, railways, canals and other transport arteries often present major physical (and sometimes psychological) barriers to human contact. An urban motorway can cut a local community in two, inhibiting the retention of long-established social ties and, on occasion, making it difficult for people to benefit from recreational and employment opportunities on the other side of the barrier. A rail line can do the same. Although it may be possible to obtain estimates of the potential pedestrian and other delays, and reassignments resulting from the impedance, suppressed trips are much harder to identify. Severance also has important links with amenity: 'the quality of a place, the way it looks, sounds, smells and feels, and it affects the way people experience a place'.[28] Quantification of community severance is not, therefore, an immediate prospect. As the UK's Jefferson Report put it in the late 1970s, 'the overall conclusion is that no acceptable way is seen of extending the assessment of severance beyond an individual examination of some of the perceived effects except, perhaps, by means of subjective statements in appropriate cases'.[29]

---

[26] A.C. Whiffen and D.P Leonard, *A Survey of Traffic Induced Vibrations*, Crowthorne: Road Research Laboratory Report, LR 418, 1971.

[27] D.J. Martin, *Low Frequency Traffic Noise and Building Vibration*, Crowthorne: Transport Research Laboratory Supplementary Report, SR. 429, 1978.

[28] S. Handy, 'Amenity and severance', in K.J. Button and D. Hensher (eds), *Handbook of Transport and the Environment*, Oxford: Pergamon, 2003.

[29] UK Department of Transport, *Report on Noise and Other Environmental Issues*, London: DOT, 1977.

6.6   Energy Use

Energy use *per se* is not strictly an environmental concern in itself; it is more a matter of the types of energy used and in what context. The various energy sources have associated with them different environmental implications. Even wind power has to be generated by man-made equipment usually involving the use of other energy sources, and wind farms can create local micro climates in their locations. There are broader issues about the non-renewable nature of oil, the main fuel used by transport.

To move anything requires energy. Transport, therefore, is by definition a user of energy. The amount and types of energy that are used, however, have varied considerably over time as technology has changed. Much of it used to be in the form of the food given to animals, beasts of burden, or simply human consumption of calories in various forms. Renewable sources of energy, wind and water power in particular, have been widely exploited and still are, although often in somewhat different ways. Wind power, for example, is more often used indirectly as a means of generating electricity than for propelling ships or Chinese wheelbarrows. Much of modern transport since the advent of the steam engine has, however, and with the exception of some less developed countries where the beast of burden often still plays a major role, relied on non-renewable sources of energy such as coal, oil and natural gas.

The levels of current and projected use of oil by the transport industries are particularly impressive. While there are national differences, Table 6.7 for example, provides some information on both the absolute and relative final demand for energy in the European Union, including forecasts of likely future use. The transport sector accounted for some 80 percent of the demand growth between 1990 and 2000, and became the largest demand-side sector. The predominant role of the transport sector in final energy demand growth is projected to continue under EU baseline assumptions until 2010, but beyond that policy initiatives and technological progress lead to a deceleration and an eventual decline of transport energy needs. Transport, however, is still expected to account for 30 percent of final energy demand in 2030, remaining the largest single consumer.

A major factor contributing to the rise in energy demand for transport is the technology changes that have taken place, and in particular the increasing use of road transport (see again Table 2.23). The number of registered cars, and trucks and buses in 2003 is approximately 589 million and 224 million worldwide, respectively, and had increased, respectively, at rates of 2.7 and 3.0 percent annually between 1993 and 2003. The US Department of Energy[30] has estimated that unchecked, the global vehicle park will increase to 3,500 million by 2050 with those in developed countries doubling and those in developing nations increasing 15-fold. The International Energy Agency reports that nearly 58 percent of global petroleum consumption was by transport in 2003, and forecasts are for this proportion growing at least to

---

[30] US Department of Energy, *Natural Gas Annual 2004*, Washington, DC: US DOE, 2004.

Table 6.7   *Final energy demand in the European Union* by sector (mtoe)*

	1990	*2000*	*2010*	*2020*	*2030*
Industry	341.1	330.1	356.4	382.4	391.6
Energy intensive	216.8	211.6	220.8	228.4	224.9
Other	124.3	118.4	135.7	154.0	166.6
Domestic	407.6	432.3	500.5	550.6	576.6
Residential	261.0	273.3	312.0	338.7	351.3
Tertiary	146.6	159.0	188.5	211.9	225.3
Transport	273.2	333.0	381.1	405.5	402.3
Total	1021.9	1095.4	1238.0	1338.5	1370.5

Note: * The data relate to the 25 member states as of 2006.

Source: European Commission, *European Energy and Transport Trends to 2030 – Update 2005*, Office for Official Publications of the European Communities, 2006.

2020.[31] In the United States, some 21 million barrels of oil are consumed daily, with 5.8 million being burned by transport, and it is forecast to rise to 26 million barrels by 2030, with gasoline accounting for about 45 percent of this.[32]

It is not just the number of vehicles that matter, but also the technical parameters. For example, the average new passenger car in Europe consumes about 6.5 liters of fuel per 100 kilometers, whereas the average passenger car in the United States uses over 40 percent more to cover the same distance. Part of this can be explained in terms of distances traveled – longer trips in America may be seen to justify more 'comfortable' vehicles – but in addition there are important taxation differences. Retail gasoline prices in Europe include taxes in the range of 60 to 75 percent, compared with only 20 to 25 percent in the United States. There may also be cultural differences in the ways various societies see large, less fuel-efficient vehicles, but these are more difficult to quantify.

Transport is not homogeneous and can be broken down in a number of ways to reflect its use of energy. The focus here is largely on the use of non-renewable energy resources, and especially oil, but the data are not always transparent in that sense. For example, electricity may be the direct energy source for many rail systems and local trams, but electricity can be generated in a variety of ways: from oil, natural gas, coal, nuclear sources, hydro power, wind power and so on. Given considerable variations in the efficiency of generating plants, one would really like an indicator of the amount of fossil fuel used to provide the energy to produce a given unit of transport. Additionally, most of the data available on energy consumed in transport relate to the final movement and offer few insights into the full costs of transport provisions that embrace the energy needed to supply and maintain transport infrastructure and the manufacture and maintenance of vehicles. We also have limited knowledge on the way transport affects use of resources in

[31] International Energy Agency, *Key World Energy Statistics 2005*, Paris: IEA, 2005.
[32] US Department of Energy, Energy Information Administration, *Annual Energy Outlook 2006: With Projections to 2030*, Washington, DC: USDOE, 2006.

Table 6.8 *Fuel consumption in the United States by the main transport modes*

	1980	1990	2000	2003	2004
Highway					
Gasoline, diesel and other fuels (million gallons)	114,960	130,755	162,555	170,069	173,750
Truck	19,960	24,490	35,229	32,696	33,968
Single-unit 2-axle 6-tire or more truck	6,923	8,357	9,563	8,880	9,263
Combination truck	13,037	16,133	25,666	23,815	24,705
Truck (percent of total)	17.4	18.7	21.7	19.2	19.6
Rail, Class I (freight service)					
Distillate/diesel fuel (million gallons)	3,904	3,115	3,700	3,826	4,059
Water					
Residual fuel oil (million gallons)	8,952	6,326	6,410	3,874	4,690
Distillate/diesel fuel oil (million gallons)	1,478	2,065	2,261	2,217	2,140
Gasoline (million gallons)	1,052	1,300	1,124	1,107	1,005
Pipeline					
Natural gas (million cubic feet)	634,622	659,816	642,210	591,492	571,853

Sources: US Department of Transportation, Federal Highway Administration; Association of American Railroads; Energy Information Administration, US Department of Energy.

the broader economy – for example, on the effect that a transport-intensive industry such as tourism has on energy consumption in final production such as hotels, restaurants and the manufacturing of souvenirs, as well as in the movement of the tourists themselves.

In terms of its immediate effects, Table 6.8 looks at energy consumption by various transport modes in the United States. The dominant role of gasoline as an energy source is clear and reflects the widespread use of automobiles for personal travel. Other countries have somewhat different relative patterns that depend, in part, on the nature and size of their national economies and geography – for example, whether they produce and move large amounts of raw materials – but also on the transport policies that have been favored – for example, whether public transport has been strongly supported and levels of fuel taxation.

While much of the interest in energy consumption until the 1990s focused on its use in developed Western economies, the subsequent rapid economic expansions of large developing countries, especially India and China, has led to a shift in focus. With rapid economic growth and aggressive expansion of transport infrastructure, for example, China saw a fourfold increase in freight traffic and a sixfold increase in passenger traffic between 1980 and 2000. Cars for short trips and planes for long trips increasingly dominate passenger traffic in the country, as growing incomes have allowed more people to utilize these fast and comfortable means of travel. From 1980 through 2002, passenger traffic grew over sixfold,

Table 6.9   *Energy consumption by transport in China (1990–2000)*

Mode	Energy consumption (ktoe)			Consumption share (%)		
	1990	*2000*	*Ratio*	*1990*	*2000*	*Change*
Railways	14,851	13,017	0.88	27.8	13.5	−14.2
Highways	25,495	65,516	2.57	47.6	68.1	+20.5
Waterways	11,407	11,988	1.05	21.3	12.5	−8.8
Civil aviation	1,222	5,090	4.16	2.3	5.3	+3.0
Pipelines	550	605	1.10	1.0	0.6	−0.4
Total	53,524	96,214	1.80	100.0	100.0	0.0

Source: China Energy Research Society, *Energy Policy Research 2002.1*, 2002.

from 228 billion to 1,413 billion person-km. Passenger highway traffic grew tenfold, its share of passenger traffic increasing from 32 to 55 percent. Passenger aviation traffic grew more than 30-fold, its share of passenger traffic growing fivefold to 9 percent. Railway passenger traffic, while nearly quadrupling in volume, saw its share of passenger traffic decline from 61 to 35 percent However, average annual growth in highway traffic share has slowed from 3.7 percent in the late 1980s to 1.9 percent in the early 1990s to 1.2 percent in the late 1990s to 0.9 percent between 2000 and 2002.

As a result of the rapid traffic growth and the changing modal split, the transport share of national energy use grew from under 5 percent in 1996 to nearly 9 percent in 1999. The share of energy used by road transport in China officially grew from roughly 48 percent in 1990 to 68 percent in 2000, and most of this is in the form of oil consumption (Table 6.9). The share of civil aviation also grew rapidly, albeit from a very much lower base.

Most of the analysis of transport energy use focuses on its importance in moving vehicles of one form or another, but both the mobile plant used in transporting goods and people and the associated infrastructure rely on significant amounts of energy in their construction and maintenance. While difficult to quantify, for example, the production of over 50 million cars, nearly 14 million light commercial vehicles, and three million heavy commercial vehicles in 2006 obviously consumed an immense amount of energy.

As with many things there is an intellectual curiosity about the links between transport and energy use, but there are also important public policy issues to be considered. Energy is used in virtually all forms of activity and there is a need to ensure that it is used to maximum effect and in ways that ensure that any external effects are not excessive. In economic terms, the market for energy is, however, far from perfect for a variety of reasons. These failures stem partly from the intrinsic nature of the 'commodity' (largely associated with market failures linked to economies of scale in supply and externalities) but can also be due to the institutional environment in which energy is provided (especially government intervention failures that often are seen in terms of allocating property rights and regulatory capture). These imperfections, in turn, affect the ways in which transport users view energy and the ways in which they use it, and the forms and quantities in which it is supplied.

Much of the energy used in transport comes from finite sources – oil reserves, coal, wood and natural gas. In economic terms, this is not a major issue if prices are appropriate and reflect the genuine, long-term opportunity cost of the use of these resources. In many cases, the drawing down of the reserves of these resources may still be consistent with a genuinely 'sustainable' scenario in the Brundtland[33] sense of ensuring that future generations enjoy the same resource base as current generations, if at the same time alternative energy sources are being created – for example, the creation of hydroelectric or wind capacity. In terms of the notion of sustainable development, future generations will still have the same resource base as the current one, albeit in a different form.

The challenge is to ensure that there are mechanisms and signals to ensure that the energy base is not diluted excessively by transport use. In the past there have been significant shifts in the energy used in transport, with coal, and then oil, taking over from oars and sails for shipping, for example. Market forces have largely driven these shifts: slaves became expensive as rowers, and sailing ships became too unreliable for expanding trade networks and hence steamships took over. One thing that has been learned, however, is that predicting the depletion rate of any resource is difficult. Stanley Jevons's famous concern in 1865 that coal supplies would soon be exhausted and, in consequence, the rail and steamship industry would, among others, become non-viable is a good example of how static analysis linking non-renewable resource depletion and transport can be misleading. But equally, the move from wood- to coal-, and then to oil-boilers on ships showed how the market can respond to potential shortages through stimulating the development of alternative technologies.

The economic problem is that for transport markets to function they must have appropriate price signals from the energy market. The semi-cartelization of many energy markets, with institutions such as OPEC (Organization for Petroleum Exporting Countries), and also of many markets that supply the hardware of transport, such as the automobile and airframe manufacturers, coupled with political involvement, means that these signals are far from perfect. Consequently, the exploitation of any non-renewable resources is seldom optimal irrespective of any externality considerations. The issue, however, is more of a generic one rather than being transport specific because market and institutional failures extend across all uses of energy.

6.7 Introduction to Traffic Congestion

The demand for transport is not constant over time. In large cities there are regular peaks in commuter travel, while on holiday routes, both within a country and to

---

[33] World Commission on Environment and Development, *Our Common Future*, Oxford: Oxford University Press, 1987 (Brundtland Report).

Table 6.10   *Traffic congestion in major US cities (2005)*

Large metropolitan areas	Annual delay per traveler (hours)
Los Angeles	72
San Francisco-Oakland	60
Washington DC	60
Atlanta	60
Dallas-Fort Worth	58
Houston	56
Detroit	54
Miami	50
Phoenix	48
Chicago	46
New York-Newark	46
Boston	46
Seattle	45
Philadelphia	38

Source: Texas Transportation Institute.

overseas destinations, there are seasonal peaks in demand. Transport infrastructure, although flexible in the long run, has a finite capacity at any given period of time. One cannot, for example, expand and contract the size of an airport terminal to meet seasonal fluctuations in demand. When users of a particular facility begin to interfere with other users because the capacity of the infrastructure is limited, then congestion externalities arise and time is wasted (Table 6.10).

Of course, some degree of congestion is almost unavoidable if facilities are not to stand idle most of the time, but the question is just how much congestion is desirable. Since people accept some level of congestion but resent excessive congestion, because of the time and inconvenience costs imposed, there is some implied notion of an optimal level of congestion.

It is not just roads that experience congestion – it can be found in most modes of transport and can be either on links or at nodes. Table 6.11, for example, looks at air traffic control delays in Europe but there are delays at airports as well. Remaining with Europe, for example, in 2006, 31.8 percent of flights were delayed by at least 15 minutes out of London's Heathrow Airport, 31.3 percent from Madrid, 30.7 percent from London Gatwick, and 28.6 percent from Paris Charles de Gaulle.

One should add, with reference to previous sections, that congestion not only imposes costs on the traveler in terms of wasted time and fuel (the pure congestion cost) but the stopping and starting it entails can also worsen atmospheric and other forms of pollution.[34] The problem is particularly acute with local forms of pollution because road traffic congestion, in particular, tends to be focused in areas where people work and live. Road traffic poses some of the greatest congestion problems and also offers a useful basis of analysis.

---

[34] J. Lin and D.A. Niemeier, 'Regional driving characteristics, regional driving cycles', *Transportation Research D*, **8**, 361–81, 2003.

Table 6.11 *European air traffic flow management delays*

	Average daily traffic	% of flights delayed*	En route delays (million minutes)	Airport delays (million minutes)
1997	19,658	7	15.5	5.4
1998	20,681	9	21.7	5.7
1999	22,064	12	36.3	7.0
2000	23,071	9	24.4	7.4
2001	23,001	8	20.8	6.8
2002	22,567	9	11.9	6.0
2003	23,197	6	8.0	6.8
2004	24,238	4	7.6	7.3
2005	25,244	4	8.9	8.7
2006	26,286	5	10.2	8.2

Note: * A delay is defined as 15 minutes or more behind schedule.

Source: EUROCONTROL Performance Review Unit.

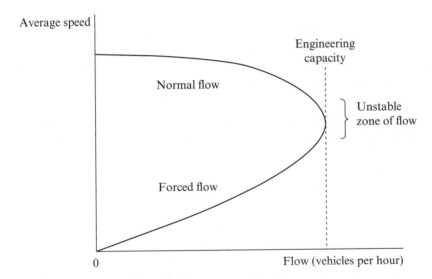

Figure 6.7 *The speed–flow relationship*

The economic costs of road congestion can be calculated using the engineering concept of the speed–flow relationship. If we take a straight one-way street and consider traffic flows along it over a period of time at different speed levels then the relationship between speed and flow would appear as in Figure 6.7. Flow is dependent upon both the number of vehicles entering a road and the speed of traffic. Hence, at low volumes of traffic, when vehicle impedance is zero, high speeds are possible, constrained only by the capability of the vehicle and legal speed limits, but as the number of vehicles trying to enter the road increases so they interact with existing traffic and slow one another down. As more traffic enters the road, speed falls but, up to a point, flow will continue to rise because the effect of additional vehicle numbers outweighs the reduction in average speed. This is the normal flow situation.

Table 6.12 *Traffic speeds in selected cities*

City	Year	Population (million)	City center traffic speed (kmph)	
			Peak hour	Off-peak
New York	1970	13.3	16.0	26.0
Detroit	1970	4.0	17.7	–
Salt Lake City	1970	0.9	27.0	–
London	1971	7.4	20.6	–
Birmingham	1965	1.1	22.1	–
Leeds	1965	0.5	18.0	–
Paris	1970	6.4	16.9	–
Athens	1971	2.7	15.5	24.0
Copenhagen	1967	1.7	14.5	–
Stockholm	1969	1.3	18.0	–
Calcutta	1971	7.5	11.0–16.0	19.0
Singapore	1972	2.2	21.0	–

Source: J.M. Thomson, *Great Cities and their Traffic*, London: Gollancz, 1977.

At the point where increased traffic volume ceases to offset the reduced speed, the road's 'capacity' is reached at the maximum flow. (This is the road's engineering capacity and differs from the economic capacity that is defined as that flow at which the costs of extending the capacity are outweighed by the benefits of doing so.) Absence of perfect information means that motorists often continue to try to enter the road beyond this volume, causing further drops in speed and resulting in the speed–flow relationship turning back on itself. These levels of flow are known as 'forced flows'. There is often a degree of 'learning from experience' that can improve the quality of decision making and in practice, without any intervention, flows would settle around the zone of instability during rush-hour periods. A cross-sectional study of the main urban centers (Table 6.12) conducted 30 years ago, though the situation is little changed today, suggests that this zone of instability occurs at speeds of about 18 kmph.

The actual form of the speed–flow relationship and the engineering capacity of any individual road will depend upon a number of factors. Clearly, the physical characteristics of the road, its width, the number of lanes and so on, are of central importance – these may be seen as the long-term influences. Short-term factors include the form of traffic management and control schemes in operation (traffic lights, roundabouts and so on). Finally, the type and age of vehicles combined with their distribution may influence capacity.

A fairly typical set of speed–flow relationships which illustrate these points are, for example, offered by Neutze[35] in his study of Sydney's arterial road system. Information obtained from over 400 locations on main roads in the city was used in the exercise, the results of which are seen in Figure 6.8. As one might expect, the capacity of six-lane roads exceeds that of either two- or four-lane roads,

[35] G.M. Neutze, 'The external diseconomies of growth in traffic', *Economic Record*, **39**, 332–45, 1963.

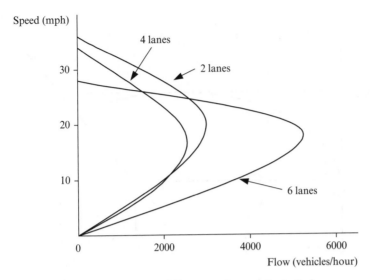

Figure 6.8 *Speed–flow relationships on different road categories in Sydney*

although at most traffic densities the speed is slightly higher on the two- rather than the four-lane roads. The explanation for this is that traffic management policies slow down flows of the four-lane roads because roadside parking is permitted and thus the capacity of curbside lanes is severely restricted, and they also tend to pass through more densely populated areas with more restrictive traffic management controls.

The speed–flow relationship provides a key supply-side input into the analysis but it is road space that is actually demanded. The type of theoretical framework that can link the two elements is described by Evans[36] although a somewhat less complete exposition is to be found in Peter Else.[37] Relaxing the basic assumptions of the model can lead to modifications to the speed–flow relationship; for example, Verhoef has shown that in some contexts it is not backward bending at the saturation level but becomes vertical.[38] The density function, the number of vehicles on a road at any one time, is also important in this type of analysis.

In Figure 6.9, element B shows the standard speed–flow relationship with the maximum flow depicted as F_{max}. This is traced round to the travel cost–flow diagram in element C. People essentially demand to join a road and this demand to enter a road is seen as the demand curve, D, in element A of Figure 6.9. This diagram also depicts the relationship between travel cost and traffic density – the MC being the rising marginal cost of congestion each additional motorist imposes on others using the road. The cost rises as the number of vehicles increases. The

[36] A.W. Evans, 'Road congestion: the diagrammatic analysis', *Journal of Political Economy*, **100**, 211–17, 1992.

[37] P.K. Else, 'A reformation of the theory of optimal taxation', *Journal of Transport Economics and Policy*, **15**, 217–32, 1981.

[38] E.T. Verhoef, 'Speed–flow relations and cost functions for congested traffic: Theory and empirical analysis', *Transportation Research A*, **39**, 792–812, 2005.

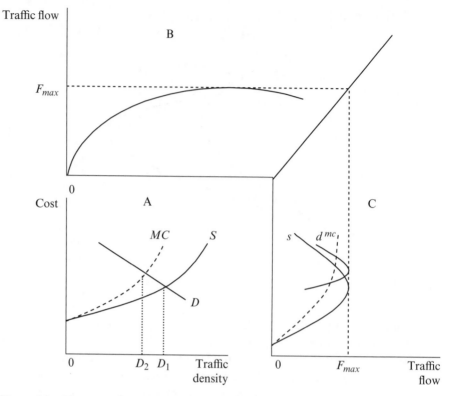

Figure 6.9   *The speed–flow relationship and the demand curve for road space*

S curve represents the cost of joining the road as seen by the additional motorist, in effect his/her cost of trip making, ignoring the consequences of his/her actions for the others on the road.

The curves in element C of the diagram, concerned with travel cost–flow relationships, are derived from elements A and B. The s curve is the average cost relating to congestion in a simple interaction model (see below) and the mc is the associated marginal curve. These relate directly back to the speed–flow relationship. Generalized costs (see Chapter 5) provide the vital link between physical traffic flows and cost. Broadly, faster travel in urban areas means cheaper travel in terms of generalized costs – vehicles are used more effectively and travel times are reduced. The s curve in element C thus represents the average generalized cost of trip making at different levels of traffic flow. It is a reverse of the speed–flow curve seen in Figure 6.7, with the positively sloped portion concerning the negatively sloped section of the speed–flow curve – this stems from the inverse relationship between speed and generalized cost. The mc curve therefore takes into account the congestion costs the additional user places on the existing traffic flow. The d curve is a derived demand curve reflecting the way in which the desired traffic flow changes as the cost of travel changes because the number of vehicles put on the road changes.

The actual traffic density that will emerge without any form of traffic

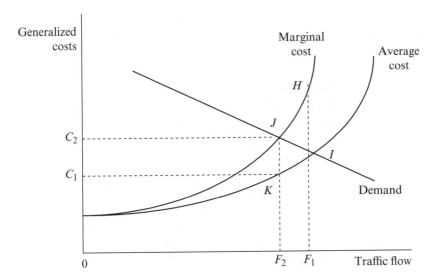

Figure 6.10   *The economic inefficiency of congestion*

restraints is where the demand for road space equals the average cost (*S*) of joining the road – D_1. This exceeds the optimal level, where road users take account of the impedance they impose on others, which is where *MC* is equated with demand. Moving across to the flow diagram, which is much more frequently found in the academic literature, the optimal traffic flow is where the *mc* curve intersects the derived demand curve.

6.8   The Economic Costs of Congestion

Most analysis of congestion focuses purely on segment C of Figure 6.9. It is usually presented in the form seen in Figure 6.10, with the *AC* curve representing the average cost of congestion at each level of traffic flow, and the *MC* curve the cost of additional traffic to existing flow. The optimal flow is, as we have seen above, where *MC* and demand are equated (F_2) while the actual flow, because road users ignore the congestion that they impose on others, tends to be F_1. A further interpretation can be placed on the *AC* and *MC* curves. The curves reflect the average and marginal generalized costs associated with different flows – they show all the time and money costs borne by road users when trip making. In this sense they may be seen as representing 'social costs' in the limited sense that they are the costs to the society (or 'club') of road users.

However, any individual user entering the road will consider only the costs he/she personally bears. The user will, in most circumstances, either be unaware of or unwilling to consider the external, congestion, costs he/she imposes on the other road users. Consequently, the individual motorist will consider only the average costs experienced by road users and take no account of the congestive impact of his/her trip on other vehicles. It is frequently argued that the *MC* curve, therefore, relates to the marginal social cost for the new trip maker and existing road users of an addition to the traffic flow while the AC curve is equivalent to the marginal private cost curve – that is, the additional cost borne and perceived by the new trip maker alone. The difference between the AC and MC curves at any traffic flow reflects the economic costs of congestion at that flow.

It is often important from a policy perspective to gain some idea of the actual costs associated with excessive congestion. From a social point of view the actual flow, F_1, is excessive because the F_1^{th} motorist is only enjoying a benefit of F_1I but imposing costs of F_1H. The additional traffic beyond the optimal level F_2 can be seen to be generating costs of F_2JIF_1, but only enjoying a benefit of (F_2JIF_1-HJI), where HJI is a deadweight loss. A traffic flow lower than F_2 is also suboptimal because the potential consumer surplus gains from trip making are not being fully exploited. Of course, this does mean that even at the optimal traffic flow there are still congestion costs, the area between the MC and AC curves up to traffic flow F_2, but these are more than offset by the benefits enjoyed by those using the road.

While the work on congestion costs is extensive, estimating the overall costs associated with excessive congestion is not simple. Work looking at the money value of lost travel time has a long pedigree – information on such costs is of commercial value to public transport suppliers who may trade off faster services against higher fares. The exact cost depends upon the mix of traffic and the reason why trips are being made. Periodically crude estimates, of the type produced by the UK's Confederation of British Industry (CBI) from 1988 onwards, are made of the costs of time wasted in congestion (about £15 billion per year for commercial traffic in the prices at the time of the first study) but these estimates, and subsequent ones based on questionnaire surveys tend to suffer from major theoretical and measurement problems. In the CBI case, the calculations were based on scaling up the responses to a small survey of distribution companies that were asked to assess the cost that traffic congestion was imposing on their operations. Besides the small size of the sample and the inherent dangers of aggregation, there was no effort to define a base-line level of optimal congestion as a benchmark for comparison, nor was there any effort to net out the costs that the distributors were imposing on others but not paying for.

A more rigorous approach is to consider the opportunity cost of lost travel time (see Chapter 5). These vary by the nature of the road involved. Using the figures adopted by the UK Department of Transport when appraising road schemes, David Newbery,[39] as the result of careful calculations, produced marginal congestion costs by road type in the UK (Table 6.13). While these figures are in themselves dated, they represent solid analysis and show the differing levels of costs imposed by an additional vehicle joining the various traffic streams. Aggregation gives an estimated annual congestion cost in the UK of about £12,750 million for 1989 to 1990.

---

[39] D.M. Newbery, 'Road damage externalities and road user charges', *Econometrica*, **56**, 295–316, 1988.

Table 6.13 *Estimated congestion costs by road type in the United Kingdom (1989)*

Road Type	Marginal cost (pence per mile)
Motorway	0.26
Urban central peak	36.97
Urban central off-peak	29.23
Non-central peak	15.86
Non-central off-peak	8.74
Small town peak	6.89
Small town off-peak	4.20
Other urban	0.08
Rural dual carriageway	0.07
Other dual carriageway	0.19
Other rural	0.05

Source: D.M Newbery, 'Pricing and congestion: economic principles relevant to road pricing', *Oxford Review of Economic Policy*, **6**, 22–38, 1990.

More recent studies of road congestion costs in the United States include Winston and Langer[40] who reviewed congestion costing methods, and using their own model came up with annual costs of $37.5 billion annually (2004 prices), a third of which consists of freight vehicle delays. Weisbrod and co-workers evaluate the economic productivity costs of congestion, particularly to businesses for distribution, and reduced economies of scale and agglomeration, finding them to range from $20 million to $1 billion a year in typical metropolitan regions. The costs vary significantly by industry, with higher costs in industries that involve significant distribution costs or rely on specialized employees.[41] More recently, the Texas Transportation Institute (TTI) has developed a congestion index to calculate congestion costs in major American cities and convert these into cost measures. The TTI estimates for 2005 are that traffic congestion in the 437 urban areas examined cost $78.2 billion.[42]

6.9   Some Refinements on the Basic Congestion Model

The analysis of congestion set out above is based upon a very simple modeling framework: a linear road, no junctions, homogeneous traffic and equally skilful drivers. In practice, as we would expect from our discussion of the speed–flow relationship, the total cost function varies with the details of the transport system under consideration. Also, considerable traffic congestion stems from 'incidents' such as accidents, emergency road repair and breakdowns that do not

[40] C. Winston and A. Langer, *The Effect of Government Highway Spending on Road Users' Congestion Costs*, Washington, DC: Brookings Institute, 2004.

[41] G. Weisbrod, D. Vary and G. Treyz, *Economic Implications of Congestion*, NCHRP Report 463, Transportation Research Board, Washington, DC, 2001.

[42] Texas Transportation Institute, *2007 Annual Urban Mobility Report*, College Station, TX: TTI, 2007.

fit comfortably into the simple framework. Traffic incidents account for up to an estimated 60 percent of delay-hours. Although they are random events, they cause significant delays where traffic volumes approach road capacity. In uncongested conditions an incident causes little or no traffic delay, but a stalled car on the shoulder of a congested road can cause 100 to 200 vehicle-hours of delay on adjacent lanes.

Vickrey[43] distinguishes five separate types of congestion relevant in this rather more complex world. While these are couched in terms of road congestion, they are equally applicable to most other modes of transport – one can quite simply substitute air-lane or waterway for roads. The types of congestion are:

- *Simple interaction*   This occurs at comparatively low levels of traffic flow where the number of mobile units is small. Delays are minimal and usually result from slow and careful driving on the part of users who wish to avoid accidents. Total delay tends to vary as the square of the volume of traffic, so that each additional motorist causes a delay to each other road user roughly equal to that which he himself suffers. This is essentially the type of congestion that we have been concerned with above.

- *Multiple interaction*   This occurs at higher levels of traffic flow where, although the road capacity is not reached, an additional vehicle causes considerably more impedance to each other vehicle than with simple interaction. Empirical evidence suggests that for every minute the marginal user is delayed, other vehicles each suffer a delay of three to five minutes.

- *Bottleneck situations*   These occur when a particular stretch of a road (or other piece of transport infrastructure) is of more limited capacity than either the preceding or subsequent links in the network. If the flow is below that of the capacity of the bottleneck then either simple or multiple interaction may occur, but once the capacity is reached, and in particular if this is sustained for any length of time, then queues develop. An exceptionally high level of congestion is then likely to arise.

- *Triggerneck situations*   When a bottleneck situation results in queues of traffic, these may impede the general flow of traffic even for those not wishing to use the section of road with limited capacity. At the extreme, congestion may become so severe that the traffic comes to a complete standstill and can only flow again after some vehicles have backed up.

- *Network and control congestion*   The efforts of traffic engineers and managers (by the introduction of different traffic control devices) may reduce congestion costs at certain times of the day or, for example, in the case of bus lanes, for specific types of traffic but increase them at other times or for other modes. This results from the general bluntness of most traffic control schemes which may help solve major problems but do, at times, create other, albeit usually less significant, difficulties. This type of congestion was not

[43] W. Vickrey, 'Congestion theory and transport investment', *American Economic Review: Papers and Proceedings*, **59**, 251–60, 1969.

fully appreciated until the mid-1970s and had earlier led to excessively high estimates of urban congestion costs. Previously it was assumed that congestion tended to be of the simple or multiple interactive kind. But as succinctly expressed in a UK policy document, 'Once account is taken of the limitations placed upon urban traffic speeds by factors such as the incidence of traffic lights and the multi-purpose nature of urban road networks, traffic speeds associated with even very low levels of congestion can be expected to be quite low – almost certainly below 20 mph in central areas'.[44]

In addition to these five types of traffic congestion that can arise when the infrastructure is fixed, Vickrey also points to the more general problem of transport congestion in the economy as a whole. In the context of urban areas, roads in the United States take up 30 percent or more of the land area of city centers, while in Western Europe the figure is between 15 and 20 percent and in Third World countries about 10 percent. The question then becomes one of whether in the long term the general welfare of urban society is being excessively reduced by too much transport infrastructure congesting city centers. The acceptance of this view makes it rather difficult to define meaningfully optimal levels of transport provision in the traditional welfare sense.

A further problem is that many travelers, and especially road users, have a very poor perception of their own private costs. Indeed, in the case of car users the perceived cost of many trips may embrace only the time involved. In such cases the perceived AC, while reflecting some of the costs to a motorist thinking of joining a traffic stream, is an inadequate basis for calculating the MC curve which embraces the congestion costs to other road users. The appropriate policy curve in these circumstances is MC^*, which is based upon the resource costs of making trips rather than just the perception of the additional user. As we see in Figure 6.11, the implication of this is that congestion may well be somewhat higher than is sometimes estimated: namely F^*F_A rather than $F_O F_A$.

Congestion, or to be more exact excessive congestion, has been shown to imply a 'deadweight' welfare loss and to reduce the economic efficiency of any transport system. In recent years there has been some debate, however, about whether this welfare loss is compensated by other beneficial effects of congestion that are not immediately apparent in the standard, static, marginal cost type of analysis. These arguments tend to follow three broad lines: those focusing on issues centering on the distributional effect of congestion on different groups in society, those concerned with more straightforward efficiency problems, and those that take other forms of cost into account.

The main costs imposed by traffic congestion are usually found to be time costs (although there may also be fuel and other components of generalized costs to be considered). Queuing up for the use of a transport facility and slowing down its consumption takes up the user's time. Measures to reduce the

[44] UK Department of the Environment, *Transport Policy: A Consultation Document*, London: HMSO, 1976.

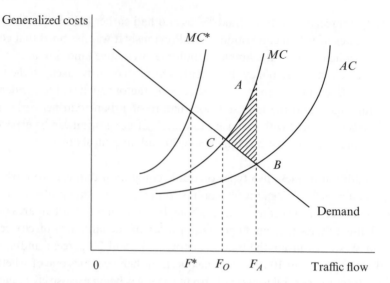

Figure 6.11 *The problems of misperceived private costs*

demand, increase the supply, or the introduction of market prices to optimize congestion (all of which will be discussed later in the book) impose some form of either financial or welfare loss which, although on very simple efficiency criteria must be lower than the congestion costs saved, still have to be borne by someone.

Those who favor the retention of a high level of congestion as a method of allocating scarce transport facilities argue that, since in the short term time is evenly distributed to everyone – that is, there are 24 hours in every person's day – it is a more equitable method of allocation than many alternative techniques. If a traveler really wants to make a journey, he/she would be willing and able to wait, whereas if a high congestion deterring charge is levied, his/her financial budget constraint may make it impossible to make the trip.

While there seem to be some grounds for this type of argument if one accepts that transport is unique in requiring a substantial time input for its consumption (a proposition that is far from self-evident), in the longer term the wider distributional issue is probably more effectively tackled by direct income redistribution measures. There seems no reason, in the general case, for singling out transport rather than a number of other economic activities for this special treatment. In addition, even when goods have in the past been provided free of charge, there is empirical evidence that, despite the equal distribution of time, it is the rich who tend to obtain them and, *ipso facto*, a disproportionate share of the benefit.[45]

Moving to the second mitigating argument in favor of allocation by congestion, we turn to efficiency considerations. Congestion is seen by some as a complementary method of allocating certain types of facility, supplementing rather than

[45] Y. Barzel, 'A theory of rationing by waiting', *Journal of Law and Economics*, **17**, 73–95, 1974.

competing with other, usually monetary price mechanisms.[46] The deadweight loss associated with congestion may in some situations, it is claimed, be outweighed by other forms of welfare benefit. In some instances people, for example those on aircraft stacked at congested airports, use time spent in queuing productively while, in others, the deadweight loss associated with suboptimally excessive congestion may be exceeded by administrative or other costs of achieving optimal utilization of the transport facility. As we shall see in Chapter 8, this has been one argument used against the introduction of sophisticated metering devices for urban road pricing.

More generally, it is argued that, since transport users are far from homogeneous, different groups of users will value time differently and hence a system with both time-allocated and financially allocated facilities could well be optimal. If analogies are made with other forms of economic activity from retailing to car manufacturing, then both money and time are used for allocation. For example, one can get fast, personal service at a small local store but prices are likely to be higher than at a large, possibly distant, supermarket where queuing is normal at checkouts.

This sort of approach is in general use for some forms of transport, with many countries, for instance, having fast, tolled motorways running parallel to slow, free trunk roads. Also one can often choose between expensive, readily available air services or cheap stand-by facilities that often involve queuing or waiting for a flight. With a given distribution of income, this increased choice necessarily increases welfare that may, in turn, offset any, or at least part of, the deadweight loss incurred on congested parts of the system. Essentially there is product differentiation taking place in response to variations in the opportunity cost of time among consumers.

The difficulty with this argument is that in many cases physical factors make it impossible to provide different types of transport service. In other cases, economies of scale are sufficient to make the provision of alternatives excessively wasteful. One approach, favored by theoreticians, may be to decide upon the optimal flow, and let only that flow on to the road or facility at any one time, leaving a queue of potential users waiting. The optimal flow in this sense is such that the length of the queue of traffic wishing to use the road would make the opportunity time cost of waiting equal to the money price at which the traffic flow is optimal. It is difficult to see how this could be put into practice on urban roads, although it may be appropriate for making optimal use of facilities such as bridges or ferries where queuing is practicable. The information costs of estimating optimal queue lengths may also prove an insurmountable practical problem.

Finally, a high level of congestion may itself be optimal (even with the deadweight losses it imposes and where neither of the former lines of argument is applicable) when other forms of cost are also considered. It may be, for example, that the transaction costs of moving from an overcongested to an optimally

[46] E. Smolensky, T.N. Tideman and D. Nichols, 'The economic uses of congestion', *Papers of the Regional Science Association*, **26**, 37–52. 1971.

congested situation exceed the conventionally defined benefits of eliminating a deadweight loss. The transition costs involved in removing an externality such as excessive congestion are of three broad types: the cost per unit of reducing the externality, initial lump-sum costs of organization, and information/enforcement costs of carrying the action through.[47]

To remove excessive congestion would, in virtually all cases, involve costs in one or more of these categories and it could well be that in many cases such transaction costs could be very high. A related point is that the actual reduction of congestion to the optimal level for transport users may mean spreading other forms of external cost (generally noise and air pollution) to a much wider group of non-users in the community. Raising landing fees at overused major airports, for example, is likely to divert traffic elsewhere and place environmental costs on people living near other, formerly underutilized and quieter airports.

In these circumstances, where the demand for transport concentrates the incidence of environmental costs on a relatively small group in the community, congestion may be felt to offer a more acceptable use of transport infrastructure than if congestion is reduced, but this results in demand being spread geographically. This is more likely if the initial congestion is concentrated in relatively insensitive areas, but its reduction would increase the environmental nuisance experienced in residential or other sensitive locations.

6.10   Some Broad Aggregate Calculations

The discussion so far has focused on individual external costs and provided, in places, some estimates of their possible magnitudes. Here we provide just a few examples of larger studies that have sought to place monetary values on a range of transport-related externalities. The problems with most of these studies are that they largely rely on secondary sources and there is, in some cases, a lack of consistency in the way various effects have been measured and evaluated. Second, placing monetary values on individual externalities at the micro, case-study level is difficult because such partial-equilibrium work assumes that 'other things remain constant', and most especially that income remains constant and that the prices of other goods remain constant. Clearly, at the macro level any effort to estimate the willingness to pay for one externality reduction will reduce the income available to pay for the optimization of another. Equally, reducing say, noise nuisance to an optimal level will affect the price of noise and thus make it difficult to evaluate the willingness to pay for, say, increased, safety. Unless these factors are embraced in the macro-level calculations there is an inherent upward bias in the valuation of external transport costs.

In addition, there are often important correlations in terms of the impact of various external factors. Reducing congestion costs, for instance, not only

[47] C.J. Dahlman, 'The problem of externalities', *Journal of Law and Economics*, **22**, 141–62, 1979.

allows transport infrastructure to be utilized more efficiently by its users but often also reduces environmental costs because, for example, automobiles are not continually stopping and starting, or aircraft do not have to circle so much before landing. The correlations are not always positive, however, and the fitting of a catalytic converter, while reducing NO_x emissions, increases fuel consumption and thus CO_2 emissions, and while smoother tires produce less road noise they have less traction and can lead to more accidents.

Notwithstanding these problems, Emile Quinet[48] first tried to use the best information available to give a general, minimum estimate of the monetary costs of the damage transport imposes on the environments of industrialized countries. His figures are seen as conservative because they cover only some of the damage done by transport, and because only lower estimates for each form of social cost considered are used in the calculations.

Table 6.14 provides a more recent assessment of the external costs (including congestion) that have been associated with the use of automobiles in the United States. Table 6.15 shows the meso level, looking at the relative external costs of car use in a European city.

It is fairly typical that the costs of congestion per mile exceed those of pollution and other environmental effects. It should be remembered, however, that congestion is only external to those using transport while the environmental costs are external to the transport system as a whole. The data suggest, therefore, that the largest social gains come from removing the imperfections within the transport system, rather than from removing the costs that are external to it.

Further Reading

Environmental data tend to be spread across a range of official publications. Data also come in a variety of different units that often makes analysis difficult. Most national governments provide some statistics in their yearly transport reports; in the case of the United States this is US Bureau of Transportation Statistics, *National Financial Statistics*, which is published annually, and for Britain it is *Transport Statistics Great Britain*. The periodic reports of the Intergovernmental Panel on Climate Change also make interesting reading.

Early attempts to specifically look at the environmental aspects of transport are found in J.-P. Barde and K.J. Button (eds), *Transport Policy and the Environment: Six Studies*, London: Earthscan, 1990. For a set of original papers looking at the economic aspects of transport and the environment see K.J. Button and D.A. Hensher (eds), *Handbook of Transport and the Environment*, Oxford: Pergamon, 2003. Many classic papers are to be found in Y. Hanyashi, K.J. Button and P. Nijkamp (eds), *Environment and Transport*, Cheltenham, UK

---

[48] E. Quinet, 'The social costs of transport: evaluation and links with internalisation policies', in *Internalizing the Social Costs of Transport*, Paris: European Conference of Ministers of Transport, 1994.

Table 6.14   *Estimated externality costs of automobile use in the United States*

	Cents per gallon	Cents per mile
Central values for marginal external costs		
Fuel-related costs		
Greenhouse gases	6	0.3
Oil dependency	12	0.6
Total	18	0.9
Mileage-related costs		
Local pollution	42	2.0
Congestion	105	5.0
Accidents	63	3.0
Total	210	10.0

Source: I.W.H. Parry, M. Walls and C. Harrington, 'Automobile externalities and policies', *Journal of Economic Literature*, **45**, 373–99, 2007.

Table 6.15   *External costs of urban car use in Brussels (€ per vehicle-mile)*

	Gasoline		Diesel	
	Peak	Off-peak	Peak	Off-peak
Congestion	1.856	0.003	1.856	0.003
Air pollution	0.004	0.004	0.042	0.026
Accidents	0.033	0.033	0.033	0.033
Noise	0.002	0.008	0.002	0.008
Total	1.895	0.048	1.933	0.070

Source: S. Proost and K. Van Dender, 'The welfare impacts of alternative policies to address atmospheric pollution in urban road transport', *Regional Science and Urban Economics*, **31**, 383–411, 2001.

and Northampton, MA, USA: Edward Elgar 1999. See also K. Small and C. Kazimi, 'On the costs of air pollution from motor vehicles', *Journal of Transport Economics and Policy*, **29**, 7–32, 1995.

Safety is a major issue in transport economics, and I.A. Savage, 'Transport safety', in K.J. Button and D.A. Hensher (eds), *Handbook of Transport Systems and Traffic Control*, Oxford: Pergamon, 2001, provides a useful overview.

A rigorous explanation of the theory of congestion is to be found in C.R. Lindsey and E.T. Verhoef, 'Congestion modelling', in D.A. Hensher and K.J. Button (eds), *Handbook of Transport Modelling*, 2nd edn, Oxford: Elsevier, 2007.

Transportation Research D, Transport and Environment the *Journal of Environmental Economics and Management* and *Resource and Energy Economics* regularly carry economics papers on the theme of this chapter.

7 Pricing of Transport Services

7.1 The Principles of Pricing

Pricing is a method of resource allocation; there is no such thing as the 'right' price, but rather there are optimal pricing strategies that permit specified goals to be obtained. The optimal price, for example, to achieve profit maximization may differ from that needed to maximize welfare or ensure the highest sales revenue. In some cases there is no attempt to devise a price to maximize or minimize anything, but rather, prices are set that permit lower-level objectives (for example, adequate security or minimum market share) to be attained. Further, prices may be set to achieve certain objectives for the transport supplier in terms of the supplier's welfare (this is normally the case of private enterprise transport undertakings) while in other fields prices may be set to improve the welfare of consumers (as has been the case with some publicly owned transport undertakings). The distinction here is a fine one and many undertakings consider that the employment of the pricing mechanisms to achieve their objectives is automatically to the benefit of customers.

One of the major problems in discussing pricing policies in practice is to decide what exactly is the objective of pricing. A good example is port pricing where there has been a traditional blurring between the 'European' doctrine of setting prices to facilitate the economic growth of the port's hinterland and the 'Anglo-Saxon' approach that attempts to ensure that ports cover their costs and, where possible, make a profit irrespective of the effects on the wider local economy.[1] In providing local transit services there are often conflicts between setting prices that allow use by lower-income groups and pricing so that the system does not get excessively congested at peak, rush-hour travel times.

When the private sector sets the price, much depends on the market power exercised by the suppliers of the transport system and those using it, and this in turn is affected by the prevailing market structure. If the supplier operates within a highly competitive market then there is no opportunity for the transport company to control the price – the market sets it. If, in contrast, and at the other extreme, there is a single monopoly supplier and numerous customers, then the transport undertaking can dictate prices to a large extent, but always has to be cognizant of losing business, and net revenue, by setting them too high. In intermediate cases, the various actors involved play 'games' with each other, jockeying to gain the most benefit, be it consumer surplus or profit.

[1] E. Bennathan and A. Walters, *Port Pricing and Investment Policy for Developing Countries*, Oxford: Oxford University Press, 1979.

Table 7.1   *Features of various market structures*

Feature	Perfect competition	Perfectly competitive	Monopoly
Profit maximization	Yes	Yes	Normally
Barriers to entry/exit	No	No	Yes
Perfect mobility of inputs	Yes	Yes	No
Ubiquitous information	Yes	Yes	No
Large number of firms	Yes	Maybe	No
Homogeneous service	Yes	Maybe	Yes
Firms confronted by the the cost function	Yes	Yes	Yes
U-shaped AC functions	Yes	Maybe	Maybe
Profits	Normal	Normal	Monopoly rent

The nature of market power and the ways that it may be exercised depend to a considerable extent on the nature of the market itself. There are many different forms of market and it is beyond this volume to explain all of them. Table 7.1, however, provides a very brief outline of the main features of competitive, contestable and monopoly markets: forms that are often said to exist in transport. They are not the only ones but the aim is to give an indication of the various parameters that determine market behavior rather than to be comprehensive.

This chapter looks at the appropriate pricing policies to adopt for transport undertakings, considering a variety of objectives and when those involved are confronted by different market conditions. While the later sections focus on criteria concerned with maximizing the social benefits of transport that embrace the interests of both suppliers and users, this section briefly reviews the prices likely to exist in situations where transport enterprises are interested in purely commercial criteria (defined here as the pursuit of their own self-interest). The chapters that follow consider, along with other things, the role of pricing of the environment and of congestion.

7.2   Matching Supply with Demand

Profit maximization is the traditional motivation of private enterprise undertakings. The actual price level in this case depends upon the degree of competition in the market. Where competition is considerable, then no single supplier has control over price and must charge that determined by the interaction of supply and demand in the market as a whole (Adam Smith's 'invisible hand'). In this perfectly competitive environment, it is impossible for any supplier to earn supernormal profits in the long term. This is because of the incentives such profits have on stimulating new suppliers to enter the market and thus increase aggregate supply. Market economics tells us that, in the long-run prices, will be equated with the marginal (and average) costs of each supplier. At these prices there is no incentive for either firms to leave the market or change their output, or for new ones to enter.

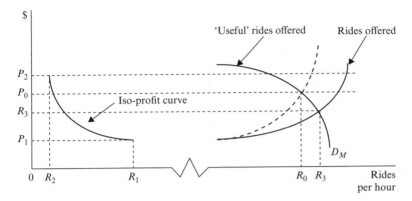

Figure 7.1   *Taxi-cab fare determination*

In contrast, a true monopoly supplier (see again Table 7.1) has no fear of new entrants increasing the aggregate supply of transport services and has the freedom either to set the price or to stipulate the level of service he/she is prepared to offer. The effective constraint on the monopolist is the countervailing power of those demanding the service which prevents the joint determination of both output and price. However, given the absence of competition and the degree of freedom enjoyed by the monopolist, it is almost certain that a profit-maximizing price will result in charges above marginal and average cost (the only exception being the most unlikely situation of a perfectly elastic market demand curve). This is one reason why governments have tended to regulate the railways, ports and other transport undertakings with monopoly characteristics.

This simple description of textbook situations does, however, hide certain peculiarities that may arise in some transport markets. Since the actual unit of supply, the vehicle, is mobile it is possible for the overall transport market to appear to be essentially competitive, but the individual suppliers to price as if they were monopolists or, at least, exercised some monopoly power. The unregulated urban taxi-cab market is an example of this.[2] In Figure 7.1, D_M is the market demand for taxi-cab 'rides' per hour in a market supplied solely by cruising taxi-cabs. The cost of taxi-cruising activities is almost constant irrespective of whether a fare is carried or not, and to stay in business the cab operator must charge fares which permit such costs to be recovered.

In the diagram, the iso-profit curve for a single operator indicates combinations of fare and ridership that allow a normal profit to be earned. It is constrained to a maximum fare (P_2) by the physical impossibility of carrying more than R_2 passengers an hour. Also, it is unlikely that a fare above P_2 would ever be feasible; potential users would simply not accept it. Further, for the market as a whole fares must exceed P_1 if taxi-cab services are to be offered, but this should not be seen as the true long-term floor level of fares. Because potential customers are seldom positioned exactly where empty cabs are cruising, there must be an

---

[2] C. Shreiber, 'The economic reasons for price and entry regulation of taxicabs', *Journal of Transport Economics and Policy*, **9**, 268–79, 1975.

excess of rides offered above total demand if sufficient rides are to be supplied – this is indicated by the 'useful' rides curve.

This lack of synchronization means, in effect, that the 'rides offered curve' in Figure 7.1 is not a true supply curve since it is dependent upon demand conditions. At higher fares, the rides offered will increase but even at the intersection with the demand curve (with R_3 rides offered) there will still be unsatisfied demand,[3] that is, the number of taxi rides taken is less than the number demanded. This is because the taxis may not be at the same location as potential customers. Only if cabs were always exactly where they were wanted would demand always be satisfied. The demand will, in normal circumstances, be fully satisfied only at a price above the intersection – say P_0 – because at this and higher prices the ratio between the number of rides demanded and the number offered will correspond to the rate of occupancy. This is so because the number demanded is then assumed to be equal to the number of rides taken, and there are no frustrated passengers who give up waiting because they are unable to obtain a ride.

The actual fare level may be set at any point above P_1 but below P_2 hence the apparently perfect taxi-cab market does not have a unique price. However, there are reasons to suspect that the final price will be nearer P_1 than P_2 thus permitting the earning of supernormal profit by the cab operators. It also means that those who still wish to pay the fare and use taxi-cab services will have a good service provided for them – the rides offered being well in excess of those demanded – although the short waiting time and abundance of capacity is likely to be wasteful in resource utilization.

The tendency towards high fares is caused by the monopoly power enjoyed by any individual taxi at the point of hire. Unlike normal perfect markets, individual suppliers are not normally confronted with perfectly elastic demand schedules for their services, but when hailed by a potential customer are virtual monopolists able to charge a high fare for their services. People seldom turn away a cab upon hearing the fare to hail another one – the low probability of a lower cab fare does not justify it. Once fares are at the higher level there is, therefore, no incentive for individual cabs to cut their fare because to customers they all appear alike and no additional business is attracted (that is, revenue for any cab acting differently will inevitably fall).

Of course, the cab market is somewhat more complicated than the simple model suggests (there are, for instance, cab ranks, and it may be possible to differentiate cabs by color schemes and so on), but the fear that cabs could exploit local monopoly power of the type described and keep fares suboptimally high is one reason why authorities in most major cities control fare levels. While this may be justified, it is hard to see why at the same time most cities outside of the United Kingdom regulate the number of taxi-cabs operating within their domain; if fares are deemed optimal at P_0 then rides offered will automatically adjust to R_0 and

[3] C. Shreiber, 'The economic reasons for price and entry regulation of taxicabs: reply', *Journal of Transport Economics and Policy*, **9**, 298–304, 1977.

there is no need for official regulation of capacity which can seriously distort the market.[4]

While it is possible that the simple picture of perfectly competitive price determination is often complicated in the transport sector, it is equally true that the basic model of monopoly also on occasions needs modification. There are few if any natural monopolies in transport; there are normally competitive modes even if the one in question tends to be monopolistic in character. Also, users of transport services often have the alternative of changing either their method of production (in the case of freight transport) or their pattern of consumption (with passenger modes) so that transport is itself competitive with different forms of human activity. In some cases where these countervailing forces are weak or the introduction of competition would mean wasteful duplication of services, government may institutionalize a monopoly, but by controlling price and other commercial aspects of its operations prevent the exploitation of customers. Much of the regulation initiated in a wide range of countries in the 1930s and 1940s, which is discussed in Chapter 14, was ostensibly introduced for this sort of reason.

The fear of potential competition, especially in the long term, tends to regulate the activities of essentially monopoly transport suppliers even when government intervention is minimal. The pricing policies pursued by liner conferences, when shipping companies combine to monopolize scheduled maritime services between major ports, offers an illustration of this. Some discussion of detailed pricing of consignments by conferences is contained in Section 7.5; here we focus on the general principles. Sturmey[5] argues that conferences do not price to maximize immediate profits but rather to maximize the present value of the flow of revenue from the market.

The emphasis on revenue reflects the concern with market size while that on the present value shows that long-term objectives dominate short-run considerations. If, in Figure 7.2, the intention were to maximize profit in each market then price would be set, assuming that the conference enjoyed a short-term monopoly position, at P_M with a monthly output of Q_M. If sales-revenue maximization (subject to cost recovery) is the objective then price P_R is charged (expanding output to where the MC curve hits the horizontal would violate the break-even constraint).

In practice, however, Sturmey argues that conference rates are found to be below P_M because the high short-term profits would encourage competition to enter the market; they are also unlikely to equal P_R because the conference looks beyond the immediate period although there is no a priori method of telling whether they will be above or below this level. The conference is likely to base its pricing policy on a relatively long time horizon – hypothesized by Sturmey to be the period over which the scale of productive enterprise is unchanged, but long enough to allow for additional capital equipment, which duplicates existing

[4] M.E. Beesley, 'Regulation of taxis', *Economic Journal*, **83**, 150–72, 1973.
[5] S.G. Sturmey, *Shipping Economics*, Basingstoke: Macmillan, 1975.

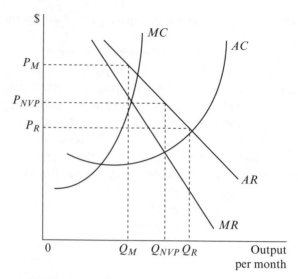

Figure 7.2 *Pricing of shipping conference services*

equipment, to be installed – although not long enough for all factors to be considered truly variable. The net revenue over this period, discounted to yield its current worth, is then seen as the key variable to maximize. The conference rate is, therefore, likely to be, say, at P_{NPV} in Figure 7.2, at which the maximum present value (the value of the flow of net revenue as perceived today) is obtained without attracting new entrants.

7.3   Marginal Cost Pricing

As was pointed out in the previous section, the pricing policy adopted by any transport undertaking depends upon its basic objectives. The traditional, classical economic assumption is that firms price so that profits are maximized. More recent variations on the theory of the firm suggest that many undertakings adopt prices that maximize sales revenues[6] when in an expansive phase, or simply price to ensure that certain satisfactory levels of profit, security, market domination and so on are achieved when a defensive stance is adopted – 'satisficing behavior'.[7]

The sales revenue-maximizing ideas of Baumol illustrate the sorts of deviation that this implies from conventional profit-maximizing ideas. In Figure 7.3, the total cost and revenues curves associated with different levels of output are depicted. The profit-maximizing business will produce an output of Q_{Π} but the sales revenue maximizer will continue producing to the point Q_R where total

[6] W.J. Baumol, 'On the theory of the expansion of the firm', *American Economic Review*, **52**, 1078–87, 1962.

[7] H.A. Simon, 'Theories of decision-making in economics and behavioural science', *American Economic Review*, **49**, 253–83, 1959.

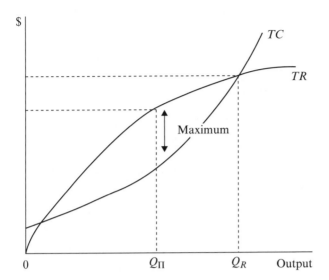

Figure 7.3   *Sales revenue-maximizing output*

revenue is highest subject to cost recovery. Costs in this case may be viewed as embracing a reasonable return for the owners of the transport undertaking.

Whatever the underlying operational objective, the theory of the firm assumes that the supplier is intent on maximizing his/her own welfare, be this defined in terms of profits or higher-level objectives.

Welfare economics takes a rather wider view of pricing, looking upon pricing as a method of resource allocation that maximizes social welfare rather than simply the welfare of the supplier. In some cases, since the good or service is actually provided by a public agency, this may be equated with maximizing the suppliers' welfare. In other instances, controls or incentives may be applied to private companies so that their pricing policy is modified to maximize social rather than private welfare. This may take the form of restrictions on pricing flexibility, or the taxing and subsidizing of firms so that their prices are socially optimal.

Social optimality has a wide variety of meanings but in broad terms it means maximizing the joint net social surplus – that is, the total revenue (*TR*) plus consumers' surplus (*CS*) generated by an undertaking minus the total cost (*TC*). We can, therefore, define the objective of public policy as the maximization of:

$$SW = TR + CS - TC \qquad (7.1)$$

Figure 7.4 takes the example of charging for rail freight capacity as an illustration of how the optimal price is arrived at. For expositional ease, assume that there are constant costs and that the railway undertaking is a monopoly. If it seeks to maximize its profits it will charge P_M, which in terms of equation (7.1) will produce total revenue of $P_M b Q_M 0$, consumer surplus of $ab P_M$ and total costs of $P_{MC} e Q_M 0$ resulting in a social welfare level of $abe P_{MC}$. While this may yield the maximum profit to the railway it is not, however, the price which maximizes social

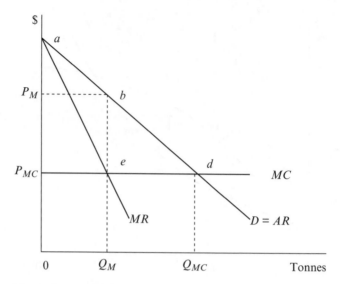

Figure 7.4 *Marginal cost pricing*

surplus. That price is the price at which marginal cost is equated with demand. At this price, the total revenue is $P_{MC}dQ_{MC}0$, consumer surplus is adP_{MC} and total costs are $P_{MC}dQ_{MC}0$ which gives a social welfare exceeding that associated with the profit-maximizing price by an amount *bed*.

In other words, social welfare is maximized when price is equated to marginal cost. What marginal cost pricing does, in effect, is to result in transport services being provided up to the point where the benefit for the marginal unit (represented by the demand curve) is equated with the costs of providing that unit. The policy is a fairly well-established one in economic theory and, indeed, formed the UK public enterprise pricing from 1967 and is the stated policy of the European Union.

Traditional theory also tells us that such a condition prevails in the long term when perfect competition exists despite the fact that each firm is attempting to maximize its own profits. The ability to exercise any degree of monopoly power, however, permits a firm to price above marginal cost so that it can achieve additional profit at the expense of reduced output and at costs to the consumers. The price charged by a profit-maximizing monopolist will force some potential consumers to forgo consumption despite their willingness to pay for the cost of their activities. Indeed, it was the fear of monopoly exploitation that led to controls being imposed on railway pricing in the late nineteenth century and has led to the United States controlling rate fixing by shipping conferences operating from its ports.

While it has been shown that adopting marginal cost pricing maximizes social welfare, the exact definition of the appropriate marginal cost has been left vague. More specifically, there is the question of whether long-run ($LRMC$) or short-run ($SRMC$) marginal cost pricing is the more appropriate (short run being when there is a fixed capacity that can be modified only in the long run). $SRMC$ pricing has the advantage in that it ensures that existing capacity is

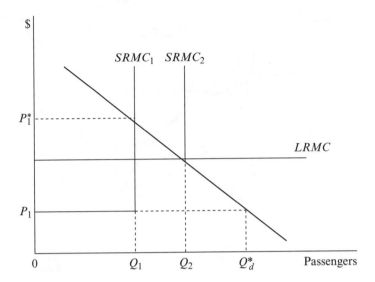

Figure 7.5   *Short- and long-run marginal cost pricing*

used optimally but does not take account of capital and other fixed cost items. Wiseman[8] was particularly concerned with this problem since, he argued, the shorter the time period under consideration, the lower will appear the *SRMC* and, *ipso facto*, the price charged to users. This concern is misguided, however, because if there is fixed capacity, as is almost always the case with transport in the short term, a premium should be added to the *SRMC* as an effective rationing device to contain excessive demand. Price is, after all, an allocative device.

Figure 7.5 shows the demand for a passenger railway service with capacity Q_1. The marginal cost of carrying each additional passenger is constant until the capacity of the system is reached whereupon the *SRMC* becomes infinite. If a price of P_1 is charged with $SRMC_1$, then demand will exceed capacity by $Q_d^* - Q_1$. In these circumstances, where demand will exceed absolute capacity using *SRMC* pricing policy, a mark-up to price level P_1^* is appropriate to ration the available seats. The extra revenue thus generated in excess of *LRMC* provides an indication that it would be beneficial for the capacity of the railway service to be expanded. The optimal scale of service will, in fact, be offering capacity Q_2 where the price charged to travelers is equated with *LRMC* (and the upturn of the $SRMC_2$ curve). We see, therefore, that the long-run optimum is where $P = LRMC = SRMC$. In some cases (for example, airports or motorway systems), indivisibilities may make it impossible to provide exactly the optimal capacity Q_2 and a choice must then be made between a suboptimally small system or a suboptimally large one. Under such conditions decisions must be based upon weighing the full costs and benefits of the alternatives against one another.

[8] J. Wiseman, 'The theory of public utility price – an empty box', *Oxford Economic Papers* (New Series), **9**, 56–74, 1957.

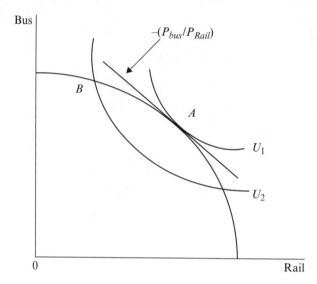

Figure 7.6   *Second-best problems*

7.4   Difficulties of 'Second-best' Situations

The preceding analysis contained a number of implicit, as well as the stated, explicit assumptions. In particular, it assumed that all other prices in the economy are set equal to marginal cost. A variety of factors – some economic, others political or institutional – mean that in reality all other prices in the economy are not equal to marginal cost. The problem, again couched in terms of the railway example, then becomes one of deciding whether marginal cost pricing is, in these circumstances, appropriate.

For simplicity we assume that there is only bus and rail transport in the economy. Further, the bus sector is under monopoly control and fares are set above the marginal costs of providing services. The issue is one of whether the railways should adopt marginal cost price or some alternative strategy that would maximize social welfare. In Figure 7.6, we have the production possibility curve for bus and rail services and, additionally, denote A as the traffic mix which would result in maximum social welfare; it is tangential to the highest attainable indifference curve.

Extending the analysis of Figure 7.4, because this combination maximizes social welfare, the two modes will be charging marginal costs at this point. Since, however, we have said that bus fares are above marginal cost ($P_{Bus} > MC_{Bus}$) the attainable position on the production possibility frontier with the actual price ratio if rail adopts marginal cost pricing ($P_{Rail} = MC_{Rail}$) is B which is on a lower utility curve; namely U_2. The question then arises as to whether the railways by deviating from marginal cost pricing and adopting a 'second-best' pricing strategy can enhance total social welfare.

The simplest approach to the second best in these conditions, as established by Lipsey and Lancaster,[9] is that rail should adopt fares which deviate by the same proportion from marginal costs as do those of bus. In other words it is possible to attain social welfare level U_1 by adopting prices that conform to:

$$\frac{P_{Rail} - MC_{Rail}}{MC_{Rail}} = \frac{P_{Bus} - MC_{Bus}}{MC_{Bus}} \tag{7.2}$$

What this effectively does is to ensure that the two modes are comparable in terms of their relative attractiveness. In practice the calculations are more complex, and Nilsson[10] offers an illustration of how second-best prices could be determined for Sweden's freight rail services in conditions where road transport is not paying its full marginal costs. A general problem is that we are looking only at transport but while the second-best rule will ensure the social optimal mix of transport use there may be problems with other prices in the economy. If they all remain set at marginal cost but both rail and bus are priced along second-best lines above marginal cost, then transport will be relatively expensive when compared to other possible expenditures. Ideally, all prices should deviate by appropriate percentages from their marginal costs in these circumstances.

Under some conditions the problem may not be serious and, from a purely pragmatic stance, it may be more efficient to charge marginal cost prices than to bear the costs of working out any optimal adjustments. In other cases, deviations from marginal cost principles elsewhere in the economy may be so remote that they have minimal influence on the demand for transport. Under such conditions, and assuming that the distortions cannot be removed, Davis and Whinston[11] demonstrate that piecemeal optimization within separate sectors of the economy using marginal cost pricing is optimal. Mishan[12] suggests that since in many cases people spend a fixed amount of their income on transport, there is, therefore, only a very low cross-elasticity of demand between transport as a whole and other goods consumed in the economy. This situation means that the issue can be reduced to optimizing the allocation of traffic between forms of transport, on a piecemeal basis, rather than having to consider the allocation of expenditure between a certain form of transport and all other goods. If, in our example, all competing forms of transport apply marginal cost pricing principles then these should also be adopted by the railway service.

While Mishan's empirical approach has a certain practical commonsense appeal for some forms of transport – such as inter-urban passenger transport – it has less applicability in the freight sector or in the context of international travel. Freight costs have a considerable bearing upon both final prices charged

[9] R.G. Lipsey and K. Lancaster, 'The general theory of second best', *Review of Economic Studies*, **24**, 11–32, 1956/57.
[10] J.E. Nilsson, 'Second-best problems in railway infrastructure pricing and investment', *Journal of Transport Economics and Policy*, **26**, 245–59, 1992.
[11] O.A. Davis and A.B. Whinston, 'Piecemeal policy in the theory of second-best', *Review of Economic Studies*, **34**, 323–31, 1967.
[12] E.J. Mishan, 'Second-thoughts on second best', *Oxford Economic Papers*, **14**, 205–17, 1962.

for products and the location of the manufacturing industry; these are also the main reasons for the attempts at the macro–macro level to develop a Common Transport Policy within the European Union and why transportation at borders has been such an issue in the creation of the North American Free Trade Area (NAFTA).

If all other inputs to industry are priced above marginal cost because, say, of the monopoly power of suppliers, but transport is priced at marginal cost, then this could lead to an overdevelopment, from the national efficiency point of view, of transport-intensive industry. (Although it is possible that the relatively 'cheap' transport could break the monopoly power of the suppliers of other inputs forcing them, in the long run, to price at marginal cost.) International air and sea transport has the complication that, except in certain well-defined areas, many nations consciously subsidize their 'flag bearers', enabling them to charge rates below *LRMC* and, on occasions, even below *SRMC*. Any single operator charging fares based on marginal cost in this situation would find itself unable to attract the optimal volume of traffic, and thus some deviation from the marginal cost principle may be necessary.

The existence of monopoly and other distorting influences in the economy has been shown to necessitate some variations to marginal cost pricing in certain transport sectors. The key to the degree to which prices should deviate from marginal cost is clearly the sign and magnitude of the cross-elasticities of demand between transport and other goods and services in the economy. The practical difficulty in many cases is not the derivation of the appropriate theoretical model but rather our inadequate knowledge of the size of the cross-elasticities. The evidence that is coming forward tends to be piecemeal. Additionally, most of the evidence is related only to intra-transport cross-elasticities with extremely few estimates of transport/other goods cross-elasticities.

7.5   Price Differentiation, Price Discrimination and Yield Management

There can be quite significant differences in the fares paid by those on a particular plane or train, but also for cargo rates on ships. Some of this is attributable to cost differences – things like superior service. But in addition to this, these different prices may be used as a rationing device to allocate out scarce resources; limited capacity being available at the last minute requiring higher prices to ration it among those seeking a late seat or berth. This is effectively yield management in its traditional sense. There is also price discrimination whereby transport service suppliers seek to gain as much revenue as each individual user is willing to pay above costs.

Second-best pricing and the like are forms of price discrimination; different users of a transport service pay different prices not entirely related to their attributed cost. So far we have discussed such discrimination largely in terms of imperfections in other markets and the need to make adjustments to marginal

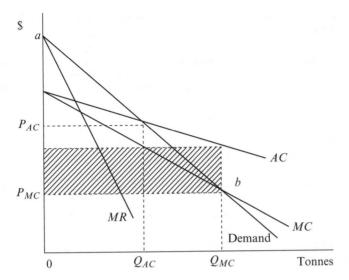

Figure 7.7   *Second-best average cost pricing with decreasing costs*

cost prices in the transport market of interest to reflect these external distortions. The adoption of marginal cost pricing can, in certain circumstances, however, also result in an undertaking making a financial loss even when other markets are working correctly. It is this type of situation that we now address.

The Basic Idea of Price Discrimination with Decreasing Costs

The classic example of this is the decreasing cost industry where, because of high initial capital costs, the setting of charges equal to short-run marginal cost will result in a financial deficit. The railways are often cited as an example of an industry where marginal cost pricing may ensure socially optimal utilization but leave the undertaking with a financial deficit. In Figure 7.7, the railways are assumed to be a monopoly supplier of freight services and, indeed, although it is not shown, if a monopoly profit-maximizing price were adopted then abnormal profits could be earned. The adoption of marginal cost pricing (P_{MC}), however, with the downward-sloping AC and MC curves, at least over the relevant range, will result in a loss shown by the shaded area. A breakeven situation could be attained by average cost pricing (that is, charging P_{AC}) but this would mean that $Q_{MC} - Q_{AC}$ potential rail travelers, willing to pay the additional costs they impose, are priced off the service.

In these circumstances the adoption of marginal cost pricing is essentially a welfare decision, and it is clear that if the undertaking does make a financial loss this is attributable to the pricing policy pursued rather than the incapacity of the service to be financially viable. The fixed costs of the service may be met in these cases by subsidy or by operating a 'club' system with potential users paying a fixed sum for the right to travel by rail and mileage rate (or some other 'cost'-related variable fee) to reflect use. It could be argued that the fixed rates of road vehicle

Table 7.2   *Road costs and user payments in Great Britain in pence per vehicle-kilometer (1998)*

Cost or revenue category	Fully allocated costs		Marginal cost	
	Low	*High*	*Low*	*High*
Costs				
Cost of capital for infrastructure	0.78	1.34	n.a.	n.a.
Infrastructure operating costs and depreciation	0.75	0.97	0.42	0.54
Vehicle operating costs (PSV)	0.87	0.87	0.87	0.87
Congestion	n.a.	n.a.	9.71	11.16
Mohring effect (PSV)	n.a.	n.an	−0.16	−0.16
External accident costs	0.06	0.78	0.82	1.40
Air pollution	0.34	1.70	0.34	1.70
Noise	0.24	0.78	0.02	0.78
Climate change	0.15	0.15	0.15	0.15
VAT not paid	0.15	0.15	0.15	0.15
Sub-total of costs	3.34	7.20	12.32	17.05
Revenues				
Fares (PSV)	0.84	0.08	0.84	0.84
Vehicle excise duty	1.10	1.10	0.14	0.14
Fuel duty	4.42	4.42	4.42	4.42
VAT on fuel duty	0.77	0.77	0.77	0.77
Sub-total of revenues	7.14	7.14	6.17	6.17
Costs–revenues	−3.79	0.07	6.15	10.88
Revenues/costs	2.13	0.99	0.50	0.36

Notes: Road sector costs exclude costs attributable to pedestrians, bicyclists, and motorcyclists; vehicle excise duty at the margin relates to heavy goods vehicles (HGV) and public service vehicles (PSV) such as buses.

Source: T. Samson, C.A. Nash, P.J. Mackie, J. Shires and P. Watkiss, *Surface Transport Costs and Charges: Great Britain 1998*, London: UK Department of the Environment, Transport and the Regions, 2001.

taxation combined with fuel duties reflect a type of club arrangement but, if so, the system is extremely imperfect. In the United Kingdom, for example, at the very crudest level of analysis, there is considerable variation in the ratio of license fee to fuel tax revenue that bears no relation to their relative expenditures on investment and maintenance (Table 7.2).[13] This is a picture repeated in virtually all countries.

Returning to Figure 7.7, if each user were charged a different price so that it reflects his/her willingness to pay, and output were limited to the point where *MC* equals demand (that is, Q_{MC}), this would yield revenue of $0abQ_{MC}$ that may

---

[13] D.M. Newbery, 'Road transport fuel pricing policy', *Annual Reviews of Energy*, **14**, 75–94, 1989.

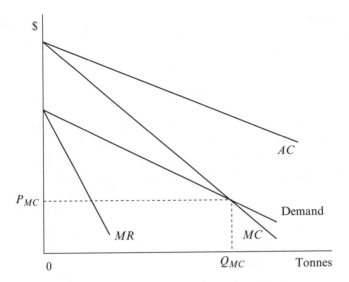

Figure 7.8 *Decreasing costs with demand always inside the average cost curve*

be compared with the total cost of providing the service, namely $0P_{MC}bQ_{MC}$. Using this first-best discriminatory pricing approach, the costs are fully recovered and a profit of $P_{MC}ba$ is being earned. Of course, price discrimination does not always guarantee full cost recovery, which depends on the revenue raised *vis-à-vis* the costs involved. Further, one should also note that perfect price discrimination as described results in the marginal cost level of output; in fact it results in social welfare maximization but with all of the benefits being derived by the provider of the transport service.

Figure 7.8 illustrates a situation, and one that does occur with certain forms of transport service, where even first-best price discrimination will not produce full cost recovery. Here at no level of output does average revenue exceed average cost. It is impossible in this type of situation for costs to be recovered by charging a single price to all users even if monopoly-pricing policies are adopted. In this case even a club arrangement is incapable of preventing the service from being unprofitable. There may be justifications for keeping the service operating with the losses financed through subsidies if there are wider benefits to be enjoyed outside of those generally linked to transport; the service may, for instance, have a strategic value or it may be deemed a 'merit good' which society ought to provide to enable isolated communities to continue in existence.

In summary, in the more conventional case, if subsidies are to be avoided, two-part tariffs are impractical and average cost pricing is deemed inappropriate then price discrimination can still be used to finance the service. Essentially, price discrimination involves charging 'what the user will bear' provided that they cover their marginal costs. In other words it involves attempting to define the maximum amount each consumer or, more realistically, each identifiable group of customers, is willing to pay for the service. The demand curve reflects willingness of users to pay (the *AR* curve becomes the *de facto MR* curve) when a transport enterprise price discriminates and a perfectly discriminating supplier will charge down this curve. First-best price discrimination is, however, rare, and more pragmatic approaches to price discrimination are pursued in practice.

Differentiation by Type of Customer/Commodity

In many cases a transport undertaking itself provides a number of different services (for example, first and second class rail services) and it also has a remit to make a prescribed level of profit, or to break even, rather than to maximize profits. Given these conditions and assuming that the cross-elasticity of demand for the different service is negligible, Baumol and Bradford[14] have stated that the price of any service should be set equal to its short-run marginal cost plus a mark-up inversely proportionate to the service's price elasticity of demand (ε). Hence, where the demand for a service is highly inelastic a substantial addition should be added to marginal cost. Where the demand is perfectly elastic, short-run marginal cost pricing is applied. In this way revenue can be obtained to meet the financial target without distorting the allocation of traffic between different services.

If cross-elasticities are not zero, which is the common case, then the simple rule must be modified to ensure that the relative quantities of goods sold respond to the proportions that would occur if marginal cost pricing were applicable. The rule, for example, for substitutes is that optimal prices should be derived so that all output be reduced by the same proportion from the quantities which are demanded at prices equal to the corresponding marginal costs. This is often called 'Ramsey pricing' after earlier work in the United Kingdom by Frank Ramsey.[15]

Assuming that the railways offer two products, express and commuter rail services, then they should, following this principle, price such that:

$$\frac{(P_{exp} - MC_{exp})}{P_{exp}} \varepsilon_{exp} = \frac{(P_{com} - MC_{com})}{P_{com}} \varepsilon_{com} \tag{7.3}$$

It is not always possible for practical reasons to discriminate perfectly: the administrative costs of operating the system may be too high or exact knowledge of the pertinent demand curves unavailable. These, for example, are the reasons cited in the 1960s by British Rail for their reluctance to adopt more sophisticated costing and policies – the diversity of services provided made it impracticable.[16] In other cases it may be felt socially undesirable to charge 'what the user will bear' because of distributional consequences. Passengers with a lower elasticity of demand may be from the poorer sections of the community and unable to transfer to alternative modes of transport. It may still be justified, even in these

[14] W.J. Baumol and D.F. Bradford, 'Optimal departures from marginal cost pricing', *American Economic Review*, **60**, 265–83, 1970.

[15] F. Ramsey, 'A contribution to the theory of taxation', *Economic Journal*, **37**, 47–61, 1927.

[16] C.D. Foster, *The Transport Problem*, London: Croom Helm, 1975.

circumstances, to provide services even if not all costs are recovered by the operator, providing that the potential revenue if discrimination were adopted exceeds
the costs of the service. If this is the case, a subsidy is required to bring actual
revenue up to potential revenue and, to some extent, the British government
accepted this in the 1968 Transport Act when, for a period, it introduced specific
social subsidies to maintain a number of railway services.

While price discrimination is relatively uncommon outside of the transport
sector it is a familiar feature of pricing policy within it, and indeed has become
more common as information systems have developed and sophisticated electronic means of actually levying fares and freights have emerged. Truelove provides an apt description of the pricing practices of British Rail in the 1990s before
privatization, illustrating that even then it was widely practiced.[17]

The distinction between first and second class can be further refined by the
exclusion of discount fares from peak weekday and holiday trains, by the limited
availability of old people's and students' discounts, and the reduction in supple-
ment for travel in first class carriages at weekends, when leisure travel is heavy and
business travel almost negligible.

Another well-documented example of third-degree price discrimination has
long been provided by shipping conferences, and now by shipping alliances. These
cartels act as monopoly suppliers of regular liner services between major ports.
The possibility of competition tends to increase the elasticity of demand for their
services to carry high-price–low-volume goods while tramp shipping becomes
competitive for low-price bulk cargoes. Consequently, one can hypothesize an
inverted S-shaped demand curve for liner services over any route. Given the high
capital costs associated with shipping, there is adequate evidence that, prior to the
widespread use of containers, without price discrimination, most conference lines
would become unprofitable.

A detailed look at the Australia–Europe Conference by Zerby and Conlon[18]
produced a breakdown of rates that clearly shows the high degree of price
discrimination exercised by these maritime cartels. Figure 7.9 reproduces their
average revenues for each type of cargo carried in 1973/74 and it is clear that
traced out this corresponds closely to the type of demand curve hypothesized.
The low-value bulk cargoes (that is, ores and metals) are carried at (or sometimes
below if ballast is required) the average incremental costs of loading and unloading. While the high-value products are carried at considerably higher rates, the
tapering off in rates caused by potential competition from air transport is seen to
be effective at the top of the price range.

Price discrimination not only permits suppliers to recover their costs, but
also helps travelers and consignors in that services can be retained even if, in
some cases, it is necessary to differentiate the quality of service provided as well
as the fare charged. International air travel offers some examples of this type

---

[17] P. Truelove, *Decision Making in Transport Planning*, London: Longman, 1992.
[18] I.A. Zerby and R.M. Conlon, 'An analysis of capacity utilisation in liner shipping',
Journal of Transport Economics and Policy, **12**, 27–46, 1978.

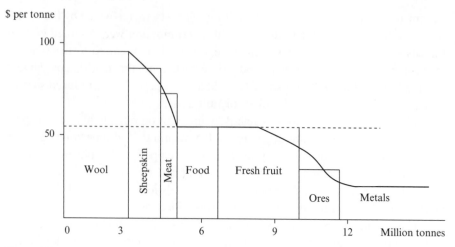

Figure 7.9   *Average revenues from cargoes carried by the Australia–Europe Conference (1973/74)*

of situation where differential prices are charged over a route according to the specifications of the types of service the travelers are willing to pay for. The gradual breakdown of the International Air Transport Association's (IATA) system of regulating airfares across the Atlantic in the 1970s was accompanied by the introduction of cut-price services such as 'Skytrain', operated by Laker Airways.[19] No-frill flights were introduced at low fares with seat allocation dependent upon the willingness of potential passengers to queue; tickets could be purchased until six hours prior to take-off. Subsequently this type of service has been modified and regular scheduled airlines now offer a variety of ticketing arrangements on their flights. A clear segmentation of the market had been recognized.

Figure 7.10 provides an illustration of the sort of situation that has emerged; for example, if there are three different groups of potential travelers with separate demand curves (D_1, D_2 and D_3) then three separate fares should be charged (P_1, P_2 and P_3) to maximize the consumers' surplus enjoyed. P_1 is charged for the highest-quality flight, equaling the marginal cost of service, with lower fares for poorer-quality flights. On the surface it appears that $0N_1$ passengers will travel first class reaping a consumer surplus of ABP_1, and N_1N_2 passengers will pay P_2 for the slightly lower quality of service and enjoy a consumer surplus of HIG. This ignores the possibility that first class travelers may switch to the poorer-quality but cheaper services (that is, there may be some 'revenue dilution'). In fact, travelers N'_1N_1 could switch and increase their welfare. Similarly, N'_2N_2 passengers appear to be the probable number of customers for the poor-quality service, but again a further N_2N_3 may be induced to join them by the lower fare. Whether people actually do take advantage of the possibility of switching to cheaper but less convenient forms of service is uncertain, but the availability of the range of

[19] M.A. Abe, '"Skytrain": competitive pricing, quality of service and the deregulation of the airline industry', *International Journal of Transport Economics*, **6**, 41–7, 1979.

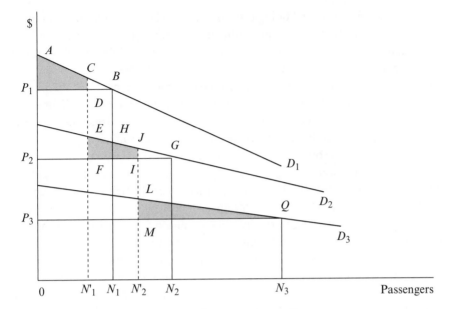

Figure 7.10   *Price discrimination according to service quality*

services means that the total potential consumer surplus (the shaded areas) will exceed that generated if only a single price and service package were available.

Dynamic Yield Management

There is also the practice of what has become known as 'yield management' in the air transport market, but is also used by other transport modes. Essentially, it is the ability of management to gain additional revenue above costs from a prede-fined activity (for example, a scheduled flight or sailing) when there is a need to ration out capacity. For example, there may be a number of people who want to book late for a flight but the number of remaining seats is small. Thus the airline will push up fares to ration out these seats to those willing to pay the most. This is not strictly the same as price discrimination because the supplier is not trying to get all of the customers' consumer surpluses but rather recover costs and allow those who gain most from a service to have access to it.

It has become a key element in, for example, the scheduled airline indus-try where the chief executive of one major operator, Robert Crandall, former President of American Airlines, stated in 1992, 'I believe that yield management is the single most important technical development in transportation manage-ment since we entered the era of airline deregulation in 1979'.[20] But it is also used elsewhere, including the maritime sector.

The use of computer reservation systems (CRSs) by airlines enables an airline to adjust the fares offered on a given flight, the seats available at each fare

---

[20] Cited in P. Davis, 'Airline ties profitability yield to management', *Society for Industrial Applied Mathematics News*, **27**, 7, 1994.

and the preconditions for booking at any fare.[21] The preconditions (combined with some relatively minor quality differentials inherent in first class, business and coach class areas of an aircraft) introduce product differentiation into the management equation while the various fares charged for what are, in many ways, very similar services represent the price differentiation element. The combinations offered, and the adjustments made by an airline as the time of any flight departure approaches, are designed to ensure the yield from the predetermined decision to offer that particular flight cover costs and allocate seats efficiently.

The technique is somewhat different from that of the classic economic model of price discrimination where management increases revenue by charging different groups of customers (differentiated by their price elasticities) different prices for the same product. The cost of serving each customer is, in the classic model, identical. There is, however, normally some qualitative or other form of product differentiation involved in yield management which implies cost differentials in the provision of services to customers – first class air travel does cost an airline more than discount travel. Equally, however, the existence of economies of scope may mean that the supplier of a range of different services can keep unit costs lower than a number of suppliers each specializing in one of the services being offered. In overall resource terms, therefore, yield management may provide for the development of a more efficient market structure.

The set of decisions confronting industries practicing successful yield management is often complex. The interactions and options available are numerous with fare levels, fare structures, constraints and capacity distribution to be decided simultaneously. This leads to a further common feature of yield management, namely sequential decision making. The form this takes varies between both sectors and firms within sectors but a broad indication of the decision sequence adopted by many airlines when considering a particular scheduled service is set out in Figure 7.11. In this case the nature of the technology does permit a degree of interaction between some of the stages (for example, discount levels and allocation of seats to different fare classes) as the time of the flight approaches.

Empirically separating out yield management, which is a resource-allocation technique, from price discrimination, which is a sales revenue-maximizing technique, is difficult in practice, and inevitably murky. But some insights into the degrees to which prices may vary for a particular service can be gleaned.

An example of what this means in practice can be seen in Figure 7.12 which looks at fares offered by regularly 'data scraping' the Web-pages of the airlines involved to see how fares are adjusted over time as departure approaches. The 'fares-offered' curves for a monopoly service indicate the degree to which available prices fluctuate, a reflection of the number of remaining seats, the fares being offered by any competitor, and the expected demand levels of potential customers at different times before take-off (last-minute business travelers, for example, tend to be willing to pay more for a seat and *de facto* compete with each other for

---

[21] B.C. Smith, J.F. Leimkuhler and R.M. Darrow, 'Yield management at American Airlines', *Interfaces*, **22**, 8–31, 1992.

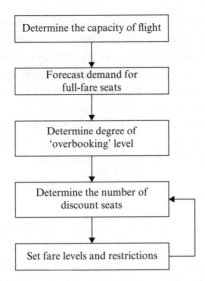

Figure 7.11 *Stages in arriving at yield-maximizing revenue in scheduled aviation*

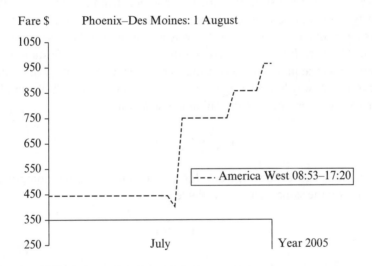

Source: K.J. Button and H. Vega, 'The temporal-fares-offered curves in air transportation', *Journal of the Transportation Research Forum*, **46**, 83–100, 2007.

Figure 7.12 *Temporal-fares-offered curves for return services from Phoenix to Des Moines: leaving August 1 and returning August 5, 2005*

them.) The fares offered rise towards take-off – but part of this may be attributable to rationing out the increasingly scarce number of unsold seats, and part to the effort of the airline to distinguish between leisure travelers who know their itinerary well in advance and are seeking cheap travel and business travelers who often have to fly at the last minute and are willing to pay more.

Another form of differentiation by time of purchase that combines second- (entailing discounts for bulk buying) and third-degree price discrimination is found in the air cargo sector.[22] The link between forwarders, who act on behalf of freight shippers, and, staying with aviation, airlines is normally initially through their acquisition of allocated or bloc one-way capacity on airlines. This entails airlines six to 12 months before a flight's departure offering capacity to freight forwarders through essentially auctioning arrangements. The freight forwarders offer 'bids' (generally in terms of price per kilogram at the point of origin) based on the anticipated demands of their customers, the shippers. The remaining capacity, the cargo capacity, is then offered for sale one month before the flight departure.

Differentiation by Length of Journey/Haul

Price differentiation is not only by type of traffic or quality of service but may also be by length of journey. Friedman[23] offers a classic example of such a policy in the context of long-haul/short-haul differentials on American railways. The practice of charging short-haul traffic a higher mileage rate on railways than long-haul, despite attempts to legislate to the contrary, was common in nineteenth-century America. Friedman's justification for this practice demonstrates that without it there may arise quite serious distortions in transport infrastructure provision.

As an example, suppose that there is a railway link between three towns, A, B and C, where B is located between the other two towns. There is also river transport (priced at marginal cost) available between A and C offering an identical service to the railway but offering no communication for town B. To simplify, we assume the fixed sunk cost of the rail link is such that:

$$C_{AC} = C_{AB} + C_{BC} \tag{7.4}$$

that is, the sunk cost of the line from A to C is the sum of the two component sub links. Also, on the same basis, the variable cost is:

$$V_{AC} = V_{AB} + V_{BC} \tag{7.5}$$

Figure 7.13 shows the respective demand schedules for transport between the different pairs of towns. The railways may maximize their profits by charging down the demand curves D_{AB} and D_{BC}, where there is no competition from riverborne transport, to the point where marginal (that is, variable) cost is reached. Where competition does exist over the long route between A and C, the railways, to attract customers, will want to charge at most the rate offered by river transport (call this R_{AC}). The railways will, however, accept traffic at rates below R_{AC} but above the variable cost. The areas WAV_{AB}, XDV_{BC} and $R_{AC}EFV_{AC}$ show the

[22] J. Bowen and T.R. Leinbach, 'Market concentration in the air freight forwarding industry', *Tijdschrift voor economische en sociale geografie*, **95**, 174–88, 2004.
[23] D.D. Friedman, 'In defense of the long-haul/short-haul discrimination', *Bell Journal of Economics*, **10**, 706–8, 1979.

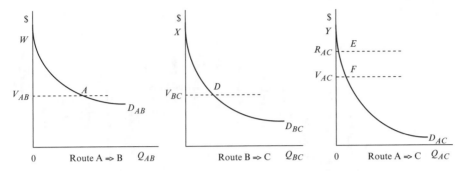

Figure 7.13 *Revenues from discriminating pricing according to length of haul*

revenues enjoyed by the railways on different links. If R_{AC} is lower than either the highest position of D_{AB} or D_{BC}, then there exists long-haul/short-haul discrimination in addition to discrimination within each type of traffic. In other words, identical goods with identical demand for transport schedules would be charged more per mile for a short haul than for a long haul.

The sum of the revenues in the diagram offers a measure of the social value of building and operating the ABC railway line. The aggregate producer surplus generated should be set against the fixed costs of provision, which together with calculations for AB and AC separately, indicate the long-term desirability of keeping the entire line open or only segments of it. Without long-haul/short-haul discrimination the railway would either have to give up some of its long-haul business or fail to capture some of the consumer surplus generated on short haul. Whatever the case, the railway's incentive to invest would be distorted and some economically desirable lines would not be operated.

Countervailing Power

The extent to which a supplier can engage in price differentiation depends on the degree to which the customer 'allows' it to price down the curve and the competition that is encountered in the market. For example, while the airline sector, where markets have been allowed to operate, has practiced extensive price discrimination, the operating margins have been well below other industries (Figure 7.14) which, in the case of the United States, have been of the order of 5.6 percent over the past two decades. This is mainly due to competition, but in other sectors, such as shipping, the power of customers is important. This ability to essentially resist the monopoly power of a large transport supplier is reflected, to a considerable extent, in the 'countervailing power' enjoyed by the potential transport user.

The development of the idea of countervailing power is usually credited to Kenneth Galbraith[24] and his book, *American Capitalism*. This very un-Galbraithian volume essentially argues that large-scale enterprises in oligopolistic or monopoly markets often have much less flexibility than conventional theory postulates to

---

[24] J.K. Galbraith, *American Capitalism: The Concept of Countervailing Power*, Boston, MA: Houghton Mifflin, 1952.

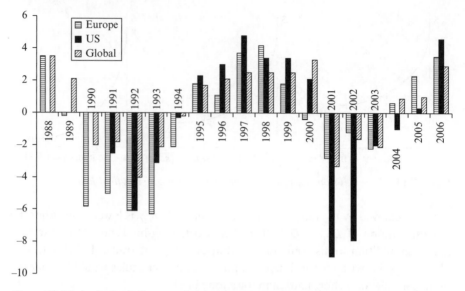

Note: (i) A lack of a bar indicates a missing observation and not a zero operating margin, (ii) Memberships of the various reporting bodies vary over time and thus the reported margins reflect the associated carriers at the time of reporting.

Sources: Boeing Commercial Airplanes, Association of European Airlines, Air Transport Association of America, International Air Transport Association.

Figure 7.14 *Airline operating margins, global, Europe and United States*

exploit their power because of the existence of monopoly power at other points in what we would now call, as we saw in Chapter 1, the 'value chain'. In particular, the interest was initially stimulated by the observation that large buyers often enjoyed significant discounts when purchasing from suppliers. While there may be cost reasons for this, such as economies of density in shipping and handling, the outcome may also be the result of the strong bargaining power of the purchaser.

Essentially, what is seen is a situation where rather than having original competition in a market, the competition is between the various buyers and sellers up and down the value chain – there are, according to this approach, bilateral monopolies or oligopolies at various points in the chain. A bilateral monopoly is a situation where there is a single buyer and one seller of a given product in a market. The level of concentration in the sale of the product results in a mutual interdependence between the seller and the buyer in price determination. The notions of price taking inherent in more standard neoclassical economics are not upheld.

Countervailing power, Galbraith argues, prevents a large business from fully exploiting customers: 'In a typical modern market of a few sellers, the active restraint is provided by competition but from the other side of the market by strong buyers . . . At the end of virtually every channel by which consumer goods reach the public there is, in practice, a layer of powerful buyers'. Basically, market power on one side of a market 'create(s) an incentive to the organization of another position of power that neutralizes it'.

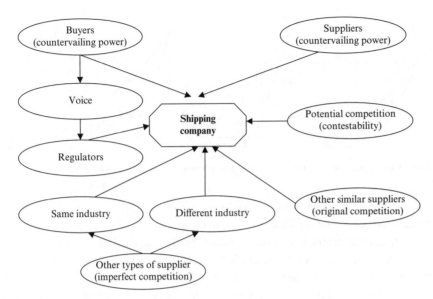

Figure 7.15   *Forces affecting a firm's pricing decisions*

It is perhaps useful to put Galbraith's ideas, together with other forms of market forces, into a wider context. Figure 7.15 offers a simple illustration of the various types of direct and countervailing powers that may affect the pricing decisions of an undertaking providing transportation services. The figure is relatively comprehensive, embracing ideas such as countervailing power, regulations, the fear of public disquiet over excessive prices (so-called 'voice'[25]), contestability and so on as well as original competition – the traditional name for competition within the market.

Not all have agreed with this outcome, and the idea of countervailing power from the time of Galbraith initiating his ideas has been the subject of some skepticism. Academics such as George Stigler,[26] and Whitney,[27] for example, questioned in a variety of ways whether the ability of large purchases of factors of production from monopolists in the value chain really had the incentive to pass on any savings to final customers; why not keep the rent themselves? Stigler was particularly strong in his criticism of the concept:

> [I]t simply is romantic to believe that a competitive solution will emerge, not merely in a few particular cases, but in the general run of industries where two small groups of firms deal with one another suddenly all the long-run advantages of monopolistic behavior have been lost sight of in a welter of irrational competitive moves.

[25] A.O. Hirschman, *Exit, Voice, and Loyalty: Responses to Decline in Firms, Organizations, and States*, Cambridge, MA: Harvard University Press, 1970.

[26] G.J. Stigler, 'The economist plays with blocs', *American Economic Review*, **44**, 7–14, 1954.

[27] S.N. Whitney, 'Errors in the concept of countervailing power', *Journal of Business of the University of Chicago*, **26**, 238–53, 1953.

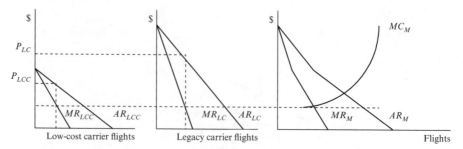

Figure 7.16   *Third-degree price discrimination between low-cost and legacy carriers*

The theory is messy in the sense that it does not, except on very stylized situations, produce a neat equilibrium, optimal outcome, but rather results in prices and outputs determined by games played by the various parties involved and influenced by their power in the market. These may be short-term equilibria but are not optimal. There is no canonical model. In particular, the degree to which the outcome approaches either monopoly or competitive outcomes depends on the strength and strategic aptitudes of the various parties involved. A variety of things can influence both of these factors.

One indicator of the extent of countervailing power is the ability of, say, an airport to price discriminate between airlines that may want to operate from it.

The ability to first-degree discriminate, involving charging different prices for each take-off or landing depending on willingness to pay, is rare and unlikely to be a practical proposition for an airport even if it does enjoy considerable monopoly power and there are numerous airlines seeking slots. The information and administrative requirements are too large. A more viable proposition to consider is third-degree price discrimination whereby the market for airport services can be segmented and where the segments have different elasticities of demand. At the most basic level we can think in terms of segmentation between low-cost and traditional, full service carriers.

We can take the simple case of a profit-maximizing airport that is serving both a low-cost carrier and a legacy carrier. In Figure 7.16 the airport decides its output by equating its overall marginal costs (MC_M) with its overall marginal revenue (MR_M). The price levied on the airlines will then be at the point on the average revenue curve directly above the flights attracted (AC_M) but not illustrated in the figure. However, landing fees are normally a larger part of a low-cost airline's costs than for a traditional, legacy carrier. This makes the former more sensitive to the level of such fees. To increase its revenues, therefore, the airport can try to charge separate fees to its two potential customer groups; for example, it may use slot auctions.[28] It would effectively do this by drawing a horizontal line through the $MC_M = MR_M$ point and carry this over to the separate markets for low-cost and legacy carriers. This intersection gives the combined profit-

---

[28] K.J. Button, 'Auctions – What can we learn from auction theory for slot allocation?', in A. Czerny, P. Forsyth, D. Gillen and H.M. Niemeier (eds), *Airport Slots, International Experiences and Options for Reform*, Aldershot: Ashgate, 2008.

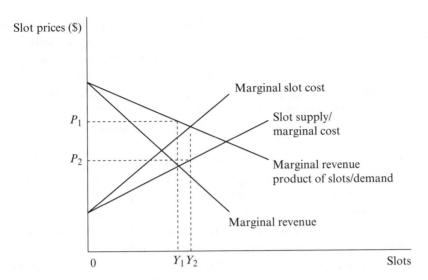

Figure 7.17   *Price and output under a pure bilateral monopoly*

maximizing output for the airport. Taking the resultant marginal cost across to the separate marginal revenue curves of the different categories of carrier optimally shares out slots between them. Prices for the low-cost carriers (P_{LCC}) and the legacy carriers (P_{LC}) are then determined by the average revenue curves corresponding to these slot numbers.

The generic types of issues that can ensue in these conditions where airlines have market power were first explored by Francis Edgeworth[29] in the nineteenth century and have subsequently attracted considerable attention within the industrial organization fraternity with an interest in game theory. Figure 7.17 provides a simple, and extreme, example with a monopsony buyer (say a large airline) negotiating landing slot charges with a monopoly airport.

Initially at one extreme, we treat the airport as a monopolist with numerous potential airlines wanting to use its slots. In this case we get the standard textbook situation where the airport will set its output where marginal cost equals marginal revenue (Y_1) and set price to clear the market (that is, price will be P_1). In contrast, if an airline (or a strong alliance of airlines) has monopsony power, and the airport is confronted with competition from alternative facilities, then the price of a slot will be P_2. This is because the market supply curve for slots will be positively sloped with a market slot curve above it. The marginal revenue product curve of slots – the additional revenue the airline obtains by buying an additional slot – is downward sloping, reflecting diminishing marginal productivity. To maximize its revenue, the airline will buy slots up to the point where the marginal cost of a slot is equated to the marginal revenue it will generate (that is, Y_2 slots) for which the market-clearing price is P_2.

The situation where there is bilateral monopoly generally leaves the outcome indeterminate with a market price somewhere between P_1 and P_2. The resultant

[29] F.Y. Edgeworth, *Mathematical Physics*, London: Kegan Paul, 1881.

price and output combination will depend on the bargaining abilities of the two parties and that, of course, will be a function of their game-playing skills. While one can relate to this in the case of a large hub-and-spoke airline negotiating slot rates at its main hub airport, there are other points in the value chain where these types of bilateral monopoly or oligopoly may emerge. Of particular relevance here, is the monopoly power of labor unions in their dealing with airports and the airframe manufacturers with the airlines. Similar situations exit for other modes of transport.

What is clear, irrespective of the power of airports and airlines in the example, is that the final consumer – passenger or shipper – does not benefit greatly from a bilateral monopoly situation further up the value chain. The sharing out of economic rents seen in Figure 7.15 between the two providers of intermediate services is an effective extraction of consumer surplus from the final users of air transport services. The situation may also pertain in other situations where there are imperfections up the value chain that result in non-competitive prices being pushed down the chain and being imposed on passengers and freight consignors.

Testing for the existence of countervailing power in any market is challenging. It is difficult to discern, for example, whether a large-scale buyer of a product from a large producer gets a discount because of the scale economies of such transactions or because the buyer can drive a hard bargain by virtue of its purchasing power. Much of the general empirical work trying to ascertain if countervailing power has any significant impacts on markets uses a structure–conduct–performance framework, looking in particular at links between supplier profits, or mark-ups, and supplier concentrations with the additional consideration of buyer concentrations. Limited work of this type, however, has been performed on the aviation sector. There has been some work trying to benchmark different airports' efficiency, generally using data envelopment methods (see Chapter 5).[30] but normalizing for the particular characteristics of airports is difficult, especially when using programming techniques.

One of the problems in exploring countervailing effects is that the market power on either side of the market varies considerably by context. The situation depicted in Figure 7.17 of a monopoly confronting a monopsony is very seldom seen; more common are oligopolistic bilateral structures where the market powers on both sides are defused by continual games being played between the buyers and suppliers. Turning specifically to aviation, in some cases groups of clustered airports are under common ownership, as with the main London airports, giving them considerable regional monopoly power, whereas in other cases there may be alternative terminals within close proximity; in the United States a 2-hour drive between airports is generally seen as providing competition. Additionally, many airports have their rates regulated – for example in the United Kingdom the British Airports Authority (BAA) is price-capped by the Civil Aviation Authority

[30] T.H. Oum, C. Yu and X. Fu, 'A comparative analysis of productivity performance of the world's major airports: summary report of the ATRS global airport benchmarking research report – 2002', *Journal of Air Transport Management*, **9**, 285–97, 2003.

– making econometric analysis of market power difficult. Also, air services are not homogeneous, and nor are the airlines providing them, making generalizations difficult.

The degree to which airports can segment in this way, however, depends on the extent to which the airlines are capable of diluting the revenue being collected by the airport – essentially, their ability to prevent differential fees. Many airports are used by a small number of airlines, and in some cases even large airports rely on a single carrier for 80 percent or more of their business. The extent to which airports practice third-degree discrimination has, however, not been rigorously examined. A study by Jacobs Consultancy[31] found differential passenger charges for low-cost terminals at Budapest, Kuala Lumpur, Marseilles and Singapore airports. While airports may exercise some forms of price differentiation by carrier type, it becomes more difficult to separate out the effects of cost variations from charging policies based upon willingness-to-pay. Even in the cases cited, low-cost carriers are often based in separate terminals that offer passengers more limited, less grandiose, and generally less well-located, facilities. For example, Richard de Neufville[32] cites Geneva, Berlin, Kuala Lumpur, Paris Charles de Gaulle, Singapore and Warsaw airports as situations where specific facilities for low-cost carriers have been provided. In effect, different fees may largely be reflecting different costs and not strict price discrimination by demand.

The fact that only a few cases of clear third-degree price discrimination would seem to exist could be suggestive of airlines being able to exercise a considerable degree of countervailing power. This would seem to be illusory however because of capacity problems at major airports in many parts of the world, and particularly Europe,[33] and regulatory regimes that force airports to set charges based upon narrow accountancy costing principles. The form exists when, given the capacity of an airport, the nature of the demand curves for potential low-cost and legacy carrier users are such that profit maximization leads to a high price that only the traditional, legacy airlines are willing to pay.

7.6   Pricing with Stochastic Demand

Our discussion of price discrimination as a method of recovering costs has to date made the rather heroic assumption that the supplier of transport – be it ship owner, railway manager, airline operator or whatever – has perfect knowledge of the demand situation being confronted. Most transport managers have, from past data and employing 'managerial intuition', some notion of the average level of demand for their services and some idea of how this demand fluctuates. With

[31] Jacobs Consultancy. *Review of Dedicated Low-cost Airport Passenger Facilities*, Burlingame: Commission for Aviation Regulation, 2007.

[32] R. de Neufville, 'Accommodating low cost airlines at main airports', *International Airport Review*, **1**, 62–5, 2006.

[33] A. Reynolds-Feighan and K.J. Button, 'An assessment of the capacity and congestion levels at European airports', *Journal of Air Transport Management*, **5**, 113–34, 1999.

yield management, regularly posting and changing the fares offered can often give a pretty good idea of short-term demand conditions. In practice, though, the assumption of complete or near-complete information is often unrealistic. This is particularly so over longer periods. The specific problem of systematic and regular known short-term peaks in demand is considered in the following section; here we concentrate on irregular fluctuations in demand of a stochastic nature. Transport undertaking may, for instance, know that fluctuations are about 20 percent of the average daily demand but have no way of telling whether tomorrow's demand will be, say, 7 percent above the average or 14 percent below it.

The introduction of this notion of 'stochastic' demand requires a slight modification to the marginal cost pricing approach. The conventional arguments for discriminate pricing revolve around the idea that simple marginal cost pricing will, because of declining average cost, result in the supplier incurring a financial loss. Turvey's[34] position is that the problem should be expressed in terms of the difficulties associated with matching the services supplied (usually vehicle journeys) with those that are demanded (usually passenger journeys) when a fixed timetable is operative.

Approached from this way, the problem is seen as one of defining a price structure which will cover all relevant costs but which will, at the same time, ensure reasonable utilization of the transport capacity available. Two broad approaches emerge. The first of these depends upon fairly reliable information about demand and its range of fluctuation, while the second is reliant upon good information on all relevant costs. Here, we concentrate on the first approach and, in particular, the load factor for a service. If fares are fixed so high that the number of people wishing to use the service never exceeds the available capacity then, as a result of the fluctuating demand condition, there will frequently be a substantial number of empty seats and resources will be wasted. Alternatively, if the fares are set so low that capacity is fully utilized all of the time then many people, who often have spent time queuing for the service, will, again because of demand fluctuations, find themselves unable to obtain a seat. Clearly, common sense suggests that a compromise between these extremes will meet the requirements of both supplier and potential traveler. Turvey's pragmatic solution is that operators should structure their fares so that on average a certain percentage of seats will remain empty.

To some extent this is the situation that has developed with yield management on the scheduled airlines where passengers have even greater flexibility by being able, via booking early, to ensure themselves a seat if they wish rather than risk disappointment, but at the cost of forfeiting the fare if they do not make the flight. The situation was also evident on the streets of central London in the past where parking meter fees were fixed so that on average 15 percent of spaces were vacant although, of course, from experience we know that at times it is impossible to find a vacant parking space while at others they are in abundance. One might also point to the 'stand-by capacity' kept by British Rail until the 1968 Transport

[34] R. Turvey, 'A simple analysis of optimal fares on scheduled transport sources', *Economic Journal*, **85**, 1–9, 1975.

Act, which it was claimed acted to cope with long-term fluctuations in demand for railway services.

To cover costs in this type of situation without recourse to either direct or cross-subsidization, it is likely that price discrimination is necessary. Any of four standard types of discrimination (that is, by type of passenger, degree of comfort, regularity of use, and/or seat availability) could be used for this.

Where knowledge of demand fluctuations is less precise, then Turvey's second and rather more pragmatic approach may be applicable. Here fares can be determined by simply dividing available costs of the service by the passengers carried and the service-only runs if such fares broadly correspond to those on the remainder of the transport system. Additional revenue may then be gained on an *ad hoc* basis by raising fares for those groups where willingness to pay exceeds the cost-based fare. The actual avoidable costs can be estimated, where there is uncertainty about initial traffic levels, using the following formula that for simplicity is couched in terms of a passenger railway service:

$$
\begin{aligned}
&[(\text{Probability that marginal passenger will necessitate an extra carriage}) \\
&\qquad \cdot (\text{Cost of extra carriage})] \\
&+ [(\text{Probability that marginal passenger will necessitate an extra train}) \\
&\qquad \cdot (\text{Cost of extra train})] \qquad\qquad\qquad (7.6)
\end{aligned}
$$

Because this probability long-run marginal cost curve represents costs as an increasing function of the number of passengers and also since this is itself a decreasing function of the fare charged, there is likely to be a fare structure where such marginal costs are recovered.

Whether the fare is optimal, however, depends upon timetable flexibility; so far we have implicitly assumed a given timetable. The overall fare is set at the level of the marginal "social" cost of an extra passenger, in other words equal to the frustration and inconvenience he/she causes to other potential but disappointed travelers by occupying a scarce seat. The combination of timetable and fare that equates the marginal cost, so defined, with the marginal financial cost is thus an overall optimum. In practice, of course, imperfect knowledge of demand situations, plus the need to make timetabling and pricing decisions simultaneously, makes it unlikely that such an overall optimum will be attained except by chance.

7.7 The Problem of the Peak

Most forms of transport, both freight and passenger, experience regular peaks in demand for their services. Urban public transport (upon which our attention will be focused later) experiences peaks in demand during 'rush hours' each weekday morning and evening. While there is considerable variation between cities, typically rush hour lasts from about 6 to 10 a.m. and from 4 to 7 p.m. local time, with some people traveling places during their lunchtime causing a mini rush hour from noon until 2 p.m. Urban freight transport also has peaks in demand to match the seasonal needs and operating practices of customers. In London, for example, the majority of deliveries have traditionally been made between 11 a.m. and noon.[35] Over a year, air, bus and rail services meet peaks in demand from holiday traffic during the summer months and over public holidays, while within a week there are marked differences between weekend and weekday demand levels. Over an even longer period, shipping is subjected to cyclical movements in demand as the world economy moves between booms and slumps.

The difficulty in all these situations is to determine a pattern of prices that ensures that transport infrastructure is used optimally, provides a guide to future investment policy, and ensures that all relevant costs are recovered. Unlike the previous section, we are concerned here with problems arising from systematic variations in demand, frequently over a relatively short time period during which adjustments cannot be made in capital equipment to ensure that price is always equated with long-run marginal cost. The problem is essentially one of indivisibility in the time dimension of supply relative to demand and is, therefore, a particular form of the joint production problem. Problems of this kind do occur in other sectors of the economy but transport, like electricity and some other forms of energy, cannot easily be stored to reconcile systematic changes in demand with smooth, even production. Reconciliation can be effectively achieved only through price adjustments or shortages and excesses in the market.

Before proceeding to look at the peak-load pricing problem it is worth noting that there exists a parallel spatial/directional problem of joint costs in transport which can be treated in an identical way to that of the peak. This involves the question of deriving appropriate rates for front- and back-hauls – a situation often found in the provision of unscheduled road haulage, or air freight and shipping services. Basically there is a high demand for a service in one direction (the front-haul) but a lower one for a return service (the back-haul); that is, demand is unidirectional in nature whereas supply consists of round-trip journeys. This situation is directly analogous to the peak-load situation, with the front-haul being the spatially directional equivalent of the peak, and simple substitution of words yields the appropriate analysis.[36]

Perhaps the most widely discussed peaking problem involves urban public transport and particularly bus services. The size of most urban bus fleets is determined by the demand for public transport services during the morning and evening commuter rush hours. Typically over half the passengers carried during a day travel during the main peak periods. In Manchester, for example, 1,090 buses were required to meet rush-hour demands in 1966 while only 400 were used during the midday period. Comparable figures for Birmingham Corporation Transport Department in 1969 were 1,500 and 327 vehicles, respectively. Bus road crews may

[35] A.W. Christie, R.S. Bartlett, M.A. Cundhill and J. Prudhoe, 'Urban freight distribution: studies of operations in shopping streets at Newbury and Camberley', Crowthorne: *Transport and Road Research Laboratory Report*, LR. 603, 1973.

[36] W.G. Waters, 'Output dimensions and joint costs', *International Journal of Transport Economics*, **7**, 17–35. 1980.

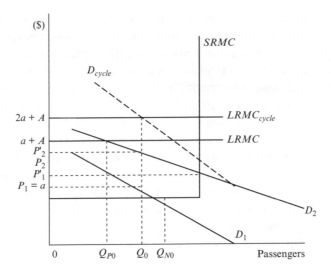

Figure 7.18   *The optimum peak price*

also be considered as a joint cost since numbers are determined by peak demand. It is seldom possible to cover both daily peaks with one shift; hence, either two shifts are required, or else split-shifts must be introduced usually involving inconvenience payments (often equal to the standard wage) being paid for time between peaks. The total wage bill for road staff, which amounts to about 50 percent of total cost of most British bus operators, is, therefore, almost invariant with demand and may be treated as a joint cost of providing peak and non-peak services.

To determine optimal prices let us assume that during a 12-hour period a bus operator is confronted by two different demand situations, each of six hours' duration. In Figure 7.18, D_1 is the low, off-peak demand situation and D_2 the peak-level demand curve. The short-run marginal costs ($SRMC$) of operations (fuel and mileage dependent depreciation) are assumed constant at level $0a$ until the capacity of the bus fleet, which initially is assumed as fixed, is filled, whereupon they become infinite. In the short term, with capacity fixed, the objective is to maximize social welfare by making optimal use of the fleet. In this case the off-peak and the peak demands should be priced at their respective $SRMCs$. The fares should, therefore, be P_1 and P_2 at the off-peak and peak, respectively, with corresponding passenger numbers Q_{P0} and Q_{N0}

Changes in capacity brought about by varying the fleet size do not influence short-run marginal costs except to the extent that the capacity constraint is pushed further to the right if vehicles are added and to the left if they are withdrawn. Long-run capacity costs ($LRMC$) are treated as constant at a level A. Since the capacity is joint to both subperiods, changes in capacity should be determined by the combined demand of peak and off-peak periods, that is, the full cycle of activities.[37] Consequently, it is D_{cycle} that is the relevant demand

---

[37] J. Hirschleifer, 'Peak loads and efficient pricing – comment', *Quarterly Journal of Economics*, **72**, 451–62, 1958.

curve (because this represents the vertical summation of D_1 and D_2). Further, it is $LRMC_{cycle}$ that is the relevant long-term cost curve because this represents the combination of the short-run costs in the two periods plus fixed costs; that is, $2a + A$. In essence the situation is analogous to that of a collective good.

The optimum long-run capacity in the case illustrated, and assuming that there are no problems of indivisibilities, involves a contraction of capacity to $0Q_0$. The non-peak travelers will then pay P'_1 and peak travelers P'_2. Given the way the D_{cycle} and $LRMC_{cycle}$ curves are derived, the combined revenues from off-peak and peak fares will exactly equal the costs involved. Also the off-peak fare now exceeds $SRMC$ and capacity is fully utilized around the clock, the pricing differences reflecting differing strengths of demand. In summary, changes in capacity, because it is joint to both periods, now depend upon the sum of the differences between price and the capacity's operating costs per period relative to the cost of providing new capacity for the entire cycle. That is, investment is justified if:

$$[(P_1 - a) + (P_2 - a)] > B. \tag{7.7}$$

It is relatively simple to extend the analysis to any number of subperiods, which may be of unequal duration, by weighting the different periods according to their fractional importance in the entire cycle.

In practice, the situation is often somewhat more complicated than that depicted, because passengers are not rigidly confined to either period but may switch trips between them if differential fares are levied. Unfortunately, little empirical work has been conducted on this but it is quite possible that our implicit assumption that D_1 and D_2 are independent is often unrealistic and allowance needs to be made both for their own and also for cross-elasticities. Also, of course, it may be necessary to take cognizance of interdependencies between the demand for urban bus travel as a whole and the possibilities of switching with private transport.[38]

While there is a firm economic basis for peak-load pricing, its implementation has been piecemeal. An early example was the pricing policy pursued in the Manchester–Salford area in Great Britain between the summers of 1970 and 1975,[39] and there are differential metro fares in American cities, such as Washington DC. Some US airports have attempted to introduce peak pricing but, as with facilities such as Boston Logan, it has met legal problems, and at other places, such as LaGuardia (Table 7.3) hardly reflects the magnitude of demand variations.[40] It is also employed at the major airports in the United Kingdom[41] although the primary objective has historically been to raise revenue for investment rather than as a strict short-term capacity rationing device. First

[38] S. Glaister, 'Generalised consumer surplus and public transport pricing', *Economic Journal*, **84**, 849–67, 1974.

[39] W.J. Tyson, 'A study of the effect of different bus fares in Greater Manchester', *Chartered Institute of Transport Journal*, **37**, 334–8, 1975.

[40] J.L. Schank, 'Solving airside airport congestion: why peak runway pricing is not working', *Journal of Air Transport Management*, **11**, 417–25, 2005.

[41] R. Doganis, *The Airline Business*, 2nd edn, London: Routledge, 2006.

Table 7.3   *Pricing structure at New York, LaGuardia Airport (2002)*

Type of charge	Minimum charge
Operation during peak (8 a.m. to 9 p.m.), non-scheduled carriers	$100
Operation off-peak, non-scheduled carriers	$25
Operation during peak (8 a.m. to 9 p.m.), scheduled carriers	$50
Operation off-peak, scheduled carriers	$20

Source: Port Authority of New York and New Jersey, Aviation Department, Schedule of charges for air terminals, 2003.

attempts to introduce peak-load pricing date back to 1972 when BAA established a runway movement charge at the busiest time of day at Heathrow. Passenger peak charges were implemented in 1976. Both the differential between peak and off-peak charges and the definition of peak periods have changed considerably over the years. The ratio of peak to off-peak fees increased until the mid-1980s. A number of differentiations for peak landing fees have been tried but these were eventually succeeded by a uniform peak-hour fee. The charter airlines in Europe in the 1990s also practiced peak-load pricing when setting their fares, in their case reflecting seasonal variations in tourism demand patterns.[42]

7.8   Transport Subsidies, Operational Objectives and Pricing

Many sectors of transport enjoy quite substantial levels of either central or local government subsidy. (Table 7.4 shows the percentage of transit costs recovered in some of the world's major cities, and Figure 7.19 provides some detail of the situation regarding recent time trends in local public transport subsidies in the United Kingdom.) Because they represent payments for transport services by non-users, subsidies complicate the pricing problem.

To some extent the type of problem created depends upon the form of subsidy given. If a central or local government provides the subsidy for a specific service, then it may be seen as representing that government's demand for that service and treated alongside the demand of other customers; the service subsidies given by local authorities to specified bus services in the United Kingdom under the 1985 Transport Act may be categorized in this way, as may many of the subsidies to franchised services in other European countries and in some American cities.[43] From a pricing/operational point of view such subsidies are relatively easily assimilated into standard economic models. This is particularly

---

[42] M. Bishop and D. Thompson, 'Peak-load pricing in aviation: the case of charter air fares', *Journal of Transport Economics and Policy*, **26**, 71–82, 1992.

[43] B.K. Morlok, 'Privatizing bus transit: cost savings from competitive contracting', *Journal of the Transportation Research Forum*, **28**, 72–81, 1987.

Table 7.4   *Levels of operational transit subsidies in various cities*

City	Percent subsidy	City	Percent subsidy
Perth	72	Brussels	27
Adelaide	60	Munich	54
Brisbane	46	Stockholm	33
Melbourne	76	Vienna	41
Sydney	45	Hamburg	38
Phoenix	72	Copenhagen	34
Denver	81	London	7
Boston	76	Paris	39
Houston	72	Singapore	−15
Washington	50	Tokyo	−5
San Francisco	65	Hong Kong	−36
Detroit	77	Kuala Lumpur	−35
Chicago	54	Surabaya	−27
Los Angeles	57	Jakarta	−1
New York	53	Bangkok	7
Toronto	39	Seoul	3
Frankfurt	55	Beijing	80
Amsterdam	60	Manila	−12
Zurich	40		

Source: P. Newman and J. Kenworthy, *Sustainability and Cities: Overcoming Automobile Dependence*, Washington, DC: Island, 1999.

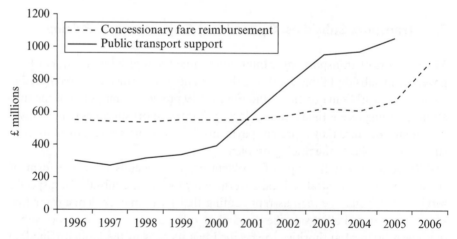

Note: Public transport support is monies spent by local authorities to provide unprofitable 'socially necessary' services generally by tendering them out to private operators. Concessionary fare reimbursements are monies paid to compensate bus operators for carrying certain types of passengers, such as the aged or physically impaired, at low or zero fares.

Figure 7.19   *Local bus subsidies in Great Britain (2006/07 prices)*

so in the UK case where the routes to be subsidized are put up for competitive tender, a process that is designed to ensure that the minimum subsidy is paid for the designated service. Further, the evidence from London, and from similar systems in the United States, is that there are cost-efficiency gains (after allowing for administrative and monitoring expenses) of about 20 percent over more general subsidy arrangements.

When lump-sum subsidies are given to transport undertakings for general revenue purposes, however, problems arise in deciding upon the best methods of using the subsidy and the appropriate charge to levy on customers. In particular, it is difficult to devise pricing and operational objectives that ensure that management uses the fixed subsidies efficiently to attain the welfare objectives for which they are intended. A number of possible objectives have been cited as offering a way around this problem.

It has been argued that commercial criteria (with profit-maximizing pricing) in this situation would lead to monopoly exploitation and be counterproductive in terms of the social objectives justifying the subsidy, while a social welfare-maximizing criterion (with marginal cost pricing) would break the link between costs, prices and output and lead to probable X-inefficiency: the provision of services at excessive costs. To circumvent these problems, and to provide clear pragmatic guidelines for lower-level management, London Transport attempted in the late 1970s to maximize passenger mileage subject to a budget constraint (that is, that costs are recovered after the fixed-sum subsidy has been taken into account). Operationally, when the criterion is applied at the margin, this means:

> Reduce price as long as the increase in passenger mileage resulting exceeds the loss of revenue multiplied by the shadow price of public funds; increase bus mileage as long as the increase in passenger mileage resulting is greater than the net addition to the financial loss multiplied by the shadow price of public funds.[44]

The criterion, therefore, permits adjustments to the system operated so that costs are met (after allowing for the subsidy) and relatively junior management can assess the desirability of alternative courses of action. The criterion is, however, demonstrably inferior in theoretical terms to a pure marginal cost pricing strategy – price discrimination and cross-subsidization may result which push fares on inelastic services above marginal operating costs so that revenue is available to finance services which exhibit a relatively high elasticity (and thus easily provide an increase in passenger-miles). It is quite possible, therefore, for a service to be operated for which the level of demand is never high enough to permit price to cover marginal costs.[45]

It is possible, at the expense of complicating the criterion, to devise weighting schemes which can be attached to passenger-miles on various routes to reflect their importance to the decision maker and schemes do exist which yield the same results as marginal cost pricing. Whether it is justified to adopt such weights must be an empirical question, depending on the loss of welfare that may accompany the simple unweighted passenger-miles maximization approach relative to the

---

[44] C.A. Nash, 'Management objectives, fares and service levels in bus transport', *Journal of Transport Economics and Policy*, **12**, 70–85, 1978.

[45] S. Glaister and J.J. Collings, 'Maximisation of passenger miles in theory and practice', *Journal of Transport Economics and Policy*, **12**, 304–21, 1978.

administrative costs of implementation. Bos[46] also pointed to the welfare distributional implications of the criterion and suggests that positive distributional effects may justify a certain level of welfare loss although, again, the exact distribution effect cannot be determined by a priori argument. (Empirical evidence in London suggests, however, that the London Transport scheme did have desirable distributional implications.)

7.9   Market Instability, Suboptimal Supply and the Empty Core

To recap, economic theory tells us that when there are no fixed costs, bargaining between suppliers and customers will ensure that prices are kept to a minimal level that allows suppliers to recover all costs over the long term. When there are no fixed costs, the marginal cost of meeting customer demand represents the entire costs of production. The problems come when there are fixed costs, or indivisibilities in the cost function.

The traditional view of fixed costs was developed when the bricks, steel and mortar of industrial plants had to be paid for. It was largely seen in relation to manufacturing, or if in the context of a services industry, in terms of the immobile hardware involved: rail track and bridges. This seemed logical at the time because fixed costs are defined as invariant with the amount of production, and the physical plant and infrastructure of the time fitted this description. Fixity is, however, a relative concept, and while, as we have seen in Chapter 5, a rail track may be seen as fixed over a long period, a railway locomotive may be seen as fixed over a shorter time until it needs replacement. In other words some costs of production are fixed over the given decision period, while the train still operates, but become variable when replacement is needed. While the locomotive keeps functioning, the use made of it will be influenced by the marginal costs of maintenance, crew, fuel and so on.

But with service industries, and especially those involving scheduled services, the fixed costs are somewhat different in detail, if not in their strict definition. While airlines and conference shipping lines, for example, do use expensive hardware, this is not their underlying fixed-cost problem. Indeed, the largest costs of airlines have traditionally been their labor. These in the traditional sense are generally, but not entirely seen as variable costs. Even aircraft are now seldom owned by the carriers but are leased, sometimes on a wet-lease that includes crew. The result is that airlines are increasingly becoming 'virtual carriers' that act to bring together packages of services owned by others and thus are encumbered with few fixed costs themselves in the traditional economic sense.

Fixed costs in a modern service industry, including airlines, however, can take a different form. An airline is committed to a particular scheduled service some 6 months or so before the flight – it is committed to have a plane, crew, fuel,

---

[46] S. Bos, 'Distribution effects of maximisation of passenger rules', *Journal of Transport Economics and Policy*, **12**, 322–9, 1978.

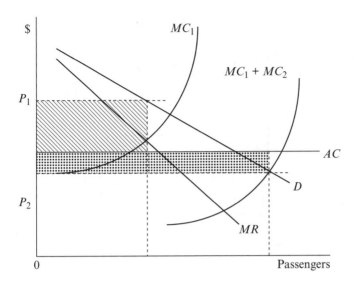

Figure 7.20   *Indivisibilities in supply*

gates, landing and take-off slots and so on available at a given time. This does
have an advantage that fares are often collected before the airline has to provide
the service, but in a highly competitive market, this is generally more than offset
by the limited amount of revenue that is ultimately collected. The commitment to
a particular scheduled take-off time poses the traditional cost recovery problem
associated with any decreasing cost situation: costs cannot be recovered by
charging a single marginal price.

The problem can be seen in Figure 7.20. Here we have a situation where
there is a single air (or ship or bus) scheduled service that has a marginal cost
curve of MC_1, an average cost curve of AC and confronted with a market
demand of D. Being a monopoly provider it will set its price at P_1 and enjoys
monopoly profits of the shaded area above the AC curve. A second carrier,
attracted by these profits, can enter the market with identical equipment and
will push out the market marginal cost curve to $MC_1 + MC_2$. The result in this
competitive situation, where price is set equal to the new marginal cost, is that
fares will decline to P_2, resulting in a combined loss for the two suppliers equal
to the shaded area under the AC curve. There must, therefore, be some mark-up
above marginal prices to sustain the two carriers. As we have seen, airlines and
other suppliers in modern deregulated markets largely engage in second- and
third-degree price discrimination and charge passengers and shippers different
prices to try to extract as much revenue as possible.

While this approach can allow revenues above marginal cost to be generated
when a service has some degree of monopoly power (for example, no competing
flight to the destination within a reasonable timeframe), the problem is that with
a fixed schedule in a competitive market, the various airlines set take-off times for
each destination at about the same time. This leads to intense competition to fill
seats and forces fares down to levels that do not allow all the costs of an individual

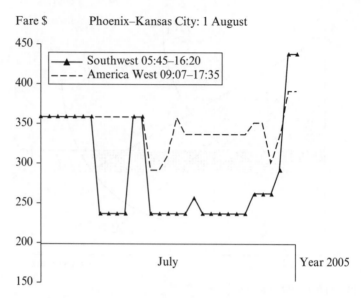

Source: K.J. Button and H. Vega, 'The temporal-fares-offered curves in air transportation', *Journal of the Transportation Research Forum*, **46**, 83–100, 2007.

Figure 7.21   *Temporal-fares-offered curves for return services from Phoenix to Kansas City, out August 1 and returning August 5, 2005*

services to be met. It is worth filling a seat once offered with anyone willing to pay for its marginal cost.

Empirical analysis supporting the logical basis of the temporal-fares-offered curve has been fairly well established in studies of European and American air transport markets. Figure 7.12 seen earlier, just as an example, looked at a US monopoly market and illustrates the fairly consistent rise in fares as the time of departure approaches. This pattern is also found on the numerous other routes where this technique has been applied, and holds irrespective of whether the monopoly airline is a low-cost carrier or pursues the traditional, full service business model.

Figure 7.21 shows the sort of temporal-fares-offer curves that emerges when two carriers offer nearly identical services, differentiated largely by a small difference in departure times. Again the pattern is consistent and has been examined in detail in other works. This is also from the United States and shows the volatility that arises, and the lack of a significant and consistent rise in fares towards take-off is clear. Other studies looking at services where there are more than two competitors show a further flattening out of the temporal-fares-offered curve, with near commonality of flat fares offered by all up to take-off as one would expect in the large numbers case.

It also leads to suboptimal levels of investment despite excess capacity during peaks in the cycle. The fact that full costs are not recovered, and that ultimately an airline will withdraw a service, or go out of business, is known as the 'empty core problem'. It is neither a new concept (it was developed in the 1880s by the largely forgotten Oxford economist, Francis Edgeworth), nor is it one that has limited application. In the long term, as potential investors become aware of this problem, they will reduce or cease to put new investment into the industry.

Overall, there are several conditions when there may be no core and, hence, a market may not be sustainable. These occur when there are relatively large fixed costs, avoidable (set-up) costs, indivisibility, network effects, or severe fluctuations in demand. An unsustainable market may also exist when some suppliers enjoy a degree of institutional or financial protection, and when there are significant variations in the costs of suppliers. In practice, many public utilities, transport industries and some manufacturing industries meet these criteria.

The lack of a core can broadly result in two outcomes depending on the reactions of the players in the market. If the transport suppliers think they can beat out competitors in the market, then there will be instability as suppliers keep entering and leaving the market. Alternatively, if potential suppliers are more rational and realize that their market entry will result in excess capacity and an inability to recover full costs, then they will not enter. The result is that there will be a suboptimally low capacity provided. Looked at in another way, there are indivisibilities in the aircraft or ships scheduled and the overall capacity will be lower than would occur if they were perfectly divisible.

The fact that this economic conundrum applies to the scheduled airlines[47] and scheduled shipping[48] industries has been appreciated for some time, but largely ignored in policy formulation. The complexity of the underlying economic model has hindered the communication of the issue to decision makers. This situation also runs counter to some traditional, often ideological, views of competition policy that hold that there can 'never be too much competition'.

7.10 Indirect Pricing

In some cases it is not possible for technical reasons, or there are excessive transaction costs involved, in directly pricing a user of a transport service. The outcome in many cases is an adjustment to the price of a complementary good; in the case of a publicly owned transport facility this means *de facto* a tax. An example of this in the United States and many other countries has been the pricing of road use from the 1930s when the road system began to be improved and largely paved. Tolls paid on turnpikes had been a traditional way of pricing many major roads, but with the advent of the widespread adoption of the motor vehicle, the excessive congestion created around manual toll booths saw a fuel tax come in as a replacement.

There are important trade-offs to consider when using indirect pricing. It

---

[47] K.J. Button, 'Does the theory of the "core" explain why airlines fail to cover their long-run costs of capital?', *Journal of Air Transport Management*, **9**, 5–14, 2003.

[48] S.C. Pirrong, 'An application of core theory to the analysis of ocean shipping markets', *Journal of Law and Economics*, **35**, 89–131, 1992.

may reduce the transaction costs of collection, which may involve savings for the supplier of transport services, other users, or third parties, but it is not an efficient price. It does not directly reflect the use of the transport system and thus does not optimize that use. A fuel tax, for example, is poorly correlated to the costs of individuals' road use; payments vary by engine size and where the vehicle is used, which may not be where the costs are incurred. There may be jurisdictional issues when, for example, fuel is purchased in one location but the driving is largely done in another. There is also the danger that because of the lack of direct account-ability, the authorities may manipulate the indirect charge to raise revenues not directly related to the costs of the facility. (This should be seen as distinct from a pure sales or purchase tax that is a clear form of government revenue collec-tion and is levied on many items.) Finally, the charge may end up serving several purposes.

There have been efforts made to see to what extent these surrogate prices do reflect actual costs of use. But this is not easy. In addition to the micro issues of how to allocate costs to particular categories of road user, trucks, cars and so, there is the issue of what items to include (for example, is air pollution a road cost in the conventional sense?), and how to value them.[49] Even when it comes to items such as capital costs there are problems. Road investments are lumpy and outlays vary considerably year by year. The 'pay-as-you-go' method simply takes the annual expenditure, which may be considered a rather simplistic approach given the volatile nature of investment. The 'public enterprise' approach looks at a road as an investment and considers how much interest would have to be paid to borrow the money required to make that investment – basically the opportu-nity cost. While there are some sound economic grounds for this methodology, it does involve somewhat strong assumptions in calculating the capital tied up in the system and the interest that would be required to finance this capital.

There are also issues about how costs should be allocated between users of common infrastructure. Trucks, for example, cause more pavement damage than do cars but because they go more slowly, design standards for bends, for example, could be more flexible. Also if the pavement depth were designed optimally for trucks then there would be less maintenance required and the allocation of oper-ating costs of the track would be less for larger vehicles. Simply looking at taxes and other non-user-based charges and treating them as prices is not helpful. In one sense, the methods of pricing much transport infrastructure is a little like charging a premium on butter to cover the costs of bread, but allowing consumers to take as much bread as they wanted. The charges do little to make consumption of bread efficient. Likewise, most surrogate charges for transport infrastructure do little to ensure that it is used optimally or to offer guidance as to when capacity needs to be adjusted.

Despite these problems, there may be practical considerations that make using indirect pricing a tractable and reasonable second-best approach. This may

---

[49] K.J. Button, 'Heavy goods vehicle taxation in the United Kingdom', *Transportation*, **8**, 389–408, 1979.

particularly be so in some countries where there are complex regulatory systems and there is a need for a significant flow of funds for investment. The distinction between the transport service and the complementary good may also be somewhat blurred.

An example of this is frequently found at airports that provide both direct services to airlines but also a variety of services on the ground to passengers. This is often referred to as the 'two till' approach to financing an airport's activities. Figure 7.22 provides an illustration of the sort of circumstances where this may arise. In more mature countries where there is a significant traffic flow, but growth in traffic is relatively slow, there is more incentive to extract extra revenue for passengers. This situation is compounded when the income of that country is high and travelers are willing to pay for additional airport services. When incomes are lower and airports are subjected to less regulation, the tendency is to rely much more on direct income from airlines – it is also easier to collect than through a multiplicity of retail concessions and the like. Whether the use of commercial revenues leads to more efficient use of resources than charging higher rates to airlines is, however, debatable. While it may be relatively easy to isolate the costs of the air services charges from commercial services offered on the ground, a differential amount of monopoly power may lead to distortions in investments and in pricing. How to handle this issue has, for example, been a major policy issue at London's airports.[50]

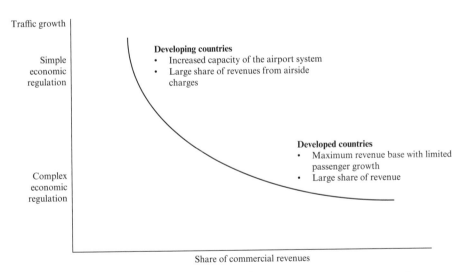

Source: E.R. Juan, *Airport Infrastructure: The Emergence Role of the Private Sector, Cofinancing and Financial Advisory Services*, Washington, DC: World Bank, 1995.

Figure 7.22   *Financing airports from two 'tills'*

50 D. Starkie, 'Reforming UK airport regulation', *Journal of Transport Economics and Policy*, **35**, 119–35, 2001.

Further Reading

Milton Friedman's *Price Theory: A Provisional Text*, New York: Aldine, 1962, is the difficult, but enduring classic, on price theory. K.E. Train, *Optimal Regulation: The Economic Theory of Natural Monopoly*, Cambridge, MA: MIT Press, 1991, provides a thorough look at the specific issue of pricing natural monopolies. Attempts to devise operational pricing rules for urban transport are reviewed both cogently and in depth by C.A. Nash, 'Management objectives, fares and service levels in bus transport', *Journal of Transport Economics and Policy*, **12**, 70–85, 1978. This reference usefully contrasts the approaches to public transport pricing. Subsidies in transport are often alluded to in the literature but, despite their quantitative importance in the real world, are seldom assessed. P.K. Else, 'Criteria for local transport subsidies', *Transport Reviews*, **12**, 291–309, 1992 and I. Elgar and C. Kennedy, 'Review of optimal transit subsidies: comparison between models', *Journal of Urban Planning and Development*, **13**, 71–8, 2005 offer useful papers on ideas behind subsidy policies. K.J. Button, 'Extraction of economic rent under various slot allocation approaches', in A. Czerny, P. Forsyth, D. Gillen and H.M. Niemeier (eds), *Airport Slots International Experiences and Options for Reform*, Aldershot: Ashgate, 2008, provides details of various forms of price differentiation that are used in the airline industry, but these are of more general applicability.

8 Containing the Environmental Costs of Transport

8.1 Introduction

Chapter 6 offered evidence on the magnitude and the diversity of the external costs associated with transport. In this chapter we are concerned with methods of confronting the externality problem and, if possible, optimizing the environmental costs of transport. It should be emphasized at the outset that the policy focus on the external costs of transport, while glaring in the developed world, is much less intense in less wealthy countries. The affluence of the Western world has transferred part of the desire from improving material living standards to that of improving (or retaining) environmental quality. The marginal utility of additional financial income, it is often argued, is, for the majority of people in the West, possibly of less value than a cleaner, quieter and safer environment in which to live. This is a comparatively recent phenomenon and books on transport economics written in the pre-war period gave scant attention to externalities.

Although increasingly concerned with matters such as deforestation and soil erosion, most Third World countries still generally retain this comparative indifference to the environmental impacts of transport – their generally poor living standards and inadequate transport systems necessitate that effort be directed almost exclusively at improving material output. This is despite mounting environmental problems.

We have seen in Figure 6.1 that ideally, externalities should be contained to the point where the costs of further reductions exceed the marginal social benefits (as stated 35 years ago, 'pollution should be reduced to the point where the costs of doing so are covered by the benefits from the reduction in pollution'[1]). It should be re-emphasized that this is unlikely to mean zero pollution or zero congestion but rather optimal levels of external cost. To achieve this optimum a number of possibilities recommend themselves, and the objective of this chapter is to evaluate the effectiveness of the main ones.

These options are largely assessed in terms of their economic implications, but in practice there are important political (most notably the lobbying power of various groups) and wider social concerns (such as 'environmental justice'[2]) that come into play when policies are being considered. There are considerable generic

---

[1] UK Royal Commission on Environmental Pollution, *First Report*, London: HMSO, 1972.
[2] J. Chakraborty, 'Evaluating the environmental justice impacts of transportation improvement projects in the US', *Transportation Research D*, **11**, 315–23, 2006.

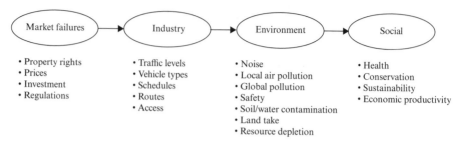

Source: Derived from, K.J. Button, 'Are current air transport policies consistent with a sustainable environment?', in E. Verhoef and E. Feitelson (eds), *Transport and Environment: In Search of Sustainable Solutions*, Cheltenham, UK and Northampton, MA, USA: Edward Elgar, 2001.

Figure 8.1   *The stages in the environmental cost chain*

analyses of these broader aspects in the economic literature, but these are not dealt with in any great detail here.

8.2   The Basic Approaches

The adverse economics effects of transport on the environment result from a chain reaction (Figure 8.1) starting with market failures, most notably negative third-party externalities, which affect the costs perceived in the transport sector, which in turn cause excessively damaging environmental effects resulting in costs ultimately being borne by society. From a policy perspective, the diagram is useful because it shows that economic policies designed to reduce, or optimize, the environmental costs associated with transport may be introduced at various points in the chain. If for political reasons, or because of transaction costs, it is not possible to tackle the market failures *per se*, there may be relatively cost-effective second-best approaches that can be applied further down the chain. For example, by building sound walls along the sides of streets to reduce excessive noise. These second-best approaches, however, may distort other markets and this needs to be borne in mind when assessing their merits.

At the more specific instrument level, a broad indication of the range of policies which can be applied to limiting the external costs of the motor vehicle are set out in Table 8.1. As can be seen, policies can broadly be divided between the market-based approaches and command-and-control measures, although in practice 'baskets' of instruments are usually employed. Further, the table reflects the ability to direct attention at various aspects of the problems and they can be aimed at the vehicle, the fuel used or affecting the level and composition of traffic.

While it is useful at times, both for illustration and to retain a link between theory and policy, to refer to actual measures employed by transport authorities, the emphasis is on the direct economic implications of the alternative approaches rather than their political or social virtues. Broadly we proceed by initially looking at the strict market approach to the subject, the 'Coasian solution' and then move

Table 8.1 *Taxonomy of main policy instruments to control the environmental impacts of motor vehicles*

	Market-based incentives		Command-and-control instruments	
	Direct	*Indirect*	*Direct*	*Indirect*
Vehicle	Emissions fee Tradable permits	Differential taxation Tax allowances for new vehicles	Emissions standards	Compulsory inspection and maintenance of emissions control systems Mandatory use of low polluting vehicles Compulsory scrappage of old vehicles
Fuel		Differential fuel taxation High fuel taxes	Fuel composition Phasing out of high polluting fuels	Fuel economy standards Speed limits
Traffic		Congestion pricing Parking charges Subsidies for less polluting modes	Physical constraints of traffic Designated areas	Restraints on vehicle use Bus lanes and and other priorities Information systems

to consider fiscal instruments, the internalizing of external costs by charging those who generate them, the 'Pigouvian solution'. Variants on both are also looked at before considering command-and-control measures.

8.3   The Coasian Solution – Tradable Permits

Much of the work of Nobel Prize-winning economist Ronald Coase[3] focused on the role that in complete or imperfect markets for property rights have in creating excessive social costs, and environmental damage. In many cases, the solution to this problem is thus seen as ensuring that individuals have more complete ownership over property rights and that they can trade these rights to maximize the efficient use of resources. As a more concrete example, the Kyoto round of negotiations regarding global carbon emissions, and *ipso facto* the release of global warming gases, gives participating countries an allocation of carbon and allows them to trade these among themselves. The countries, or individuals and firms within them that can make the most effective use of carbon, will then buy

[3] R.H. Coase, 'The problem of social cost', *Journal of Law and Economics*, **3**, 1–44, 1960.

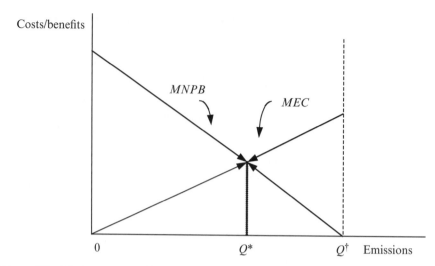

Figure 8.2 *The importance of property rights*

additional amounts on the market from those that have allocations but cannot use them effectively. In this way the allocations end up in uses that yield the greatest economic gains.

The way in which this works can be illustrated by looking at Figure 8.2. In this diagram, the *MNPB* curve, drawn linearly purely for the sake of simplicity, shows the net benefits that the perpetrator of the externality (emissions in our example) gains from that activity. There are diminishing returns as more emissions are generated. The *MEC* curve reflects the marginal costs of emissions that are assumed to rise as emissions increase – for example, small emissions of NO_2 cause little damage but as they mount up, increments become more serious.

If there are no property rights, in other words, the perpetrators can use up as much of the environmental resources as they wish at no cost, then emissions will rise to the point $Q^\dagger$ irrespective of the costs involved. There are also no incentives to emit beyond this level – it is an equilibrium. If on the other hand, those affected by the pollution have the rights to clean air then there will be no pollution – again an equilibrium point, despite the net benefits that would be generated if a degree of pollution were allowed.

Ideally, when the optimum level of emissions is at Q^* the net benefits are maximized. To reach this point, and for it to be an equilibrium, Coase argues that rights to the atmosphere should be created and trade in them permitted. Assume that those adversely affected were given these rights, then some of the individuals would be willing to sell these rights to the emitters who would have a willingness to pay. Trade would continue as long as there were enough potential emitters willing to buy rights from the polluted that were not so severely affected; in other words until an equilibrium is reached with emission levels at Q^*. Alternatively, the initial allocation of rights could be given to the emitters. The marginal emitters would be willing to be bought out by the most severely affected polluted and this trade would again continue until emissions are at Q^*.

It does not matter in this context from a long-run perspective who is initially granted the property rights to the atmosphere. The ultimate trading leads to an optimal outcome. The initial allocation could be by an auction (in which case the government would get a windfall once-and-for-all gain), it could be by lottery, it could be according to current use, and so on. This is more of a political than an economic matter because it has obvious distributional effects – those with the initial allocation (or the government in the case of auctions) make a short-term financial gain – but no long-term resource efficiency effects.

While theoretically the Coasian approach has intellectual merit, it has limitations. To allocate property rights to, in the example, the atmosphere, there is a need to be able to define the units being traded. While this can be proxied in the case of something like greenhouse gas emissions by using tons of carbon, this is not so easy with things like noise or visual intrusion. There is also the issue of policing to ensure that contracts agreed upon are upheld, and there are the transaction costs involved in the buying and selling of the rights themselves. Efficient trade also assumes that markets work perfectly, and there is no monopoly power present.

Despite these challenges, tradable permits, or at least policies containing their main elements, have been used to deal with specific transport-related externalities, in addition to more generic problems such as global warming gas emissions. In particular, they were used in the US to remove lead from gasoline.[4] The United States decided that lead was an undesirable additive and in 1982 established a trading program, which in 1985 was modified to allow banking (the holding over of allocations from one period to another). Lead credits were allocated according to the existing use of lead and standards regarding the lead content of gasoline. (For example, if the standard was 1.1 grams per gallon then a firm producing 100 gallons of lead would receive up to 110 grams which it may either use or sell.) The standards and, thus the amount of lead available, declined to zero by 1987.

In terms of property rights, the system, because current production is correlated to past production, implies that the existing distribution is taken as the starting point. Whether the program created net environmental benefits beyond the standards set is difficult to determine, although trading was extensive (about 15 percent of the total allocation) indicating that the transition was achieved relatively efficiently in terms of which refineries were used. Those with more efficient capacity had an incentive to buy from those with less efficient capacity.

A less strict market approach is that inherent in the CAFE (corporate average fuel economy) standards on the fuel efficiency of vehicle fleets discussed below. Here there is no monetary trading but car manufacturers can adjust the types of vehicles being made (intra-company trading) as long as average fuel burn standards are met, which allows for flexibility in their production to reflect costs and market demand.

---

[4] R.W. Hahn, 'Economic prescriptions for environmental problems: how the patient followed the doctor's orders', *Journal of Economic Perspectives*, **3**, 95–114, 1989.

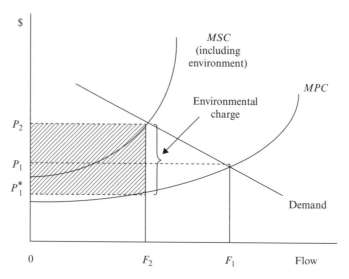

Figure 8.3   *The Pigouvian environmental tax*

8.4 The 'Polluter-pays' Principle

There is an inevitable problem with optimizing externalities, as pointed out by Coase himself, and this involves the perspective with which one looks at an externality. Coase argued that externalities could theoretically be removed by allocating environmental property rights, either to polluters or to those adversely affected, and allowing trade in these rights to take place. There are clear practical problems of doing this, not least of which is that of policing the system, but the idea does pinpoint the symmetrical nature of externalities. Should those who suffer be protected or should those who benefit be compensated for desisting from their current transport activities? While from an efficiency perspective there is no clear answer, international agencies such as the OECD have taken the line that morally those who pollute should pay for the excessive damage they cause the environment.

The idea is not a new one and the publication of Arthur Pigou's seminal work, *The Economics of Welfare*,[5] caused a large number of economists to examine the merits of adopting emission charges. The idea is that the authorities take responsibility for the environment – in effect they become the property right holders, and charge users of the environment an appropriate price (or tax) for that use. Figure 8.3 provides a fairly standard type of visual illustration of how such a charge would apply to road transport. We see the marginal cost of using a road rising (*MPC*). Because road users only take account of the cost of trips they incur themselves they will keep making trips until the flow is F_1. The traffic, however, creates, as an example, noise that when added to the costs of fuel and time in making trips pushes up the full marginal cost at each level of flow to the

[5] A. Pigou, *The Economics of Welfare*, London: Macmillan, 1920.

MSC. If this were taken into account, then motorists would reduce their traffic and the flow would fall to F_2. The optimal environmental charge designed to reflect the noise costs on the local residents is the difference between the *MSC* and the *MPC* at this flow – $P_2 P_1^*$. The road users, by having the marginal costs of their trips pushed up from P_1 to P_2, are discouraged from making trips that do not cover this full cost and thus the flow falls to F_2.

Strictly this diagram could be a little deceiving. It assumes that imposing a pollution charge will affect traffic flow, which it may, but in fact there may be other ways in which a road user could deal with an environmental charge. In terms, of say, a charge on noise, a road user could suppress the noise without making fewer, or at least not significantly fewer, trips or with a carbon tax buy a smaller-engined vehicle to conserve fuel but not seriously affect travel patterns. In other words, part of the impact of an emissions charge would be to pull the *MSC* cost down in Figure 8.3.

The more technically correct diagram would be to have emissions on the horizontal axis to directly link the charge with the *de facto* effect on the environmental cost. One can easily trace out that the environmental result would be exactly the same as when emissions are perfectly correlated with traffic flow. It is deliberately drawn this way, however, to allow the discussion to move to the need to target policies and to measure their impacts in relation to the externality involved. For example, high fuel taxes may be a good way of reducing certain emissions, such as CO_2, but the ability to change vehicle types means that traffic flows may be unaffected. For handling congestion problems, as we shall see in the next chapter, there is a need for direct measures affecting trip making.

Pigouvian-style charges, while not common, are increasingly being used in transport, the best-known example being the differential tax on leaded petrol that virtually all industrialized countries outside the United States adopted in the 1980s, but some airports also vary landing/take-off fees according to the noise nuisance created by aircraft.[6]

While the basic concept is not difficult to appreciate, it has been refined and argued over for the past 70 years. Perhaps the most important of these debates reflects the fact that it is the authorities who impose the Pigouvian tax who are the main beneficiaries of them. Unlike tradable permits where markets allow for compensation through the pricing mechanism, there is no such automatic structure with charges because the on-going revenues collected go to government. It is then a political matter regarding who subsequently enjoys them. Historically, it has often been debates over the use of revenues that have been the main obstacles to the use of environmental charging, for example, in the case of French airlines.[7]

---

[6] C.-I. Hsu and P.-H. Lin, 'Performance assessment for airport noise charge policies and airline network adjustment response', *Transportation Research D*, **10**, 281–304, 2005.

[7] J.-P. Barde, *Use of Economic Instruments for Environmental Protection*, ENV// ECO/86.16, Paris: Organisation for Economic Co-operation and Development, 1986.

There are also problems in the calculation of the optimal pollution charge or price, since it is necessary to have reliable information about the MPC and MSC curves. As we have seen in Chapter 6, knowledge in this area is scant and although the use of, for example, hedonic house price indices may shed some light on the monetary importance of noise nuisance, they are far from perfect and normally offer little insight into the shape of the curves involved or the responsiveness of people to financial incentives.

At a rather more theoretical level, it is possible to question whether the polluter-pays principle is being correctly applied in Figure 8.3. We have implicitly assumed that the road users should buy the right to pollute in the area, but this could be turned on its head, and the proposition presented that road users should buy the right to relatively clean air, that is, the road users should be paid a subsidy of an amount equal to the emissions charge ($P_2P_1^*$) depicted in the diagram to curtail their activities. Again as with the Coase case, the question is essentially a moral–legal one involving property rights; although there may also be practical considerations involving administrative costs of introducing either prices or subsidies, these should also be considered.

As William Baumol and Wallace Oates[8] have stressed, one of the problems of charging polluters is that information about the MSC curve is imperfect, and that, even if some initially arbitrary price is charged, there is no indication of whether this is too high or too low. The usual 'trial and error' method of pricing used in industry is, therefore, not appropriate.

Since information about the MSC curve is necessary for virtually all optimal containment of noise and emissions, irrespective of the method used, Baumol and Oates, however, argue in favor of pricing on the grounds that it will cause less distortion than other policies. Their arguments found favor with the OECD[9] which argues, 'The costs of these measures (to ensure that the environment is in an acceptable state) should be reflected in the cost of goods and services that cause pollution in production and/or consumption'. Figure 8.4 considers two modes of transport, trucking (A) and railways (B), and relates the marginal net private benefits associated with using each mode to the noise nuisance emitted.

These curves are unknown to the authorities but it may be decided that it would be beneficial to do something about noise pollution rather than leave it at a high level. In these circumstances one may wish to reduce noise emissions by say 15 percent, and to use polluter charges to achieve this. Baumol and Oates demonstrate that a uniform charge on both road haulage and railway noise is the appropriate 'second-best' policy to pursue. In the figure the marginal abatement costs (MAC) of reducing noise emissions by one unit for each of the two modes are plotted. These curves are not known with any degree of exactitude to policy makers. A mandatory reduction of 15 percent for each

[8] W.J. Baumol and W.E. Oates, *The Theory of Environmental Policy*, Cambridge: Cambridge University Press, 1988.

[9] Organisation for Economic Co-operation and Development, *The Polluter Pays Principle*, Paris: OECD, 1975.

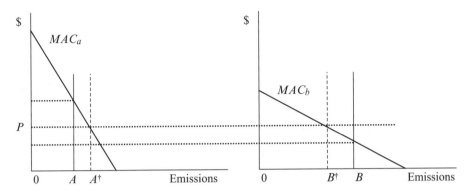

Figure 8.4   *The advantage of fiscal instruments when there is uncertainty*

mode would result in emissions being reduced to A and B for trucking and railroads, respectively.

While the desired objective has been satisfied, what one sees is that the MAC costs involved differ as between the modes – they are higher for road than for rail. It would be more cost effective to reduce noise by a greater amount on the railways than on roads quite simply because it is cheaper per unit to cut emissions in the former. A noise emissions charge of P per unit per decibel would automatically achieve the aimed-for improvement because it would be more of an incentive to cut pollution where it is cheaper to do so (a level $B^\dagger$ for rail) and have smaller reductions where the costs of abatement are higher (to $A^\dagger$ in the case of road haulage).

The Baumol and Oates argument highlights that if a particular standard is to be aimed for, then the most efficient way of attaining it is by using fiscal instruments. One can see the particular importance of this in many transport contexts. Because of its very nature, much transport activity is a mobile source of environmental intrusion but the domains in which it operates often differ in their sensitivity to its presence. Different airports, for example, because of their location and prevailing wind conditions, impose different noise envelopes on their surrounding populations. The actual physical noise associated with any aircraft type may, therefore, impose different costs at different airports.

To set a standard that all aircraft should reduce noise levels by a specified amount would thus be inefficient. On the other hand, a charge that would bring about the same overall noise reduction would give the flexibility to airlines to use their quieter aircraft at locations where noise is a major nuisance and their older, noisier ones where the problem is less severe.

The polluter-pays principle tends to be favored by many academics but it is not without its critics. Sharp,[10] for example, questions the distributional implications and argues that in some instances an environmental improvement may be obtained as efficiently by means of progressive taxation without the possible regressive effects of pollution charges. Essentially, the argument revolves around

[10] C.H. Sharp, 'The environmental cost of transport and the public interest', *Journal of Transport Economics and Policy*, **13**, 88–191, 1979.

Table 8.2   *Cost–benefit analysis of 1970 – Clean Air Act on automobile emissions*

Benefit estimate	% Control level			Benefit (10^9)	Cost (10^9)	Net benefit (10^9)
	HC	CO	NO			
Low	0.98	0.97	0.94	9	65	−56
Prime	0.98	0.97	0.94	34	65	31
High	0.98	0.97	0.94	102	65	37

Source: R.C. Schwing, B.W. Southwark, C.R. von Buseck and C.R. Jackson, 'Benefit–cost analysis of automobile emission reductions', *Journal of Environmental Economics and Management*, 7, 44–64, 1980.

the fact that the benefits from any environmental improvement are closely related to income. A poor person would probably have a preference for no pollution charges (and *ipso facto* lower final money prices) than a wealthier person whose marginal utility of income is lower. Hence, from a distributional point of view, a subsidy of $P_2P_1^*$ in Figure 8.3 to the airport to suppress aircraft noise, financed from a progressive taxation system, will have the same environmental effect but none of the regressive features of the pollution charge.

While hardly common, pollution charges have been used in transport with some success. One clear illustration of where fiscal incentives (in this example, coupled with regulation) have proved particularly effective has been in reducing the levels of lead (Pb) pollution. Many countries have introduced significant tax differentials between leaded and unleaded gasoline but, equally, many have also initiated regulations regarding the fuels that can be sold. In particular, the banning of normal gasoline (providing the tank capacity for garages to stock unleaded fuel and leaving only the more expensive super) has effectively further reduced the real choice open to most automobile users in the Netherlands, Switzerland, the United Kingdom and Germany. The combined impact of these measures in the United Kingdom was a rise in vehicles using unleaded gasoline from 0.1 percent of the vehicles in the country, the 'car park', in March 1988 to 25.9 percent in October 1989. Similarly, in the pre-unified Federal Republic of Germany the percentage of automobiles using unleaded rose from 11 percent in 1986 to 28 percent in 1987.

To date, however, fiscal policies have tended to be piecemeal, usually focusing on modes of transport rather than directly on transport externalities and, generally, with the explicit objective of reducing the effect of different modes rather than optimizing them. This suggests that the social objective of government policy has been one of satisficing rather than optimizing, although it has been argued that the actual effect of some regulations has been excessive. Schwing et al. (see Table 8.2), for instance, have suggested that the US Clean Air Act of 1970 imposed car exhaust emission levels that were far too stringent, with a consequential welfare loss. The table presents the results of their cost–benefit study. While the high benefit estimate suggests some welfare advantage from the Act, the underlying assumptions required to reach this conclusion are deemed very unrealistic. The optimal levels for the toxic exhaust emissions were estimated to be 0.73, 0.31 and 0.82 percent control for nitrogen oxide (NO), carbon monoxide (CO) and hydrocarbons (HC), respectively.

The acceptability of this type of work would be questioned by environmentalists in terms of both the items included in the cost–benefit calculations and the valuations placed upon them. The problem, common to most studies of environmental aspects of transport, is the inadequacy of knowledge both about the actual physical impact of the various external effects generated by transport and about the values that society places upon them. Until some clear understanding of these matters is obtained it is difficult to see how the external effects of transport are likely to approach the optimal level.

8.5   More on Environmental Standards

Figure 8.3 indicated that charging a pollution price might optimize external costs. It is equally possible, however, as we have seen that rather than operate through the pricing mechanisms the desired, environmentally optimal level of traffic could be obtained by using command-and-control instruments; that is, the establishment of legal, or in some cases voluntary standards, covering pollution, noise and safety.

The setting of environmental standards is long established, as the oft-cited night-time banning of chariots in classical Rome illustrates. Their use is now extensive and covers such wide-ranging things as establishment of 'noise abatement zones' in the United Kingdom, and the controls embodied in a series of Road Traffic Acts that have, since 1973, laid down regulations regarding car silencers and exhausts. The CAFE standards define the fuel efficiency of new vehicles in the United States (see Section 8.8) and most industrial countries now insist that gasoline-powered cars are fitted with catalytic convertors and have to use unleaded fuels. There are controls over where oil tankers may clean their tanks and when aircraft are allowed to take off. Individuals are required to wear seat belts in many countries and the use of cell phones while driving is often illegal. The list of standards and regulations is long and continues to grow.

Standards also change over time, as we shall see later regarding vehicle fuel efficiency. As another example, noise standards were introduced in Britain at the manufacturing stage for new lorries in 1970 with limits of 91 dB(A) for vehicles with engines over 200 hp and 89 dB(A) for less powerful lorries, while from March 1983 new vehicles coming into production had to meet more stringent requirements of 88 dB(A) and 86 dB(A), respectively. Supranational legislation has gained in importance recently with the European Union setting vehicle noise limits from the early 1990s.[11] The Civil Aviation Act 1971 laid down regulations about night movements over built-up areas in the country, and specifies overfly patterns for aircraft. The speed limits operative on roads in virtually all countries

[11] S. Vougias, 'Transport and environmental policy in the EC', *Transport Reviews*, **12**, 219–36, 1992.

are primarily designed to reduce accident risk – with some supplementary positive effects, on occasions, on fuel economy.

The compulsory wearing of seat belts in many countries is also to reduce accident costs. Similarly, the periodic testing of vehicles and the licensing of lorries, aircraft and so on are to ensure that minimum safety and environmental standards are achieved. In many overseas countries the regulations are more stringent (for example, the removal of lead from petrol in the United States, and stricter annual checks on pollution emissions from internal combustion engines in states such as New Jersey and Oregon) or take different forms (such as airbags in cars in the United States) but their intended effect is the same, to reduce the marginal environmental, including external accident, costs of transport.

While all the above represent physical regulations to contain pollution, they should strictly be divided between those controls that act directly to contain the externality (for example, noise emission legislation), the third component of Figure 8.1, and those that control transport in such a way as to reduce the external costs (for example, lorry routes and aircraft flight path regulations). The effects of these alternative broad sets of physical controls are not the same.

Actual emission standards act directly to limit the external effects, permitting other characteristics of operations to be adjusted freely. The operational regulations impose much more stringent controls, severely limiting the alternative courses of action open to the operator. With noise emission standards for aircraft flying over an area, for instance, an airline can either conform and pay the costs of suppressing noise or avoid the area in question; with operational controls only the latter option is available. This point should be borne in mind during the more general discussion of physical controls, which follows. We shall return to the question of operational restrictions, traffic calming and vehicle routing in more detail later.

One justification for adopting command-and-control methods is that they can have lower administrative costs. For example, the imposition of a zero lead content requirement for gasoline is relatively easy to understand and to enforce. It may not be optimal, and the effects across different users may not be fully efficient, but the transaction costs are relatively small. Allowing different individuals to have different amounts of lead in their fuel according to, say, their willingness to pay is quite clearly going to be difficult to price and to administer. In more strict economic terms, the transaction costs of pricing *a là* Pigou, or marketable permits along Coasian lines is just not cost effective. But there may be other reasons for adopting standards or prices.

While in the simple case illustrated in Figure 8.3 the effect of an optimal standard produces an identical level of road transport activity (and, *ipso facto* environmental intrusion) to an optimal pollution charge, it can be argued that, with more realistic assumptions, the pricing approach offers a superior solution to the externality problem even where administrative costs are similar.

When information about the exact shape of the *MEC* curve is poor, the use of standards is demonstrably less efficient than the Baumol–Oates charging approach seen in Figure 8.4. If, to achieve the 15 percent reduction in transport noise used in our example, both road and rail were compelled to cut their noise emissions (that is, to $0A^\dagger$ and $0B^\dagger$, respectively), then it is clear from the diagram that the marginal net private benefits generated by the two modes are no longer equal (at the new emission levels, $MAC_a > MAC_b$). Consequently, social welfare could be improved by lowering the standard for road haulage and increasing it for rail. Unfortunately, in the real world lack of perfect knowledge of the MAC curves means that the optimal differentiation of standards is likely to be impossible to define. Thus in this imperfect situation, fiscal measures are almost certainly going to prove superior to the use of emission standards.

It is also probable that pollution pricing will prove more flexible than standards. While transport infrastructure may impose external costs of visual intrusion, it is normally the mobile unit that generates the greatest external costs. Given the differing income levels and preference patterns in various parts of the country one could re-interpret the MAC curves in Figure 8.4 in terms of the marginal abatement associated with a single mode, but operating in different parts of the country. In this case the uniform emissions charge would be both theoretically superior and, in addition, reduce the costs to transport undertakings of reducing their noise emissions. The imposition of different standards for each area means that operators must either ensure that vehicles moving between areas conform to the most stringent standards or have specific, variously suppressed vehicles designed to conform to local regulations. Both options are likely to be wasteful. With a charging regime, the operator can select a vehicle mix that minimizes his/ her overall costs of operation – vehicles may be suppressed or pay the emissions price *or* they may be subjected to a combination of the two.

Moving to a more dynamic situation, where technology is variable, Maler[12] has suggested that pollution prices have important advantages over regulations for the encouragement of a rapid adoption of cleaner technologies. His argument rests upon the implicit assumption that transport suppliers, when confronted with either a pollution price or an emissions standard, assume this price or standard to be fixed in the medium term irrespective of their individual action. Consequently they will always assess the benefits to themselves of adopting new operating methods or technologies against existing prices or standards. In Figure 8.5 we show the marginal private costs of reducing exhaust fumes for a truck operator confronted with the existing technology (MC_1) and with the new technology (MC_2). The MC_2 curve is inside MC_1 because it is cheaper to suppress vehicles with the new technology at all noise levels. On the assumption that the authorities have full information on MEC and can, therefore, define the optimal level of traffic noise we see that either a pollution charge of $0P$ or a standard of $0C$ will ideally be in force.

If the pricing policy is pursued the trucker will find it financially worthwhile to quieten his vehicle by CD_1 (costing CD_1B) and pay $0CBP$ in charges. With a

---

[12] K.G. Maler, 'Environmental policies and the role of the economist in influencing public policy', in J.G. Rothenberg and I.G. Heggie (eds), *Transport and the Urban Environment*, Basingstoke: Macmillan, 1974.

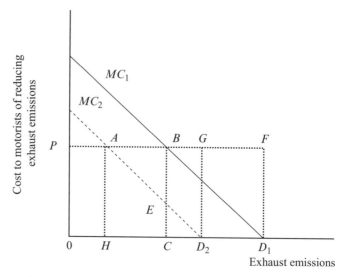

Figure 8.5 *Pollution charges, emission standards and technical change*

standard he pays no pollution charges but it costs him CBD_1 to conform to the noise regulation. However, if the new technology is available an individual trucker will perceive, *ceteris paribus*, the benefits of adopting it as ABD_1D_2 if there is a charging policy operative, that is, he will reduce his emissions with the new technology to $0H$ (costing AHD_2) and pay charges of $0PAH$. The incentive to adopt the alternative technology with the emissions standard is only D_2EBD_1, that is, the cost of conforming to the standard with the new technology rather than the old. Thus the pollution charging policy offers an incentive of the ABE, in excess of an emissions standard to move to the cleaner technology.

One possible option is a combined environmental tax/standards approach whereby all vehicles are obliged to meet a set standard and there is a scale of emissions-related 'fines' for vehicles that exceed this. If the standard were rigorous and well below the existing level of emissions (that is, consistent with the optimal level of pollution with the cleaner technology in our example above), then this would be as effective as the pricing approach and at the same time offer a firm target for vehicle operators to aim at. Such a tax/standards approach may, however, be particularly appealing at the vehicle manufacturing stage where new technology can most easily be injected into the transport sector in a gradual manner.

8.6 Transport Subsidies and the Environment

To try to stimulate the greater use of less 'polluting' transport, in the broadest sense, there has traditionally been a fairly widespread use of subsidies. These are politically attractive, largely because they involve a diffuse contributor base but a focused receptor base. We exclude here the plethora of subsidies that are designed primarily to meet social objectives, such as ensuring acceptable levels of mobility, meeting the needs of the physically disadvantaged, and providing access to remote regions, but are concerned explicitly with subsidies aimed at changing travel patterns with the objective of encouraging more environmentally benign forms of transport.

In practice, however, it is important to note that these are not normally 'Pigouvian subsidies' that are explicitly paid to individuals to desist in generating external costs, but rather indirect subsidies to encourage the adoption of other activities that are associated with lower levels of external or other adverse economic impact. In terms of surface, personal travel the conventional wisdom is that, for example, an efficient public transport system with adequate load factors is more energy efficient than the automobile.

There are general issues regarding subsidies of any kind, such as whether it is reasonable to use taxes collected from the general public to essentially subsidize public transport and car users, and whether it is possible to have an efficient subsidy regime that is not highly X-inefficient and captured by the transport-providing agencies and their employees. But from a pure efficiency perspective for the types of subsidies given to stimulate less environmentally intrusive modes of transport, there has to be a significant cross-elasticity of demand between modes for public transport subsidies to be effective. We shall return to this later.

Thus, an alternative to operating directly upon the transport undertaking generating externalities (either pollution or congestion) is seen to be the offering of a carrot to transport users to switch to more socially desirable modes. This line of reasoning has been widely used as a partial justification for the large subsidies given to support the railways and urban transport services. In the United Kingdom, the Railways Act 1974, for example, permitted government grants of up to 50 percent of the costs to be paid to British Rail customers for the installation of sidings and provision of rolling stock, on the basis of an assessment of the environmental harm of the lorry movements which would be avoided if the investment concerned went ahead. The 1968 Transport Act initiated a system of centrally and locally financed public transport operating and capital subsidies (the latter of which has subsequently been abandoned) with the objective of containing the growth in private motor traffic in the large urban areas.

In the United States, net federal subsidies from 1990 to 2002 meant that for every thousand passenger-miles, transit received $118 in subsidy, although not all of this was justified on environmental grounds. In addition there were extensive state and local support initiatives for public transport, although their motivations have not always been clear.[13]

In a perfectly competitive world there would be no justification for this type of policy, but in a situation where marginal cost pricing is not universal and where political expediency leans against the introduction of measures such as emission fees, subsidies may offer a pragmatic second-best approach to the externality problem.

---

[13] D.B. Hess and P. Lombardi, 'Governmental subsidies for public transit history, current issues, and recent evidence', *Public Works Management and Policy*, **10**, 138–56, 2005.

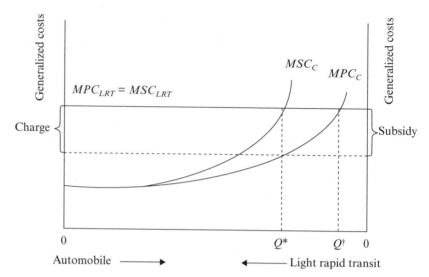

Figure 8.6 *Optimal subsidy to a non-polluting substitute mode with fixed aggregate demand for travel*

Where the cross-elasticity of demand between transport and other goods is negligible and the overall demand for transport is totally inelastic – a situation not unrealistic in the context of commuter travel in many large urban areas – the optimal subsidy to a zero externality-generating transport mode will have the same effect on the use of an externality-generating mode as pollution charges.

In Figure 8.6, the overall demand for transport, which is supplied by a combination of private cars and a light rapid transit system, is fixed. Cars have associated with their use external costs that can be expressed as the difference between the MPC_C and the MSC_C. The light rapid transit system has no such externalities associated with its use (that is, $MSC_{LRT} = MPC_{LRT}$) and for simplicity we assume that its marginal costs are constant. The free market outcome, where no cognizance is taken of externalities, will be a division of traffic at point $0Q^\dagger$ in the diagram. The optimal solution is a split of Q^* that may be brought about either by charging a Pigouvian pollution charge of the level indicated in the figure or, alternatively, by subsidizing the public transport mode by an identical amount. The modal split effects are the same.

If aggregate demand is not perfectly inelastic then the optimal subsidy is more difficult to define, although it may still offer a second-best solution to the externality problem. Figure 8.7 shows the cost conditions for the externality-generating mode (the car) with a demand curve for its services of D_C. It also shows the cost (C_{PT}), (D_{PT}) and patronage (Q_{PT}) for public transport. A subsidy for the public transit mode will cause D_C to shift to the left (say to D'_C), reducing the deadweight welfare loss associated with the initially suboptimally high level of car usage. Unless, however, the demand for car use is pushed so far left that it intersects the cost curves in some area where $MPC_C = MSC_C$, a deadweight loss will remain.

As with Figure 8.6, the subsidy will also change the welfare enjoyed by bus users. The fall in the cost of car use as people switch to public transport (initially

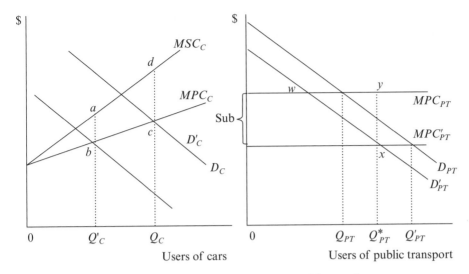

Figure 8.7   *Optimal subsidies with elastic aggregate demand for travel*

to Q'_{PT}) will have the effect of pulling back the demand for the latter to D'_{PT} (and use to Q^*_{PT}) and thus reduce the amount of funds needed to fund the subsidy. In simple terms, the subsidy makes the public mode cheaper, this reduces the demand, and use of the car, but will also have an off-setting effect in terms of the relative quality of services of the modes. The ultimate cost of the subsidy is the amount per transit user times Q_{PT}, which exceeds the area of net consumer surplus enjoyed at the subsidized fare level by *wxy*. If we denote the deadweight loss saving associated with the reduced level of demand for cars as *abcd* (that is, the area between MSC_C and MPC_C as D_C shifts to the left) then the optimal subsidy can be defined as that which maximizes the difference between the gain from reducing the deadweight loss of excessive congestion minus the efficiency cost of the subsidy. In the diagram, this is the subsidy that will maximize $(abcd - wxy)$.

The practical difficulty with this approach is that the optimal subsidy may be extremely large and, theoretically, if the cross-elasticity of demand between modes is low, may even result in negative fares. The use of public transport subsidies in urban areas has been questioned for this very reason. This is a topic that we covered in Chapter 4, where it was found that price cross-elasticities, in particular between bus and car, are generally low, with service cross-elasticities somewhat higher.

Specifically on modal transfers, in an early survey, Kemp[14] found that in general the direct fare elasticity for urban public transport was low (–0.1 to –0.7), suggesting that substantial subsidies are necessary to attract passengers to public transport irrespective of whether they constitute new travelers or those diverted from private cars. Baum's[15] work looking at the possible effects of

[14] M.A. Kemp, 'Some evidence on transit elasticities', *Transportation*, **2**, 25–52, 1973.
[15] H.J. Baum, 'Free public transport', *Journal of Transport Economics and Policy*, **7**, 3–19, 1973.

offering free urban bus transport was even less optimistic, his analysis yielding elasticities in the range from –0.1 to –0.4 for Britain, the United States and West Germany. After surveying some 50 empirical studies of both long- and short-term cross-elasticities, however, Goodwin[16] concluded,

> Thus in the short term, bus demand remains, as traditionally thought, inelastic enough to make revenue raising by fare increases an effective policy, but demand increases by fare reductions . . . rather limited. But in the longer run the effectiveness of the first policy is reduced, and of the second is increased.

This problem is compounded by two further points. First is the issue of the degree to which there may be leakage from subsidies into, for example, X-inefficiency in the management of the system. There are methods of tendering which, for example, are being used in the UK to minimize such losses but it is not altogether certain that they may not meet problems in the longer term as incumbent subsidized operators essentially enjoy economies of experience over potential new suppliers. Second, there is the question of the nature of the subsidy required. Fare subsidies, for example, may be of social importance in income distribution terms but often it is quality of service (that is, frequency, reliability, amenities and so on), that is of more importance to commuters.

8.7   Protecting the Sufferers

The strategies examined so far have relied upon either forcing the generators of externalities to change their production process or encouraging the adoption of a different method of operation. We have only touched upon the idea of insulating the public from environmental intrusion (that is, in the context of aircraft landing path controls and lorry routes). Insulation in the short term may be achieved either by directing traffic away from sensitive areas or by physically protecting people and property (for example, with double glazing for sound insulation) while in the longer term new investment permits a more efficient separation of transport from those sensitive to its wider impact (the main reason for the official rejection of the Roskill Commission's recommendations on the siting of a Third London Airport in the 1970s was that an inland site would be excessively damaging to the country's environment – see Chapter 11).

Fairly typical of the approaches favoring command and control was the Armitage Report produced 25 years ago in the United Kingdom,[17] it goes as far as to recommend the establishment of 'lorry action areas' to protect residents living in a limited number of areas but who suffer from the worst

---

[16] P.B. Goodwin, 'A review of new demand elasticities with special reference to short and long run effects of price changes', *Journal of Transport Economics and Policy*, **26**, 155–70, 1992.

[17] UK Department of Transport, *Report of the Inquiry into Lorries, People and the Environment*, London: HMSO, 1980.

environmental effects of road freight transport. Specifically such areas would involve:

- the installation of double glazing in houses, which would reduce considerably the major problem of noise in homes;
- grants for repairs to houses physically damaged by lorries;
- maintaining road surfaces to high standards, which would reduce vibrations;
- minor road improvements to reduce accidents and to reduce noise, for example, by the use of noise-absorbing road surfaces;
- the building up of pavements or erection of bollards to reduce the problems of vehicles cutting corners and of damage to buildings through physical contact; and
- in the worst cases of intense local nuisance by a specific generator of lorry traffic, compensation for discontinuance action taken by a planning authority in respect of a site with planning permission or existing use rights.

The difficulty with protective options, both long and short term, is that their effects are often much wider than simply protecting sensitive groups in the community, and their overall cost may be considerable. Limiting the flight paths of aircraft can both increase the risk of accident (by forcing the adoption of less safe climbing and turning patterns) and increase the cost, including environmental costs, of operations (especially energy use). Similarly, lorry routing both necessitates higher infrastructure costs and often leads to longer trip distances.

In the longer term it should, theoretically, be easier to design the spatial economy so that transport's effect on the environment is significantly lower. Following Foster and Mackie,[18] many options are available including:

- sterilization of land between nuisance and dwellings;
- using non-sensitive buildings (for example, light industry) as barriers between nuisance and sensitive areas;
- designing dwellings so that little-used rooms confront the nuisance rather than living rooms or bedrooms; and
- making use of self-protecting developments – for example, patio-style housing – to reduce intrusion.

Such designs obviously generate additional costs and only provide a partial solution to the environmental problem. Like most of the shorter-term protective measures they only ameliorate those aspects of environmental costs that are inflated while people are at home. Land-use planning may offer some limited protection at other times, especially in the reduction of accident risk – but it is unlikely to separate completely transport from the non-traveler.

[18] C.D. Foster and P.J. Mackie, 'Noise: economic aspects of choice', *Urban Studies*, **7**, 123–35, 1970.

One should also perhaps include under protective measures the notion of traffic calming. This entails the use of such things as road humps, speed tables, raised junctions, reduced carriageway widths and 'changed road surfaces' both to slow traffic flows and to encourage the use of particular 'suitable' links in the network or alternative modes. Essentially the idea is to make streets more attractive and liveable. In Europe, traffic calming has tended to come about as part of wider packages and has often been tied to legal speed limits of 30 kph and, in the Netherlands, to a walking pace limit. The latter is part of the country's *Woonerven* – where all road users have equal rights to road space. In the UK, traffic calming schemes have come about more as part of a policy to reduce urban traffic speed for safety reasons – about 70 percent of schemes have this as a primary objective. Evidence from Germany suggests that serious casualties fell by up to 50 percent in areas where it has been introduced, for example by 44 percent in Heidelberg after traffic calming was initiated.

There are also some wider positive environmental externalities associated with some types of urban design. In particular, obesity and many forms of illness are associated with a lack of physical activity. The way that cities are built and the way individuals move about them influence the amount of physical activity that citizens 'enjoy'; lack of facilities within walking or cycling distance necessitates the use of mechanized transport with minimal physical activity.[19] The design of urban areas can thus be seen as a way of alleviating some of the adverse effects on personal well-being by fostering a healthier lifestyle.[20]

8.8   Energy Use

We now spend some time looking in detail at some economic aspects of transport energy policy. In many cases the instruments used are from the generic toolkit outlined above, but their role is of particular importance because of the very high correlation between energy use and form and different components of atmospheric pollution. Ensuring that there is no excessive use of a scarce, finite resource such as oil is also of importance.

There is theoretically a wide range of policy tools that can be deployed to affect the energy use of transport. Each has its particular characteristics and usefulness depending on the background assumptions that are adopted. Here we are selective and focus on some of the more important efforts that have been made to influence fuel consumption in transport. In particular, longer-term policies involving land use such as 'compact-city' design are explicitly omitted. These are large and multidimensional topics in their own right and take us beyond the boundaries of a chapter such as this.

[19] L.D. Frank, P. Engelke and T. Schmid, *Health and Community Design: The Impact of the Built Environment on Physical Activity*, Washington, DC: Island Press, 2003.

[20] D.A. Rodrigues and J. Joo, 'The relationship between non-motorized mode choice and the local physical environment', *Transportation Research D*, **9**, 151–73, 2004.

Although theoretically there are numerous ways to influence energy use, a wide range of practical and political factors determine the policies that have been initiated to influence the energy consumption in transport.[21] In some cases the costs of introducing, monitoring and policing some policies, as with some specific environmental policies, simply make them impractical, or at least in the purest forms. In other cases there may also be trade-offs between improving energy efficiency and meeting other objectives, such as removing pollutants from the atmosphere or ensuring an acceptable level of traffic safety. An example of the former has been the removal of lead from gasoline in many countries which reduces the fuel efficiency of internal combustion engines.

The policy tools that are in place, or have been used, to influence the type of fuel used in transport, as well as the aggregate consumption, are, nevertheless, quite extensive. The following is not intended to be comprehensive in its coverage but rather should be viewed as illustrative of the types of measures that have been put in place.

Leaving Things to the Market

One policy option that is often forgotten is to leave things to the market. After all while there are market failures, there are also government intervention failures that may either worsen an original market failure or cause serious and unexpected distortions elsewhere in the system.[22]

In practice, the market has been a significant influence on the types and amount of energy used by transport. Historically, for example, changes in prices have demonstrable medium- and long-term impacts on overall energy consumption in transport, most of which have only appreciated in retrospect. Not all these, however, have been directly related to the price of fuel. A simple transmission mechanism illustrates the difficulty of policy makers trying to foresee energy changes and plan for the development of new technologies.

At the beginning of the twentieth century, automobiles were expensive and coal powered (either directly or after transformation into electricity) and railway systems dominated surface transport. The energy effect was brought about by the introduction of mass production, initially by Fiat in Italy, but on a larger scale by Henry Ford in the United States, to take advantage of the high car prices of the time; this brought down the costs of car production and subsequently the price of cars (from $910 for a touring Model-T in 1910 to $367 in 1925). In turn, this led to more use of cars and trucks (sales of the touring models were 16,890 units in 1910 rising to 691,212 in 1925) with a resultant switch in transport away from coal and the primary energy source to oil.

In contrast, in the East German economy of the 1960s, market forces were

---

[21] P.C. Flynn, 'Commercializing an alternative vehicle fuel: lessons learned from natural gas for vehicles', *Energy Policy*, **30**, 613–19, 2002.

[22] Organisation for Economic Co-operation and Development, *Market and Government Failures in Environmental Policy: The Case of Transport*, Paris: OECD, 1992.

Table 8.3   *Fuel efficiency of US cars following the 1973 and 1979 'oil crises'*

Year	Miles per US gallon		Harmonic mean	Real price of gasoline (1967=100)
	City	Highway		
1968	12.59	18.42	14.69	97.3
1969	12.60	18.62	14.74	95.4
1970	12.59	19.00	14.85	98.0
1971	12.27	18.18	14.37	87.6
1972	12.15	18.90	14.48	85.9
1973	12.01	18.07	14.15	88.7
1974	12.03	18.23	14.21	108.3
1975	13.68	19.45	15.79	106.0
1976	15.23	21.27	17.46	105.3
1977	15.99	22.26	18.31	103.7
1978	17.24	24.48	19.89	100.5
1979	17.70	24.60	20.25	122.2
1980	20.35	29.02	23.51	149.6
1981	21.75	31.12	25.16	150.8
1982	22.32	32.76	26.06	134.7
1983	22.21	32.90	26.01	126.1
1984	22.67	33.69	26.59	119.2

Source: R.W. Crandall, A.K. Gruenspecht, T.E. Keeler and L.B. Lave, *Regulating the Automobile*, Washington, DC: Brookings Institution, 1986.

largely ignored when policy moves towards greater car ownership at administered prices were initiated. The resultant centrally planned outcomes were the Wartburg and Trabant cars, and, by the time the Berlin Wall came down, there was a waiting time of nearly 10 years to receive your not very comfortable, reliable, or efficient vehicle. The complexity of planning the design and production of cars proved too complex for even the highly skilled planners of East Germany.

Fuel prices themselves are also powerful influences on consumption. Where there have been shortages of some forms of energy, either because of physical or institutional factors, markets can bring about changes. In the past there have been shortages of oil for political reasons. While there are short-term adjustment issues, the long-term effect of fuel shortage and price rise is that it is used more efficiently.

For example, Table 8.3 shows the impact on the fuel efficiency of the US "car park" after the oil crises of 1973 and 1979. It is clear that the average energy efficiency of vehicles (and possibly the way they are driven) rose following both crises, albeit with a lag as the adjustment took place. A more recent survey bringing together work on long-term gasoline fuel price elasticities indicates that about 20–60 percent appears to be due to changes in the vehicle miles driven, with 40–80 percent being due to changes in fleet composition.[23] A more general rule of

[23] I.W.H. Parry, M. Walls and W. Harington, 'Automobile externalities and policies', *Journal of Economic Literature*, **45**, 373–99, 2007.

thumb, suggested by Goodwin and colleagues[24] after reviewing numerous empirical studies, is that fuel consumption elasticities are greater than traffic elasticities, mostly by factors of 1.5 to 2.00.

Fuel Taxation

Energy, because of the relative inelasticity of aggregate demand for its use, has traditionally been the subject of taxation. In many cases this has been for purely sumptuary purposes, but in other cases, as with the federally earmarked gasoline tax in the United States, it has been used as a proxy charge for some related consumption items: in the US case to pay for the use of the road. In other cases, there have been environmental motivations, for example the differential taxes applied to gasoline and diesel fuels in many countries.

Examples of taxes on the energy used by transport abound, although as mentioned earlier the exact motivations underlying them are not always clear. The US Energy Tax Act of 1979, for instance, was a law passed as part of the National Energy Act. One element of the act created the 'gas-guzzler' tax applying to sales of vehicles with official estimated gas mileage below certain levels. In 1980, the tax was $200 for a fuel efficiency of less than 14 to 15 miles per gallon, and was increased to $1,800 in 1985. In 1980, the tax was $550 for fuel efficiencies of 13 mpg and below, and was changed in 1986 to $3,850 for ratings below 12.5 mpg. The gas-guzzler tax only applied to cars under 6,000 lbs, which made sports utility vehicles and other large passenger cars exempt.

In terms of using taxation as an instrument for encouraging energy conservation, or changes in the energy source used for environmental reasons, carbon taxes have been adopted in a number of countries. These are not transport specific but are more holistic in their intent of making optimal use of resources more generally, although their impacts on transport are often large. In 1991, Sweden, for example, placed a tax of $100 per ton on the use of oil, coal, natural gas, liquefied petroleum gas, petrol and aviation fuel used in domestic travel. Industrial users paid half the rate (between 1993 and 1997, 25 percent of the rate), and certain high-energy industries such as commercial horticulture, mining, manufacturing and pulp and paper were fully exempted from these new taxes. In 1997 the rate was raised to $150 per ton of CO_2 released. Finland, the Netherlands and Norway also introduced carbon taxes in the 1990s.

In other cases, however, efforts at introducing such policies have failed. In 2005, New Zealand proposed a carbon tax to take effect from April 2007, and applied across most economic sectors but the policy was abandoned in December 2005. Similarly, in 1993, US President Bill Clinton proposed a British Thermal Unit (BTU) tax that was never adopted.

---

[24] P. Goodwin, J. Dargay and M. Hanly, 'Elasticities of road traffic and fuel consumption with respect to price and income: a review', *Transport Reviews*, **24**, 275–92, 2004.

Table 8.4   *New automobile emissions standards (grams per mile)*

Model year	Hydrocarbons	CO	NO_X
Pre-control; vehicle	10.6	84.0	4.1
1970–71	4.1	34.0	–
1972	3.4	39.0	–
1973–74	3.4	39.0	3.0
1975–76	1.5	15.0	3.1
1977–79	1.5	15.0	2.0
1980	0.41	7.0	2.0
1981–93	0.41	3.4	1.0
1994–2003	0.25	3.4	0.4
2004	0.09	4.2	0.07

Vehicle Standards

Rather than directly regulate the composition of fuels, or use the pricing mechanism, there have been efforts to influence energy consumption and pollution by legislating on the design of vehicles. The details adopted vary and here we just highlight some of the issues by looking at the European and North American cases.

There have been somewhat different approaches adopted in different countries. Returning to Figure 8.1, the approach of the Europeans has been to act largely on the environmental emissions themselves by stipulating in three agreements with their own industry and manufacturers in Japan and South Korea, the maximum levels of pollution that new vehicles may emit (Table 8.4).

In contrast to this, the corporate average fuel economy (CAFE), first enacted by the US Congress in 1975, are federal regulations that have sought to improve fuel economy in the wake of the 1973 Arab oil embargo (Table 8.5). In other words, in terms of Figure 8.1 they impact on the industry. The regulations initially applied to the sales-weighted average fuel economy, expressed in miles per gallon, of a manufacturer's fleet of current model year passenger cars or light trucks with a gross vehicle weight rating of 8,500 lbs or less, manufactured for sale in the United States. Light trucks not exceeding 8,500 lbs gross vehicle weight rating do not have to comply with CAFE standards; some half a million vehicles in 1999. From early 2004, the average new car has had to exceed 27.5 mpg and light trucks exceed 20.7 mpg. Trucks under 8,500 lbs must average 22.5 mpg in 2008, 23.1 mpg in 2009, and 23.5 mpg in 2010. After this, new rules set varying targets based on truck size 'footprint'.

Whereas the US regime is statutory, the Canadians have a voluntary scheme to foster fuel economy; the company average fuel consumption (CAFC) agreement that was established between government and auto manufactures in 1978. Details of the joint goals set are seen in Table 8.5.

The US National Highway Traffic Safety Administration (NHTSA) regulates CAFE standards and the US Environmental Protection Agency (EPA) measures

Table 8.5   *CAFC goals and the US CAFE standard (liters/100 km)*

Model year	Passenger cars		Light-duty trucks	
	CAFC	*CAFE*	*CAFC*	*CAFE*
1978	13.1	13.1	–	–
1980	11.8	11.8	–	–
1982	9.8	9.8	–	13.4
1984	8.7	8.7	–	11.8
1986	8.6	9.1	–	11.8
1988	8.6	9.1	–	11.7
1990	8.6	8.6	11.8	11.8
1992	8.6	8.6	11.6	11.8
1994	8.6	8.6	11.5	11.7
1996	8.6	8.6	11.4	11.7
1998	8.6	8.6	11.4	11.7
2000	8.6	8.6	11.4	11.7
2002	8.6	8.6	11.4	11.7
2004	8.6	8.6	11.4	11.7
2006	8.6	8.6	11.4	10.9

Source: Adapted from A. Perl and J.A. Dunn, 'Reframing automobile fuel economy policy in North America: the politics of punctuating a policy equilibrium', *Transport Reviews*, **27**, 1–35, 2007.

vehicle fuel efficiency. Congress specifies that CAFE standards must be set at the 'maximum feasible level' given consideration for technological feasibility; economic practicality; the effect of other standards on fuel economy; and need of the nation to conserve energy. If the average fuel economy of a manufacturer's annual fleet of car and/or truck production falls below the defined standard, the manufacturer pays a financial penalty; thus a very crude pricing mechanism is involved. Fuel efficiency is highly correlated to vehicle weight, but weight has been considered by many safety experts to be correlated with safety, intertwining the issues of fuel economy, road-traffic safety, air pollution, global warming and greenhouse gases. Hence, histori-cally, the EPA has encouraged consumers to buy more fuel-efficient vehicles while NHTSA has expressed concerns that this leads to smaller, less safe vehicles. More recent studies tend to discount the importance of vehicle weight to traffic safety, concentrating instead on the quality of engineering design of vehicles.

While there have been changes in the standards over time, the table shows that these have tended to be infrequent and that by, for example, European stand-ards, the American fleet is relatively fuel inefficient. Part of the problem seems to be difficulties in building political alliances strong enough to carry though meas-ures that tighten the prevailing standards.[25]

A further problem within the CAFE standard approach is that it may actu-ally lead to an increase in highway externalities. While the standards, and disre-garding any effects that they have on the sales of light trucks (and most notably

[25] A. Perl and J.A. Dunn, 'Reframing automobile fuel economy policy in North America: the politics of punctuating a policy equilibrium', *Transport Reviews*, **27**, 1–35, 2007.

sports utility vehicles) that are much less rigorously controlled, may increase the fuel efficiency of vehicles, because of their greater fuel efficiency they also make them cheaper to drive per mile. This adds, for example, to congestion and local environmental damage associated with, for example, noise nuisance.[26]

Speed Limits

Engines of all types perform differently at different speeds and each has an optimal fuel performance speed. Given the operational cycle of any transport activity, as a generalization more energy is expended at the beginning of a movement, and in some cases at the end, than during cruise, although there is normally an optimal cruising speed. It is possible, therefore, to influence the energy efficiency of a transport system by regulating the speeds at which individual units operate over it. Privately supplied transport operations, such as shipping and airlines, have a financial incentive to conserve energy and, other things being equal, route ships and planes accordingly set fuel-efficient schedules. The public authorities, cognizant of the wider impacts of transport, often offset these energy goals to attain other objectives. The most obvious cases are the take-off and landing patterns at airports that seldom are energy efficient but take particular cognizance of noise nuisance envelopes.

While speed limits are usually imposed for reasons of improving traffic flows and for safety, there are examples of explicit, speed-based energy policies in transport. As an emergency response to the 1973 oil crisis, the US Congress effectively imposed a national 55 mph speed limit in 1974 under the Emergency Highway Energy Conservation Act by requiring the limit as a condition of each state receiving highway funds. The limit was unpopular, especially in western states that have long distances between cities or points of interest. Subsequent analysis was somewhat unclear on the implications of the measure on energy consumption.[27] Congress lifted all federal speed limit controls in the November 28, 1995 National Highway Designation Act, fully delegating speed limit authority to the states.

Fostering Alternative Technologies

Taxation, vehicle design standards, and other measures, in addition to market forces, can, and have in many cases, affected the technology of transport and, *ipso facto*, energy use and efficiency. The higher fuel prices after the Israeli wars of the 1970s led to lighter vehicles using alternative materials for bodywork, and more fuel-efficient engines. In addition, however, there have also been a number of other explicit policies aimed at technology shifts with the aim of reducing the use of oil-based fuels.

---

[26] A.N. Kleit, 'Impacts of long-range increases in the fuel economy (CAFE) standard', *Economic Inquiry*, **42**, 279–94, 2004.

[27] T.H. Forester, R.F. McNown and L.D. Singell, 'A cost–benefit analysis of the 55 mph speed limit', *Southern Economic Journal*, **50**, 631–41, 1984.

There has been a long history, for example, of policies aimed at developing viable electric cars that can effectively be powered from a variety of energy sources, including hydro-generated electricity. Historically, in the early days, electric-driven cars were as numerous as gasoline, steam or diesel cars, the first electric car being developed somewhere between 1832 and 1839, but seem to have gone out of favor because of maintenance issues and the cost of mass production. These are sometimes called, as in California, 'zero-emissions vehicles', although from the wider geographical perspective, given the primary source of energy, this is very seldom the case, and even if solar panels are used on vehicles, there is still the pollution associated with the production of these panels. National governments have regularly tried to foster the development of economically feasible electric car technologies by investing in research and development (R&D) programs.

At a more local level, the California Zero Emission Vehicle (ZEV) program, initiated in 1990, and followed in some other states as a Partial Zero Emissions Vehicle (PZEV) program, was designed to catalyze the commercialization of advanced-technology vehicles that would not have any tailpipe or evaporative emissions. It initially required that 2 percent of new vehicles produced for sale in 1998 and 10 percent of new vehicles produced for sale in 2003 would be zero emission vehicles. After automakers argued that they could not meet the 1998 deadline, full implementation of the program was delayed until 2003 with interim measures to encourage the use of more PZEVs. In 2002, automakers sued the state over the program and were granted a preliminary injunction barring its implementation pending a final court ruling. In the midst of the ensuing legal debate, the state decided to go ahead and make revisions to the rule to sidestep the legal challenge, with the aim of restoring the ZEV program by 2005.[28] Overall, these types of policy have not been conspicuously successful in bringing about sea-changes in transport technology. For example, of the 4,000 to 5,000 electric cars built for California's ZEV mandate in the late 1990s, only about 1,000 remain on the road.

The European Union, through Joint Technology Initiatives in the 7th Research Framework Programme running from 2007 to 2013, is providing increasing levels of funding for research into fuel cells and hydrogen with the intention of reducing the time needed to market such technologies by between two and five years.

While fully electric or hydrogen-propelled vehicles have proved elusive to develop on a commercial scale, the hybrid vehicle such as the Honda Insight and the Toyota Prius which combines electric propulsion with, generally, a gasoline engine, has proved more successful. They offer, at prevailing prices, fuel efficiency, although at a higher capital cost, and in many cases are economically justified in the marketplace. Policy has been instrumental by both financing part of the R&D costs of the underlying technology, but in many cases local policies have provided an added inducement for its uptake. In the United States many local jurisdictions,

---

[28] California Air Resources Board, *California's Air Quality History Key Events*, Sacramento: CARB, 2005.

for example, allow hybrids to use high-occupancy vehicle (HOV) lanes on highways even if they do not meet passenger requirements.

There are also initiatives to foster the use of telecommunications as an alternative to trips that are primarily for information exchange. This can apply to such things as teleworking (rather than commuting to work in an office) and teleshopping, including telebanking.[29]

While the question of whether advances in telecommunications have added to travel because of the complementary nature of the 'product', or reduced it because of its substitutability features, is still the subject of much debate, policy makers have put forward a number of initiatives to increase its use as a transport energy policy initiative. Some of this has been in the form of information – for example, The US Office of Personnel Management and the General Services Administration have established a joint website on Telework to provide access to guidance issued by both agencies – and facilitation, for example, under US law, federal executive agencies must establish policies under which eligible employees may participate in telecommuting to the maximum extent possible. Again in the United States, in 1996 the Clean Air Act, among other things, required companies with over 100 employees to encourage telecommuting. The European Union also reached a framework agreement to encourage more teleworking and to put in place laws that would help facilitate it across the member countries.

The difficulty is assessing whether telecommuting and similar activities, while unquestionably enhancing social welfare by giving firms and individuals more choices, results in less travel. There are inevitable 'buyback effects', as time formerly used (for example, in physically commuting) can be used for other forms of trip making. Additionally, telecommunications may simply add to the conventional travel behavior of people and the way firms use their employees' time. This type of situation is illustrated in Figure 8.8.[30]

There are assumed to be physical limits to the amount of travel an individual can do and the number of physical interactions possible. Improved transport and communications has undoubtedly improved the situation, but logic would suggest that there is some asymptote. While one may pull down this asymptote, or modify the growth path in physical interpersonal communications by fostering telecommunications after time T, there is also the possibility that the new technology will lead to a higher number of interpersonal communications, pushing up the overall communications asymptote without reducing the growth in personal movements. The telecommunications gap reflects this. If so, then the impact on the environmental damage associated with transport is left unaffected. Indeed, if there is a degree of substitution within the physical travel aggregate, then this may

---

[29] I. Salomon and P.L. Mokhtarian, 'Can telecommunications help solve transportation problems? A decade later: are prospects better?', in D.A. Hensher and K.J. Button (eds), *Handbook of Transport Modelling*, 2nd edn, Amsterdam: Elsevier, 2008.

[30] K.J. Button and R. Maggi, 'Video conferencing and its implications for transport: an Anglo-Swiss perspective', *Transportation Reviews*, **15**, 59–75, 1995.

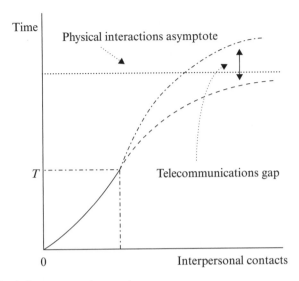

Figure 8.8   *The 'telecommuncations gap'*

be more damaging to the environment if it involves trips through more sensitive areas of cities or at times of day when citizens are more sensitive to noise.

8.9   Safety and Accidents

Safety is a major concern in modern transport. Any form of movement of individuals and goods involves a degree of danger, but that has not stopped the development of modern transport. Indeed, while the opening of the Liverpool and Manchester Railway in the United Kingdom, the world's first intercity railway, in September 1830 saw William Huskisson, the popular Member of Parliament for Liverpool, run over by the engine, the *Rocket*, and killed, this actually heralded the beginning of a period of 'railway mania'.

Earlier, Table 6.6 provided data on fatal transport accidents in the United States, and the text offered details of accidents elsewhere. The direct economic cost of global road crashes alone has been estimated at $518 billion a year, with $207 billion accruing to the EU countries and $230 billion to the United States. There are many reasons for accidents,[31] but many are the result of irresponsible behavior by vehicle operators.[32] In particular, on the roads, young and older drivers are more prone to accidents, but there is a strong correlation between drinking and driving. There are also some people who are quite literally for no apparent reason 'accident prone'. Although many factors contribute to the frequency and severity of road crashes, drunk driving is among the principal reasons for crashes in many countries; for example, 40 percent of fatal crashes in the United States in 2003 were

[31] P. Loeb, 'The determinants of automobile fatalities', *Journal of Transport Economics and Policy*, **21**, 279–87, 1987.

[32] L. Evans, *Traffic Safety and the Driver*, New York: Van Nostrand, 1991.

alcohol related, a percentage that has remained relatively stable over the past few years. Consistent with this, the NHTSA, in a study based on 2000 US crash data, estimated that alcohol-related crashes imposed a $114.3 billion cost on society.[33]

Safety is partly an externality and partly it is not. One policy approach is to internalize more of the costs of safety. This is done by such measures as legal responsibility for the cost of accidents in the form of compensation, a measure that is often accompanied by compulsory insurance. Such actions can, however, in some contexts because of moral hazard prove counterproductive. Moral hazard is the prospect that a party insulated from risk, by in this case insurance, may behave differently from the way it would behave if it were fully exposed to the risk. It can arise because an individual does not bear the full consequences of his/her actions, and therefore has a tendency to act less carefully than would otherwise be the case, leaving another party to bear some responsibility for the consequences of those actions. With insurance, it is the other premium payers who bear the burden. For example, an individual with insurance against automobile theft may be less vigilant about locking his or her car, because the negative consequences of automobile theft are partially borne by the insurance company.

One way of reducing the moral hazard problem is to change the insurance market, and one modification, the pay-as-you-drive (PAYD) insurance, which embraces actual miles driven for premiums, rather than a flat period sum, has been suggested. The aim would be to limit trips rather than encourage them as the more traditional approaches do. Aaron Edlin[34] has estimated that this would reduce the externalities associated with driving, including accidents.

If such internalization is not possible, or thought to be ineffective or impractical, a number of other policies are commonly used to handle safety concerns. Focusing on road transport to keep the material manageable, although the experiences extend in general across all modes, policy initiatives often revolve around keeping some groups off the road entirely – for example, a minimum driving age – and deterrent measures such as driving bans if caught with alcohol in the system above a 'safe' level, fines for speeding or dangerous maneuvers, and imprisonment for extreme offences. Training and testing of drivers is also common practice, and educational initiatives to discourage dangerous driving are common, although it is not clear that they always meet their objectives.[35]

After reunification of East and West Germany, one important change for East German motorists was a relaxation of the legal blood alcohol concentration limit with no change in the legal limit for West German motorists. This offered the opportunity to analyze the immediate-, short- and longer-term effects of raising

[33] P. McCarthy and R. Tay, 'Road safety, alcohol and public policy', *Transportation Research E*, **41**, 373–76, 2005.

[34] A.S. Edlin, 'Per-mile premiums for auto insurance', in R. Arnott, B. Greenwald, R. Kanbur and B. Nalebuff (eds), *Economics for an Imperfect World: Essays in Honor of Joseph E. Stiglitz*, Cambridge, MA: MIT Press, 2003.

[35] R. Tay, 'The relationship between public education and enforcement campaigns and their effectiveness in reducing speed related serious crashes', *International Journal of Transport Economics*, **31**, 251–55, 2004.

the blood-alcohol concentration (BAC) limit in East Germany between 1992 and 1994. A major finding was that the relaxed concentration limits led to an increase in blood-alcohol levels among East German drivers but generally did not increase the frequency of drinking and driving. The exception was younger drivers who not only increased their alcohol consumption subsequent to the relaxation in the legal limit but also increased their frequency of drinking and driving.[36]

Also focusing upon drinking and driving policy, Mathijssen[37] conducted a retrospective analysis of anti-drunk-driving campaigns that the Netherlands implemented between 1970 and 2000. The study found significant deterrent effects following the introduction of a statutory alcohol limit, random breath testing and evidential breath testing, and changes in the enforcement level; but mixed effects for publicity and educational campaigns; and little effect for changes in penalties and driver improvement programs.

Speed is generally highly correlated with accidents, and speed limits are common for that reason. In April 1987, the US federal government enacted the Federal Highway Bill which, among its other provisions, permitted states to increase speed limits on rural sections of their interstate highways. Forty states responded to the enabling legislation by raising their speed limits, fueling an ongoing debate regarding the highway safety effects of higher speed limits. The results of annual cross-section–time series covering 1981 to 1989 for California, which raised speed limits in May 1987, found the higher speed limits to have no system-wide effects on fatal, injury-related, or property damage accidents.[38] Redistribution effects, however, were identified in that counties with 65 mph highways experienced a significant increase in each accident category. Ted Keeler[39] also found when looking at data for 1970 and 1980, that lower rural speed limits did little to reduce fatal automobile accidents.

Vehicle design and 'fittings' may also affect safety. These types of measures include such things as seat belts, air bags, crash helmets on motorcycles, the quality of brakes and suspension, the types of windshield glass and head lighting, and so on. There is an economic problem forcing regulatory measures to ensure that the safest engineering technology, or at least a minimum standard, is adopted. People react to the new technical requirements. Lester Lave and Warren Weber, for instance, suggested that mandated safety devices (seat belts, better bumpers, collapsible steering wheels) might lead to faster driving which could offset the safety gains.[40] More

---

[36] M. Vollrath, A.-P. Krüger and R. Löbmann, 'Driving under the influence of alcohol in Germany and the effect of relaxing the BAC law', *Transportation Research E*, **41**, 377–93, 2005.

[37] M.P.M. Mathijssen, 'Drink driving policy and road safety in the Netherlands: a retrospective analysis', *Transportation Research E*, **41**, 395–408, 2005.

[38] P. McCarthy, 'An empirical analysis of the direct and indirect effects of relaxed interstate speed limits on highway safety', *Journal of Urban Economics*, **36**, 353–64, 1994.

[39] T. Keeler, 'Highway safety, economic behavior, and driving environment', *American Economic Review*, **84**, 684–693, 1994.

[40] L.B. Lave and W.E. Weber, 'A benefit–cost analysis of auto safety features', *Applied Economics*, **2**, 265–76, 1970.

generally, Sam Peltzman[41] finds that while technological studies in the mid-1970s implied that annual highway deaths would be 20 percent greater without legally mandated installation of various safety devices on automobiles, offsetting effects of non-regulatory demand for safety and driver response to the devices virtually offset these. In other words, safety regulation had not decreased highway deaths. Other studies have not been quite so pessimistic.

Sass and Zimmerman,[42] for example, studied the impact of US state laws mandating helmet use by motorcyclists over a 22-year period and found helmet laws to be associated with an average 29 to 33 percent decrease in per capita motorcyclist fatalities. However, since voluntary helmet-wearing rates are higher in harsher climates, the efficacy of helmet laws varied directly with the warmth of a state's climate. Repeal of helmet laws in the 1970s and subsequent re-adoption in the late 1980s and early 1990s has had roughly symmetrical effects on fatalities. It was also found that alcohol consumption and the number of police available to enforce traffic laws also significantly affect motorcyclist fatalities.

The effects of piecemeal approaches and policy conflicts involving packages of measures have been studied by Crandall et al.[43] They were concerned about the conflicts which arose in the United States between the determination of safety standards (set by the NHTSA), emissions standards and fuel economy measures (both set by Congress and administered by the EPA). While static conflicts emerge as technically unavoidable (for example, the safety regulations initiated in the United States between 1968 and 1982 pushed average car weights up by 136 lbs and increased fuel consumption by 3.5 percent which conflicted with measures aimed at fuel efficiency and emissions controls), the dynamic effects of uncoordinated policies, for instance, slowing down replacement of older, less socially desirable cars was a serious administrative failure.

An important point is that the level of safety expected from transport systems does tend to vary between countries. In part this is due to income differentials. As seen earlier in the book, the value society puts on reducing the chance of a fatal accident depends to some extent on the income of the people involved. There is ample evidence that when it comes to transport safety, poorer countries, in part because of their limited resource base, but also because of the shadow prices involved, spend less on meeting what in other countries are seen as minimum safety standards.[44]

[41] S. Peltzman, 'The effects of automobile safety regulation', *Journal of Political Economy*, **83**, 677–725, 1975.

[42] T.R. Sass and P.R. Zimmerman, 'Motorcycle helmet laws and motorcyclist fatalities', *Journal of Regulatory Economics*, **18**, 195–215, 2000.

[43] R.W. Crandall, A.K. Gruenspecht, T.E. Keeler and L.B. Lave, *Regulating the Automobile*, Washington, DC: Brookings Institution, 1986.

[44] K.J. Button, A. Clarke, G. Palubinskas, R. Stough and M. Thibault, 'Conforming with ICAO safety oversight standards', *Journal of Air Transport Management*, *10*, 251–57, 2004.

Further Reading

K.J. Button, *Transport, the Environment, and Economic Policy*, Aldershot, UK and Brookfield, VT, USA: Edward Elgar, 1993, although dated adds depth to many of the arguments found in this chapter, and I.W.H. Parry, M. Walls and C. Harrington, 'Automobile externalities and policies', *Journal of Economic Literature*, **45**, 373–99, 2007, updates many of the ideas. A. Schäfer, J.B. Heywood, H.D. Jacoby and I.A. Waitz, *Transportation in a Climate-Constrained World*, Cambridge, MA: MIT Press, 2009, provides a somewhat broader perspective of policy, taking account of engineering and technology considerations.

A useful set of papers on transport and environmental policy is E. Verhoef and E. Feitelson (eds), *Transport and Environment: In Search of Sustainable Solutions*, Cheltenham, UK and Northampton, MA, USA: Edward Elgar, 2001. I. Savage, 'Transport safety', in K.J. Button and D.A. Hensher (eds), *Handbook of Transport Systems and Traffic Control*, Oxford: Pergamon, 2001, is a good survey of the economics of this subject.

9 Optimizing Traffic Congestion

. . . .

9.1 The Economic Approach

As we have seen in Chapter 6, excessive congestion leads to the inefficient use of transport infrastructure. Throughout the world, there have been a *pot-pourri* of initiatives over the years to optimize congestion, not only on city streets but also on inter-urban roads and at sea- and airports. These initiatives have not proved conspicuously successful, as we can observe in most cities and at many airports. Many of the policies that have been pursued have been devoid of serious economic content, and the aim of this chapter is to examine the types of approach that economists have advocated for reducing excessive levels of traffic congestion.

It is not only in the context of pollution that economists have advocated externality pricing. One idea for optimizing the level of congestion is to use the price mechanism to make travelers more fully aware of the impedance they impose upon one another. The idea is that motorists should pay for the additional congestion they create when entering a congested road or that aircraft should pay a premium to land at busy times of the day. In the case of road traffic, ideally, as with pollution charges, they should pay the actual road users affected but in practice this is quite clearly impossible, so the idea is that the relevant road authority or agency should be responsible for collecting the charges. We spend some time looking at the theoretical and practical issues involved in congestion pricing, and assess some of the schemes that have been introduced into cities such as London and Stockholm.

Other measures of a less direct, and second-best, kind such as parking charges, public transit subsidies, the deployment of an intelligent transport system (ITS) and investment in additional infrastructure are also considered. In technical terms, while congestion charging or Road Pricing seeks to equate the demand for transport use with the full costs of use, including the costs on other transport users (environmental costs are a separate matter), alternatives such as capacity expansion and the wider use of an ITS seek to push the costs of transport use down, whereas measures such as transit subsidies seek to decrease the demand for the congestion-causing mode through substitution effects.

While much of our attention is on the congestion seen on roads, congestion is a problem found in many other transport activities, as discussed in Chapter 6. While the general economic approach to developing and assessing remedial policies is common across the various forms of transport, there are various nuances and we shall consider some of these later in the chapter.

Further, the aim of this chapter is not to provide an encyclopedic coverage of all the literature that has been generated on Road Pricing and other forms of congestion charging, nor to catalog all the efforts that have been made, largely failures with a few successes, to adopt Road Pricing. It is definitely not the intention to go into the finer points of obtuse microeconomic theory. Rather, the aim is to consider some of the challenges that confront the adopting of efficient fiscal policy instruments within the transportation system using Road Pricing as an illustration. In doing this, examples and case studies will be used so that readers unfamiliar with the idea of adopting user charges as a means of improving traffic management will not find it difficult to understand the basic concepts involved.

9.2 'Road Pricing'

Traditionally the methods of charging for road use have taken one of two forms. There have long been tolled roads, of the type initiated in Britain in the seventeenth century, where users pay a fee for use. These tolls, and the same is true where they are used today, are set to recover the cost of constructing and physically maintaining the road. Such tolls are not designed to allocate the road space or to optimize congestion – when the tolls vary it is normally related to the physical damage done by a vehicle to the pavement, and not to the impedance that such a vehicle may impose on other road users. More widely, as we noted in the chapter on pricing, road users are charged even less directly for their use of infrastructure through a variety of taxes that may (as in the case of the US federal gas tax) be hypothecated to be spent on the road network (often through a road fund mechanism) or flow into the general coffers of the treasury to be spent as government wishes. In general, these taxation systems have little to do with making good use of road assets.

The role of an economic price, however, is threefold: to allocate what is available; to indicate where that capacity needs to be changed; and to provide the resources for financing that change. Traditional tolls may serve the last of these purposes by recovering investment costs but they seldom meet the other two. Table 9.1 provides some guidance as to the tasks that various forms of road charging are set to perform.

The adverse effects of inappropriate charges for the use of one asset, in this case a road, are felt in complementary and competitive sectors. They also occur when authorities seek to contain the primary problem with a second-best approach involving either restricting the use of complementary services (for example, controls over parking) or stimulating the use of alternatives (such as public transit). These types of initiatives seldom works.

On the expenditure side, road investments are made for a variety of reasons, often with quasi-economic justifications added as a veneer. Cost–benefit analysis, which is discussed in detail in Chapter 11, is widely used in one of its variants to provide a social assessment, but the technique is far from perfect and subject to political manipulation. More powerful in the age of the car has been the engineering approach of providing capacity to meet demand. While there may be justification for this in some situations, the fact that there is no direct economic price per trip paid by road users for their activities means that 'demand' in this context

Table 9.1 *Technical tasks for various forms of road charging*

Road charging scheme	Entering/ exiting facilities	Presence in area	Position on road network	Distance traveled	Time/ congestion level	Vehicle class/ weight	Charges owed	Data communication	Data storage	Payment billing	Enforcement
Facility congestion tolls	●				●	○	●	●	●	●	●
Cordon congestion tolls		●			●	○	●	●	●	●	●
Weight–distance truck tolls	○	○	○	●	○		●	●	●	●	●
General distance tolls		●	○	●	○	○	●	●	●	●	●

Note: ● Required for the task; ○ Optimal but not required for the task.

Source: Adapted from P.A. Sorensen and B.D. Taylor, 'Innovations in road finance: examining the growth in electronic tolling', *Public Works Management and Policy*, **11**, 110–25, 2006.

is nothing like the notion of effective demand used by economists. The outcome is likely to be excess capacity and a geographical maldistribution of roads. The reluctance of citizens to accept the environmental effects of more large-scale investments in roads, coupled with the increasing costs of construction as successive projects move down the marginal returns on investment curves, have to some extent stymied this build-to-meet-demand philosophy.

The distortions that result from inappropriate charges for the use of one asset, in this case a road, have also been felt in complementary and competitive sectors as the authorities have sought to initiate second-best policies to contain congestion. Attempts to discourage car trips terminating in a congested area by means of parking restrictions and fees leads to higher levels of through-traffic as well as additional congestion as terminating drivers seek the limited parking capacity that is available. A significant amount of car movements in many cities involves drivers looking for somewhere to park.[1] Subsidies to public transport reduce the incentive for it to be provided efficiently and at the lowest cost – the X-inefficiency problem.

To reduce urban road traffic congestion, national and local authorities have gradually been turning to policies with a degree of economic rationale underpinning them, rather than simply trying to build their way out of problems or providing ever-increasing amounts of subsidies to public transport. In particular, there have been moves to use Road Pricing as a tool for rationing scarce road space to those who gain most from its use.

The importance of appropriate pricing to make the best use of transport infrastructure is certainly not new: the principles can be found in the work of French engineering economists of the 1840s.[2] Unfortunately, for a variety of reasons, both practical and due to a lack of understanding by many of basic economic principles, road space is seldom priced in a way that optimizes congestion and, as a result, social welfare is not maximized. The modern principles of Road Pricing, which go back over 80 years to the work of Arthur Pigou,[3] were expanded upon by the Nobel Prize-winning economists James Buchanan[4] and William Vickrey,[5] and by the former British Prime Minister, Margaret Thatcher's main economic advisor, Alan Walters.[6]

The idea is simple: since roads are not privately owned and access to them is not determined by the market, there is a need, if roads are to be used efficiently,

---

[1] D. Shoup, *The High Cost of Free Parking*, Chicago, IL: Planners Press, 2004.

[2] J. Dupuit, 'On the measurement of the utility of public works', *Annales des Ponts et Chaussées Mémoires et Documents*, 2nd Series, **8**, 332–75, 1844 (translated by R.H. Barback, *International Economic Papers*, **2**, 83–110, 1952).

[3] A. Pigou, *The Economics of Welfare*, London: Macmillan, 1920.

[4] J.M. Buchanan, 'Private ownership and common usage: the road case re-examined', *Southern Economic Journal*, **22**, 305–16, 1956.

[5] W.S. Vickrey, 'Statement on the Pricing of Urban Street Use', Hearings, US Congress Joint Committee on Metropolitan Washington Problems, 1959.

[6] A.A. Walters, 'The theory and measurement of private and social cost of highway congestion', *Econometrica*, **29**, 676–97, 1961.

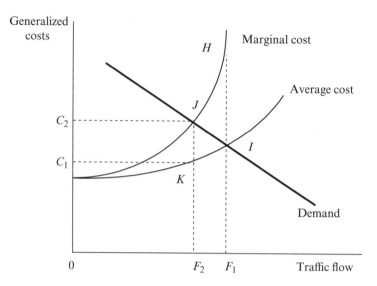

Figure 9.1   *Simplified diagram of the effects of Road Pricing*

for the authorities to set a user charge which, for any given capacity, ensures that socially optimal flows are attained – the Road Price. There is often confusion about what this means. Road Pricing is concerned solely with making the best use of roads from the narrow perspective of users and is not concerned with third-party effects such as pollution which should be treated separately. Congestion may or not be related to environmental damage; 20,000 solar-powered cars per hour on a road may congest it but cause minimal environmental damage whereas 500 old, badly maintained diesel vehicles may cause no congestion but a lot of pollution.

Second, as another Nobel Prize-winning economist, Ronald Coase, so ably famously demonstrated, policies such as Road Pricing are not market solutions but the most effective way of achieving an externally determined target traffic flow. This flow is independently determined and is not the result of any market-based process.

The standard economic diagram illustrating the basic principles of Road Pricing is that originally found in the works of Walters and Vickrey, and although this is now seen as a gross simplification, it serves well to illustrate the essential aims of congestion charging. In Figure 9.1, we take the basic case of a straight, single lane road with a single entry and single egress point, and with homogeneous traffic entering the road at regular intervals, although the intensity of entry can change. The average cost curve shows the generalized costs (a composite of money and time costs) of using the road for existing traffic, and is the cost observed by a potential additional user. The demand curve represents the utility that potential road users enjoy by joining the traffic flow at different levels of generalized cost. Individuals will join the traffic flow as long as they feel the benefits to be enjoyed exceed the costs. In the diagram, this leads to a traffic flow of F_1.

The problem, however, is that by undertaking the very act of joining the traffic stream, a vehicle slows all succeeding vehicles by some small amount unless there is excess capacity on the road. This may be only a few seconds for each vehicle, but when the flow is large this mounts up. This combination of the cost borne by the vehicle driver and the cost imposed on other vehicles is depicted as the marginal cost curve in the diagram. If motorists take these combined costs into account then the flow would fall to F_2. The idea of the Road Price is to make motorists cognizant of the congestion cost element by imposing a charge of $C_2 - C_1$ on each road user, this being the additional congestion cost associated with the marginal user at the optimal traffic flow. The result of this is a welfare gain amounting to HJI – traffic flow F_1F_2 only generated benefits to road users equal to the areas F_1F_2JI but at a cost of F_1F_2JH.

The optimal road price is relatively simple to calculate, and may seem to require little information. Taking the average cost of making a trip to the vehicle user as:

$$AC = a + (b/v), \qquad\qquad (9.1)$$

where a is the cost per vehicle in $ per mile, b is the value of travel time in $ per hour, and the total cost of the traffic flow of q vehicles is $TA = ACq$, then the additional vehicle joining the flow increases the overall cost to road users by:

$$MSC = \frac{dTC}{dq} = AC + \frac{dAC}{dq}. \qquad\qquad (9.2)$$

The congestion externality is given by $q(dAC/dq)$.

It takes little imagination to realize that over a complex network with numerous junctions, various road types, different vehicle mixes and so on, the case in the diagram and equations is simple in the extreme and that calculating the optimal charge would be challenging. Indeed, this is sometimes used as a reason for not charging. In reality, however, the pricing of a computer, a car, or any other sophisticated product or service is far from easy but it is done, albeit far from ideally, and companies like Microsoft and Apple seem to be held in much higher esteem than many local politicians and traffic engineers. Private sector companies in Western-style economies make an educated guess at the appropriate direct price for their products and then adjust them in the light of experience; if there is a large demand for their product then they raise prices and use the revenue to invest in additional capacity that will ultimately reduce costs and pries. They do not charge a low price and then let queues allocate the output.

The figure, despite its simplicity, also provides a way of looking at alternatives to Road Pricing as congestion containment policies. Expanding the capacity of a road by adding physical capacity, or initiating better traffic management through intelligent transport initiatives, will shift the cost curves down and out and thus reduce the divergence between them at the point where demand equates with the average cost. Such actions are clearly not costless and still leave a divergence between the new actual traffic flow and the optimal flow, given the added capacity. Effectively, traffic increases to fill the additional road capacity available. Subsidizing public transport will, as we saw in the context of environmental policies, pull the

Table 9.2   *Characteristics of eight major road pricing schemes*

City	Electronic system starting date	Entry charge for a small vehicle	Toll ring area (km²)	Average daily crossings	Annual revenue (million)
Trondheim	1991	$2.40	50.0	74,900	$25.00
Oslo	1991	$2.40	64.0	248,900	$196.00
Bergen	2004	$2.40	18.0	84,900	$36.00
Stockholm	2006	$1.33 – $2.66	29.5	550,000	n/a
Singapore	1998	$0.33 – $2.00	7.0	235,000	$80.00
Rome	2001	$3.75	4.6	75,000	$12.30
London	2003	$15.0	22.0	110,000	$320.00
Santiago	2004	$6.42	n/a	250,000	n/a

demand curve for road use to the left but again will still leave, albeit smaller, a traffic flow in excess of the optimum. Limiting or charging for parking will have the same effect. We shall look at these effects in more detail in Section 9.9.

9.3   Examples of Urban Road Pricing

What is so surprising is that the principles of using pricing to allocate scarce resources, indicate where more are needed, and provide revenues to fund expansions – very simple economic ideas, so central in other parts of market economies – have taken so long to be applied to roads. Basically, if there is a shortage of something, prices rise to allocate out what you have to those who benefit most from its use. The higher prices indicate that more capacity is needed, and generate revenue to finance it.

Although it seems unlikely that many of the policy makers who have moved towards Road Pricing as a means of reducing congestion are aware of the finer points of economic theory, a combination of desperation at the failure of traffic engineers to provide solutions to what is an economic issue, combined with a tightening of public funding, concerns about the environmental implications of continued massive infrastructure expansion, and the emergence of new technologies for fee collection, have created settings conducive to congestion pricing. We review some of these here and Table 9.2 offers a few more details.

In 1975, Singapore implemented a cordon-based variable pricing scheme with the aim of reducing congestion in the city's central business district. In 1999, the scheme was extended and now charges are applied to users on certain expressways and outer ring roads as well. Charges are in effect on weekdays, from 7:30 a.m. to 7:00 p.m. in the business districts, and from 7:30 a.m. to 9:30 a.m. on outer roads. Automated electronic road pricing was implemented in 1998.

Cordon tolling has been a widely used strategy, with some initiatives that were first intended to finance additional engineering works evolving toward congestion charges. The deployment of cordon tolling, for example, was popularized by its use in a number of Norwegian cities primarily for revenue-generating purposes. In 1986, Bergen established the first urban toll ring as a supplementary funding mechanism for new roads, public transport, parking space, pedestrianization, and an environmentally improved city center. The cordon-based scheme requires payment only on entering the city center. There are seven toll points around the city with fees collected between 6:00 a.m. and 10:00 p.m. on weekdays. Approximately 13 percent of the revenue is used to cover operating costs. Enforcement is dependent on digital video control. Because of the level and structure of the charges, there has been little impact on traffic levels and the system is not really a demand management tool in its current form. The toll ring is expected to cease operating in 2011.

A toll-ring scheme was initiated in Oslo in 1990 with the objective of financing additional road capacity. Charges are in effect seven days a week at all times of the day. Electronic collection started in 1991. The current toll ring is expected to cease operations in 2011 but there is interest in having the Oslo system evolve into a genuine congestion pricing scheme. Trondheim introduced an area-wide variable pricing scheme in 1991 again to finance road infrastructure and public transport. Since its inception, Trondheim has opted for electronic fee collection, with differential rates being charged for the morning and evening rush hours and a lower rate between 10:00 a.m. and 6:00 p.m. An innovation to this system that was originally cordon based only, was the introduction of inter-zone charging in 1998. The pricing scheme, as originally conceived, stopped at the end of 2005.

In 1998, Rome implemented a cordon-based pricing scheme with the aim of preserving its historical areas. Payment is required to enter the city center and only residents and employees working in the area with a secured parking space are allowed to enter. Authorized non-residents, about 35,000, are charged a flat rate. Charges are in effect six days a week, from 6:30 a.m. to 6:00 p.m. on weekdays, and from 2:00 p.m. to 6:00 p.m. on Saturdays. Electronic pricing started in 2001 with 22 toll points around the city.

Santiago de Chile's scheme consists of a network of toll roads that cross the city from north to south and also surround it. In 2004, the first of four major toll road concessions involved the implementation of a pricing mechanism, and in 2006 two additional projects were completed. The main purpose has been reducing air pollution in the city with the alleviation of excess congestion a secondary concern. There are three levels of charge depending on traffic speeds, the lowest being effective when the speeds are above 70 km/h and the highest when speeds fall below 50 km/h. Payment is required at all times when using any of the road concessions.

More recently, Central London has been the subject of an area-pricing regime.[7] The charges apply to vehicles using roads in the city's core area between 7.00 a.m. and 6.30 p.m. on weekdays with a 90 percent discount for those living

[7] J. Leape, 'The London congestion charge', *Journal of Economic Perspectives*, **20**, 157–76, 2006.

in the area, buses and some other groups. Payment is made through a variety of channels and there is the opportunity for retrospective payment.

During the first seven months of 2006, a full-scale cordon-based road pricing trial was implemented in Stockholm with the objective of reducing congestion and improving environmental quality. This was followed by a referendum in September 2006 to test views on making the scheme permanent – a proposal that received over 50 percent of the vote. Road users were obliged to install a free-of-charge transponder on the windshields and a smartcard could be bought at different locations, recharged, or linked to a bank account to make payments. Charges were in effect on weekdays from 6:30 a.m. to 6:00 p.m., and on Saturdays from 2:00 p.m. to 6 p.m. A limit of $8.30 was set as the maximum a user could be charged per day. As in other schemes, users were able to make a payment after they used the roads. Violations were considered tax evasion as the scheme was classified as a governmental tax.[8]

Table 9.2 focuses on urban pricing schemes but some semi-urban schemes have involved a somewhat different approach that sets a particular level of service on a road and then adjusts the price to attain this. This has been deployed in the Interstate 15 (I-15) scheme in California. In this case, the toll varies with traffic to maintain a target traffic speed with the road users being given the option of a 'free' road alongside the priced one. Information on average tolls for various times of the day is made available to help in route-choice decision making. Tolls can change every 15 minutes from 5:45 a.m. to 7.00 p.m. as well as by day of the week. The minimum toll was 50 cents and under normal conditions it could go up to $4.00, although if road sensors detected extremely heavy traffic it could be as high as $8.00. The project was a 3-year demonstration starting in 1996 that allowed single-occupant vehicles to use the existing I-15 high-occupancy vehicle, express lanes for a fee. With the aim of maximizing the use of the existing I-15 express lanes, to fund new transit and road improvements in the I-15 corridor, and to use a market-based approach to set tolls. The pricing project met its primary objectives.

9.4   Some Difficulties with Road Pricing

Theoretical economics, with its love of abstraction and mathematical exactitude, has long been drifting away from more traditional ideas of political economy. It is easy to show, as seen above, that with a few equations or diagrams, there are benefits to be gained by manipulating road user charges to contain excessive congestion. Implementation of such strategies, however, has been confronted by a plethora of practical and political challenges. In addition, these have not always been independent of one another, with opponents to Road Pricing using techni-cal imperfections of any scheme as justification for attacking the concept in its entirety.

---

[8] Stockholmsforsöket, *Facts and Results from Stockholm Trials*, Congestion Charge Secretariat, City of Stockholm, 2006.

Thus despite the adoption of a number of more economically based road charging systems in recent years, and indeed more economically based congestion pricing systems in other contexts as we shall see later, Road Pricing is not the norm. There are many reasons why this is the case, some of which have been explored in detail by academics, but others that remain speculative. From a review of public service attitudes, Peter Jones,[9] for example, listed the following reasons for opposition to Road Pricing:

- Drivers find it difficult to accept the idea of being charged for something they wish to avoid (congestion), and also feel that congestion is not their fault but rather something that is being imposed on them by others.
- Road Pricing is not needed, either because congestion is not bad enough or because other measures are superior.
- Pricing will not get people out of their cars.
- The technology will not work.
- Privacy concerns.
- Diversion of traffic outside the charged area.
- Road Pricing is just another form of taxation.
- Perceived unfairness.

We have touched lightly on some of the issues, such as those associated with distributional impacts and the expenditure of revenues, when discussing the rationale for the systems that are now being used. The topic is a large one, however, and some more scratching is attempted regarding several of the other factors that have proved impediments to improving the way that roads are used. Additionally, it should be remembered, there is no single, ideal way of implementing Road Pricing, and the rejection of some schemes that have been put forward in the past may have related more to their particular details than the acceptability of the concept itself. While the basic theory of Road Pricing is, thus, comparatively straightforward, its detailed implementation has been subject to debate.

Political Ideology

Reluctance to adopted economic pricing principles may in part be due to a feeling that individuals have some form of inalienable right to mobility and that pricing would restrict this. Matters of 'inalienable rights' are complex, and this is not the place to discuss them in any detail. What is perhaps germane, however, is that rights are not free goods: there is an opportunity cost involved in acquiring and retaining them. The costs of providing ubiquitous mobility are high and, while some may see ubiquitous mobility as desirable, the opportunity costs of achieving

---

[9] P.M. Jones, 'Urban road pricing; public acceptability and barriers to implementation', in K.J. Button and E.T. Verhoef (eds), *Road Pricing, Traffic Congestion and the Environment: Issues of Efficiency and Social Feasibility*, Cheltenham, UK and Lyme, NH, USA: Edward Elgar, 1998.

it are opaque in a world where there are inappropriate signals of the wider economic and social costs involved. Nevertheless, notions such as the 'freedom of the King's Highway' still persist and many are reluctant to pay for the use of roads irrespective of the economic consequences of current and future generations of excessive congestion.

In some ways related to this notion of a right to mobility, is the position taken in some countries that once a road has been built using public money, normally financed by taxation, then the public have the right to freely use the facility. This, for example, is a common argument voiced in the United States, and one of the reasons why Road Pricing in California has been limited to new facilities offering a better quality of service to the existing public roads; hence the charging regime is called 'value pricing'. The argument that once paid for, a facility should be open to all runs against the basic ideas of economic resource allocation but has emotive appeal. In reality, unless there is optimal capacity whereby user charges should just reflect upkeep costs, then there is a need to somehow ration the scarce road space so that its benefits are not diluted; pricing is the way this is normally done in market economies and seems to work well.

Calculating the Road Price and Its Impact

The simple analysis of the sort seen in Figure 9.1, as we have seen, assumes a lot, and in particular that the demand for road space may be represented by a continuous function. In practice there may be kinks or discontinuities and indeed, theoretically, there may be no optimal road price because the demand situation is such that pricing would result in either too much traffic or too little depending upon the levy charged. This is a theoretical possibility. After all, the smooth curves used in basic analysis are only expositional aids and the actual form of the demand function is an empirical question that can be resolved only in the light of practical experience.

It is clearly difficult, perhaps impossible, however, to calculate the optimal road price, especially because it is often context specific. Indeed, Table 9.3 provides a very wide range of calculations from some of the main studies. To begin with, the road price is simply the efficient way of attaining a traffic-related objective – particular flow, speed, or traffic density. This objective is set by the authorities, often based on the views of traffic engineers who take into account such things as safety and road wear and damage in their estimates. It is largely a subjective indicator of the type of performance that is wanted from the road. The road price is then set to limit traffic to attain the objective.

What this charge will need to be will depend on the costs perceived by motorists of using the road; and this is largely a combination of direct costs and the implicit money costs of travel time. In practice neither is easy to calculate. The problem is that people's demand elasticities depend on their perceptions and not on objective measures. Hence, while the money costs of a trip will embrace such things as fuel costs and wear and tear on the vehicle, because these involve infrequent outlays, the road user tends to ignore most of them when deciding

Table 9.3   *Early estimates of optimal road prices*

Study	Place	Road price at peak times (current prices)
Walters (1961)	Generic US urban expressway	$0.10–0.15/auto-mile
UK Ministry of Transport (1963)	Urban areas in Great Britain	£0.375/auto-mile
Greater London Council (1974)	Central London	£0.60/auto-day
Elliott (1975)	Los Angeles	$0.03–0.15/auto-mile
Kraus et al. (1976)	Twin-cities expressways 1970	$0.03–0.15/auto-mile
Keller and Small (1977)	Bay Area expressways 1972	$0.027–0.343/auto-mile
Dewees (1978)	Toronto 1973	$0.04–0.38/auto-mile
Cheslow (1978)	Berkeley 1977	$2.00/auto-trip
Spielberg (1978)	Madison 1977	$1.00/auto-trip
Mohring (1979)	Twin-cities	$0.66/auto-trip
Gómez-Ibáñez and Fauth (1980)	Boston	$0.5–1.0/auto-trip
Viton (1980)	Bay Area bridges 1972	$0.154/auto-mile
Starrs and Starkie (1986)	Adelaide arterial roads 1982	AU$0.025–0.22/auto-km
Cameron (1991)	Los Angeles expressways	$0.15/auto-mile

Sources: K.J. Button, 'Road pricing – an outsider's view of American experiences', *Transport Reviews*, **4**, 73–98, 1984; and S.A. Morrison, 'A survey of road pricing', *Transportation Research*, **20A**, 87–97, 1986. (Full references are contained in these articles.)

on a particular journey. Travel time poses a different sort of problem because, although it is recognized that 'time is money' to adopt the old saying, exactly how much money a minute of travel time saved is worth is open to some debate. As we have seen, there are a variety of techniques available for putting a valuation on time savings but issues arise about such things as the appropriateness of the methods used (generically between stated and revealed preference techniques) and whether one can sum the value of many small savings to get the value of a large saving.

Difficulty in Devising a Practical Method of Collection

Congestion varies across road networks but it is quite clearly impossible to make a separate charge for each segment of a road network. The pioneering Singapore area licensing scheme was, for example, simple and just involved vehicles having to display a card to show that the driver had paid to enter the core area during designated times. From an economic perspective, this procedure had low transaction costs – the production and sales of permits was cheap and enforcement at entry points to the city became part of normal policing – and provided drivers with prior knowledge of potential costs upon which to base decisions regarding entering the city. It did not, however, provide any direct link to the congestion caused by a vehicle once in the city, and its application elsewhere in urban areas with far more entry and exit points would make enforcement more difficult and costly.

Some general attempt at reflecting congestion more accurately is found in the Stockholm scheme where there are differential charges, but difficulties arise if this is taken too far because motorists are only retrospectively made aware of the congestion costs of their trip. Such systems are also likely to be more expensive to install and administrate, although recent advances in 'smart-card' technology have reduced this problem.[10]

Crude area licensing, even if enforced electronically as in London, is cheaper and, since permits must be purchased before entering specified urban zones, the full cost of a journey is made known to motorists before they enter congested streets – if they are still prepared to do so. The disadvantage of this simpler system is its insensitivity to changes in traffic conditions throughout the day. It is a trade-off between the price accurately reflecting the full economic costs of a trip and the ability to relay this to the potential road user.

Manual charging systems also inevitably lead to 'step tolls' in the sense that you either pay or you do not pay, and even when there is payment the price goes up in discrete jumps. The academic evidence is that there are considerable efficiency losses when such crude charges are imposed.[11]

The Smeed Report[12] recognized the limitation of this type of simple fee collection over 40 years ago and discussed various electronic options. The technology of the day was, however, limited and expensive. Things have changed and now a variety of alternatives are available, many of which have been adopted.

There are two broad ways of implementing more sophisticated forms of electronic road pricing. The first uses automatic vehicle identification (AVI), which records centrally the congestion costs of individual trips for each vehicle. The second does not identify individual vehicles but deducts the cost of using congested roads from a stored value medium (similar to the current use of telephone cards) where the proprietor of the system is not able to establish who is using the facility. This latter approach, which might usefully be called 'non-smart-card technology', can be extended to the use of smart cards, similar to credit cards, which automatically debit the costs of trips directly from bank accounts or charges them to a credit card account (such as VISA or Mastercard).

There was early experimentation with equipment and operational practices in Hong Kong.[13] On the operational side, the two-year experiment during the

[10] K.J. Button and H. Vega, 'The costs of setting up and operating electronic road pricing in cities', *Traffic Engineering and Control*, **48**, 6–10, 2007.

[11] R. Arnott, A. de Palma and R. Lindsey, 'A structural model of peak-period congestion; a traffic bottleneck with elastic demand', *American Economic Review*, **83**, 161–79, 1993.

[12] UK Ministry of Transport, *Road Pricing: The Economic and Technical Possibilities*, London: HMSO, 1964.

[13] J.A.L. Dawson and I. Catling, 'Electronic road pricing Hong Kong', *Transportation Research A*, **20**, 129–34, 1986.

mid-1980s involved fitting over 2,500 vehicles with AVIs together with the setting of electronic loops in the road surface at the edge of charge zones. When a vehicle crossed a boundary, a power loop energized its AVI which sent a message, via inductive receiver loops, to a road-side recorder. The technical and economic feasibility of the system used was found to have achieved 99 percent effectiveness and reliability against the criteria set it.

There are, however, practical difficulties with the system. An early concern that emerged involved confidentiality of the information gathered. The issue is still a sensitive one. Keong,[14] for example, argues that the issue of privacy is inevitable when implementing electronic Road Pricing. The Hong Kong experiment, while successful in showing that the technology used was reliable and that real-time adjustments to charges were possible, also raised concerns that the information collected could infringe on personal liberties.[15] The electronic congestion charging schemes in Stockholm, London and elsewhere that have been initiated since that time have taken care to minimize the possibility of them being used for 'tracking', with powerful legal protections being built in to the institutional structures in which they operate.

The London system makes use of off-the-shelf camera-based automated number plate recognition technology to enforce speed limits. Video recognition closed-circuit television cameras target optical characters on the number plates of vehicles at a rate of one per second even if the vehicle is traveling up to 100 mph. Charging is automated through computerized systems that deduct funds from the smart cards or through billing.

The systems now deployed in Stockholm, Norway and Santiago use AVI involving the installation of a transponder and/or a smart card that are detected by beacons installed at toll booths and other checkpoints. The exchanges of information between the tag and radar are possible using simple radio frequency identification technology. Regular users have their vehicles fitted with an electronic tag while visitors can make cash payments using specific lanes. Violators are identified through camera-based recognition of the vehicles' license plates and charged a retrospective fee.

Singapore's second generation scheme does not require a centralized computer system to keep track of vehicle movements since all charges are deducted from an inserted smart card at the point of use, with records of transactions kept in the memory chip of the card belonging to the individual. As a further step to assure the public of privacy, all records of transactions required to secure payments from the banks are erased from the central computer system once this is done – typically within 24 hours.

In a sense, these types of device are often just more efficient ways of cordon

---

[14] C.K. Keong, 'Road pricing: Singapore's experience', paper presented at IMPRINT-EUROPE Thematic Network: Implementing Reform on Transport Pricing: Constraints and Solutions: Learning from Best Practice, Brussels, 2002.

[15] T.D. Hau, 'Electronic road pricing: developments in Hong Kong 1983–1989', *Journal of Transport Economics and Policy*, **24**, 203–14, 1990.

charging. While it is possible to develop these types of technologies to provide real-time charging, which reflects the actual levels of congestion when a vehicle is using a particular part of the road network, they still suffer the major economic drawback that consumers should know the price of something before coming to the purchase decision. The problem is that the drivers' own actions affect the price that should be paid, and this makes real-time charging extremely difficult in practice.

Efforts at circumventing this problem have been made. One approach is to provide advanced information on local traffic conditions so that a driver has more insight as to the likely road price to pay. Modern technology facilitates the provision of real-time traffic information on relevant parts of the network. Another approach is the one that has been deployed in the I-15 scheme in California. In this case, the toll varies with traffic to maintain a target traffic speed with the road users being given the option of a 'free' road alongside the priced one. Information on average tolls for various times of the day is made available to help in route choice decision making.

Distributional Effects

Technically, in economic terms, Road Pricing leads to a Hicks–Kaldor societal welfare improvement (a subject we shall return to when looking at investment criteria in Chapter 11). What this means is that overall, while some people will be worse off as a result of the price (if they were not it would be a Pareto improvement), those who benefit would be in a position to compensate them and still retain some gains from the scheme. In the case of road pricing, it is the authority that imposes the charge that benefits from the revenues collected (represented by C_2JKC_1 in Figure 9.1) with the average road user being worse off. This leads to two related issues: first, defining exactly which road-using groups lose and by how much, and second, if and by how much the authorities should provide compensation. The first of these issues is dealt with here, and the second in the subsection that follows.

Under a Road Pricing regime, road use depends on the capabilities of potential users to pay the congestion charge. Whether this would result in undesirable regressive effects on social welfare is an empirical question. It is likely that surface public transport, as we shall see below when discussing London, would move more freely, and would provide a better service for the lower-income groups that tend to patronize it. Also, the wealthy are likely to benefit from being able to 'buy' uncongested road space, a situation they value because of the importance they attach to time savings. In contrast, middle-income groups could be forced to switch from private to public transport, a mode they consider inferior.[16]

Interpersonal welfare comparisons of this type are difficult to make but it is possible, for example, that if some of the revenue from road pricing were directed

---

[16] H.W. Richardson, 'A note on the distributional effects of road pricing', *Journal of Transport Economics and Policy*, **8**, 82–5, 1974.

towards further improvements in public transport (which may or may not mean heavily subsidized fares), then the adverse effects on the middle-income group could be substantially reduced. Whether this is socially acceptable or desirable is a political question.

All forms of pricing inevitably lead to differential consumption patterns that are to some extent influenced by income levels. Western-style economies accept this partly because it prioritizes what people want to consume but also because income is itself seen as reflecting the endeavors of individuals. If there are concerns about the income distribution, this is treated as a normative issue that should be handled through redistribution as part of a political process. Road Pricing is no exception to normal pricing principles. Much of the debate about the distributional effects of congestion charging centers on the ability of poorer individuals to be able to buy road space, but the poor are unable to buy many things. Thus the problem is really one of income distribution *per se*, rather than of the price mechanism.

There is a second area of distributional interest, namely how the impacts of Road Pricing are spread over geographical space. In some cases there is a clear link between this and the income distribution issue because of the correlation between land-use patterns and household incomes. In another context, however, there are concerns that Road Pricing will penalize businesses in areas where road users have to pay for their congestion effects as opposed to those that do not. The evidence on this is limited, but a study of the London road charging scheme by Quddus et al.[17] found that although individual stores were adversely impacted by the road price, it did not affect overall retail sales in Central London. Isolating the implications of the congestion charge is, however, not easy because of a failure of the Central underground line during the initial period of its introduction, the heightened fear of terrorism at the time, and the onset of a general macroeconomic downturn.

Expenditure of Revenue

Linked to the distributional issue, Sharp[18] pointed out that the revenues from road pricing need to be reallocated with a degree of circumspection. In particular, a distinctive outcome of the road price is that the revenue does not normally go to a private company that then makes commercially oriented decisions on how to spend it, but rather to a public agency that has less clear-cut criteria regarding using the revenue flow. This poses short-term practical as well as intellectual challenges. Sharp himself assessed some alternatives for using the revenues, including reducing other road user charges, which has an intuitive appeal provided that they are not being used to fulfill other policy objectives, such as reducing CO_2

---

[17] M.A. Quddus, A. Carmel and M. Bell, 'The impact of the congestion charge on retail: the London Experience', *Journal of Transport Economics and Policy*, **41**, 113–34, 2007.

[18] C.H. Sharp, 'Congestion and welfare, an examination of the case for a congestion tax', *Economic Journal*, **76**, 806–17, 1966.

emissions from carbon fuels or acting as a sumptuary tax to finance other, socially approved expenditures.

In strict efficiency terms, the revenues should be used for purposes that yield the highest social return. Since in most cases large revenues from optimal congestion charges themselves indicate inadequate capacity, a strong case can be made that some should go into providing additional road capacity.[19] A related, but slightly different argument, is that the $F_1 - F_2$ motorists priced off the roads in Figure 9.1 should receive some compensation. Direct transfers back to former motorists, however, pose the problem that they are likely to use at least part of the money to 'buy back' road space. An alternative method of compensating motorists adversely affected may be to use the road pricing revenues to construct more roads, but there are issues here. Daniel Graham and Stephen Glaister,[20] for example, take a wide geographic perspective of Road Pricing across the entire UK road network and find that while its introduction in urban areas would increase the revenues enjoyed by the relevant road authorities, revenues would fall on other parts of the network that are far less used.

Given that investment decisions should be based upon a much wider range of criteria than simply the revenues raised from road pricing (see Chapter 11), an alternative approach would be to treat the revenues as a pure tax income and to use them as part of general public expenditure, and in this way wider problems of efficiency and distribution may be tackled. In this vein, from a pragmatic, political economy perspective of forming coalitions of interests that would endorse Road Pricing, Phil Goodwin[21] and Kenneth Small[22] looked at spreading the expenditure of revenues across different interest groups including road users (in the form of investment in additional capacity and intelligent transport technology to better manage what there is), public transport authorities (in the form of capital and operating subsidies), and the general public (in the form of reduced taxation or increases in public endorsed non-transport expenditures). The trick, of course, would be to find the appropriate balance of this redistribution between the various groups that would carry local political opinion. However, this has proved difficult in many cases.

A number of efforts have been made to ask those affected how they would like to see the revenues from Road Pricing spent. Erik Verhoef and colleagues[23] did an extensive survey in the Netherlands, and found that, in decreasing order,

---

[19] K.J. Button, 'How should the revenues from congestion pricing be spent?', in G. Roth (ed.), *Street Smart: Competition, Entrepreneurship, and the Future of Roads*, Washington, DC: The Independent Institute, 2006.

[20] D.J. Graham and S. Glaister, 'Spatial implications of transport pricing', *Journal of Transport Economics and Policy*, **40**, 173–201, 2006.

[21] P.B. Goodwin, 'The rule of three: a possible solution to the political problem of competing objectives for road pricing', *Traffic Engineering and Control*, **29**, 495–7, 1989

[22] K.A. Small, 'Using revenue from congestion pricing', *Transportation*, **19**, 359–81, 1992.

[23] E.T. Verhoef, P. Nijkamp and P. Rietveld, 'The social feasibility of road pricing; the case study of the Randstad area', *Journal of Transport Economics and Policy*, **31**, 255–67, 1997.

the preferences were for investment in more road capacity, reduction in vehicle taxation, reduction in fuel taxation, investment in public transportation, subsidies for public transportation, investment in car pooling facilities, general taxation cuts, and expansion of other forms of public expenditure.

In practice, most Road Pricing schemes do involve a high degree of earmarking of revenues either because the local authority has needed to do this to get policies through or because central government has mandated it as part of its wider policy agenda. In the case of the toll roads in Norway, although not strictly a Road Pricing scheme, the revenues were specifically earmarked for local transport expenditures on roads and buses. In the UK, the revenues from London's congestion charging must, by national law, be spent on transport in London; in fact much of it goes to subsidize bus services.

Road Pricing is a First-best Solution in a Second-best World

Marginal cost pricing of road space is strictly optimal only if all other goods in the economy are also marginal cost priced; it forms a benchmark. To deal with situations where marginal cost pricing is not universal there is a need to adjust the Road Price to reflect distortions elsewhere in the system. For example, if the costs of public transport are set above their costs inclusive of congestion, then the charges imposed on roads should also be set above the simple calculation of the road price.

While this concept is relatively simply to follow, operationalization can be difficult, as shown by Verhoef.[24] The nature of pricing imperfections can be complex and extensive; they may also be positive, in the sense of reinforcing the road price, or they may conflict with it. They may also be within the road system; for example, introducing congestion pricing on some roads but not others affects the relative attractiveness of various routes and the economic activities located about them. At the micro level, charging for only some routes may deflect some traffic onto unpriced 'rat-runs' which not only has adverse effects for congestion, but also may have adverse environmental implications. There is a danger that one region or city may not introduce Road Pricing, hoping to attract business from adjacent areas that do. A similar problem arises when it comes to air- and seaport pricing, which will be discussed later.

This type of problem can easily be seen in a diagram. Figure 9.2 shows a situation where there are two roads linking A and B: one free and the other with an optimal road price in place. (One could easily interpret the unpriced route as an alternative mode and the arguments would remain valid.) The roads are pure substitutes for each other in the sense of the generalized costs, using the sum of the monetized travel cost, c, plus the toll r where it is levied. The costs will be equal for both roads (following the so-called 'Wardropian' equilibrium principle) with people trading off lower monetized costs of a non-priced trip against the

[24] E.T. Verhoef, 'Second-best congestion pricing in general static transportation networks with elastic demands', *Regional Science and Urban Economics*, **32**, 281–310, 2002.

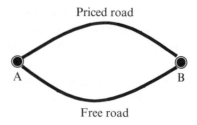

Priced road

A   B

Free road

Figure 9.2   *The classic two-route second-best case*

higher-priced, but faster facility. Drivers are nearly identical in their preferences (for example, their values of time savings are the same) except when demand is not perfectly elastic.

Given the different prices, the challenge is to set a second-best charge for the priced road that maximizes the efficiency with which both roads are used. In general this will be below the optimal road price when only one link has to be considered. This is because the charge on the priced road will improve the situation over conditions when there is no access fee. But this charge will divert some traffic to the other, unpriced road, adding to the level of congestion there. Thus there is a trade-off in terms of improving travel conditions on the facility that is road priced but worsening them on the route that remains free. Ideally both routes should have a congestion charge, but we are assuming that that is not possible. It is the establishment of the optimal trade-off in this constrained case that necessitates the second-best pricing.

9.5   Outcomes of Road Pricing Implementation

There are numerous academic and official studies that have examined the potential effects of using road user charges of one form or another to reduce urban traffic congestion. Rather than rehash these, or try to produce some meta-analysis of their statistical conclusions, here we look briefly at what has actually transpired when Road Pricing has been adopted. One thing is clear, the evidence from the various road pricing schemes that have been initiated, and heavily studied, to date shows that drivers do respond to prices and that traffic congestion can be controlled through direct user charges. Besides the direct traffic effects on congestion, the initiatives have exerted a number of secondary influences, many that were generally anticipated but not on the scale that they have occurred.

Inevitably, there are problems in assessing the pure impacts of Road Pricing. All the schemes that have been introduced to date have been part of larger packages, and isolating the effects of any element is difficult. The Singapore area licensing, for example, was accompanied by additional bus capacity and investments in park-and-ride facilities as well as exemption for high-occupancy cars. Also the charges themselves have inevitably embraced political compromise that, for example, in the London case resulted in significantly lower charges for residents

Table 9.4   *The effects of major road pricing schemes*

City	Traffic effects	Congestion effects	Public transport effects
Singapore, 1975–1998[1]	−44%; −31% by 1988	Average speed increased from 19 to 36 km/h	Modal shift, from 33% to 46% trips to work by city bus, 69% in 1983
Trondheim, 1991	−10%	n.a.	+7% city bus patronage
Singapore, 1998[2]	−10 to −15%	Optimized road usage, 20 to 30 km/h roads, 45 to 65 km/h expressways	Slight shift to city bus
Rome, 2001	−20%	n.a.	+ 6%
London, 2003	−18% 2003 vs 2002, 0% 2004 versus 2003	−30%. 1.6 min/km typical delay 2003, 2004 versus 2002 (2.3 min/km)	+18% during peak hours bus patronage 2003, +12% in 2004
London, 2005[3]	Small net reductions −4% 2005/06	−22%. 1.8 min/km typical delay	Bus patronage steady
Stockholm, 2006	−30% 2006 versus 2004	−30 to −50% journey time	+ 6%

Notes:
1. Although called an area licensing scheme, the system was a cordon toll rather than an area license.
2. Electronic fee collection introduced.
3. New rate introduced.

and some types of road users such as taxis, trucks and two-wheeled vehicles. Added to this, there can be particular circumstances that affect the system, such as the closure for a period of the main underground railway line in London at the time when congestion charging was initiated.

The world is also not static and traffic growth takes places over time. Consequently, there is a need for the level of congestion charges to change with circumstances. However, this makes it hard to estimate anything but very short-term *ex post* elasticities because of the problem associated with allowing for these background growth trends. Thus the outcomes of any scheme at any particular point in time will depend upon exactly how recently Road Pricing has been imposed and the extent to which it has been modified in the light of experience.

Table 9.4 provides details of the outcomes of some of the major urban Road Pricing schemes in terms of the direct effects on automobile traffic, on the traffic situation more generally, and on public transport. The pattern that emerges is pretty clear and does not need much in the way of elaboration; Road Pricing where it has been employed has reduced the use of cars, improved traffic flows, and led to a modal shift toward public transport during peak periods.

There have also been secondary benefits, such as reduced traffic-generated environmental pollution, although this is difficult in practice to quantify and evaluate because people allocate their time saved from not being held up in traffic in a number of ways that in themselves can result in adverse environmental consequences. Just as an example, it has been estimated that the Stockholm scheme reduced CO_2 by 10 to 14 percent in the inner-city area and by 2 to 3 percent in the surrounding area, although there was little impact on noise levels, while the London charging scheme produced an annual $6 million benefit in terms of reduced CO_2 emissions, and $30 million in lower accident costs.

Not all the systems described are strictly Road Pricing: the Norwegian ones, for example, were introduced primarily for revenue raising. In addition, while the Singapore scheme showed that Road Pricing can reduce congestion successfully, it also showed that the effect of any scheme seems rather more difficult to forecast than some advocates suggested. The actual details of this scheme are obviously tailored to the geography and political climate of Singapore and have not been exactly replicated elsewhere. It was also questionable whether the actual prices charged are truly optimal or whether they are excessively high,[25] acting as a method of revenue collection for the government as much as an instrument of microeconomic resource allocation. Quite clearly, transport may be a legitimate field for pure indirect taxation but in assessing the effectiveness of a Road Pricing scheme it is important to isolate the price efficiency aspect from that of taxation *per se*.

Of course not all outcomes have been exactly as predicted. In very many cases, the authorities have underestimated the power of pricing and the reduction in traffic has exceeded forecasts, and the revenue collected has been less than expected. Equally, public transport has generally been found to be a more popular substitute than expected once travelers are aware of the congestion costs of using cars – the park-and-ride facilities introduced in Singapore being a notable exception to this. This poses some operational challenges in terms of budgeting, scheduling and in the provision of public transport more generally, but has not seriously brought any scheme into difficulties.

Enforcement has posed challenges to the authorities responsible for some schemes, although there seems to have been a learning process. Transport for London,[26] for example, reported that the number of penalty charge notices fell throughout 2005 with 21 percent fewer charges overall. Nussio[27] reports that in Rome, violations to the zone resulting in fines have fallen from an initial 22 percent of the overall access flow to about 7 percent of those registered in 2005–06. Reductions in traffic flows were actually mainly achieved through this reduction of illegal traffic entering the limited traffic zone. Better monitoring was made possible by the installation of electronic gates in 2001; illegal traffic decreased from an estimated 36 percent before their activation to under 10 percent after a year and a half.

[25] R. Toh, 'Road congestion pricing: the Singapore experience', *Malayan Economic Review*, **22**, 52–61, 1977.

[26] Transport for London, *Fourth Annual Monitoring Report: June 2006*, London: 2006.

[27] F. Nussio, *Rome and the Limited Traffic Zones*, Rome: EU Civitas Initiative, 2007.

9.6   Parking Policies

In some cases, often for political reasons but also possibly because it is more cost effective to operate, a parking charging policy may appear preferable to Road Pricing as a means of containing congestion externalities. This is particularly true if much of the traffic is terminating in the area concerned and there is a lot of circulating traffic seeking parking spots because of inadequate signage. Again, while the most extensive coverage of parking is in the context of urban car traffic, the principles can be equally valid for stands at airports or berths at seaports; for example, high stand charges for aircraft at air terminals can stimulate changes in flight patterns and traffic concentrations.

Parking is seldom provided and operated in an economic manner, and optimal fees are rare.[28] Parking can be considered either in a first-best world, where there is appropriate pricing elsewhere, including Road Pricing, or in a second-best context as a means of limiting traffic congestion when appropriate prices are not charged for other goods and services.[29]

The first-best approach is simply to set the parking charge equal to the marginal cost of parking, including the congestion costs of seeking a parking space. In practice, their detailed effects can be influenced by the institutional structure of an area; for example, any attempt to influence the parking market in one part of a city will influence the scale and nature of the induced externalities in adjacent boroughs by, depending on the nature of the policy, attracting or discouraging terminating traffic and affecting such things as the land value of office premises with parking facilities. Institutionally this can also lead to game playing by employers who argue for favorable parking concessions as a pre-requisite for them locating in any particular local administrative unit. These longer-term costs are generally more difficult to handle because of hysteresis. Once people change their activity patterns it is often difficult to encourage them to adjust to optimal behavior; there are stranded cost considerations and uncertainties to contend with.

A simple way to look at the role of parking fees in a second-best context is set out in Figure 9.3.[30] Quadrant **A** has the marginal cost and average cost curves (where we assume simple interaction congestion to be the only externality) of car use but added to this is the cost of parking (reflecting the opportunity costs of parking space and assuming for simplicity that each individual's parking duration is identical). This gives the combined costs curve of *TMC*. The optimal Road Price plus parking fee, with regard to traffic density, then become *RP* in the diagram. We now take the extreme case that for some reason the Road Price element of *RP* cannot be collected.

On the assumption that all vehicles paying appropriate prices which enter

[28] W. Young, 'Parking and traffic control', in K.J. Button and D.A. Hensher (eds), *Handbook of Transport Systems and Traffic Control*, Oxford: Pergamon, 2001.

[29] K.J. Button, 'The political economy of parking charges in "first" and "second-best" worlds', *Transport Policy*, **13**, 470–78, 2006.

[30] E.T. Verhoef, P. Nijkamp and P. Rietveld, 'The economics of regulatory parking policies', *Transportation Research A*, **29**, 141–56, 1995.

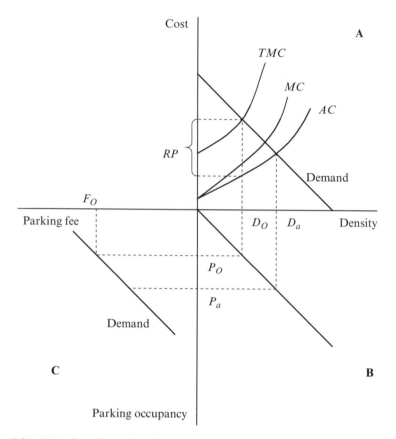

Figure 9.3   *A simple analysis of parking charges*

during the study period will find parking, then we can draw the 45° line in quadrant **B** of the diagram which relates traffic density to parking occupancy. The parking fee for the period, *F*, required to achieve this is then mapped out in quadrant **C**. This demand curve again assumes that willingness to pay the set fee will guarantee a parking place; if this assumption is not valid because of suboptimal capacity, the analysis requires modification.[31] The demand curve for parking places is derived from the difference between Demand and the *AC* in quadrant **A**. The optimal parking fee here (F_O) is acting as a rationing device and its size could be adjusted accordingly if a suboptimal Road Price were initiated at some later date.

Parking policy has its own limitations. It obviously has little impact on through-traffic and, indeed, by terminating stopping traffic, may actually encourage it in city centers. It also has distributional consequences. In particular, it bears more heavily on those making short journeys since the parking fee will form a relatively larger part of the overall cost of their trips compared to those driving a greater distance. The policy is also likely to be relatively insensitive to actual levels of congestion since it is acting as a complement to road use rather than road use itself. From a practical

---

[31] R.W. Douglas, 'A parking model – the effects of supply on demand', *American Economists*, **19**, 85–6, 1975.

Table 9.5   *Parking elasticities in Sydney*

	Preferred CBD	Less preferred CBD	CBD fringe
Car trip, preferred CBD	−0.541	0.205	0.035
Car trip, less preferred CBD	0.837	−0.015	0.043
Car trip, CBD fringe	0.965	0.286	−0.476
Park and ride	0.363	0.136	0.029
Ride public transit	0.291	0.104	0.023
Forgo CBD trip	0.469	0.150	0.029

Source: D.A. Hensher and J. King, 'Parking demand and responsiveness to supply, price and location in Sydney central business district', *Transportation Research A*, **35**, 177–96, 2001.

perspective, many parking places are privately owned and hence direct control of prices is difficult for policy makers although indirect measures, such as taxing land used for parking, provide a mechanism for tackling the problem.

There is also the question of just how sensitive parking decisions are to charging – the elasticity of demand. Table 9.5 provides some calculations for Sydney, Australia, dividing parking locations up into more or less preferred sites. It provides both direct elasticities, and also cross-elasticities between locations. It shows, for example, that while a 1 percent rise in parking charges at preferred urban locations will reduce parking there by 0.54 percent, it will increase parking at less preferred sites by 0.84 percent and fringe parking by 0.97 percent. In other words, simply raising parking charges at the most congested parts of the city can spread the demand for parking to other locations.

9.7   Congestion Pricing at Airports

Congestion in air transport arises at airports and during flights. As with road transport, the lack of a genuine benchmark for measuring congestion means that estimating congestion costs at different traffic levels or excess congestion levels in either context is difficult. The US Federal Aviation Administration and many other civil aviation organizations use a 15-minute delay on the published schedule as an indication of congestion, and on this basis 25 percent of flights suffered from excess congestion at major US airports in 2006.

The economic cost of these delays is difficult to estimate because, unlike road traffic congestion where car drivers are trying to minimize their travel time and vehicles costs, commercial airlines are the direct customers for most airport slots, and in a deregulated world airlines are largely motivated by profit. In other words, the nature of the opportunity cost associated with congestion is perceived differently when the user of a facility is a commercial entity from when it is an individual – the effects of congestion on an airline affect its bottom line, the effects of road congestion on an individual are on that person's utility, which is usually modeled in terms of financial costs and the monetary value of lost time.

Table 9.6 *Delays suffered by major European airlines at large airports (2006)*

Airport	Departures		Arrivals	
	Flights (%)	Minutes (average)	Flights (%)	Minutes (average)
London Heathrow	31.8	34.9	30.3	38.9
Madrid	31.3	45.7	33.1	44.3
London Gatwick	30.7	32.5	31.5	37.8
Paris CDG	28.6	38.1	23.4	37.4
Barcelona	27.2	43.4	28.0	41.2
Rome	26.3	41.8	22.8	42.0
Athens	25.2	40.2	27.7	41.0
Frankfurt	25.0	36.9	24.6	40.0
Dublin	24.4	44.6	29.5	39.7
Larnaca	24.3	50.9	30.1	49.8
Milan Malpensa	24.2	44.3	22.1	41.6
Lisbon	24.1	42.6	30.2	37.5

Source: Association of European Airlines.

Airports vary in their physical form, ownership, and in their motivations. While there has been a gradual trend towards privatization in Europe, and especially in the United Kingdom, and modifications to the regulations regarding how they operate, US airports are largely owned by local authorities of one kind or another. There are few, if any, fully privately owned airports in the world driven purely by unrestrained profit motives and this may, in part, explain why their efficient operations are often an issue of public interest.

Many airports are already congested (Table 9.6 gives data for major European facilities) and it is unlikely that runway capacity will in the foreseeable future expand in line with the projected increase in traffic, and certainly there will be many facilities where capacity will remain stagnant or grow much more slowly. EUROCONTROL estimates that traffic will double by 2020 and that 60 airports will be congested and 20 saturated for 8 to 10 hours a day if policies remain as they are. These are often airports where demand is high but additional runways will not be constructed because of local opposition to adverse local environmental effects. There are also few quick-fix technologies on the horizon. Enhanced air navigation equipment and air traffic control practices are likely to offer only temporary relief in terms of controlling flows into and out of airports. The challenge in these circumstances is to make the best use of the capacity that is available, and to stimulate the adoption of efficient management practices.

The existing mechanisms for allocating take-off and landing slots generally rely upon administrative procedures. Many countries, or groups of countries such as the European Union, have regulations governing the ways slots are allocated, embracing a combination of formal and informal arrangements often overseen by a scheduling committee that includes incumbent users. It is normal to have some grandfathering element that favors existing users, and often there are limitations on the ability of incumbents to trade their slots with other carriers. To assist in coordination across airports, every flight requires a take-off and landing slot. There are also various inter-airport and -airline meetings and, for international routes, since 1947 the International Air Transport Association (IATA) has held twice yearly schedule conferences now involving some 300 airlines and 200 airport representatives.

The situation is different in the United States where anti-trust laws mean that airlines simply schedule flights taking into account expected air traffic control and airport delays. An exception initiated in 1969 under the High Density Rule temporarily designated five 'slot-controlled airports' (JFK and LaGuardia in New York, O'Hare in Chicago, Newark, and Washington Reagan National) where the federal government limited the number of aircraft movements during certain hours although the airlines from 1986 could buy and sell, or lease, the slots designated for domestic use among themselves. This regime has been modified several times since.

Although there are variations by country and airports, the fees charged for a slot are based largely on the size of aircraft, with some variations that reflect, for example, noise emissions, and determined on cost recovery criteria. This is a sort of unequally weighted Ramsey pricing concept.[32] Where there are fee differentials, they seldom embrace a full consideration of congestion costs. There is thus no reason to assume that this type of arrangement results in anything like the optimal use of slots at one airport, let alone across a network. There are few incentives for reallocation between carriers as the demand for their services fluctuates even when this is permitted. While there are wide variations, it is often difficult for new carriers to enter specific markets, and especially those dominated by a major airline. Equally, there are less than maximum incentives for incumbents to make efficient use of slots they retain in terms of the congestion that is imposed on other operators. Indeed, congestion may be used as an entry deterrent measure to limit competitive market entry.

While there is a temptation to simply transfer the Road Pricing concept to air transport infrastructure, there are differences. Roads are, for example, used by an atomistic set of independent 'customers' which cannot control the trips of others, whereas air transport facilities are used by a relatively small group of airlines that often have significant control over their actions. In some cases a carrier is a near monopsonist buyer of services at an airport. (This is particularly so at the hub-airports in the United States, but there is still considerable concentration in Europe; Table 9.7.) What one has in these circumstances are bilateral monopolies or oligopolies with airlines providing countervailing power to the airports. Further, while it may be reasonable to apply continuous functions to the estimation of road traffic congestion, although cars are clearly discrete units, this is less sensible regarding aircraft movements which are far less numerous.

As alluded to earlier, there are also other differences that affect the measurement of congestion costs. While the analysis of production externalities is similar

---

[32] S.A. Morrison, 'The efficiency and equity of runway pricing', *Journal of Public Economics*, **34**, 45–60, 1987.

Table 9.7   *Market share of passengers by airline at Europe's 10 largest airports (2002)*

Airport	Carrier 1	Carrier 2	Carrier 3
London Heathrow	British Airways 41.6%	bmi 12.1%	Lufthansa 4.8%
Frankfurt	Lufthansa 59.4%	British Airways 3.6%	Austrian 2.9%
Paris Charles de Gaulle	Air France 56.6%	British Airways 5.15	Lufthansa 4.9%
Amsterdam	KLM 52.2%	Transavia 5.5%	easyJet 4.3%
Madrid	Iberia 57.0%	Spanair 12.7%	Air Europa 7.1%
London Gatwick	British Airways 55.1%	easyJet 12.8%	flybe 5.6%
Rome	Alitalia 46.2%	Air One 10.0%	Meridiana 3.9%
Munich	Lufthansa 56.8%	Deutsche BA 6.6%	Air Dolomiti 6.5%
Paris Orly	Air France 64.2%	Iberia 8.2%	Air Littoral 3.6%
Barcelona	Iberia 48.5%	Spanair 9.4%	Air Europa 5.5%

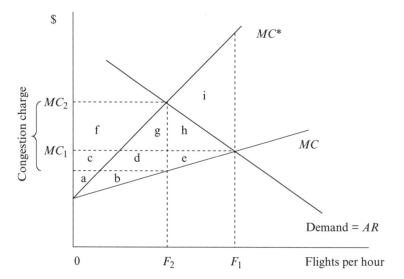

Figure 9.4   *Congestion costs at airports*

to the user-on-user externalities that form the basis of the economic analysis of road congestion, the motivation of the actors involved is not consumer surplus maximization (usually dominated by travel time costs) but rather producer surplus maximization. Commercial airlines in most markets are concerned only with profits when making operational decisions, and may well impose significant time costs on large numbers of their own passengers if this ensures high profits from the remainder, including those using connected services.

Figure 9.4 provides a simplified version of the use of a congestion charge regime for take-offs on a single runway on the premise that there are numerous airlines seeking rights – the atomistic case. The airport just charges an account-ancy fee to cover costs. Functions are linear for ease of drafting and this does not affect the argument. With each additional flight the marginal aircraft impacts other flights that the initiating airline does not take into account in its decision making – seen as the divergence of the MC and the MC^* curves. The result is a flow through the runway of F_1 involving a marginal cost of MC_1. The flight, however, will impose congestion on other carriers' activities, affecting their profitability as their costs rise and as customers' lower willingness to pay for a poorer service adversely affects revenues. The outcome is an aggregate producer surplus for the airlines at the airport of $\{a + c\} - \{g + h + i\}$ when there are F_1 flights. This will be zero if there is an atomistic market.

If there were a monopsony airline at the airport bearing congestion effects internally, it would take MC^* as its reaction function and manage a flow of F_2. Such an airline can prioritize flights for take-off at the airport and, to a lesser extent, en route by allowing overtaking. The resultant producer surplus to the airline is then $\{a + c + f\}$ which will be above zero. Similarly, with an airport employing marginal cost pricing akin to a road congestion charge, and thus levying a take-off fee that embraces congestion, the flights would be F_2.

While this simple analysis, essentially just a transfer of the Pigouvian framework to a situation where the infrastructure users are interested in economic rent maximization, can be insightful it does miss some essential elements of runway economics. In the analysis, the degree to which any individual flight by an airline affects other flights depends on the nature of the carrier operating the services – basically upon the number of slots an airline uses. In many cases, where there is a dominant carrier, the impact of any flight is on the other operations of that carrier. What this intuitively means for charges is that when there is a single dominant carrier operating from a not-for-profit airport not actively seeking to exploit monopoly power, there is no need to initiate congestion charges. There are potential problems, however, if the airport is itself rent seeking. As with most bilateral monopoly situations, the slot prices will be bounded, but indeterminate, in this case. This is because a market dominated by a profit-maximizing monopoly tends to have high prices from users, whereas a market dominated by a profit-maximizing monopsony tends to seek lower prices for these services.

When combined into a bilateral monopoly, the buyer and the seller cannot both maximize profit simultaneously and are forced to negotiate. The resulting price could be anywhere between the higher monopoly and the lower monopsony prices depending on the relative negotiating power of each side. What theory suggests, however, is that, in formulating its case, the monopoly airline will think in terms of being able to internalize its congestion costs.

Where there is a degree of competition among airlines, however, congestion costs are not fully internalized and congestion pricing become relevant. In reality, most airports are used by several airlines of different sizes with diverse scheduling desires leading to some degree of imperfect competition. In these cases there will be some internalization of congestion costs but, from a social welfare maximization perspective, a need for congestion charges remains to internalize the remainder. The situation is made more difficult to analyze because the airports themselves usually confront some degree of competition from other airports or, and especially in Europe, high-speed rail services.

In addition to this issue of pure market power, the air transport network is generally more complex than a road system in a very particular way. While most road movements are point to point (car drivers seldom change vehicles *en route*), most large airlines operate hub-and-spoke systems where people make trips via a hub and changes of hardware for them are the norm. This means that carriers are concerned about not only the immediate implications of flight delays but also the effects of this on connecting traffic and its own further network operations.

Further, whereas a car can wait almost indefinitely in traffic, an aircraft cannot be airborne indefinitely, reducing the flexibility of infrastructure to handle connecting traffic flows. Passengers would also be less than happy if an airborne flight were diverted to an alternative airport because its congestion fees were lower at that particular time.

Added to this is an issue examined initially by Jan Brueckner, and in more detail by Eric Pels and Erik Verhoef,[33] namely the possibility in an oligopolistic environment for strategic interaction between competitors that leads to non-competitive pricing. Basically, without congestion this will lead to prices in excess of the Pareto optimum for the airlines that collude with the policy implication that, in the absence of any direct remedial action on the part of the authorities, there is a second-best case for subsidies.

But perhaps the biggest difference is that literature on road pricing generally makes simplifying assumptions of homogeneous traffic and identical types of driver, which allows the MC curve also to be the cost curve related to the MC^* curve. This gives a determinant solution for the congestion charge. Put another way, with MC also representing the congestion embracing average cost curve, MC_1 is both the average revenue in equilibrium F_1 and the average cost. The types of assumption made regarding roads, however, seem less applicable to runways, and the MC curve is unlikely to be identical to the AC curve. We just list a few of the complications.

First, as noted previously, it may not seem reasonable to assume that the curves are continuous: with 5,000 cars an hour on a road continuous functions may seem an acceptable assumption, but with 40 landings an hour on a runway it is much less justifiable. Second, many runways involve mixed flows of take-offs and landings with different time and fuel requirements. Third, typically air traffic is highly heterogeneous involving different sizes and types of aircraft. Fourth, because of laws regarding flying hours, the crew costs may vary between flights if connecting movements are missed. What these, and other inconveniently realistic features, would typically mean is that there would be no stable AC and MC curves (that is, adding a marginal flight may change the average cost for infra-marginal flights, so the curve is not stable). In this case there is no way of estimating an optimal congestion charge.

While in some ways more complex than roads, air transport infrastructure is also simpler in many dimensions, making some forms of congestion charging, and especially auctioning, easier. It involves relatively small networks compared

[33] E. Pels and E.T. Verhoef, 'The economics of airport congestion pricing', *Journal of Urban Economics*, **55**, 257–77, 2004.

to the complexity of most urban road systems and, despite some differences in technical requirements, has a much more homogeneous set of users. A look at the vast number of theoretical papers on urban networks seeking optimal traffic flows, and *ipso facto* charges, all of which are based on a plethora of simplifying assumptions, illustrates the complexities involved. Further, while this work no doubt maximized the adrenalin flow of the authors that accompanies dancing an intellectual jig, it would seem to have little impact on policy. The road prices introduced in places such as Singapore and London involve nice round numbers, and the speed targets on I-15 in California's variable charging projects have been equally robust rather than being founded in economic science.

Considerable intellectual effort has been expended on defining appropriate pricing principles for airport slots, focusing mainly on the ways in which administrative fees could be modified to make better use of them. The resultant output has included looking at making greater use of pricing for cost recovery when there is no congestion,[34] but has largely been focused on situations where there are at least some periods where demand under the current charging regime exceeds the capacity of the system.

Moving to the empirical analysis of airport congestion, much of this has involved looking at whether dominant airlines do internalize their costs. Daniel's pioneering work (Table 9.8) suggests that there is very little internalization by the larger carriers but his analysis suffers from being based on a single airport and focusing on just Northwest Airlines within a narrow cost-minimization context. The focus on one airport may be a reasonable approach if it is the only one subjected to serious congestion, but if there are other facilities in a similar situation then a network analysis becomes germane. Additionally, the simulation models deployed do not have a closed-form solution and thus it is not possible to discern what drives the non-internalization.

Subsequent work, notably by Brueckner[35] and Mayer and Sinai,[36] as well as that by Daniel and co-workers,[37] has looked across a range of airports to gain empirical breath, and modified the models they used to meet the technical limitations of earlier formulations. New data sources also allow for econometric analysis of causes for different behavior patterns of airlines rather than just simulations. Using the number of flights that are delayed for 15 minutes or more as the indicator of excess congestion, Brueckner finds that delays do decrease where there is airline domination at an airport, but the degree of internalization is small.

Adopting the excess of flight time over the minimum feasible flight time as their indicator of delay, Mayer and Sinai come to the same conclusion. Where

34 R.R. Martín-Cejas, 'Airport pricing systems in Europe and an application of Ramsey pricing to Spanish airports', *Transportation Research E*, **33**, 321–7, 1997.
35 J.K. Brueckner, 'Airport congestion when carriers have market power', *American Economic Review*, **92**, 1357–75, 2002.
36 C. Mayer and T. Sinai, 'Network effects, congestion externalities, and air traffic delays: or why not all delays are evil', *American Economic Review*, **93**, 1194–215, 2003.
37 J.I. Daniel, 'Congestion pricing and capacity of large hub airports, a bottleneck model with stochastic queues', *Econometrica*, **63**, 327–70, 1995.

Table 9.8   *Econometric studies of internalization of congestion at airports*

Study	Case	Model	Findings
Carlin and Park (1970)	LaGuardia Airport, New York, 1967–1968	Numerical calculation and regression	While full marginal cost pricing is not possible, proportional marginal cost pricing does offer some efficiency gains
Morrison (1987)	US technical data on airline costs for 1980	Numerical calculations	Equal weighted Ramsey pricing would redistribute welfare from commuter and local service carriers to cargo, international, and trunk carriers
Morrison and Winston (1989)	US delay data for May 1988	Looked at a Road Pricing regime type model of atomistic pricing	Atomistic pricing would generate significant welfare benefits
Daniel (1995)	Minneapolis-St Paul airport in 1990	Bottleneck congestion model and a time-homogeneous stochastic queuing model	Demand peaking means that congestion pricing can generate large savings by smoothing out demand
Martín-Cejas (1997)	Uncongested Spanish airports	Simulations looking at Ramsey pricing	Allows for cost recovery
Daniel (2001)	Minneapolis-St Paul airport in 1990	Stochastic bottleneck model	Congestion pricing would transfer welfare back from private aircraft operators and their high-income passengers to common travelers on commercial aircraft
Daniel and Pahwa (2000)	Minneapolis-St Paul airport in 1990	Standard peak-load pricing model Deterministic bottleneck model Stochastic bottleneck model	Similar traffic patterns are produced by the models using weight-based fees, but a variety of patterns emerge when congestion pricing is used
Brueckner (2002b)	25 most congested airports in the US in 1999	Econometric analysis of delays using six different specifications	When an airport is dominated by a monopoly airline then the costs of congestion are fully internalized
Mayer and Sinai (2003)	Flights between airports with at least 1% of US flights, 1988–2000	Econometric analysis of delays using regression with and without fixed effects	Hubbing is the primary cause of traffic delays and this largely reflects optimal use of runway capacity
Harback and Daniel (2007)	27 major US airports, 2003	Deterministic bottleneck model of congestion	The notion that dominant carriers internalize self-imposed congestion costs is rejected and full congestion pricing is found to be optimal
Morrison and Winston (2008)	74 US airports for 2005	Morrison/Winston (1989) congestion measure	Optimal and atomistic congestion pricing generate welfare gains with the latter being slightly greater

Source: K.J. Button, 'Issues in airport runway capacity charging and allocation', *Journal of Transport Economics and Policy*, **42**, 563–85, 2008. This paper contains full details of the studies cited.

there is competition between airlines at an airport then each should take a share of the congestion costs imposed on others in proportion to their market share – for example, American and United Airlines both have roughly half the traffic at Chicago O'Hare International Airport, and should thus each pay half of the costs that it imposes.

This is not, however, the finding of Harback and Daniel,[38] who look at 27 large US airports using structural models of landing and take-off queues rather than using econometric techniques for empirical verification. It also differs from Brueckner's and Mayer and Sinai's findings in that an input measure of delays (the delays generated by each aircraft) is used rather than an output measure (delays experienced by each aircraft). The result, tested on data for 2003, is that in most cases there is no internalization of congestion costs by dominant airlines. The rationale seems to stem from Stackelberg oligopoly game theory, although other gaming models may be relevant. Essentially, the dominant carrier uses its ability to manipulate congestion to deter market entry by competitors, a limit pricing, which leads the dominant firm to act as if it had the costs of its rivals or potential rivals. If it were to internalize its congestion it would release capacity that could be taken by a competitor, allowing the latter the potential of reaping economies of scope and density, and of market presence.

What much of the work on airport congestion pricing does not completely embrace is the issue of full cost recovery.[39] In conditions of a competitive supply of runway capacity and constant cost, the link is a simple one: appropriate charges indicate where capacity is needed and provide the revenues to complete new works. This quickly breaks down where supply is not competitive and there are obvious technical non-linearities in the long-term cost function – runways are not divisible. The empirical work on this is limited, but Morrison and Winston[40] indicate that only charging for congestion caused to other carriers *a là* Brueckner would lead to $4.6 billion less revenue at US airports than a regime of atomistic congestion charges akin to road pricing. Cost recovery then poses a range of additional issues in terms of the supplementary methods of finance, be these subsidies of one kind or another or Ramsey pricing.

There are difficulties in the general approach of these studies, besides specific limitations inherent in each. Here we focus on the data and definitional problems in trying to determine congestion costs. Consideration of transaction costs and information availability is, as Coase pointed out, important in determining the best mechanisms for asset allocation. Much of the slot analysis work focuses on the operating impacts of congestion on airlines' costs and time costs for passengers, but airlines are the final purchasers of the infrastructure.

Airlines are rent seekers and use a variety of practices to extract rent from

[38] K.T. Harback and J.I. Daniel, '(When) do hub airlines internalize their self-imposed congestion delays?', *Journal of Urban Economics*, **63**, 613–30, 2007.

[39] T. Oum, A. Zhang and Y. Zhang, 'Alternative forms of economic regulation of airports', *Journal of Transport Economics and Policy*, **38**, 217–46, 2004.

[40] S.A. Morrison and C. Winston, 'Another look at airport congestion pricing', *American Economic Review*, **97**, 1970–7, 2008.

their customers – in particular, second-degree price discrimination with frequent flyer programs that offer effective discounts for multiple flights and a combination of second- and third-degree price discrimination through yield management practices that involves posting a menu of fares, but where this menu changes by user groups according to their preferences about timing of bookings. Because airlines take advance bookings, the immediate effects of congestion charges on revenue would be minimal, but the longer-term implications may be larger. In this context, even if an airline is profit maximizing, it may prioritize its actions by net revenue flow rather than cost savings in terms of the ways it adjusts its flight sequencing. The empirical problem is that suitable information on revenues per flight is not available, although this is needed to estimate the congestion cost.

Added to this, as Brueckner[41] points out in a theoretical contribution, on the cost side there are indivisibilities in the provision of airline services that make assessments of flight prioritization difficult, and especially so when there are hub-and-spoke operations. There are problems of scheduling different sizes of aircraft over various stage lengths and ensuring equipment compatibility as well as fulfilling technical requirements regarding such things as periodic refueling and maintenance inspections. In addition, crew changes have to meet statutory flying hour regulations and there are operation constraints such as gate availability. Much more than in the road traffic congestion case, the internalization process within this context is inevitably one of a constrained optimization process, and assessment of the degree to which this is done requires more complex assumptions about relevant functions. While these considerations may be built into theoretical models, they are difficult to incorporate into empirical analysis and, in turn, into estimation of actual charges.

As mentioned earlier, one difference between road and airport congestion is that the airline market is not atomistic and this difference offers an alternative practical approach to handling congestion. An underlying problem with congestion charging, and its analysis, is that it involves making external judgments about the optimal congestion charge. While the approaches examined in Table 9.8 are essentially about situations where there is excess demand under current charging regimes, and the role a Pigouvian style price may play in optimizing this, they do not focus on how optimal slot charges may be implemented. In particular they do not look at arrangements that would automatically reveal these fees and impose them on users. The alternative approach to setting congestion charges is to create appropriate institutional structures that coincidentally reveal optimal prices while allocating efficiently a given capacity.

One suggestion for significantly improving the slot allocation situation is the adoption of some form of auctioning system.[42] This is a mirror image of

[41] J.K. Brueckner, 'Internalization of airport congestion: a network analysis', *International Journal of Industrial Organization*, **23**, 599–614, 2005.

[42] K.J. Button, 'Auctions – what can we learn from auction theory for slot allocation?', in A. Czerny, P. Forsyth, D. Gillen and H.M. Niemeier (eds), *How to Make Slot Markets Work*, Aldershot: Ashgate, 2007.

congestion charging where some 'expert' sets a congestion charge and users willing to pay this price purchase capacity. Instead, the expert sets a level of capacity and then allows bidding for that capacity, generally in the form of an auction. Auctions have become a subject of increasing interest as markets have been deregulated and authorities have become interested in attracting more private finance. Indeed, the idea of using auctions for allocating airport slots is not new, and Vernon Smith and his associates[43] used the problem in early work on experimental economics. Their use for allocating air transport facilities is now attracting the interest of the European Union and some national governments.

Strictly, the standard Coasian line of reasoning implies that the initial allocation of slots, be it by lottery, auction, a handover to incumbents, or whatever, should, if subsequent secondary markets are permitted, make no difference to the long-run efficiency with which they are used. Auctions are but one way of allocating property rights. There is no need for an expert economist or engineer to externally set congestion prices once the allocation has been made. There will be a short-term transfer of rents between airports and carriers, and subsequently between various carriers after secondary trading, but the outcome is that carriers that can make the most efficient use of slots will be able to obtain the numbers they require through either their bidding at an auction or secondary trading, and will subsequently buy and sell slots as markets change.

In practice, there are matters of political economy to consider as well as the technical nature of subsequent secondary markets. The way that slots are allocated is a concern; windfall gains accrue if incumbents are given property rights that would not be enjoyed by those wishing to join the market. It is thus no accident that many legacy carriers find voice in supporting this give-away approach. Lotteries by definition spread the windfall rents randomly but issues arise about who can participate and whether there are any payments to be made by winners. There is also the matter of whether the lotteries should be for pairs, combinations, or groups of slots. An extensive secondary market would be needed because the initial allocation is likely to be far from optimal.

But even if auctions are adopted there are issues akin to those inherent in Road Pricing, including that of ensuring that costs of maintaining existing capacity are recovered and how to finance and prioritize capacity expansion. With charges this problem involves notions of maintenance cost allocations between users and cost recovery that have to be embraced within the charging regime. While auctions of runway slots are certainly not free from problems, they do partially circumvent the need for excessive calculations.

The primary aim of a well-structured periodic auction of slots is to make sure that the winner is the carrier that will generate the most profit from the use of a slot or bundle of slots. Ideally, it is a neutral process whereby exogenous information has no influence. In addition, an appropriately structured auction, through the revenues it raises, both provides signals as to whether additional capacity is

---

43 S.J. Rassenti, V. Smith and R. Bulfin, 'A combinational auction mechanism for airport time slot allocation', *Bell Journal of Economics*, **13**, 369–84, 1982.

needed and also provides initial resources for capacity expansion. Indeed, the collection of a bid from the auction transfers the value of a slot to the airport and avoids the concerns with arbitrary initial allocations whereby airlines enjoy the wide-fall gains. Incorporating secondary markets into the structure allows for fine-tuning as markets evolve and making technical adjustments for imperfections in the auction procedure.

As with congestion charging, auctioning of runway slots has its problems and it is perhaps helpful to discuss these in a comparative context. The number and duration of slots that are seen as making efficient use of a runway has to be determined and this, like a congestion charge, is an external judgment. But it is very much akin to the real economic decisions made by industry every day – coffee is normally sold in cafes in cups and there is the issue of defining exactly what constitutes a 'cup'. While modeling, by definition, abstracts from reality, there are institutional constraints that implicitly shape both, including the definition of slots as well as 'coffee cups'. Roads are designed to engineering standards that affect, for example, the speeds at which one can drive and remain on the surface, and this is in addition to institutional issues such as speed limits and driving restrictions for safety and environmental reasons. These are largely taken as axiomatic in the Road Pricing analysis.

Runways are similarly restricted, with stall speeds limiting the number of take-offs and landings per hour, as well as institutional requirements dictating headways and hours of operation. While in the road case these factors can be incorporated in the assumptions needed for a continuous traffic flow (for example, in the maximum engineering flow) without much disruption, they are important for runways that involve only 60 or so movements an hour. The technical and institutional constraints that are part of airport operations essentially determine the capacity in terms of very discrete units. This makes the modeling of congestion pricing difficult.

If auctions are adopted, there are further issues to consider. One approach is a once-and-for-all auction with rights transferred to the airlines, and the other is a concession arrangement with periodic auctions of slots but with airports retaining property rights. The former has considerable theoretical attraction in that there is no requirement to externally determine the optimal frequency of auctions for concessions but may well be preferable to avoid the 'New York cab medallion problem', whereby existing holders resist any expansion in capacity to protect their monopoly powers, which highlights difficulties in increasing and allocating new capacity. However, the airlines have no incentive to support more slots.

In practice, slot delineations, again as with estimation of a Road Price, cannot be treated as independent of wider considerations. In the case of Road Pricing, there is the problem of the allocation of capacity to non-vehicles users, most notably pedestrians. Their pricing seems to be singularly ignored in the academic literature but they, and cyclists in some countries, probably constitute the largest number of movements on urban roads and, through their cross-automobile paths, the greatest congestion. The parallel at airports are non-aircraft movements on aprons. Added to this, there are matters of interactions between traffic at junctions and how this should be handled. In the case of urban traffic systems, light sequencing is partly designed to facilitate high flow but also take into account access needs of those on secondary roads and the overall safety of road users. The use of complicated runway configurations and the need to use runways for both take-off and landings are the aviation parallels.

Another difficulty often raised is the matter of how auction revenues should be used; they effectively transfer economic rent from carriers to the airport authority (be that a private or public agency). This is not a difficulty absent from congestion charging in atomistic markets, and deciding what to do with Road Pricing revenues has generated a small library of publications. If the airport is a rent maximizer then the auction becomes a form of price discrimination, with each slot being sold at a price that reduces its value to the purchasing airline to that yielding a normal profit. The airline holding a slot would use it efficiently, including taking account of any internal congestion considerations. The airport would use the revenue to make investments that offer the highest return irrespective of the sector involved. Strictly, if an airport is congested then there are grounds for using the revenue for capacity expansion, and the return would justify this.

Finally, while the general economic literature, which is not considered here, on auctions is extensive, no fully efficient and practical auction structure for allocating slots emerges, just as there is no ideal form of congestion charging. Although it poses some problems of its own, secondary trading in slots can provide a viable adjustment mechanism to correct for the worst misallocations of a primary auction and allow airlines to adjust their slot portfolios to meet take-off and landing requirements.[44] But these also have to be structured. As institutional economists frequently point out, markets do not arise and function in a vacuum but rather operate within a structure of formal laws and governances.

In practical terms, normally there is a place for trade to take place – in the twenty-first century this can be an electronic exchange – and there is the need for oversight of transactions, and methods of recording to ensure that property rights are transparent. These are not problematic and, indeed, exist in embryonic forms in several airport slot markets already and seem to impose minimal transaction costs. A more important concern is the possibility that the market will prove to be imperfect with monopoly power distorting its efficient functioning. In particular there may be concerns that participants will 'bank' certain slots that other airlines need to make efficient use of those slots they already have. The extent to which this can occur often depends not only on the underlying nature of the airline market and the details of the secondary slot market but also on the generic nature of competition laws in the country.

---

[44] UK Civil Aviation Authority, *The Implementation of Secondary Slot Trading*, London: CAA, 2001.

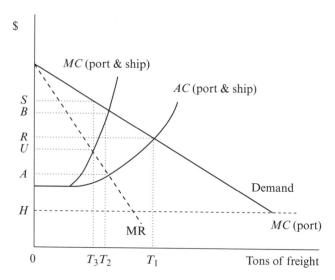

Figure 9.5   *Port congestion pricing*

9.8   Congested Seaports

Roads and airports are not the only areas where congestion pricing has been advocated. Walters,[45] for example, has argued that appropriate marginal cost pricing (including congestion charges) is 'no panacea for ailing or congested ports, but it does supply a useful set of principles to deploy in the discussion of port pricing policy'. Focusing on ports, the general principles are identical to Road Pricing, but in some circumstances the nature of the shipping industry may result in complications.[46] In the road context there is a monopoly supplier adopting social pricing policies coupled with competition for road space among many, uncoordinated potential users. While the majority of ports conform to this type of market situation, in some instances the port authorities are confronted by a monopoly (or, more likely, a cartel) of shipping companies.

Figure 9.5 shows the demand curve for shipping (the demand for port services may he seen as proportional to this) in terms of import and export traffic. The port is assumed to have constant marginal handling costs, $0H$, which are passed to the ship owners as port charges. The shipping companies, if competitive, would then charge these customers an additional amount, RH, to reflect their own average costs, to give a total shipping rate of $0R$. The AC of shipping will itself rise after a certain point as port congestion forces queuing to load and discharge. Since the AC curve does not reflect the true costs of increasing traffic, the port authority should, on welfare economic grounds, levy a congestion charge of AB.

[45]   A.A. Walters, 'Marginal cost pricing in ports', *Logistics and Transportation Review*, **12**, 99–105, 1976.

[46]   A.H. Vanags, 'Maritime congestion: an economic analysis', in R.O. Goss (ed.), *Advances in Maritime Economics*, Cambridge: Cambridge University Press, 1977.

Assuming that there is no potential for modifying the types of ship in service or methods of cargo handling, this will reduce the tonnage passing through the port from to the optimal level $0T_2$. This is identical to the Road Pricing case.

Suppose that instead of a competitive shipping market, the port was used exclusively by a closed liner conference. There are now two important differences. First, the conference, being the sole operator, will bear the costs of congestion itself – the congestion costs are internalized. Second, the conference is likely to act as a monopolist (although, as we have seen in previous chapters, countervailing powers act as a limited constraint in practice) and be more concerned with the marginal revenue curve than with demand. Thus the ship owner will charge customers a rate of $0S$ for his services which comprise port fees, $0H$, his own costs, including that of congestion, HU, and economic, monopoly, rent, US. The tonnage passing through the port is now suboptimally small at $0T_3$.

Although one might argue that in this situation the optimal use of the port could, technically, in some situations, be achieved by not charging a congestion toll and by reducing port fees below $0H$,[47] this rather evades the real problem, namely the monopoly power of the shipping conference. Such a policy also places excessive power in the hands of the conference when negotiating with port authorities the fees (and, *ipso facto*, the subsidy) to be charged. The solution here is to tackle distortions at source, namely, in the shipping market, rather than maladjusted port prices.

9.9   Non-congestion Pricing Options

The traditional approach to handling traffic congestion, be it on the roads or elsewhere, in the absence of appropriate economic pricing has been to increase capacity (which may entail civil engineering works or softer options such as the use of informatics) or to try to attract passengers or freight to less congested facilities such as public transport or the railways. These approaches have largely been advocated in part because they do not alienate road users, who, in terms of coalition theory form a powerful lobbying group, and in part because of the capture of the system by engineers and others that have a vested interested in infrastructure investments. We look at the implications of some of these alternatives.

Invest in More Capacity

As we have seen in Chapter 6, and earlier in this chapter, because there is congestion it does not necessarily mean that there is a shortage of capacity; it is often the result of inappropriate use and incorrect pricing. Adding capacity in these circumstances can be wasteful and seldom reduces the congestion problem in the long run.

---

[47] E. Bennathan and A.A. Walters, *Port Pricing and Investment Policy for Countries*, Oxford: Oxford University Press, 1979.

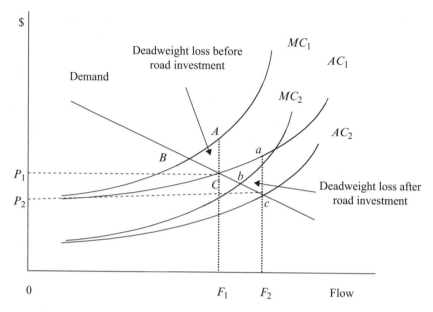

Figure 9.6   *The effects of expansion capacity on road congestion*

Figure 9.6 replicates the standard congestion diagram (essentially Figure 9.1) with a suboptimal traffic flow of F_1. An optimal road price would bring traffic levels back to the flow where MC_1 is equated to Demand (that is, at point B). In efficiency terms this means that without an appropriate charge the traffic flow F_1 results in a social, or 'deadweight' loss equal to the area ABC.

Increasing capacity affects the cost curves in the diagram; it pushes them down and to the right because at any flow the generalized cost is lower. The extra capacity need not come from physical investment but may be the result of introducing improved traffic control or information systems. If the additional investment pushes the marginal and average costs down to AC_2 and MC_2 then traffic flow will increase to F_2. At this flow, however, there is still excessive congestion resulting in a deadweight loss of abc, quite simply because the optimal use of the road after its expansion or the introduction of some enhanced informatics would be where MC_2 is equated with demand (that is, at point b in the figure).

Since mixing traffic (buses, cars, trucks, bicycles and so on) can worsen traffic flows because of their different engineering features, such as speed and acceleration, compound the problems of vehicle interaction, one policy approach is to segregate traffic and to construct mode-specific infrastructure. Truck-only lanes, for example, are under study as tools to combat road congestion, enhance safety and reduce other external costs of road traffic. The benefits of separating cars and trucks depend on several factors: the relative volumes of cars and trucks, the congestion delay and safety hazards that each vehicle type imposes, values of travel time for each type, and lane capacity indivisibilities. The optimal assignment of vehicles to road capacity can be supported using Road Pricing that differentiates by vehicle type and lane. Lane access restrictions, however, were found by Andrà de Palma and colleagues not to be that useful and a priced lane for one vehicle type is generally more effective.[48] The benefits of all forms of intervention, though, are sensitive to whether the proportions of cars and trucks are commensurate with lane capacities.

One way of looking at the effects of infrastructure on traffic congestion is to examine the effects of national construction programs. In an econometric study of highway spending and the cost of traffic congestion (as measured by the Texas Transportation Institute) in 74 urban areas in the United States covering 1982 to 1996, Winston and Langer,[49] found that, 'on average, one dollar of highway spending in a given year reduced the congestion costs to road users only eleven cents in that year'. Part of this may, of course, be because the investments were not optimal, but nevertheless, the congestion-reducing effects do not appear large.

One of the reasons why capacity expansion has often been seen as a way of optimizing congestion is that an implicit assumption of many traffic forecasting models is that the demand curve for road use is perfectly inelastic, whereas in reality the evidence from the Road Pricing schemes that have been initiated suggests that this is far from the case. We shall return to this issue when discussing the economic aspects of transport forecasting modeling.

Improved traffic management, including the adoption of electronic ITSs, has the same effect as building more capacity. It allows more vehicles to use a road, but without any system of limiting entry, simply leads to additional traffic bringing the flow back to the initial level. As an example, the perennially congested south-western stretch of the M25 ring road around London has been fitted with an experimental automated traffic control system called Motorway Incident Detection and Automatic Signalling (MIDAS). This consists of a distributed network of traffic and weather sensors, speed cameras and variable-speed signs that control traffic speeds with little human supervision, but it has done little to alleviate traffic problems.

Subsidize Fewer Congestion-causing Modes

Some modes of transport can technically make more efficient use of infrastructure than others, and thus there are arguments advanced for stimulating their use rather than congestion-inducing modes such as the motorcar.[50] In the road context, the most common approach is to subsidize public transport modes. Buses, trams and metro systems can in most circumstances when fully loaded move more people than the motorcar for a given land-take. In terms of the standard congestion diagram, subsidizing, say a bus service, shifts the demand for car use down and to the left as seen in Figure 9.7. The welfare implications are that,

---

[48] A. de Palma, M. Kilani and R. Lindsey, 'The merits of separating cars and trucks', *Journal of Urban Economics*, **64**, 340–61, 2008.

[49] C. Winston and A. Langer, 'The effect of government highway spending on road users' congestion costs', *Journal of Urban Economics*, **60**, 463–83, 2006.

[50] D.A. Hensher, 'Modal diversion', in K.J. Button and D.A. Hensher (eds), *Handbook of Transport Systems and Traffic Control*, Oxford: Pergamon, 2001.

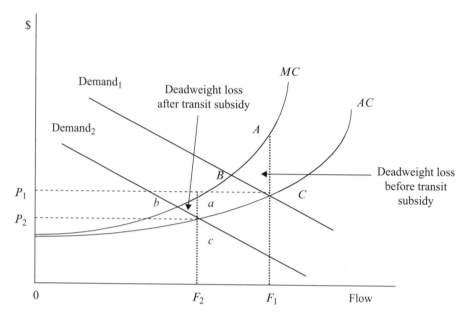

Figure 9.7   *The effects on road traffic of subsidizing rapid transit*

whereas without out any congestion initiatives, there is a loss of *ABC*, by attracting some travelers from the car to a bus the loss declines to *abc*. Excess congestion
costs remain, because the lower generalized costs of road use will cause some
people who did not travel before to make trips.

This type of policy has attractions, especially in circumstances when the subsidies also benefit low-income public transport services. Often, however, there are
difficulties. For the subsidies to stimulate a significant traffic effect, there must, as
discussed earlier, be a relatively high-fare cross elasticity of demand. As we have
seen in Chapter 4, the cross-elasticities between modes often tend to be relatively
low. The general evidence suggests that lowering fares often has little impact when
it comes to attracting traffic to buses; at the extreme one can witness the reluctance
of schoolchildren in the US to use free and convenient 'yellow buses' once they can
drive a car. There is some limited support for the position that improved service
(speed, frequency and reliability), and especially in terms of rapid transit systems,
can affect modal transfers to some extent, but this is an expensive option.

The second issue is that there are generally deadweight losses associated with
subsidies that we touched upon in Chapter 7, and just highlight again in a slightly
different way.

First, a subsidy will result in a simple loss in terms of waste in the public
transport sector. In Figure 9.8 it is assumed that the public transit undertaking,
which for simplicity we assume has its own track, is run effectively and is economically priced. Further, and just for ease of exposition, it is assumed that the
marginal cost of each public transport passenger is constant, thus giving an initial
fare of F_1. A subsidy is then introduced to reduce fares to F_2 to attract travelers
from their automobiles. The cost of that subsidy is the shaded area F_1F_2bc; the

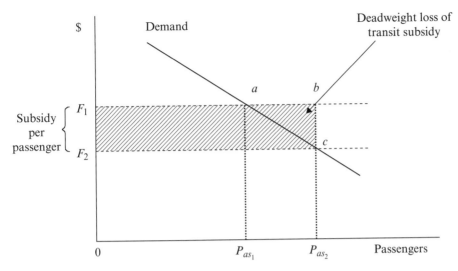

Figure 9.8   *The deadweight losses of subsidies*

subsidy times the number of passengers that ultimately use the public transport. Part of the subsidy goes to the P_{as_1} passengers who are already riders and the rest to those who actually give up their cars. Those already on the public transport enjoy a transfer of money from taxpayers; this has no resource effects if prices elsewhere in the economy are optimal, although there are differential effects on bus riders and taxpayers.

The amount that is needed to stimulate the $P_{as_1} - P_{as_2}$ transfer to public transport entails a degree of waste. In this case it is equal to an amount *abc* in the figure. This is a loss because while the P_{as_1}th transfer needs the full subsidy to cause the transfer, the P_{as_2}th person needs very little. But in addition to this, there is also the potential significant X-inefficiency in terms of the ways that subsidies are actually used. Much depends, as we saw in Chapter 7, on the way in which subsidies are awarded to public transport suppliers.

Further Reading

A rigorous discussion of congestion pricing is to be found in R. Lindsey and E. Verhoef, 'Traffic congestion and congestion pricing', in K.J. Button and D.A. Hensher (eds), *Handbook of Transport Systems and Traffic Control*, Oxford: Pergamon, 2001. A useful summary of the diverse forms of pioneering quasi-road pricing schemes that have been deployed is to be found in J.A. Gómez-Ibáñez and K.A. Small, *Road Pricing for Congestion Management: A Survey of International Practice*, Washington, DC: National Academy Press, 1994. Collections of largely readable papers dealing with congestion optimization include: G. Santos (ed.), *Road Pricing: Theory and Evidence*, Research in Transportation Economics, 9, Amsterdam: Elsevier, 2004; K.J. Button and E.T. Verhoef (eds), *Road Pricing, Traffic Congestion and the Environment*, Cheltenham, UK and Lyme,

NH, USA: Edward Elgar, 1998; and G. Roth (ed.), *Street Smart: Competition, Entrepreneurship, and the Future of Roads*, Washington, DC: The Independent Institute, 2006. For a discussion of airport congestion issues, see K.J. Button, 'Issues in airport runway capacity charging and allocation', *Journal of Transport Economics and Policy*, **42**, 563–85, 2008.

In terms of the various technologies that can be used for congestion charging, see D.N. Cottingham, A. Beresford and R. Harle 'Survey of technologies for the implementation of national-scale road user charging', *Transport Reviews*, **27**, 499–523, 2007.

10　Some Economics of Transport Logistics

· ·

10.1　Introduction

Economists have long recognized that transport services are not provided in isolation. Indeed the very fact that they appreciate that transport providers are confronted by a derived demand curve makes this explicit. It has also been made clear in our earlier discussion of the value-chain concept. For a variety of reasons, not least of which were the technical ability to actually do it and a rapidly growing demand for international trade facilitation, the larger notion of transport logistics began to be developed in the 1990s. This is effectively a more holistic way of looking at transport; in effect redefining its boundaries to move outside of the simple movement of, in the case of freight logistics, goods from A to B.

The analysis of optimal supply chains is very much a matter of maximizing the efficiency of resource allocations and considering the best way of using scarce resources. It is about opportunity costs and thus it is about economics. Many of the findings of the work that has been done in the supply-chain field, however, have tended to appear in the management literature, or specialized logistics publications, rather than in mainstream economics journals. This is not the place to consider why this is so, although there has certainly been an element of the practical leading the theoretical in many of the developments that have taken place in supply-chain management, and much of the recent economic literature has tended to be rather abstract in its orientation. Here we focus on the main areas where there are particular differences or refinements in the way that economics is applied compared to that often covered in the more conventional transport economics texts.

The chapter is largely about the private provision of logistics services, but this provision is always within particular institutional and policy frameworks. These are largely taken as given, and discussed only when of immediate relevance to the economics of an issue. But they are important and it is clear that one reason why modern transport logistics has grown in importance in business is that there have been significant changes in the legal constructs under which transport services, and trade more generally, can be delivered.

In addition, the focus is largely on the private sector businesses, but as David Quarmby[1] and others have pointed out, there are also issues involving the

---

[1] D.A. Quarmby, 'Developments in the retail market and their effect on freight distribution', *Journal of Transport Economics and Policy*, **23**, 75–87, 1989.

provision and management of public sector transport infrastructure. For example, the scale and quality of road and rail networks affect such things as warehouse distribution and the extent to which just-in-time management of the supply chain is possible. This also raises economic issues of a different kind, namely how to appraise public infrastructure investments; the conventional cost–benefit procedures that we consider in the following chapter would appear inadequate to the extent that they do not fully encapsulate the benefits throughout the supply chain. This is not a topic dealt with in any depth here, but really reflects the partial equilibrium nature of the economic cost–benefit approach.

10.2   What Is 'Transport Logistics'?

Transport logistics has a long history, and in many ways is the adoption of transport economic principles within a larger supply-chain concept. Definitions of what transport logistics entails are not always precise, but one useful idea put forward by the British logistics expert, Jim Cooper, is that it is the 'relationship between transport and integrated approaches to logistics and supply chain management'. In other words, it involves the movement of goods through the supply chain, but is more than just the freight transport aspect and embraces the full commercial and operational frameworks within which the movement of goods is planned, managed and finally carried out.

The modern, large-scale academic study of civilian transport logistics started in the early 1990s, when many of the current approaches were originally developed, but there was both an implicit interest in it going back centuries, and a more systematic study of military logistics from classical times.

Logistics has always been important for the military, and transporting men and equipment to the battle-front in a timely and coordinated fashion has since the time of Alexander the Great given armies a decided advantage. The advent of mechanized transport and of massive, often conscript, armies has made the task more complex but possibly also more important. One reason for the failure of the German army to capture Paris in 1914, for example, was the inadequacy of transport logistics support; in effect, it was impossible to move the number of men and their supplies through Northern France to conform with the needs of the Schlieffen Plan. More recently, the overwhelming military success of Operation *Desert Storm* in Kuwait in 1990 was in part due to the transport logistics expertise of US General William (Gus) Pagonis.

More recently, the crucial role of logistics in the civilian sector has been recognized by the appointment of logistics experts to the boards of many major corporations – positions formerly largely reserved for financial, marketing and production executives. There are also many companies that specialize in transport logistics, in addition to the in-house divisions of companies, and in many cases this involves international activities as the 'global economy' grows and the supply chains grow longer and more complex. The educational establishment has also not been slow to recognize the modern role of logistics, and many of the prestigious business schools around the world offer options in logistics as elements of their MBA programs.

This change has come about for a variety of reasons: some are economic in their nature and others stem from the emergence of new technologies. Before looking at some of these in a little more detail, two overriding trends have been important in shaping the form of modern logistics. First, the length of freight hauls has increased due to wider outsourcing and new approaches to centralization, inventory holding and terminal capacity. This means that production is now more transport intensive. Second, there has been a 'time-compression' in production and distribution that has put pressures on the system for more rapid delivery of intermediate and final goods. This, in turn, has reduced inventory holdings, making the production chain more vulnerable to disruptions in the transport system.

At the more meso-level, in terms of technology, the advent of the container in the 1960s, and the fact that Malcom McLean did not seek any patent on his invention, revolutionized the way that movement of semi-bulk cargoes could be conducted, reducing the costs of movement almost immediately. In 1983, US foreign ocean-borne commerce was 694.4 million metric tons; 10 years later, this had increased to 884.4. Ten years after that, it had magnified to 1,167.9 million metric tons, nearly doubling in just 20 years. Growth of this magnitude is physically possible only through the use of containers.

The container not only cuts the costs of individual movements by a single mode of transport, but speeds up and cuts the cost of trans-shipment and consolidations between modes, making intermodal transport a viable form of freight movement. Intermodal freight transport is movement of cargo in a container using multiple modes of transport (rail, ship and truck) without any handling of the freight itself when changing modes. It also allows for easier handling of mixed types of cargo on a single mode – a container can have its own refrigeration unit or can be a 'tank' within a container-size frame. The standardization of the unit being carried allowed for economies of scale in the cost of manufacturing ships, wagons and so on. A container is also relatively easy to track, and can be sealed to enhance security.

The types of goods being carried have also changed, in part because of the availability of container transport and on-vehicle storage facilities (for example, refrigeration). There are more high-value, less-bulky commodities being moved, and their origins and destinations are more dispersed than with most primary products. Their value means that holding large inventories can be costly and also, that there are often economies in minimizing warehousing and storage. Inventory management requires reliable delivery to ensure that goods and components are available at the right time and undamaged. 'Just-in-time production' requires complex logistics, including information systems, to ensure that the generalized cost of the supply chain is minimized.

Supply chains vary in their form and scale depending on factors such as whether they are domestic or international, involve perishable goods, are mainly bulk commodities, the costs of inventory holding, and whether special services

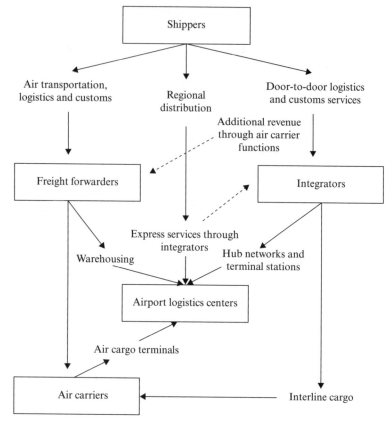

Source: Derived from J.D. Kasarda, J. Green and D. Sullivan, *Air Cargo: Engine of Economic Development, Center for Air Commerce*, Chapel Hill, NC: University of North Carolina, 2004.

Figure 10.1 *The supply chain for air cargo*

are required, such as refrigeration. They can also vary by direction, for example involving the movement of bulk commodities in one direction and exotics, such as agricultural products, in the other. They are also frequently multimodal, often involving collection and delivery by one mode but trunk haul by another. In some cases there may be considerable interaction between the freight supply chain and passenger transport; for example, trucks and cars share road space, and many 'passenger' aircraft carry freight in their belly holds.

In terms of economics, the logistics supply chain may be thought of as a set of interdependent markets, or in some cases a single market, for transport services. Figure 10.1 provides a very simple illustration of the air cargo supply chain. In depicting this, we assume that air is the chosen mode of transport, which will itself be an economic decision; in some cases road or rail may also be an option, and in a few cases, maritime transport. The shippers may send goods directly through their own regional distribution centers, may engage an integrated carrier, such as UPS or Federal Express that offers door-to-door multimodal services, or they may go to a freight forwarder that basically offers wholesale services.

The decision on the option to take is economic and involves considering the generalized costs of the alternatives *vis-à-vis* their respective services. This is a market decision. But there are also submarkets in the chain. While the shipper may select a particular airfreight forwarder, that forwarder will obtain capacity on air cargo carriers by bidding for space.

Looked at from the supply side, the various air cargo chains that coexist reflect the different business models that exist which in turn can be explained in economic terms. Ronald Coase,[2] many years ago, provided the classic economic reason for different types of industrial structure, and in particular why firms exist. The main reason stems from the existence of transaction costs. He argues that a firm's interactions within a market may not be under its control, but the firm's internal allocation of resources are. Consequently, the integrated suppliers that manage the chain internally cater mainly for small, high-value goods that require rapid and reliable service, whereas, the use of forwarders reflects the need for less-structured, but cheaper services that accompany more general cargoes.

10.3   Transport Costs, Warehousing and Inventory Holdings

Savings in freight travel time are an important, although not always the crucial, indicator of improvements in the efficiency of freight transport. The methods of valuing such savings for use in the economic analysis of firms or for forecasting aggregate traffic flows in transport infrastructure planning, are similar to those that are used in valuing passenger travel time savings (see Chapter 4). The savings, however, can be related to a number of units – for example, to truck trips, ship sailings, or rail wagons – in addition to the actual item being transported. Table 10.1 offers a survey of the sorts of results that have emerged across a range of studies covering inland waterways, air transport, railroads and trucking, taking account of the country to which the study relates, the type of data used and the methodology adopted.

There are wide variations in the results, and drawing general conclusions is not simple. Much depends on what is being carried, saving a few hours for a ton of coal may not be worth a great deal, but delays in supplying a crucial component for a damaged piece of equipment may be very costly. Modes of transport can also be important because of their particular security and safety features as well as their position in the supply chain. We also note that most of the studies that have been undertaken have used stated preference techniques, and these would in general seem to generate relatively higher values for time savings than the small number of revealed preference studies cited.

Freight is not always on the move in the logistics supply chain, but is periodically held in storage. The economics of warehousing is essentially about efficient inventory holding. The role of a warehouse is that of storage. Referring back to Figure 1.2 in Chapter 1, warehouses can also be seen as providing for

---

2 R.H. Coase, 'The nature of the firm', *Economica*, **4**, 386–405, 1937.

Table 10.1   *Value of time in goods transport by rail, inland waterways, trucking and air transport*

Publication	Country	Data	Method	Value of travel time savings
				€ per transport hour
Rail transport				
Transek (1990)	Sweden	SP	Logit	1 (wagon)
Inregia (2001)	Sweden	SP	Logit	0 (shipment)
de Jong et al. (2004)	Netherlands	SP	Logit	918 (train)
Air transport				
Inregia (2001)	Sweden	SP	Logit	13 (shipment)
de Jong et al. (2004)	Netherlands	SP	Logit	7,935 (full carrier)
				€ per tonne-hour
Trucking				
Transek (1990)	Sweden	SP	Logit	2
de Jong et al. (1992)	Netherlands	SP	Logit	35
Widlert & Bradley (1992)	Sweden	SP	Logit	7
de Jong et al. (1995)	France	SP	Logit	32
Fosgerau (1996)	Denmark	SP	Logit	29–67
Small et al. (1999)	USA	SP	Logit	174–267
Kawamura (2000)	USA	SP	Logit+OLS	22–25
Bergkvist (2001)	Sweden	SP	Logit+WML	3–47
de Jong et al. (2001)	France	SP+RP	Logit	5–11
Fowkes et al. (2001)	UK	SP	Logit	40
Inregia (2001)	Sweden	SP	Logit	0–32
Fowkes et al. (1991)	UK	SP	Logit	0.08–1.18
Kurri et al. (2000)	Finland	SP	Logit	1.53
De Jong et al. (2004)	Netherlands	SP	Logit	4.74
Rail transport				
Fowkes et al. (1991)	UK	SP	Logit	0.08–1.21
De Jong et al. (1992)	Netherlands	SP	Logit	0.81
Vieira (1992)	USA	SP/RP	Ordered logit	0.65
Widlert & Bradley (1992)	Sweden	SP	Logit	0.03
Kurri et al. (2000)	Finland	SP	Logit	0.09
De Jong et al. (2004)	Netherlands	SP	Logit	0.96
Inland waterways				
Roberts (1981)	USA	RP	Cost model	>0.05
Blauwens & Van de Voorde (1998)	Belgium	RP	Logit	0.09
de Jong et al. (2004)	Netherlands	SP	Logit	0.05

Notes: SP are stated preference models and RP are revealed preference models. OLS = ordinary least squares and WML = weighted maximum likelihood.

Source: Adapted from G. De Jong, 'Value of freight travel time savings', in D.A. Hensher and K.J. Button (eds), *Handbook of Transport Modelling*, 2nd edn, Amsterdam: Elsevier, 2008. Full references to the studies are contained therein.

consolidation and points between elements in the value chain, but we leave discussion of that role to the next section. Warehousing, within the narrow, traditional-context, serves a number of functions:[3]

[3] K.B. Ackerman and A.M. Brewer, 'Warehousing: a key link in the supply chain', in A.M. Brewer, K.J. Button and D.A. Hensher (eds), *Handbook of Logistics and Supply-chain Management*, Oxford: Pergamon, 2001.

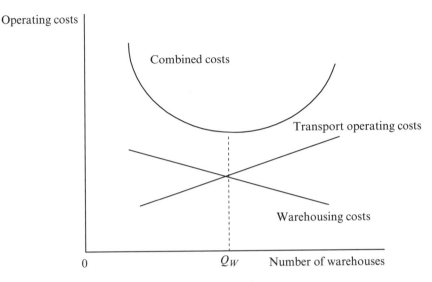

Figure 10.2   *Trade-off in transport and warehouse operating costs*

- Accumulations of raw materials for distribution further down the supply chain.
- Storage of in-process inventory at various points in the logistics pipeline.
- Storage of finished goods near the point of production.
- Storage of wholesale or retail inventory pending distribution to final customers.

From an economics perspective, warehousing is a clear cost. There are the fixed and variable costs of the warehousing activity itself, but there are also the costs of holding inventory in the system. These are the direct costs of having assets sitting in a warehouse, but added to these are the costs of physical decay of the products, its potential redundancy in the supply chain, a major concern for fashion items, and the danger of theft or damage being done. The benefits of warehousing come in reducing risk in the system, for example, by having spare stock to meet contingencies, and in allowing economies of scale in production and in the transport. In the context of the last, it allows larger units to be transported less frequently.

One aspect of inventory optimization that has gained in importance in recent years relates less to the area served by a producing unit and rather more to the area served by warehouses. Changes in transport technology and information systems combined with the increased importance of high-value, low-weight manufactures in the economy have brought forth new physical distribution systems. The traditional model (Figure 10.2) assumed a trade-off between warehousing and transport, with the costs of operating warehouses rising with their number but transport costs falling, assuming a constant throughput of goods. The optimal number of warehouses would be determined by minimizing the combined costs of warehousing and transport (that is, Q_w).

Table 10.2   *The benefits of just-in-time production*

Area of improvement	Description
Productivity	Manufacturing productivity can improve by 20 to 40%
Lead times	Lead times can be reduced by more than 90%, reducing the need to carry finished goods inventories
Flexibility	Improves production flexibility, by allowing changes to the manufacturing schedule to meet changes in market demand
Market power	Market position is strengthened by the ability to supply on short notice, with greater flexibility and greater reliability
Quality	Consistency of quality improves
Inventories	Substantially reduces inventories, often by 60 to 80%
Floor space	Manufacturing floor space requirements are reduced by 30 to 40% because there is no 'waiting' inventory stacking on the floor
Investment	Capital required to operate a business is significantly reduced, estimated reductions being 25 to 50%

Source: J. Warne, M.J. Rowney and Technology Transfer Council, *The Toyota Just in Time Production System and Early Experience with ZIPS (Zero Inventory Production System)*, Canberra: TTC, 1986.

Modifications have incorporated the costs of holding inventories, essentially warehousing and handling, into the calculations that, in the simplest of terms, argue that variations in the costs of holding inventories follows the 'square root law'. This law effectively says that safety and cycle inventory requirements are related to the square root of the number of warehouses in the system. Hence, moving from a system of 10 depots to an entirely centralized system would reduce inventory requirements by 68 percent. This has provided justification for companies reducing the number of warehouses and with this the market area served by each. The breakeven point for degrees of warehousing, however, is sensitive to prevailing costs of holding inventories; in effect to the interest rate.

Reducing warehousing essentially means that more inventory is being held in the narrower transport system, in containers on trucks or rail cars, or in the holds of ships or aircraft (transit inventory). This has been made more attractive as the costs of tracking and tracing have fallen as telecommunications and related technologies have advanced in sophistication and fallen in cost. This has not only made the transport system more internally efficient, but by providing more information to consignors, has given the ability to reduce inventory holdings. This is the basis for just-in-time production, or 'lean logistics'. Some of the claimed gains that can result optimal from just-in-time, as opposed to conventional, production are listed in Table 10.2.

The challenge is to find the optimal mix between using more transport to facilitate more frequent deliveries and greater reliability in those deliveries and the reduction in inventory holdings. What a manager is trying to do is to optimize his/her stock, which consists of three elements:

Target stock = Forecast demand next period + Forecast demand in lead time + Safety stock.

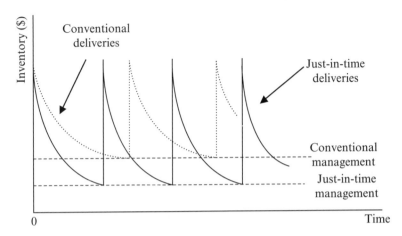

Figure 10.3   *The economics of just-in-time production*

The problem is that the forecast elements have inherent uncertainty in them, and so the safety stock acts as a buffer. Improved transport systems, packaging and information systems have effectively reduced the scale of inventory holdings required for safety purposes. Much of the rise in just-in-time practices came with the advent of 'dependent demand inventory' systems from the late 1960s which, rather than traditional approaches that relied on forecasts premised on overall demand being made up of a large number of independent separate demands, focused attention on the interdependent needs for delivering a target near-term output.

The possibility of more frequent deliveries means that the period over which demands are made is shorter and thus uncertainty is reduced. It is not just reduced lead times (the period between which an order is placed and the delivery of that order) that are important, but also the reliability of delivery. Rail transport, for example, in the United States is often used in just-in-time manufacturing systems because of its reliability rather than its speed. Of course, higher costs of meeting short lead times have to be taken into account in the arithmetic. Figure 10.3 offers a fairly simple illustration of the situation.

Conventional management requires that there is always a fairly large safety stock of inventory to cope with unexpected contingencies. On the other hand it has large and infrequent deliveries of stock that it holds in its warehouses. Just-in-time inventories are small in magnitude but the number of deliveries is larger. To maximize efficiency, the manager requires to set the cost of alternative delivery patterns against the level of stock that is being warehoused.

10.4   Consolidation and Trans-shipment

Warehousing is simply a storage function and adds little value to the supply again other than providing insurance through the holding of safety stocks. A more dynamic form of warehousing involves consolidation and trans-shipment:

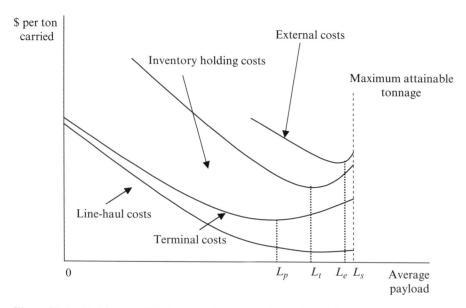

Figure 10.4   *Freight consolidation costs (represented cumulatively)*

a direct element of value added to the logistics supply chain. When warehousing is used in this way, it becomes part of a hub-and-spoke structure that enables the suppliers in the system to benefit from economies of scope and density in the logistics chain just as airports do in the provision of air passenger services (see Chapter 5).

To look at the optimum level of consolidation, it is useful to break down the costs involved along the lines of Figure 10.4. The diagram considers the problem in terms of the optimal payload for a delivery vehicle and in this case we use trucks as an example. The line-haul costs of moving goods to and from the consolidation point fall with the size of consignment carried due to scale effects, until the maximum physical or legal average payload on a vehicle is reached. If only haulage costs were to be considered in the warehousing decisions, then this would represent the optimal payload. However, there are also the resource costs involved with warehousing and consolidation itself – the provision of depots, handling staff, administrative costs and so on. These terminal costs are likely to rise with the level of warehousing and trans-shipment. Consequently, the logistics supply chain manager, when considering options and taking both broad elements of cost into account will feel that the optimal level of consolidation would imply an average payload of L_p in the diagram.

So far we have looked at only the terminal and movement costs confronting the transporter; however, the final customer awaiting delivery will also have costs that vary with trans-shipment levels. The greater the amount of warehousing, and the larger the final average payload per vehicle, then the fewer the number of deliveries that will be needed. Longer frequencies between deliveries push up the costs of stockholding for customers and the overall level of inventories held. Thus the time costs of increased consolidation rise with average payload suggesting that, overall, final recipients of goods would prefer a level of consolidation consistent with an average payload of L_t in Figure 10.4.

The diagram shows a clear distinction between the direct costs influencing the transporter's optimum and those factors affecting the final customer of the service, and it is the bringing together of these elements that supply-chain logistics embraces.

As we have seen in Chapter 6, there are also wider external costs influencing those not directly concerned with transport operations; these include those affected by vehicle noise or fumes or who have their own travel disrupted by freight vehicles. Generally, increased consolidation and higher payloads will reduce these costs, because fewer trips are needed, even if just-in-time production is part of the process, to transport the same volume of goods, and consolidation generally means that less environmentally intrusive vehicles can be used in sensitive areas.[4] Hence, from society's point of view, the optimal level of consolidation in the diagram is when all costs are minimized, that is, at point L_e.

10.5   The Mode Choice

Logistics is not a transport mode-specific activity and entails the use of a diversity of modes, either within a single logistics provider's own fleet or through the use of forwarders and consolidators who make use of third-party transport suppliers. The way mode choices are made within a supply chain are, in economic terms, not that conceptually different from the way individuals make decisions whether to, say, make a trip by car or by bus. It is all about opportunity costs. We consider the more technical aspects of modeling and forecasting in more detail in Chapter 12 and here just provide a flavor of the type of models that are used. We also focus on the more micro models, rather than those that are used, for example, in national network planning.[5]

One way of looking at the decision-making process of logistics services providers is to treat the alternative modes as a bundle of attributes – availability, speed, cost, capacity, security, safety and so on – and then select the mode that comes closest to meeting the providers' requirements, given their financial and other constraints. This is the approach adopted by Baumol and Vinod[6] when considering a situation where speed and economy of service are important; adding more factors complicates the mathematics but not the logic.

Speed is important to minimize the amount of 'inventory on wheels',

[4] K.J. Button and A.D. Pearman, *The Economics of Urban Freight Transport*, Basingstoke: Macmillan, 1981.
[5] K.J. Button, 'Can freight transport models be transferred across the Atlantic?', in A. Regiani and L. Schintler (eds), *Methods and Models in Transport and Telecommunications: Across Atlantic Perspectives*, New York: Springer-Verlag, 2005.
[6] W.J. Baumol and H.D. Vinod, 'An inventory theoretical model of freight transport demand', *Management Science*, **16**, 413–21, 1970.

essentially the lead time, and regular services to termini are usually preferred by consignors for their own production purposes – the possibility of delays necessitating keeping a larger safety stock. Initially the problem of safety stocks is assumed away and an iso-cost equation of the general form is used:

$$e = vp/(Kvp - 1) \tag{10.1}$$

where:

e is the reciprocal of the shipping cost per unit of commodity;
v is the reciprocal of the average time required to complete a shipment;
p is the reciprocal; and
K is set equal to the expected annual variable cost of handling.

Allowances need to be made for uncertainty in delivery and safety stocks, and doing this provides an operational model of the form:

$$C = T/e + T/(pv) + a/s + wsT/2 + wh\{[s + (1/v)]\} T^{0.5} \tag{10.2}$$

where:

C is the expected annual variable cost of handling;
T is the amount transported per year;
a is the cost of ordering and processing per shipment;
w is the warehousing cost per unit per year;
s is the average time between shipments; and
h is a parameter derived from the Poisson distribution used to simulate the stochastic elements of the problem.

The final items in equation (10.2) reflect the fact that when the timing of deliveries is uncertain, slow deliveries require larger safety stocks which increase the costs of warehousing. A shipper will select the mode of transport that will complete the delivery at the lowest annual variable cost of handling.

This approach provides guidance as to the mode that would be selected for a particular consignment, but not the demand for the services of any given mode. The latter may, however, be of interest for the providers, either in the public or private sectors, which provide infrastructure and operational capital (truck fleets, rail cars, ships and so on). Aggregate demand can be assessed if it is assumed that profit maximization is the goal of the providers (which is largely realistic, say for US railroads but not for state-owned roads); that the demand curve is linear of the form $\Delta c = \alpha - \beta T$; and that the safety stock is proportional to the total volume of shipments (rather than the square root specification used in equation (10.2)). This then gives:

$$T = (1/b)\{\Delta c - 1/e - 1/(pv) - ws/2 - wh[s+(1/v)]^{0.5}\} \tag{10.3}$$

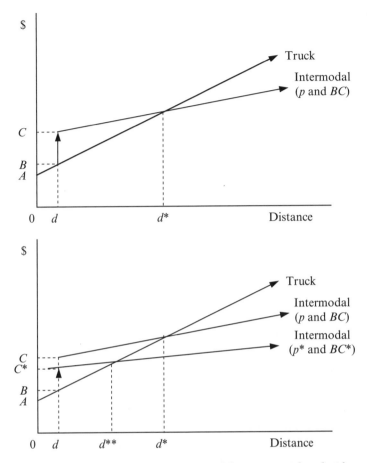

Figure 10.5   *The costs per ton of direct and intermodal transport with and without support for trans-shipping and rail rates*

where: Δc is the price difference between origin and destination and b is a constant equal to $-d\Delta c/dT$.

This illustrates the fact that the annual tonnage shipped will be larger, the greater the price difference between the destination and the origin, the smaller the time taken between shipments, the smaller the time taken by a shipment and the flatter the slope (b) of the demand curve for the commodity. However, these intuitively satisfying conclusions come at a price. The linear specification of the model is convenient for estimation purposes but may deviate significantly from reality.

The analysis of William Baumol and Vinod is really about warehousing and inventory management; it does not fully take account of consolidation and trans-shipment which is an integral part of many supply chains. This is often a multimodal (intermodal) activity – for example, using shipping for the long haul and trucks and rail for access and egress to and from ports. The question then often becomes one of whether to use the same transport mode for the entire trip – say the truck as in Figure 10.5 – or to use a combination of modes and trans-shipments or consolidate at some point in the system.

Table 10.3   *Reasons for electing to use a company's own truck fleet*

Factor	Score
Reliability	14.9
Control	13.0
Customer relations	9.4
Speed of delivery	9.2
Flexibility	7.8
Cost versus price	7.4
Ability of 'own account' to meet timing constraints	6.6
Price is subordinate to service considerations	6.5
Specialized capacity	5.5
Speed of response	5.1
Adaptability	3.6
Consistency	3.5
Avoidance of damage of consignment	3.4
Security	2.6
Other (non-financial)	1.1
Other (financial)	0.5

Source: UK Department of Transport (1979), *Road Haulage Operators Licensing Report of the Independent Committee of Enquiry into Road Haulage Operators' Licensing*, London: HMSO, 1979.

Figure 10.5 offers a fairly simple example of what this means and the implications of technical change, or policy shifts, in terms of mode split.[7] This considers an option of moving freight from A to B using either a truck or a rail/truck combination. The top diagram shows a comparison between trucking which is a load/unloading cost of $0A$ plus a trucking rate of r per mile. The cost by intermodal road and rail is $0A$ plus AB (the cost of using a truck over distance $0d$) plus the trans-shipment cost of BC plus a rail rate of p per mile. The cut-off point in the figure when intermodal transport become less costly than rail is at $0d^*$. The relative mile rates of the r and p, combined with the trans-shipment costs, determines this point. If there are technical changes, which one may think of in terms of the advent of container technology, whereby these parameters are reduced so that $BC^* < BC$ and $p^* < p$, then this will shift the comparative advantages of the alternatives; the threshold distance would decrease to $d^* < d$ for intermodal transport.

A further aspect of mode choice is the extent to which third-party logistics, the employment of an outside transport operator and logistics suppliers, should be engaged and the degree to which a company should operate its own transport fleet ('own account operations' in the United Kingdom). Surveys conducted over the years, such as that in the United Kingdom and reported in Table 10.3, suggest that simple cost of carriage does not dominate decisions regarding third-party carriage use, but broader notions of costs and quality of service, such as

[7] M. Beuther and F. Kreutzerberger, 'Consolidation and trans-shipment', in A.M. Brewer, K.J. Button and D.A. Hensher (eds), *Handbook of Logistics and Supply-chain Management*, Oxford: Pergamon, 2001

reliability, security and flexibility also play a role. While the exact weights placed on the individual items inevitably vary with industrial sector, the size of companies, and change over time, the items listed remain much the same. Globalization, lead-time reductions, customer orientation and outsourcing have, for example, been important considerations since the 1990s. Further, new firms from different fields have entered the market, competing with the traditional transport and warehousing firms to offer different packages of service attributes.[8]

10.6   Urban Logistics

Many of the challenges in logistics involve collection and delivery in urban areas – often called the 'last-mile problem'. This may be misleading because urban freight transport can involve four types of movement – in, out, within and through – and clearly the last two may not be the last mile of a trip. At the same time, because collection and delivery are often done by road transport which uses a common infrastructure with passenger modes, and can involve numerous stops, urban distribution can add more than proportionately to larger traffic congestion problems.

What constitutes urban freight transport in this context is not, however, clearly defined. There has, for example, been a considerable reduction compared with 50 years ago, in the number of household deliveries of goods; people collect goods from stores, and in particular large hyper- and supermarkets. Should this be treated as part of this 'last-mile problem' or is it part of consumption behavior?[9] The issue may be seen in terms of whether the purpose of a trip is explicitly to transport freight, but even here it is not always easy to separate out the urban logistics part of a multipurpose trip from say, that part involving getting to or from work.[10] We have a joint product situation in these circumstances.

Table 10.4 provides a categorization of the various commercial transport segments serving the urban market. It shows quite distinct market segments meeting the demands for carriage of various types of commodity. From a transport economic perspective, no single market structure emerges. Couriers, for example, which often include integrated suppliers such as FedEx, DHL and UPS, offer extensive networks of service with multiple local pick-up and delivery points – often a *de facto* personal service – and there are clear economies of scope and density involved. Other, more specialized types of service, have simpler networks and are thus more amenable to competitive supply.

Improving urban logistics can have significant economic benefits for their users. Table 10.5 offers a few examples of both the importance of local freight transport, and also some of the gains that have come about by enhancing the

---

[8] S. Hertz and M. Alfredsson, 'Strategic development of third party logistics providers', *Industrial Marketing Management*, **32**, 139–49, 2003.

[9] P.B. Goodwin, *Car Dependence*, London: RAC, 1995.

[10] G. D'Este, 'Urban freight movement modeling', D.A. Hensher and K.J. Button (eds), *Handbook of Transport Modelling*, 2nd edn, Amsterdam: Elsevier, 2008.

Table 10.4   *The market sectors of urban freight*

Market sector	Truck type	Commodity	Load type	Route	Trip type
Courier	Small	Mixed	LTL	Variable	Very complex linked trips
General carrier	Intermediate size	Mixed	LTL or FTL	Variable	Variable – simple or linked trips
Specialist commodities (e.g., bulk liquid)	Large	Specific	FTL	Regular	Mostly simple trips
Over-sized/ hazardous	Large	Specific	FTL	Fixed	Simple trips
External	Large	Mixed or specific	FTL	Regular	Simple trips – external to/from a single point

Note: LTL is less than truck load; FTL is full truck load.

Table 10.5   *The estimated benefits of improved urban distribution systems*

Supply-chain study	Scope of study	Estimated savings
Kurt Salmon Associates	US dry grocery sector	10.8% of sales turnover (2.5% financial, 8.5% cost) Total supply chain $30 billion, warehouse supplier dry sector $10 billion. Supply chain cut by 41% from 104 to 61 days
Coca-Cola supply chain	127 European companies focused on cost reduction from the end of manufacturing line	2.3–3.4% of sales turnover (60% to retailers, 40% to manufacturers)
ECR Europe	15 value-chain analyses (10 European manufacturers, 5 retailers) 15 product categories, 7 distribution	5.7% of sales turnover (4.8% operating costs, 0.9% inventory cost. Total supply-chain saving of $21 billion. UK savings $2 billion

Source: Adapted from C. Fiddis, *Manufacturer–Retailer Relationships in the Food and Drink Industry: Strategies and Tactics in the Battle for Power*, London: Pearson, 1997. Full references to the studies are contained in this book.

system. Of course, there have also been failures when inappropriate changes have been made. As with any activity, the costs of change must be set against the benefits, and in the urban logistics case there are such issues as the relative costs of changing the entire distribution network as opposed to making marginal changes to elements of it. The more complex the network, the more difficult it is generally to change the entire system.

The nature of urban logistics systems, and in particular retail systems, differs between countries and this can partly be explained in terms of the market power within the specific supply chain, and the motivations of the various actors. For example, Mitchell[11] points to the fact that most German and French retailers tend to be privately owned or franchised operations, largely motivated by volumes of sales and price when planning their strategic positioning.

In contrast, UK firms tend to be publicly quoted companies motivated by margins and thus have a more constructive approach to their suppliers, including transport services. The US system also differs because there is greater market segmentation, wholesalers have more power in the supply chain, and there is more focus on customer promotions, and greater government intervention in the market, especially regarding anti-trust issues. These factors determine the bargaining ability of the transport suppliers in the market and the types of service that are demanded from them. In the United Kingdom, for example, the shift has largely been to one controlled by retailers, with their needs being pushed through to the transport market. This, combined with the long-established deregulated trucking market (following the 1968 Transport Act) which offers significantly lower-cost services, has meant the widespread use of third-party logistics in the United Kingdom, but a slower uptake in the United States.

10.7   Green Logistics

Chapters 6 and 8 focused on some of the major environmental challenges imposed by transport, and on the economic implications of some of the ways of reducing, if not always removing, them. Here we focus specifically on the economic aspects of reducing the environmental costs of the larger, freight supply chain. This has been a subject of increasing interest as trade, both within and between countries, has grown and the supply chain has become more extended. Interest has expanded beyond traditional environmental groups and government to embrace trade bodies.[12]

The supply chain makes use of a diverse range of transport inputs that in turn impact on the environment. These differ sometimes from the environmental externalities associated with passenger modes, because they can involve what is carried as well as the pure transport-generated environmental externalities, but from an economic perspective can largely be treated in the same way. While there are market incentives for the private sector to adopt greener logistics supply chains, official policies have also been deployed, mainly to reduce energy

---

[11] A. Mitchell, *Efficient Consumer Response: A New Paradigm for the European FMCG Sector*, London: Pearson, 1997.

[12] International Road Transport Union, *Guide to Sustainable Development*, Paris: IRU, 2000.

Table 10.6 *Macro studies on fuel consumption of impacts of alternative logistics structures*

Country	Time period	Main measures	Changes in energy consumption	
			Business as usual	With rationalization
Netherlands	1990–2015	Increased fuel efficiency Consolidation of loads Reduced empty running Large modal shift to rail	+47	−46
Germany	1988–2010	Improved fuel efficiency Large modal shift to rail Higher vehicle utilization Shorter distances traveled	+55	+28
United Kingdom	1995–2020	Halving the rate of ton-miles growth to 10% per decade Large modal shift to rail and water	+56	−4.4

Source: Adapted from A.C. McKinnon, 'Logistics and the environment', in K.J. Button and D.A. Hensher, *Handbook of Transport and the Environment*, Oxford: Pergamon, 2003.

consumption. A range of policy options are available, but while there are a variety of approaches, the pros and cons of the alternatives, with some minor nuances, are largely the same as with passenger transport.[13] They often entail the types of measures outlined in Chapter 8 for transport more generally, but in addition there are often specific measures covering elements of the logistics supply chain. Table 10.6 provides details of the potential impact of some strategies that have been considered to foster lower fuel consumption and thus also CO_2 emissions. What they do not show, however, are the detailed mechanisms for bringing this about, or the costs that these changes would impose on the supply chains involved.

Logistics also serves a reverse role in the larger production process in terms of product returns, source reduction, recycling, material substitution, reuse of materials, waste disposal, and refurbishing, repair and remanufacturing.[14] This is known as 'reverse logistics'. The combination of making the transport element of the overall supply chain more environmentally benign, and the role of reverse logistics in optimizing the use of resources in the entire production process through the facilitation of recycling, refurbishment and so on of products is known as 'green logistics'. It is a wider approach to the interactions of transport and the environment than just simply making transport *per se* less environmentally

[13] D. Martin, W. Cannell and K.M. Gwillian, 'Reducing the impact of freight transport on global warming: the potential of technical solutions', *World Transport Policy, and Practice*, **1**, 11–7, 1995.

[14] J.R. Stock, *Developing and Implementation of Reverse Logistics Program*, Lombard, IL: Council of Logistics Management, 1998.

Table 10.7   *Amounts of hazardous goods moved in the United States (1997)*

Mode	Thousand tons	Thousand ton-miles
For-hire truck	336,363	45,244
Private truck	522,666	28,847
Rail	96,626	74,711
Water	143,152	68,212
Air (inc. truck and air)	–	95
Pipeline	432,075	–
Multiple modes	6,022	3,061
Other	17,459	1,837

Source: Adapted from US Department of Transportation and US Department of Commerce, *United States Hazardous Materials, 1997 Economic Census, Transportation, 1997 Commodity Flow Survey,* Washington, DC: USDOT/USDOC, 1999.

intrusive.[15] From a narrow economic perspective, the commercial advantage to the transport industry of such things as recycling and refurbishment is that it can provide return loads and thus reduce the back-haul problem.

Recycling and refurbishment is growing in importance, not just for environmental reasons but also as a simple commercial proposition. Some examples of the gains from recycling compared to entirely new extraction and processing include 95 percent in both energy and air pollution savings for aluminum, 40 percent and 73 percent for paper; between 5 and 30 percent, and 20 percent respectively for glass and 60 percent savings in both for steel. The amount of recycling that takes place varies by commodity and between countries; for example, the United Kingdom recycled 42 percent of steel packaging in 2002, with Belgium recycling 93 percent, Germany 79 percent, and the Netherlands 78 percent. The European average was 60 percent. Outside of Europe, the figure for Australia was 43 percent, Korea 47 percent, the United States 59 percent, South Africa 63 percent and Japan 86 percent.

Some materials moved are also hazardous – especially certain chemicals – and command-and-control instruments involving routing, timing and packaging are often adopted to minimize any external costs of spillage.[16] This applies to cargoes carried by water, pipeline and air as well as road and rail. The amounts involved are quite large, about 10 percent of the total ton-miles of freight movement done in the United States. Table 10.7 offers some indication of the ways in which hazardous goods are moved.

Command-and-control instruments are preferred over pricing largely because of the transaction costs involved. It is relatively easy to highlight hazardous loads by signs on vehicles, and this makes enforcement of such things as routings and use of specified infrastructure such as designated lanes on freeways relatively

15 J.-P. Rodrigue, B. Slack and C. Comtois, 'Green logistics', in A.M. Brewer, K.J. Button and D.A. Hensher (eds), *Handbook of Logistics and Supply-chain Management*, Oxford: Pergamon, 2001.

16 K.L. Hancock, 'Hazardous goods', in A.M. Brewer, K.J. Button and D.A. Hensher (eds), *Handbook of Logistics and Supply-chain Management*, Oxford: Pergamon, 2001.

easy. There is clearly, however, a quasi-pricing mechanism involved through the insurance market, and in many cases compulsory insurance coverage is used to complement command-and-control instruments.

10.8   International Logistics

The major growth in international trade has been both facilitated by innovations in international logistics and a driving force for new approaches to logistics. The introduction of the container from the late 1960s significantly cut both the financial and the time costs of freight movements. Institutional changes, both at the global level including tariff reforms under the auspices of such agencies as the World Trade Organization, and domestically in many countries, which has enhanced the efficiency with which goods can be moved to and from gateway, international ports, have been complementary to this.

There has also been a move towards internationalization of freight transport service suppliers. This has involved the formation of strategic alliances in shipping and cargo airlines, and in the United States and abutting countries between the freight railroads. The economic rationale for this is parallel to economies of scope, density and market presence found in the passenger airline sector discussed earlier in the book. In addition, there have been direct international mergers and take-overs that have brought about even greater integration. Some of these have involved very large companies, such as the mega-shipping lines P&O Nedlloyd and AP Moller Maersk which merged in 2005.

Figure 10.6 offers a very stylized picture of what generally has happened regarding freight movements before and after technology changes, such as the adoption of the container, mergers, or more often, relaxation of institutional barriers to international trade. (The broken line represents a national border.) Not only is there a shift to more cross-border trade, but also the amount and complexity of goods movements within the nations involved increases.

This type of pattern has been observed in the European Union after the removal of internal restrictions of trade from the early 1990s and also as additional countries have joined periodically since 2000. While the creation of the European Economic Community under the Treaty of Rome in the late 1950s had intended to introduce free trade between member states, progress was slow. After 30 years, as we see in more detail in Chapter 14, there remained serious obstacles to the movement of goods. Some indication of the administrative costs of international border crossings within Europe prior to the Single European Market initiative are seen in Table 10.8. Estimates made by the European Union in 1996 after the removal of border controls under the Single European Market initiative, which came into effect in 1992, suggest that logistics costs fell by as much as 27 percent between 1987 and 1992. About half of this saving was realized in the transport sector as idle time at borders was reduced and service reliability improved.

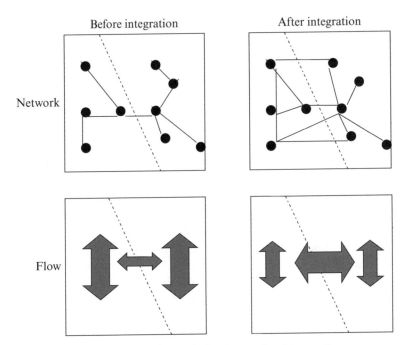

Figure 10.6   *Freight movements before and after international integration*

Table 10.8   *Estimated annual cost of administrative formalities and border controls in Europe prior to the Single European Market initiative*

	$ billion (1988)
Administration	9
Delays	1
Public spending on customer operations	1
Lost business opportunities	5 to 19
Total	16 to 30

10.9 Security

Security has always been a concern in the supply chain. Various elements of transport networks have historically found themselves prone to attack both in conventional wars and by terrorists (broadly defined). While the focus of these attacks has in the past often involved links and terminals in inter-urban networks – airlines/airports, railway lines/railway stations and so on – the local, urban and suburban elements of logistics chains have not been left unscathed. Security is a large subject and the focus here is on the vulnerability of shopping malls – important urban and suburban interfaces between inbound flows of goods to retail outlets and outbound flows from retail outlets to final consumption.[17] They are

---

[17] K.J. Button, 'The economics of shopping mall security', *Journal of Transportation Security*, **1**, 127–39, 2008.

an integral part of the supply chain and also an element that is both high profile and difficult to secure.[18] We also add a few words on shipping matters.

Shopping malls provide important retail outlets that offer shoppers economies of scale and scope in their purchasing and economies of market presence for retailers in their selling. They have grown significantly in number in the United States and in many other countries over recent years, with increases in their size and range of facilities provided. They also often act as major recreation centers containing cinemas and food outlets in addition to stores selling commodities to take away. Strolling and 'hanging out' in malls can also provide a distraction for teenagers. Overall, from a security perspective, they represent large gatherings of citizens that offer possible targets for terrorists. Indeed, the US Department of Homeland Security categorizes shopping centers, along with other easily accessible public places, as 'soft targets'.

Traditional concerns with security involving theft and attacks on individuals have focused on the location of malls. Older malls located in middle-income areas and accessible only by automobile were previously considered relatively 'safe', but with increasing suburbanization and changing demographics this is now less the case – 65 percent of US and Canadian malls of over 400,000 square feet are located in areas with above-average crime risk, with 25 percent being in areas having three times or more the national crime risk. Mall design and that of its surrounding area also play a role in crime rates. Crime tends to be higher in malls with spots that are attractive to juveniles and 'non-shoppers', and where there are crowded stores offering easy access.

Much of the discussion of mall security and terrorism has relied on anecdotal evidence – perhaps not unexpectedly given the nature of the 'games' that are played with potential terrorists. Their features would seem to make them very vulnerable to terrorist attacks of various kinds – they have multiple entrances and exits, are open to the public, have numerous potential places for concealment, often have adjacent car parking, have frequent deliveries, attract numerous shoppers, and employ large numbers of workers. Additionally, since their initial introduction in 1956, many of the larger malls in the United States (some 1,200 or so) and elsewhere are enclosed, with extensive air-conditioning and ventilation systems making them potential targets for toxic chemical or biological attacks. Other developments in the supply chain have seen the greater containerization of consignments, reducing considerably the transparency of what is being delivered.

Security has thus always been an issue at malls and it is the emphasis that has changed.[19] Traditional security has been focused on preventing petty crimes of theft, minor material damage to the fabric of buildings, and assaults on individuals – collectively called 'crimes' hereafter for brevity. These problems

---

[18] O.K. Helferich and R.L. Cook, *Securing the Supply Chain*, Lambard, IL: Council of Logistics Management, 2002.

[19] E. Romano, 'Making shopping centres safer', *Journal of Property Management*, **59**, 46–51, 1994.

continue. For example, in a 1995 survey for the National Retail Federation, the University of Florida found that the average discount store in 1994 had 0.09 crimes against customers, ranging from simple assault to rape and murder. That translates into a rate of about 20 crimes against customers per year for chains the size of Wal-Mart and Kmart. This problem of criminality is now overlapped by concerns about the possibility of terrorist attacks.

Worldwide, malls have not been immune from attacks in the past – there have been over 60 terrorist or terrorist-inspired attacks of various size at shopping malls since 1998 in 21 countries, including the UK, Turkey, Israel, Russia and Spain.[20] The majority of these attacks have involved explosives of various types, but there have also been incidents involving firearms and chemicals. The events of September 2001 have heightened concerns in the US and elsewhere that shopping malls may more frequently become explicit targets for major attack. There is also increased concern about other forms of major assault at malls. For example, a bombing took place in October 2002 in Vantaa, Finland in a local Myyrmanni shopping mall, killing seven people, including the bomber, and injuring 166. The shopping center was particularly crowded, with almost 2,000 people, including many children who had come to see a clown perform.

There have already been some actual and thwarted terrorist attacks at US malls, although on a relatively minor scale. Five people were killed and four injured in a shooting at a Salt Lake City mall in 2007 by a Bosnian, for example. There have also been abortive attempts at terrorism. In November 2007, Nuradin Abdi, a Somali living in Ohio pleaded guilty to planning, with other al Qaeda operatives, to blow up a Columbus shopping mall.

Nevertheless, and for a variety of economic, political and social reasons, the attention paid to shopping mall security has been much less than to many other parts of the transport supply chain such as airports, airlines, and chemical and oil movements.

One of the problems is that the retail industry has trod warily for commercial reasons. Customers expect shopping centers to be free and open, and mall owners and operators have been reluctant to introduce stringent security measures, as airports have done, that might limit shoppers' access, or scare them off altogether. Although security officers are usually uniformed, for example, they are not intended to appear threatening and frequently serve a variety of roles as well as security.

Although the Nobel Prize-winning economist, Gary Becker[21] and others have enhanced our understanding of crime prevention in general, the analysis of terrorism and its prevention is a relatively new area of study for economists – much of the social science interest in the field coming from sociologists and political

[20] T. LaTourrette, D.R. Howell, D.E. Moshes and J. MacDonald, *Reducing Terrorism Risk at Shopping Centers: An Analysis of Potential Security Options*, Chicago, IL: RAND Corporation, 2006.

[21] G. Becker, 'Crime and punishment: an economic approach', *Journal of Political Economy*, **76**, 169–217, 1968.

scientists. Much of traditional economic analysis of crime has focused on deterring criminals, but this is of limited relevance in situations where the perpetrator is intent on committing suicide. Inevitably there has been some theoretical economic analysis of the appropriate role of public and private sector insurance, essentially revolving around the degree to which the threat of terrorism constitutes risk or uncertainty, on the moral hazard issues, various compensation policies, and on the optimal ways to allocate the cost of counter-terrorism measures. There has also been applied analysis seeking to estimate the macro costs of terrorism on economic performance. Here we are more concerned with embracing some of these things within an assessment of how optimal security levels may be defined.

One of the problems in trying to apply economics to a subject such as mall security is that many of the actions are driven by subjective factors, often influenced by only partial information, which are difficult to quantify given the lack of large amounts of prior data. This makes it difficult to work out probabilities of attacks and their costs.

The situation is compounded because, unlike the consideration of safety where there is no feedback mechanism, the perpetrators of terrorist acts modify and adjust their methods and targets as security measures reduce the vulnerability of previous types of target. They essentially play games with the security agencies; for example, in some cases they switch targets because they have achieved their objectives, having diverted considerable security efforts to the old category of target. This means that much of the difficulty lies in the uncertain nature of terrorism, in Frank Knight's[22] sense of there being no easily calculable probability distributions associated with attacks. Initially, however, we look at a Gaussian approach and assume that such probabilities can be calculated.

Figure 10.7 provides a simple abstract diagrammatic representation of the situation, with security measured in some undefined way. This allows an assessment of the optimal level of security that should be provided in simple cost–benefit terms. C is an upward-sloping marginal cost of security curve based on the reasonable assumption that each increment of security costs more as the most basic measures are exhausted. The B curve indicates the marginal benefits of additional security, with the flattening of the slope reflecting the decline in additional benefits associated with the more detailed security measures. The optimal level of security in this case is at S.

These curves, however, can for analytical purposes usefully be decomposed. Increased security provides benefits in terms of both a reduced threat of material (including physical injuries to people) damage in the mall (separated out as B^*) and greater psychological 'comfort' to those shopping, or having family or friends shopping in the mall (the distance between the B and B^* curves). The extent to which this psychological 'comfort' exceeds the actual dangers that exist depends to a large extent on the information that is available to potential shoppers. While there may be no good estimate of the reduced chance of being involved in an attack on a mall, there are benefits from simply seeing security measures in place

[22] F.H. Knight, *Risk, Uncertainty and Profit*, Boston, MA: Houghton Mifflin, 1921.

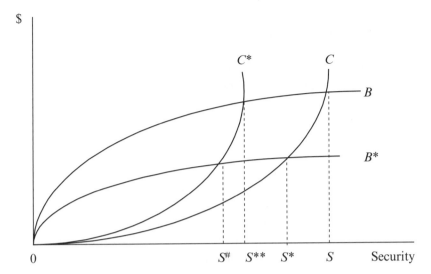

Figure 10.7   *The determinants of optimal security provision*

even if there is no objective method of assessing their effectiveness, although conversely people are sensitive to such things as media coverage of threats that push out the mental benefits of greater security actions. There may also be benefits that are external to those using and working in a mall, for example to those living in the neighborhood.

The cost curve also has its complexities. Attacks on malls can inflict both material damage on the fabric of the buildings and the vitality of the shops in it, and injury and death on individuals. The C^* curve is drawn to separate out the minimum marginal costs of incremental units of security, including the additional inconvenience costs to all parties as well as financial outlays, but the actual full economic costs may deviate from this. (While the B and C curves are drawn as smooth functions, in practice there may well be kinks if, for example, shoppers have threshold tolerance levels to the degrees of intrusion that security will impose on them.) The incentive to provide security at the lowest cost may not be there and, in consequence, X-inefficiency may be present in providing security measures, pushing up the cost curve. Potential inefficiency arises in these types of situation because objectives tend to be opaque and many of the costs are only indirectly borne by those responsible for the security provided.

The problems of providing security on the lowest-cost curve are compounded if there is asymmetrical information concerning the effectiveness of security measures – for example, security experts and consultants have an incentive to exaggerate the challenges being faced; consultants are after all rent-seeking economic agents operating in a commercial market. In effect, there is the potential for a degree of 'regulatory capture' of the security system by those involved in providing it.

On the other hand, the costs of security measures may reduce insurance premiums and also other forms of crime in the mall. The costs may also be offset to some extent by the supply chain adjusting at other points, either up or down, as other actors modify their behavior. In these cases the actual cost curve will be lower than that depicted in the figure. The trade-offs involved are empirical questions and inevitably will differ between malls.

Given these complexities, a number of suboptimal outcomes may emerge. For simplicity, we assume that gains at other points in the supply chain will offset some of the costs of enhanced security and any X-inefficiency associated with it. In other words, $\{C^* - C\}$ is the difference between the actual and the narrowly defined minimum cost curve of on-site security.

If the attention were purely on the commercial damage that can be caused by acts of terrorism, as for example may be the case of private insurance companies, then security will be undersupplied by $\{S - S^*\}$. But even if the psychological benefits of more assured security are not ignored, then there may be inefficiencies in the provision of security measures leading to inadequacies of $\{S - S^{**}\}$ in their provision if the agencies responsible do not minimize their costs. If both full benefits are underestimated and costs and the provision of security measures are not done efficiently, then the resultant level of security, $S^{\#}$, could be well below the social optimum.

The conventional public policy approach to this sort of optimization problem is to apply cost–benefit or cost-effectiveness analysis but this is difficult in this case because terrorism involves both uncertainty, because of the limited number of previous events, and game playing, because of the reactive function of the terrorists. To get a genuine handle on the shapes of these curves, perhaps the best tools available are experiments. These may involve some form of conventional simulations that can help assess static uncertainty, or more interactive approaches deploying experimental economics that can capture the adaptive behavior of terrorists to security measures.

While it is generally impossible to identify and quantify many of the costs and benefits of securing transport facilities, there are important questions about who should pay the costs if the terrorist threat is to be handled efficiently.

Shopping malls, as our continuing example, are generally owned by the private sector and traditionally they have provided significant amounts of security within their facilities. Indeed, most of the protection is provided by private security.[23] Mall owners and operators have had a vested interest in doing this, and in cooperating with police forces and other private parties (for example, the security personnel employed by individual retailers in a mall and the transport companies involved in deliveries). Public confidence in the security of people and property is an important marketing tool for a mall operator.

Given the nature of traditional crime, mall operators have the option of passing on some of the risk of any breakdown in this type of security – for example, compensation claims – through insurance markets. They can also, as

---

[23] R.C. Davis, C. Ortiz, R. Rowe, J. Broz, G. Rigakos and P. Collins, *An Assessment of the Preparedness of Large Retail Malls to Prevent and Respond to Terrorist Attack*, Washington, DC: US Department of Justice, 2006.

most have done, internalize some of the risk by enhancing their private policing.[24] On the premise that they act rationally, shoppers in the mall also have a personal interest in protecting themselves (after all, compensation for being killed by a mugger is hardly ideal!) and their property, and also often have the option of taking out insurance. Individual shops within malls have differing levels of attraction to criminals and may thus add additional security.

In another context, namely international freight movements, the US government (but also authorities in other countries have adopted similar policies) have played upon this private sector interest and developed initiatives such as the Customs–Trade Partnership Against Terrorism (C-TPAT) which fosters public/private cooperation throughout the global supply chain.[25] Firms that participate conduct a comprehensive self-assessment of their security practices using guidelines developed after consultation with the national government. This avoids excessive checking by the government and affords the logistics supply flexibility in its operations on the premise that any failure in the security arrangements will hit the supplier commercially.

The general problem with security is that the threat posed by terrorists is different in that it largely involves uncertainty, with little knowledge about any underlying probability functions, if indeed any exist, rather than risk. The actuarial approach to the challenge is thus far from perfect, and certainly incomplete. The potential costs of a major terrorist incident are also extremely high. Returning to our primary example, these factors make it virtually impossible for a mall operator to completely insure, either internally or through the financial market, against terrorist attacks. This is one reason why Figure 10.7 is very broad in its nature; the precise quantification of any of the curves shown is virtually impossible. We can point to some costs associated with security measures in a number of transport contexts (Table 10.9, for example, provides a comparison of the costs directly borne by airline travelers for security measures) but these are only partial and are not easily transferable.

There is the added problem that a major attack on a terminal facility or interchange point such as a mall could have serious and much wider economic and geographical repercussions than those simply relating to the shopping facility. This can be seen and treated as a standard externality problem if these effects have relatively small impacts on overall price levels and incomes in the larger economy, but, and this may well not be the case, if this is not so then the conventional tools of microeconomics break down. The standard *ceteris paribus* assumptions of neoclassical analysis do not hold. The issue becomes one of so-called 'political risk', although strictly, given the subjective nature of the issue, it is more about 'political uncertainty'.

These market failures necessitate a degree of public involvement in terms

[24] J. de Ward, 'The private security industry in an international perspective', *European Journal of Criminology Policy and Research*, **7**, 143–74, 1999.
[25] M.R. Brooks and K.J. Button, 'Market structure and shipping security', *Maritime Economics and Logistics*, **8**, 100–120, 2006.

Table 10.9   *Average security charges per traveler at airports (2002)*

Country	Average charge per passenger ($)
Canada	14.50
Germany	10.57
Israel	8.03
France	6.88
Australia	5.19
United States	5.00
Netherlands	4.13
Russia	2.04
Italy	1.90
United Kingdom	0.00

Source: W.G. Waters and C. Yu, 'Air security fees and highway safety', Proceedings of the 38th Canadian Transportation Research Forum Annual Conference', Ottawa, 2003.

of specifying and, possibly, providing security and, if this fails, resources to cope with many of the aftermath effects. These are obviously not problems unique to transport security but they certainly do exist when it comes to looking at appropriate economic strategies concerning transport infrastructure and operations.

Where the line is drawn between private sector responsibility and the public is partly a technical one, largely depending on where uncertainty becomes the dominant concern, but also embodies normative judgment involving public perception of what the exact role of government should be. While normally the actual implementation of policies is seen in terms of narrower economic efficiency considerations – essentially the undertaking of a cost–benefit calculation of the effectiveness of public and private actors – when security arises there is often a high degree of subjectivity involving public perceptions. This was seen in the debates in the United States over whether private operators should implement new airport security measures after the 2001 terrorist attacks or whether this should be done by a federal agency. Also indicative of this is that, while there is evidence that private security does not reduce security in malls, many shopping mall operators in the United States actively seek a local police presence in their facilities, often a police station, to give added public confidence.

Further Reading

A classic volume that illustrates the links between economics and operations research, which are the basis of much of logistics, is W.J. Baumol, *Economic Theory and Operations Analysis*, Englewood Cliffs, NJ: Prentice-Hall, 1962. For a good, solid, although slightly dated, basic overview of logistics and supply-chain management, see A.C. McKinnon, *Physical Distribution Systems*, London: Routledge, 1989. A collection of classic articles on logistics is contained in A. McKinnon, K.J. Button and P. Nijkamp, P. (eds), *Transport Logistics*, Cheltenham, UK and Northampton, MA, USA: Edward Elgar, 2002, while A.M.

Brewer, K.J. Button and D.A. Hensher (eds), *Handbook of Logistics and Supply-chain Management*, Oxford: Pergamon, 2001, offers a set of original papers that cover most aspects of supply-chain management. For a more rigorous assessment of freight network modeling, see T.L. Friesz and C. Kwon, 'Strategic freight network planning models and dynamic oligopolistic urban freight networks', in D.A. Hensher and K.J. Button (eds), *Handbook of Transport Modelling*, 2nd edn, Amsterdam: Elsevier, 2008. An assessment of the various models of the global supply chain is found in M.J. Meixell and V.B. Gargeya, 'Global supply chain design: a literature review and critique', *Transportation Research E*, **41**, 531–50, 2005.

Most of the articles dealing with the economic aspects of logistics are scattered in the *Management Science* and *Operational Research* journals, however, *Transportation Research E: Transportation and Logistics Review* often carries papers directly relevant to the subject matter of this chapter.

11 Investment Criteria – Private and Public Sector Analysis

● ●

11.1   The Importance of Infrastructure

Adam Smith in his classic book, *The Wealth of Nations*, certainly thought that transport in 1776 had a major and positive role to play in fostering economic well-being, and spends considerable time explaining this, and also that government has an important responsibility in ensuring that adequate transport infrastructure is provided:

> The third and last duty of the sovereign or commonwealth is that of erecting and maintaining those public institutions and those public works, which, though they may be in the highest degree advantageous to a great society, are, however, of such a nature that the profit could never repay the expense to any individual or small number of individuals, and which it therefore cannot be expected that any individual or small number of individuals should erect or maintain.

The preceding chapters have been primarily concerned with making the best use of an existing transport network or fleet of vehicles. They have, therefore, principally focused on short-term problems involving the management, regulation and pricing of an established transport system. In particular, they were concerned with emphasizing the central role of marginal cost pricing (including social costs) in encouraging the optimal utilization of transport facilities. The discussions have thus largely taken the stock of transport infrastructure as given and been concerned with making the most efficient economic use of it.

There is, however, a longer-term aspect to be considered, namely possible changes in the size or nature of the basic transport system by either investment or disinvestment. (The latter may take the form of allowing quality deterioration by reduced maintenance rather than a physical removal of a link, such as a road closure, from a transport network.) In the case of road-haulage, airline and shipping operations, the commercial nature of decision-making bodies means that changes are normally analyzed in terms of their financial repercussions. With road track, railways and port authorities, which in most countries are owned by public agencies, the provision of basic infrastructure is usually determined by looking at much wider considerations.

Before moving on to look at some of the key techniques employed in investment analysis, it is perhaps helpful to consider the actual scale of transport infrastructure that exists, and to provide some factual information on variations in modal provision and technology. We have already seen in Chapter 2 the

Table 11.1   *Investment in transport infrastructure in European countries*

Country	Infrastructure investment as % of GDP	
	Road	*Rail*
Belgium	0.67	0.29
France	0.65	0.09
Germany	0.79	0.26
Italy	0.62	0.27
Spain	0.50	0.27
United Kingdom	0.04	0.09

considerable amount of transport infrastructure – roads, railway track and so on – that has been developed over the years; basically, the stock of network capital. It is also clear from what we saw in Tables 2.7 and 2.8 that road infrastructure provision far exceeds that of rail in most of the larger wealthier industrial nations. This stock is also growing. The US railroad network, for example expanded from 178.0 thousand kilometers in 1993 to 205.6 in 2004, and that in Japan from 20.3 to 23.7 thousand kilometers in the decade to 2004. Perhaps more pronounced has been the investments in road networks.

The global situation is, however, variable. For example, the picture is slightly different in the former communist states in Europe (and even more so in many less developed countries) which have relatively extensive rail networks *vis-à-vis* their road systems, although things are changing. In addition, it is not simply a matter of the quantity of the capital stock; its quality is also of considerable importance.

When compared to Organisation for Economic Co-operation and Development (OECD) states, only a relatively small percentage of their networks were double tracked in the 1990s; for example, 23 percent in each of Bulgaria, Hungary and Poland and 15 percent in Hungary, compared to 63 percent in the Netherlands, 69 percent in the United Kingdom and 45 percent in France. Taking another parameter, while there are considerable variations in the electrification of rail networks in industrialized countries because of the type of traffic they carry, and in particular the freight/passenger mix, they generally still have more extensive systems than in the post-communist states. For example, of 31,000 kilometers of line, nearly 12,000 were electrified in the western states of pre-1990 Germany, but out of 14,024 kilometers in the former East Germany only 3,475 kilometers were electrified, and in Poland, of 26,545 kilometers only 6,296 were electrified. Today, Poland has about 11.9 thousand kilometers electrified, and Hungry has increased its electrified system from 2.3 to 2.8 thousand kilometers.

There have always been significant variations between countries in terms of the proportion of national resources that are invested in transport infrastructure. This can be explained in terms of different geographies and industrial needs. As can be seen in Table 11.1, which relates to Europe in the 1990s, this is not simply in terms of the modal division of expenditure but also in the absolute proportion going to transport as a whole.

While the capital stock of transport infrastructure is large and huge sums are spent on its expansion and maintenance, the evidence is that investment in transport, and especially rail transport, has actually tended to slow down in the latter part of the twentieth century compared to the 1960s and 1970s, and, in some cases, disinvestment may well have taken place. In the case of rail this manifested itself in a 4.1 percent reduction in the rail network of OECD countries between 1970 and 1985, although effective capacity may well have increased as electrification and double-tracking programs were carried through. One reason for this is that many networks, such as the US Inter-state Highway System neared completion, and most industrialized countries had extensive transport networks in place by the 1990s. The growth in globalization and removal of trade barriers at the macro level, and the spread of urbanization at the more local levels, have added some impetus to the notion that additional capacity is needed in the early part of the twenty-first century. The changes in Europe, and in particular the EU TENs initiative that we shall discuss in Chapter 13, can also be likened to the development of transport networks of the kind fostered in Canada and the United States in the nineteenth century as a tool for political integration.

Economists look at transport investment from two broad perspectives. At the macro and meso levels there is interest in the ways and extent to which it contributes to the economic advancement of a region or a country – a topic we shall address later in the book. In the 1930s, for example, the construction of the autobahns in Germany was used as way to stimulate employment and the construction of the Federal Highway System in the United States was seen as a major macroeconomic stimulus. At the microeconomic level, which is our main concern here, the interest is in the efficiency of individual transport investments, and the returns that they generate either in narrow financial terms or in wider, social terms. Project appraisal is necessary because investment resources are not infinite and there are many potential options in terms of the ways in which they may be used. Looking at the efficient use of these resources is our focus here.

11.2   Basic Principles

Simple economic theory provides straightforward guidelines for investment decision making; essentially, they involve pricing and output decisions where the constraints of a fixed production capacity (for example, a given fleet or rail network) cease to be binding. In Figure 11.1, for example, we consider a profit-maximizing airline with a fleet exhibiting short-run average and marginal cost characteristics of $SRAC_1$ and $SRMC_1$, respectively, and confronted by the demand curve D (with marginal revenue MR). Ideally, a price P_1 will be set and seat-kilometers Q_1 offered. The long-run marginal cost ($LRMC$) is, however, below marginal revenue at this output and, with this size of fleet and gives an inducement to expand output in the long term by acquiring more capacity.

Greater seat availability will, however, force price down but, and this is important in the example, it may also make it more economical to increase the

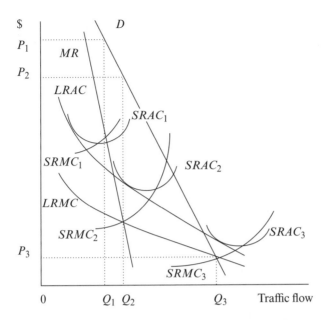

Figure 11.1   *Optimal investment: profit maximization and social surplus maximization*

aircraft fleet size. In the diagram, and assuming throughout that profit maximizing prices are charged, the fleet could be expanded to correspond to $SRAC_2$ and
$SRMC_2$. Here the long-run optimum situation is achieved with marginal revenue
equated to long- and short-run costs, and with profit maximization resulting. If
the firm were concerned with social rather than commercial profit-maximization
criteria and adopted instead marginal cost pricing, then the $SRMC_3$ and $SRAC_3$
curves become relevant because with this objective function it is the setting of
$D = LRMC = SRMC$ which is important. Greater capacity still is needed for
this (hence the $SRMC_3$, and $SRAC_3$ curves) and optimal long-run output will be
higher at Q_3 seat-miles with fares lowered to P_3. At this price and output, social
surplus is maximized although, since $P_3 < LRAC$, in the long run a financial loss
will be made (that is, $<RAC > P_3$).

The basic principles are simple, and come straight from the elementary economic literature; the difficulty comes in the transport context in putting them into
practice. In many cases investments are not divisible and, hence, the $LRAC$ and
$LRMC$ curves are disjointed segments, or even points, which do not intersect with
demand. This is an extremely common situation in transport and it does pose
serious problems in many operational cases.

It is not difficult, for example, to envisage routes where the available vehicles (be they planes, buses or whatever) are either too small or too large to be
optimal and it is even more common in the case of infrastructure where, for
instance, a two-lane motorway may be inadequate to cope with normal demand
but a three-lane one is too capacious; you also have to build a complete runway
at an airport because planning to construct 20 percent of one does not make
a great deal of sense. Further, there is the problem of what exactly is meant

by 'cost'; is it simply the costs borne by the investor or are there, because of market imperfections such as externalities, other costs that should be taken into account? There is also the matter of how inclusive the number of alternative investments to be considered is; in many cases there are a wide variety of alternative ways in which resources can be invested and selection processes become important.[1]

While we have treated the commercial and social criteria of profit maximization and marginal cost pricing as amenable to presentation on one diagram, in practice most socially oriented undertakings look at a much wider range of costs (notably many of the externalities discussed in Chapter 6) when deciding upon investment than do those motivated by purely financial considerations. Coupled with this is the fact that the diagrammatic analysis assumes that, irrespective of the operational criteria, prices are optimal in the short term and thus can act as an aid and guideline to investment decision making. Also, despite the sophistication of forecasting techniques (see Chapter 12) it is unlikely that the transport provider is completely aware of the exact form of the long-run demand curve confronting him/her, and may have a very poor idea of the full costs of constructing new facilities. Indeed, the fluctuating nature of demand for transport (especially long-term cycles in demand associated with national and international economic conditions) means that it is rather more of a stochastic concept than a deterministic phenomenon as depicted.

There is the added institutional problem that transport investments are seldom made in isolation from other changes to the transport system. For example, larger suppliers of transport services in the private sector that have the potential to exercise monopoly power are generally subjected to economic regulations to prevent such exploitation. Regulatory policies regarding external costs may also change during the construction of a large project. The result is that in practice a sort of 'muddling through', to use Charles Lindblom's[2] jargon, turns out to be the reality, with continual modifications being made to the project even after its construction has begun.

Given all these difficulties, together with the general inadequacy of information enjoyed by most transport suppliers of their current levels of cost, let alone future costs, it is not surprising that investment analysis in transport has received considerable interest. The high costs and long-term implications of infrastructure investments in road and rail track, and sea- and airports has led to particular attention being directed at these areas. At the academic level they also pose especially difficult questions because, in many cases, facilities are provided at prices unrelated to cost, or made freely available to users. Additionally, there are frequently widespread ramifications for transport users elsewhere or for the non-users living in surrounding areas.

[1] P.J. Mackie and D. Simon, 'Twenty-one sources of error and bias in transport project appraisal', *Transport Policy*, **5**, 1–7, 1998.
[2] C.E. Lindblom, 'The science of muddling through', *Public Administration*, **19**, 79–88, 1959.

11.3   Commercial and Social Approaches to Investment

Transport infrastructure is provided in a variety of institutional settings, ranging from purely commercial structures to ones that are totally socially oriented, and is financed in many different ways, ranging from user fees to taxes. Just considering air traffic control systems, the US Federal Aviation Administration is financed largely from taxes and has no strict financial remit, whereas NAV Canada is a non-profit, private corporation that levies user fees, the Australian air traffic control body is a government corporation financed from user fees, and the UK's National Air Traffic Services (NATS) is a price-regulated, for-profit, public/ private partnership that imposes user fees.[3] But there is also diversity within countries, and sectors within them.

The administrative structure of transport in many countries means that most types of infrastructure are supplied with the intention of maximizing overall economic efficiency; that is, they are appraised in terms of their social value assuming that they are optimally utilized at marginal cost prices. There are clearly exceptions to this where profit maximization is seen as the primary objective, as with the US railroads. Even when conducting an assessment of a single project, or a series of closely related ones, the complexity of funding mechanisms can mean that a combination of techniques are adopted to meet the requirements of different stockholders; and this can even involve different approaches by various levels of government that have a financial stake in the project.[4] A simple review of the ways in which highways are financed in the United States (Table 11.2) highlights the complexity of the problem.

Financial Appraisal

Historically a lot of transport infrastructure has been provided by the private sector, and even some that has been publicly provided has been done so using commercial criteria. Indeed there are arguments that there are cycles in which the private sector, and, *ipso facto*, financial considerations, have played a greater or lesser role in transport investments.[5] While this may apply when there are new modes emerging, for example the railroads taking over from canals for the movement of freight in the mid-nineteenth century, there have also been shifts of emphasis within modes. An example is the private engagement in turnpike investments in the eighteenth and early nineteenth centuries, reverting to government investments in highways in the early twentieth century, to the concessions for private investors that became common in the 1990s.

---

[3] K.J. Button and G. McDougall, 'Institutional and structural changes in air navigation service-providing organizations', *Journal of Air Transport Management*, **12**, 236–52, 2006.

[4] K.J. Button and D.W. Pearce, 'Infrastructure restoration as a tool for stimulating urban renewal – the Glasgow Canal', *Urban Studies*, **26**, 559–71, 1989.

[5] D. Levinson, *Financing Transportation Networks*, Cheltenham, UK and Northampton, MA, USA: Edward Elgar, 2002.

Table 11.2 *Sponsors and features of highway financing in the United States*

Sponsor	Major features of financing	Examples
Private equity investors	Finance and develop the project using private resources	Dulles Greenway (VA) 91 Express Lanes (CA)
Private, non-profit entity	Issues tax-exempt debt backed by tolls (and without recourse to taxes) and oversees the project under the terms of the agreement between the state and a private developer	TH 212 (MN) Southern Connector (SC) Interstate 895 (VA) Tacoma Narrows Bridge (WA) Arizona toll project (AV)
Special-purpose public	Issues tax-exempt debt backed by tolls (and without recourse to taxes) and oversees the project under the terms of the agreement with the private developer	E-470 (CO) Orange County transportation corridor agency (CA)
State agency	Issues tax-exempt debt backed by tolls (and without recourse to taxes)	Some turnpikes
State agency	Issues tax-exempt debt backed by taxes	Most highway projects that are financed by debt
State agency	Finances highways on a pay-as-you-go basis using state taxes and fees plus federal aid	Most highways

Source: US Congressional Budget Office, *Innovative Financing of Highways: An Analysis of Proposals*, Washington, DC: US Congress, 1998.

Differences in the perspective of the investors depend largely on whether the focus is on the stockholding (concerning only the people who make the investment) or the stakeholding (embracing those who not only put the finance into the system but also are affected by its larger outcomes). The former focuses primarily on commercial criteria, and the financial returns that an investment can generate, and the latter on wider social criteria.

In technical terms, the simple differences between the basic commercial and social welfare-maximizing approaches are seen in Figure 11.2. The profit maximizer is only interested in 'producer surplus', the difference between money paid out to make the investment and the subsequent revenue earned, whereas the broader approach takes account of both the 'producer surplus' and the 'consumer surplus', the amount society would have been willing to pay for the investment beyond the actual costs incurred – the combination forming the social surplus.

The distinction between the two approaches may be seen in more detail by contrasting the discounting approach used by large profit-oriented firms (and public corporations instructed to operate commercially) with the discounting approach of undertakings concerned with economic efficiency. (The discounting process is a simple weighting of different items of cost and income according to the time period at which they occur, more distant items being given less emphasis in the calculations.)

More formally, a commercially motivated firm will, in the absence of a

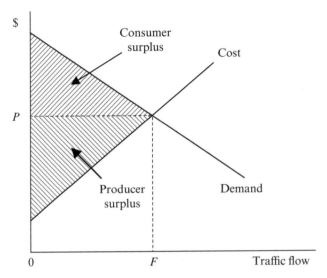

Figure 11.2   *The simple difference between the financial and social cost–benefit approaches*

budget constraint, accept investments when the financial net present value is positive, that is,

$$NPV_P = \sum_{t=1}^{t=k} \left[\frac{P(R_t) - P(C_t)}{(1 - r)^t} \right] \tag{11.1}$$

where:

  NPV_P is the financial net present value;
  $P(R_t)$ is the probable revenue that would be earned in year t from the investment;
  $P(C_t)$ is the probable financial cost of the investment in year t;
  r is the rate of interest reflecting the cost of capital to the undertaking; and
  k is the anticipated life of the investment.

A positive NPV_P therefore, tells the businessperson that it is worthwhile undertaking an initial investment, that is, it tells him/her that a movement from zero output in Figure 11.1 to output Q_1 with the associated short-run costs of $SRAC_1$ and $SRMC_1$ is commercially desirable and that a profit above both long- and short-run costs will be earned. A more normal case, where an expansion of operations is being considered involving some new capital outlay, requires the additional discounted profits from the investment to be compared with the additional discounted costs. If the resultant incremental NPV_P is positive, then the investment is justified on profitability grounds. In terms of the diagram, a movement down the $LRMC$ curve to output level Q_2 with the short-run marginal costs of $SRMC_2$ would yield a positive incremental NPV_P but subsequent investment to take one down the $LRMC$ curve to say output Q_3 would not.

The Cost–Benefit Approach

In contrast to the stockholder approach, investments involving the public sector generally involve economic efficiency being assessed using some form of cost–benefit (or 'benefit–cost') analysis (CBA)[6] which, again in the absence of a budget constraint, suggests that schemes with a positive social net present value should be undertaken where:

$$NPV_{SW} = \sum_{G=1}^{G=X} \sum_{T=1}^{T=K} \left(\frac{a_m P(B_{GT}) - b_m P(L_{GT})}{(1-i)^T} \right) \qquad (11.2)$$

where:

> NPV_{SW} is the social net present value;
> $a_m P(B_{GT})$ is the probable social benefit to be enjoyed by individual m in year T as a result of the investment's completion. B_{GT} is given a weighting a, to reflect society's welfare preference;
> $b_m P(L_{GT})$ is the probable social cost imposed on individual m in year T as a result of the investment's completion. L_{GT} is given a weighting b, to reflect society's welfare preference;
> i is the relative social weight attached to a cost or benefit occurring in a given year;
> K is the anticipated life of the investment; and
> G is the number of individuals affected.

Again, in terms of Figure 11.1, a positive NPV implies that the social surplus associated with an investment exceeds the discounted costs – that is, the demand curve at the final output is equal to or above the $LRMC$ curve. An additional investment will be economically justified as long as the discounted value of incremental social benefit exceeds incremental costs. Contrasting this with the commercial criteria, the NPV_P, associated with moving down the $LRMC$ curve from output Q_2 to Q_3 is negative but the incremental NPV would be calculated to be positive.

Not only is the cost–benefit type of analysis more comprehensive in terms of the items considered but it also redefines many of the items retained from commercial criteria. For example, the costs of imported raw materials used in a potential road construction project in a Third World country would be valued at market prices if a commercial undertaking were responsible for road investment decisions.

If a public body undertakes road investment using wider social criteria, then it would look beyond the immediate financial indicators and at the 'shadow' prices of imports so that the scarcity of foreign exchange and the limitations of adequate finance for imports is reflected in the decision making. In some investments, use

---

[6] P. Mackie and J. Nellthorp, 'Cost–benefit in transport', in K.J. Button and D. Hensher (eds), *Handbook of Transport Systems and Traffic Control*, Oxford: Pergamon, 2001.

is made of formerly unemployed factor services – for example, unemployed labor where the opportunity cost of employment in a transport scheme is really zero or the opportunity cost of the leisure they now forgo. A commercial concern would cost such inputs as the wages that have to be paid, but in a cost–benefit study they may not be considered a cost at all or, more probably, would be costed so that genuine resource costs are incorporated in the calculations.

A further very important distinction is that the social efficiency approach takes cognizance of the distributional effect of the investment (the a_g and b_g terms in equation (11.2)). This is often difficult to do in reality although various schemes for weighting costs and benefits have been advanced by theoreticians.[7] In practice there is a tendency to employ rather crude methods. Often, as in the case of the planning balance sheet approach discussed below, such methods have been used in urban infrastructure investment appraisals,[8] which involve the simple setting out in tabular form of the impacts of a scheme on the different user and non-user groups affected or, as with the COBA inter-urban road appraisal methods used until recently in the United Kingdom,[9] which carried out a partial CBA with no allowance for distributional effects but subjecting the results of this to further debate at public inquiry.

In other cases, the social analysis may not be complete – it may focus only on the internal social efficiency of the transport system and ignore its wider implications on the environment and so on. In an evaluation a new mode of high-speed ground transport, the magnetic levitation rail system (Maglev), Elhorst and Oosterhaven[10] compare the results of an integral CBA that embraces environmental and wider economic effects, with those of a conventional partial CBA that looks only at transport effects, and conclude that the additional economic benefits due to market imperfections vary from −1 to 38 percent of the direct transport benefits, depending on the type of regions connected and the general condition of the economy. Initially, however, it is useful to explain in a little more detail the broad differences between a financial appraisal and a social analysis of an investment.

11.4 The Theory of Cost–Benefit Analysis

While there are many complexities in undertaking commercial investment appraisal (for example, allowing for risk of unexpected changes in demand,

---

[7] M. McGuire and H. Gain, 'The integration of equity and efficiency criteria in public project selection', *Economic Journal*, **79**, 882–93, 1969.

[8] N. Lichfield and W. Chapman, 'Cost–benefit analysis and road proposals for a shopping centre – a case study: Edgware', *Journal of Transport Economics and Policy*, **2**, 280–320, 1968.

[9] UK Department of Transport, *Urban Road Appraisal: Report of the Standing Committee on Trunk Road Appraisal*, London: HMSO, 1986.

[10] J.P. Elhorst and J. Oosterhaven, 'Integral cost–benefit analysis of Maglev rail projects under market imperfections', *Journal of Transport and Land Use*, **1**, 65–87, 2008.

deciding upon appropriate methods of raising capital and so on), it is public sector transport investment that has attracted the greatest attention. The wide-ranging and long-term effects of most major changes in transport infrastructure necessitate the employment of sophisticated methods of project appraisal and of comprehensive techniques for decision making. The underlying notion of CBA that forms the explicit (and, on occasions, implicit) foundation for much of this work has already been alluded to in previous sections. While the algebra set down there suggests a comparatively simple set of standard calculations, the theoretical model is itself based upon a set of much more complex assumptions which makes the application a far more tortuous exercise than it might at first appear. Indeed, there is evidence that the optimism once felt for CBA as the panacea for all trans-port investment appraisal problems has gradually evaporated and the confidence felt in the strength of CBA calculations no longer exists.

This and the following sections attempt, in broad terms, to explain the CBA methodology and to point to recent innovations in theory and practice. The subject matter of CBA has now become so vast that the treatment here must, by necessity, be rather limited. We begin by looking at the basic welfare economics underlying the technique. This highlights some of the key assumptions upon which it is based.

The simple outline of CBA in the previous section emphasized the notion of selecting investments that maximize social surplus rather than just pecuniary returns. One of the major problems in this is that of interpersonal comparisons of welfare. Is it really possible to say that social welfare has risen if one group becomes better off at the expense of another? This represents a common situation in transport where users tend to benefit at the expense of non-users, or among users, travelers using one mode gain at the expense of another. CBA attempts to circumvent this conceptual problem by making use of 'hypothetical compensa-tion tests'. Strictly, since we only have a notion of the ordinal ranking of indi-viduals' priorities, interpersonal welfare comparisons can be made only in very limited circumstances. The Pareto criterion, which underlies most modern welfare economics, states that an action can only definitely be said to be socially desirable if at least one agent benefits and no one suffers any diminution of welfare.

Diagrammatically, in the upper portion of Figure 11.3 we have two individu-als, A and B, who enjoy various levels of welfare recorded on the horizontal and vertical axes as U_A and U_B. If we have a finite collection of goods and services available (including transport services) together with a fixed level of costs, then the well-being of A and B will depend upon how these goods, services and costs are distributed between them.

The utility possibility frontier represents the maximum possible welfare they could enjoy given different distributions of the goods, services and costs. Initially, the goods and so on are distributed so that point X on the pre-investment frontier is achieved (that is, A enjoys a utility of $0U_A^*$ and B of $0U_B^*$). The goods, services and costs could be redistributed so that any other point on the pre-investment frontier could be obtained but no point outside of it. Suppose now a transport investment results in the bundle of goods, services and costs changing and that position Y beyond the pre-investment frontier is reached. This would be deemed

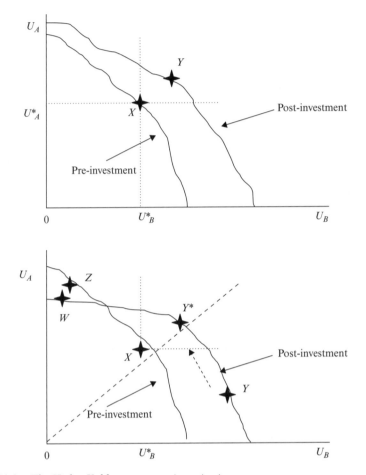

Figure 11.3   *The Hicks–Kaldor compensation criteria*

a Pareto improvement because both *A* and *B* are better off. Indeed, any *ex post* position within the 90° zone marked (such as *Y*) in the upper part of the figure would be Pareto superior to *X* since, even on one of the limits, at least one person is better off while the other at worst retains his/her original utility level.

The strict Pareto criterion is of little use in practice as most transport schemes have either direct or indirect net adverse effects on some members of the community. The suggested method of allowing for this, developed 70 years or so ago, is to adopt a hypothetical Pareto criterion and decide whether after the investment it would be possible to redistribute the impacts in such a way that no one is worse off but there is still some residual gain to others. Whether such redistribution actually occurs is felt to be a normative issue and should be treated as within the domain of politics rather than economics.

There are two broad approaches to the hypothetical compensation criteria. The first, initially advanced by Nicholas Kaldor,[11] forms the basis for most CBA

[11] N. Kaldor, 'Welfare proposition and interpersonal comparisons of utility', *Economic Journal*, **49**, 549–52, 1939.

studies and suggests that a scheme is socially desirable if the beneficiaries could compensate the losers and still remain better off. In the lower part of Figure 11.3, Y is Kaldor superior to X (although not strictly Pareto superior) because Y is on the post-investment utility possibility frontier that passes outside of X. Hence, the bundle of goods, services and costs which generate the post-investment frontier could be redistributed from Y to Y^* which is Pareto superior to X.

Whether the government instigates a tax/subsidy scheme to cause such a movement along the post-investment frontier is considered a political issue; Kaldor (in a discussion of the repeal of the nineteenth-century Corn Laws!) simply argues that it could be done. Sir John Hicks[12] favors a similar approach but adopts pre-investment weights for his criteria. Specifically, he argues for a project's acceptance if those who lose as a result of its implementation cannot bribe the gainers not to do it without becoming worse off themselves. In the figure, Y is Hicks superior to X because, with the pre-investment package of goods, services and costs that permitted the post-investment frontier to be attained, it is impossible for A (the loser) to bribe B (the beneficiary) not to support the investment.

The problem with the Kaldor and Hicks approaches is that they may, in some circumstances, contradict one another. For example, in Figure 11.3, although combination W is Kaldor superior to X, we can see that X is Hicks superior to W. Further, even if one used only the Kaldor test and the investment was completed and position W attained, it then becomes possible to show that it is, again following the Kaldor criteria, socially beneficial to disinvest and return to X. (Similar types of problem exist with the Hicks test.) Paul Samuelson,[13] argues that the problem will always exist as long as the pre- and post-investment utility possibility frontiers cross and that comparisons in such circumstances are invalid.

This is an extremely restrictive view. As long as the two actual positions being compared are on the same side of any intersection of the frontiers, then the two criteria give consistent assessments and there are no problems of so-called 'Scitovsky reversibility'.[14] Figure 11.3, for instance, shows a situation where Y meets both the Hicks and the Kaldor hypothetical compensation tests and may, therefore, be considered socially superior to X. There is also no question of advocating reversibility once the investment leading to Y has been undertaken. Whether, in practice, transport analysts need to test for these problems is an empirical question that has, to date, been inadequately explored. At least one experienced economist in the CBA field suggests that the Scitovsky criteria may be violated on more occasions than is sometimes supposed.[15]

A different problem may arise when appraising a series of piecemeal

[12] J.R. Hicks, 'The valuation of social income', *Economica*, **7**, 105–24, 1940.
[13] P.A. Samuelson, 'Evaluation of social income, capital formation and wealth', in P.A. Lutz and D.C. Hague (eds), *The Theory of Capital*, New York: St Martins, 1961.
[14] T. Scitovsky, 'A note on welfare propositions in economics', *Review of Economic Studies*, **9**, 77–88, 1941.
[15] J. de V. Graaf, 'Cost–benefit analysis: a critical view', *South African Journal of Economics*, **44**, 233–44, 1975.

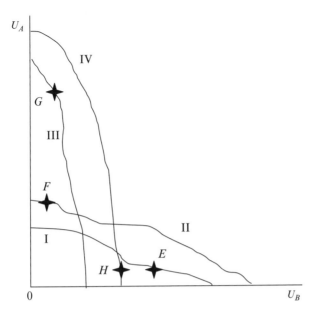

Figure 11.4   *The problem of assessing a series of small investments*

investments. It is possible, because of the relative nature of consumer surplus that underlies all these tests, for a series of small investments each to pass the Scitovsky test but for the eventual outcome to be socially inferior to the initial position.[16] In Figure 11.4, if we have an initial position of E on the pre-investment frontier (I), then an investment that permits F on frontier II to be reached satisfies the Scitovsky criterion (and, indeed, Samuelson's); further, a move from F to G, following additional investment, may be approved and, likewise, a subsequent move from G to H, which again meets the Scitovsky test. However, despite the fact that we have seen that $E < F < G < H$ in terms of hypothetical compensation tests, it is clearly evident in Figure 11.4 that E is preferable, on Scitovsky grounds, to H on frontier IV. Each of the series of small changes appear desirable but the final, overall outcome leaves society worse off than before.

If this problem was only a theoretical curio there would be no need for concern; unfortunately this does not seem to be the case. Numerous examples of piecemeal decision-making leading to a subsequent diminution of social welfare can be cited in urban planning, but in the context of transport perhaps the most worrying problem concerns the growth in car use since the Second World War at the expense of urban public transport.[17] For simplicity, we take a concentric-shaped city with employment concentrated in the center. The urban core is surrounded by a ring of residential estates. The analysis is short term and assumes that this land-use pattern is fixed. It is now possible to define three phases:

[16] W.M. Gorman, 'The intransitivity of certain "criteria" used in welfare economics', *Oxford Economic Papers* (New Series), **7**, 25–35, 1955.
[17] E.J. Mishan, 'Interpretation of the benefits of private transport', *Journal of Transport Economics and Policy*, **1**, 184–9, 1967.

- *Phase I*   All commuters have only one mode of transport available to them and travel to work by means of public transport – taking 10 minutes – is the norm.
- *Phase II*   One commuter buys a car and drives to work taking 5 minutes, leaving the other travelers unaffected by his/her action and still taking 10 minutes to reach their work by public transport.
- *Phase III*   Many commuters, observing the advantage enjoyed by the car driver, begin to buy and use cars that, with the congestion they generate, increase driving time to work to 15 minutes and, due to the impedance caused by the cars, slows public transport so that commuters using this mode now suffer a 25-minute journey. In the longer term, because of the technologically unprogressive nature of public transport, the service may be withdrawn (following the syndrome of few passengers ⇒ higher fares and poorer service ⇒ even fewer passengers and so on) leaving a choice of car purchase or walking to work. The result is a 'prisoner's dilemma' type of situation where individually each commuter would prefer the original situation, rather than the new undesirable equilibrium, but cannot attain it by unilateral action.

The example illustrates the difficulties which may arise as the result of decisions based upon relative welfare measures: each commuter thought that he/she would benefit by investing in a car because he/she did not take cognizance of the whole set of decisions being made. Ideally, a CBA study should appraise all the systems or sequences of potential investments rather than assess individual components of a program of events. The urban planning process, discussed in Chapter 12, is an area where this is particularly relevant.

While most CBA studies of transport projects have concentrated on efficiency considerations, relying upon the hypothetical compensation criteria, it has been suggested by Ian Little[18] that some allowance for distributional impact should be incorporated. Specifically, it is argued that a project should only be accepted using the hypothetical type of criteria if the final outcome improves the income distribution. For example, in the lower part of Figure 11.3, we assume that an improved income distribution means greater equality of welfare and thus corresponds to a movement closer to the 45° line depicted. Thus, Y, on the post-investment policy frontier, is Scitovsky superior to X but Little inferior because it is further from the 45°, equal utility, line. It is important to note that with Little it is the actual outcome that is being considered and not potential redistributed packages of the post-investment collection of goods, services and costs such as Y^*. As we shall see in Section 11.5, there are several ways in which this distributional element may be incorporated within CBA studies.

[18] I.M.D. Little, *A Critique of Welfare Economics*, Oxford: Oxford University Press, 1950.

11.5   Coping with Network Effects

The discussion above applies to all CBA applications but a particular difficulty of applying the technique to transport investment decisions is the need to incorporate adequately the wide-ranging effects that a change in one part of the transport system has on the rest of the network. Most transport infrastructure forms a link in a much larger, interacting network and, consequently, changes in any one link tend to affect demand on competitive and complementary links. Although this sort of complexity exists for virtually all forms of transport, the problem of assessing the overall effect on road transport of improving a single link has, because of the dominance of this form of transport in modern society, attracted most attention.

If there are two roads, one from X to Y and the other from X to Z, where Y and Z are to some degree substitute destinations, then an improvement in route XY will affect three groups. We shall assume for simplicity that all demand curves are linear and that the pre-investment traffic flows on XY and XZ are T_{XY} and $(T_{XZ} + R)$, respectively. The three groups of users to consider are then:

1   Existing users who remain on their original routes (that is, T_{XY} and T_{XZ}). These will enjoy a gain in consumers' surplus because those on route XY will now be using a higher-quality facility while those on XZ will benefit from reductions in demand for this route as some former users switch to the improved XY. If this latter traffic which has diverted from XZ to XY is denoted as R, then the benefit to those remaining loyal to their initial routes may be represented as:

$$T_{XY}(C_1 - C_2) + T_{XZ}(C_1^* - C_2^*) \tag{11.3}$$

where C_1, C_2, C_1^* and C_2^* are the pre- and post-investment costs by roads XY and XZ, respectively.

2   Generated traffic consisting of people who did not previously travel (that is, G_{XY} and G_{XZ}). On average (given the linear demand curves) each of these groups of new road users will benefit by half as much as existing, non-switching traffic. (Some will obviously be marginal trip makers and only just gain by making a trip while others are intra-marginal and enjoy nearly as much additional consumer surplus as the non-switchers.) The benefit of the investment to this group will thus be:

$$0.5G_{XY}(C_1 - C_2) + 0.5G_{XZ}(C_1^* - C_2^*) \tag{11.4}$$

3   Diverted traffic that switches from route XZ to route XY as a consequence of the investment (that is, R). The switch, given the free choice situation open to travelers, must leave this group better off – they would not have switched otherwise – and the additional welfare they enjoy can be seen to equal half of the difference in benefit between the cost reductions on the two routes, that is,

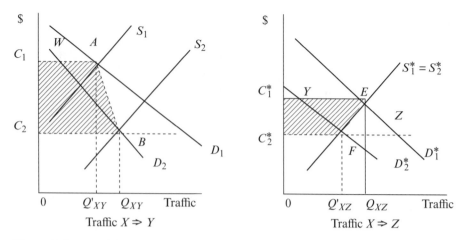

Figure 11.5   *Social benefits over a transport network*

$$R\{(C_1^*-C_2^*) + 0.5[(C_1 - C_2) - (C_1^* - C_2^*)]\},$$

which may be reduced to:

$$0.5R[(C_1 - C_2) + (C_1^* - C_2^*)]. \tag{11.5}$$

The total benefit of the investment is the summation of these three elements namely:

$$TB = T_{XY}(C_1 - C_2) + T_{XZ}(C_1^* - C_2^*) + 0.5G_{XY}(C_1 - C_2)$$

$$+ 0.5G_{XZ}(C_1^* - C_2^*) + 0.5R[(C_1 - C_2) + (C_1^* - C_2^*)]. \tag{11.6}$$

Figure 11.5 shows this diagrammatically. The left-hand part of the figure represents the supply and demand situations on route XY and right-hand segment those on route XZ. On route XY we see that demand has increased the supply of road space but that demand for its use has declined because the relative generalized cost of using XZ changes as traffic diverts from it to the improved facility.

Using the notation in the diagram, we know that $Q_{XY} = T_{XY}$ and that $Q'_{XY} = (T_{XY} + G_{XY} + R)$, therefore:

$$0.5(Q_{XY} + Q'_{XY}) = (T_{XY} + 0.5G_{XY} + 0.5R)$$

Similarly, since $Q_{XZ} = (T_{XZ} + R)$ and $Q'_{XZ} = (T_{XZ} + G_{XZ})$ we know that:

$$0.5(Q_{XZ} + Q'_{XZ}) = (T_{XY} + 0.5G_{XY} + 0.5R)$$

Substituting this into equation (11.6) we discover:

$$TB = [0.5(Q_{XZ} + Q'_{XZ}) (C_1 - C_2) + 0.5(Q_{XZ} + Q'_{XZ})(C_1^* - C_2^*)]$$

or more generally, this can be seen as the oft-cited 'rule of half',

$$TB = 0.5 \sum_N (Q_n + Q_n^*)(C_n + C_n^*) \qquad (11.7)$$

This net benefit is equivalent to the shaded areas seen in Figure 11.5. The rule of half can be applied to all transport schemes that interact with other components of the transport system where demand curves are linear. (It must, however, be used with a degree of circumspection when routes are complementary, where demand for the non-improved links may shift to the right, but the broad principle applies.)

The method of handling the interdependencies outlined above was initially developed in the late 1960s as part of the London Transportation Study, but it does rely upon a rather strong implicit assumption that the income elasticities of demand for routes XY and XZ are equal. The problem is that there are many possible sequences in which price changes on routes XY and XZ could follow; each would yield a different level of aggregate social welfare. For instance, if the chain of price changes is $(C_1, C_1^*) \Rightarrow (C_2, C_1^*) \Rightarrow (C_2, C_2^*)$ then the consumer surplus gain in the diagram would be $\{(C_1 AXC_2) + (C_1^* YFC_2^*)\}$. But if the sequence is $(C_1, C_1^*) \Rightarrow (C_1, C_2^*) \Rightarrow (C_2, C_2^*)$ then the aggregate benefit would be $\{(C_1 WBC_2) + (C_1^* EXC_2^*)\}$.

The general measure set out in equation (11.7) assumes that the demand fluctuations are linear in their own prices and with respect to cross-price effects – if this is so then the measure would give identical results to both the sequences outlined above (which would themselves yield identical benefit estimates). Whether such assumptions are valid is debatable, but Foster and Neuburger[19] argue that any deviation is unlikely to be of any practical significance in actual evaluation exercises. Certainly, given the other major difficulties of evaluation and measurement, the 'rule of half' provides a robust and useful guide to the user benefits of transport schemes.

11.6   CBA in Practice and Variations on the Theme

Our attention, to this point, has focused on the theoretical ideas and concepts underlying CBA. We now turn to look more directly at its actual application in transport fields. Equation (11.2) set out above gives a formal mathematical definition of CBA, while Prest and Turvey[20] give the verbal counterpart: CBA is a practical way of assessing the desirability of projects, where it is important to take a long view (in the sense of looking at repercussions in the further as well as the nearer future) and a wide view (in the sense of allowing for side-effects of

---

[19] C.D. Foster and H.L.I. Neuburger, 'The ambiguity of the consumer's surplus measure of welfare change', *Oxford Economic Papers*, **26**, 66–77, 1974.

[20] A.R. Prest and R. Turvey, 'Cost–benefit analysis – a survey', *Economic Journal*, **75**, 683–735, 1965.

Table 11.3   *The nature of transport infrastructure decision making in European*
Countries

Country	Systems approach	Master plan	Intermodal cooperation	Time horizon	Private financing
France	S	M	S	Long	M
Germany	M	W	M	Long	S
Italy	S	M	S	Short	S
Belgium	S	S	S	Short	S
Sweden	M	M	S	Medium	S
Denmark	M	M	M	Short	S
Norway	M	M	S	Medium	S
Finland	S	S	S	Medium	S
Switzerland	W	W	M	Long	S

Notes: S = scarcely developed; M = partially developed; W = well developed.

many kinds on many persons, industries, regions and so on) that is, it implies the enumeration and evaluation of all the relevant costs and benefits.

CBA has, over the years, formed the basis of investment appraisal of many major transport schemes in the United Kingdom (for example, the Ml motorway, the Victoria Line underground railway, the Channel Tunnel, London's system of ringway or beltway urban motorways and the siting of a Third London Airport) and elsewhere. It has also become a tool in more routine decision making (for example, to assess UK railway social service subsidies in the late 1960s and as a component of inter-urban road investment appraisal in the form of COBA and its subsequent modification, New Approach to Appraisal, or NATA[21]). The UK situation, however, is a particular case and there are quite important variations in the form of appraisal used to assess transport projects in industrialized countries, some more comprehensive and others less so. Table 11.3 offers a broad over-view of the differing nature of decision-making processes in a number of major European countries in the 1990s. The United States, being a federal system, has both a manual for conducting CBA for national highway investments[22] as well as each state having its own approach.

The Third London Airport Study completed by the Roskill Commission[23] established the traditional textbook CBA approach although here, since it was assumed that a new facility was necessary anyway, the benefits were deemed vir-tually equal for all possible sites, that is, the questions posed involved considering where and when an airport should be built – not whether. This meant that in some ways it became a social cost-effectiveness study – finding the site with the lowest social costs attached to it. The present values of the various cost and benefit items

[21] S. Glaister, 'Observations on the new approach to the appraisal of road projects', *Journal of Transport Economics and Policy*, **33**, 221–6, 1999.

[22] US Federal Highway Administration, *Economic Analysis Primer: Benefit–Cost Analysis*, Washington, DC: FHWA, 2003.

[23] Commission on the Third London Airport, *Report*, London: HMSO, 1971.

Table 11.4   *Social costs and benefits (£millions in 1970 prices) associated with alternative sites for a Third London Airport*

	Cublington	Foulness	Northampstead	Thurleigh
Capital costs				
Construction of airport	184.0	179.0	178.0	166.0
Airport services	14.3	9.8	14.5	11.6
Extension/closure of Luton Airport	−1.3	10.0	−1.3	−1.3
Road and rail development	11.8	23.4	15.5	6.5
Relocation of defense and public scientific establishments	67.4	21.0	57.9	84.2
Loss of agricultural land	3.1	4.2	7.2	4.6
Impact on residential conditions	3.5	4.0	2.1	1.6
Impact on schools, hospitals, etc.	2.5	0.8	4.1	4.9
Other	3.5	0.5	6.7	10.2
Total	*288.8*	*252.7*	*284.7*	*288.3*
Current costs				
Aircraft movements	960.0	973.0	987.0	972.0
Passenger users	931.0	1,041.0	987.0	931.0
Freight users	13.4	23.1	17.0	13.9
Airport services and operations	60.3	53.1	56.2	55.6
Travel costs to/from airport	26.2	26.5	24.4	25.4
Other	12.4	7.5	8.5	7.2
Total	*2,003.3*	*2,124.2*	*1,988.1*	*2,005.1*
Benefits (relative to Foulness)				
To common/diverted traffic (net of costs)	–	n.a.	–	–
To generated traffic	44.0	n.a.	27.0	42.0
Total (cost less differential benefits	*2,248.1*	*2,376.9*	*2,245.8*	*2,251.4*

Note: The table is only a partial reflection of the results obtained and does not, for example, reflect the sensitivity analysis conducted.

Source: Commission on the Third London Airport, *Report*, London: HMSO, 1971.

for each alternative discounted from 2006 back to 1975 values are given in Table 11.4. While the study team favored Cublington as marginally superior to the other sites, subsequent parliamentary debate overruled this in favor of Foulness (that is, Maplin). Although even this revised proposal was later abandoned, the study proved useful in showing up some of the practical difficulties in conducting a CBA study of a scheme which has extremely wide-ranging and diverse impacts – many of them posing serious problems of evaluation.

A less comprehensive approach than that devised by Roskill is the COBA computer program[24] which was for many years employed as part of the inter-urban road appraisal process in the United Kingdom from the 1960s, although, it should be emphasized, only as part of a more extensive procedure. The emphasis here has been rather more on consistency than on comprehensive coverage. The program makes use of traffic forecasts derived from a standardized procedure and uses them to compare discounted monetary valuations of travel time changes, variations in vehicle operating costs and impacts on accident rates with the capital and maintenance costs of a project. While this provides an indication of the costs and benefits to traffic and the exchequer, additional information on third-party effects, such as environmental impacts, were, until the early 1990s, been treated separately.

Despite the widespread adoption of CBA by the transport sector, there has been a gradual disillusionment with the all-embracing, stereotype appraisal implied by Prest and Turvey (see note 20). This has manifested itself most strongly since the rejection of the Roskill Committee's recommendation regarding the siting of a Third London Airport and became particularly noticeable at public inquiries into new road proposals in the late 1970s and early 1980s. While the criticisms of CBA as a method of socially evaluating transport investments have been extensive, they are perhaps most adequately summed up by Wildavsky,[25] 'Although cost–benefit analysis presumably results in efficiency by adding the most to national income, it is shot through with political and social value choices and surrounded by uncertainties and difficulties of computation'. A former Chairman of British Rail summarized the attitude evolving in the United Kingdom when he argued that there is a need for an approach

> [that] can be understood by ordinary intelligent people . . . incorporates the methods of analysis developed by welfare economists over the last decade or so . . . gets away from the naive position adopted by the early cost–benefit men which seemed to imply that every consideration could be perfectly weighted and that, therefore, there was a single best solution.[26]

The responses of analysts to these dissatisfactions with mechanical CBA procedures have taken two broad lines. The first is an attempt to modify the original CBA framework (as exemplified by equation (11.2)) so that some allowances are made for the major criticisms. In particular, greater effort has been put into evaluating the externality items included in a CBA account and to placing more reliable values on time-saving attributes of schemes. Advances on this front have been more rapid in some countries than in others. Sweden, for example,

[24] UK Department of Transport, *COBA 9 Manual*, London: HMSO, 1992; UK Department of Transport, *Assessing the Environmental Impact of Road Schemes, Report of the Standing Committee on Trunk Road Assessment*, London: HMSO, 1989.

[25] A. Wildavsky, 'The political economy of efficiency: cost–benefit analysis', systems analysis and program budgeting', *Public Administration*, **26**, 292–310, 1966.

[26] P. Parker, 'A Way to Run a Railway', Haldane Memorial Lecture, University of London, 1978.

uses a variety of techniques to enable a diverse range of effects, often expressed in monetary terms, to be brought into the appraisal process. The position in the UK is that a more consistent process is taking rather longer to emerge, although experimentation in embracing a limited number of environmental factors within the COBA framework began after the publication of a report by the Standing Advisory Committee on Trunk Road Appraisal.[27]

Additionally, techniques have been evolved that introduce allowances for the distributional effects of schemes – an area neglected in earlier work which concentrated on overall impact – and for the risk and uncertainty that the predicted cost and benefit streams will diverge from that forecast. Theoretically, distributional effects can be allowed for by weighting the costs and benefits according to the different groups affected. Unfortunately, it has been demonstrated at the theoretical level[28] that in many investment situations the applications of such weights (which may, in particular, be based upon measures reflecting income tax liability) to cost and benefit items can still lead to the acceptance of projects which benefit the rich to the detriment of the poor. Consequently, there is a case for treating distributional considerations independently of efficiency.

Risk and uncertainty about probable outcomes pose even more difficult problems. With risks there is some knowledge about the likelihood of errors in forecasts and this can be incorporated in the analysis by indicating the range of probable long-term effects of investment, together with an indication of the probabilities of different levels of costs and benefits occurring. Unfortunately, there is no such knowledge of possible error with uncertainty and consequently adjustments tend to be made according to intuition or 'skilled judgment'. With many transport projects, the costs of under-engineering are likely to be higher than those of comparable over-engineering (the 'premature' physical disintegration of the UK motorway system being a good example) and thus there is a tendency to over-react to the possibility of uncertain outcomes.

While these advances in traditional CBA techniques go some way towards meeting criticism of early studies in the field, they tend to complicate the estimation and decision-making frameworks and, hence to move even further from the openness sought by the Transport Ministry, and also the Leitch Committee on trunk road investment appraisal.[29] One offshoot of CBA which retains the notion of social welfare maximization but also makes the CBA account accessible to the proverbial 'educated layperson' is the planning balance sheet (PBS) which was initially devised and developed over a series of case studies to help urban planners. We shall discuss the PBS in more detail below.

The second response to the critics is to move entirely away from the notion of a social welfare maximization CBA approach and to adopt a lower-level, but

[27] UK Department of Transport, *Assessing the Environmental Impact of Road Schemes: Standing Advisory Committee on Trunk Road Appraisal*, London: HMSO, 1992.

[28] E.J. Mishan, 'Flexibility and consistency in cost–benefit analysis', *Economica*, **41**, 81–96, 1974.

[29] UK Department of Transport, *Report of the Advisory Committee on Trunk Road Assessment*, London: HMSO, 1978.

possibly more operational and manageable, approach to investment appraisal. This, for example, is the approach that has increasingly been followed in France since the late 1960s.[30]

Broadly, it is argued that, like most large private companies, public transport undertakings have insufficient information about the stream of costs and benefits (including social items) associated with the different policy options open to them and should, therefore, attempt to meet broad minimum levels of achievement rather than to maximize net benefits. This notion of 'satisficing' fits in with the attitude of most mature industrial concerns towards managerial decision making.[31] Although this second type of response to the critics of CBA is, to date, still comparatively under-researched in the transport field, a number of multi-criteria investment appraisal techniques have been developed, often only at an abstract level, in related areas of study such as regional and national resource planning.

The PBS approach mentioned above, although firmly founded in the CBA tradition, offers a methodology that is sufficiently flexible to adaptation for both maximizing and satisficing frameworks. It has two main merits: first, it shifts the emphasis of analysis away from the total measurement of net benefit to the distribution of the costs and benefits among affected groups and second, it circumvents many of the problems associated with expressing all costs and benefits in money terms.

The technique involves setting down, in tabular form, all of the pros and cons associated with alternative investment options. These socioeconomic accounts are expressed in monetary values wherever possible but should this prove impracticable then physical values are used and, if quantification is not possible, ordinal indices or scales. The accounts are subdivided to show the effect of different schemes on the groups affected and this offers guidance to distributional implications. The accounts are compared with predetermined planning goals (and these instrumental objectives may imply either maximization or satisficing objectives) which are selected as reflective of community preferences. Alternative investment plans are ranked under each objective heading using ordinal ranking procedures and the ranks are then added together to produce a ranking of the investments with respect to the objectives taken as a whole.

A technique of this general kind met with approval from the Leitch Committee in the UK as a tool in inter-urban road investment appraisal. The Committee felt 'the right approach is through a comprehensive framework which embraces all the factors and groups of people involved in scheme assessment'.[32] The 'project impact matrix', as the Leitch Committee called their variation, sets out a 'general framework' of about 80 relevant measures of the effects of transport

[30] E. Quinet, 'Can we value the environment?', in D. Banister and K.J. Button (eds), *Transport, the Environment and Sustainable Development*, London: E.&F.N. Spon, 1993.

[31] H.A. Simon, 'Theories of decision-making in economics and behavioral science', *American Economic Review*, **49**, 253–83, 1959.

[32] UK Department of Transport, *Urban Road Appraisal: Report of the Standing Committee on Trunk Road Appraisal*, London: HMSO, 1986.

Table 11.5 *The project impact matrix suggested by the Leitch Committee in the United Kingdom*

Incidence group	Nature of effect	Number of measures	
		Financial	*Other*
Road uses directly affected	Accident savings	1	3
	Comfort and convenience		
	Time savings	6	
	Vehicle operating cost savings	5	
	Amenity		2
Non-road users directly affected	Demolition or disamenity to owners of residential, commercial and industrial properties		22
	Demolition or disamenity to users of schools, churches, public open space		15
	Land-take, severance and disamenity to farmers		7
Those concerned with the intrinsic value of an area	Landscape, scientific and historical value	3	
		(+ verbal description)	
Those indirectly affected	Sterilization of natural resources, land-use planning effects on other transport operators	6	
		(+ verbal description)	
Financial authority	Cost and financial benefits	19	7
Total		19	59

Source: Adapted from, UK Department of Transport, *Report of the Advisory Committee on Trunk Road Assessment*, London: HMSO, 1978.

schemes. As with most PBS studies the final account produced was extensive, but Table 11.5 provides a summary. The intention is to use such an account to make pair-wise comparisons between the magnitude of the effects associated with different investment alternatives or, where the problem is deciding upon a specific project in isolation, to compare them with some instrumental objectives.

The PBS type approach has, despite its attractions, some inherent limitations. In particular it depends upon crude ranking criteria and scaling methods. The selection of instrumental objectives is itself highly subjective and, although it does force the decision taker to make his/her underlying value judgments explicit, it can result in some conflict between interested parties. There is also the danger that the subjectivity of these objectives and trade-offs is forgotten in the mass of data incorporated in the accounts. The PBS has the advantage over some of the more mechanical CBA approaches where numbers are simply fed into a computer program (such as COBA as was used in the UK for trunk road investment appraisal) in that the construction of the initial socioeconomic account can often, in itself, be educational and shed considerable light on salient questions the decision taker should be asking.

While PBS has been seen as an extension of CBA, it may also be viewed as a primitive form of a 'multi-criteria decision-making technique'. Multi-criteria decision-making techniques fall into the second category of advances outlined above in that they are concerned more with the meeting of certain low-level aims than maximizing social welfare. They involve weighting the different effects of an investment to reflect social priorities, but the weights reflect the success at attaining certain objectives rather than maximizing an output.

A number of multi-criteria approaches have been devised, each attempting to achieve a multidimensional compromise between the wide diversity of goals and objectives that are embodied in any form of public choice.[33] Approaches differ in their methods of presentation, the level of mathematical sophistication involved and the amount of data input required. Several of the techniques rely upon geometrical representation to produce multidimensional scalings while others involve a considerable degree of intuition. Of greatest practical value in transport are some of the weighting techniques, of which there are numerous variations. Hill's[34] goals achievement matrix, for example, offers an explicit treatment of various goals and applies a set of predetermined weights to them so that each option can be assessed in terms of goals achieved. To facilitate this, the goals are related to physical measures (for example, minimum traffic speeds, acceptable accident rates, and reduced levels of specified toxic exhaust emissions) to reflect the extent to which they have been achieved. The final goals achievement account employs the weighted index of goal achievement to determine the preferred course of action.

The problem with all useful multi-criteria procedures is the derivation of weighting schemes that reflect the relative importance of physical 'goals' or 'objective instruments' – seldom will a public sector transport scheme do all that is hoped for. The traditional CBA approach, albeit in a maximizing context, avoids this problem by using monetary values as weights. While there is evidence that those actually responsible for decision making in the publicly controlled sectors of transport favor movement towards multi-criteria appraisal techniques, the practical problems are unlikely to permit the widespread use of such approaches – beyond the project impact matrix type of analysis – in the near future.

These types of modification to the cost–benefit approach are also likely to lead to a more consistent treatment of environmental effects but there is a more fundamental point about infrastructure provision. It has been argued that the conventional CBA approach to appraisal, because of its inherent assumptions regarding pricing, can lead to overinvestment in transport infrastructure and excessive transport use. In Figure 11.6 we show various combinations of prices

[33] P. Nijkamp and A. van Delft, *A Multi-criteria Analysis and Regional Decision-making*, London: Martinus Nijhoff, 1979.

[34] M. Hill, 'A goal achievement matrix for evaluating alternative plans', *Journal of the American Institute of Planners*, **34**, 19–29, 1968.

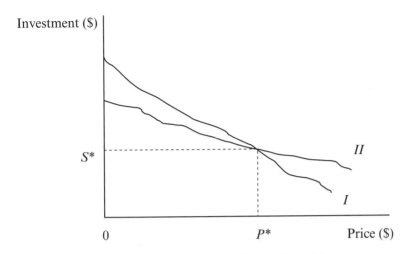

Figure 11.6   *Second-best investment with suboptimal congestion pricing*

charged for road use and, on the vertical, various levels (in money terms) of investment. There will be some optimal price–investment mix such as P^*/S^*. This would be the socially efficient outcome if road users were charged optimal prices (embracing all external considerations) for their journeys.

Suppose, however, that the price in effect does not fully reflect costs; then, since there would be a heavy demand for road use, the conventional CBA approach would imply that more investment than S^* is required. Curve I traces out the relevant optimal price–investment combinations that would emerge. In fact, the low price is generating demand beyond the optimal level and thus the overall amount of traffic on curve I at points to the left will be suboptimally large. Wheaton[35] argues, therefore, that investment should be limited along a P/S curve such as II. The additional congestion occurring at any price below P^* because of the limited additional investment in capacity will in effect constrain traffic flows to the optimal level. The reasoning behind this conclusion is summarized by Wheaton in the following way:

> Such a reduction will increase congestion, and this helps to discourage the demand that has been 'artificially' induced by under pricing. It is important to remember that second-best investment does not call for building fewer roads as the price of driving is lowered. That would result in 'excessive' congestion. Rather it requires accommodating less of the induced demand than would be met if a simple cost–benefit analysis were applied.

Applying this to the question of, say, environmental policy, the relevance is mainly in terms of just how much investment in new infrastructure is economically justified when transport prices do not reflect true costs. The standard methodology tends to ignore the imperfections which exist in terms of transport users not

---

[35] W.C. Wheaton, 'Price-induced distortions in urban highway investment', *Bell Journal of Economics*, **9**, 622–32, 1978

paying for the full costs of their activities and thus to favor high levels of investment. Wheaton's analysis essentially implies that in these conditions where money prices are ineffective, second-best criteria determined by travelers' time costs (that is, congestion) can be used to limit travel to a level closer to the optimum. The actual conditions for achieving this second-best situation may, however, prove to be rather complex.[36] In terms of equity there may be a further argument in favor of such an approach in that time is allocated evenly across individuals. In practice, there are difficulties in working out the optimal second-best strategy and, in overall environmental terms, given the proportionately higher pollution, noise and other costs associated with congested roads, it is not altogether clear what the ultimate overall social outcome would be.

11.7   Comparability between Appraisal Techniques

If scarce investment funds are to be allocated to best effect within the overall transport sector and between it and the rest of the economy, it is clearly important that in some way comparisons are made between the potential effect of using funds in projects evaluated on commercial criteria and using them where social evaluation techniques such as CBA are employed.

Accepting that for institutional or administrative reasons there is no hope of a common method of assessment being employed in practice, then one possible method of comparing projects between sectors is to develop comparability criteria that reduce social and financial costs and benefits to a common denominator. Essentially a mathematical relationship between net social and net financial returns must be found. In certain, highly restrictive, situations this may prove to be feasible.[37] It is theoretically possible, under simplistic assumptions, to reduce everything to either a common financial or a common social basis; we shall assume, however, that we are assessing a potential investment aimed at improving an intercity passenger rail service (where profit-maximizing levies are charged) and wish to convert the net reserves obtained into social welfare terms. Social welfare is assumed here to refer to social surplus (that is, combined consumer and producer surpluses) as is standard practice in welfare economics.

Figure 11.7 shows the demand curve for the existing rail service to be linear (D_1 with marginal revenue curve MR_1) and that the improvement will result in a parallel shift of this curve to D_2. The average and marginal costs of using the service are assumed constant irrespective of custom with MC_1 ($= AC_1$) being the relevant curve prior to improvement and MC_2 ($= AC_2$) being operative afterwards.

With these assumptions, the demand curves are easily represented: D_1 as $P =$

---

[36] A.F. Friedlaender, 'Price distortions and second best investment rules in the transportation industries', *American Economic Review, Papers and Proceedings*, **71**, 389–93, 1981.

[37] A. Peaker, 'The allocation of investment funds between road and rail: a conversion factor linking financial and surplus rates of return', *Public Finance*, **75**, 683–735, 1974.

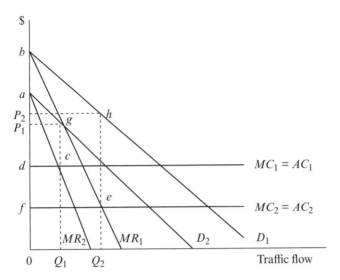

Figure 11.7 *Comparability between commercial and social investment criteria*

$a - kQ$ and D_2 as $P = b - kQ$ where P is price, Q is the level of traffic flow and k is the slope of the parallel demand curves. With profit maximization (that is output at the point where $MC = MR$) it is seen from Figure 11.7 that $Q_1 = (a - d)/(2k)$ and $Q_2 = (b - f)/(2k)$. Integrating under the relevant marginal revenue curves shows that the improved rail service would increase profits by {Area (bef) – Area (acd)}. This equals:

$$0.5(b - f)Q_2 - 0.5(a - d)Q_1 = \frac{1}{4k}[(b - f)^2 - (a - d)^2]. \qquad (11.8)$$

The increase in consumers' surplus associated with the improved rail service is obtained from integrating under the relevant demand curves but above price. In this case the integration yields Area (bhP_2) – Area (agP_1) which equals:

$$0.5(b - P_2)Q_2 - 0.5(a - P_1)Q_1 = \frac{1}{8k}[(b - f)^2 - (a - d)^2]. \qquad (11.9)$$

Since social surplus is composed of producers' surplus (that is, profit) plus consumers' surplus it is apparent from adding equation (11.8) to equation (11.9) (and then comparing back to equation (11.8)) that the gain in social welfare as a result of the rail investment in this profit maximizing situation is 1.5 times the profit which would be earned. It seems possible, therefore, in the circumstances to be able to convert profits earned into a comparable social surplus by multiplying by 1.5.

How useful is this conversion factor likely to be in practice? It is clear that it applies only to user costs and does not permit the inclusion of external factors, in terms of either pollution or congestion, which limits its usefulness in urban transport appraisal or for certain types of infrastructure, such as airports, which are particularly environmentally intrusive. Further, even within the strict confines of user-benefit analysis the conversion factor crucially depends upon a series of limiting assumptions. The factors which have been found to influence the ratio include:[38]

- the shape of the MC curve before and after the investment;
- the shapes of the demand curves before and after the investment;
- the extent of price discrimination;
- the pricing policy actually pursued and the nature (if any) of its deviation from profit maximization;
- the consistency of the pricing policy employed as investment alters the cost and demand conditions;
- the incidence of externalities including network effects; and
- the extent to which revenue and benefit streams differ in their availability for reinvestment.

Given the sensitivity of the '1.5 rule' to these various factors, it can hardly be seen as a practicable method of introducing comparability into transport investment decision making.

The comparability ratio approach assumes that an investment is undertaken and then prices set to achieve some economic objective, usually profit maximization. Financial returns are then compared to social returns. David Starkie[39] argues that a more practicable approach is to determine a common basis for pricing first and then adjust capacity accordingly. The basic idea stems from work on the UK railways by Joy,[40] who looked exclusively at freight investment, but Starkie generalizes the approach to all forms of transport investment. It is assumed that the correct economic price for each mode is determined along the second-best pricing lines formalized by William Baumol and David Bradford,[41] and that investment, or disinvestment, should be adjusted until long-run marginal costs are equated with the revenues obtained. This means that prices are set to cover short-run marginal cost with a mark-up in proportion to the inverse of the price elasticity of demand for each mode. The mark-up then reflects 'what the user will bear' towards the cost of capacity provision (that is, consumer surplus above $SRMC$). If this mark-up, combined with the revenue covering $SRMC$, does not meet the full $LRMC$ then capacity should be reduced until an equality is established. If such a pricing regime produces a surplus in excess of $LRMC$ then, *ceteris paribus*, there is a case for expanding capacity.

The fundamental idea is that if sufficient price discrimination is applied then all potential consumers' surplus is transferred to the supplier and, *ipso facto*, net

[38] A.J. Harrison and P.J. Mackie, *The Comparability of Cost Benefit*, Civil Service Occasional Paper 5, London: HMSO, 1973.

[39] D.N.M. Starkie, 'Allocation of investment in inter-urban road and rail', *Regional Studies*, **13**, 323–36, 1979.

[40] S. Joy, 'British Railways' back costs', *Journal of Industrial Economics*, **13**, 74–89, 1964.

[41] W.J. Baumol and D.F. Bradford, 'Optimal departures from marginal cost pricing', *American Economic Review*, **60**, 215–43, 1970

revenue can be equated with social surplus. Its main advance is the importance which it places on pricing and the recognition that in the long run it is possible to fine-tune investment at the margin. Such an approach obviously removes the need to conduct comparability studies but it has its limitations. The main difficulty is that while it may be possible in some areas to apply the discriminate pricing Starkie advocates, and mainly those undertakings directly controlled by government, in other cases private provision of transport facilities makes it rather difficult to ensure that the Baumol/Bradford rules are being applied. Consequently, it is difficult to see how it could be decided what is the correct level of overall investment in the publicly owned sector of transport *vis-à-vis* the aggregate for the private sector. Because much public investment is assessed on social criteria and virtually all private sector investment on commercial criteria, many of the problems of comparability remain. (This problem is avoided in Starkie's empirical work which focuses on road and railway track investment.) Further, the approach once again emphasizes user benefits but does not allow for external factors, especially the environmental effects of transport on non-users.

11.8 Assessing the Effect on National Income

It has been suggested that rather than expand financial surplus by a comparability ratio, or force some form of common pricing on all sectors of transport, an entirely different measure of the net value of investment, applicable to all forms of transport project irrespective of ownership, may be preferable. The effect of transport on national income, for example, could be used as a substitute for the combined consumers' and producers' surplus generated.[42] However, besides the practical difficulties involved in estimating the change in national income associated with alternative transport investments, the measure throws up an additional problem that involves the more fundamental question of whether the national income approach really does offer a reasonable and acceptable guide to the relative desirability of alternative investments. (We should perhaps note at this stage that national income, in this context, refers to the accountancy concept used in macroeconomics rather than the wider notion of national income referred to by Wildavsky earlier in the chapter; see note 25)

We can consider Figure 11.8 and assume that demand will not shift following a change in capacity Further, if we assume that the transport undertaking acts as a monopolist in its pricing policy, then we can see that an investment that reduces marginal costs from MC_1 to MC_2 will increase consumer surplus by ($hgcd$) in the diagram and profits by ($hdef$) – ($gcba$). The reduction in costs will also produce a higher gross national income. If the Laspeyres index is used (that is, the change in output valued at the pre-investment price), the rise will be measured as Q_1,cjQ_2. If the Paasche approach is favored (that is, the change in output is valued at the

[42] A.F. Friedlaender, *The Interstate Highway System: A Study in Public Investment*, Amsterdam: North-Holland, 1965.

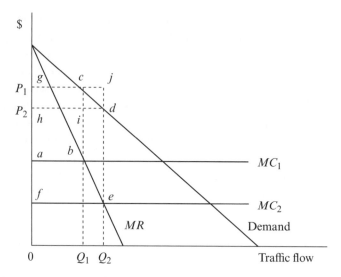

Figure 11.8 *The national income change approach to transport investment appraisal*

post-investment price), however, the addition to gross national income is found to be only $Q_1 i d Q_2$.

There is no reason for the social surplus measure to correspond to the national income measure (or for different estimates of the latter to correspond) except in rather unrealistic circumstances. Nor indeed need it correspond to the profit generated. Of more practical importance, there is no reason why alternative investment possibilities will be ranked consistently by the different methods.

The reason why social surplus and national income measures (and, indeed, financial measures) need not correspond, or rank consistently, stems from the fact that they measure entirely different things. Social surplus both includes leisure benefits emanating from a project and explicitly incorporates allowances for the diminishing marginal utility associated with the increased consumption of travel. The national income measure does neither: it concentrates exclusively on goods and services traded in conventional markets, and assumes either a fixed pre- or post-investment price level. The national income measure is also a general equilibrium measure.

Mohring[43] has demonstrated that the only time the two types of measure yield identical numerical results is '*If* a change takes place which increases the output obtained from a given set of primary resources, and *if* the primary resources allocated to market activities do not themselves change, and if the same pricing rules are used in consumers' surplus as in national income change benefit calculations' (emphasis original). Clearly, this means that the national income measure is likely to differ in practice from either the financial or social surplus measure of benefit and, hence, is simply an alternative method of ranking and appraisal, different but not necessarily superior. Given the practical difficulties of

[43] H. Mohring, *Transportation Economics*, Cambridge, MA: Ballinger, 1976.

estimation in most advanced economies its usefulness seems limited. In less developed countries, though, it may be seen as a more viable appraisal technique if distributional and welfare considerations are felt to be of secondary importance to boosting the national product. Transport projects that help stimulate national income growth in these circumstances may be given priority over others.

The practical problem of incomparability between investments in different transport sectors has not gone unnoticed by UK and other transport authorities. The problem is particularly acute in publicly owned inland inter-urban transport where government policy in countries like the United Kingdom has distinguished among different types of service, some of which must show a financial return and others a social return. While the moves towards privatization and deregulation from the 1970s (see Chapter 14) have rather blurred the distinction, the problem of allocating resources between commercial and social transport services remains.

Certain measures have been introduced in the United Kingdom that attempted to standardize some elements of appraisal procedures across the two groups. From the late 1960s, for example, discounting techniques were employed in all sectors using a nationally stipulated rate of discount.[44] Some minor changes in the basis of calculation took place subsequently but such techniques remained the main tool of appraisal for a long period. The differences among sectors are really just the actual items discounted; in one case it is simply the fare revenues, while in the other it is user benefits (usually calculated in terms of the financial value of the money, accident rate and travel time changes associated with the investment).

The official position, until relatively recently, was that, although there may be a need to take distributional or environmental factors into account when doing either type of calculation, the pricing policies pursued mean that revenue may be equated with social surplus in the financially based calculation. Comparability then becomes unnecessary. The rationale behind this view was summarized by the Department of the Environment in evidence to a UK House of Commons Select Committee,[45] the argument being that although 'the mechanics of assessment differ . . . in ordinary circumstances British Railways pursue a policy of market pricing which ensures that *most benefits to users are fully reflected in the revenue collected*' (emphasis added). The Select Committee was not convinced, however, that inconsistencies did not remain, and advocated the establishment of an Interurban Directorate to tackle the problem.

The Leitch Committee in the United Kingdom, when looking at trunk road investment, examined comparability in more detail and recommended that consistency could be achieved only if those undertakings employing financial techniques extended their analysis to embrace the wider social surplus-based procedures of appraisal. As we have seen, the type of CBA envisaged, however, is

---

[44] UK Treasury, *Nationalised Industries: A Review of Economic and Financial Objectives*, Cmnd 3437, London: HMSO, 1967.

[45] UK House of Commons Select Committee (1974), *First Report from the Expenditure Committee Session 1974, Public Expenditure on Transport*, HC 269, London: HMSO, 1974.

somewhat more comprehensive and transparent than that currently used for road investment appraisal in the UK or elsewhere which concentrate solely on user benefits. Further, to gain an even greater degree of consistency, there is a need to bring port and airport investment into the general CBA framework and widen the scope of appraisal away from the purely financial aspects which tend (with some significant exceptions) to dominate decision making in these spheres.

While the notion of common CBA techniques being applied throughout the publicly controlled inter-urban transport system may have certain apparent advantages – in Germany and some other European countries it is used for all inter-urban road, rail and waterway analysis – the Leitch study recognized the private ownership of coastal shipping and pipeline limits the degree of comparability. Essentially, the widespread use of CBA within the publicly owned sector (which, in fact, goes beyond the road/rail situation considered by Leitch) may produce consistent investment decisions within this sector but does not determine the optimal size of public *vis-à-vis* private sector investment. In effect, very limited progress has been made towards a common method of economic assessment for road and rail investments in the United Kingdom and most other countries, despite the findings of the Standing Advisory Committee on Trunk Road Appraisal over 20 years ago,[46] that:

> It is possible to have a consistent approach to economic assessment along the lines we have recommended which is equally appropriate to the evaluation of road public transport investments.

11.9   Some Institutional Considerations

From a policy perspective, while there are good reasons to ensure that adequate transport is available to facilitate economic development, and thus infrastructure investments are made efficiently, there are market imperfections that can present this from happening. One serious set of constraints in most countries is that associated with planning requirements. These can delay the construction of a facility and affect its design and operations. We shall not deal directly with these issues here, because they vary considerably between countries, but rather focus on issues of finance and efficient operations. Financing can pose particular problems in poorer countries, or even regions within more prosperous nations if they do not have an adequate tax base, or access to more sophisticated money markets. The scale of much transport investment also means that they often get entangled in macroeconomic policy and the cycles of public expenditure expenditures that accompany this.

Just taking the example of airports, but roads or seaports would serve equally well: airports are relatively expensive to build and, because of their monopoly status in many locations, are often not operated efficiently. To reduce the

---

[46] UK Department of Transport, *Urban Road Appraisal: Report of the Standing Committee on Trunk Road Appraisal*, London: HMSO, 1986.

X-inefficiency, there have been moves in many countries to make airport operators more commercially oriented. The national approaches aimed at injecting more commercial pressures into the provision of airport services have varied. Much of the interest that is now emerging is either in the privatization of some aspects of airport activity or engaging the private sector in some partnership arrangement with the state. In part this is because an airport is effectively a composite entity comprising units offering a variety of services – land access, parking, concessions, terminals, runways, ground handling, fire and response units, security and so on. Commercialization does not have to be applied to all these activities, and may be pursued in a piecemeal way if politics or economics dictate.

Approaches differ according to the state of the local air transport market that is, in turn, often linked to the stage in economic development of the region concerned. For example, airports can vary in terms of their potential revenue flow from different sources – slot fees and concessions and so on – and this can affect the degree of privatization or deregulation that is possible and the form it is most likely to take. Similar arguments apply to other forms of transport infrastructure.

Much depends on the state of the regional air transport market. The forecasts of relatively slow longer-term growth in air traffic in and between the developed countries (for example, estimated at about 3.6 percent a year to 2025 within North America, 3.4 percent within Europe, and 4.5 percent between North America and Europe) means that their major airports will increasingly become dependent on commercial or non-aeronautical revenues to enhance their revenue stream. This in turn can pose problems in terms of regulation, as has already been seen in the debates over the imposition of the price-capping regime used in the United Kingdom.

While still relatively small, the protected growth of many air markets involving regions of developing countries offers the potential for increased airside revenue in situations where there are potentially fewer social constraints involving such things as noise and land-take on building additional capacity or where there is already adequate capacity. The scope for raising significant commercial income is much less, however, because of lower initial traffic bases. It also suggests, though, that the regulatory regime overseeing a privatized airport system needs to be less sophisticated because it has to deal only with airside issues, making the potential for various forms of regulatory capture smaller.

The problem for regions of the poorest developing countries, however, is that even though their air traffic flows may in aggregate be growing, this is from a low base and they still seldom generate sufficient revenue to cover the full costs of operations let alone investments. Airports are essentially decreasing cost entities for which cost recovery can be difficult, especially in a situation where there is competition from other airports. This makes pure privatization options less tenable and the need for outside assistance from aid agencies or from government more relevant. Private/public partnerships offer another alternative.[47]

---

[47] K.J. Button, 'Air transport infrastructure in developing countries: privatization and deregulation', in C. Winston and G. de Rus (eds), *Aviation Infrastructure Performance: A Study in Comparative Political Economy*, Washington, DC: Brookings Institution, 2008.

The wide variety of circumstances around the world has led to a diversity of approaches to commercialization of airports. Some have involved complete divestiture of former state assets to the private sector, albeit with some oversight of how the airport is operated, but in other instances the withdrawal of the state has been less complete.

The management contract approach retains government control, but involves contracting out specified elements of airport services – parking, hotels, retail concessions and so on – for periods of time. This normally involves some form of auction. The system is in line with the notion of 'competition for the market'. Long-term contracting involves giving over the operational side of an airport, sometimes including investment commitments in additional capacity, for an extended period with the authorities retaining a degree of strategic control. The financing required normally entails bringing in specialized international companies with the expertise to manage an airport, or system of airports, together with finance houses that can provide the necessary support for large-scale service activities. These types of concessions are widespread in South America, where local expertise and finance is limited, but there is reluctance for the state to divest itself of aviation assets.

Many developed countries have also pursued similar philosophies when expanding the involvement of private enterprise, but falling short of complete divestiture.[48] Many US airports have adopted various concessionary schemes – for example Boston, Pittsburgh and Reagan National Airport, Washington have entered into concessionaire agreements for the entire operations at Pittsburgh and for specific terminal buildings at the other airports. At Chicago O'Hare airport, parking has been contracted out, and the Port Authority of New York and New Jersey, which owns a number of airports, has a variety of agreements covering such things as the operation of terminal buildings and the supply of heating and cooling at some of its facilities. There is also a tradition in the United States of significant airline involvement in providing check-in facilities and baggage systems.

Complete privatization of major airports is uncommon, although increasing. In most cases there is concern that a privately owned airport will exercise its monopoly power to extract rent from customers and under invest. The challenges are to devise and operationalize appropriate regulatory regimes to monitor and direct these large companies in the public interest – often price-capping is deployed. The ongoing debates about full privatization concern such things as whether single airports or, as with the UK's BAA, systems of airports, should be privatized and when they are privatized what should be regulated; should it be all airport activities or just those directly aviation related?

In their overview of various governance options, Carney and Mew[49] focus

---

[48] K.J. Button, 'The Implications of the commercialization of air transport infrastructure', in D. Lee (ed.), *The Economics of Airline Institutions, Operations and Marketing 2*, Amsterdam: Elsevier, 2007.

[49] M. Carney and K. Mew, 'Airport governance reform: a strategic management perspective', *Journal of Air Transport Management*, **9**, 221–32, 2003.

correctly on the government being involved in both seeking to improve the efficiency of their airports, but at the same time trying to direct the gains to particular groups rather than leaving management with full autonomy in their actions. This involves complexities that, while common to businesses in developed countries, are unfamiliar in many parts of the world. As a result, this has added to the growth in international firms specializing in airport management, including ownership and financing, to allow the development of common, best-practice methods of operation while at the same time being innovative in creating bespoke models for different circumstances.

Further Reading

C. Winston, 'Efficient transport infrastructure policy', *Journal of Economic Perspectives*, **5**, 113–27, 1991, provides a good survey of efficiency in transport infrastructure provision. The available technical literature on investment appraisal is immense. E.J. Mishan and E. Quah *Cost–Benefit Analysis*, 5th edn, London: Taylor & Francis, 2007, is an updated classic volume on cost–benefit analysis and is almost encyclopedic in its coverage – it can be hard going! A. Boardman, A. Vining and D.L. Weimer, *Cost Benefit Analysis: Concepts and Practice*, 3rd edn, Englewood Cliffs, NJ: Prentice-Hall, 2005, is another comprehensive volume. The contributions by C.A. Nash, 'Cost–benefit analysis of transport projects', in A. Williams and E. Giardina (eds), *Efficiency in the Public Sector: Theory and Practice of Cost–Benefit Analysis*, Aldershot, UK and Brookfield, VT, USA: Edward Elgar, 1993, and K.A. Small, 'Project evaluation', in J.A. Gómez-Ibáñez, W.B. Tye and C. Winston (eds), *Essays in Transportation Economics and Policy: A Handbook in Honor of John R. Meyer*, Washington, DC: Brookings Institute, 1999, provide a more explicit introduction to the subject.

In terms of more-specific topics, K.J Button and D.W. Pearce, 'Infrastructure restoration as a tool for stimulating urban renewal – the Glasgow Canal', *Urban Studies*, **26**, 559–71, 1989, is a discussion of the problems of defining the exact boundaries of a transport investment appraisal and, in particular, the requirements of different institutional bodies involved in an investment decision. Specific consideration of investment in transport infrastructure is to be found in H.A. Adler, *Economic Appraisal of Transport Projects*, Washington, DC: World Bank, 1987, which is particularly strong on approaches that are relevant in Third World countries. K.J. Button, 'Models for decision-making in the public sector', *OMEGA*, **7**, 399–409, 1979, provides a brief résumé of alternatives to the conventional CBA approach and has an extensive set of references.

12 Transport Planning and Forecasting

12.1 The Development of Transport Planning

The preceding chapters have concentrated primarily upon pricing and invest-ment decisions for individual modes of transport in isolation – the pricing of public transport, urban car users and so on. Little has been said about the coor-dination of pricing and investment decisions across whole sectors of transport. Coordination, as Adam Smith pointed out, will come about automatically in a perfectly competitive market framework where marginal cost pricing principles are universally applied. Indeed, there has been considerable emphasis on coor-dination through the market in the development of inter-urban transport policy in countries such as Britain and the United States, but extending more broadly, from the late 1970s as we shall see in Chapter 14. Concern over safety and the environment is now often considered to be the main interest of the authorities and, within a quality licensing and quality regulatory framework, competition both within and among inter-urban modes is often encouraged.

Generally, however, either by central or by local government, there is some planning of infrastructure provision in most countries and, indeed, at the inter-national level there are coordinated plans for strategic highway, air traffic control, and high-speed rail developments within the European Union and other such groupings. The extent and nature of this planning varies considerably between countries, as well as modes and regions within them. The main objective in these cases is often the avoidance of duplication, especially in relation to major development projects with a long period of gestation, and the adoption of a high degree of technical consistency.

In other areas of transport activity, and particularly in the urban context, there is still a strong feeling that it is necessary to engage in a high degree of planning, with central and local government intervention to improve the overall efficiency of local transport provision. The role that transport may play in other spheres of economic activity is one reason for this (improved transport, for example, may form part of a social welfare policy and is currently seen as central to the revitalization of local economies in depressed inner-city areas), but a more general explanation may be found in the magnitude of the imperfections of the urban transport markets. The justification for urban transport planning in this context was usefully summarized some years ago in a UK policy document, *Transport Policy*:[1]

---

[1] UK Department of Transport, *Transport Policy*, Cmnd 6836, London: HMSO, 1977.

The many activities concentrated in urban areas must be accessible to people and the economic and social life of cities depends on enormously diverse and complex patterns of travel and destination. Yet there is not enough road space in large towns and cities for people to travel as much as they like and how and when they like. This in itself can be one source of grievance. Another is that intrusion of dense traffic brings objectionable and sometimes intolerable noise, fumes and vibration.

We have already seen, in Chapter 6, the extent of the external effects of transport and subsequently considered ways in which they may be tackled individually. A comprehensive marginal pollution-pricing regime combined with comparable social investment criteria could, for example, ensure optimality. Political resistance to such an approach combined with disquiet over the possible distributional repercussions and the practical problems of implementation have so far tended to rule out the full-scale use of market mechanisms to regulate the urban transport sector. This does not mean that the pricing mechanism is not used but rather that it forms part of a much larger package of policy instruments which are combined with the intention of improving the overall efficiency of urban transport in meeting the objectives of society.

Planning history and philosophies differ between countries, but there are some general themes that are common.[2] Technology changes have often been a driving force – for example, the advent of the steam locomotive brought with it the need for strategic planning as fixed networks of rail had to be laid; this led to early traffic surveys and forecasts of traffic flows to enable priorities to be developed and costs to be calculated. The emergence of street cars and underground transport systems from the late 1850s meant that urban transport planning began to emerge, with government acting as facilitator for the private sector.

By the end of the nineteenth century, transport planning had reached a stage that would be recognized today. It had become a sequential process:[3]

- *Political*   This is planning at the conceptual level and considers broad social and economic goals.
- *Development*   This is planning at the strategic and systems level, embracing factors such as land-use and service levels.
- *Transport*   This is conducted at the corridor level, considering transport demand management and infrastructure provision.
- *Facility*   This entails the implementation of the plan with the provision of track capacity and its design.

In more detail, the recent history of urban transport planning in the United Kingdom, as an illustrative case study, is comparatively short, originating in the recognition that urban lifestyles and cities themselves would change

---

[2] M.G. Lay, 'The history of transport planning', in K.J. Button and D.A. Hensher (eds), *Handbook of Transport Strategy, Policy and Institutions*, Oxford: Pergamon, 2005.

[3] E. Weiner, *Urban Transportation Planning in the United States, History, Policy, and Practice*, New York: Springer, 2008.

once ownership of private cars became widespread. The physical planners of the immediate pre- and post-Second World War periods were concerned with redesigning cities and transport infrastructure to meet the requirements of an automobile age. Patrick Abercrombie, in the County of London Plan of 1943, for example, typified much of the philosophy of the period in his proposals for the university quarter of Bloomsbury and the area around Westminster where he advocated the application of the 'precinctual principle'. Traffic was to be diverted around these areas on good-quality, arterial roads, with the precincts served by a limited number of local, access routes. While this idea, which was American in origin, was never applied to the two sites studied by Abercrombie, the broad principle was employed in the post-war reconstruction of Coventry.

The 1947 UK Town and Country Planning Act institutionalized planning by making anyone wishing to develop land seek permission from the local authority. The basis for decision making regarding land-use changes was a series of proposal maps which traced out proposed land uses for a horizon of 10 years or more. The 'Town Map' was a legal document that both took time to prepare and required cumbersome procedures to be gone through prior to changes being accepted.

The system had the advantage that it allowed land to be set aside for schools, residential development and so on, but only limited land was allocated to road construction. Further, since funds were not always available for rapid construction programs, in many places where land was allocated for transport corridors it led to blight and lack of maintenance of buildings that might at some unspecified future date be taken for road building. These were particular problems since a central theme of the physical planning approach to the urban transport problem was that improving the local transport network could alleviate excessive traffic congestion.

As traffic grew, alternative solutions were sought. While the initial approach to urban planning had been a narrow one, two important developments occurred in the 1950s and 1960s which strengthened the concept. First, although some planners, such as Abercrombie, took a broad geographical view of urban problems, the focus of most early planners tended to be local, seeking piecemeal solutions to specific traffic problems. In the 1950s there was a widening out. Local highway authorities were encouraged by central government to produce joint plans for local road networks and the joint plans produced by the authorities in the Manchester area (the SELNEC Highway Plan of 1962) and by the Merseyside area authorities (in 1965) bear witness to the success of this policy. Second, and not entirely independent of coordinated highway planning, came the recognition of the strong links between land use and transport planning.

The Buchanan Report[4] in the early 1960s provided firm evidence of the need to coordinate the two areas of planning. Colin Buchanan was particularly concerned about the environmental cost of traffic, and argued that urban road networks should not be expanded to the extent needed to reduce congestion to some predefined levels, as was then the accepted practice, but rather changes in

[4] UK Ministry of Transport, *Traffic in Towns*, London: HMSO, 1963.

transport and urban land-use systems should be assessed in terms of the costs of reducing congestion while maintaining some predefined environmental standard. If the costs of expanding the transport network without violating the environmental standard prove excessive to the community, then traffic must be restrained until the environmental limit is attained.

Once it became recognized that not only was there a need to consider objectives other than simply congestion in transport planning, especially since transport is an integral part of a much wider urban economic system, it became apparent that physical planning needed to be replaced by a more comprehensive planning framework. The coordinated approach which resulted embodied 'structure planning' which sets out policies for the development of land, transport and the local environment.

The UK's Town and Country Planning Act of 1968 embodied the idea of structure planning while the creation of the Department of the Environment in 1970 integrated overall responsibility for urban and transport planning in one organization. The 1968 Transport Act created a number of passenger transport authorities (PTAs) in major conurbations that were given responsibility for public transport operations within their area. The PTAs were themselves committed to drawing up policies (within a year) and plans (within two years) to provide 'a properly integrated and efficient system of public transport to meet the needs of [the] area'. While the commitment to draw up structure plans necessitated liaison and coordination between local planning and highway departments and the PTAs, in practice land-use, road-building and public transport responsibilities remained separate – indeed in some cases the agencies had different boundaries.

The Local Government Act, 1972, integrated the existing PTAs, plus three newly created ones, into a reformed local government structure. The Act placed further emphasis on the need for coordinated transport planning in urban areas, and each urban authority was compelled to produce a Transport Policy and Programme (TPP) setting down the strategy and objectives that were being followed. The TPPs were used after 1975 as a means of assessing the level of central government financial aid to local urban transport undertakings (via the Transport Supplementary Grant) and emphasis was placed on integrating transport planning with the wider issues of land-use planning and social policy in the area. The aim of this structure, therefore, was to distribute grants to reflect local transport needs, and to reduce central government control.

The move to structure planning, which still forms the basis for local transport policy today, resulted in two major changes in the types of approach adopted by local transport agencies. First, there has been a trend towards more structured and phased planning; the Tyneside Study of 1968, for instance, produced an immediate action program, a transport plan for a 15-year horizon and a general urban strategy plan to the end of the century. The TPP framework encouraged a continual monitoring and updating of plans within a rolling framework. Second, planning was no longer viewed simply in terms of investment but embraced the short-term management of existing resources. In part this may be a reflection of the changing objectives of urban transport planning, but it was also the consequence of a greater economic awareness in planning that there is an opportunity cost associated with all actions involving the employment of scarce resources.

12.2 The Theory of Transport Planning

The movement away from physical transport planning to structure planning in the 1960s increased the economic input into the transport planning process, although the development of modern planning methods must be attributed mainly to civil engineers, statisticians and mathematicians rather than economists. One of the main problems of urban land-use/transport planning is the enormous range of possible options available, although this is much less of a difficulty in countries such as Britain or the US, where urban land-use patterns are established and not susceptible to rapid change – in such cases one is seeking the optimal transport system for the existing urban structure. A sequential approach to urban transport planning may, therefore, be appropriate with the four different levels of planning outlined in Section 12.1 taking place viewed as system designs:

1   design of broad land-use plan;
2   design of strategic transport plan;
3   design of detailed land-use plan; and
4   design of detailed transport plan.

(There may be some feedback between (3) and (4) in the sequence.)

The transport planning process itself is complex and entailing far more complex institutional and technical issues than can be fully considered here. In general, as we have seen it can be broken down into a number of stages, each involving a certain amount of economic input. There is no firm or accepted best-practice method of drawing up a transport plan – different agencies favor different detailed approaches. Broadly, however, the process may be typified by the various stages set out in Figure 12.1, but this must be seen very much as a stylization intended rather more to show where economics can contribute to the transport planning process, than as a representation of any actual planning procedure. A few comments are justified on each of the stages.

Goals and Objectives

As we have seen above, the objectives of urban transport planning tend to change over time, periods when there is an emphasis being placed upon social and environmental considerations are often followed by a focus on improving the efficiency of the system. The general objectives of policy need to be made specific to permit trade-offs among alternative goals at a later stage of the planning process. The economist's contribution at this stage is that of a balancing agent, often counteracting engineering pressures for the emphasis of the plan to be on improving traffic flow or adopting capital-intensive solutions to environmental

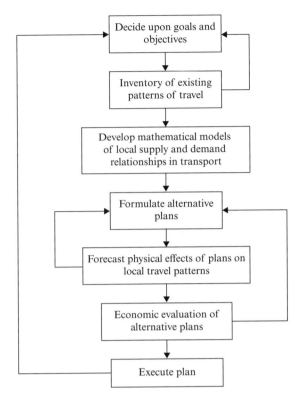

Figure 12.1 *The urban transport planning process*

problems. The notion of 'opportunity cost' is essential if resources are to be used efficiently. The economists may also act as a filter, pointing out the incompatibility or contrary nature of certain goals. Since goals and objectives are often formulated at the beginning of the planning exercise before full information on existing transport problems has been obtained, they may be redefined after later stages in the sequence.

Inventory of Existing Transport System

Information is gathered about the nature of the local transport system and travel patterns both by sampling and counting people actually in the act of using transport and by obtaining information from firms and households about their travel behavior and requirements.[5] Additional information is often extracted from official sources such as the Census, national travel surveys and consumer expenditure surveys. The types of surveys conducted and the questions asked have changed over the years as a result of important developments in transport forecasting. As we shall see in later sections, much more emphasis is now placed on understanding why people travel rather than on simply modeling flows of traffic.

---

[5] P.R. Stopher, 'Survey and sampling strategies', in D.A. Hensher and K.J. Button (eds), *Handbook of Transport Modelling*, 2nd edn, Amsterdam: Elsevier, 2008.

Consequently, more detailed information of household characteristics is now sought, although the greater efficiency of modern measuring techniques means that the actual sample size has tended to fall (from over 10,000 households in the large studies of the late 1960s – the last substantial household survey in the United Kingdom, that of the West Yorkshire Transportation Studies, sampled 12,322 addresses – to considerably less than 1,000 today).

The broad-brush approach has given way to seeking greater insights into representative travel behavior. For example, while the US Federal Highways Administration set out guidelines for surveying household trip-making patterns in the 1970s,[6] more recently there have been advances for collecting broader information on household activity patterns to allow these to be linked with travel behavior.[7]

One reason for this is that the types of planning issue under review have changed with time, and in particular large road-building programs have tended to be replaced by traffic management and public transit policies. But modeling has also evolved. In particular, there has been a shift away from the more mechanical types of approach to travel patterns, and more of a focus on understanding factors that influence them. The development of stated preference techniques in recent years, for example, has in particular furthered our understanding of the underlying nature of travel decisions. Quite clearly, since the basic aim is to seek information on existing conditions of supply and demand for urban transport services, economists can contribute to formulating the types of questions to ask as well as the forms of model in which information will be fed.

Mathematical Simulations of the Local Transport Market

The following sections look at modeling and forecasting techniques, and in particular their economic underpinnings, but it is important to emphasize at this stage the basic requirements of the simulation models. Transport markets are complex and to produce models which replicate all their details is both difficult and, more importantly, likely to be too cumbersome for totally accurate forecasting. Ian Heggie[8] suggests that the prerequisites of a good transport model are that it:

- assists in understanding and explaining behavior;
- aids policy formulation; and
- provides robust predictions.

The models of travel and transport demand are used for forecasting; therefore it is important that the explanatory factors can themselves be predicted with

[6] US Federal Highways Administration, *Urban Origin–Destination Surveys*, Washington, DC: USDOT, 1973.

[7] P.R. Stopher, 'Use of an activity-based diary to collect household travel data', *Transportation*, **19**, 159–76, 1992.

[8] I. Heggie, 'Putting behaviour into behavioural models of travel choice', *Journal of the Operational Research Society*, **29**, 541–50, 1978.

some degree of certainty. The models are also used to assess the effects of differ-ent planning options; thus it is important that they are simple to use and permit the effect of several alternative strategies to be explored. One of the major limita-tions of early models was that they were cumbersome to manipulate, limiting the possible policy options that could be assessed.

Formulating Alternative Plans

The complex and wide-ranging effects of any change in an urban transport system make it very difficult in practice for more than a limited number of detailed plans to be fully formulated. A comprehensive plan consists of a package of projects and schemes, and for a large city the possible combinations forming such a package is immense. In some cases only one planning alternative is drawn up in detail after a preliminary sifting of other possibilities at an earlier stage in the planning process.

Usually the planning alternatives considered are a little more numerous and, besides the 'do-nothing' situation, which may act as a benchmark, generally involve at least one public transport-oriented package, one private transport-based proposal and probably one rather more central alternative, offering a mix of private and public transport. Since the plans themselves are later evaluated, this approach should not be as restrictive as it appears. Following the forecasting and/or the evaluation stage, new light may be shed on the detailed effect of alternative plans, and new compromise packages of projects emerge. Without feedback of this kind it would be quite possible, given the vast range of alternative plans that are feasible for most large cities, to miss the potentially most beneficial option.

Forecasting the Physical Effects of Alternative Plans

Transport forecasting will be looked at in detail in Sections 12.3 to 12.6, the mod-eling and forecasting stages being both central to the planning process and having a very substantial economics component. The key aspect of forecasting is that it provides the planner/decision maker with useful information about the long-term implications of plans, emphasizing in particular those areas where there are sig-nificant differences in the consequences of the alternative plans. Given the fact that transport is going to exist in the urban setting, irrespective of the plan adopted, and providing that a 'do-nothing' option is assessed, then it is the relative perform-ance of plans that is important. Additionally, it is important that the final decision makers are aware of the underlying assumptions of the forecasts so that they can assess their reliability and strengths. To this end, most forecasts are now presented as a range of likely outcomes under alternative assumptions.

Economic Evaluation

The economic evaluation of plans normally involves employing some variant, albeit in a less formalized format, of the cost–benefit analysis approach outlined in Chapter 11.[9] The comprehensive nature and emphasis on distributional effects which characterizes the Planning Balance Sheet makes it a particularly attractive technique in the urban planning context. It is also sufficiently 'open' to permit the various consequences of plans to be related directly to the objectives of the planners.

With traditional CBA, not only are there problems of placing monetary values on many items but also members of the urban community often view the final output of a single net present value of benefits with suspicion. General practice involves the inclusion of public participation at the evaluation stage, often in the form of public inquiries. In some cases – such as the Layfield Inquiry into the Greater London Development Plan in the United Kingdom[10] – such inquiries can result in quite substantial revisions of the plan to be adopted. Evaluation of something as complex as a transport plan is, by necessity, a political process, but economists can assist the decision maker by ruling out plans which are clearly inferior to others while at the same time giving a systematic presentation of the pros and cons of the final short-list of alternatives.

The inherent explicit value judgments built into all forms of CBA in many ways makes it a powerful aid in evaluation, but it is unlikely ever to provide an automatic, purely technical decision-making calculus; indeed, it is debatable whether such a mechanical approach is to be desired.

Implementation

While it is often possible to implement some parts – usually traffic management components – of a transport plan almost immediately upon acceptance, other components – usually those involving infrastructure changes – are much more long term in nature. It is important, therefore, that actions are phased so that costs are kept at a minimum. Additionally, over time objectives change and 'errors' in forecasts become apparent and this may necessitate revisions of the plan. Consequently, there are feedbacks from the implementation stage back to the early stages of the planning process; in other words, modern planning is seen as an ongoing, rolling process of adaptation and change. It is often important, in this context, to ensure the maximum flexibility in the implementation program.

The preceding paragraphs have painted a thumbnail sketch of the transport planning process, highlighting the role that economics can play. It is thin on detail and hides many of the subtleties of the planning exercise: readers interested in this specific aspect of transport economics are strongly advised to refer to one of the excellent texts now available on the subject. The following sections consider the economic problems of transport modeling and forecasting. These areas, together with plan evaluation, have become increasingly the preserve of economists and involve the application of modern microeconomic theory.

[9] P. Truelove, *Decision Making in Transport Planning*, London: Longman, 1992.
[10] UK Department of the Environment, *Report of the Panel of Inquiry into the Greater London Development Plan*, London: DOE, 1973.

12.3 Traffic Modeling and Forecasting

At the outset is should be said that the objective here is not to provide anything like a comprehensive account of how traffic is modeled for planning purposes; that is a subject that extends well beyond our scope. What we do is to provide an indication of the types of models that have been adopted, their limitations from an economic perspective, and some information on some of the more economically oriented approaches that are gradually coming to the fore. In the past, much of the work in this area has been dominated by engineers who have been rather neglectful of how travelers make decisions, relying instead on notions of flows derived from the physical sciences.

To conduct successful planning exercises, or indeed many other forms of policy development, it is, however, essential to have reliable forecasts of the probable effect of different policy options. General qualitative assessments can often provide useful insights into the effects of different policies, but good planning decisions require that we have more exact information of the detailed quantified relationship between travel and transport and the factors that influence them. Engineers, for example, need projections of future traffic flows when designing roads and other infrastructure. Recent years have witnessed a substantial growth in work attempting to specify and calibrate econometric travel demand models. Not everyone feels that economists are making great progress. As a general comment on economic forecasts John Kenneth Gailbraith observed, 'The only function of economic forecasting is to make astrology look respectable'.[11]

In the United States the increased role of the federal authorities in funding both inter-state transport facilities and local, urban transit systems had a similar effect. The need to allocate large sums to durable transport infrastructure schemes in the Third World motivated the World Bank to pursue a similar course. More recently still, the general move towards more careful project appraisal at the micro level has led to the development of stated preference techniques employing market research-style procedures to transport forecasting.

Accuracy of Transport Forecasting

Having noted the growth of work in the field, it is only fair to deviate and point to the quantitative limitations of what has been done before moving on to the technical details of methodology. In his classic paper on the methodology of positive economics, Milton Friedman[12] emphasized the need for a good model to predict relatively well. In practice, however, very little retrospective work is done assessing the predictive abilities of models in transport economics.

[11] J.K. Galbraith, *Money: Whence it Came, Where it Went*, Boston: Houghton Mifflin, 1975.
[12] M. Friedman, 'The methodology of positive economics', in M. Friedman (ed.), *Essays In Positive Economics*, University of Chicago Press, 1953.

An early assessment of traffic forecasting in the UK[13] did not paint a very complimentary picture of the engineering-based methods used at the time: 'an assumption of zero change from the base year would not have produced larger forecast errors . . . for trips the errors would have been considerably less [than those obtained from a transport model]'.

A study in the late 1980s of 41 road schemes in the United Kingdom concluded from a comparison of actual and projected flows that only in 22 cases were the actual flows within 20 percent of the original forecast. Of the remainder, flows ranged from 50 percent below to 105 percent above the original estimate.[14] The forecasts for the M25 London orbital road, for instance, were that on 21 of the 26 three-lane sections the traffic flow would be between 50,000 and 79,000 vehicles a day in the fifteenth year, whereas the flow within a very short time was between 81,400 and 129,000.

A noted exception is found in Dan McFadden's forecasts. These deployed a random utility mode split model to examine the construction of the Bay Rapid Transit System (BART) in the San Francisco area.[15] The quality of his results may help explain why he was awarded the Nobel Prize in Economic Science, although it has not stopped the continued use of engineering consultants' four-stage modeling sequence for transport forecasting. Capture is as endemic in transport work as elsewhere. (While the conventional aggregate gravity model forecast a 15 percent mode share for BART, McFadden's disaggregate forecast was 6.3 percent and the actuality was 6.2 percent. Despite this, BART has never adopted disaggregate modeling as a policy tool.)

More recently, Flyvbjerg et al.[16] looking solely at cost estimations for 258 transport infrastructure projects (including rail, fixed-link and roads) found that they are generally underestimated and are systematically misleading. Rail projects had the largest error, where actual costs were 45 percent higher than estimated.

Don Pickrell's[17] (1989) study of grant programs funded by the US Federal Urban Mass Transportation Administration found that all 10 urban public transport projects examined produced major underestimates of costs per passenger (for example, the costs for the Miami heavy rail transit were 872 percent of those forecast, for Detroit's downtown people mover they were 795 percent and for Buffalo's light-rail transit project they were 392 percent). While inaccurate costing was one element of the problem, the forecasts of patronage in all cases was overoptimistic. Indeed, only the Washington heavy-rail transit project produced actual patronage that is more than half of that which was forecast. Some of the differences can be explained by difficulties in predicting future values of

---

[13] I. Mackinder and S. Evans, *The Predictive Accuracies of British Transport Studies in Urban Areas*, TRRL Report, Crowthorne, SR 699, 1981.

[14] UK House of Commons Committee of Public Accounts, *Road Planning*, London: HMSO, 1988.

[15] D. McFadden, 'Economic choices', *American Economic Review*, **91**, 351–78, 2001.

[16] B. Flyvbjerg, M. Holm and S. Buhl, 'Underestimating costs in public work projects: error or lie?', *Journal of the American Planning Association*, **68**, 279–95, 2002.

[17] D.H. Pickrell, *Urban Rail Transit Projects: Forecast Versus Actual Ridership and Costs*, Washington, DC: US Department of Transportation, 1989.

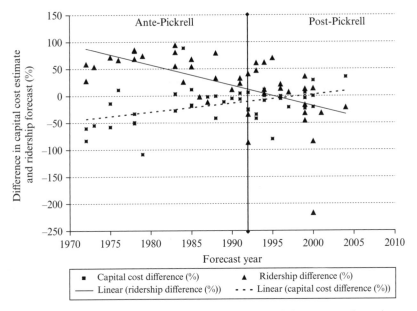

Source: M.H. Hardy, S. Doh, J. Yuan, X. Zhow and K.J. Button, 'The accuracy of transit system ridership forecasts and capital cost estimates', paper presented to the 50th Transportation Research Forum Annual Meeting, 2009.

Figure 12.2 *Ridership forecast and capital cost estimate trends*

explanatory variables such as demographic changes, automobile costs and the service level which the public transport service would offer, but Pickrell argues that important questions must also be raised over the structure of the models employed, the ways in which they were used and the interpretation of output during the planning process.

Updating this work by looking at cost and ridership forecast for 47 US transit systems indicates only limited improvements over time. Figure 12.2 provides details of the forecast versus out-turn investment costs. A positive value indicates overestimation, while a negative value is underestimation. Visual inspection shows that most transit systems do not perform as well as forecast in terms of ridership, nor are they constructed consistent with their estimated costs; there are significant over-runs. For example, in the case of the Los Angeles Orange Line, ridership was underestimated by more than 200 percent.

But there have been changes. During the period prior to Pickrell's study, visual inspection clearly suggests that ridership was overestimated while capital costs are underestimated. However, during the post-Pickrell period, there are slight improvements. Post-Pickrell values are smaller than ante-Pickrell values (generally within 50 percent difference), implying an overall improvement in the forecasting and estimation process. The linear trend lines showing the differences in ridership forecasts and capital cost estimates reinforce this notion of improved forecast: the differences moved closer to the 0 percent line. Of course, external factors change with time (including land-use characteristics, transit

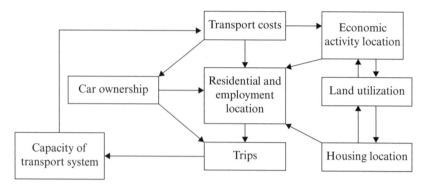

Source: F.V. Webster, P.H. Bly and N.J. Paulley (eds), *Urban Land-use and Transport Interaction*, Aldershot: Avebury, 1988.

Figure 12.3   *Urban land-use and transport interaction model*

system types, and transit technology) and corrections are needed to reflect this. Such adjustments suggest the improvements have been modest.

The Challenges of Forecasting

It is quite clear from these findings that forecasting traffic is far from easy. While these problems are diverse and sometimes rather technical, a number of general comments on the application of econometric analysis to transport forecasting highlight the difficulties that have been encountered in constructing travel demand models.

First, transport is by its nature a derived demand but equally, as we have seen in previous chapters, it interacts with land-use and location patterns. There is, therefore, logic in developing a forecasting model that allows for these very close linkages. This is obviously not an easy thing to do, but it is unlikely that reliable long-term forecasts will be forthcoming if transport and land-use models are treated in tandem rather than developed within an interactive framework. Indeed, using the type of interlinked land-use and transport model set out in Figure 12.3, it was shown that interactive effects over time account for a significant portion of the economic benefits of a transport scheme.[18]

Moving on to the actual transport modeling framework, traditional micro-economic analysis specifies a demand relationship relating quantity demanded to price, and assumes that this relationship changes (that is, shifts) only when factors other than price vary. In transport demand analysis it is fairly easy to incorporate the 'shift' variables into a modeling framework because their values are essentially determined outside the transport system (for example, income changes or changes in taste). The control price variable is much more difficult. As we have seen, price is a broad concept in transport, embracing time, comfort and other factors, in addition to simply the monetary cost of a trip. While generalized cost offers one

[18] J. Berechman and P. Gordon, 'Linked models of land use–transport interactions: a review', in B. Hutchinson and M. Balty (eds), *Advances in Urban Systems Modelling*, Amsterdam: North-Holland, 1986.

method of reflecting the multidimensional nature of the price variable, there is a tendency in forecasting work to employ changes in the ease of access as a proxy for price. Accessibility is nothing more complicated than an index that reflects the ease with which people can achieve the various activities they wish.

Transport systems are extremely complicated, comprising many modes of travel, varieties of routes and combinations of different potential travel patterns. The sheer number of links and possibilities in any non-trivial transport network has inevitably resulted in simplifications having to be adopted by forecasters to permit calculations to be reduced to manageable proportions. Further, the 'product' being offered by the transport system is also unique in that a passenger-mile at a particular point on the network at a specific time may be performing a completely different function from another passenger-mile at another time and at a different point in the system.

While not always designed to handle the land-use/transport interaction effects, these latter types of problems have resulted in the emergence of three broad types of forecasting framework, each with its own characteristics and each with its particular advantages and defects. Each of these has many variants but they can generally be thought of as sequential, disaggregate and interactive frameworks. They are looked at in turn. While the discussion is couched primarily in terms of forecasting the demand for person movements, much of the traffic carried by the transport system is freight. The demand to move commodities differs quite substantially from person movements in the sense that it is, normally, unidirectional while person trips are usually circular (that is, from home to work to home). The types of forecasting frameworks used to look at goods traffic are, however, essentially the same as for person movements, modified usually only in terms of the actual variables used. The three main approaches are now reviewed in turn.

12.4   Sequential Travel Demand Forecasting

Sequential models attempt to reduce the complexity of travel demand forecasting and make the handling of large databases easier by breaking the complicated patterns of demand for travel into, usually, four submodels.[19] This approach has a long history, starting with the Detroit and Chicago Transportation Studies of the 1950s, and is still, despite serious limitations, the dominant form of modeling used today; for example, it is used within the US Government's Urban Public Transport Planning System (UTPS). The four stages are:

- First, the trip generation/attraction model (the trip-end model) is used to forecast the number of trips originating and ending within predefined geographical zones of the study area (these might be countries in international travel studies or smaller areas within a city in urban land-use studies).
- Second, the total zonal trips are then 'distributed' between origin–destination pairs of zones.

[19] M.G. McNally, 'The four-step model', in D.A. Hensher and K.J. Button (eds), *Handbook of Transport Modelling*, 2nd edn, Amsterdam: Elsevier, 2008.

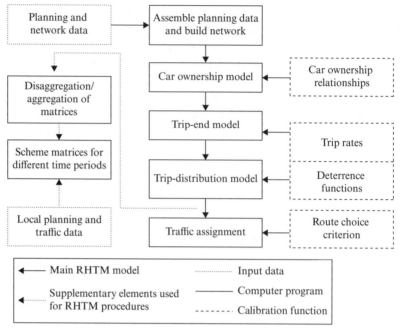

Figure 12.4   *The UK Regional Highway Traffic Model*

•   Third, for each flow between different zones, a modal choice model is calculated to explain the split of traffic between the alternative forms of transport available.

•   Finally, the traffic flows between each pair of zones and by each mode of transport are assigned to specific routes on the transport network.

In the context of freight modeling, which we discussed in the logistics chapter (Chapter 10), the parallel submodels represent transactions, flows, mode changes and network assignments, with an industrial location model added to make the links between industrial activities and freight vehicle movements explicit. A vehicle-loading submodel is also sometimes added to shift the emphasis from the vehicle to the consignment.

Figure 12.4 provides an example of the sequential approach as developed by the Regional Highway Traffic Model (RHTM) team in the United Kingdom, and used to assist specifically in national road planning. It is typical of the series of sequences used in most other countries, including the United States. Mode choice submodels are excluded because of the dominant position filled by motor-car traffic. The approach set out is particularly useful in distinguishing between the data analysis, computer simulation and calibration aspects of the overall modeling and forecasting process.

The sequential framework may, therefore, be seen as moving from an aggregate overall traffic model to quasi-disaggregate forecasting with each successive submodel in the sequence acting as a check on the one following. In econometric terms the sequence is recursive. Attempts have been made (for example, in work

forming part of the appraisal of the Greater London Development Plan) to introduce feedbacks from later to earlier submodels in the sequence on the grounds
that one cannot really forecast, say, mode choice without knowing probable levels
of congestion on each route and this latter knowledge becomes available only
after the assignment stage. A land-use forecasting model that attempts to describe
the effect of changing land-use patterns on transport usually precedes the transport model sequence. Ideally, because land use is itself partly affected by transport conditions, there should also be feedbacks from the assignment submodel to
land-use patterns, but to date this has proved to be practicably impossible.

Trip-end submodels are usually estimated on a household basis using either
multivariate regression techniques or category analysis. The former statistically
relates the number of trips made by households to the socioeconomic characteristics of the households (for example, income, number of residents, car ownership,
social status and so on) and the type of environment in which they are located.
The concentration on the household is now widely accepted as standard practice
to reduce statistical problems that appear when data are grouped excessively
(for example, by geographical zone). Category analysis is simpler, involving the
construction of a multidimensional matrix with each dimension representing a
socioeconomic variable stratified into a number of discrete classes or categories.
For example, households may be divided into four income classes, three car-
ownership classes and two location classes, giving in total 24 categories of household, each with its own average trip-generation level. Forecasts are obtained by
predicting the number of households falling into each category at the target date,
and multiplying by the relevant average trip-generation rate. The total zonal trips
in the example above would be predicted as:

$$T = \sum_{t=1}^{24} n_k r_k \qquad (12.1)$$

where: n is the future number of households in category k, and r is the corresponding trip-rate.

Revealed preference approaches to trip distribution models are of two broad
types. Growth factor models involve extrapolating existing patterns of trips
between alternative origins and destinations with projected trip-end estimates
acting as constraints on the number of trips leaving or entering any individual
zone. They are little more than mechanical procedures based upon past behavior
patterns and suffer, in particular, from the inability to allow for new zones being
created. They have also gone out of favor because they require a substantial
amount of data input.

The second group, simulation models, are more overtly economic in their
nature. The gravity model is the most commonly used member of this group and
has the attraction of having a precise economic interpretation.[20] The underlying concept is also widely used in other areas of transport analysis such as when

[20] R.A. Cochrane, 'A possible economic basis for the gravity model', *Journal of Transport Economics and Policy*, **9**, 34–49, 1975.

looking at the importance of transport costs in labor mobility which will be discussed in Chapter 13.

Gravity models differ in form but all exhibit terms reflecting the relative attractiveness of different destinations and terms that measure the effect of impedance caused by the nature of the transport system. In early work, attractions were specified simply in terms of the population sizes of the zones of attraction, but in more recent studies a multiplicity of factors have been included, frequently varying with the journey purpose under consideration. Similarly, the crude notion that distance is a full reflection of impedance has given way to the incorporation of various forms of generalized cost measures.

The interactive version of the gravity model takes the general form:

$$T_{ij} = T_i T_j A_i A_j B_j f(C_{ij})$$ (12.2)

subject to: $A_i = \left[\sum_j T_j B_j f(C_{ij}) \right]^{-1}$ and $B_j = \left[\sum_i T_i A_i f(C_{ij}) \right]^{-1}$ where:

T_{ij} is trips between zones i and j;
T_i is the number of trips originating in zone i;
T_j is the number of trips destined for zone j;
C_{ij} is the generalized cost of travel between zones i and j; and
A and B are 'fuzz factors' – sometimes justified as indices of inverse accessibility – to ensure that trips distributed across the whole study area originating from i do not exceed T_i and those destined for j do not exceed T_j.

This doubly constrained model assumes that trip makers are competing for a limited number of opportunities in any specific zone, and has clear applications to modeling the demand for work or school trips where job and educational opportunities can be assumed to be independent of the transport system. In many cases only one constraint (either T_i or T_j) is imposed; for example, with interurban freight demand, one is often only interested either in the way movements fan out from a city or depot or in the way they converge on it. Urban non-work demand models are also often based upon origin-constrained models with less concern about destinations. On other occasions it may prove necessary to relax the constraints to facilitate easier fitting of the models – constrained versions of the gravity model usually requiring specific computer software for calibration. An alternative simulation model considers the opportunities available in different zones to meet the needs of travelers.

The intervening opportunities model assumes that people try to keep their trips as short as possible and lengthen them only if nearer destinations do not prove acceptable to their needs. Individual residents in a given zone are assumed to consider opportunities for the location of their conduct of specific activities (residence, work, shopping and so on) at various places, starting from the base zone and fanning out to other zones in increasing order of difficulty in reaching them. Each time an opportunity is considered, there is a given, constant chance that it will be selected. The model takes the general form:

$$T_{ij} = T_i[\exp(-LV_j) - \exp(-LV_{j+1})] \qquad (12.3)$$

where:

> V is the possible destination just considered; and
> L is a constant representing the probability of possible destination being accepted (if considered).

While this type of approach has an intuitive appeal, it does suffer from the problem that, empirically, L seems to vary with V rather than remaining constant. Adjustment techniques to correct for the 'wandering' of L values are available but their use seems to violate the notion of constancy. Empirical studies indicate that the results obtained using the intervening opportunities model are no better than those from gravity models. Attempts to develop the opportunities framework by considering competing rather than intervening opportunities (by basing the underlying probability function on the ratio between the trip opportunities in a zone and its competing opportunities) offer no improvements in a forecasting context but complicate the estimation process considerably.

In some instances, as for example with inter-urban road traffic forecasting in the United Kingdom, there had been a tradition to employ a 'fixed trip matrix' when distributing traffic which assumes that the total number of trips (the trips generated and attracted) is unaffected by the new transport scheme. The total traffic, which may well grow due to changing socioeconomic conditions, is simply redistributed as a result of the change in transport policy or infrastructure invest-ment. If new traffic is generated, however, this result may prove distortive.

In Figure 12.5, Demand represents the true aggregate relationship between the cost of travel and the traffic flow. As a result of, say, a road investment the cost of trip making falls from P to P^* with traffic increasing to F^*. Assuming that there has been no shift in demand due to changing income or other socioeconomic factors, the traditional model would assume that demand had remained fixed at the all-traffic flow – in other words that the implied demand curve is Demand*. This means that the benefit enjoyed by the generated traffic ($F^* - F$), and repre-sented by the shaded area in the diagram, would be excluded from the subsequent appraisal stage. This is another reason why there are often feedback links which, in this case, result in the trip-end models being rerun, incorporating some allow-ance for this generation effect that results from redistribution of traffic.

Modal split models allocate traffic flows to particular types of vehicles. In some cases, for example, with urban freight transport or long-distance inter-national passenger transport, one mode so dominates a particular sphere of transport activity that no mode choice submodel is required, although this is exceptional. The traditional method of splitting origin–destination traffic flows by mode involves the use of diversion curves. These show the proportion of traffic likely to favor a particular mode, given its relative cost or other advantage over alternative modes. If we are concerned with two forms of transport, a and b, then a typical model might be:

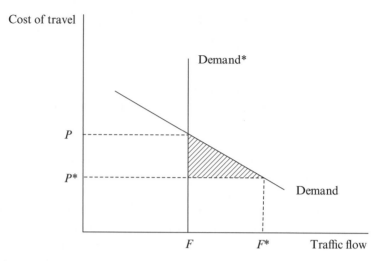

Figure 12.5   *The fixed trip matrix*

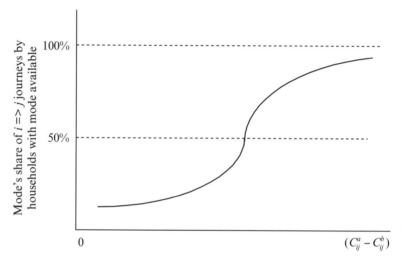

Figure 12.6   *Diversion curve of traffic between modes 'a' and 'b'*

$$\frac{T_{ij}^a}{T_{ij}^a + T_{ij}^b} = \frac{1}{1 + e^{-\lambda(C_{ij}^b - C_{ij}^a)}} \tag{12.4}$$

This yields a diversion curve of the general form seen in Figure 12.6. Normally a series of curves are estimated by subdividing the traveling population (for example, by income) and modes (for example, by service ratios).

In some studies, mode choice is modeled prior to distribution using trip-end or interchange models. The former are often used in highway-oriented origin and destination studies where the emphasis is on car travel, with public transport being treated as little more than a residual to be subtracted from the trip-end predictions prior to assignments being made. The emphasis on variables such as car ownership and income, and the general neglect of public transport characteristics, limits the usefulness of this approach in urban transport planning. Interchange models are more commonly used in public transport feasibility studies and, consequently, concentrate on comparative time, cost and service differentials between competing modes. Models of this type take the form:

$$T_{ijm} = \alpha_0 X_{ij}^{\alpha 1} (F_{ij}^M)^{\alpha 2} (F_{ij}^b)^{\alpha 3} (H_{ij}^M)^{\alpha 4} (H_{ij}^b)^{\alpha 5} \qquad (12.5)$$

where:

X_{ij} is a matrix of exogenous economic and social variables;
F_{ij}^M is the financial cost by mode M;
H_{ij}^M is the time cost by mode M; and
the superscript b indicates the money/time cost by the best mode.

Models of this type have a foundation in economic theory but estimation of parameters $\alpha_1 - \alpha_5$ poses serious statistical problems.

The final submodel, route assignment, compares the travelers' preferences for routes with the characteristics of the routes available. Early approaches relied upon diversion curves similar to those used in modal choice work, but the development of minimum-path algorithms combined with improved computing facilities has permitted the introduction of more sophisticated techniques. A major problem in assignment is the possible need to constrain traffic flows on each link in the transport network to the capacity of the link. If the capacity constraint is omitted then an 'all-or-nothing' assignment results and no allowance is made for the congestion that accompanies high traffic volumes. In reality, travelers use all routes, both the initially cheap and the not so cheap, especially when overall cost differentials are small. The introduction of capacity constraints permits this to be reflected in the model by adjusting link speeds, and hence costs, as the assignment proceeds and congestion levels rise.

In summary, the sequential method of forecasting broadly involves developing a series of mathematical models taking the general form:

$$T_i = f(X_i); \; T_i = f(X_j), \qquad (12.6a)$$

$$T_{ij} = f(T_i, T_j, C_{ij}), \qquad (12.6b)$$

$$T_{ijm} = f(T_{ij}, C_{ijM}, C_{ijM'}) \qquad (12.6c)$$

$$T_{ijMP} = f(T_{ijMP}, C_{ijMP}, C_{ijMP'}) \qquad (12.6d)$$

where the prime notation refers to alternative modes (M') or routes (P').

While widely used, the sequential modeling approach has serious limitations.[21] Clearly, the series of calculations required to calibrate this set of equations

---

[21] US Department of Transportation, *Activity-based Travel Forecasting Conference Proceedings*, USDOT-T-97-7, Washington, DC: 1997.

places tremendous strains on the databases available and, in most studies, large and expensive surveys are needed to gather the necessary information. Also, as pointed out above, it is difficult to incorporate the desirable feedback from assignment and other stages to trip generation so that quality of service variables are adequately and consistently reflected in each submodel of the sequence. Statistically, while it is generally possible to test the significance of the individual models in the sequence, it is not possible to undertake statistical tests of the overall recursive system. The approach is also deficient in that it does not embrace the fundamental tenet of travel demand, namely that it is derived from the desire to participate in some final activity.

One of the reasons why disaggregate economic models have been developed is to avoid some of these problems and to approach more closely to the basic decision-making unit, the household.[22]

12.5 Disaggregate Modeling

The substantial data input required to calibrate satisfactorily the submodels and the difficulty of transferring models once estimated from one data area to another, combined with dissatisfaction with the basically mechanistic and physical nature of the sequential approach, has resulted in an alternative mathematical approach being developed.[23] This second generation of models employing disaggregate methods of travel demand forecasting emphasizes the economic–psychological influences on travel behavior at the individual household level.

The idea is that households are utility maximizers which, mainly for mathematical convenience, are considered to make travel decisions in isolation from other activities. The emphasis is on short-run decisions rather than long-run mobility decisions. Small stratified samples of households (700 or less) provide the data input into the models which tend to be probabilistic, rather than deterministic, in nature (that is, they forecast the probability of particular household travel patterns rather than the average number and type of trips to be undertaken).

A personal disaggregate model of trip making would be of the general form:

$$P(f, d, h, m, t) = P(f)P(d/f))P(h/f, d)P(rn/f, d, h)P(r/f, d, h, m) \qquad (12.7)$$

where $P(f, d, h, m, r)$ is the probability that an individual will undertake a trip with frequency (f) to destination (d) during time of day (h) using mode (m) and via route (r) out of a choice set comprising all possible combinations of

[22] M. Ben-Akiva and S. Lerman, *Discrete Choice Analysis: Theory and Application to Travel Demand*, Cambridge, MA: MIT Press, 1985.

[23] R.E. Quandt, 'The theory of travel demand', *Transportation Research*, **10**, 411–13, 1976.

frequencies, destination, time of day, modes and routes available to the individual. For actual planning or assessment, the forecasts produced from such models must be aggregated up to the level of the geographical zone – it is the inter-zonal level, for example, that determines the level of public transport demand. While there are claims that the approach can be used in comprehensive transport planning, its main role to date has been in policy assessment (for example, looking at car pooling proposals, pollution controls, and public transport subsidies).

Broadly, disaggregate models are characterized by two main features. First, they explicitly recognize that travel decisions emerge out of individuals' optimizing behavior and, if it is pointed out that the final goods consumed as a result of travel are normal, then at a very minimum the demand for travel ought to be related positively to disposable incomes and negatively to the prices of transport services. Second, most have their origins in the 'attribute theory of demand' associated with Kelvin Lancaster.[24] This approach to human behavior assumes that people desire to maximize a utility function that has, as its arguments, commodity attributes rather than the quantities of the actual goods consumed. In other words, if we represent the amounts of attributes by the vector z, the amounts of commodities (in this case travel alternatives) by the vector x, posit a utility function, $U(z)$, and a production of attribute function, $G(x)$, which reflects the attributes of different travel alternatives, and assume that potential travelers are constrained by income, y, and the price of travel, p, then we can reduce the problem to solving:

$$\max U(z) \tag{12.8}$$

subject to $z = G(x)$, $x \geq 0$, $p \cdot x \leq y$

The selection of the attributes can also be seen diagrammatically in Figure 12.7 which looks at a very simple mode choice situation. Potential travelers have a fixed budget, and a choice of three modes (car, train and bus) which have different attribute supply characteristics in terms of speed and economy. With a given budget the traveler can enjoy the combination of attributes seem on the frontier – for example, if all trips were made by train then the bundle of attributes would be S_T and E_T. Of course combinations of modes may be consumed for the budget. The final selection will depend on the consumers' preferences for speed and economy and, since the aim is to maximize utility, this will be at the point where the highest possible constrained indifference curve (I_2) is reached. By using a combination of train and car the traveler will enjoy E of economy and S of speed.

As an example, if one is considering air transport between the United Kingdom and the United States, then the alternative commodities would be the different fare packages offered by the airlines, and the attributes of each would be characteristics such as money costs, speed, period of advance booking,

[24] K.J. Lancaster, 'A new approach to consumer theory', *Journal of Political Economy*, **74**, 132–57, 1966.

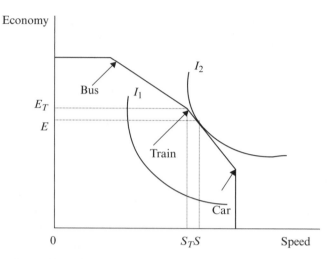

Figure 12.7   *The attribute choices in mode selection*

timing, type of aircraft, on-plane service (such as food, drink and films), stopover regulations, required length of stay at destination and so on.

In terms of application, direct attempts were initially made to apply Lancaster's theory at the aggregate level by Quandt[25] and others in the context of abstract mode modeling. At the inter-urban level Quandt and Baumol[26] developed an abstract mode model for air, bus and car journeys between 16 city pairs in California using cost and time (both absolute and relative) as the determining attributes, but the results were inferior to those obtained from more conventional trip-distribution models. Howrey's[27] early study of air travel out of Cleveland produced an abstract mode model with correct signs, significant coefficients and a good overall fit to survey data. However, while its explanatory power proved statistically superior to a conventional gravity model it turned out to be inferior in terms of *ex post* forecasting quality. Talvitie[28] concentrated on developing the framework to handle inter-urban travel while, as we saw in Chapter 10, Baumol and Vinod, by combining the attributed theory of demand with an inventory theory of goods handling, have adapted the approach to deal with urban freight transport demand.

While some of the calibration problems that were associated with the early aggregate abstract mode models have been resolved, it has been the introduction of disaggregate approaches that has marked the greatest advances. The major advance in this context was the realization that each individual has a different utility function, partly because of quantifiable differences in their personal characteristics

[25] R.E. Quandt, 'The theory of travel demand', *Transportation Research*, **10**, 411–13, 1976.

[26] R.E. Quandt and W.J. Baumol, 'The demand for abstract transport modes: theory and measurement', *Journal of Regional Science*, **6**, 13–26, 1966.

[27] E.P. Howrey, 'On the choice of forecasting models for air travel', *Journal of Regional Science*, **9**, 215–24, 1969.

[28] A.P. Talvitie, 'A direct demand model for downtown work trips', *Transportation*, **2**, 121–52, 1973.

but also partly because of random factors. While the heterogeneous nature of the population poses serious problems, the work of Domenich and McFadden[29] in modeling the random factors, and especially their theoretical work on justifying the use of 'multi-nomial logit models', forms the basis of much modern disaggregate analysis. The forms of disaggregate model that have been developed along these lines, and the range of applications to which they have been applied, are many.

Most of the recent work on disaggregate modeling has centered on mathematical and calibration issues and there is no intention of taking discussion of such matters any further in this book. The mathematical complexity stems from the fact that one is looking at discrete choices – that is, whether a person makes a trip or not – and this involves complications not normally encountered when considering continuous functions.

12.6   Interactive and Stated Preference Modeling

While the sequential and disaggregate approaches to transport demand analysis concentrate on developing sophisticated mathematical simulations, recently there has been a growth of interest in 'behavioral realism', and an emphasis on 'understanding the phenomenon'.[30] Sometimes called the 'activity-based approach',[31] because it has sought to embrace a richer, holistic framework in which travel behavior is analyzed as a daily or multi-day pattern of behavior related to lifestyles and participation in various activities.

The idea is that the demand for travel is derived from the activity patterns of individuals and households. The basic idea has much to do with the concept of time-geography developed by Hägerstrand[32] in which an individual's choice of a specific activity pattern is viewed as being the solution to an allocation problem involving limited resources of time and space. In this sense actual behavior is not that useful, but rather there is a need to put more emphasis on the constraints that limit people's behavior.

These approaches to modeling have also been tied in with the greater use of stated preference techniques that we have already encountered in Chapter 6 in the context of contingency evaluation procedures. This latter approach which, to adopt Kroes and Sheldon's[33] definition, is 'a family of techniques which use

[29] T. Domenich and D. McFadden, *Urban Travel Demand – A Behavioural Analysis*, Amsterdam: North Holland, 1976.
[30] M.C. Dix, 'Report on investigations of household travel decision making behaviour', in E.J. Visser (ed.), *Transport Decisions in an Age of Uncertainty*, Dordrecht: Martinus Nijhoff, 1977.
[31] M.G. McNally and C.R. Rindt, 'The activity-based approach', in D.A. Hensher and K.J. Button (eds), *Handbook of Transport Modelling*, 2nd edn, Amsterdam: Elsevier, 2008.
[32] T. Hägerstrand, 'What about people in regions?', *Papers of the Regional Science Association*, **24**, 7–21, 1970.
[33] E.P. Kroes and R.J. Sheldon, 'Stated preference methods: an introduction', *Journal of Transport Economics and Policy*, **22**, 11–26, 1988.

individual respondents' statements about their preferences in a set of transport options to estimate utility functions', is often claimed to be helpful when:

- there is insufficient variation in revealed preference data to examine all variables of interest;
- there is a high level of correlation between the explanatory variables in a revealed preference model, making statistical estimation of parameters difficult;
- a radically new technology or policy takes the analysis outside of the realms where current revealed behavior is relevant; and
- variables are not easily expressed in standard units (for example, when the interest is in the effects on demand of less-turbulent travel by air).

The aim of interactive modeling is to develop models that get closer to the essential decision process underlying travel behavior. Rather than simply incorporate variables such as household status in mathematical models because the statistical 'explanation' of the model appears to be improved, interactive modeling seeks to explain why status affects travel behavior. Theoretically, travel is seen as one of a whole range of complementary and competitive activities operating in a sequence of events in time and space. It is seen to represent the method by which people trade time to move location in order to enjoy successive activities. Generally, time and space constraints are thought to limit the choice of activities open to individuals. The technique is still far from fully developed, and it has been applied in only a relatively limited number of small-scale forecasting studies (for example, by Peter Jones,[34] in the United Kingdom to school bus operations, and by Tony Fowkes and John Preston,[35] to new local rail services; and by Phifer et al.,[36] in the United States to energy constraints).

The emphasis of interactive models is upon the household (or individual) as the decision-making unit. According to Ian Heggie, ideally, an interactive model should exhibit six main properties:

- It should involve the entire household and allow for interaction between its members.
- It should make existing constraints on household behavior quite explicit.
- It should start from the household's existing pattern of behavior.
- It should work by confronting the household with realistic changes in its travel environment and allowing it to respond realistically.
- It should allow for the influence of long-term adaptation.

[34] P.M. Jones, 'School hour revisions in West Oxfordshire: an exploratory study using HATS', *Technical Report*, Oxford University Transport Studies Unit, Oxford, 1978.

[35] A.S. Fowkes and J. Preston, 'Novel approaches to forecasting the demand for new local rail services', *Transportation Research A*, **25**, 209–18, 1991.

[36] S.P. Phifer, A.J. Neven and D.T. Hartgen, 'Family reactions to energy constraints', paper presented at the Transportation Research Board Annual Meeting, Washington, DC, 1980.

- It should be able to tell the investigator something fundamental that he/she did not know before.

In general, the approach is typified by a fairly small sample and careful survey techniques, often involving such things as 'board games' (such as the 'household activities travel simulator' (HATS) developed by the Oxford University Transport Studies Unit) or other visual aids, frequently computer based these days, to permit households to appreciate the full implications of changes in transport policy for their own behavior. In a sense it represents an attempt to conduct laboratory experiments by eliciting responses in the context of known information and constraints.

The HATS approach, for example, was to confront a household with a map of the local area together with a 24-hour 'strip representation of colored pieces' showing how current activities of the household are spread over space and throughout the day. Changes to the transport system were then postulated (for example, reduced parking availability in the local urban center) and the effects on the household's activities throughout the day were simulated by adjustments to the strip representation. In this way changes in the transport system could be seen to influence the entire 24-hour life pattern of the household, and apparently unsuspected changes in 'remote' trip-making behavior can be traced back to the primary change. It makes clear the constraints and linkages that may affect activity and transport choices. The emphasis is on the micro unit with the aim of being able to develop fairly simple models that permit much clearer insights into the overall effects of transport policy. By asking respondents to trace the effect of changes in transport provision on the entire set of activities undertaken during a day (or week), information on important travel intentions can be seen and the relationships between travel and non-travel activities become explicit.

More recent studies have adopted rather more sophisticated experimentation procedures, often involving computers, which provide for greater flexibility and easier interaction with those being 'interviewed'. Examples of programs of this genre include ALBATROS (A Learning-Based Transportation Oriented Simulation System), the first computational process model of the complete activity scheduling process that could be fully estimated from data, and TRANSIMS, an attempt to replace the entire traditional transport paradigm, has an activity-based front end linked to a population synthesizer and integrated with a micro simulation of modeled travel behavior.

While this aspect of the approach has been refined, important technical issues remain regarding using the information gathered from stated preference-type experiments for forecasting. There is still, for example, much to be learned about why some households give strategically biased responses; in particular there are difficulties in handling habit, inertia and hysteresis in an experimental framework. At a more technical level, John Bates[37] points to our lack of knowledge

---

[37] J. Bates, 'Econometric issues in stated preference analysis', *Journal of Transport Economics and Policy*, **22**, 59–70, 1988.

about the error structures associated with stated preference data and the particular problems of pooling data across individuals.

In contrast to the more traditional revealed preference schools, advocates of this approach, however, point to both the specific recognition that travel is a derived demand and the fact that transport policies have qualitative, as well as quantitative, effects on people's lives. In the longer term, when operational models are more fully developed, the framework may offer the much-sought-after basis for integrating land-use and transport planning assessment. In the short term, the approach has offered useful insights and a method for cross-checking the validity of conventional statistical analysis of behavioral data.

Further Reading

A number of seminal papers on planning issues are contained in Y. Shiftan, K. Button and P. Nijkamp (eds), *Transportation Planning*, Cheltenham, UK and Northampton, MA, USA: Edward Eldgar, 2007, while I.G. Heggie, *Transport Engineering Economics*, New York: McGraw-Hill, 1972, offers a useful extension to this chapter by setting out in more technical detail the traditional methodology of transport planning and by outlining some of the basic techniques. There are numerous papers in D.A. Hensher and K.J. Button (eds), *Handbook of Transport Modelling*, 2nd edn, Amsterdam: Elsevier, 2008, that provide more details of the various approaches to transport modeling and forecasting. World Bank, *A Decade of Action in Transport: An Evaluation of World Bank Assistance to the Transport Sector, 1995–2005*, Washington, DC: World Bank, 2007, offers a perspective on the approach to transport planning in the developing world, and R.S. Timberlake, 'Traffic modelling techniques for the developing world: case studies', *Transportation Research Record*, **1167**, 28–34, 1988, provides useful case-study material in this context. I.S. Jones, *Urban Transport Appraisal*, Basingstoke: Macmillan, 1977, provides a terse, but very useful guide to the contribution that economics may make to the transport planning process and also sketches out in more detail than has been possible above the various methods of transport demand forecasting.

The set of papers edited by D.A. Hensher and P.R. Stopher (eds), *Behavioural Travel Modelling*, London: Croom Helm, 1979, supplies overviews of transport modeling and forecasting, as does J. de Dios Ortúzar and L.G. Willumsen, *Modelling Transport*, 3rd edn, Chichester: John Wiley, 2001, and although the mathematics in both is at times formidable, a careful and selective 'picking' through the pages should prove invaluable to a reader specifically interested in this branch of transport economics. E.P. Kroes and R.J. Sheldon, 'Stated preference methods: an introduction', *Journal of Transport Economics and Policy*, **22**, 11–26, 1988, offers a good introduction to the use of stated preference approaches to forecasting.

13 Transport and Development

13.1 Transport and Economic Development

Economists have long been concerned with assessing the links between changes in the transport sector and the evolving pattern of economic development within the area that it serves. While the importance of transport in economic growth and development has never seriously been questioned, its exact role and influence have been subjected to periodic reappraisals. The subject is made more difficult, because the impacts of transport are not always intended, and thus can have unforeseen consequences. The underlying problem is, however, a more general one in that our understanding of what causes economic development is poor. This point was very clearly made by Charles Kindleberger[1] over half a century ago:

> We have suggested that there is no agreement on how economic development proceeds and have implied that this is because the process is not simple. There are many variables involved, and there is a wide range of substitutability among ingredients – land, capital, and the quality and quantity of labor, and technology can substitute for one another, above certain minima, although there are at the same time certain complementary relationships among them. The will to economize and organization are probably the only indispensable ingredients. For the rest, none are necessary, and none sufficient.

The interest in the topic, though, is not purely an academic matter; public concern with regional disparities within countries and more in economic performance, and the considerable differences in national economic prosperity between the 'North' and the 'South', has brought forth efforts to stimulate growth in lagging economies by investing in various forms of infrastructure. The creation of the World Bank, the Inter-American Development Bank, various United Nations agencies, and a plethora of other bilateral and multilateral organizations is a tangible institutional manifestation of these concerns at the macro level. This is also setting aside any consideration of the use of transport investment programs as part of a Keynesian-style macroeconomic stimulus package.

The form and scale of the measures that could be taken, and indeed their general desirability, are matters of practical interest. In consequence, while Kindleberger is still correct in that our knowledge is in many respects very limited, efforts to clarify the situation continue. The work on development economics and the role that transport can play in the economic development process is extensive.

[1] C.P. Kindleberger, *Economic Development*, New York: McGraw-Hill, 1958.

To provide some context for our discussions we begin by considering the theories of economic development and how transport fits into them. Without an understanding of how economic development takes place, it is not possible to study transport's contribution. We move to look at more specific issues, beginning with a longstanding debate in economics about the role that public transport infrastructure can play in stimulating economic productivity. This has largely been an empirical debate that was initiated in the 1980s regarding questions about the role that infrastructure policies should play in macroeconomic policy. This leads on to questions regarding the ripple effects on economic performance of individual transport initiatives. We then move on to consider the more macro problems of stimulating economic growth in the Third World, before proceeding to consider the problems of formulating a common transport policy to foster the economic growth ambitions of the member states of the European Union (EU). At a more micro level, there are also questions concerning the ways in which transport provision can stimulate economic growth within certain parts of a country or for a given urban area.

While the discussion of transport and economic development has been sectionalized for expositional convenience, it is important to emphasize that in practice considerable trade-offs may be necessary between, say, devising a transport policy to stimulate national growth and one designed to assist the development of specified backward regions. The poorest countries, especially, often feel that they must attempt to increase their national income. Indeed, if one were to accept the 'growth pole' approach to economic development,[2] then national growth is achieved by concentrating effort in several strong regional centers. Hence, interregional inequality of growth is an inevitable concomitant and condition of growth itself. Consequently, although it may be possible to design a national transport strategy or investment program that assists in the maximization of national economic growth, it may need modifying to ensure that an acceptable degree of equity is retained among the different regions of the country.

13.2   Economic Growth Theory and Transport

First a little background. In the neoclassical economic framework, which we shall consider in more detail below and which largely represents an extension of eighteenth century trade theory, transport is not really considered at all. The existence of optimal transport services is assumed and, if they are lacking in the short term, then it is assumed that a perfectly functioning market would soon supply the optimal amount. The more recent endogenous approach to economic development assumes imperfect markets that need not result in socially optimal outcomes. Again with reference to transport, these imperfections may entail lack of adequate financial markets to construct appropriate infrastructure and

---

[2] H.W. Richardson, 'Growth pole spillovers: the dynamics of backwash and spread', *Regional Studies*, **10**, 1–9, 1976.

imperfect markets in making use of the roads, ports and so on that are available, due to either market or government failures.

Traditionally, it was argued by Adam Smith and others that transport exerted a strong positive influence on economic development and that increased production could be directly related to improved transport. In the UK context, for example, over a century ago, Baxter[3] argued that 'Railways have been a most powerful agent in the progress of commerce, in improving the conditions of the working classes, and in developing the agricultural and mineral resources of the country'. Fifty years later we still find Lord Lugard[4] writing, 'the material development of Africa may be summed up in the one word, transport'. Perhaps the strongest advocate of the positive role of transport, however, is Rostow[5] who, in accounting for economic growth, maintains that 'The introduction of railroads has historically been the most powerful single indicator to take-offs. It was decisive in the United States, France, Germany, Canada and Russia'.

A broader brush approach is adopted by Andersson and Stromquist[6] who claim that all the major transitions in the European economic systems were accompanied, or initiated by major changes in transport and communications infrastructure. Four main transport and logistics revolutions can be distinguished:

- the period from the thirteenth century, in which water transport emerged as a new logistic system connecting cities along the rivers and coastal areas (the Hansa economy);
- the period from the sixteenth century (the Golden Age), characterized by a dramatic improvement in sailing and sea transport and by the introduction of new banking systems which stimulated trade to the East and West Indies (with Lisbon, Antwerp and Amsterdam as major centers);
- the middle of the nineteenth century, marked by the Industrial Revolution, in which the invention of the stream engine generated new transport modes, thereby creating new market areas such as North America; and
- from the 1970s, which is marked by increased information and flexibility; just-in-time systems and material requirements planning have evolved within this framework.

Positive linkages between transport provision and economic development can be divided between the direct transport input and indirect, including multiplier, effects. Good transport offers low shipping costs that have permitted wider markets

[3] R.D. Baxter, 'Railway extension and its results', *Journal of the Statistical Society*, **24**, 549–95, 1866.
[4] F.D. Lugard, *The Dual Mandate in British Tropical Africa*, Edinburgh: Blackwoods, 1923.
[5] W.W. Rostow, *The Stages of Economic Growth*, Cambridge: Cambridge University Press, 1960.
[6] A. Andersson and U. Stromquist, 'The emerging C-society', in D.R. Batten and R. Thords (eds), *Transportation for the Future*, New York: Springer, 1988.

to be served and the exploitation of large-scale production in an extensive range of activities. In the past, Hunter,[7] for example, postulated a causal linkage between low-cost transport and economic growth. The Industrial Revolution was successful because of a prior revolution in transport technology. Similarly, Owen[8] argued that a widening of domestic markets through improved transport services is a necessary prerequisite for national economic development. Further, most undeveloped countries are, for a variety of geographical, economic and historic reasons, dependent upon international trade, and an expansion of this trade is an essential prerequisite for growth. In these circumstances the provision of efficient port facilities will, according to this school of thought, positively assist development.

The indirect effects stem from the employment created in the construction of transport infrastructure and the jobs associated with operating the transport services. Further, there may be multiplier effects stemming from the substantial inputs of iron, timber, coal and so on required to construct a modern transport system and which, at least in the context of development in the nineteenth century, were supplied by indigenous heavy industries. Transport also often provided some initial experience of business for many industrialists of the period. The potential multiplier effects for Third World countries today are likely to be substantially less given the growth (itself a function of improved transport) of international trade and tied development aid. Additionally, the technical expertise required to engineer and plan modern transport systems is often unavailable in less developed countries and must be bought from more advanced nations.

The broad theories that underlie these views of the role of transport have evolved over time, and can be divided into two broad conceptual approaches, each seeing transport as impacting on development in somewhat different ways.

Neoclassical Economics

Economists have struggled over many years to explain why some regions' economies, or indeed national economies, perform better than others. Traditional neoclassical, long-run macroeconomic growth theory of the type espoused by Robert Solow[9] and others argues that per capita income in a region or country depends on local factor endowment, the savings rate, and the impact of exogenously determined 'technical progress'. Transport is seen as one of the inputs in this context, on a par with other industries.

More formally, an exogenous growth model of the so-called Solow type can be formulated by taking a simple Cobb–Douglas production function of the form,

$$Y = A(t)K^{1-b} L^b \tag{13.1}$$

[7] H. Hunter, 'Transport in Soviet and Chinese development', *Economic Development and Cultural Change*, **14**, 71–2, 1965.

[8] W. Owen, *Strategy for Mobility*, Washington, DC: Brookings Institution, 1964.

[9] R.M. Solow, 'Technical change and the aggregate production function', *Review of Economics and Statistics*, **39**, 312–20, 1957.

where:

   Y is net national product;
   K is the capital stock;
   L is the labor stock; and
   A is the level of technology.

The fact that A is a function of time (t) indicates the standard neoclassical assumption that technology only improves over time for reasons external to the model.

Where regional, as opposed to macro, neoclassical growth models differed from this to some extent is that they treat labor and other factor supplies as dependent on both the internal demographics and an inherent resource base of a region and also on factor movements between regions. While most national economies experience relatively small flows of factors of production between them, the much laxer border restrictions within a region tend to foster such flows. This makes factor growth in a region more elastic.

Basically, this spatial mobility of factors of production can help to compensate for an initial shortage of a factor in a region. Hence, a specific region may grow when there is capital abundance by 'importing' labor from other regions. This, combined with the natural growth in labor supply within the region, can lead to growth through more-efficient use of the complementary capital stock, although in the long run there will be convergence in per capita income between the regions, albeit at a higher average wage rate. One can consider parallel movements of capital but this is less relevant to air transportation.

Figure 13.1 offers a simple illustration of the larger point. There are two regions, **A** and **B**. Region **A** enjoys high income and low unemployment ($Y+$: $U-$) while **B** is the mirror image of this. There are decreasing returns to factors of production, including capital. The neoclassical economic model assumes that with zero costs of migration (including zero transportation costs) and a homogeneous labor force, labor will move from **B** to **A** seeking work and higher pay whereas, on the assumption of uniform commercial risk across regions, capital will move from **A** to **B** where it can be combined with abundant, cheap labor to maximize returns.

Wages will fall in **A**, unemployment will increase, and the return on capital will rise as the labor supply grows and capital becomes scarcer. The additional capital and the decreasing size of the labor force in **B** will push down the marginal return on investment and concurrently push up wages. The process continues until labor costs and unemployment levels are equalized. This equalization is achieved in a world of zero transport costs and full information about opportunities.

The problem with this way of looking at regional development is that it relies on a number of relatively strong assumptions. Factor movement is not frictionless: there are distance, information and money costs. Also, factors of production are not homogeneous, and some are more mobile than others. Young, skilled, highly educated workers, for example, tend to be more mobile than those lacking these characteristics. Investors consider returns on their capital relative to risk

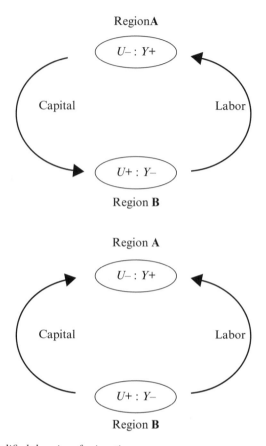

Figure 13.1 *Simplified theories of migration*

incurred – they are not risk neutral. There is also the issue of technical progress that is simply treated as a sort of residual and uncontrollable factor in the neo-classical framework. This seems excessively fatalistic.

In addition, empirical analysis hardly gives solid support for the neoclassical idea. Testing the validity of the alternative theories, in the absence of easily quantifiable counterfactuals, has frequently involved looking at secondary evidence, and in particular at evidence shedding light on whether there is convergence in the economic growth paths of regions or, at the macro level, nations. The empirical question that is explored becomes one of whether there is convergence in regional economic growth rates in, generally, per capita income or productivity as is an outcome of the neoclassical model.

The extensive empirical analysis that has emerged has been assisted by the improved data made available in recent years, as well as new models, enhanced econometric techniques, and better understanding of how to measure convergence. In particular, there has been the development of the concept of β-convergence measures that has allowed a more rigorous analysis of economic convergence than the more traditional σ-convergence measure that looks for changes in standard statistical indicators of dispersion – normally the variance.

The estimation of possible β-convergence involves a mean-reversion calculation, which occurs if there is a negative relationship between the growth rate of income per capita and the level of initial income. Much of this type of analysis has been done at the national level, but it, and the more limited body of analysis that has been conducted at the regional level, does offer some insights into the validity of the idea of "endogenous" economic growth.

Much of the early work on spatial economic convergence relied upon aggregate, national data sources and focused on σ-convergence measurements. The findings indicated that labor productivity, and with it per capita income in the world, was converging in the long run and thus rendered support to the neoclassical growth theory. The difficulty with this work was that the datasets used only contained countries that had already industrialized, and even for those there were periods of divergence. Improved data subsequently indicated a lack of any general economic convergence.

The more recent work that has made use of β-convergence measures, and embraces a number of subnational studies, tends to find little support for overall convergence, and *ipso facto* the neoclassical model. Robert Barro and Xavier Sala-i-Martin[10] in a number of studies that, for example, have examined the economies of American states and EU regions, find that while there is evidence of convergence in per capita income, it is slow – about 2 percent per annum and well below the 12 percent or so that neoclassical theory would suggest. These are also conditional convergence measures that allow for homogeneity between, for example, the regional economies within a European economy, but diversity between countries that would suggest potential differences in steady-state growth rates for the regions within them. Hence, overall there is little support in this body of work for the exogenous growth idea.

'New Economic Growth Theory'

An alternative to the neoclassical model attempts to circumvent some of these intellectual problems by embracing such things as transport costs. In endogenous growth models, growth over time entails increasing returns to scale for a region. A proportionate increase in labor and capital gives rise to more than proportionate gains in output. This, when embodied into the 'New Growth Theory' or 'New Economic Geography', is consistent with divergence in economic growth along the traditional lines of Gunnar Myrdal's[11] ideas of 'circular-and-cumulative causation', albeit for somewhat different reasons.

The situation can be illustrated by returning to Figure 13.1. Taking the initial starting positions for two regions, the endogenous growth approach argues that not only will equalization of real wages and employment levels not be attained, but that there may be cases where they diverge further. Labor mobility between regions

---

[10] R.J. Barro and X. Sala-i-Martin, 'Convergence across states and regions', *Brookings Papers on Economic Activity*, **1**, 107–82, 1991.

[11] G. Myrdal, *An American Dilemma*, New York: Harper & Row, 1944.

A and **B** may be impeded by the various costs of migration – embracing social and search costs as well as simple financial costs and transport considerations – and heterogeneity in the labor market – the jobs available in region **A** not being compatible with the skills and knowledge of labor in region **B**.

Equally, capital does not always move from region **A** to **B** because of the higher returns due, not to an actual shortage of capital, but rather to the lesser uncertainty that is to be found in regions that already have a high level of prosperity and a pool of complementary skilled labor. While the earlier regional models of Nicholas Kaldor[12] in particular, focused largely on divergent growth rates in the context of traditional-style industries, the more contemporary form of the theory pays particular attention to the endogenous growth that occurs in regions that have an established highly skilled workforce and the ability to further develop their knowledge-based industries.[13]

The relevance of the new thinking, and the empirical analysis that has been found to support at least parts of it, is that it gives a role for government in regional and transport economic policy. If there is circular-and-cumulative causation caused by scale effects of one kind or another, combined with imperfections in the mobility of factors of production, very broadly defined to embrace knowledge, then policies can be devised to compensate. Part of this policy may embrace appropriate transport elements, and especially those relating to infrastructure provision.

13.3 Transport Infrastructure Investment and Economic Productivity

Large transport infrastructure investments, such as the US Federal Highway System, have often been credited with having major impacts on the economic efficiency of a country. Fogel's work questioned whether that was always the case, but the issue resurfaced in the late 1980s in the context of the role of public investment, when David Aschauer[14] produced work suggesting that the return on public infrastructure investment, of which transport works form the largest element, exceeded by a large margin that found for private investment over the period from 1949 to 1985 in the United States. Analysis by Biehl[15] relating to European regions came to the same basic conclusion.

Aschauer's analysis took a simple macro national time-series production function for the United States of the general form:

$$Y = f(L, K, J) \tag{13.2}$$

[12] N. Kaldor, 'The case for regional policies', *Scottish Journal of Economics*, **17**, 337–48, 1970.

[13] R.E. Lucas, 'Making a miracle', *Econometrica*, **61**, 251–72, 1993.

[14] D.A. Aschauer, 'Is public infrastructure expenditure productive?', *Journal of Monetary Economics*, **23**, 177–200, 1989.

[15] D. Biehl, *The Contribution of Infrastructure to Regional Development*, Regional Policy Division, European Communities, 1986.

Table 13.1   *Summary of estimated output elasticities of public infrastructure investments*

Study	Level of aggregation	Output elasticity of public capital
Aschauer (1989)	National	0.39
Holtz-Eakin (1988)	National	0.39
Munnell (1990)	National	0.34
Costa et al. (1987)	States	0.20
Eisner (1991)	States	0.17
Munnell (1990)	States	0.15
Mera (1973)	Regions	0.20
Duffy-Deno & Eberts (1989)	Urban areas	0.08
Eberts & Fogarty (1987)	Urban areas	0.03

Source: K.J. Button, 'Infrastructure investment, endogenous growth and economic development', *Annals of Regional Science*, **29**, 189–206, 1995. This paper contains full references to the studies cited.

where:

    Y indicates output;

    L is labor;

    K is the stock of private capital; and

    J is the stock of public capital;

Aschauser used a Cobb–Douglas specification to estimate the output elasticity of public sector investment. Later work sometimes modified the production framework by adding additional variables, for example, Prud'homme[16] used a function of the general form $Y = f(L, K, J, F)$ where F reflected employees in the public sector. Some studies have used a cost, rather than a production, function of the form $C = f(IP, Q, PK)$,[17] while other studies have used varying levels of aggregation and some have taken cross-sections of data, often by region, rather than a single national time series. Table 13.1 provides a listing of the results of the main studies. These do not refer specifically to transport investments, but transport is by far the major component in each.

The early studies indicated that at the time they were conducted, infrastructure expansion would significantly enhance productivity: a 1 percent increase in the public capital stock would raise total factor productivity by 0.39 percent. Later studies, and especially as the level of aggregation moved down from national to state to urban level, brought this into question. As Ronald Fisher[18] put it,

[16] R. Prud'homme, 'Assessing the role of infrastructure in France by means of regionally estimated production functions', in D.F. Batten and C. Karlsson (eds), *Infrastructure and the Complexity of Economic Development*, New York: Springer-Verlag, 1996.

[17] C. Lynde and J. Richmond, 'Public capital and long-run costs in UK manufacturing', *Economic Journal*, **103**, 880–93, 1993.

[18] R.C. Fisher, 'The effects of state and local government public services on economic development', *New England Economic Review*, March/April, 53–82, 1997.

The research is all over the board and somewhat inconsistent in its results as to whether investments in public services can increase levels of economic development. For example, the relationship between transportation investments and development is generally positive (but not overwhelming), and it is statistically significant only half of the time.

A number of technical points have also been raised about the way this sort of analysis has been conducted:[19]

- While the various studies have thrown up positive correlations between economic performance and the quantity of infrastructure, the direction of causality is not immediately clear. Wealthier areas, or times of greater economic growth, may simply provide more resources to be put into public projects. Testing for causality is difficult, and unfortunately the econometric work that has been done is not conclusive. Looking at tourism, a transport-intensive activity, for example, studies of Spain by Balanguer and Cantavella-Jorda[20] and of Turkey,[21] has suggested that there is a causal link running from tourism to economic development, but contrarily Narayan[22] finds the linkage to be in the other direction for Fiji.
- The term 'infrastructure' is flexible; there is no agreed definition and taking accountancy data may disguise important measurement, qualitative and definition factors. In the United States, for example, Alan Aschauer, Alicia Munnell[23] and others used a 4-category core subset of the nine US Bureau of Labor Statistics infrastructure categories, whereas other studies have employed the full set.
- The way that infrastructure is managed, used and priced may be as important as the level of investment involved. In terms of impact, therefore, account needs to be taken of the short-term levels of utilization, maintenance and so on in addition to the stock of, and investment in, capacity.[24]
- While transport is the largest element of most nations' infrastructure, it is not the only one, and ideally one should separate it out from energy, education, health, defense and so on.
- As Morrison puts it: 'A clear consensus about the impacts of infrastructure investment has as yet been elusive, at least partly because different

[19] E.M. Gramlich, 'Infrastructure investment: a review essay', *Journal of Economic Literature*, **32**, 1176–96, 1994.
[20] J. Balanguer and M. Cantavella-Jorda, 'Tourism as a long-run economic growth factor: the Spanish case', *Applied Economics*, **34**, 877–84, 2002.
[21] L. Gunduz and A.-J. Hatemi, 'Is the tourism-led growth hypothesis valid for Turkey?', *Applied Economics Letters*, **12**, 499–504, 2005.
[22] P.K. Narayan, 'Economic impact of tourism on Fiji's economy: Empirical evidence from the computable equilibrium model', *Tourism Economics*, **10**, 419–33, 2004.
[23] A.H. Munnell, 'Is there a shortfall in public capital investment?', *New England Economic Review*, September/October, 11–32, 1990.
[24] C. Winston, 'Efficient transportation infrastructure policy', *Journal of Economic Literature*, **5**, 113–27, 1991.

methodologies generate varying results and implications'.[25] From an econometric perspective, for example, Sturm and de Haan[26] looking at American and Dutch data series on the economic effects of public investment found them to be neither stationary nor co-integrated, suggesting that the estimation techniques used in many time-series studies are often inappropriate.
- From a purely *a priori* perspective some of the studies have thrown up rates of return that are outside of normal expectations, and well outside of what have been found in most individual micro projects.

13.4   The Multiplier Impacts of a Transport Investment

While at the macro level there seems, from the empirical evidence, to be only a very general link between transport provision and economic development, at best, it is at the more meso level that investment decisions are actually made. Major transport investments are generally neither simple in engineering terms, nor in their economic implications. Chapter 11 dealt with the microeconomic matters of assessing the pros and cons of a transport investment; here we look at transport provision in terms of its implications for stimulating economic activity at a higher level of aggregation.

A new airport, which for specificity is what we shall consider, goes through a number of stages from its planning to becoming fully operational and heavily used. Each of these phases generates its own particular type of income multiplier effect on the region. Figure 13.2 offers a simple diagram tracing out the temporal and spatial impacts together with some indication (the size of the arrows) of their respective magnitudes. The following discusses each multiplier in turn:

- *Primary*   The primary multiplier stems from the income that is associated with the multiplicand inherent in construction of the facility, and the rounds of expenditure that emanate as part of that money is recycled through the local economy. The size of the local multiplier is often tempered in the case of an airport, if there is a need for significant inflows of labor, raw materials, and equipment to plan and construct the facility. Leakages of this kind are often substantial because new airports or major extensions are rare events in aggregate let alone in a particular region. As a result, there is seldom either adequate local expertise or equipment available. Even when local resources are used, there may be crowding-out effects if these are taken from other sectors of the regional economy and, thereby, the multiplier effects of these sectors are reduced.

[25] J.C. Morrison, 'Macroeconomic relationships between public spending on infrastructure and private sector productivity in the United States', in J.M. Mintz and R.S. Preston (eds), *Infrastructure and Competitiveness*, Kingston, Ontario: John Deutsch Institute for the Study of Economic Policy, 1993.

[26] J.E. Sturm and J. de Haan, 'Is public expenditure really productive? New evidence from the USA and the Netherlands', *Economic Modelling*, **12**, 60–72, 1995.

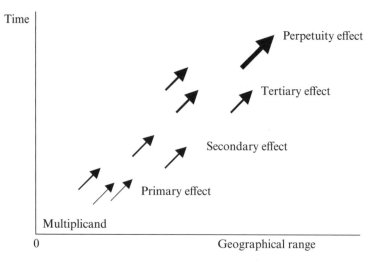

Figure 13.2 *The various economic multipliers associated with an airport investment*

- *Secondary*   Once an airport is operational, it pumps money into the local economy through the staff that it directly employs and the activities of the airlines that make use of the facility. This income, in turn has multiplier effects on the regional economy. Airports can be major employers but there is a largely bimodal distribution in the labor force. While airports do employ many highly skilled and, thus, generally highly paid workers, many jobs are unskilled or semi-skilled (for example, in terms of drivers, aircraft cleaners, workers in concessions and baggage handlers). Equally, while the airlines using the airport may maintain a staff to handle ticketing and aircraft maintenance, as well as have aircrew stopping overnight at local hotels; the numbers are generally relatively small compared to the land-take and investment in infrastructure and operational equipment.
- *Tertiary*   The tertiary multiplier is the one that normally attracts most attention in the economic development literature. It is concerned with the amount of economic activity drawn to the region by the existence of an airport, and with the subsequent ripple effects that result as this pumps income into the area. These regional economic effects can be substantial. For example Memphis Shelby Airport, the major US hub for FedEx, is surrounded by warehouse and distribution facilities – one of the largest concentrations in the world. These facilities house products as varied as just-in-time surgery and orthopedic devices, home decor products, and DVDs, all of which are shipped from Memphis to destinations around the world. But elsewhere, and at much smaller facilities, the presence of air services is important for many industries not only in their cargo needs but more often in terms of allowing their employees and customers easy access to their facilities and markets. High-technology industry makes extensive use of air transport, as do tourists.
- *Perpetuity*   While the tertiary multiplier effect can often be pronounced when an airport is suitably located and an extensive range of destinations

offered, its effect largely stems from a movement up the local production function. The airport itself, or extensions to an existing facility, is justified because there is an existing demand for air transport services. The perpetuity effect is often, although not always, associated with the development of a large airport that shifts the regional production function upwards. Essentially it changes the structure of the regional economy. For example, many islands in the Caribbean and the Mediterranean have had their entire economies changed, usually from fishing and agriculture, to tourism as the result of the construction of a large airport. Air travel, after the construction of airport infrastructure, was also vital to the growth of tourism in larger regions, such as the coasts of Spain and of Miami. Additionally, as alluded to earlier, high-technology corridors have emerged at locations that had either been farmland before or dependent on more traditional industries.

The empirical evidence has not always been very helpful in sorting out these rather diverse ideas concerning the links between specific transport initiatives and the economic development, as can be seen from the summaries of studies conducted of surface transport in industrial countries in the 1980s and set out in Table 13.2. One of the difficulties is that economic development itself is not easy to define, and as can be seen from the table, a number of different measures can be used in addition to simply the impact on local GDP.

There are also some serious caveats that can often lead to overestimations using income or employment multipliers at the regional level.[27] Multipliers were derived as part of demand-side macroeconomics at a time when factor supply constraints were not an issue. In practice, regions, and especially those where the economy has been performing poorly, often have particular supply constraints that limit the size of multiplier effects. Most empirical work tends to use macro parameters that may not be relevant for the region under consideration.

While multipliers are often useful for considering the impacts on the region enjoying the new air transport services, they consider only the gross effects. The initial injection of resources is often from outside the region; the multiplicand has to come from somewhere, and there are opportunity costs associated with resources drawn in during successive multiplier rounds, and this means that there is an opportunity cost involved. In the case of an airport intended to open up a tourist area, for example, this may stimulate more tourism in aggregate, but some of the visitors will be attracted from alternative destinations. As with any activity that allows trade, airports have both a traffic generation and a traffic diversion effect.

In addition, while there may be positive multiplier effects, the closure of an airport or airline service may produce a downward spiral as income circulation is reduced. This can lead to retention of a facility or service that may not be justified. Investment, therefore, should be viewed over a fairly long horizon, and simply to assess the short-term effects of, say developing a small airport to

---

[27] K.G. Debbage, 'Airport runway slots: limits to growth', *Annals of Tourism Research*, **29**, 933–51, 2002.

Table 13.2   *Summary of findings looking at transport and development in industrialized countries*

Study	Geographical scale	Infrastructure	Conclusions
Botham (1980)	28 Zones (UK)	Changing nature of highways	Small, centralizing on employment
Briggs (1981)	Non-metropolitan counties (US)	Provision of highways	Presence of interstate highway is no guarantee of county development
Clearly & Thomas (1973)	Regional level (UK)	New estuarial crossing	Little relocation but changes in firms' operations
Dodgson (1974)	Zones in North (UK)	New motorway	Small effect on employment
Eagle et al. (1987)	87 counties (US)	New highway	No increased employment
Evers et al. (1987)	Regional level (Netherlands)	High-speed rail	Some effect on employment
Forrest et al. (1987)	Metropolitan areas (US)	Light rapid transit	Property blight – good for urban renewal
Judge (1983)	Regional level (UK)	New motorway	Small economic impact
Langley (1981)	Highway corridor (US)	Highway	Devalued property in areas
Mackie et al. (1986)	Regional level	New estuarial crossing	Small overall effect
Mills (1981)	Metropolitan areas (US)	Interstate highways	No significant effect on location patterns
Moon (1986)	Metropolitan areas (US)	Highway crossings	Existence of 'interchange villages'
Pickett (1984)	Local districts (UK)	Light rapid transit	Properties close to the line benefited
Stephandes (1990)	87 counties (US) expenditure	New highway	Could affect employment – depends on county
Stephandes et al. (1986)	87 counties (US)	New highway expenditure	Some positive association with employment
Watterson (1986)	Metropolitan area (UK)	Light rapid transit	Modest growth in land use
Wilson et al. (1982)	Regional level (US)	Existing highways	Transport affects location decisions but not development

Source: K.J. Button, S. Leitham, R.W. McQuaid and J.D. Nelson, 'Transport and industrial and commercial location', *Annals of Regional Science*, **29**, 189–206, 1995. This paper contains full details of the studies cited.

stimulate local residential development or tourism may not be enduring and may leave the area with significant stranded-costs. Reliance on one industry that is in turn dependent on another is also a risky development strategy.

This causal view of transport and economic development has come under question in recent years. The cliometrics (the systematic application of economic theory, econometric techniques and other mathematical methods to the study of history) work of Fogel[28] in the United States, for example, offers evidence that American growth in the nineteenth century would have been quite possible without the advent of the railways – waterways supplying a comprehensive transport system at comparable costs. The view that the railways were the motive force behind American economic development has given way to a weaker position, namely that good transport permits economic expansion.

Economic development is, thus, now generally seen as a complex process with transport permitting the exploitation of the natural resources and talents of a country; it is, therefore, necessary but not sufficient for development. Transport can release working capital from one area that can be used more productively as fixed capital elsewhere, although a necessary prior condition is the existence of suitable productive opportunities in potential markets. Public infrastructure in this sense should be set in the context of the availability of private capital: many parts of the world, for example, would not benefit from more transport infrastructure because of the lack of private resources.[29]

Looked at from a slightly different perspective, improved transport can help overcome bottlenecks in production and thus further foster economic expansion.[30] This is, for example, the underlying position taken by Roger Vickerman[31] and Button[32] when examining the regional impacts of the Channel Tunnel between the United Kingdom and France. A difficulty, of course, if this is true, is that the bottleneck may be some distance from the region and superficially appear unconnected with it. Accepting this caveat, the basic view of this school of thought is that transport is seen more as a facilitator than a generator of development:

> In many developing countries the inadequacy of transport facilities is one of the major bottlenecks to socio-economic development and a national integration. Often the lack of transport makes it difficult to introduce other social infrastructure such as education and medical services. The dissemination of the modern techniques and inputs of agricultural production and the linking of agriculture to other sectors of the economy through the market is hampered by the absence or inadequacy of transport facilities. As a result of these and other factors, the productivity of agriculture – the dominant sector in developing economics – is deplorably low.[33]

[28] R.W. Fogel, *Railroads and American Economic Growth: Essays in Econometric History*, Baltimore, MD: Johns Hopkins University Press, 1964.

[29] D. Biehl, 'The role of infrastructure in regional development', in R.W. Vickerman (ed.), *Infrastructure and Regional Development*, London: Pion, 1991.

[30] P. Rietveld, 'Infrastructure and regional development: a survey of multiregional economic models', *Annals of Regional Science*, **23**, 255–74, 1989.

[31] R.W. Vickerman, 'The Channel Tunnel: consequences for regional growth and development', *Regional Studies*, **21**, 187–97, 1987.

[32] K.J. Button, 'The Channel Tunnel – the economic implications for the south-east of England', *Geographical Journal*, **156**, 187–99, 1990.

[33] Y. Ahmed, P. O'Sullivan, Sujono and D. Wilson, *Road Investment Programming for Developing Countries: An Indonesian Example*, Evanston, IL: Northwestern University Press, 1976.

While the approaches sketched out above ascribe a positive role to transport in economic development, albeit in different ways, there is a feeling among some economists that an excessive amount of scarce resources sometimes tends to be devoted to transport improvements. As with any scarce input, it is possible to define an optimal provision of transport to facilitate development so that resources being drawn from other activities are not wasted. Excess provision can have an economic cost such as reduced or missed opportunities elsewhere; the aim is thus to optimize 'crowding-out'.

At a given point in economic development, a country requires a certain level of transport provision so that its growth potential is maximized – hence there is an optimum transport capacity for any development level. It has been argued, however, that there are economic forces that tend to lead to an excess of transport provision (especially high-cost infrastructure) at the expense of more-efficient and -productive projects. More specifically, Wilson[34] has pointed to the lumpiness of transport capital that, together with its longevity and associated externalities, makes it particularly difficult to estimate future costs and benefits. Consequently, decisions to devote resources to transport are not easily reversible or readily corrected.

The political acceptability of transport has been highlighted by Albert Hirschman[35] who feels that the sector attracts resources quite simply because it is difficult for mistakes (of an economic nature) to be proved even after major projects have been completed. Also, development planners tend to be mainly concerned with allocating public investment funds and it is, therefore, natural that they should claim transport, communications, energy, drainage and so on as being of overriding and fundamental importance. Further, given the industrial composition of wealthier developed countries with an established heavy industrial base, tied aid for transport schemes has a firm attraction. Those adopting this rather skeptical approach to the role of transport, therefore, accept that an adequate basic transport system is an obvious *sine qua non* for modern economic development, but question whether the opportunity costs involved in further improving transport are necessarily justified.

13.5   Transport Economics in Less Developed Countries

Transport investment forms a major component of the capital formation of less developed countries, and expenditure on transport is usually the largest single item in the national budget. Up to 40 percent of public expenditure is devoted to transport infrastructure investment, with substantial supplements coming

---

[34] F.W. Wilson, 'Towards a theory of transport and development', in F.W. Wilson, B. Bergman, L.V. Hirsch and M.S. Klein (eds), *The Impact of Highway Investment on Development*, Washington, DC: Brookings Institute, 1966.

[35] A.O. Hirschman, *The Strategy of Economic Development*, New Haven, CT: Yale University Press, 1958.

from outside international agencies such as the World Bank or in direct bilateral assistance from individual countries. At one level it is important to know whether this is, in aggregate terms, the most practical and efficient method of assisting the poor countries of the world, while at another level it is necessary to be able to assess the development impact of individual transport schemes.

Broadly, transport may be seen to have four functions in assisting economic development in poorer countries:[36]

- First, it is a factor input into the production process, permitting goods and people to be transferred between and within production and consumption centers. Because much of this movement is between rural and urban areas, it permits the extension of the money economy into the agricultural sector.
- Transport improvements can shift production possibility functions by altering factor costs and, especially, it reduces the levels of inventory tied up in the production process.
- Third, mobility is increased, permitting factors of production, especially labor, to be transferred to places where they may be employed most productively.
- Transport increases the welfare of individuals, by extending the range of social facilities to them, and also provides superior public goods such as greater social cohesion and increased national defense.

Transport economists have made significant contributions in assessing in detail the role that transport may play in assisting economic development in Third World countries. At the microeconomic level they have developed techniques of project appraisal that permit a more scientific assessment of the costs and benefits of individual transport projects to be conducted. Many of the techniques of investment appraisal employed in the developed parts of the world (see Chapter 11) are applicable in Third World conditions but local situations often require changes of emphasis. This is not surprising considering that these techniques were devised to look at transport systems based almost entirely upon mechanical modes, while head-porterage and canoes still account for a great proportion of goods movement in many less developed countries.

Basic data are also often not so readily available or reliable in the Third World as in most developed countries, thus limiting the precision of any analysis. Nevertheless, the development of investment appraisal techniques of the type set down by Little and Mirrlees[37] permits consistent analysis across investment alternatives both within the transport sector and between the transport sector and other areas of economic activity. Such techniques emphasize the importance of estimating appropriate shadow prices for both inputs into transport and the

[36] G. Fromm, 'Introduction: an approach to investment decisions', in G. Fromm (ed.), *Transport Investment and Economic Development*, Washington, DC: Brookings Institution, 1965.

[37] I.M.D. Little and J.A. Mirrlees, *Project Appraisal and Planning for Developing Countries*, London: Heinemann, 1974.

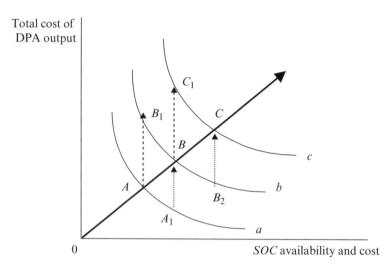

Figure 13.3   *Balanced and unbalanced growth paths*

benefits derived from it. In particular, the shortage of foreign exchange suffered by many less developed countries is highlighted, while it is recognized that higher levels of underemployment and unemployment require adjustments to the wage costs of labor. (The shadow price of labor, estimated as any lost production by diverting it from elsewhere in the economy, is usually negligible, plus an allowance for the disutility associated with the work in the transport sector.)

At the macroeconomic level economists have pointed to the general influence that appropriate transport planning can have in assisting overall economic development.[38] While it may be argued that ideally one should expand transport provision to balance developments elsewhere in the economy, this is not always possible. The balanced growth approach maintains that if transport services are inadequate, then bottlenecks in the economy will curtail the growth process, but if the services are excessive this is both wasteful, in the sense that idle resources could be earning a positive return elsewhere, and can become demoralizing if the anticipated demand for transport does not materialize relatively quickly (Nath offers a general defense of the balanced growth model[39]). Hirschman takes a somewhat different view, arguing that the relationship between economic development and the provision of social overhead capital, such as transport, is less flexible than members of the balanced growth school believe.

In Figure 13.3, the horizontal axis shows the provision and cost of social overhead capital (which is normally provided by the public sector and will embrace transport as a major component) while the vertical axis measures the total cost of direct productive activities (which are normally undertaken on purely commercial criteria). The balanced growth approach assumes that *DPA* output

---

[38] T.R. Leinbach, 'Transport and Third World development: review, issues, and prescription', *Transportation Research A*, **29**, 337–44, 1995.

[39] S.V. Nath, 'The theory of balanced growth', *Oxford Economic Papers*, **14**, 138–53, 1962.

and *SOC* activities should grow together (that is, along the growth path represented by the ray from the origin), passing through the various curves from *a* to *c* representing successively higher amounts of *DPA/SOC* output.

Hirschman, however, argues that less developed countries are in practice not in a position to follow such a path – partly because of the lack of necessary expertise to ensure that the balance is maintained and partly because of inherent indivisibilities in the social overhead capital schemes available. Consequently, growth is inevitably unbalanced and may follow one of two possible courses – one based upon excess capacity of *SOC* (that is, path $A \Rightarrow A_1 \Rightarrow B \Rightarrow B_2 \Rightarrow C$) the other upon a shortage of *SOC* (that is, path $A \Rightarrow B_1 \Rightarrow B \Rightarrow C_1 \Rightarrow C$). If a strategy of excess *SOC* capacity is preferred, it is hoped that this will permit *DPA* to become less expensive and encourage investment in that sector. Alternatively, with the second approach, *DPA* expansion occurs first and *DPA* costs will rise substantially. As a consequence, considerable economies will be realized through the construction of more-extensive *SOC* facilities. The actual effectiveness of the alternatives depends upon the strength of the profit motive in the *DPA* sector, and the responsiveness of the public authority in the *SOC* sector to public demand.

The type of transport provision most suited to developing economies is often of as much importance as the aggregate level of provision. Many developing countries tend to spend scarce development funds on prestige projects to demonstrate visually their capacity to emulate the performance of more developed nations; in other words X-efficiency is sacrificed for a modern, if superficial, image. More critical is the way in which funds are spent on internal transport provision and, in particular, whether there are advantages in concentrating limited capital resources in either the road or rail modes.

The appropriateness of different modes often depends upon the geographic–demographic nature of the country. Following Fromm, most less developed countries may be categorized as one of the following:

- densely populated tropical lands;
- tropical land with low population density;
- mountainous, temperate lands with a low overall density of population but a concentration on a coastal plain or altiplane; or
- thinly populated desert areas with population concentrated along irrigated channels.

The appropriateness of different transport modes changes according to the type of country under consideration, thinly populated, tropical lands having different transport problems from heavily urbanized countries with high population densities.

While the railways were important in the development of nineteenth-century economies and characterized colonial development, in many countries the emphasis in recent years has switched to the provision of adequate road infrastructure. This is particularly true in areas where a skeleton of roads already exists and resources can be devoted to improving and extending an established, if rudimentary, network. This approach may be especially fruitful if it links isolated agricultural communities both with each other and with the more advanced areas of the economy. Fifty years ago, Millard[40] argued that, unlike economically advanced countries, in Third World nations 'the benefits from road construction are almost entirely in the form of new development from traffic which the new road will generate'. The effect is not purely on immediate output but can stimulate a propensity for further development.

Wilson strongly supported road development in Third World countries for this reason, arguing: 'Investment options might usefully be analyzed in terms not only of their direct economic pay-off but also in terms of their influence on attitude' and 'The educational and other spill-over effects of road transportation appear to be greater than those of other modes of transport. This is especially significant at low levels of development'. Having said this, however, there is a danger if integrated planning is not pursued that while improved road facilities may stimulate the agricultural economy, the new links between rural and industrial– urban areas could lead to increased polarization in the spatial economy with an enhanced geographical, as well as sectional, dualism resulting.

To keep the discussion manageable, it is useful to look at a specific case of transport enhancement and the ways it may affect the performance of economies. Externally, improved port and shipping facilities permit less developed countries to export their products to wider markets and gain foreign exchange, although, as we shall see later, there are some dangers here. Since the demand for shipping services is derived from that for the final product, we can illustrate the benefits to less economically advanced countries from reducing maritime shipping costs by looking at the quantities of exports from a Third World country and the imports into the market of a higher income economy. Figure 13.4 shows a back-to-back diagram (after Shneerson[41]) where S_i, D_i are the supply and demand schedules for the commodity in the developed country and S_j, D_j the supply and demand curves in the less economically developed nation. Demand for imports and supply of exports is obtained by subtracting horizontally the domestic supply from demand. The demand for imports (exports) at each price being the difference between the quantity supplied and demanded, assuming that domestic and import commodities are perfect substitutes. D_e and S_e in Figure 13.4 are derived in this fashion; the vertical difference between these curves then represents the demand for shipping shown as D_T. (If shipping charges were zero, for example, then the free trade equilibrium would be Z.) Suppose actual shipping rates were P_{T1}, then at that rate the price of imports from country i confronting country j is seen to be P_m^* (the cif price) while the cost of exports to country j would be seen in country i to be P_e^* (the fob price). Country i would then import an amount ab equal to country j's (the less developed country's) exports of AB.

[40] R.S. Millard, 'Road development in the overseas territories', *Journal of the Royal Society of Arts*, **107**, 270–91, 1959.

[41] D. Shneerson, 'On the measurement of benefits from shipping services', *Maritime Policy and Management*, **4**, 277–80, 1977.

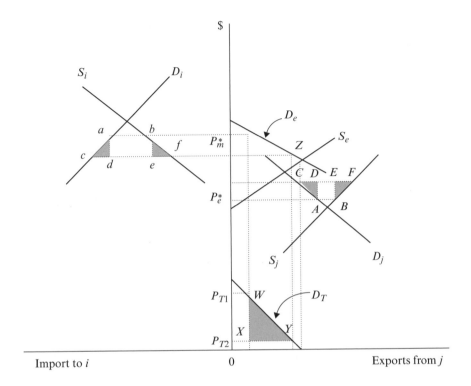

Figure 13.4   *Welfare gains from improved maritime services*

There is now an improvement in shipping services; this may take the form of better port facilities or more efficient ships or it may be administrative (for example, relaxation of high conference shipping rates). The effect is that shipping costs fall to P_{T2} resulting in exports from j rising to CF to match the higher imports of cf into the developed country i. Trade has expanded for the less developed country. The benefit of this trade to the two countries is represented by areas in the figure. Area adc is the extra consumption enjoyed by the developed, importing country as a result of the fall in the cif price while bef is a positive production effect resulting from a contraction of i's relatively high-cost industry. The areas ADC and BEF are the symmetrical benefits to the less developed country. (The sum of these benefits can also be measured directly as the area WXY under the demand curve for shipping services.)

While it can be demonstrated that improved shipping facilities in our example can aid development, it should be noted that the analysis is crucially dependent upon the elasticities of demand for goods in developed and underdeveloped countries, and the relative costs of supply. This often poses serious problems for less developed countries, as pointed out by the United Nations Conference on Trade and Development (UNCTAD),[42] with the less developed nations often paying much of the costs of transport, that is:

[42] UNCTAD, *Level and Structure of Freight Rates, Conference Practices and the Adequacy of Shipping Services*, New York: United Nations, 1969.

> For many of the world's agricultural products, on which developing countries rely for much of their export earnings, supply elasticities are low in the short run . . . Although overall demand elasticities for most of these commodities are also low, the elasticity of demand facing the individual supplier or the whole group of suppliers in a single country is likely to be relatively high, unless that country is the only source of supply, and there is no ready substitutes for the commodity . . . The supplier in these cases therefore normally bears the bulk of the transport costs.

In practice, the world is also a little more complicated, with trade involving not simply the production and transport sectors but also the system of international finance operating and the tariff barriers in effect.

One of the perceived problems experienced by many less developed countries has been the fact that shipping lines have combined in conferences and alliances to regulate prices and this has often led to shipping costs, which are often borne by the less developed countries, being higher than in a free market situation. There are also arguments that the existence of non-pricing competition within conferences in itself produces a much higher quality of service (and *ipso facto* cost) than would prevail without collusion[43] and that this is again detrimental to Third World countries. Empirical evidence produced by Devanney et al.,[44] looking at trade between the East Coast of the United States and Chile, Columbia, Ecuador and Peru, suggests that the conference system on these routes pushed up shipping rates by about $20 per ton in 1971, most of which would have been borne by the poorer countries.

It may not seem surprising that in these circumstances UNCTAD negotiated a Code of Conduct for Liner Conferences that allocated maritime traffic on 40:40:20 basis with 40 percent of the trade allocated to the merchant marine of each of the trading nations and 20 percent to cross-traders.[45] This was intended to give underdeveloped countries the chance to reap some of the financial rewards from shipping and also exert a more immediate influence on their own development. In 1978, for example, Third World countries were in the disadvantaged position of only having 8.6 percent of the world deadweight tonnage of shipping but generating over 30 percent of the bulk cargoes and over 90 percent of the tanker cargoes.

In the short term, lack of capacity prevented some nations from enacting the full implementation of the Code. Zerby[46] estimated, for instance, that of the 26 less developed countries he studied, only nine had merchant fleets large enough to handle 40 percent of their exports in 1975 and only 15 had sufficient capacity to handle 40 percent of imports (Third World nations, as we saw in Chapter 2,

---

[43] J.J. Evans and A. Benham, 'A forked tariff system for liner freight routes', *Journal of Transport Economics and Policy*, **9**, 62–6, 1975.

[44] J.W. Devanney, V.W. Livanos and R.J. Stewart, 'Conference rate-making and the west coast of South America', *Journal of Transport Economics and Policy*, **9**, 154–77, 1975.

[45] S.C. Neff, 'The UN code of conduct for liner conferences', *Journal of World Trade Law*, **14**, 398–423, 1980.

[46] J.A. Zerby, 'On the practicability of the UNCTAD 40–40–20 code for liner conferences', *Maritime Policy and Management*, **6**, 241–51, 1979.

physically export about twice as much as they import – that is, 440 million tons compared to 242 million tons in 1973). Attempts to expand the fleets of less developed countries to fulfill 40 percent of the market would, therefore, result in excess capacity in the fleets of the developed countries, but more importantly, given the imbalance in the volume of imports and exports, attempts to meet 40 percent of shipping demand both into and out of Third World nations would lead to a 50 percent excess capacity within their own fleets. Zerby, therefore, feels 'that a rigid adherence to the 40:40:20 principle is likely to be an extremely costly method of reducing the developing countries' dependence on conference services'. Only with cooperation both between the developed and the underdeveloped nations and between the less economically advanced countries themselves, Zerby argues, will benefits be reaped.

13.6   The Transport Policy of the European Union

A number of national groupings have emerged in both the developed and less developed world where countries have come together into strong or loose economic unions with the aim of fostering their common economic interests. The European Union (this term is used throughout for simplicity; the actual title has changed several times) is one example, the North American Free Trade Agreement (NAFTA) is another. Each has its own priorities and has set about achieving these in its own way. The development of transport policies within the framework of the European Union provides some indication of the importance that is increasingly being attached to transport by these groupings and also to some of the problems of creating pan-national transport policies. (Indeed, the challenges are often similar to those trying to develop a transport strategy in a national federal structure.) The European case also provides a useful illustration of the problems of devising an international transport policy designed primarily to foster economic growth.[47]

The objective of the European Union is 'to promote throughout the Community a harmonious development of economic activities, a continuous and balanced expansion, an increase in stability, an accelerated raising of the standard of living, and closer relations of member states'. A 'Common Transport Policy' was seen as important in facilitating the attainment of this aim. The difficulties of agreeing on how to achieve this from a political economy perspective can be illustrated in Figure 13.5. Before integration there are a number of "access points", both physical and institutional, that allow interactions between two countries (either side of the dashed line) with internal movements combining to influence location, traffic and production. Most movement is internal and the subject of domestic, national rules and standards. After integration brought about by a common transport policy there is more international trade that affects levels of production, the routes used for transport, and the relative importance

---

[47]   K.J. Button, 'Transport policy', in A.M. El-Agraa (ed.), *The European Union; Economics and Politics*, 8th edn, Cambridge: Cambridge University Press, 2007.

Before Economic Union

Country A Domestic	International	Country B Domestic
Regulated prices/market access	Few "gateways"	Regulated prices/market access
National licensing	Document checks	National licensing
National establishment	Bilateral license	National establishment
National labor laws	Split tariffs	National labor laws
National technical standards	Different "gauges"	National technical standards
Split tariffs	Different labor laws	Split tariffs
	Different laws of establishment	

After Economic Union

Country A Domestic	International	Country B Domestic
Competitive markets	Open borders	Competitive markets
National/EU licensing	European licenses	National/EU licensing
EU establishment	Open access to infrastructure	EU establishment
EU/national labor laws	Through tariffs	EU/national labor laws
National/EU technical standards	Different "gauges"	National/EU technical standards
EU licenses	Coordinated labor laws	EU licenses
EU/national infrastructure policy	EU laws of establishment	EU/national infrastructure policy
	Coordinated EU infrastructure	

Figure 13.5   *EU international and domestic transport1960 and 2009*

of domestic and international markets. The institutional structure had completely changed. The final outcome is difficult to foresee, and although aggregate economic welfare will continue to rise, the ultimate distribution of the welfare across locations and industrial sectors is uncertain.

Each member state also had its own set of transport objectives that must be modified to conform with commonly agreed goals and objectives, and each has its own sets of institutions and policy tools that often conflicted with the criteria favored by the grouping as a whole. Many countries in Europe had traditionally used transport subsidies to protect specific industries or regions, but this may run counter to the EU's objectives of increasing overall economic efficiency or be thought to result in undesirable redistributions of welfare.

Problems with the creation of a transport policy began early.[48] The initial Rome Treaty of 1957 contained an entire chapter on transport, although limiting itself initially to movement of freight by road, rail and inland waterways. It was not until 1961, however, that a memorandum appeared setting out clear objectives and not until the following year that an Action Programme was published. The emphasis of these initiatives was to remove obstacles to trade posed by the institutional structures governing transport and to foster competition once a level playing field of harmonized fiscal, social and technical conditions had been established. That it took over 40 years to make significant progress towards a substantive policy is in part due to the nature of European geography and the underlying

[48] K.J. Button, 'Transport policy in the United Kingdom: 1968–1974', *Three Banks Review*, **103**, 26–48, 1974.

transport market, although continued insistence on nation states pursuing their individual agendas did not help.

Examination of a map of the European Union provides insights on some of the problems of devising a common transport policy. Ideally, as we have seen, transport functions most effectively on a hub-and-spoke basis with large concentrations of population and economic activity located at corners and in the center and with the various transport networks linking them. The central locations act as markets for transport services in their own right, but also as interchange and consolidation points for traffic between the corner nodes. In many ways the United States fits this model rather well, but the European Union never has. When there were initially six members the bulk of economic activity was at the core, with limited growth at the periphery. The various enlargements over the years have added to the problems of serving peripheral and often sparsely populated areas. The geographical separation of some states and the logical routing of traffic through non-member countries, together with the island nature of others, posed further problems.

The common policy was also not initiated with a clean slate – member states had established transport networks and institutional structures that could not rapidly be changed even if a common set of principles could have been established.[49] At the outset, countries such as France and West Germany carried a significant amount of their freight traffic by rail, whereas others, such as Italy and the Benelux nations, relied more on road transport. The resultant differences were also not simply physical (including variations in railway gauges, vehicle weight limits and different electricity currents). They also reflected fundamental differences in the ways transport was viewed.

At a macro, political-economy level there are two broad views on the way transport should be treated. Following the Continental philosophy, the objective is to meet wide social goals that require interventions in the market through regulations, public ownership and direction. This approach particularly dominated much of twentieth-century transport policy thinking in Continental Europe. Its place has been taken by a wider acceptance of the Anglo-Saxon approach to transport policy. This treats the sector as little different from other economic activities. Transport provision and use should be efficient in its own right, with efficiency normally best attained by making the maximum use of market forces. Of course, the extremes of either of the approaches never existed; it has been a matter of degree. Even in countries such as the United Kingdom, which was been seen as a bastion of the Anglo-Saxon ideology, there existed extensive regimes of regulation and control and large parts of the transport system were in state or local government ownership.

The situation can also be looked at from a more analytical perspective in terms of the ways that efficiency is viewed.[50] The approach until the 1970s was

---

[49] K.M. Gwilliam, 'Realism and the Common Transport Policy of the EEC', in J.B. Polak and J.B. Van der Kamp (eds), *Changes in the Field of Transport Studies*, Dordrecht: Martinus Nijhoff, 1980.

[50] K.J. Button, 'Transport in the European Union', in J.B. Polak and A. Heertje (eds), *Analytical Transport Economics: An International Perspective*, Cheltenham, UK and Northampton, MA, USA: Edward Elgar, 2000.

to treat efficiency in transport largely in terms of maximizing scale efficiency while limiting any deadweight losses associated with monopoly power. Most transport infrastructure was seen as enjoying economies of scale that could only be exploited by coordinated and, *ipso facto*, regulated, often subsidized, development and in many cases was state owned. Many aspects of operations were also seen as potentially open to monopoly exploitation and hence in need of oversight. This situation changed. From a pragmatic perspective, the high levels of subsidies enjoyed by many elements of the transport sector became politically unsustainable. Economists began to question whether the regulations deployed were actually achieving their stated aims. Government failures, it was argued, were often larger than the market failures they were trying to correct.

New elements also came into play in the 1970s. Attitudes towards environmental intrusion, for example, changed in part as part of a wider effort to improve the overall environment and fulfill larger, global commitments on such matters as reducing emissions of global warming gases. Local environmental effects were largely left to individual countries, but as the implications of regional and global environmental intrusions have become more widely appreciated so the EU's transport policy has become proactive in these areas.

The early thinking regarding a Common Transport Policy (CTP) centered on harmonization so that a level playing field could ultimately be created on which competition would be equitable. The European Coal and Steel Community had initiated this approach in the early 1950s[51] and it continued as EU interest moved away from primary products. The ECSC had removed some artificial tariff barriers relating to rail movements of primary products and the EU's policy initially attempted to expand this idea in the 1960s to cover the general carriage of goods and especially those moved on roads. Road transport was viewed rather differently from railways. It was perceived that the demand and supply features of road haulage markets could lead to excessive competition and supply uncertainties.

Early efforts included seeking to initiate common operating practices (for example, relating to driving hours and vehicle weights) and accounting procedures, and standardizing methods of charging. A forked tariff regime for trucking, with rates only allowed between officially determined maxima and minima, was aimed at meeting the dual problems of possible monopoly exploitation in some circumstances, and of possible inadequate capacity due to excess competition in others. Such rates were stipulated on international movements within the EU. There were practical problems in setting the cost-based rates and questions were raised concerning a policy that was aimed at simultaneously tackling monopoly and excess competition.[52] Limitations on the number of international truck movements across borders were marginally reduced by the introduction of

---

[51] J.E. Meade, H.H. Liesner and S.J. Wells, *Case Studies in European Economic Union: The Mechanism of Integration*, Oxford: Oxford University Press, 1962.

[52] D.L. Munby, 'Fallacies of the Community's transport policy', *Journal of Transport Economics and Policy*, **1**, 67–98, 1962.

a small number of Community quota licenses, authorizing the free movement of holders over the entire European road network.[53]

The 1973 enlargement to nine member states stimulated a renewed interest in transport policy and offered the opportunity to review a whole range of policy areas. The new members – the United Kingdom, Ireland and Denmark – are more market oriented in their transport policy objectives. At about the same time, the European Commission raised legal questions concerning the inertia of the Council of Ministers in creating a genuine CTP. It also followed a period of rapid growth in trade within the EU bringing infrastructure capacity issues to the fore and pressures for more flexible regulation of road freight transport.

The outcome was not dramatic although new sectors entered the debates, most notably maritime transport, and wider objectives concerning environmental protection and energy policy played a role. Overall, the actions in this period were a gentle move to liberalization by making the quota system permanent and expanding the number of licenses increased international intra-EU road freight capacity. The option of using reference tariffs rather than forked tariffs was a reflection of the inherent problems with the latter. A major element of the measures involved transport infrastructure in terms of improving decision making regarding its provision and with regard to consideration of the way that charges should be levied for its use. The importance of transport links outside of the EU, but part of a natural European network, also began to play a part in policy formulation, with the EU beginning to develop mechanisms for financing investment in such infrastructure.

The enlargements of the EU as Greece, and then Spain and Portugal, joined had little impact on the CTP. It still essentially remained piecemeal. The only significant change prior to major developments in the early 1990s was the gradual widening of the modes covered. There were, for example, moves to bring maritime and air transport policy in line with EU competition policy.

The accession to membership in the 1970s and early 1980s of countries such as the United Kingdom and Greece with established shipping traditions, brought maritime issues to the table and then the Single European Act of 1986 provided a catalyst for initiating a maritime policy.[54] A series of measures were introduced aimed at bringing shipping within the EU's competition policy framework. This came at a time when major changes were beginning to permeate the way in which maritime services were provided. Technical shifts, such as the widespread adoption of containerization, had begun to influence the established cartel arrangements that had characterized scheduled maritime services. (These initial arrangements were 'conferences' that coordinated fares and sailings but later were more integrated 'consortia'.)

The size of the EU's shipping sector declined significantly in the 1980s in

---

[53] K.J. Button, *Road Haulage Licensing and EC Transport Policy*, Aldershot: Gower, 1984.

[54] M. Brooks and K.J. Button, 'Shipping within the framework of a Single European Market', *Transport Reviews*, **12**, 237–52, 1992.

the face of competition from Far East and Communist bloc fleets. The 'First Package' of measures in 1985 sought to improve the competitive structure of European shipping by giving the Commission power to react to predatory behavior by third-party ship owners, and reinterpreted competition policy to allow block exemptions for shipping conferences, albeit with safeguards. In 1986 a 'Second Package' set out to establish a common registry, although this did not prove successful. Also, as part of the general effort to liberalize the market, agreement on cabotage (the provision of a domestic service within a country by a carrier from another nation) was reached but with exceptions in some markets, for example, the Greek Islands.

Port policy was largely *ad hoc*.[55] Initial concerns in the early 1990s centered around modernizing European ports to ensure that they could handle the large ships that were being introduced. Progress was relatively slow until 2000 when sea and inland ports were incorporated into the Trans-European Networks (TENs) initiative with the objective of integrating and prioritizing investment in transport infrastructure.

The European bilateral system of air service agreements covering scheduled air transport between member states was, like those in other parts of the world, tightly regulated. Typical features of a bilateral agreement meant that: only one airline from each country was allowed to fly on a particular route with the capacity offered by each bilateral partner also often restricted; revenues were pooled; fares were approved by the regulatory bodies of the bilateral partners; and the designated airlines were substantially state owned and enjoyed state aid. Domestic air markets were also highly controlled. Air transport in general, however, since the liberalization of US domestic markets in the 1970s, was moving away from a tradition of strict regulation. Until the early 1980s, it had been thought that European aviation policy was outside of the jurisdiction of the European Commission and a matter for national governments.[56] This changed, following a number of legal decisions by the European Court of Justice beginning in 1979.

The basic philosophy became that deregulation would take place in stages (an approach to regulatory reform we shall discuss in more detail in Chapter 14), with workable competition being the objective and a series of 'packages' was subsequently enacted. The 1987 package aimed at relaxing existing intra-EU bilateral regimes by, for example, allowing deviations from the traditional air services agreement that set a 50/50 split of traffic between the two member countries. The decision also required member states to accept multiple designations on a country-pair basis by another member. It also became easier for countries to allow more than one of their airlines on routes. This was extended in the 1989 'Second Package' when all capacity limits between bilateral partners were to dis-

[55] C.I. Chlomoudis and A.A. Pallis, *European Union Port Policy: The Movement Towards a Long-term Strategy*, Cheltenham, UK and Northampton, MA, USA: Edward Elgar, 2002.

[56] K.J. Button, K.E. Haynes and R. Stough, *Flying into the Future: Air Transport Policy in the European Union*, Cheltenham, UK and Lyme, NH, USA: Edward Elgar, 1998.

appear, and, further, only if both civil aviation authorities refused to sanction a fare application could an airline be precluded from offering it to its passengers. Governments could no longer discriminate against airlines of other member states provided that they met safety criteria, effectively removing national airline identities with the EU.

The enactment of the Single European Market in 1992 and subsequent moves towards greater political integration brought important changes to the CTP and related transport policies. Broadly, the 1986 Single European Act removed institutional barriers to the free trade in transport services. At about the same time, efforts at further political integration and economic development led to major new initiatives to provide an integrated European transport infrastructure – for example, the TENs. While there were moves to liberalize industries such as air transport from the late 1980s, the broad basis of European transport policy was established in *The Future Development of the Common Transport Policy*[57] which advocated as a guiding principle the need to balance an effective transport system for the EU with a commitment to the protection of the environment.

The changes reflected developments in economic theories that provided new ways of thinking about transport markets. There was also a switch away from concern about problems of optimal scale and monopoly power that had been the intellectual justification for state ownership and regulation of such industries as railways and air transport, to seeking ways of creating conditions favorable to X-efficiency and dynamic efficiency. Technically, this was largely but not exclusively a concern with reducing costs replacing that of containing consumer exploitation. In particular, there was mounting concern about the costs of regulated transport that had macroeconomic implications for the overall economic development of the EU.

Although terms such as multi-modalism abound in the official literature of the EU, and, indeed, some initiatives have transcended the conventional bounds of modal-based actions, a useful and pragmatic way of treating these recent developments is by mode.

Road Transport

Road transport is the dominant mode of both freight and passenger transport in Europe; the share of freight going by rail, for example, has fallen from 32 percent in the EU in 1970 to about 14 percent. Over the period, the freight tonnage in Europe has increased 2.5 times and the share of this going by road has risen from 48 to 74 percent. The initial efforts to develop a common policy regarding road transport, however, proved problematic. Technical matters on things like driving hours were more easily solved than those of creating a common economic framework of supply, and economic controls lingered on as countries with less efficient

---

[57] Commission of the European Communities, *The Future Development of the Common Transport Policy, A Global Approach to the Construction of a Community Framework for Sustainable Mobility*, Brussels, COM(92) 494 Final, 1992.

road haulage industries sheltered them from the more competitive fleets. There were also more legitimate efficiency concerns throughout the EU over the wider social costs of road transport, regarding both environmental matters and questions of infrastructure utilization.

The single market initiative, also later influenced by the potential of new trade with the post-Communist states of Eastern and Central Europe, many of which have joined the EU, has resulted in significant reforms to economic regulation in recent years.[58] Earlier measures had helped expand the supply of international trucking permits in Europe and, as part of the Single Market initiative from 1992, a phased liberalization was initiated that gradually removed restrictions on trucking movements across national boundaries and phased in cabotage which had hitherto not been permitted. There was also a considerable reduction in cross-border documentation.

Railways

Rail transport, while largely filling a niche market in many countries, is an important freight mode in much of Continental Europe and provides important passenger services along several major corridors. At the local level, it serves as a key mode for commuter traffic in larger cities. The European Coal and Steel Community undertook considerable economic reform of Europe's freight railways in the 1950s, including the removal of discriminatory freight rates. From the late 1960s and 1970s the emphasis had shifted to the rationalization of the subsidized networks through more effective and transparent cost accountancy. The recent focus has been more with widening access to networks and with technological developments, especially regarding the development of a high-speed rail network as part of the TENs initiative. The EU has also instigated measures aimed at allowing the trains of one member to use the track of another with charges based upon economic costs. The implementation of the strategy has been slow and has had limited impact.

The EU has found it difficult to devise practical and economically sound common pricing principles to apply to transport infrastructure despite the proposals of the Oort Report.[59] With regard to railways, the gist of the overall proposals is for short-run marginal costs including environmental and congestion costs as well as wear and tear on the infrastructure) to be recovered. Long-run elements of cost are to be recovered only in narrowly defined circumstances, and only in relation to passenger services. This clearly has implications, especially on the freight side, if genuine full cost-based competition is to be permitted with other transport modes.

---

[58] K.J. Button, 'The development of East–West transport in Europe', in D. Banister and J. Berechman (eds), *Transportation in Unified Europe: Policies and Challenges*, Oxford: Elsevier, 1993.

[59] C.J. Oort and R.H. Maaskant, *Study of the Possible Solutions for Allocating the Deficit Which May Occur in a System of Charging for the Use of Infrastructure Aiming at Budgetary Equilibrium*, Brussels: European Economic Community, 1976.

Rail transport has also received considerable support as an integral part of making greater use of multi-modal transport systems. Such systems would largely rely upon rail (including piggy-back systems and kangaroo trains) or waterborne modes for trunk haulage, with road transport used as the feeder mode. This is seen as environmentally desirable and as contributing to containing rising levels of road traffic congestion in Europe.

The success of some of the French TGV services, and especially that between Paris and Lyons, where full cost recovery has been attained, has led to a significant interest in this mode. In 1990 the Commission set up a high-level working group to help push forward a common approach to high-speed railway development, and a master plan for 2010 was produced. The EU's efforts to harmonize the development of high-speed rail has not been entirely successful and there are significant technical differences, for example between the French and German systems.[60]

Inland Waterway Transport

Inland waterway transport has been important for the European Union from the beginning. This is mainly because it is a primary concern of the Netherlands and Germany, with France and Belgium also having interests in the mode. Progress in formulating a policy has tended to be slow, in part because of historical agreements covering navigation on the Rhine (for example, the Mannheim Convention), but mainly because the major economic concern has been that of overcapacity which in 1998 was still estimated at between 20 and 40 percent at the prevailing freight rates. Retraction of supply is almost always inevitably difficult to manage, both because few countries are willing to pursue a contraction policy in isolation and because of the resistance of barge owners and labor.

As in other areas of transport, the EU has sought technical standardization, and principles for social harmonization were set out in 1975 and 1979. Economic concerns took over in the 1990s, and in 1990 a system of subsidies designed to stimulate scrappage of vessels was adopted. The introduction of new vessels into the inland fleet is allowed only on a replacement basis. The labor subsidies given in the Netherlands, Belgium and France (the 'rota system') were phased out by 2000.

These measures were coupled with an initiative in 1995 to coordinate investment in inland waterway infrastructure (the Trans-European Waterway Network), designed to encourage, for environmental reasons, the greater use of waterborne transport. Subsequently, in *European Transport Policy for 2010: Time to Decide*,[61] the Commission has put emphasis in its Marco Polo Programme on integrating

---

[60] J.M. Viagas and U. Blum, 'High speed railways in Europe', in D. Banister and J. Berechman (eds), *Transportation in Unified Europe: Policies and Challenges*, Oxford: Elsevier, 1993.

[61] Commission of the European Communities, *European Transport Policy for 2010: Time to Decide*, Brussels: CEC, 2001.

inland waterways transport with rail and maritime transport for the movement of bulk consignments within an intermodal chain.

Maritime Transport

Much of the emphasis of the EU's maritime policy in the late 1990s was on the shipping market rather than on protecting the EU's fleet; that is, it was user rather than supplier driven. Globally, the sector became increasingly concentrated as, first, consortia grew in importance, mergers took place and then the resultant large companies formed strategic alliances. An extension of the 1985 rules to cover consortia and other forms of market sharing was initiated in 1992, and subsequently extended as maritime alliances become more complex.

In 1994 the Commission acted to ban the Transatlantic Agreement reached the preceding year by the major shipping companies to gain tighter control over loss-making North Atlantic routes. It did so because the agreement manipulated capacity and rates and contained articles covering pre- and on-carriage over land. It also fined 14 shipping companies that were members of the Far East Freight Conference for price fixing because the prices embodied multi-modal carriage, and while shipping *per se* enjoyed a block exemption on price agreements, multi-modal services did not.

Ports also attracted attention in the 1990s, mainly because advances in technology had led to significant concentrations in activities as shipping companies have moved towards hub-and-spoke operations. The main European ports were working at about 80 percent capacity with many at or near their design capacity. Whether this is a function of a genuine capacity deficiency or reflects inappropriate port pricing charges that do not contain congestion cost elements is debatable. In 2001 the Commission launched an initiative to improve the quality of services offered by ports which involves tightening access standards for pilotage, cargo handling and so on, and to make more transparent the rules of procedure at ports with the particular aim of bringing ports more fully into an integrated transport structure.

Air Transport Policy

The final reform of air transport, the 'Third Package', came in 1992 and was phased in from the following year with the aim of having a regulatory structure by 1997 similar to that for US domestic aviation. From 1997, full cabotage has been permitted, and fares are generally unregulated. Additionally, foreign ownership among EU carriers is permitted, and these carriers have, for internal purposes, become European airlines. One result has been an increase in cross-share holdings and a rapidly expanding number of alliances among airlines within the EU. This change did not initially apply to extra-EU agreements where national bilateral arrangements still dominated the market. A ruling by the European Court of Justice in 2002 gave the Commission the authority to negotiate with the United States on liberalizing the transatlantic market. Negotiations subsequently took place, but while there was some initial progress through compromise in a number of technical areas, little substantive agreement emerged for some time regarding the key and fundamental economic issues. The interests of the domestic coalitions of the military and the air labor unions that influence the American stance strongly favor an 'Open Skies' arrangement with free airline access to markets, while the EU has favored a much more free market approach that allows for cabotage and flexible movement of capital, via an 'Open Aviation Area'. The impasse was broken in 2007 with a compromise, short-term agreement that effectively opened the skies over the North Atlantic but not the factor markets.[62]

The EU Enlargement

The phased enlargement of the EU under the Treaties of Nice and Madrid has had implications for transport by affecting the demands placed on the networks of existing member states and those that have acceded. The accession states are reforming their economic structures – important for influencing what is transported and where – and their transport systems. Nevertheless, the difficulties to be overcome are not trivial and many are likely to be long-term:

- *Geographical*   Enlargement has had implications for the economics of long-haul transport operations as well as necessitating investment in infrastructure. What the enlargement has not done is to create a 'natural' transport market. The spatial distribution of economic activities still does not have the structure of the United States where the overall physical market is essentially rectangular with centres of population and economic activities at the corners and in the center that allow exploitation of efficiency benefits from long-haul carriage and hub-and-spoke structures. In the EU, economic activity is dichotomously distributed and enlargement has added to its central/peripheral nature.
- *Legal*   There are issues concerning the role of central legal responsibilities and the degree of local national autonomy will inevitably arise. This is shaping the wider legal structure in which macroeconomic policies regarding transport are being formulated, and is influencing the external policies of the EU – important for transport in a world of global economies and global trade.
- *Economic*   In 2002 the EU's Commission President raised the issue of the need for a common fiscal policy within Europe, or at least that part of it in the eurozone. Economists have long understood that a common currency requires a common fiscal policy as a concomitant. This involves the EU having responsibility for fiscal transfers above that it now controls. While the exact amount is debated, and depends on the extent to which the center considers distribution as well as macroeconomic stabilization as part

---

[62] K.J. Button, 'The impact of US–EU "Open Skies" agreement on airline market structures and airline networks', *Journal of Air Transport Management*, **15**, 59–71, 2009.

of its function, it may well be considerable. This would take away much national autonomy over major transport infrastructure works and influence short-term public expenditure patterns.

These are not trivial changes, and it is impossible to talk about any one in isolation from the others, or without considering the background and the current state of existing EU transport policy. The countries that gained membership in 2004 (Poland, the Czech Republic, Hungary, Slovakia, Lithuania, Latvia, Slovenia, Estonia, Cyprus and Malta) also offer a variety of different challenges from a transport perspective. Adding Bulgaria and Romania has compounded the diversity.

The nature of the economies of the post-Soviet, transition states, and their relationships to the EU has already changed considerably. Nevertheless, there are numerous ways in which their transport systems differ from much of the older EU. They are largely distant from the core, making railways a potentially more viable mode for long-distance freight transport. Indeed, the physical area of an enlarged EU offers the prospects of haul lengths comparable with those in the United States where deregulated railways have at least been maintaining their market share. However, the rail freight networks within transition economies are largely based on dated technologies and are not oriented to meeting transport demands for movements to and from the EU. They have traditionally been excessively labor intensive and serve as job creators rather than transport suppliers.

Car ownership is considerably lower in the accession countries than in the older ones, but this is changing. This is putting strains on urban infrastructure and poses mounting environmental problems. Smaller states, and some regions within the larger ones, are also themselves subjected to significant transit traffic flows, raising issues of infrastructure capacity and environmental degradation but also matters of charging and pricing – a subject the EU has been singularly poor at addressing. The transition economies also have poorly maintained transport networks largely directed to moving bulk, raw materials to Russia. The road freight sector has begun to develop in response to the needs of modern just-in-time production and some countries are making use of the limited infrastructure links to the West. Transition economies with maritime access and inland waterways make considerable use of them. Enlargement comes at a time of technical change in the sector, with the increasing deployment of a post-panamax fleet exploiting scale economies and putting pressures for more hub-and-spoke operations and fleet rationalization.

13.7 Transport and Regional and Urban Development

We move from macro issues, to look at some of the meso-level effects that transport may have on economic development. The interregional spread of economic activity within a country is of major concern to national governments. Geographical variations in unemployment, income, migration and industrial structure are of importance because they both result in spatial inequalities in welfare and, in many cases, reduce the overall performance of the national economy. For these reasons, many countries actively pursue policies that attempt to stimulate economic activity in depressed areas and to contain damaging explosive growth in prosperous regions.

The policies, which have varied both in intensity and in form over time, and differ in their nature across countries, have generally concentrated on giving direct financial assistance to industry and on improving the mobility of labor. In addition there have been attempts at improving the economic infrastructure of what are seen as particularly depressed areas, or in some cases proactive policies where depression is anticipated, with specific emphasis being placed on providing better transport facilities. The policy of biasing transport investment in favor of depressed regions has been subjected to considerable debate over the years.[63]

In the United Kingdom, skepticism about the effectiveness of such a policy as a regional economic development aid was initially expressed by A.J. Brown in a Minority Report of the Hunt Committee Inquiry into the Intermediate Areas[64] as long ago as 1969 and was supported by the findings of the Leitch Committee.[65] A common thread in these studies is that in a country such as Britain where infrastructure is already relatively comprehensive, transport is seldom an important factor explaining disparities in regional economic performance. It is now accepted by many such countries that transport policy motivated by regional policy objectives must be pursued with circumspection and that, in many cases, improved transport facilities may prove counterproductive for development areas.

A simple hypothetical example illustrates the difficulty.[66] We have two regions, A and B, producing a single homogeneous commodity. The centers of the regions (see Figure 13.6) are M miles apart and the commodity can be transported over the area at a constant money cost per mile of $f - t$ per ton. The markets served by the regions differ, however, because it costs $\$C_A$ to produce a ton of the commodity in region A and $\$C_B$ per ton in region B. Consequently, and assuming that no production centers exist between the regions, a distribution boundary can be drawn (shown by the dashed line in the figure) which is m_A miles from the center of A and m_B miles from the center of B (where $m_A + m_B = M$). The boundary is determined by the relative production costs of the regions and the costs of transport (that is, $C_A + tm_A = C_B + tm_B$). Basic manipulation of the algebra gives:

$$mA = \left(M + \frac{C_B - C_A}{t} \right) \qquad (13.3)$$

[63] G. Giuliano, 'Research Policy Review 27, new directions for understanding transportation and land-use', *Environment and Planning A*, **21**, 145–59, 1989.

[64] UK Department of Economic Affairs, *The Intermediate Areas*, London: HMSO, 1969.

[65] UK Department of Transport, *Report of the Advisory Committee on Trunk Road Assessment*, London: HMSO, 1978.

[66] C.H. Sharp, 'Transport and regional development with special reference to Britain', *Transport Policy and Decision Making*, **1**, 1–11, 1980.

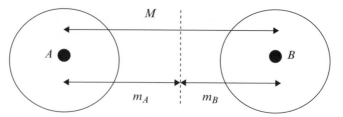

Figure 13.6   *Market areas served by centers A and B*

If, therefore, production is relatively cheaper in region A, then m_A will increase if infrastructure reduces the cost of transport. Thus if A is a depressed area, then transport improvements could assist in expanding its potential market and, therefore, generate more income and employment, but region A must be a low-cost producer for this to be automatically true. If region B is the depressed one, then quite clearly investment in improved transport will only worsen the regional problem by contracting the market area served by the region. Indeed, at the extreme (where $(C_A - C_B) > M_t$) region B may be forced from the market entirely by the expansion of the low-cost region's market area.

Of course, the model is a considerable simplification. Regions do not normally, for instance, specialize exclusively in the production of a single commodity but produce a range of goods. Thus a transport improvement, while damaging certain industries, may increase the competitiveness of others. The final effect of the improved transport facility will then depend upon relative production costs between regions and the importance of transport *vis-à-vis* production costs in the overall cost functions for the various commodities.

Further, costs of production may vary with output and thus (following the 'infant industry argument') it may be beneficial to reduce transport costs if the government's regional policy also involves using grants and subsidies for encouraging the establishment of decreasing cost industry in a depressed area. Supplementary measures of this kind may be necessary if the depressed area is sparsely populated and, to be successful, its industry needs to penetrate the markets of other, more populous, regions to benefit from scale economies. It should be noted, however, that in these circumstances transport improvements must be accompanied by other regional aids if the natural gravitation of decreasing cost industries to centers of population is to be counteracted. Additionally, transport costs tend not to increase linearly with distance because of discontinuities and fixed cost elements in the overall cost function (see Chapter 5). Consequently, the influence of any transport infrastructure improvement is much more difficult to predict than the simple analysis implies.

A good example of misplaced transport investment is Montreal-Mirabel International Airport, near Montreal that was opened in 1975 as the second-largest airport in the world in terms of surface area ever envisaged. It was intended to replace the existing Dorval Airport (now Montreal-Pierre Elliott Trudeau International Airport) as the eastern air gateway to Canada, and from 1975 to 1997, all international flights to/from Montreal were required to use Mirabel.

However, its distant location and lack of transport links, as well as Montreal's economic decline relative to Toronto, made it unpopular with travelers, so Dorval was not closed as originally planned. Eventually, Mirabel was relegated to the role of a cargo airport.

In summary, there is no general case for thinking that investment in transport infrastructure will automatically improve the economic performance of depressed regions. In a country such as Britain, where the transport cost difference between the least and the most accessible regions has traditionally been only about 2 percent across industries,[67] the effect of transport investment on regional policy is, in general, unlikely to be substantial. This is particularly true if industrial location is influenced by objectives other than cost minimization (for example, on satisficing principles) or where there is a high degree of X-inefficiency. The situation may be different in larger countries like the US or China.

While in Table 13.2 a number of important studies were cited, it is nevertheless true that empirical evidence on the specific regional effect of transport policies is scant, and that which is available is often weakened by the difficulties of isolating transport effects from those of other regional policy measures. By conducting a counterfactual exercise, Botham[68] suggests that road investment in Britain between 1957 and 1972 had little effect although there was some tendency for it to have a centralizing effect on the distribution of employment in the country. At a more micro level, Linneker and Spence[69] concluded from their study of the impact of the M25 motorway around London that while it has improved accessibility (and regional market potential) much of this has subsequently been eroded by generated traffic. This study, however, did not allow for the substantial range of other aid measures then operative, or for intra-regional movements between subregions adjacent to the new facility and those more distant. A study of the high-speed TGV rail system in France by Bonnafous[70] suggests that, while facilitating development, the overall impact has been small. Studies of airports have suggested that they may have significant regional impacts that extend beyond the immediate area, but this varies on a case-by-case basis.[71]

Turning to a slightly lower level of spatial aggregation, changes in transport technology have, over time, exerted a strong influence upon the shapes and forms of the urban areas in which we live. The development of steam locomotion in the second half of the nineteenth century substantially improved inter-urban

---

[67] M. Chisholm and P. O'Sullivan, *Freight Flows and Spatial Aspects of the British Economy*, Cambridge: Cambridge University Press, 1973.

[68] R.W. Botham, 'The regional development effects of road investment', *Transportation Planning and Technology*, **6**, 97–108, 1980.

[69] B.J. Linneker and N.A. Spence, 'An accessibility analysis of the impact of the M25 London orbital motorway on Britain', *Regional Studies*, **26**, 31–47, 1991.

[70] A. Bonnafous, 'The regional impact of the TGV', *Transportation*, **14**, 127–37, 1987.

[71] K.J. Button, 'High-technology employment and hub airports: infrastructure's contribution to regional development', in Y. Higano, P. Nijkamp, J. Poot and J.J. van Wijk (eds), *The Region in the New Economy: An International Perspective on Spatial Dynamics in the 21st Century*, Aldershot: Ashgate, 2002.

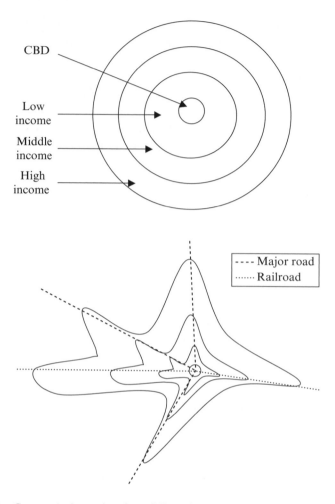

Figure 13.7 *Concentric (upper) and axial (lower) city geographies*

transport and permitted urban growth. Local, distributional services evolved much more slowly, leading, in most cities, to a concentric pattern of development around the main rail (or occasionally port) terminal of the type we saw associated with bid–rent curves in Chapter 3. The wealthy tended, because they could afford transport which was available, to live in the outer rings of housing while industry, being dependent upon good inter-urban transport, and the working-class poor concentrated near the urban core, the central business district (CBD) – the upper element in Figure 13.7.

   The introduction of motorized local public transport (initially the tramcar and later the omnibus) followed by the motor car encouraged the growth of an axial pattern of urban land use with the former succession of concentric rings of housing being extended (star-like) in ribbon developments along the main road arteries (see lower element of Figure 13.7). Finally, the widespread adoption of the automobile, combined with improved road systems, limited traffic restraint and more efficient road freight transport, has led to the growth of multi-nucleus cities where there are numerous subcenters and suburbs – Los Angeles is often cited as the extreme example, as is Phoenix. While this simplified account of urban development misses many important subtleties it serves to highlight the historical role which transport has had in shaping urban growth.

More recently, the difficulties of most large urban areas in the United States and Europe, unlike rapidly developing countries such as China or India, have not been ones of containing or molding growth but rather of reversing decay. The concern once focused on the role of transport in stimulating urban development has been, since the early 1970s, transformed into concern for inner-city revitalization and redevelopment. There were substantial outflows of population from the centers of virtually all major cities from the 1960s. This has been accompanied by an even faster exodus of industry. The result of this has been a decay in inner-city public economies (the tax base of such areas has fallen while the composition of the population has become increasingly biased towards the old, disabled and poor) and unemployment (not only have firms left more quickly than the population but also it has primarily been manufacturing industry which has left behind large numbers of unemployed, unskilled workers).

The causes of the decline of inner-city areas are complex,[72] regional and urban planning policies are partly responsible but there have also been changes both in the lifestyles aspired to by the population (urban life becoming less attractive as incomes have risen) and in the production functions confronting industry (the land–output ratio in particular has been rising). Improved personal transport, especially higher car ownership levels, has also encouraged more commuting from more-distant suburbs.

Official policy to counter the decline of the inner-city areas and to stimulate the redevelopment of urban cores has incorporated a substantial transport component. For example, the UK's white paper, *Policy for the Inner Cities* published in 1977 made specific reference to the fact that 'Commerce and industry in inner areas need to be served by transport conveniently and efficiently' and points to the need for local authorities 'to give weight to the implications for local firms when designing traffic management schemes to improve access for central traffic, to ensure efficient loading and to provide adequate and convenient parking'. Additionally, it is argued that movement, notably in terms of journey-to-work trips, needs to be made easier, especially for certain groups of travelers.

At the theoretical level, the bid–rent curve analysis set out in Chapter 3 would seem to imply that cheaper and better public transport would lead to a spread of cities (that is, the residential bid–rent curves would shift up and to the right) while traffic restraint policy would lead to greater concentration of economic activity at the urban core. As Goldstein and Moses[73] have shown, however, this type of analysis rests upon the assumption of a single central business district with

---

[72] K.J. Button, 'Employment and industrial decline in the inner city areas of British cities; the experiences of 1962–1977', *Journal of Industrial Affairs*, **6**, 1–6, 1978.

[73] G.S. Goldstein and L.N. Moses, 'Transport controls and the spatial structure of urban areas', *Papers and Proceedings of the American Economics Association*, **85**, 289–94, 1975.

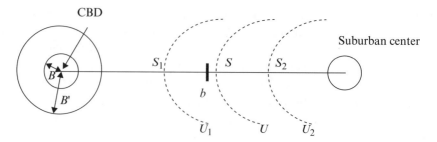

Figure 13.8   *The impact of traffic restraint and public transport subsidies on the urban core*

no allowance for possible competing suburban centers. This is unrealistic in the context of most modern conurbations. Figure 13.8 depicts a more typical urban situation with a major urban center – the CBD – serving as the focal employment point dominating the suburban center to which it is linked by road.

The urban core itself is served by good local public transport with people for up to *B* miles away being able to travel into work by bus. But there are other modes available for workers and they may opt for one of three main employment/ residential location choices. The situation we consider is one of equilibrium, with every household achieving the same utility level:

- Live within the immediate commuting area (radius *B*) and travel to work at the CBD by bus.
- Live outside the immediate commuting area and travel to work in the CBD by car.
- Commute to the subcenter by car.

In this situation – and excluding residents of the city who elect to take a fourth option, namely working at home – the boundary *U* will separate those workers employed at the core and those with a job at the suburban center. This state of affairs is one in which no household can improve its utility by changing its place of work, residential location or mode of transport. We now assess the impact of two alternative strategies on the economy of the central core area of the city.

1   The generalized cost of car travel in the central city area is increased, say, by either higher parking charges or the imposition of road pricing. This will tend to cause a rapid decline of the urban core in this model. Higher motoring costs will cause the immediate bus commuting belt to widen out (say to a radius of *B'* in Figure 13.8) with a reduction in real income for those living (*B'* − *B*) miles from the CBD. This will encourage more people either to work at home or to cease to be active in the labor force (if there are other cities in the economy, there may also be some out-migration), leading to a decrease in the labor supply function at the CBD. Also some car travelers confronted by higher costs will seek work at the suburban center, shifting the employment boundary to, say, U_1. The increased competition for jobs at

the subcenter will depress real income there leading, once again, to a general reduction in the overall labor supply in the city. Generally, therefore, traffic restraint in the CBD makes labor conditions less favorable which will, in the long term, make non-core sites more attractive for industry. The empirical fact that skilled labor tends to be more mobile (between both jobs and locations) is likely to magnify this effect on industrial location.

2   A subsidized express bus service running in bus-only lanes is introduced from a depot at location b to run non-stop into the urban core. This is unlikely to have an effect on those using the existing commuter public transport services around the CBD although, if fewer car trips and less congestion result, the speed of their journeys may rise – but if the service is, in general cost terms, cheaper than car travel, this will widen the employment market for the urban core. Former car travelers from as far out as S_2, will find that by driving to b and transferring to the express service they reduce the overall cost of traveling to the CBD. Consequently, the boundary marking employee catchment areas will shift to U_2. People living to the left of U_2 will find that their real income has risen as a result of lower transport costs (indeed, many people to the left of b may drive out to the depot to catch the bus into the core) and the labor supply function at the core will have shifted out, making the CBD a more attractive place for industry. People formerly inactive or working at home may also now find it attractive to seek employment in the CBD. The labor supply for the subcenter has fallen, and wages will have to rise to generate the real income increase anticipated by employees there. In the long term the subcenter will become less attractive for employers.

This theoretical analysis suggests that while one common effect of both the traffic restraint policy and the public transport improvement policy is to increase local bus service utilization, the long-run effects on the distribution of population and economic activity are likely to be quite different. Goldstein and Moses argue, therefore, that even if transport policy in itself cannot cure the malaise of inner-city areas, improved public transport provision can at least slow down the decline.

Further Reading

A set of classic papers linking transport and land use is contained in J. Berechman, H. Kohno, K.J. Button and P. Nijkamp (eds), *Transport and Land Use*, Cheltenham, UK, and Brookfield, VT, USA: Edward Elgar, 1996. A useful, if rather difficult-to-obtain, survey of what we understand about the links between transport and economic development is contained in D.W. Slater, 'Transportation and economic development: a survey of the literature', in Canadian Royal Commission on National Passenger Transportation, *Directions*, Volume 3, 1992, while V. Dugonjic, 'Transportation: benign influence or an antidote to regional inequality?', *Papers of the Regional Science Association*, **66**, 61–76, 1989, reviews the influence of transport on regional inequalities. The importance of transport in encouraging the development of Third World economies is looked at in A.R. Prest, *Transport Economics in Developing Countries*, London: Weidenfeld & Nicolson, 1969 which offers a good, general, if dated introduction to the subject. I.M.D. Little and J.A. Mirrlees, *Project Appraisal and Planning for Developing Countries*, London: Heinemann, 1974, is difficult, but fruitful reading, and provides a comprehensive treatment of investment appraisal (including transport) in less developed countries.

The European Union periodically publishes pamphlets outlining changes in its transport policy, but for further analysis of the philosophy underlying the Common Transport Policy and also for some critical comments on its more recent developments, see K.J. Button, 'Transport policy', in A.M. El-Agraa (ed.), *The European Union; Economics and Politics*, 8th edn, Cambridge: Cambridge University Press, 2007. Transport and regional policy is well assessed in K.M. Gwilliam, 'Transport infrastructure investments and regional developments', in J.K. Bowers (ed.), *Inflation, Development and Integration – Essays in Honour of A.J. Brown*, Leeds: Leeds University Press, 1979, which contains careful theoretical arguments outlining conditions where transport policy may affect regional economic performance as well as reference to a body of applied literature. P. Nijkamp, 'Infrastructure and regional development: a multi-dimensional policy analysis', *Empirical Economics*, **11**, 1–21, 1986, contains some useful theoretical discussion of the links between transport and land-use patterns, while Transportation Research Board, 'Transportation and Development Conference', *Transportation Research Record*, **1274**, 1990, contains a useful, even if relatively old, collection of articles linking transport and development.

14   The Economic Regulation of Transport

14.1   The Broad Issues

A comprehensive chapter concerned with the economic regulation of transport activities must inevitably involve some overlap with chapters in this volume. Thus this chapter is less than comprehensive in that sense. Economic regulation is also a very large and complex topic and there is no pretense that the coverage here is complete or thorough. It is also a topic that transcends the transport sector in many ways as nations have modified the ways in which they look at economic regulation more generally since the 1970s.[1]

For instance, space has already been devoted to policies for containing pollution, and for the control of traffic congestion. We have also implicitly considered the implications of some forms of intervention regarding pricing and market entry. Transport, however, has been a sector that has been subjected to various forms of economic regulation throughout history, and this in itself justifies a more specific examination. Wider questions concerning such matters as why regulations have been imposed, how they have operated, and how they can be appraised have not been examined in any depth so far. Equally, there are different ways in which transport is supplied with differing degrees of public sector participation in ownership – the ultimate form of regulation – that impact on efficiency and equity implications. Just why this occurs and how it differs between countries raises a further set of economic questions.

Besides the general issues of the various types of regulation and ownership of transport, there have also been significant changes in the way in which many countries approach these regulatory policy issues.[2] We saw, for instance, a considerable relaxation of long-standing entry and price controls in markets as diverse as the US domestic aviation and the UK bus transport industries in the 1970s and 1980s, and it is a trend that has extended to the new market economies of the post-communist states and to many developing nations. We have also seen extensive privatization of transport infrastructure (for example, airports in Britain and in many other European countries, and the growth of build, operate and transfer initiatives in the road and other sectors) and of transport operations (for example, of airlines and railways). Private sector involvement at a second tier is also growing with the franchising out of operations (for example, London's

---

[1] K.J. Button and D. Swann (eds), *The Age of Regulatory Reform*, Oxford: Oxford University Press, 1989.

[2] A.E. Kahn, *The Economics of Regulation: Principles and Institutions*, Cambridge, MA: MIT Press, 1991.

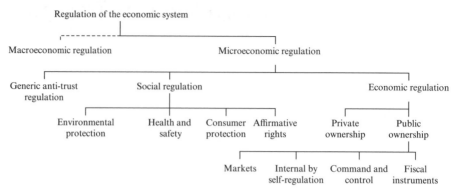

Figure 14.1 *The basic breakdown of types of regulations affecting transport*

bus services) and the greater use of private sector funds in the financing of infrastructure investments (for example, the Channel Tunnel and the French TGV network). The subject, therefore, is an important one and is likely to remain so for some time to come.

What we do not consider here in any detail are the generic laws and controls that are imposed in most countries, and thus inevitably affect transport. For example, many countries have minimum wage laws, anti-trust and monopoly regulations, and consumer protection legislation. These apply to all sectors, including transport, although in some cases there are specific exemptions. The implications of such regulations on transport are often far from trivial, but discussion of them is moving us away from the main theme of this book.

While it is often difficult precisely to define the rationale and nature of regulations, a simple flow chart is seen in Figure 14.1, which gives some broad indication of the types of measures involved. Transport is inevitably affected by macroeconomic policies, such as monetary and trade policies, which can influence the aggregate size of the economy and thus the total demand for transport services. But this is a large subject and really outside the scope of this book. More important are the micro and meso economic regulations that affect the economic and social environments in which transport services are demanded and supplied. Since we have spent some time on the challenges of dealing with areas of social regulation, and especially the environment, the focus here is on the nature of economic regulation. What we do not do, however, although it can be very important, is to offer any overview of generic anti-trust or mergers regulations that affect all types of industry. We essentially push that to one side and direct our attention to that economic regulation that is specifically focused on transport matters.

The objective of this chapter is not to describe all of the changes in regulation and ownership of transport that have taken place, although some of the more important developments are reviewed, but rather to explore the economic arguments underlying the various positions that policy makers have taken. Some contextual historical information is helpful in doing this. Initially, however, a little time is spent looking at the various economic theories of regulation and setting trends in transport policy in the context of these theories.

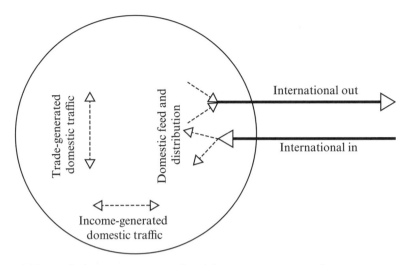

Figure 14.2 *Links between international and domestic transport markets*

In doing this, we not only look at domestic policies and their effects but also international policy, a matter of increasing importance as globalization takes place. Changes in international transport regulations, which may range from the removal of transport barriers within the European Union and NAFTA to the spread of Open Skies agreements in air transport, have implications for international markets.

In Figure 14.2, for example, if international air services are deregulated then they have direct effects on traffic into and out of the country of interest. But this action also has secondary effects on airlines and other modes within the country that take traffic to and from the international airport. This in turn, because of economies of scope and density, will lower the costs of some purely domestic services and hence the use made of them. The additional markets that are now opened up will lead to further changes in both domestic and international traffic as industries such as tourism and high-technology companies that use air transport change the scale and nature of the products they supply. In effect, it will have a macro-income effect of increasing national income, inducing a further positive ripple effect on the demand for air transport.

14.2 Theories of Regulation

Economists have long recognized that markets may, in practice, suffer from serious imperfections; indeed, some discussion of this has been set out in previous chapters. Most obviously, these imperfections, or market failures, could adversely affect the users of transport services, perhaps because fares would be suboptimally high or the service offered dangerous. But equally, they may harm third parties through, for example, generating excessive environmental pollution, or the predatory pricing behavior of incumbent operators may reduce the potential viability of other firms wishing to supply transport services and thus deter them from entering the market.

A wide range of arguments, some of doubtful economic logic, have been drawn into debates over transport regulation. Broadly, the types of market failure that have attracted most attention embrace:

- *The containment of monopoly power*   Transport often involves large, indivisible, and specialized infrastructure that lends itself to monopoly provision to maximize scale economies. This has led to long-standing concerns about the potential economic exploitation of monopoly power.[3] This was particularly seen to be an issue in the case of the railways, which dominated inland transport for nearly a century from the late 1830s, but while some monopoly power still persists today in certain areas of transport activity, technical advances across a range of transport modes have reduced the potential for pure monopoly exploitation, at least in most developed countries. More common, perhaps, is the fear that suppliers of transport services may combine in cartels to limit output and prevent new entrants coming into the market.

- *The control of excessive competition*   Unregulated competition may limit the quality of service offered to customers and result in instability in the industry – in technical terms there may be no sustainable equilibrium; as we have seen an empty core may exist. The actual problem is not competition *per se* but rather the possibility that externalities may result or that some sections of the community may not be provided with adequate services. Additionally, in some instances, notably trucking and inter-urban passenger transport, the potential for conditions of monopolistic competition developing also pose problems with the capacity being supplied.

- *The regulation of externalities*   Imperfections in the market mechanism may result in transport activities imposing costs that are not directly included in the private sector's decision making – pollution and congestion being the main causes for concern. This subject has been explored more fully in earlier chapters and we do not dwell on it here. It is, however, becoming an aspect of regulation that is attracting increasing attention at the global as well as at the national and local levels.

- *The provision of public goods*   Because certain items of infrastructure, such as roads, are thought to exhibit public goods characteristics (that is, non-excludability, whereby use cannot be controlled, and non-rivalry, whereby congestion cannot arise) their provision, it is argued, would be at best inadequate without government intervention. In effect, suppliers could not charge for their use. The fact that one cannot exclude use makes it difficult to price the facilities. The degree to which such infrastructure should be seen as conforming to a public good, however, often depends upon the initial

---

[3] J.A. Gómez-Ibáñez, *Regulating Infrastructure: Monopoly, Contracts, and Discretion*, Cambridge, MA: Harvard University Press, 2003.

policy in place – for example, it is relatively easy to exclude cars from a road if wished.

- *The provision of high-cost infrastructure*   The sheer cost, long payback period, and complexity, combined with possible high levels of risk, makes it unlikely that all major pieces of economically justifiable infrastructure would be built or expensive transport engineering research undertaken without some form of government involvement. Adam Smith, as we saw earlier, even conceded that on occasions the government may need to actually directly provide such facilities, but there are also ways of regulating the private sector to ensure that it provides appropriate infrastructure.
- *The assistance of groups in 'need' of adequate transport*   As was seen in Chapter 4, the idea of 'need' embraces the notion that, for a variety of reasons, including faults in the existing pattern of income distribution, effective demand is not an adequate guide to transport resource allocation and wider, social criteria should, therefore, be sought. The market thus needs regulations to meet this objective.
- *The existence of high transaction costs*   While free markets may theoretically be capable of optimizing output, this may involve high transaction costs – the costs of 'doing business'. Drivers confronting each other on a road could bargain as to who has right of way but a simple rule, say giving priority to the right, is likely to prove more efficient. The problem may also be linked to the difficulties of negotiating for rights of way to construct transport infrastructure.
- *The integration of transport into wider economic policies*   Land use and transport are clearly interconnected and some degree of coordination may be felt desirable if imperfections exist in either the transport or the land-use markets. Additionally, intervention in the transport sector may form part of a wider government macroeconomic strategy (for example, price controls or investment programs) or industrial policy. The traditional notion of Keynesian fiscal macroeconomic policies of the type adopted in the United States in 2008–09 to counteract economic recession, for example, often involve significant public investments in transport facilities.
- *The need to reflect the genuine resource costs of transport*   In the case of certain finite, non-renewable resources (for example, mineral fuels) the market mechanism may fail to reflect the full social time preference of society. The government may, therefore, intervene to ensure that the decision maker is aware of the true long-term shadow price.
- *The improvement of transport coordination*   Because there are numerous suppliers of transport services, inefficient provision may result if their decisions are made independently. There is also the prospect of duplication of transport facilities, and consequential wastage of resources, without some degree of central guidance. This is a topic that we shall return to in more detail later.

Of course, in practice most official policies claim to cover a range of different problems although conflicts may and do emerge. For example, policies designed primarily to contain externalities may have adverse effects on income distribution or could run counter to a national economic policy that is pursuing a course of maximizing gross national product. Similarly, measures to ensure that adequate high-cost research is conducted may mean conferring monopoly powers on private suppliers (for example, through the patent system or in terms of government contracts to purchase the fruits of a new technology). Consequently, there is an inevitable blurring across these justifications for government involvement when various policy measures are discussed or introduced. Even more uncertain than the detailed justification or objectives underlying some policies are the exact effects that the different policy tools employed by policy makers are likely to exert.

The instruments of transport policy are sometimes broken down into those which, adopting American jargon, are aimed at economic regulation, and those aimed at social regulation – quantitative and qualitative regulation in the English vocabulary. The former are concerned with controlling the amount supplied in transport markets, who supplies it and the price that consumers pay. Social regulation specifies the nature of the transport services provided relating, for instance, to vehicle design, maximum emissions levels, driving hours, and training of personnel. In practice there is an inevitable overlap between the two sets of instruments. Limiting market entry, for example, can contain many adverse environmental effects of transport, while strict quality controls can act to contain competition.

It is perhaps more useful, therefore, simply to provide a listing of the various policy instruments under the following general headings:

- *Taxes and subsidies*   The government may use its fiscal powers either to increase or to decrease the costs of various forms of transport or services over different routes – or, indeed, the cost of transport in general. While they may be designed in some cases to consciously affect the costs of transport (for example, subsidies to promote transit use or fuel taxes to finance road construction) in other instances they are pure sumptuary taxes aimed at raising revenue from sources where demand is less price sensitive. Generally this involves taxes on transport services used by higher-income groups.
- *Price controls*   Concerns that a monopolist transport service supplier may exploit its ability to price above marginal costs has led to wide-ranging price regulations over the years. These have taken a variety of forms ranging from rate-of-return regulation (which sets prices allowing a particular profit level to be attained) to price-capping (which allows average prices to rise regularly but at a rate less than general cost levels), each with its particular advantage and challenges.[4]
- *Direct provisions*   Local and central government are direct suppliers, via municipal and nationalized undertakings, of a wide range of transport services. They are also responsible for supplying a substantial amount of trans-

---

[4] K.E. Train, *Optimal Regulation: The Economic Theory of Natural Monopoly*, Cambridge, MA: MIT Press, 1991.

port infrastructure, notably roads, and supplementary services, such as the police. In the context of bodies such as the European Union, the supply may be by pan-national agencies. The link between supply, the infrastructure and its use may also involve direct public provision of both, as was often the case with airport and state-owned airlines, but this is decreasingly so.

- *Laws and regulations*   Government (and to a lesser extent, local authorities) may legally regulate the transport sector and there has grown up an extensive body of law that, in effect, controls and directs the activities of both transport suppliers and users. Linked with this there are generic laws that govern financial, labor and other markets that provide essential inputs into transport industries and thus affect the way in which it functions.

- *Competition policy and consumer protection legislation*   It is useful to distinguish general industrial legislation, governing such things as restrictive practices and mergers, and consumer protection legislation, covering such things as advertising, which embrace all forms of activity in the economy and not just transport. Obviously, as we mentioned earlier, they generally apply to transport. In addition, many countries have specific transport-oriented policies aimed at protecting users.

- *Licensing*   The government may regulate either the quality or the quantity of transport provision by its ability to grant various forms of licenses to operators, vehicles or services. The system of driving licenses for cars and trucks also influences the demand for private transport. A specific form of licensing may be seen in franchising whereby a private sector undertaking may operate a publicly owned transport facility for a designated period. At the much broader level, there have been long-standing policies in international transport that have, *de facto*, imposed a licensing structure to limit the supply of transport services, or to restrict the carriers involved in the trade.

- *The purchase of transport services*   Various non-transport activities of government require the use of transport services – for example, to move military personnel and to supply medical services. Hence, by means of its position as a large consumer, government may exert a degree of countervailing power over transport suppliers. This is often more relevant at the local level of administration where large fleets of vehicles can be loaned or leased. More indirectly, by purchasing one type of transport service a government may influence the larger market for these services. For example, the purchase of military transport equipment may allow economies of scale in production, which reduces the cost of producing related civilian products. Aircraft engine and frames and often seen in this context.

- *Moral suasion*   In many instances this is of a weak form, usually being educational or the offering of advice on matters such as safety (for example, advertising the advantages of the wearing of seat belts), but it may be stronger when the alternative to accepting advice is the ultimate exercise, by government, of others of its powers (for example, the refusal of a license or withdrawal of a subsidy).

- *Research and development*   Government may influence the long-term development of transport through its own research activities. These are, in part, conducted by its own explicit agents (for example, the Transport Research Laboratory in the United Kingdom or the Transportation Research Board in the United States) and, in part, through the funding of outside research via contracts. There are also fundamental research initiatives overseen by such bodies as the National Science Foundation in America, which can impact significantly on transport.
- *Provision of information*   The government through various agencies offers certain technical advice to transport users and provides general information to improve the decision making within transport. Many of these services are specific to transport (for example, weather services for shipping and air transport) while others assist the transport sector less directly (for example, information on trading arrangements overseas). In terms of safety and security, most governments offer warnings of any severe dangers that may exist in other countries.
- *Policies relating to inputs*   Transport is a major user of energy, especially oil, and also utilizes a wide range of other raw materials and intermediate products. Government policy relating to the energy and other sectors can therefore have an important indirect bearing on transport. It can, for instance, stipulate the types of fuel that may be sold – lead-free gasoline being required in many countries.

It seems logical, therefore, that if market imperfections can be identified, it is in the 'public interest' to intervene and reduce their distortive effects. This is not a particularly contentious view. Difficulties arise, however, not from the notion of public interest as such but rather to the degree to which intervention can, in practice, produce public benefit. In the 1970s, as we shall see below, a growing body of opinion emerged that regulation had become excessive and no longer served the public interest. In particular, the ideas of the Chicago School of economists questioned the motivation underlying the actions of regulators – most notably that they tend to act as rational economic entities and pursue policies aimed at furthering their position rather than necessarily that of the public interest.[5] Others considered the power of the regulated industries and argued that because of their control of information flows (for example, regarding cost data which are needed to regulate fares) and their power to lobby, there was a tendency for them to capture the regulatory process.

Even if regulation is initiated in the public interest it is not free from problems. Ideally, policy makers like to match one policy instrument with one objective, but this is seldom possible in transport. The problems of interdependence of objectives have already been alluded to but, in addition, the instruments themselves frequently have diverse effects. Taxation policies to reduce the use of a

---

[5] G.J. Stigler, 'The theory of economic regulation', *Bell Journal of Economics and Management Science*, **2**, 3–19, 1971.

specific mode of transport may prove regressive, while licensing to contain externalities may result in quasi-monopoly powers being given to certain suppliers.

Actually forecasting, monitoring and appraising the effects of alternative policy instruments also usually proves difficult. Transport policy is pursued through a package of instruments and policy changes usually resulting in several of these instruments being varied in their intensity at once. The effects of such changes are also only likely to be fully felt after a lag as agents in the transport market gradually respond and adjust to the new situation. In the short term a trucker, for instance, may do little in response to higher fuel taxation (save pay the additional money) but in the longer term he is likely to modify the method of operation employed and, in the very long term, he may even change the type of vehicle fleet used.

Even if one could isolate occasions when a change is made to a single policy instrument it is unlikely that the full effect could be recorded before further changes take place. Finally, there is the problem of determining the counter-factual – the course of events which would have ensued if policy had not been changed. Government is frequently reactive in its approach – suggesting that changing circumstances are already observable by the time policy is enacted – but on other occasions, policy changes represent initiatives and actually anticipate change. One can never simply assume that events would have continued on the course set prior to a major policy change.

14.3   The Regulation of Monopoly Power

Although economic regulations have been motivated by a variety of factors, concern over the exercise of monopoly power has dominated much of the debate and legislation. The large-scale infrastructure that is needed to support most forms of transport, and the various forms of network economies that can exist in providing transport services, suggest that concentrated supply can minimize cost. Such a concentration, however, allows for the opportunity for suppliers to exploit users by pushing up prices, or it can lead to them not having adequate incentive to manage the system efficiently.

These problems have long been recognized and regulations have been commonplace. Direct public provision has often been used to ensure that users are not exploited by keeping user prices in line with costs. This has widely been used in the provision of track but also, as we shall see below, in the provision of services in some countries. The issue of 'government failure', and in particular the capture of systems by politicians and management, has led to other options being pursued in some cases. In particular, countries such as the United States have sought to control the prices at which the private sector may offer transport services. The traditional methods used, for example by the Civil Aeronautics Board (CAB) and the Interstate Commerce Commission until the 1980s, relied upon rate-of-return regulation. This set transport prices so that suppliers could earn a 'fair rate of return' on their investments. This allows the transport undertaking to choose its use of inputs, levels of output and prices as long as there is no excess above the officially defined fair rate of return. In other words with only one non-capital input labor, L, the rate of return is:

$$(PQ - wL)/K \qquad (14.1)$$

where P is price, Q is output, w is wages, and K is capital and this must not exceed the "fair rate of return":

$$f \geq (PQ - wL)/K \qquad (14.2)$$

The main difficulties with this approach involve the incentive structure it offers to overcapitalize (the 'Averch–Johnson effect'[6]) and, as discussed in the previous section, the ease with which the system may be captured both by the industry under regulation and the regulators seeking to serve their own ends.

The Averch–Johnson effect is the tendency of companies to engage in excessive amounts of capital accumulation to expand the volume of their profits. If companies' profits to capital ratio is regulated as in equation (14.2), then at a certain percentage there is a strong incentive for companies to overinvest to increase profits overall. Specifically, the main Averch–Johnson result is that the capital–labor ratio selected by a profit-maximizing, regulated firm will be greater than that consistent with a cost-minimizing one for any output it chooses to produce. If the fair rate of return is greater than the cost of capital, a firm will have an incentive to invest as much as it can consistent with its production possibilities, because the difference between the allowed rate and its actual cost of capital is pure profit. This goes against any optimal efficiency point for capital that the company may have calculated, as higher profit is almost always desired over and above efficiency.

Concern with rate of return regulation's economic efficiency has also been supported by empirical analysis, and in particular with the way it affected American transport provision and prices in the 1960s and 1970s. Table 14.1 provides a brief summary of a series of studies conducted on the rate-of-return regulation of the CAB. In particular, the fact that only intra-state services were regulated whereas many state systems were not allowed enabled comparisons to be made.

An alternative to rate-of-return regulation developed initially for telecommunications regulation, but subsequently adopted in numerous transport contexts is 'price-capping'.[7] The aim of this policy is to squeeze out inefficiencies, and in particular X-inefficiency, by forcing transport industries to provide their services at increasingly lower real prices. It has, for example, been applied to privatized airports in the United Kingdom and to the National Air Traffic Control System.

[6] H. Averch and L. Johnson, 'Behavior of the firm under regulatory constraint', *American Economic Review*, **52**, 1053–69, 1962.

[7] M.A. Crew and P.R. Kleindorfer, 'Incentive regulation in the United Kingdom and the United States: some lessons', *Journal of Regulatory Economics*, **9**, 211–25, 1996.

Table 14.1 *Results of US studies on the implications of airline regulation prior to 1978*

Study	Data	Comparisons	Conclusions
Caves (1962)	CAB routes	Structure, conduct & performance	Problems with the industry's performance that required changes in the regulatory structure but did not oppose regulation
Levine (1965)	Intrastate & CAB routes	Fares	Regulation caused higher fares & resulted in lower load factors
Jordan (1970)	California & CAB routes	Fares Fares	Regulation caused excess capacity, benefited aircraft manufacturers, labor unions & airlines
Keeler (1972)	California & CAB routes	Fares	Regulation caused excess capacity that dissipated any profits from fares set at cartel levels by the CAB
Douglas & Miller (1974)	CAB routes	Fares & flight frequency	Regulation resulted in high fares & suboptimal high qualities of service being offered
DeVany (1975)	California & CAB routes	Fares & flight frequency	Regulation protected the consumer with fares set close to the output maximizing level
Keeler (1978)	California & CAB routes	Fares	CAB regulation led to excess charges amounting to $2.7 billion per annum

Source: K.J. Button, 'The deregulation of US interstate aviation: an assessment of causes and consequences, Part 2', *Transport Reviews*, **9**, 189–215, 1989, which also contains full references cited in the table.

In more detail, price cap regulation adjusts the transport operator's prices according to a price cap index that reflects the overall rate of inflation in the economy, the ability of the operator to gain efficiencies relative to the average firm in the economy, and the inflation in the operator's input prices relative to the average firm in the economy.

Price cap regulation is sometimes called '*CPI-X*', (in the United Kingdom '*RPI-X*') after the basic formula employed to set price caps. This takes the rate of inflation, measured by the consumer or retail price index and subtracts an expected efficiency savings X. The system provides an incentive for greater efficiency, as any savings above the predicted rate X can be passed on to shareholders until the price caps are next reviewed. The rate X is based not only on a firm's past performance, but also on the performance of other firms in the industry and is intended to be a proxy for a competitive market, in industries which are natural monopolies. The problem is that where there is manifest inefficiency, it is relatively easy to generate a reasonable value for X, but as a transport undertaking moves towards a quasi-competitive situation, X approaches a normal profit margin. In other words, it converges on rate-of-return regulation.

There have been other perspectives on regulating what are often seen as natural monopolies in transport. William Baumol's[8] idea of contestable markets

[8] W.J. Baumol, J.C. Panzar and R.D. Willig, *Contestable Markets and the Theory of Industry Structure*, New York: Harcourt Brace Jovanovich, 1982.

which was touched upon in Chapter 7, for example, argues that with free market entry and exit, effectively the absence of any 'sunk costs', the forces of potential competition temper the monopoly powers of any incumbent transport suppliers. This logically moves to notions of unbundling of those elements of transport supply that may be subject to contestable forces and focusing regulation on those that are characterized by elements of sunk costs. This was, for instance the rationale underlying the deregulation of US and European airlines and more generally, modes such as buses and trucking.

Although some studies have supported a weak notion of contestability,[9] the evidence supporting this, however, tends to show that the forces of contestability are weaker than those of actual competition. In particular, scheduled airlines do not seem as affected by potential competition as initially thought. Gale Moore,[10] for example, found that in the United States, fares were lower in markets with more actual carriers, while Steve Morrison[11] found that actual competition with Southwest Airlines produced aggregate fare savings of \$12.9 billion in 1998 whereas potential and adjacent competition produced a saving of only \$9.5 billion. As a result, even some of its strongest initial supporters have questioned the limits of its usefulness: 'We now believe that transportation by truck, barges, and even buses may be more contestable than passenger air transportation'.[12]

Where there are sunk costs, there have been arguments that the monopoly power of the transport undertakings may be controlled through initiating 'competition for the market', rather than trying to stimulate competition in the market.[13] This essentially involves auctioning off the rights to provide the transport service. This may, for example, be used to supply infrastructure such as roads whereby a concession to build, operate and toll the facility may be auctioned off with the state taking back the road after some specified period. Basically, the competition is in the rights to have the market for road space rather than in the market for road use.

A number of different auctioning methods, with numerous variants, each with their advantages and limitations, are available and have been used in various contexts in the transport sector:

- *English or ascending-bid auction*   This is the most common form of auction for the sale of goods with an auctioneer allowing successively higher bids

[9] K.J. Button, 'Contestability in the UK bus industry, and experience goods and economies of experience', in J. Dodgson and N. Topham (eds), *Bus Deregulation and Privatisation: An International Perspective*, Aldershot: Avebury, 1988.

[10] T.G. Moore, 'US airline deregulation; its effects on passengers, capital and labor', *Journal of Law and Economics*, **29**, 1–28, 1986.

[11] S.A. Morrison, 'Actual, adjacent, and potential competition: estimating the full effects of Southwest Airlines', *Journal of Transport Economics and Policy*, **35**, 239–56, 2001.

[12] W.J. Baumol and R.D. Willig, 'Contestability: developments since the book', *Oxford Economic Papers*, **38**, 9–36, 1986.

[13] H. Demsetz, 'Why regulate utilities?', *Journal of Law and Economics*, **11**, 55–65, 1968.

until only a single bidder is left. At each point in the auction, the various potential bidders know the prevailing highest bid.

- *Dutch or descending-bid auction*   In this model, the auctioneer gradually lowers the price until a bidder accepts it.
- *First-price sealed-bid auction*   This approach involves bidders submitting sealed bids and the 'winner' is the one with the highest bid when they are opened. In this case the bidders have no idea what the competing bids are when they make their offer.
- *Vickrey*[14] *or second-price sealed-bid auction* This variant on the sealed-bid model awards the 'prize' to the highest bidder but the winner only pays the amount of the second-highest bid.

The difficulty with any auction is that it involves game-playing between the auctioneer and those bidding, but in transport there can be particular challenges. In many cases, because transport is essentially a network activity, there are issues of the boundaries of the auction – for example, should it be for a single highway or a set of highways? There is the physical longevity of much transport infrastructure and the problems that may arise if for a variety of reasons the demand for its use declines significantly during the period of the contract, making it impossible for the company that has won the auction to make a viable return. This may involve the need for renegotiations. Nevertheless, competition for the market has been widely adopted in many transport contexts, ranging from auctions for subsidized bus routes in the United Kingdom (the bid with the lowest subsidy requirement winning) to auctions for airport concessions in many South American countries.

14.4   Priorities in Transport Policy

It now seems appropriate to examine the various landmarks and phases of transport policy. This is intended to highlight the way in which transport policy has evolved to match both the changing technical and organizational structure of the sector and also the differing attitudes of society to transport over the past century and a half. It is in no way intended as a comprehensive piece of economic history. While much of the focus is on the UK situation, changes elsewhere in the world, and in particular in the United States, are also examined. The 'story' is also slanted in favor of the more recent developments.

The Anti-monopoly Phase, Pre-1930

Government has always taken some interest in transport. Historically, military, political and fiscal factors were the prime motivation, but over the past century

[14] W. Vickrey, 'Counter-speculation, auctions, and competitive sealed tenders', *Journal of Finance*, **16**, 8–37, 1961.

and a half this concern has broadened out. Previously, it was not the efficiency of the transport market that was the principal concern but rather the assurance that adequate transport was available to permit the fulfillment of the major commitments of defense, administration and internal stability. The Industrial Revolution placed greater emphasis on the need for an economically efficient transport system which, combined with the rapid technical changes that took place in transport during the later years of the eighteenth century and, more importantly, the early decades of the nineteenth, resulted in rather more official intervention. (Indeed, even the Duke of Wellington called for a National Transport Plan for the United Kingdom at one stage.)

While much of the early involvement was to permit canal and railway facilities to be constructed, there was also a political awareness of the potential monopoly powers which canals, but railway companies in particular, could exercise. The 1844 Railway Act in the United Kingdom, for example, gave government the option of purchasing newly formed companies after 21 years (a power never exercised) and maximum rates were normally included in the enabling acts. In all, over 200 regulatory acts were passed before 1930 to appease public concern about the private control exercised over the monopoly of the railway companies.

By the 1920s the UK railway companies had to publish their rates, were subject to common carrier obligations, were not allowed to show undue preference, had to present accounts in a prescribed manner and were subjected to controls over wage bargaining. An element of social service obligation was also apparent in some of this legislation with, initially, railway companies required by law to provide specified cheap services and, subsequently, workmen's tickets.

This type of situation was not unique to the United Kingdom. At the extreme, the majority of Continental European countries, partly for strategic reasons but also in part because of their general approach toward natural monopoly, had developed their rail systems as public enterprises from the outset. The United States, while fostering private ownership and finance, had passed its first legislation on rate regulation in 1856 and the Interstate Commerce Commission came into being in 1887. Equally, in Canada the inherent advantage of the railways led to concern about the abuse of their powers, including discriminatory practices, and to the passing of the Railway Act of 1903.

The Anti-competition Phase, 1930–45

The advances in trucking and passenger transport in the period after the First World War substantially eroded the near-monopoly that had been enjoyed by the railways for the previous 80 or so years. The nature of road transport, and especially the relative ease of entry, and low capital requirement necessary, changed the focus towards the regulation of dangerous operating practices and excessive competition. The political pressures of the railway companies, still hampered by numerous restrictions on their commercial freedom, to contain cheap road transport, added emphasis to the debate. Besides the financial strains on the regulated railway industry, fears were expressed that excessive competition produces dangerous operating practices and results in inadequate and unreliable services for those situated away from the main transport arteries. The UK's Salter Conference which reported on trucking in 1932 found:

> Any individual at present has an unlimited right to enter the haulage industry without any regard to the pressure on the roads or the existing excess of transport facilities . . . This unrestricted liberty is fatal to the organization of the industry in a form suitable to a carrier service purported to serve the public.

(It should perhaps be said that the composition of the Salter Conference – it was made up of railwaymen and representatives of established truckers – may have colored its conclusions.)

The legal manifestations of this policy were the passing of the Road Traffic Act, 1930, and of the Road and Rail Traffic Act, 1933, which introduced, respectively, quantity licensing into road passenger transport and trucking. In addition to trying to temper the competitive environment of road transport, the operation of the licensing system for road passenger transport also encouraged the provision and cross-subsidization of unprofitable social bus services by virtue of the method of license allocation. Other measures designed to produce greater equality in the operating conditions encountered on the roads and railways included relaxation of certain constraints on railway pricing and the introduction of minimum wage rates and specified employment conditions into the industry.

Elsewhere a plethora of similar regulations were appearing. In the United States, federal legislation was introduced controlling coastal shipping (1933), inter-urban bus operations (1935), trucking (1935), airlines (1938), inland waterways (1940) and freight forwarders (1942), and many states also tightened their regulatory regimes. Canada initiated regulations over its aviation industry under the 1938 Transport Act and encouraged coordination, rather than competition, between its two main railway operators under the 1933 Canadian National–Canadian Pacific Act.

Central Control and Nationalization in Europe, 1945–51

The years immediately following the end of the Second World War saw, under the newly elected Labour government, a period of reconstruction and an industrial policy emphasizing the nationalization of UK industry. The 1947 Transport Act, for the first time outside of war years, brought a substantial part of the British transport system under direct government control. (Although it should be pointed out that peacetime nationalization was not entirely new nor a Labour Party monopoly and, indeed, the British Overseas Airways Corporation was formed in 1939 by a Conservative administration.)

The objectives of the 1947 Act were clearly stated, namely to 'secure the provision of an efficient, adequate, economical and properly integrated system of public inland transport and port facilities'. The earlier success of the London Passenger Transport Board gave credence to this view and the British Transport Commission (BTC) (with five functional executives) was established to emulate this success. It was given the responsibility of coordinating the newly nationalized railways, long-distance road haulage, sections of public road transport, London Transport and publicly owned ports and waterways.

Unfortunately, the BTC was given no rules of economic behavior as guidelines. It was recognized that, for the railways to compete efficiently, a much closer price–cost relationship was required, but it was impossible for a new set of freight charges to be set before 1955 and, in the meantime, the BTC was impotent to direct traffic to the mode for which it thought it was best suited. The difficulty was compounded by the fact that consignors had a free choice of transport mode, and that own-account trucking vehicles were free from government control. Further, the 1947 Act had little opportunity to work because of, first, the lack of sufficient time needed to develop the necessary administration and to reorganize the newly nationalized undertakings and, second, the inadequate funds available to carry out the necessary investment required in the rail sector after the wear and tear of war.

A Competitive Framework, 1951–64

The period of successive Conservative administrations between 1951 and 1964 witnessed a movement away from a regulatory approach to transport coordination in Britain towards one based upon competition, that is, by making use of 'the natural interplay of economic forces'. A policy of decentralized control was pursued and, under the 1953 Transport Act, the railways were freed from many of their long-standing statutory obligations (for example, they were relieved of the status of 'common carrier' and the burden of having to publish their rates and charges). Large sections of nationalized trucking were also returned to private ownership. The basic argument for this competitive approach was that even if integration in the fullest sense were practicable, it would result in a large, unwieldy machine, ill-adapted to meet with promptitude the varying and instant demands of industry.

The culmination of these policies was the 1962 Transport Act which freed the railways from most of their remaining legal constraints, regionalized their boards, separated their overall administration from that of trucking and recognized that commercial viability required some rationalization of the rail network. Nationalized road haulage (which was composed of British Road Services and several specialist undertakings) was given terms of reference requiring it to perform as though it was a 'private enterprise concern'.

The general policy of 'coordination by competition' pursued by the Conservative government met with considerable problems after 1962. The railways and public transport in general ran into increasing financial difficulties, while public concern began to grow about both the need to provide additional road space for the growing number of motor vehicles and the actual environmental effects of this growth, especially on urban areas. The established method of providing social services by cross-finance from profitable services ceased to be financially viable. Further, there were questions arising concerning the most appropriate ways of exploiting new transport technologies, especially containerization.

Controlled Competition, 1964–74

The socialist, Labour administration elected in 1964 undertook a series of detailed policy studies in transport that culminated in the 1968 Transport Act. This, in conjunction with the 1968 Town and Country Planning Act, attempted to produce a policy based upon 'controlled competition'.[15] It hoped to combine the advantages afforded by the automatic processes of the market mechanism with those of direct control. The policy was comprehensive, setting up passenger transport authorities (PTAs) to control and coordinate urban public transport, devising new systems of quality licensing for trucking, providing specific finance to support socially necessary transport, drawing up a national road-building program and reconstructing the accounts and activities of the railways. It used all means of policy: market measures, such as taxation and subsidy, as well as 'administrative' measures such as licensing and the establishment of new institutions.

The Act was also liberal in the sense that the framework of legislation and licensing that was introduced was intended to provide a basis for 'fair' competition, leaving the actual coordination of modes, in the majority of sectors, to market forces. The PTAs were introduced in the major conurbations to control urban public transport, but this was in a market where externalities are widespread and competition felt to be unlikely to solve problems of congestion and environmental decay. The inter-urban market was left to competitive forces with intervention limited to preventing excess instability or dangerous practices.

The Conservative government, returned to office in 1970, pledged itself to the repeal of many of the clauses in the 1968 Act although, in practice, few of the measures they found exceptionable – such as quantity licensing for long-distance trucking – had in fact been implemented.[16] Indeed, the 1972 Local Government Act set up authorities that logically extended the PTA concept and further integrated the long-term planning of overall urban development. The Civil Aviation Authority, which was set up in 1971, rather than reversing the philosophy of the 1968 Act, was designed to control operating practices and improve the stability of the sector. As the government minister said at the time, 'There are close links between the economics and the financial health of the airlines and the safety of their operations and between operational safety, air worthiness, air traffic control and navigational services'.

---

[15] D.L. Munby, 'Mrs Castle's transport policy', *Journal of Transport Economics and Policy*, **2**, 135–73, 1968.

[16] K.J. Button, 'Transport policy in the United Kingdom 1968–7', *Three Banks Review*, **103**, 26–48, 1974.

The Search for Efficiency, 1974–80

The policies of the UK's Labour government from 1974 to 1979 were spelt out in *Transport Policy*:[17]

> First, to contribute to economic growth and higher national prosperity . . . Second, to meet social needs by securing a reasonable level of personal mobility. . . . Third, to minimize the harmful effects, in loss of life and damage to the environment, that are the direct physical results of the transport we use.

In many ways the policies, which reduced government expenditure considerably, moved further towards the free market than the 1968 Transport Act, with greater emphasis now placed on allocative efficiency. Although government expenditure on 'roads and transport' fell from £3,820 million to £3,023 million per annum (at 1978 prices), between 1974 and 1978, this does not mean that official intervention was ignored. The 1974 Railway Act, for example, had already introduced the idea of a 'Public Service Obligation' and subsidies were made available to provide services 'comparable' to those existing at the time of the legislation.

Methods of allocating public monies were also modified with the introduction of transport supplementary grants and the need, from 1974, for the production of transport policies and programs by local authorities to demonstrate the evolution of coherent local transport policy. This latter idea was later extended in the 1978 Transport Act to embrace public transport services (the Public Transport Plans) at the shire level. But, on the other hand, grand strategies for road-building were replaced by piecemeal assessments, emphasizing a further shift from the active policy of the Labour administration of the 1960s to rather more reactive policy making.[18]

The emphasis on allocative efficiency and market mechanisms was further strengthened in the 1980 Transport Act introduced by the Conservative government returned the previous year. Quantity licensing in the express coach sector was abolished and free competition (with quality controls) was permitted. Further relaxation of sharing and lift-giving laws also allowed more opportunity for private transport to offer limited forms of public service in rural areas, while policies of denationalization have resulted in sales of limited amounts of publicly owned transport assets to private industry. (It is interesting to compare this trend towards both reactive policy making and a greater reliance on market forces with the developments in the EU Common Transport Policy discussed in Chapter 13.)

[17] UK Department of Transport, *Transport Policy*, Cmnd 6845, London: HMSO, 1977.
[18] K.M. Gwilliam, 'Institutions and objectives in transport policy', *Journal of Transport Economics and Policy*, **13**, 11–27, 1979.

The Age of Regulatory Reform, 1980 to late 1990s

The past 30 or so years have witnessed major reforms in transport regulation. While there are marked national differences in the nature and pace of change, this process has, in the case of public transport modes, been characterized by moves toward more liberal regimes and a withdrawal of government from the ownership of transport operating companies. In contrast, there has been an increasing emphasis on the containment and the management of automobile use both on environmental grounds and because of congestion problems.

The liberalization measures that have been adopted not only represented legal reforms, but also embraced *de facto* changes in interpretation and enforcement of regulations. In addition, they have extended across national boundaries with, for instance, the removal of institutional barriers to free transport operations being an explicit element of the European Community's 1992 initiative. Whereas previously the majority view was that, because of scale economies and the potential for serious market failure, it was in the public interest for government to take an active role in regulating the industry, the prevailing wisdom is now that intervention failures are often potentially more damaging than market imperfections.

The generality of the regulatory trends across industrialized countries raises questions concerning the underlying causes of change. Certainly, in more recent years one can point to the demonstration effects exerted mainly by the deregulation of US domestic aviation, but there also seem to be more fundamental issues that need addressing.

The first American economists to oppose regulation did so for a straightforward reason. Most subscribed (and still do) to the basic theorem that welfare is maximized when the price of each good or service equals its long-run social marginal cost, but evidence mounted in the 1950s, 1960s and 1970s that regulatory agencies caused prices to diverge from long-run social marginal costs, rather than converge to them. Economic studies of US aviation provided a cornerstone in this debate. It was the combination of direct evidence that the Civil Aeronautics Board kept long-haul, high-density fares high and evidence of low fares in the unregulated intra-state markets in California that provided the first evidence that deregulation of intercity air passenger transport was justified. Indeed, in the case of airlines, the California markets provided evidence against airline regulation, evidence that could be understood not only by economists, but also by the general traveling public (see again Table 14.1).

By the mid-1960s, a strong case existed for transport deregulation in the United States, but there was much research needed to get a full picture: for example, early studies disagreed as to whether the costs of excess rail capacity resulting from closure regulation were high or low. A number of subsequent studies considered these issues, as well as the more basic issue as to how high the social loss from transport regulation was in the United States.

There were also theoretical developments in economics that encouraged deregulation. The Chicago models of regulation made it clear that the public interest is not necessarily served by regulation. However, these models also implied

Table 14.2   *Major legal changes in US transport regulation (1976–89)*

1976	Railroad Revitalization and Reregulation Reform Act – removed many regulations over rate setting
1977	Air Cargo Deregulation Act – initiated free competition for air cargo services
1978	Airline Deregulation Act – initiated a phased removal of fare setting and market entry controls
1980	Staggers Rail Act – removed many regulations over line abandonments and gave further freedom over rate setting
1980	Motor Carriers Service Act – increased entry and rate-setting freedom and reduced the role of rate-fixing bureaux
1981	Northeast Rail Reform Act – enabled Conrail to abandon little-used lines
1982	Bus Regulatory Reform Act –eased conditions of market entry and exit and phased in relaxation of rate controls

that existing regulations were the result of a rational process, and by the interpretation of some they could be thought to work against deregulation, because they implied that regulation was itself a result of social optimization. Nevertheless, subsequent analyses have extended the analysis to indicate how it could indeed explain regulatory reform. The reason is that changes in technologies, markets and the balance of political power among different groups can easily stimulate regulatory reform, even in a Chicago-type model, This has been examined in the context of the bus[19] and airline industries.[20]

Another theory which supported deregulation was that of contestability, which asserted that with sufficiently easy entry and exit in a market (there are no sunk costs but there are lags in matching price cuts), even a natural monopoly could have a zero-profit, competitive outcome.[21] The model, however, served more as an after-the-fact rationale for deregulation than as a stimulus, because it was developed fully only after deregulation occurred in most US industries. Furthermore, subsequent empirical evidence for the US airline industry has not fully supported the contestability hypothesis.[22]

The resultant changes that have taken place around the world since the mid-1960s have not been uniform across either countries or modes. Part of this stems from the different starting points that existed in the early 1970s. In very general terms, the United States led the way in legal change with a rush of liberalizing measures during the 1970s and early 1980s which removed much government control from its domestic transport system – see Table 14.2. Other countries have followed the trend, in part because of demonstration effects that indicated

[19] K.J. Button, 'Economic theories of regulation and the regulation of the United Kingdom bus industry', *Anti-trust Bulletin*, **34**,489–515, 1989.

[20] T.B. Keeler, 'Theories of regulation and the deregulation movement', *Public Choice*, **44**, 103–45, 1984.

[21] E.E. Bailey and J.C. Panzar, 'The contestability of airline markets during the transition to deregulation', *Law, and Contemporary Problems*, **44**, 125–45, 1981.

[22] S.A. Morrison and C. Winston, *The Economic Effects of Airline Deregulation*, Washington, DC: Brookings Institution, 1986.

significant benefits can come from change, but in some cases because of the direct impacts of changes in the United States – Canada, for example, was so affected.

In effect, the systems of boards and committees, which regulated the industry, have gradually had their powers curtailed, and transport industries are increasingly being treated like other commercial undertakings. Where controls remain there has been a shift in their emphasis. In inter-state trucking, for example, the 1980 legislation shifted the burden of proof for market entry from the applicant to the protester and this effectively eliminated the major entry barrier. It also created a zone of reasonableness within which rates could vary. Equally, with respect to freight railroads, the reforms gradually removed rate controls, allowed rationalization and facilitated reorganization, especially mergers.

This quest for efficiency was emulated in the United Kingdom as, first, the 1980 Transport Act and then the 1985 Transport Act liberalized bus markets and introduced new financial mechanisms for providing social services. *De facto* reform was brought about in domestic aviation as the Civil Aviation Authority adjusted its position on licensing in 1982. Developments within the European Union meant that there was further *de jure* changes as cabotage was phased in within the Community by 1997. Indeed, as outlined in Chapter 13, the creation of a Single European Market meant that cabotage rights, albeit initially often in rather limited forms, extend across all transport modes within the European Union.

Similar changes occurred elsewhere with the domestic Canadian trucking market, partly as a result of increased competition from the more efficient American carriers being liberalized in 1987 and its aviation market, after some *de facto* changes in 1984, being legally deregulated in 1988. Reforms of a similar nature ended Australia's 'two airline' domestic aviation policy in 1990 but liberalization of surface transport has progressed more slowly.

Gradually the effects of reform strategies, especially through the influence of agencies such as the World Bank and the Asian Development Bank, are also being felt in developing countries.

The extensive public ownership of transport that existed in countries such as Canada, Australia and Japan, and in most of Europe has meant that reforms have often also involved elements of privatization. The privatization process, while reducing the direct control of government, has however stimulated the creation of new regulations, for example, to limit market power and to meet social objectives. Many of these relate to quality of service, especially safety, and to the nature of ownership (such as governing allowable foreign ownership of shares) but economic regulations have also been imposed.

The sale of transport undertakings through stock market flotation (for instance, British Airways and the British Airports Authority) attracted considerable attention and raised large sums of money for the UK Exchequer (Table 14.3). Privatization in transport has also taken a diversity of other forms.[23] The

[23] K.J. Button, 'Privatization in the transport sector: some of the key issues', *Economisch en Sociaal Tijdschrift*, **45**, 29–48, 1992

Table 14.3 *Transport privatization proceeds in the United Kingdom*

Undertaking	Year	Amount (current prices)
National Freight Corporation	1982	£7 million
British Rail Hotels	1983	£30 million
Associated British Ports	1983–84	£34 million
Sealink	1984	£66 million
British Airways	1987	£892 million
British Airports Authority	1987	£1,200 million
National Bus Company	1988	n.a.

former National Bus Company in the United Kingdom, for instance, was broken up and privatized mainly through management buyouts. In France and Japan, private money is increasingly being used to finance railway operations through commercial loans and investments. Open tendering for formerly publicly supplied bus services is now widespread in the United Kingdom and franchising systems, albeit on a somewhat different basis, exist in a number of Continental European states. In a similar way, Sweden attempted to increase efficiency on parts of its railway network by separating operations from track and allowing private operating companies to tender for services. Actions were also initiated in the United Kingdom although extended, for a period, to embrace privatization of the rail track with somewhat less success.[24] Overall, the experiences have been mixed.[25]

The Notion of 'Sustainable Development', Late 1990s to Date

We saw in previous chapters the impact that transport can inflict on both the built and natural environments. Regulations of various kinds have long been used to minimize these problems, but the nature of the problems being addressed and the forms of regulation deployed have, as we have seen in Chapter 8, been changing. The use of regulation, and to a lesser extent pricing policy, have reduced, if not necessarily optimized, many of the local and regional adverse external effects. There seems every indication, however, that the political economy of optimizing such things as global warming gas emission will remain challenging.[26]

In broad terms this fits with a wider policy shift that focuses on sustainable development, within which transport policy plays a significant role.

The past three decades have witnessed a complete transformation in the way

---

[24] D. Tyrrall, 'The UK railway privatization: failing to succeed', *Economic Affairs*, **24**, 32–8, 2008.

[25] J.D. Bitzan, 'Railroad costs and competition – the implications of introducing competition to railroad networks', *Journal of Transport Economics and Policy*, **37**, 201–25, 2003.

[26] D. Banister and K.J. Button (eds), *Transport, the Environment and Sustainable Development*, London: E & FN Spon, 1993.

in which policy makers think about regulating transport markets. The role of government in regulation has moved from directing the operational sides of the sector, to looking for innovative ways to finance its infrastructure and control its wider impacts on society. Part of this stems from wider developments concerning the perceived role of government *per se*, but the changes in transport have also come about because of particular concerns. The outcome has seldom been as predicted and certainly the more liberal conditions which now exist in most transport markets around the world are not without their problems. In general, however, the changes have afforded the opportunity for users to express their preferences through the market and for regulators to pinpoint specific distortions where intervention can be justified.

In summary, if there is a single conclusion to be drawn from the experience of regulatory reform in transport, it has been that reform has, in general, been an economic success. Although there have been areas in which the policies need improvement (anti-trust, infrastructure, franchise arrangements and so on), these are small matters of 'fine tuning' compared with the broad picture of overall success in improving the efficiency of transport provision. What has been lacking have been comparable reforms in the regulation of private transport use.

14.5   Alternative Paths for Regulatory Reform

Regulations are continually changing as we saw in our discussion of institutions in Chapter 1. This reflects a variety of factors but here the focus is more on the ways in which the regulatory reforms are enacted. We saw in Chapter 13 that the European Union, for example, staged its reforms of aviation and shipping policy over a series of 'Packages'. This was not the way the United States approached the challenge. This raises issues about the speed at which change in transport regulations is optimal from an economic perspective. Linked to this is the matter of how the transition is best managed, and the role that different incentives and instruments may play in this.

'Big-bang Approach' versus 'Phased Reform'

There are two basic ways in which regulatory reforms are initiated: they either come in at once as a 'big bang' or they are phased in in stages. There are economic advantages and disadvantages of each.[27] The big-bang approach, typified by the individual modal regulation changes in the United States in the late 1970s and early 1980s, involves a comprehensive legal change in regulations that comes into effect very rapidly. There are potential costs in this (Figure 14.3).

First, the reforms may leave significant 'stranded costs' in the industry. For

---

[27] K. Johnson and K.J. Button, 'Incremental versus trend-break change in airline regulation', *Transportation Journal*, **37**, 25–34, 1998.

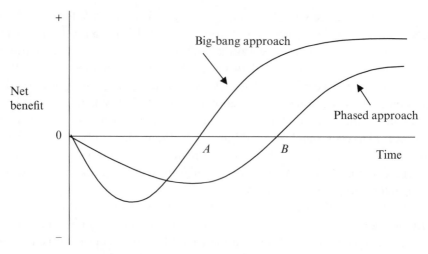

Figure 14.3 *The 'big-bang approach' versus 'phased reform'*

example, the infrastructure and hardware of the industry will be designed for the prior regulatory regime and some of it will be redundant under the structures of supply that emerge after reforms, or at least not be ideal in the new situation. Second, the new measures may not themselves be optimal. Changes in regulatory structures impose a wide variety of unforeseen costs on any industry, and some of these may be larger than anticipated. Equally, some of the possible benefits of reform may be lost if the reforms are not optimal.

The advantages, on the other hand, are that a big-bang change removes considerable uncertainty from the market about the nature of future institutional structures and should, therefore, remove some of the challenges in making invest-ments. It also means that there is less opportunity for those in the industry, or for others with related interests, to manipulate the various stages in the reform process, as may be the case if the changes are phased in over a period of time. Additionally, there is the expectation of a significant flow of benefits once the reforms have worked their way through the system.

In contrast, a series of smaller changes phased in allows for stranded costs to be minimized as transport hardware is physically worn out before it needs to be replaced and it allows modification to the new regulatory structure in the light of the experiences gained in the previous phases. But it is prone to capture by vested interests seeking to protect their position and it takes longer for the benefits of the new regime to work their way through.

In practice, the decision regarding which approach to adopt is often more to do with political economy than the simple calculation of costs and benefits. Reform generally requires a common perspective of a coalition of interests, and this shapes the pattern of change.

Considerable attention is paid in economics to comparative-static compari-sons, normally in terms of efficiency, between the implications of one regulatory regime and another, and to a lesser extent to the merits of the big-bang and phased approaches, but there are also more detailed issues of the transition process.[28] Much depends on the peculiarities of the situation. The matter is seldom purely economic in nature and, for example, there are often long-standing legal contracts that make sudden change difficult, or can only be circumvented by expensive buyouts. There are also equity considerations. The loss of sunk costs is not just a matter of efficiency but adversely impacts on those who had incurred them under the old regulatory regime, whereas the gains of change are enjoyed by new investors.

An Example of Phasing: US–EU Transatlantic Aviation

The development of international air transport markets on the North Atlantic routes offers an example of the ways phasing of regulatory changes may occur and their economic implications.[29] The restrictive bilateral air service agreements that typified the institutional structure of international airline markets from the Chicago Convention of 1944 have gradually been eroded by multilateral actions of entities such as the European Union and the advent of the Open Skies initiative by the United States (see Table 14.4 for details). This initially involved a loosening up of individual bilateral agreements between countries such as Germany and the Netherlands and the United States, but this was done in an *ad hoc* fashion, and agreements with countries such as the United Kingdom remained restrictive.

Negotiations to reach a more comprehensive structure emerged when the European Commission was given authority to negotiate on behalf of all EU airlines. The effects of such changes have not been easy to isolate but Figure 14.4 offers a general representation of the issues that are involved in looking at what has happened. In particular, it highlights the potential fare and output implications of the various types of transatlantic regulatory regimes that have been considered.

The initial position of the demand curve for transatlantic services under the pre-1980s regulatory regime is assumed linear and shown as D_1 in the figure, and the average cost curve per passenger, which for simplicity is assumed to rise more than linearly with quantity, as C_1. Market forces, however, because of the institutional interventions in place, did not determine fares and capacity across the Atlantic. Capacity under this system was limited (seen as the 'capacity constraint') and fares were regulated. If we assume that the terms reached under the bilateral agreement regarding fares allowed for at least cost recovery by the partners' airlines, this implies a fare level up to F_1. The removal of both this capacity constraint and of negotiated pricing, as happens under the Open Skies arrangements, results in competition for air services, and a move toward cost-recovery pricing strategies by the carriers. This would reduce fares to F_1^*.

[28] J.R. Meyer and W.B. Tye, 'The regulatory transition', *American Economic Review, Papers and Proceedings*, **71**, 268–72, 1981.

[29] K.J. Button, 'The impact of EU–US "Open Skies" agreement on airline market structures and airline networks', *Journal of Air Transport and Management*, **15**, 59–71, 2009.

Table 14.4   *Main features of United States bilateral air service agreements*

Pre-1978 bilateral air service agreements	*1978–1991 Open Market bilaterals*		*Post-1991 Open Skies bilaterals*
	US airlines	*Foreign airlines*	
Market access	Only to specified points	From any point in the US to specified points in foreign countries	Access limited to a number of US points	Unlimited
	Limited 5th freedom rights granted to US carriers. Charter rights not included	Extensive 5th freedom rights granted		Unlimited 5th freedom rights
			Unlimited charter rights	
		7th freedom rights not granted. Cabotage not allowed		
Designation	Single – some multiple		Multiple	
	Airlines must be 'substantially and effectively controlled' by nationals of designated state			
Capacity	Capacity agreed or shared 50:50. No capacity/frequency controls in liberal bilaterals, but subject to review	Break of gauge permitted in some agreements	No frequency or capacity controls	Break-of-gauge rights granted
				Free pricing
Tariffs	Approval by both governments (double-approval) or as agreed by IATA	Double-disapproval (filed tariffs operative unless both governments disapprove) or country of origin rules		
Code sharing		Not part of bilateral		Code sharing permitted

Open Skies policies that free up market entry by carriers and the fares they may levy, coupled with the permitting of strategic alliances, not only removes the capacity constraint but also affects both the demand and supply curves for transatlantic air travel. The ability of airlines to more effectively feed their transatlantic routes and coordinate their activities, through the restructuring of their business and networks, will reduce the average cost of carriage to C_2 in the figure. The effect is often reinforced due to downward pressure on costs because, although not strictly part of the Open Skies framework, the wider competitive environment within Europe, and the privatization of many carriers, by heightening commercial pressures, reduces the amount of both static and dynamic X-inefficiency in the airline industry. In other words, there is the combined competitive pressure of both free airline markets across the Atlantic and within the two feeder markets at either end.

The Open Skies policy also has stimulation effects on the demand side. By allowing more effective feed to the long-haul stage of transatlantic services through the concentration of traffic at international hub airports, it increases the geographical market being serviced and generates economies of market presence. The larger physical market demand, combined usually with the improved

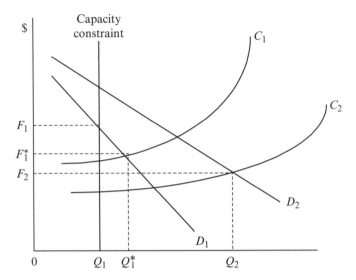

Figure 14.4   *The simple economics of Open Skies policies*

quality of the 'product' that accompanies more integrated services, such as code sharing, interchangeable frequent flier programs, common lounges, and through-baggage checking, pushes out the demand for international air services to D_2 in the figure.

The outcome of the lowering of costs and the outward shift in demand is that the number of passengers traveling increases to Q_2 and, because Open Skies allows price flexibility, the fare falls to F_2 in the way our example is drawn. It should be noted that fares might not actually fall; indeed they may rise as the result of the freer market conditions. The reason for this is that the outward shift in demand reflects a better 'quality' of service – for example, more convenient flights, transferability of frequent flier miles, and seamless ticketing – and that, on average, potential travelers are willing to pay more for this than the generic portfolio of features that were found under the old bilateral air service structure. (The shift out in demand may counteract the fall in costs resulting in a fare above F_1^*, that is, the final outcome may be $F_1^* < F_2$.)

What does become pertinent, however, is the extent to which the fare structure is influenced by the market power of the airlines. The analysis presented in Figure 14.4 assumes that, in the Open Skies environment, fares are set to recover costs; in other words, competition and mergers policy can effectively fulfill the role of regulation. This raises issues as to the nature of a market served by a relatively small number of network carriers. A degree of competition exists between the various alliances for the trunk-hauls market, and there is also competition at either end of routes with many other, including low-cost, carriers competing for passengers in overlapping feeder and origin–destination traffic to international hub airports. There are also theoretical reasons derived from game theory, suggesting that the outcome in a market with three players approaches that of competition. Nevertheless, each alliance by dint of product differentiation (for example, they serve different airports) inevitably enjoys some degree of monopoly power. This could lead to fares somewhat higher than F_2 and a smaller output than Q_2 with consequential reductions in consumer surplus.

The effects of a full Open Aviation Area – a genuine Open Market – can be seen as an extension of this framework. Free capital markets, together with the ability to have more-flexible feeder networks owned by the truck carrier at both ends of transatlantic services, would further lower costs and may generate additional economies of market presence, although this latter effect is unlikely to be large. The ability to invest across national boundaries provides for short-term support in situations of local market fluctuations and more integrated long-term planning of infrastructure; it would in effect produce air networks akin to those enjoyed by US railroads which can move investment funds across states rather than have separate rail companies each limited to intra-state operations. In terms of Figure 14.4, it would mean lower fares and larger air traffic volumes with concomitant increases in society benefits.

14.6   Studying Regulatory Reform

The impacts of reforms in the economic regulation since the late 1970s have been extensively researched, but the impossibility of accurately guessing counter-factuals – what would have happened in the absence of regulatory change – leaves much room for debate. Furthermore, many markets have not yet reached long-run equilibrium. In particular, while some sectors such as the UK bus and the US domestic aviation industries were liberalized some time ago, many international transport sectors are still in the process of change, merging and shaking out. Infrastructure regulations have also generally been more recent and, because of the physical nature of the assets involved, take longer to have an effect.

Experience so far, however, provides some insights on the working of transport markets and the benefits and costs of regulation, but it is not complete, and in particular infrastructure often remains heavily regulated and some of it is still state provided. Also, there have been problems with some of the reforms initially introduced, as for example with rail track in the United Kingdom, and thus there have been subsequent modifications that make assessment murky.

Overall, however, simply looking at the crude data indicates that regulatory liberalization during this period conferred significant benefits on the users of transport services as efficiency gains from 'deregulation' and privatization were passed on to consumers in more competitive markets. A simple indication of this is seen in the pattern of European air transport costs throughout the 1990s when reforms were taking place (Figure 14.5); fares and rates fell to the benefit of customers.

One important issue in the working of transport markets, as we have seen in Section 14.3, is that of contestability. Evidence so far indicates strongly that actual competition is considerably more effective in reducing market power than is potential competition. But even those skeptical of the contestability of

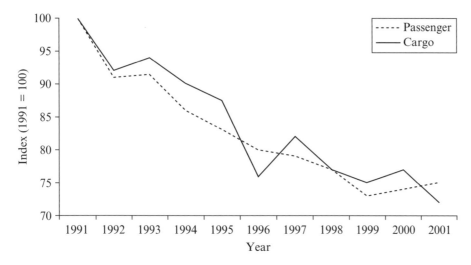

Figure 14.5   *Air fares and cargo rates for European airlines*

transport markets nevertheless find evidence that the market power of firms in these markets is nowhere near strong enough to justify regulation. That is, it can be argued that unregulated markets in transport function quite well by reasonable measures of market performance, compared with other sectors of market economies, and more efficiently than they did under regulation.[30]

There is, in fact, a strong body of evidence that regulatory reform has substantially enhanced economic efficiency in the United States, the United Kingdom and many other intercity transport markets, and that the benefits of that efficiency have been passed on to consumers, as we shall summarize below. The evidence on more limited experiments in deregulating markets in urban transport is not so clear, but is still encouraging.

Although almost all studies trying to analyze the effects of regulatory liberalization for intercity transport in the United States and the United Kingdom find positive benefits from change, there is nevertheless some controversy surrounding the proper methods for evaluating the costs of excessive regulation. Traditionally, regulation is seen to affect efficiency by imposing static deadweight loss, encouraging excess capacity, and stifling technological change. The implications of regulation, however, extend beyond these considerations. For example, regulatory change can have a dynamic effect on productivity change, rather than just a one-shot effect on static efficiency. Further, regulatory change will likely redistribute income across different groups and industries, affecting geographical areas and stakeholders differently, as well as changing national productivity.

As regards dynamic shifts in productivity, there have been far fewer studies than of static efficiency. Nevertheless, some studies have been done, including for airlines and for American trucking. They conclude that deregulation caused

[30] K.J. Button, 'Is the debate over the contestability of airline markets really dead?', in B. Jourquin, P. Rietveld and K. Westin (eds), *Towards Better Performing Transportation Systems*, London: Routledge, 2006.

acceleration in the improvement of productivity in their industries, at least for a period.[31]

Concerning redistribution, existing studies clearly indicate that the effects of deregulation in this area are substantial. Early work in the United States, for example, indicated that deregulation of US aviation benefited the user by some $6 billion per year (1977 prices) with profits rising to $2.5 billion,[32] subsequent mergers and structural changes have altered these figures, but not significantly.[33] In the area of freight, American deregulation seems to have had powerful effects on efficiency and distribution. Winston and colleagues found $20 billion (1988 prices) in annual benefit to shippers and their customers.[34] Yet investors in trucking are estimated to have lost over $5 billion per annum, with losses of similar magnitude to labor employed in the industry. On the other hand, investors in railroads appeared to have gained from deregulation. In some cases, such as with the UK buses and US railroads and airlines, there were overall declines in real wages from deregulation.

While the privatization of transport-supplying industries has been somewhat more recent than many other measures of liberalization, the evidence seems to be that it has enhanced efficiency. In the case of air transport, simple comparisons of productivity between the privately owned major US carriers in 1987 and the mainly state-owned European carriers indicate the former to be significantly more efficient.[35] The privatization of British Airways unquestionably improved the company's productivity *vis-à-vis* its nationally owned European rivals. Equally, the privatized UK bus companies have increased productivity. The application of more rigorous analysis to those transport industries still under public ownership tends to indicate that levels of subsidy and intervention in management decision making lead to technical inefficiency.

In nearly all cases of liberalized regulation, there were concerns on the part of some observers that regulatory change would come at a cost to society in terms of safety and externalities, because the need of firms to minimize costs under a competitive market situation would require them to pay less attention to these considerations. Although it is always difficult to distinguish between long-run trends and short-run fluctuations in transport safety, nevertheless, considerable time has now passed since regulatory reform, especially in the United States. Virtually all evidence regarding deregulation and safety in the United States goes in one direction: there has been no change to existing trends.

[31] K.J. Button and T.E. Keeler, 'The regulation of transport markets', *Economic Journal*, **103**, 1017–28, 1993

[32] S.A. Morrison and C. Winston, 'Empirical implications and tests of the contestability hypothesis', *Journal of Law and Economics*, **30**, 53–66, 1987.

[33] S.A. Morrison and C. Winston, *The Evolution of the Airline Industry*, Washington, DC: Brookings Institution, 1995.

[34] C. Winston, T. Corsi, C. Grimm and C.A. Evans, *The Economic Effects of Surface Freight Deregulation*, Washington, DC: Brookings Institution, 1990.

[35] F. McGowan and P. Seabright, 'The deregulation of European airlines', *Economic Policy*, **9**, 283–344, 1989.

In the case of airlines, perhaps the greatest concern of many, not only did deregulation not harm safety (in terms of fatalities per passenger-mile), but the trend towards increased safety did not significantly shift with the Airline Deregulation Act of 1978; fatalities continued to decline at basically the same rate. Of course, to the extent that deregulation induced intermodal shifts in traffic, the effects could be complicated. But even here, the most evident effect is positive: low airline fares have induced passengers away from a less-safe mode (the private car) to the safer mode of air transport.

The effects of transport deregulation on the wider environment are, at best, ambiguous. Greater freedom of entry and exit has removed much excess capacity from markets everywhere; this goes for trucking, airlines and railroads, both in the European Union and in America. Fuller planes, lorries, trains and railway track should be positive in their effects on the environment. Furthermore, to the extent that freedom of the railroads to compete in the United States takes traffic from roads, that could be thought to be an environmental improvement as well. The major polluter in most contexts is the private car, and little if anything has been done to liberalize the market for car use.

What the recent phase of liberalization has revealed is that, although less regulation may be beneficial, there is still a need for government intervention. A degree of 're-regulation', or modifications to the liberalized structures, is already being considered by some, and adopted by a few,[36] although in practice the process is one of tidying up and adjusting to new circumstances. Specifically, it is concerned with removing serious market imperfections.

With some notable exceptions, the recent liberalization of transport has tended to focus on operations. Transport infrastructure investment has in contrast continued to be controlled, and in many cases owned, by government. How to achieve optimal utilization of this infrastructure and, specifically, the development of appropriate user-charging mechanisms that minimize distortions in liberalized markets, is attracting increasing attention. At one level there are matters relating to investment coordination and policy appraisal, especially in international markets, which have attracted little attention from economists.

At another level there is the matter of efficient use and financing. The separation of infrastructure from operations, as has been the tradition with road and air transport and is being considered by more countries in the context of railways, is seen as one approach to achieving greater efficiency. In North America, recent history has seen monopoly passenger services (such as VIA Rail in Canada) hiring track capacity from freight companies. An alternative approach, however, is simply to offer available capacity to the highest bidder along the lines suggested by Harold Demsetz,[37] although this can raise a variety of technical problems.[38]

---

[36] H.F.A.J. Bettini and A.V.M. Oliveira, 'Airline capacity setting after re-regulation: the Brazilian case in the early 2000s', *Journal of Air Transport Management*, **14**, 289–92, 2008.

[37] H. Demsetz, 'Why regulate utilities?', *Journal of Law and Economics*, **11**, 55–65, 1968.

[38] UK Department of Transport, *The Franchising of Passenger Rail Services: A Consultation Document*, London: DoT, 1992.

Sweden and the UK, however, has already gone some way in this direction as have other countries.[39]

An alternative is to develop economic charging regimes. Important in this is the question of cost attribution. In terms of rail transport, the past 25 years have seen considerable advances in cost allocation procedures. Equally, at airports, our improved understanding now provides a more rational basis for determining landing fees. With respect to road track cost allocation, studies in the United States[40] and the United Kingdom[41] provide a similar foundation for more rational user-charging regimes. Indeed, in New Zealand road freight transport taxation is on a broad user-costs basis. The foundation is, therefore, now laid for more rational charging for infrastructure use.

Anti-trust and mergers have posed serious challenges for regulators both at the domestic and international levels, and brought forth a significant body of analysis. Where mergers have not been prohibited entirely, *ex post* assessment has often within legal–economic work deployed structure, conduct and performance analysis. This involves analyzing the broad structure of the industry (for example, the degree to which it is inherently monopolistic), the ways in which firms behave within it (for example, in terms of fixing prices), and the performance of the industry (for example, in terms of whether consumers benefit from the merger). This is inevitably a rather subjective exercise but does allow a multidimensional approach to the subject.

Econometric and programming approaches of the type set out in Chapter 5 have been deployed in academic work. Table 14.5 offers a brief summary of some of the analysis on airline alliances under which carriers coordinate some of their activities. This provides a more quantitative assessment of the implications of collusion, although it inevitably misses out some of the less tangible or quantifiable elements of supplying, in this case, air transport services.

In summary, the period since the 1970s has seen considerable change in the way that economic regulations are viewed and how they are applied, and with this have come innumerable studies analyzing what has happened. Given the differences in the timing of changes, the sectors affected, and the nature of the reforms, these studies have often sought to see the extent to which the experiences in one country, or relating to one mode, are transferable to other countries or modes. For example, the early move towards lighter regulation in the United States was seen as an opportunity for other countries to learn lessons.[42]

The degree to which there has been, or can be, a successful learning experience is not always, however, clear. While it is interesting to speculate over whether, for example, the EU approach with its emphasis on gradualism is optimal, in

---

[39] L. Hansson and J.-E. Nilsson, 'A new Swedish railroad policy: separation of infrastructure and traffic production', *Transportation Research A*, **25**, 153–60, 1991.

[40] K.A. Small, C. Winston and C.A. Evans, *Road Works – A New Highway Pricing and Investment Policy*, Washington, DC: Brookings Institution, 1989.

[41] D.M. Newbery, 'Road user charges in Britain', *Economic Journal*, **90**, 161–76, 1988.

[42] K.J. Button and D. Swann, 'Transatlantic lessons in aviation deregulation: EEC and US experiences', *Antitrust Bulletin*, **37**, 207–55, 1992.

Table 14.5 *Studies of the effects of strategic airline alliance*

Study	Alliances	Period	Findings
Gellman Research Associates (1994)	BA/US Air, KLM/NW	1994	Profits increased for all parties with BA and KLM gaining more than their partners
Youssef & Hansen (1994)	Swissair and SAS	1989–91	Increases in flight frequency; variations in fare levels; the strongest service levels had the lowest fare increases
US General Accounting Office (1995)	KLM/NW, USAir/BA, UAL/Lufthansa UAL/Ansett, UAL/BMA	1994	All carriers enjoyed increased revenues and traffic gained at competitors' expense, not industry growth
Dresner et al. (1995)	Continental/SAS, Delta Swissair, KLM.NW	1987–91	Mixed successes with traffic volumes; in general alliances did not benefit partners
Park (1997)	KLM/NW, Delta/Swissair/Sabena	1990–94	Traffic increases at the expense of rivals. Complementary alliances lowered fares while parallel alliances increased fares
Oum et al. (2000)	Star Alliance, oneWorld Skyteam, KLM/NW	1992–94	Increased traffic on alliance routes
Brueckner & Whalen (2000)	US international alliances	1999	Fares are some 18% to 20% lower on international alliance, inter-lining routes

Source: K.J. Button, 'The Impact of EU–US "Open Skies" Agreement on airline market structures and airline networks', *Journal of Air Transport Management*, **15**, 59–71, 2009, where full references to the studies are to be found.

practice it is very difficult to reach any firm conclusions. Just taking air transport as an example, there was, and remain significant differences the American and European markets (Table 14.6). These differences in the geography, history, structure and use of the network can make it hard to discern what lessons are relevant, and to decide the extent to which transfers have been successful.

14.7 Coordination via the Market, or by Direction?

A number of potentially useful insights emerge from the previous sections. First, governments in virtually all countries find the transport sector extremely difficult to handle; this is perhaps most clearly seen if one reflects on the fact that major pieces of transport legislation appeared on the UK's statute books every seven or eight years during one half-century period (that is, 1930, 1933, 1947, 1953, 1962, 1968, 1974, 1980, 1985). These have been supplemented by numerous pieces of

Table 14.6   *Difference between the US and European air transport markets*

- *Domestic/international traffic split*   The vast majority of European carriage and historically its airlines have largely operated in regulated international markets, and the natural inclination for rent protecting may take longer to erode than it did in the United States
- *The non-scheduled market*   European aviation involves a large charter component. In 1999, the revenue from passengers by non-scheduled services in America was 12 billion out of 772 billion – comparable figures for Europe were 120 billion out of 337 billion
- *Market size*   The average route length in Europe is 720 kilometers; in the United States it is 1,220 kilometers. The average number of passengers per scheduled route is about 100,000 in Europe but virtually double that in the United States
- *Airline size*   The scale of the European market is also reflected in the actual size of the EU's airlines. The merger of British Airways (46.3 billion scheduled passenger-kilometers) and British Caledonian (8.8 billion) in 1987 made it the largest European carrier in terms of passenger-kilometers. The situation has not changed significantly since that time and while there are some large European carriers, the world's largest passenger airlines and cargo carriers as measured by conventional parameters are American based
- *Ownership of airlines*   While the US commercial airline industry has always been in private hands, most major European carriers have been state owned and a number of carriers still remain state owned or have a significant state involvement
- *Approaches to bankruptcy*   Chapter 11 arrangements in the United States are less stringent than most European bankruptcy regimes and allow for existing management, under supervision, to restructure a company's finances rather than have the assets of the undertaking realized
- *Subsidies*   America had no tradition of explicitly subsidizing airlines until 2001, except in limited cases of social air services. There has been a tradition of subsidizing European flag carriers but EU policy on state subsidies has now been tightened and criteria made explicit under which subsidies may be given
- *Intermodal competition*   There is substantial intermodal competition in Europe from high-speed train services
- *Infrastructure availability*   US air traffic control is centralized, whereas air traffic control in Europe has been a national concern. The EU system comprises a patchwork, while the US has less than half the number of centers and standardized mainframe computers. Airport capacity in Europe is rapidly being reached at many major terminals whereas this is a more limited problem in America. More than 50 percent of traffic in Europe passes through 24 airports and, although figures are somewhat subjective on the issue of airport capacity, all of these have reached their technical capacity or are very close to it
- *Advantage of hindsight*   European policy makers and airlines have the United States as an example to warn them against some of the difficulties to be avoided

minor legislation. There have been substantial shifts both in the way that transport has been viewed and the type of policy approach pursued.

Second, the changes in policy have exhibited systematic swings between attempts at making greater use of market forces and a more comprehensive level of central control or direction. Intervention has always existed, but the degree and nature of this intervention has differed according to whether more or less confidence was felt in market processes. Recent changes in policy, from the late 1970s, have reflected a greater market orientation while the nationalization of the immediate post-war period had followed philosophies of direction. The respective merits of market-oriented policies *vis-à-vis* ones of planned allocation of resources are subjects of considerable debate. While much of the discussion is political (often doctrinal) there is, nevertheless, an important area of economic controversy involved.

It is quite possible that in theory a variety of approaches with quite significant differences in their degree of market orientation could achieve the basic objectives of transport policy, but the standard economic problem of integration or 'coordination' remains difficult in practice. (Coordination is here used in its economic context and is best defined by Peterson:[43] 'Coordination is the assignment by whatever means of each facility to those transport tasks which it can perform better than other facilities, under conditions which will ensure its fullest development in the place so found'.) In practice, reliance is never placed entirely on the market mechanism to achieve the desired coordination, or upon direction. The issue is rather one of degree and emphasis. It seems useful, however, to look initially at some of the arguments that are advanced for adoption of the extreme position.

The price mechanism is the main instrument of the market and offers an obvious method of coordination – each consumer being in a position to purchase transport services at the lowest cost. Arguments that transport is a public utility, on a par with street lighting or the police force, are dismissed by advocates of this school who point out that transport, unlike genuine utilities, would be provided even if government did not exist.

There may be cases (for example, quasi-public goods) where government must act as the supplier, if provision is to be optimal, but providing the rules of marginal cost pricing are pursued no difficulties arise. If externalities exist then these can be handled adequately by means of ensuring that property rights are allocated according to fairly accepted rules, while lump-sum transfers could tackle social difficulties associated with hardship. (At the extreme one may argue that income differences are themselves the result of market forces and should, therefore, be left.) Insurance markets would handle the longevity of transport infrastructure, and the associated risks. Safety would be ensured by travelers/consignors selecting operators with a good safety record or alternatively they may prefer a higher risk but at a lower charge for the trip. Perfection in the 'safety market' may require government intervention to ensure that users are cognizant of the dangers involved – in this sense information becomes the only 'merit good' to be provided in the transport sector.

Advocates of market approaches to coordination point to the automatic mechanisms involved, and to the freedom of the system from political manipulation.

[43] G.S. Peterson, 'Transport coordination: meaning and purpose', *Journal of Political Economy*, **38**, 660–81, 1930.

John Hibbs,[44] in particular, suggested that the direction of resources by some overriding body is likely to be less efficient at coordination because 'The administrative mind is not likely to possess the qualities of imagination and flair that are necessary if the consumer's interest is to be served'. Cooter and Topakin[45] produce evidence from the Bay Area Rapid Transit System in the San Francisco Bay area that provides tentative confirmation of this type of bureaucratic hypothesis; namely, that the technostructure places its interest before that of customers. The validity of this view is, however, debatable and it has been suggested that the managers of any large undertaking, irrespective of the type of purpose they are charged to pursue, will be motivated by their own self-interest – in particular they will attempt to maximize their power and security. Self-interest at the expense of customer interest, therefore, seems to be a function of the scale of management rather than of ownership or the objectives that are set.

But even if there are potential managerial problems associated with the central direction of resources, these may well be outweighed by the possible benefits. Strictly, planned resource allocation involves the direction of traffic as well as factors of production actually employed in providing transport services. In general, however, UK and US policy has seldom attempted to direct traffic, leaving the consumer free to choose his/her mode, route, service, and so on. (There are exceptions such as one-way streets and barriers to trucks, but these are rather outside of the main thrust of the debate.)

The most important UK case, where some degree of direction was intended, concerned the proposed introduction of quantity licensing into long-distance trucking under the Transport Act, 1968. The broad argument here was that it was to the consignor's benefit to be directed to rail in certain instances because of his/her own misperception. ('Inertia and habit will play their part and some consignors may not even be aware of the advantage to them of the new rail services, nor of the true economic cost of their present arrangements', according to the UK transport ministry.[46]) The difficulty with this line of argument, and possibly one of the main reasons why the system was never implemented, is that the administrators, in making their allocation, may themselves misperceive the priorities and needs of the consignor.

On the more central issue of service provision, it has been suggested that without directed coordination it is often impossible or prohibitively wasteful for many of the wider goals to be fully achieved. Direct income transfers, for example, may rectify differences in the spending power of households, but it is often a subgroup within a household (for example, housewives) whom one is trying to assist, and direct transfers may not reach them. Further, with so many operators in the transport market, there are suggestions that technical coordination of services would be less efficient (for example, bus services would not act as

---

[44] J. Hibbs, 'Transport without Politics?', Hobart Paper 95, London, 1982.
[45] R. Cooter and G. Topakin, 'Political economy of a public co-operation – pricing objectives of BART', *Journal of Public Economics*, **13**, 299–318, 1980.
[46] UK Department of Transport, *Transport Policy*, Cmnd 6845, London: HMSO, 1977.

local distributors to trunk rail services). Private firms may not be willing to undertake substantial capital projects because, unlike government, they cannot spread risk adequately, even where insurance markets do exist. In more simple terms, advocates of direction feel that it is likely to prove overall to be more efficient than an optimally maintained market environment.

Quite clearly the substance of these lines of argument is likely to vary among transport sectors. It is not surprising, therefore, that in general the allocative mechanism favored for inter-urban transport (especially freight) is that of the market and of price, while intra-urban transport tends to be subjected to considerable planning and control. The widespread occurrence of externalities, the more immediate distribution issues, the interaction of an imperfect transport market with that of an imperfect land market and so on make it particularly difficult to remove the impedance that exists to the efficient function of a pure market for urban transport.

One exception, which should be noted, to the dominance of the market in allocating inter-urban resources, is the public provision of roads. Here, as we have seen elsewhere, there are important differences between the way in which road and rail track costs are passed on to users. Comparable pricing policies are the clear market solution, but increasingly economists have taken the argument further and have suggested that both sets of track should be publicly owned and then users should pay on an identical basis for the services rendered – a situation that exists with parts of Sweden's rail network and one that has been actively pursued in the United Kingdom. Open access and economic charging for rail infrastructure is also part of the EU's transport policy.

Finally, it is becoming increasingly apparent that the tools of direction or control are, in effect, so numerous, sophisticated and subtle that the distinction between market-oriented policy and control is rapidly ceasing to be a meaningful one. By manipulating price, licensing, operating laws and work conditions, government is in effect directing resources and ultimately influencing the traffic patterns that evolve. The tools of policy outlined earlier are all, in effect, tools of direction but at the same time they may operate as tools to improve the workings of the market. Would road pricing, for example, be extending the market to embrace congestion or would it be a direction of traffic? In this context the extremes of market versus direction cease to be helpful; one moves to a rather more basic debate concerning the desirability of goals and the relative merits of different policy tools for achieving them.

Further Reading

A good general overview of the role of government in markets is found in C. Winston, *Government Failure Versus Market Failure*, Washington, DC: Brookings Institution, 2006. The recent literature relating specifically to transport regulation is extensive, diverse, and the recommendations offered here are but a small sample of what is available. K.J. Button and D. Gillingwater, *Future Transport Policy*,

London: Routledge, 1986, provides a historical perspective up to the 1990s. Sets of papers examining the experiences of liberalizing transport regulation across a number of countries and covering virtually all modes of transport are to be found in D. Banister and K.J. Button (eds), *Transport in a Free Market Economy*, Basingstoke: Macmillan, 1991 and K.J. Button and D.E. Pitfield (eds), *Transport Deregulation: An International Movement*, Basingstoke: Macmillan, 1991. In terms of mode-specific studies, see K.J. Button (ed.), *Airline Deregulation: International Experiences*, London: David Fulton, 1991, which contains papers on aviation; T.E. Keeler, *Railroads, Freight and Public Policy*, Washington, DC: Brookings Institution, 1983, which is concerned with US railroad regulation; J.S. Dodgson and N. Topham (eds), *Bus Deregulation and Privatisation*, Aldershot: Avebury, 1988, which looks at aspects of UK bus regulatory reform, and K.J. Button and G. Chow, 'Road haulage regulation: a comparison of the Canadian, British and American approaches', *Transport Reviews*, **3**, 237–64, 1983, which provides a comparative study of US, UK and Canadian trucking regulation. An interesting discussion of some of the problems associated with privatizing transport infrastructure is contained in J.A. Gómez-Ibáñez, J.R. Meyer and D.E. Luberoff, 'The prospects for privatizing infrastructure: lessons from US roads and solid waste', *Journal of Transport Economics and Policy*, **25**, 259–78, 1991, and a useful overview of experiences with bus deregulation is contained in J.R. Meyer and J.A. Gómez-Ibáñez, 'Transit bus privatization and deregulation around the world: some perspectives and lessons', *International Journal of Transport Economics*, **18**, 231–58, 1991. Matters of financing policy, albeit in the context of freight, are considered in Transportation Research Board, *Funding Options for Freight Transportation Projects*, Washington, DC: National Academy of Sciences.

Index

· ·